INTRODUCTION TO CLASSICAL ETHIOPIC

HARVARD SEMITIC MUSEUM

HARVARD SEMITIC STUDIES

Number 24

INTRODUCTION TO CLASSICAL ETHIOPIC
by
Thomas O. Lambdin

Thomas O. Lambdin

INTRODUCTION TO CLASSICAL ETHIOPIC (GEʿEZ)

Scholars Press

Distributed by
Scholars Press
PO Box 5207
Missoula, Montana 59806

INTRODUCTION TO CLASSICAL ETHIOPIC
by
Thomas O. Lambdin

Library of Congress Cataloging in Publication Data

Lambdin, Thomas Oden.
Introduction to Classical Ethiopic (Geʿez)

(Harvard Semitic studies ; v. 24 ISSN 0147-9342)
Bibliography: p.
1. Ethiopic language—Grammar. I. Harvard University. Semitic Museum. II. Title. III. Series: Harvard Semitic series ; v. 24.
PJ9023.L3 492'.8 78-12895
ISBN 0-89130-263-8

Printed in the United States of America
1 2 3 4 5
Edwards Brothers, Inc.
Ann Arbor, Michigan 48104

TABLE OF CONTENTS

Preface ix

Abbreviations and Conventions x

Introduction 1

Phonology 2

- A. The Vowels 2
- B. The Consonants 3
- C. Stress 5
- D. Root and Pattern 5
- E. The Ethiopic Alphabet 6
- F. Special Phonological Rules 7
- G. Manuscript Errors and Normalization 13

1.1 Absence of Definite and Indefinite Articles 15

1.2 Prepositions 15

1.3 Third Person Forms of the Verb (Perfect) 15

2.1 Noun Plurals 18

2.2 Syntax (Verb plus Noun Subject) 18

3.1 Noun Plurals (cont.) 21

3.2 Collectives 21

4.1 The Construct State 23

5.1 Gender 26

5.2 Number 27

5.3 Some Demonstrative Adjectives 27

6.1 The Personal Pronouns (Independent Form) 29

6.2 Non-verbal Sentences with a Nominal Predicate 29

6.3 The Plural Demonstratives 30

7.1 The Accusative Case 33

7.2 Word Order in a Verbal Clause 33

7.3 The Accusative of Goal 33

7.4 The Accusative Forms of the Demonstratives 34

8.1 Interrogative Pronouns and Adjectives 36

8.2 Interrogative Adverbs 36

8.3 The Particles *-nu* and *-hu* 36

8.4 The Remote Demonstratives 37

8.5 Accusative of Time 37

9.1 The Noun with Pronominal Suffixes 40

10.1 Prepositions with Pronominal Suffixes 44
10.2 The *waldu la-neguš* Construction 44
10.3 *K^well-* 45
11.1 Types of Verbs 49
11.2 The Full Inflection of the Perfect 50
12.1 The Perfect: Roots II-Guttural 53
13.1 The Perfect: Roots III-Guttural 56
13.2 The Perfect with Object Suffixes 56
14.1 The Perfect: Roots III-W/Y 60
15.1 The Perfect: Roots II-W/Y 63
15.2 The Perfect with Object Suffixes (cont.) 63
15.3 The *qatalo la-neguš* Construction 64
16.1 Adjectives 68
16.2 Attributive Adjectives 68
17.1 Adjectives: The Pattern *Qetul* 72
17.2 Adjectives as Predicates 73
17.3 Adverbial Predicates 73
18.1 Adjectives: The Pattern *Qatil* 76
18.2 The Comparative 76
19.1 Adjectives: The Pattern *Qattāl* 79
19.2 Adjectives in -*āwi* and -*āy* 79
19.3 Adjectives: Miscellaneous Types 79
19.4 Qualification 79
19.5 Substantivization 80
20.1 *La-* with Pronominal Suffixes 83
20.2 Object suffixes in a Dative or Prepositional Sense 83
20.3 Partitive Apposition 85
21.1 Medio-passive Verbs: Gt 88
22.1 Medio-passive Verbs: Dt, Lt, Qt 93
23.1 Cardinal Numbers (1-10) 97
23.2 Ordinal Numbers (1-10) 97
23.3 Cardinal Adverbs (1-10) 98
24.1 Associative (Reciprocal) Verbs: Glt 101
25.1 Relative Pronouns and Relative Clauses 106
25.2 *ʾAma* and *xaba* 108
26.1 Causative Verbs: CG, CD, CL, CQ 111
26.2 The Meaning of CG Verbs 111

27.1 Causative Verbs: CG (cont.) 117
27.2 Causative Verbs: CD, CL, CQ 118
27.3 General Remarks on the Verbal System 118
28.1 *Ba-* with Pronominal Suffixes 122
28.2 *Ba-* Indicating Possession 122
28.3 *Bo(tu)* Indicating Existence 123
28.4 *Bo za-* as the Equivalent of an Indefinite Pronoun 123
28.5 *ʾAlbo ... zaʾenbala*: Only 123
29.1 Interrogatives with *za-* 128
29.2 Indefinite Pronouns 128
29.3 *ʾAkko* 129
30.1 The Infinitive: Form 134
30.2 The Infinitive: Uses 134
31.1 The Perfective Active Participle 140
32.1 The Imperfect: G Verbs from Sound Roots 144
32.2 Independent Uses of the Imperfect 144
32.3 Dependent Uses of the Imperfect 145
33.1 The Subjunctive: G Verbs from Sound Roots 149
33.2 The Uses of the Subjunctive 149
34.1 The Imperative: G Verbs from Sound Roots 154
34.2 The Agent Noun *qatāli* 154
35.1 The Verbal Adjective *qetul* 159
35.2 Further Remarks on Complements 160
36.1 The Verbal Noun (G Verbs) 164
36.2 The Cognate Accusative 166
37.1 Nouns of Place: The Pattern *meqtāl* 170
37.2 Nouns of the Pattern *maqtal(t)* 170
38.1 G Verbs from Roots I-Guttural: Remaining Forms 174
39.1 G Verbs from Roots II-Guttural: Remaining Forms 180
39.2 The Verb *behla* to say 181
40.1 G Verbs from Roots III-Guttural: The Remaining Forms 186
41.1 G Verbs from Roots I-W: The Remaining Forms 191
42.1 G Verbs from Roots II-W/Y: The Remaining Forms 195
43.1 G Verbs from Roots III-W/Y: The Remaining Forms 200
44.1 Gt Verbs: Imperfect, Subjunctive, and Imperative 205
44.2 Glt Verbs: Imperfect, Subjunctive, and Imperative 205
44.3 *Hallawa* with the Subjunctive and Imperfect 206

45.1 CG Verbs: The Remaining Forms 209
46.1 D Verbs: Imperfect, Subjunctive, and Imperative 214
46.2 The Names of the Months 214
46.3 The Numbers Above Ten 215
47.1 D Verbs: Verbal Adjectives 218
47.2 D Verbs: Agent Nouns 218
47.3 D Verbs: Verbal Nouns 219
47.4 D Verbs: Nouns with Prefixed *m-* 220
48.1 Dt Verbs: Imperfect, Subjunctive, and Imperative 222
48.2 Dt Verbs: Verbal Nouns 222
48.3 CD Verbs 223
48.4 Independent Personal Pronouns (Secondary Forms) 223
49.1 L, CL, and Lt Verbs: The Remaining Forms 225
49.2 CGt, CDt, CLt, and CGlt Verbs 226
50.1 Quadriliteral Verbs: The Remaining Forms 228
50.2 Quinquiliteral Verbs 229
50.3 N Verbs 229
50.4 A Special Adjective Type: *Qataltil* 230
51.1 Conditional Sentences 231
51.2 Optative Sentences 232
51.3 The Syllogistic Construction *Za ... 'efo* 232
51.4 The Sentence Particles 232
51.5 The Repeated Prepositions *ba-ba-*, *la-la-*, *za-za-* 234
51.6 A Special Use of the Third Person Singular Pronominal Suffixes 234
51.7 The Periphrastic Passive 235
51.8 Attributive Adjectives in Construct Phrases 235

Texts in Transliteration with Glosses 236
Lives of the Saints (from the Synaxarion) 236
The Book of Baruch 276
The Gospel of Matthew 298
Matthew V, 1-24, in Ethiopic Script 377
A Selected Bibliography 378
Glossary 381
Principal Part of G Verbs 450
Synopsis of the Sound Triliteral Verb 451

PREFACE

The present work was developed during more than a decade of teaching Classical Ethiopic on the elementary and intermediate levels. It is designed to provide a detailed but carefully graded introduction to the grammar and basic vocabulary of the language. The material covered in this book should be adequate in itself for those who, as Semitists or students of textual criticism, require only a working knowledge of the language as a tool within a wider discipline. I hope too that beginning Ethiopicists will find it an orderly and comprehensive introduction to their study of the classical language.

Because the grammar is presented entirely in transliteration, the student is urged to familiarize himself with the Ethiopic alphabet as soon as possible and to copy out and study at least the vocabulary of each lesson in the native script. In this way he will considerably lessen the difficulty in making the transition to the reading of published texts and manuscripts.

It is a pleasure to acknowledge my gratitude to the many classes which have worked with me through the successive drafts of this grammar. I have profited greatly from their criticism, questions, and corrections, but most of all from the practical experience of teaching so many interested and gifted students.

I also wish to express my sincere thanks to Miss Carol Cross for the great care and professional skill which she exercised in preparing the copy for publication. Her patience with a tedious manuscript and author is undoubtedly registered in the *Maṣḥafa Ḥeywat*.

Lastly, I cannot let go unexpressed my deep appreciation for the genius and diligence of August Dillmann, whose grammatical, textual, and lexical work in the last century laid the firmest possible foundation for all subsequent scholarly investigation in the field. It is on that foundation that the present work is based.

Thomas O. Lambdin

Cambridge, Massachusetts
June 1978

Abbreviations and Conventions

a. d. o.	accusative direct object
a. n.	agent noun (also an.)
acc.	accusative
adj.	adjective
adv.	adverb
c.	common gender
caus.	causative
coll.	collective
compl.	complement
coord.	coordinated
dat.	dative
dem.	demonstrative
dir.	direct
e.g.	for example
encl.	enclitic
esp.	especially
ex(x).	example(s)
exclam.	exclamation
f.	feminine
fem.	feminine
fig.	figuratively
foll.	following, followed
Gk.	Greek
i.e.	that is.
imperf.	imperfect
indef.	indefinite
indir.	indirect
inf.	infinitive
interrog.	interrogative
introd.	introductory
lit.	literally
m.	masculine
masc.	masculine
n.	noun
N. T.	New Testament
neg.	negative
o. s.	object suffix
O. T.	Old Testament
obj.	object
part.	particle
pass.	passive
perf.	perfect
pers.	person
pl.	plural
pred.	predicate
prep.	preposition
pron.	pronoun
q. v.	which see
rel.	relative
subj.	subjunctive, subject
s.	singular
sing.	singular
suff.	suffix(es)
v. n.	verbal noun (also vn.)
voc.	vocative
w.	with
/	or (used in listing alternate constructions, transcriptions, or meanings)
idem	"has the same meaning(s) as the preceding entry"
etc.	"has the same range of meanings as the main entry"
=	"is completely equivalent to in regard to meanings and constructions"
±	with or without

In the reading of plurals, suffixes are to be added to the preceding item: *te'mert* (pl. *-āt, ta'āmer, -āt*) = *te'mert* (pl. *te'mertāt, ta'āmer, ta'āmerāt*).

Introduction

Classical Ethiopic, or Geʿez, is the literary language developed by missionaries for the translation of the scriptures after the Christianization of Ethiopia in the 4th century. The new written language was presumably based on the spoken language of Aksum, the commercial and political center at the time. Some inscriptional material survives from this earliest period of the language, but our main source is the extensive religious literature which was translated into Geʿez during the ensuing centuries. As the official language of the church, the written language survived the demise of its spoken counterpart in a manner analogous to the survival of Latin in Europe.

Although evidence is sparse and scholarly opinion is not unanimous, the Semitic presence in Ethiopia is most plausibly explained as the result of migrations from South Arabia in the form of commercial colonizations beginning possibly as early as the middle of the first millennium B.C. Geʿez is linguistically a member of the South-east Semitic family, but does not seem to be derivable directly from Old South Arabic as known from Sabaean, Minaean, Qatabanian, and other inscriptions during this time. The real ancestral language on Arabian soil is irretrievably lost to us, but we do have its descendants in the modern South Arabic dialects such as Mehri, Soqotri, and Shahri, when these can be extricated from their North Arabian admixtures.

Because the Ethiopic script is fully vocalized, the main features of the grammar are clear from the texts themselves. The orthography, however, has two defects: (1) consonantal doubling (gemination) is not indicated, and (2) the presence of one of the vowels (*e* in our transliteration) is not clearly indicated. These problems may be resolved in two ways: the first is to examine the evidence of corresponding forms in other Semitic languages; the second is to consult the reading tradition preserved by scholars in the modern Ethiopic Church. Neither of these, if taken alone, is conclusive: Semitic historical linguistics is itself ambiguous on certain crucial questions because of insufficient data; the modern reading tradition, as published by various European scholars, contains many contradictions and is heavily influenced by the informants' own modern languages (usually Amharic). In developing the grammar of Geʿez in the following lessons I have followed as closely as possible the traditional pronunciation as studied and published by E. Mittwoch, *Die traditionelle Aussprache des Äthiopischen* (Berlin 1926). All major deviations from this tradition are noted in the appropriate sections of the lessons; these result either from a choice among variant forms or from an attempt to minimize the influence of Amharic present in the pronunciation. Since all deviations involve either consonantal doubling or the presence of an *e*-vowel, the reader is not likely to be seriously misled by my interpretation of a particular form. To attempt a harmonization of all published material would be far more confusing. The interested reader may consult the Bibliography.

Phonology

A. The Vowels

The distinction between long and short vowels, a property of earlier Semitic according to standard reconstruction, probably persisted into the period when Geʿez was first reduced to written form, but because this cannot be proven except by appeal to certain structural features, an argument that not all scholars would accept, and because the modern reading traditions do not recognize vowel length as a significant vowel feature, reference to long and short vowels in the following discussion should be regarded as a classification which the writer finds convenient for the description of the phonology rather than a universally accepted fact about the Geʿez vowel system.

There are seven vowels:

short: *a*, *e*   Long: *ā*, *i*, *u*, *ē*, *o*

Only *ā* and *ē* are marked with macrons in our transcription, since no confusion can result from leaving *i*, *u*, and *o* unmarked. The vowels *ē* and *o* usually result from the contraction of the diphthongs *ay* and *aw* respectively. There are many situations where *aw* and *o* alternate optionally (e.g. *taloku*, *talawku* I followed). Optional alternation between *ay* and *ē* is less common but not problematic.

The modern reading pronunciation of these vowels is indicated by their position on the following standard chart. Brackets enclose standard phonetic symbols.

	Front	Central	Back
High	i [i]	e [ɨ]	u [u]
High-Mid	ē [e]		o [o]
Mid			
Mid-Low		a [æ, ä]	
Low		ā [a,ɑ]	

ē and *o* are very often preceded by palatal and labial glides respectively: for example, *bēton* is pronounced [$b^y et^w on$]. This feature is not represented in the script, and unless the student is determined to imitate the modern reading pronunciation in every detail, it may be ignored. The correct pronunciation of *e* and *a* is very difficult for the speaker of English. Since Geʿez is no longer a spoken language, the following approximations should prove adequate:

a	as in father, short	*i*	as in machine, long
e	as in let, short	*o*	as in boat, long
ā	as in father, long	*u*	as in boot, long.
ē	as in bait, long		

The length distinction between *a* and *ā* is not difficult to make. For those who have no concept of vowel length, however, *a* may be pronounced like the vowel of *up*, and *ā* like the first vowel of *father*, in order to maintain this important distinction.

B. The Consonants

Most of the Ethiopic consonants have an approximate counterpart in English and offer no problems in pronunciation:

b	as in boy	*k*	as in king	*š*	like sh in should
d	as in dog	*l*	as in leaf	*t*	as in tea
f	as in foot	*m*	as in man	*w*	as in wall
g	as in goat	*n*	as in no	*y*	as in yet
h	as in hope	*s*	as in so	*z*	as in zoo

No distinction is made between *s* and *š* in the modern tradition; both are pronounced as *s*. *b* tends to be pronounced as a voiced bilabial spirant [β], in medial positions when not doubled.

The five sounds ʾ ʿ *h ḥ x* will be referred to collectively as gutturals. Three of the gutturals *(h ḥ x)* are pronounced simply as *h* in the modern tradition. The reader is urged to make a clear distinction among these three sounds:

h is ordinary [h], as in hope.

x is the voiceless velar fricative [x], as in German *Bach* (Arabic خ).

ḥ is the voiceless pharyngeal continuant [H], an *h*-sound accompanied by a tense narrowing between the base of the tongue and the back of the throat (Arabic ح).

Two of the gutturals (ʾ ʿ) are not pronounced at all in word-initial position in the modern tradition, and both are pronounced as a glottal stop internally. They were originally distinct sounds, and to avoid mistakes in spelling, the reader should make a clear distinction between them:

ʾ is the glottal stop [ʔ].

ʿ is the voiced laryngeal (pharyngeal) continuant [ʕ], i.e. the voiced counterpart of *ḥ* above (Arabic ع).

The consonants *ṭ ḍ ṣ* and *q* have the common feature of glottalization: the flow of air is cut off completely at the glottis and the sound is made by a forcible ejection of the air already in the oral cavity. These sounds have a very sharp, click-like character.

ṭ is glottalized *t*,

ṣ is glottalized *s* (sounding almost like *ts*),

q is glottalized *k*.

The older pronunciation of *ḍ* has not been preserved, since it is now pronounced exactly like *ṣ*.

There are two *p*-sounds, both of which occur only in words of foreign origin. The sound transcribed simply as *p* in this text occurs mainly in Greek names (e.g. *Pēṭros* Peter) and loanwords and is pronounced in the modern tradition as a *glottalized p*. The second *p*-sound is now pronounced as ordinary *p*, but is so rare that it occurs only once or twice in this entire book, transcribed as *ṗ*.

The labialized sounds k^w x^w g^w q^w are simply *k x g q* pronounced simultaneously with *w*, precisely like English [kw] in *quick* or [gw] in *Guam*.

All of the consonants may occur simple or doubled. [The reader should note that doubling a consonant merely means holding it noticeably longer than its single counterpart.] The modern pronunciation does not preserve the doubling of the guttural consonants, but there is no reason to suppose that they were an exception in the classical language. A sequence of two labialized consonants is realized as a doubled simple consonant plus labialization and is transcribe accordingly: $-k^w k^w- > -kk^w-$.

C. Stress

According to the tradition adopted in this text, stress (accent) for the vast majority of words may be described by two simple rules:

(a) All finite verbal forms without object suffixes are stressed on the next-to-last (i.e. penultimate) syllable. Thus: *nabắra*, *qatắlat*, *yeqắttel*, *yeqattḗlu*. The sole exception is the 2nd person feminine plural of the Perfect in *-kḗn* (e.g. *nabarkḗn*).

(b) Most other words, including nouns, adjectives, and adverbs, are stressed on the last syllable unless this ends in final *-a*, in which case the stress is on the preceding syllable.

The relatively few exceptions to these rules are in the pronominal system, including the pronominal suffixes on nouns and verbs. All deviations from the two basic rules given above will be noted in the lessons where appropriate. Words in construct (see Lesson 4) tend to lose their stress or, at most, retain only a secondary stress. The same is true of the proclitic negative *ʾi-* and of prepositions before a noun.

D. Root and Pattern

In Ethiopic, as in Semitic languages in general, most verbs, nouns, and adjectives may be analyzed into a sequence of three consonants and a vowel pattern, with or without a prefixal or suffixal element. For example,

		Consonant Base	Vowel Pattern	Additional Elements
negušš	king	*ngš*	$C_1eC_2uC_3$	none
negešt	queen	*ngš*	$C_1eC_2eC_3$-	suffix *-t*
berhān	light	*brh*	$C_1eC_2C_3$-	suffix *-ān*
manbar	throne	*nbr*	$-C_1C_2aC_3$	prefix *ma-*

The consonantal sequence (C_1-C_2-C_3) is called the root of the set of words which share that sequence and can usually be assigned a meaning common to the set; compare, for example, *neguš* and *negešt* above with *negš* (rule, reign), *nagāši* (king), *mangešt* (kingdom), *nagša* (he became king), all sharing the common notion of "ruling."

Because most of the morphology is devoted to a study of the triliteral root and the patterns (nominal, adjectival, and verbal) associated with it, it is convenient to have a way of specifying "any triliteral root" in a less clumsy fashion than C_1-C_2-C_3. For this purpose Semitists generally employ the "dummy" root *qtl*. Thus,

neguš, berur, beluy	are of the pattern	*qetul*
berhān, rešʾān, q^w erbān		*qetlān*
manbar, manfas, marxo (from **marxaw*)		*maqtal*

and similarly for all the words in the language that can be associated with a triliteral root. The extreme usefulness of this device will become apparent in the lessons. When discussing roots or sequences of more than three consonants, we shall employ $C_1C_2C_3C_4$ (and similarly for more than four), since no other convention exists.

The vocalic patterns, together with prefixes and suffixes, form the subject matter of the grammar. Very few patterns have a completely predictable meaning, but a large number of them belong to the "almost predictable" category. For example, *qetul* is almost always adjectival in meaning (see Lessons 17 and 35), but the two frequent nouns cited above (*neguš* and *berur*) are exceptions to this rule. Close attention to the formative patterns and the relationships among them will give the reader a proper feeling for the derivational processes at work in the language.

E. The Ethiopic Alphabet

The Ethiopic alphabet was borrowed directly from the Old South Arabic monumental script, gradually modified for book use. Genuine cursive forms are modern; manuscripts consistently (and happily) employ a more or less hand-printed form, with separation of all the letters. The individuals responsible for the borrowing of the alphabet and its adaptation to their literary purposes showed an orthographic acumen rare in the Semitic world: the consonantal alphabet was altered into a fully vocalized syllabary by the addition of various strokes and modifications to the individual letters. The resulting "alphabetic syllabary" is given in Table A. The order of the letters is traditional and does not include the labialized consonants, which are given in Table B. The columns are sometimes numbered (from left to right), and a letter, e.g. ኪ *(ki)* is spoken of as *k* with a vowel of the third order. We shall not adopt this awkward terminology.

The forms of the letters in the first column (read with the vowel -a) are the basic forms of the borrowed consonants. These should be mastered thoroughly before taking up the remaining forms. Each column should then be analyzed separately, since there is a great deal of consistency in the way particular vowels are indicated. Note that the signs for the labialized sounds are secondary modifications of the non-labialized counterpart.

To express numbers in numeral form the Greek alphabet was employed, written within a top and bottom frame. The numerical values are the same as those known from Greek sources. See Table C. Note the combinations: 1000 = 10 hundred; 10,000 = 100 hundred.

Several new letters were developed for the writing of Amharic by modifying certain forms of the Geʿez alphabet. These sometimes occur in Geʿez manuscripts in writing native personal and place names. See Table D.

The Old South Arabic monumental script regularly employed a vertical stroke as a word divider. This too was borrowed and appears after every single word in an Ethiopic text as ፡ (see the specimen text for examples). The sign ፤ is used as a colon or semicolon within a sentence, and ። is used as a period. Other more elaborate devices are sometimes used to mark off paragraphs and longer sections.

F. Special Phonological Rules

These rules are taken up in detail in appropriate lessons of the Grammar; they are summarized here for convenience in reference and need not be studied before beginning the lessons. The presentation is purely synchronic, dealing only with forms as they can be paired in the language, without reference to antecedent reconstructed forms. The treatment of the latter would take us too far afield.

1. The presence of a guttural consonant *(ʾ ʿ h ḥ x)* often produces an alteration of a given word pattern. Many of these are according to fixed rules:

(a) **-aG-* > *-āG-*, where G is any guttural that closes a syllable. Compare:

Table A: The Ethiopic Alphabet

	Ca	Cu	Ci	Cā	Cē	C,Ce	Co
h	ሀ	ሁ	ሂ	ሃ	ሄ	ህ	ሆ
l	ለ	ሉ	ሊ	ላ	ሌ	ል	ሎ
ḥ	ሐ	ሑ	ሒ	ሓ	ሔ	ሕ	ሖ
m	መ	ሙ	ሚ	ማ	ሜ	ም	ሞ
š	ሠ	ሡ	ሢ	ሣ	ሤ	ሥ	ሦ
r	ረ	ሩ	ሪ	ራ	ሬ	ር	ሮ
s	ሰ	ሱ	ሲ	ሳ	ሴ	ስ	ሶ
q	ቀ	ቁ	ቂ	ቃ	ቄ	ቅ	ቆ
b	በ	ቡ	ቢ	ባ	ቤ	ብ	ቦ
t	ተ	ቱ	ቲ	ታ	ቴ	ት	ቶ
x	ኀ	ኁ	ኂ	ኃ	ኄ	ኅ	ኆ
n	ነ	ኑ	ኒ	ና	ኔ	ን	ኖ
’	አ	ኡ	ኢ	ኣ	ኤ	እ	ኦ
k	ከ	ኩ	ኪ	ካ	ኬ	ክ	ኮ
w	ወ	ዉ	ዊ	ዋ	ዌ	ው	ዎ
‘	ዐ	ዑ	ዒ	ዓ	ዔ	ዕ	ዖ
z	ዘ	ዙ	ዚ	ዛ	ዜ	ዝ	ዞ
y	የ	ዩ	ዪ	ያ	ዬ	ይ	ዮ
d	ደ	ዱ	ዲ	ዳ	ዴ	ድ	ዶ
g	ገ	ጉ	ጊ	ጋ	ጌ	ግ	ጎ
ṭ	ጠ	ጡ	ጢ	ጣ	ጤ	ጥ	ጦ
p	ጰ	ጱ	ጲ	ጳ	ጴ	ጵ	ጶ
ṣ	ጸ	ጹ	ጺ	ጻ	ጼ	ጽ	ጾ
ḍ	ፀ	ፁ	ፂ	ፃ	ፄ	ፅ	ፆ
f	ፈ	ፉ	ፊ	ፋ	ፌ	ፍ	ፎ
ṗ	ፐ	ፑ	ፒ	ፓ	ፔ	ፕ	ፖ

Table B. Labialized Consonants

	Ca	Ci	Cā	Cē	C,Ce
q^W	ቈ	ቊ	ቋ	ቌ	ቍ
x^W	ኈ	ኊ	ኋ	ኌ	ኍ
k^W	ኰ	ኲ	ኳ	ኴ	ኵ
g^W	ጐ	ጒ	ጓ	ጔ	ጕ

Table C. Numerical Signs

1	፩	6	፮	11	፲፩	20	፳	70	፸
2	፪	7	፯	12	፲፪	30	፴	80	፹
3	፫	8	፰	13	፲፫	40	፵	90	፺
4	፬	9	፱	14	፲፬	50	፶	100	፻
5	፭	10	፲	15	፲፭	60	፷	200	፪፻

1000	፲፻
10000	፼
100000	፲፼

Table D. Amharic Modifications

	Ca	Cu	Ci	Cā	Cē	C,Ce	Co
š	ሸ	ሹ	ሺ	ሻ	ሼ	ሽ	ሾ
č	ቸ	ቹ	ቺ	ቻ	ቼ	ች	ቾ
ñ	ኘ	ኙ	ኚ	ኛ	ኜ	ኝ	ኞ
k̲	ኸ	ኹ	ኺ	ኻ	ኼ	ኽ	ኾ
ž	ዠ	ዡ	ዢ	ዣ	ዤ	ዥ	ዦ
j	ጀ	ጁ	ጂ	ጃ	ጄ	ጅ	ጆ
ç̌	ጨ	ጩ	ጪ	ጫ	ጬ	ጭ	ጮ

Pattern	Typical Example	Guttural Example
yeqtal	*yegbar*	*yesmāʿ*
qatl	*gabr*	*bāḥr*
maqtal	*manfas*	*māxdar*
qatalt	*ṣaḥaft*	*samāʿt*
yetqattal	*yetgabbar*	*yetballāʿ*

One important situation where this change does not take place (at least graphically) is after word-initial ʾ:

ʾaqtala	*ʾanbara*	*ʾaʿbaya* (not *ʾāʿbaya*)
ʾaqtāl	*ʾagmāl*	*ʾaʾbān* (not *ʾāʾbān*).

But see below, G2.

(b) In the patterns *-*aG(G)i*- and *-*aG(G)e*-, *a* > *e*:

qatil	*ṭabib*	*lehiq*
yeqattel	*yenabber*	*yelehheq*

Exceptions to this rule are rare. Note, for example, the subjunctive and imperative forms *mahher*, *yemahher* (Lesson 46). The rule does not apply across certain morpheme boundaries (e.g. prefixes, prepositions):

taʾexza	he was taken	not **teʾexza*
ba-ʾegara	at the feet of	not **be-ʾegara*.

(c) In the pattern *-*eG(G)a*-, *e* > *a*

yeqattel	*yenabber*	*yaḥawwer*
qetal	*nebar*	*laʾak*.

Note that this does operate across a morpheme boundary, as in the case of the prefix *ye*- in *yaḥawwer* above. It does not apply, however, across the boundary of a stem and its suffix:

yesammeʿ + *aka* ⟶	*yesammeʿaka*	he will hear you
ʾabāgeʿ + acc. -*a* ⟶	*ʾabāgeʿa*	sheep

(d) The peculiar behavior of the stem vowel before a final guttural radical of a verbal stem is the result of various analogies at work during an earlier stage of the language. In the inflection of the Perfect there is an *e* before the third root consonant when the preceding syllable is long (Cv̄, CvC):

ṣawweʿa	he summoned
ʾasmeʿa	he caused to hear.

This *e* is deleted when the preceding syllable was short (Cv):

samʿa	(not **sameʿa*)	he heard
tasamʿa	(not **tasameʿa*)	he was heard.

This zero or *e* alternates regularly with *ā* when an ending beginning with a consonant is added to the stem:

samʿa but *samāʿku* *ṣawweʿa* but *ṣawwāʿku*.

The *ā* which results from the rule given in paragraph (a) above is regularly replaced by *e* when any vowel is added to the stem:

yesmāʿ but *yesmeʿu*, *yesmeʿani*, etc.

2. The long vowels *u* and *i* may be shortened to *e* when the syllable in which they occur becomes doubly closed by the addition of the feminine ending -*t*. This change is frequent in the case of *u* (see Lesson 17) and rare in the case of *i*:

kebur	+ *t*	⟶	*kebert*	mighty
qeddus	+ *t*	⟶	*qeddest*	holy
lehiq	+ *t*	⟶	*leheqt*	old, eldest.

The long vowel *ā* may remain in such positions or be shortened to *a*:

šannāy	+ *t*	*šannāyt*, *šannayt*	good, beautiful
šalās	+ *t*	*šalast*- (in *šalastū́*)	three
samān	+ *t*	*samānt*- (in *samāntū́*)	eight.

3. The alternations *i*~*ey* and *u*~*ew* occur regularly at the end of verbal stems from roots whose third radical is *w* or *y*. If no inflectional ending or object suffix is added, *u* and *i* are usually written:

yetallu he will follow *yesatti* he will drink

But with the addition of any element beginning with a vowel:

yetallewu	they will follow	*yesatteyu*	they will drink
yetallewani	he will follow me	*yesatteyo*	he will drink it.

But the final syllables of nouns and adjectives are normally written -*ew* and -*ey*:

maxātew lamps *layāley* nights *ʿelew* perverse *lāḥey* beautiful.

With the addition of the feminine ending *-t* to adjectives, *-ewt* regularly becomes *-ut*, as in **ʿelewt* > *ʿelut*. Final *-eyt* may remain, as in *lāḥeyt*, but usually appears as *-it*; this is especially true if *-eyt* results from **-uyt* by rule 2 above:

beluy old, worn out   **beluyt* > **beleyt* > *belit*.

Nouns and adjectives ending in *-āwi* show a frequent variation between *-āwiy-* and *-āwey-* when the plural endings *-ān* and *-āt* are added.

4. In adjectives of the pattern *qetul* from roots whose second radical is *w*, the sequence *-ewu* alternates optionally with *-ewe-* (perhaps to be read as *-ewwe-*), e.g.

mewut or *mew(w)et* dead   *dewuy* or *dew(w)ey* sick.

5. The behavior of final *-aw* and *-ay* is inconsistent. *-aw* at the end of a verb (where *w* is the third radical) may optionally be replaced by *-o*, as in *yetraxxaw* or *yetraxxo* (it will open); *-ay* usually remains in this situation. At the end of a noun, *-aw* and *-ay* usually contract to *-o* and *-ē* respectively, as in *marxo* (for **marxaw*, key) and *ferē* (for **feray*, fruit). When the plural ending *-āt* is added to nouns ending in *-ē*, the result is either *-ēyāt* or *-eyāt* (e.g. *ferēyāt*, *fereyāt*); the "historically correct" form occasionally shows up, as in *dasēt*, pl. *dasayāt*.

6. The treatment of final *-āw* (where *w* is the third root consonant) is also inconsistent: Sometimes it remains, as in *ḥeyāw* (living), and sometimes it is lost, as in *tasfā* (for **tasfāw*, hope), *ʿedā* (for **ʿedāw* debt).

7. Consonant assimilations are relatively rare except for the behavior of prefixal and suffixal *ṭ*:

(a) Suffixal *-t* (a feminine adjectival and nominal ending) is regularly assimilated to a preceding dental stop *d* or *t*.

kebud + *t* ⟶ *kebedt* > *kebedd*
šeṭuṭ + *t* ⟶ *šeṭeṭt* > *šeṭeṭṭ*.

Remember that the Ethiopic script shows no doubling of consonants in any forms.

(b) Prefixal *-et-* (in the Imperfect and Subjunctive forms of Gt, Dt, Lt, Qt, and Glt verbs) is assimilated regularly to a following dental stop or sibilant *(ṭ, d, ḍ, s, š, ṣ, z)*:

**yetsammay* > *yessammay* he will be named
**yeṭṭammaq* > *yeṭṭammaq* he will be baptized.

For further examples see Lesson 44.

8. The *-k-* of the verbal subject suffixes *-ku*, *-ka*, *-ki*, *-kemu*, , *-ken* is regularly assimilated to a preceding *q* or *g*:

**wadaqku* > *wadaqqu* I fell
**xadagka* > *xadagga* you left
**ʿaragkemu* > *ʿaraggemu* you (pl.) went up.

See Lesson 11 (end).

9. In the causative prefix *ʾa-* (see Lesson 26) and the prefix *ʾa-/ʾe-* of the first person (Imperfect and Subjunctive) the ʾ regularly becomes *y* after the proclitic negative *ʾi-*:

ʾafqara he loved	*ʾi-yafqara* he did not love
ʾaḥawwer I shall go	*ʾi-yaḥawwer* I shall not go
ʾenabber I shall sit	*ʾi-yenabber* I shall not sit.

To facilitate recognition, this secondary *-y-* will be transcribed as *-ỷ-* throughout this text.

G. Manuscript Errors and Normalization

The gradual evolution of spoken Geʿez and its ancient sister dialects into the modern languages of Ethiopia led to the introduction of systematic errors into manuscript copying by scribes who applied their own pronunciation to the ancient language and misspelled accordingly. Roughly in chronological order, these errors are the following:

1. The earliest was the confusion of *ḍ* and *ṣ*, as the former merged with the latter. This change was so early, in fact, that it contaminated nearly all manuscripts, and our choice of *ḍ* or *ṣ* (or vice versa) in spelling a particular root is sometimes arbitrary. The normalization of *ḍ* or *ṣ* in this text usually follows that of Dillmann's *Lexicon*, but in a few instances (e.g. *bḍʿ/bṣʿ*, *ḍbʾ/ṣbʾ*) the alternate forms have been retained because they are so frequent.

2. Probably next in order was the loss of contrast between *a* and *ā* after a guttural consonant, with *a* becoming *ā*. The spelling errors produced by this change are ubiquitous: any syllable beginning *Ga-* may be written *Gā-*, and vice versa. This error has been corrected

in our texts. Occasional ambiguities remain, however: e.g. are *se-b(e)-ḥa-t* and *se-b(e)-ḥā-t* the same word? Should the latter be read as *sebbeḥāt*, a D verbal noun?

Because the initial sequence *ʾa-* was later always pronounced as *ʾā-*, the prefixing of the negative *ʾi-* (F,9 above) often resulted in the spelling *ʾi-y̓ā-*:

ʾi-ʾafqara > *ʾi-y̓afqara* spelled *ʾi-yāfqara*
ʾi-ʾaʾmero > *ʾi-y̓aʾmero* spelled *ʾi-yāʾmero* (ignorance).

3. Almost equally common in all but the best manuscripts is the confusion among the three *h*'s *(h ḥ x)*, although a given manuscript may show consistency in the spelling (wrong or right) of a particular root. Here again we have followed the lexical norm established by Dillmann; in only a few roots (e.g. $hg^{w}l$) is there any real uncertainty about the correct form.

4. Many texts show a confusion between *š* and *s*, reflecting the merger of these two sounds in Amharic, as noted above (p.).

5. Perhaps the most recent error is the confusion between ʾ and ʿ, an error which is not present in many manuscripts at all, but frequent in others. Normalization here is not problematic, since the earlier and correct spellings are, for the most part, known.

The cumulative effect of the preceding errors can be quite bewildering unless one has a firm grasp of the forms and lexicon of the older language as it has been recovered by Dillmann and other scholars. The failure of modern editors of Ethiopic texts to normalize spelling is puzzling (unless, of course, a word is unknown or genuinely ambiguous); even more reprehensible is the burdening of a critical apparatus with such trivial and predictable pronunciation errors.

....

Lesson 1

1.1 There is no definite or indefinite article in Ethiopic. Thus,

hagar	a city	or	the city
neguš	a king		the king.

1.2 Prepositions. Most prepositions are written as separate words before the noun they govern:

westa hagar	in/into/to the city
diba dabr	on the mountain.

The exceptions are

ba-	in, with (location, agent, manner)
la-	to, for (dative)
ʾem-	from (ablative, source),

which are always written as a unit with the following word: *baxayl* with strength *(xayl)*, *laneguš* to the king, *ʾemhagar* from the city. For the sake of clarity we shall always transcribe these with hyphens: *ba-xayl*, *la-neguš*, *ʾem-hagar*. There is also an independent (unbound) form of the preposition *ʾem-*, namely *ʾemenna*:

ʾemenna hagar = *ʾem-hagar* from the city.

Ba- and *ʾem-* are freely combined with the other prepositions. *Ba-*, as in *ba-diba* and *ba-westa*, seldom alters the meaning of the second preposition. *ʾEm-* has its usual force: *ʾem-diba* from on, *ʾem-westa* from in. These various compounds will be noted in the vocabularies as they are required.

1.3 Although we shall defer full treatment of the verb until later, it is necessary here to introduce the 3rd person forms of the inflection called the Perfect:

	Singular		Plural	
3rd pers. masc.	*nabara*	he sat	*nabaru*	they (m.) sat
3rd pers. fem.	*nabarat*	she sat	*nabarā*	they (f.) sat

The four endings, *-a*, *-at*, *-u*, *-ā*, are used on all verbs in the language to mark these four forms of the Perfect, regardless of the shape of the stem: *mot-a* he died, *re'y-a* he saw, *'anbar-a* he set, *'astabq^{w}e'-a* he implored. Note that the pronominal subject (he, she, they) is included in the verb form itself and need not be expressed separately. The Ethiopic Perfect corresponds to the English simple past (he went, wrote, etc.) or present perfect (he has gone, he has written, etc.).

The basic lexical form of the Ethiopic verb is the 3rd pers. masc. singular of the Perfect. In the lesson vocabularies and in the Glossary we shall always give the English meaning in the infinitive form; thus: *nabara* to sit.

With verbs of motion the goal is expressed by various prepositions, the most frequent of which are *westa* and *xaba*. *Westa* is used if the goal is a place, as in

Ḥora westa hagar.	He went to the city.

Xaba is used with both persons and places:

Ḥora xaba neguš.	He went to the king.
Ḥora xaba bēt.	He went to the house.

Whether a preposition like *westa* means "to," "into," or "in" depends on the verb with which it is employed: *nabara westa* to dwell in, *bo'a westa* to enter into, *ḥora westa* to go to.

Vocabulary 1

Nouns:

hagar city.
neguš king.
bēt house.
dabr mountain.

Verbs:

nabara to sit, sit down; to stay, remain, continue; to live, dwell.
warada to descend, come down, go down.
'arga to ascend, come up, go up, climb.
ḥora to go.

Prepositions:

'em/'emenna from, out of, away from.
westa or *ba-westa* in, into, to (a place); *'em-westa* from in, from within.
diba or *ba-diba* on, upon, onto; *'em-diba* from on, from upon.

xaba or *ba-xaba* by, with, at, near (person or place); to, toward, unto; *'em-xaba* from with, from the presence of.

ba- in, into; by, with (of agent).

Exercises

A.

1. westa hagar
2. diba dabr
3. 'emenna bēt
4. 'em-westa bēt
5. ba-westa bēt
6. 'em-diba dabr
7. 'em-neguš
8. ba-xaba neguš
9. diba neguš
10. 'em-westa hagar

B.

1. Nabara westa bēt.
2. Nabarat ba-westa bēt.
3. ʻArgu diba dabr.
4. ʻArga westa hagar.
5. ʻArgā xaba bēt.
6. Ḥora westa dabr.
7. Ḥorā westa bēt.
8. Waradu 'em-diba dabr.
9. Waradat 'em-diba bēt.
10. Warada 'emenna hagar.

Lesson 2

2.1 Noun Plurals. In general, the plural of a noun is formed in one of two ways:

a. Pattern replacement: *dabr* ⟶ *ʾadbār*

b. Addition of an ending: *ʿāmat* ⟶ *ʿāmatāt*

Plurals formed by pattern replacement are often referred to as "broken" plurals or "internal" plurals; those with suffixes, as "external" plurals. Because there is no sure way to predict the form of the plural from that of the singular, it is necessary to learn both forms from the outset. These will be given in the lesson vocabularies. Some nouns have more than one plural form, though they may not be of equal frequency.

The patterns used for noun plurals are for the most part distinctive and seldom occur in singular nouns. For reference only, the following list of plural noun types includes all but the rare forms:

qetal	e.g. *ʾegar*	the plural of	*ʾegr*	foot
ʾaqtāl	*ʾadbār*		*dabr*	mountain
ʾaqtul	*ʾahgur*		*hagar*	city
ʾaqtel	*ʾabter*		*batr*	rod, staff
ʾaqtelt	*ʾagbert*		*gabr*	servant
qatalt	*nagašt*		*neguš*	king
$C_1aC_2āC_3eC_4t$	*malāʾekt*		*malʾak*	messenger, angel
$C_1aC_2āC_3eC_4$	*ʾanāqeṣ*		*ʾanqaṣ*	gate
ʾaqātel	*ʾabāgeʿ*		*bagʿ*	sheep

2.2 Syntax. The nominal subject of a verb normally follows it immediately. The problem of the agreement between verb and subject will be discussed in Lesson 5. It is sufficient here to note that nouns denoting male human beings are masculine and those denoting female human beings are feminine. The verb agrees with these nouns in number and gender:

Ḥora neguš.	The king went.	*Ḥoru nagašt.*	The kings went.
Ḥorat beʾsit.	The woman went.	*Ḥorā ʾanest.*	The women went.

See the exercises for further examples.

Vocabulary 2

Nouns:

hagar (pl. *'ahgur*) city.

neguš (pl. *nagašt*) king.

bēt (pl. *'abyāt*) house.

dabr (pl. *'adbār*) mountain.

gabr (pl. *'agbert*) servant.

be'si (pl. *sab'*) man, husband; the pl. also means people in general.

be'sit (pl. *'anest*) woman, wife.

ḥamar (pl. *'aḥmār*) boat, ship (of any size).

Verbs:

maṣ'a to come

waḍ'a to go/come forth, emerge; with *'em*: to leave, depart from; to spring from, originate in.

bo'a to enter *(westa, ba-)*.

wadqa to fall, fall down, collapse.

Adverbs:

heyya/ba-heyya there, in that place; *'em-heyya* from there, thence.

zeyya/ba-zeyya here, in this place; *'em-zeyya* from here, hence.

Conjunction:

wa- and (written as part of the following word, e.g. *be'si wa-be'sit* a man and a woman).

Exercises

A. 1. xaba gabr
2. ba-xaba be'sit
3. diba ḥamar
4. 'emenna be'si
5. diba 'adbār
6. ba-diba 'aḥmār
7. 'em-westa 'abyāt
8. xaba nagašt
9. 'emenna 'ahgur
10. ba-xaba sab'

B. 1. Nabaru 'agbert heyya.
2. Nabarat be'sit ba-heyya.
3. ʻArga be'si diba dabr.
4. Waradu sab' 'em-diba bēt.
5. Ḥoru nagašt westa 'ahgur.
6. Maṣ'a gabr xaba neguš.
7. Maṣ'ā 'anest xaba neguš.
8. Wadqa be'si 'em-diba bēt.
9. Wadqu sab' 'em-diba dabr.
10. Waḍ'u sab' 'em-heyya.
11. ʻArgat 'em-zeyya.
12. Bo'a westa bēt wa-nabara heyya.

13. Warada ’em-westa ’adbār wa-bo’a westa hagar.
14. Maṣ’u westa hagar wa-bo’a xaba negš.
15. Waḍ’u ’agbert ’em-hagar wa-ḥoru westa dabr.
16. Maṣ’ā ’em-heyya wa-nabarā zeyya.
17. Wadqa bēt.
18. ‘Argā ’anest westa ḥamar.

Lesson 3

3.1 Noun Plurals (cont.). The two endings used to form external plurals are *-ān* and *-āt*. *-ān* is, for the most part, restricted to nouns denoting male human beings:

maša̮gger	plural:	*mašaggerān*	fishermen
liq		*liqān*	elders, chiefs.

-āt has no such restriction:

nabiy	plural:	*nabiyāt*	prophets
negešt		*negeštāt*	queens
gadām		*gadāmāt*	wildernesses.

It is by no means uncommon to find broken plurals further pluralized by the ending *-āt*, but because these forms are sporadic and easily identified, they will not be listed in the lesson vocabularies.

Several biconsonantal nouns have plurals ending in *-aw*:

ʾed	pl.	*ʾedaw*	hands	*ʾaf*	pl.	*ʾafaw*	mouths
ʿeḍ		*ʿeḍaw*	trees	*ʾab*		*ʾabaw*	fathers
ʿed		*ʿedaw*	males	*ʾex^{w}*		*ʾaxaw*	brothers.

Beʾsi (man) and *beʾsit* (woman) have the plurals *sabʾ* and *ʾanest* respectively. The word *sabʾ*, which as a plural may be translated "men" or "people," may also be used as a singular noun in the sense of "a man" or "mankind."

3.2 Collectives. Some nouns, formally singular, designate groups or species as well as a single item. For example,

ʿeḍ a tree (pl. *ʿeḍaw*); a group of trees, a grove, woods. It also denotes the material "wood."

ʿof a bird (pl. *ʾaʿwāf*); fowl in general.

ḥezb a people or nation (pl. *ʾaḥzāb*); people (as a plural).

daqiq offspring, progeny, children.

When there is a conflict between form (singular) and meaning (plural), the noun may be construed either way: *maṣʾa ḥezb* or *maṣʾu ḥezb* the people came.

Vocabulary 3

Nouns:

mašagger (pl. *-ān*) fisherman.

liq (pl. *-ān, liqāwent, liqānāt*) elder, chief.

nabiy (pl. *-āt*) prophet.

gadām (pl. *-āt*) wilderness; any remote, uninhabited area.

ḥezb (pl. *ḥezab, 'aḥzāb*) people, nation; crowd; also with the nuance of gentiles in the N. T.

Verbs:

roṣa to run.

gʷayya to flee.

gab'a to return, come/go back.

baṣḥa to arrive.

Preposition:

mesla with, in the company of.

Exercises

1. Roṣu 'agbert 'em-bēt.
2. Gʷayyu sab' westa 'adbār.
3. Gab'u nagašt westa hagar.
4. Baṣḥu ḥezb mesla nabiy.
5. Gʷayya nabiy westa gadām.
6. Gʷayyā 'anest 'emenna bēt.
7. Gab'a mašagger 'emenna ḥamar.
8. Bo'u liqān xaba neguš.
9. Waḍ'a nabiy 'em-hagar.
10. Ḥoru mesla nabiy wa-'agbert.
11. Maṣ'u nabiyāt westa hagar.
12. Nabaru mašaggerān heyya.
13. Nabara liq heyya mesla ḥezb.
14. Gʷayya ḥezb westa gadām wa-nabara heyya.
15. Baṣḥat be'sit xaba bēt.
16. Roṣu 'em-zeyya wa-gʷayyu heyya.
17. Gab'u 'em-heyya wa-nabaru zeyya.
18. Wadqa mašagger 'em-diba ḥamar.

Lesson 4

4.1 The Construct State. A modifying relationship between two nouns is indicated by adding the ending *-a* to the first noun in the sequence $Noun_1$ + $Noun_2$. It is the second noun that modifies, limits, or qualifies the first. $Noun_1$ is said to be in construct with $Noun_2$, or in the construct state. Study the following examples:

negušа hagar	the king of the city
walda neguš	the son *(wald)* of the king
qāla nabiy	the voice *(qāl)* of the prophet
sema malʾak	the name *(sem)* of the angel *(malʾak)*
felsata Bābilon	the Babylonian Exile *(felsat)*
liqa kāhenāt	the chief of the priests *(kāhen)*
maʿāra gadām	wild honey; lit. honey *(maʿār)* of the wilderness
fenota bāḥr	the sea road; lit. the road *(fenot)* of the sea *(bāḥr)*

Most such combinations may be translated, at least roughly, by the use of the preposition "of." This exceedingly common construction will pose little difficulty to the reader; expressions that are not transparent literally will be given in the vocabularies.

Two formal points should be noted:

(a) Most nouns ending in *-i* have their construct in *-ē*:
ṣaḥāfi scribe *ṣaḥāfē ḥezb* the scribe of the people

(b) Nouns ending in the long vowels *-ā*, *-ē*, *-o* remain unchanged in the construct.

The construct state of plural nouns is formed in exactly the same way:

nagašta hagar	the kings of the city
weluda neguš	the sons of the king
qālāta nabiy	the words of the prophet

Construct sequences of three or more nouns occur but are rare. In most instances a subset of the sequence is a fixed expression (i.e. a frequent compound), such as *bēta maqdas* the Temple in Jerusalem, literally "the house of the holy place," in the sequence *tadbāba bēta maqdas* the top *(tadbāb)* of the Temple.

Note also the curious, but not rare, expression

walda ʾegʷāla ʾemma-ḥeyāw the Son of Man,

where *ʾemma ḥeyāw* "the mother *(ʾemm)* of the living *(ḥeyāw)*" is an epithet of Eve, and *ʾegʷāla ʾemma-ḥeyāw*, lit. "the offspring of Eve," denotes mankind. Also in fixed expressions one may find a compound $Noun_2$, such as *samāy wa-medr* heaven and earth in

ʾAmlāka samāy wa-medr the Lord of heaven and earth.

Vocabulary 4

Nouns:

ʿeḍ (pl. *ʿeḍaw*) tree, wood.
fenot (pl. *fenāw, fenāwē*) road, way, path (lit. and fig.).
ʾarwē (pl. *ʾarāwit*) animal, wild beast.
samāy (pl. *-āt*) heaven, sky.
barad hail.
zenām (pl. *-āt*) rain.
qʷaṣl (pl. *ʾaqʷṣel*) leaf, foliage.
bēta neguš palace, royal residence.

Prepositions:

ʾenta via, by way of.
tāḥta under, below.

Adverb:

ʾi- the general negative, prefixed directly to the verb in a verbal sentence.

Exercises

A. 1. neguša hagar
2. hagara neguš
3. bēta neguš
4. fenota dabr
5. gabra nabiy
6. beʾsita mašagger
7. fenota gadām
8. ʾaḥzāba hagar
9. ʾahgura neguš
10. ʾahgura nagašt
11. ḥamara mašaggerān
12. ʾaḥmāra mašagger
13. ʾarāwita dabr
14. ʾarāwita gadām
15. qʷaṣla ʿeḍ
16. ʾaqʷṣela ʿeḍaw

17. ʿeḍawa ʾadbār
18. zenāmāta samāy
19. fenāwē gadām
20. negušа samāyāt

B. 1. Nabara tāḥta ʿeḍ.
2. Gabʾa ʾenta fenota dabr.
3. Wadqa ʾem-westa ʿeḍ.
4. Maṣʾa ʾem-westa samāy.
5. G^{w}ayya ʾemenna ʾarāwita gadām.
6. Warada barad wa-zenām.
7. Ḥora nabiy ʾem-zeyya wa-ʿarga westa samāy.
8. Waḍʾa ʾarwē ʾem-tāḥta bēt.
9. Wadqa ʿeḍ diba bēta nabiy.
10. Gabʾu ʾagberta neguš.
11. Baṣḥā ʾanesta hagar.
12. G^{w}ayyā ʾanesta mašaggerān.
13. Warada zenām ʾem-westa samāy.
14. Ḥora ʾenta fenota gadām.
15. Wadqu ʾaq^{w}ṣela ʿeḍaw westa fenot.

Lesson 5

5.1 Gender. The gender of a given noun is not based on formal criteria, such as the presence or absence of a particular ending. Gender is apparent only in the agreement that exists, for example, between a noun and a modifying adjective or between a noun subject and its verb. When we consistently find *zentu be'si* for "this man" and *zāti be'sit* for "this woman," we may identify *zentu* as the masculine form and *zāti* as the feminine form of the demonstrative adjective. Then, because a noun like *fenot* will appear sometimes with *zentu* and sometimes with *zāti*, we are led to observe that the gender of *fenot* is variable, or perhaps better, irrelevant.

In general, gender usage is fixed (i.e. predictable) only for nouns denoting human beings, where grammatical gender coincides with natural gender (sex). Nearly all other nouns occur in either gender, but for many nouns there is a definite preference. The following rules are sometimes cited in this connection, but they cover an insignificant range of nouns and admit of numerous exceptions:

(a) Nouns denoting the names of months, stars, meteorological phenomena, rivers, metals, and weapons tend to be treated as masculine.

(b) The names of towns, cities, districts, and paired parts of the body tend to be treated as feminine.

In the vocabularies and Glossary the gender of non-personal nouns will be indicated in the following way:

m. or f. alone means that the noun is almost exclusively treated as marked.

m.f. or f.m. means that the noun occurs in both genders, but that the first gender indicated is the more frequent.

These designations must be considered as only approximate, since they would doubtlessly be subject to some revision if a full tabulation were made. Such a study, however, would hardly be worth the enormous effort required, since gender usage varies markedly from one text to another, and in some cases it may even be dependent on the gender of the underlying Greek noun. In other cases, variation in gender appears to have an expressive function (feminine = diminutive, familiar, individualizing) and depends on the personal predilections of a given translator.

The genders of the non-personal nouns in Vocabularies 1-4 are as follows:

hagar f.m.	*ḥamar* f.m.	*fenot* f.m.	*barad* m.
bēt m.f.	*gadām* m.	*ʾarwē* m.f.	*zenām* m.f.
dabr m.	*ʿeḍ* m.f.	*samāy* m.f.	*qʷaṣl* m.f.

5.2 Number. Agreement in number is similar to that of gender. Only nouns denoting human beings regularly have verbal and adjectival agreement in the plural. The plurals of all other nouns may have either singular or plural verbs and modifiers, with no clear preferences.

5.3 Some Demonstrative Adjectives.

this	masc.	*ze-*	fem.	*zā-*
		zentū́		*zātī́*
that	masc.	*weʾétu*	fem.	*yeʾéti*

These regularly precede the noun they modify. *Ze-* and *zā-* are written proclitically *(ze-beʾsi, zā-beʾsit)*, but if preceded by another proclitic element, such as the preposition *ba-*, the two proclitic elements may be written together as a single word: *ba-ze bēt* in this house; *ba-zā hagar* in this city.

Vocabulary 5

Nouns:

makʷannen (pl. *makʷānent*) judge, administrator, high official.

qāl (pl. *-āt*) m.f. voice, word, sound; saying.

nagar (pl. *-āt*) m. speech, account, narrative; thing, affair, situation.

malʾak (pl. *malāʾekt*) angel, messenger.

ṣaḥāfi (pl. *ṣaḥaft*) scribe; a literate (hence learned) person.

wald (pl. *welud*) son, child, boy, lad; the pl. form is also used as a singular.

walatt (pl. *ʾawāled*) daughter, girl.

And the demonstrative adjectives given in the lesson.

Exercises

A. 1. tāḥta zentu ʻeḍ
2. mesla weʼetu ʼarwē
3. ʼenta zā-fenot
4. ʼem-westa zāti hagar
5. ba-westa weʼetu gadām
6. mesla zentu mak^{w}annen
7. ba-xaba ze-nabiy
8. ʼem-ze bēt
9. ba-diba zentu dabr
10. tāḥta yeʼeti ḥamar

B. 1. liqa ṣaḥaft
2. qālāta nabiyāt
3. nagara mak^{w}annen
4. ʼabyāta mak^{w}ānent
5. qāla zentu malʼak
6. walda mašagger
7. weluda ṣaḥāfi
8. ʼawāleda weʼetu mak^{w}annen
9. ʼarāwita zentu dabr
10. ṣaḥāfē neguš

C. 1. ʼI-wadqu ʼaq^{w}ṣela yeʼeti ʻeḍ.
2. Warada zenām ʼem-westa samāy wa-ʼi-warada barad.
3. ʻArga qālāta nabiy westa samāy.
4. Ḥorat walatta neguš xaba weʼetu nabiy.
5. Maṣʼa beʼsē yeʼeti beʼsit xaba neguš.
6. Waḍʼa malʼak ʼem-westa samāy wa-baṣḥa xaba bēta yeʼeti beʼsit.
7. Roṣu weluda mak^{w}annen westa fenota hagar.
8. Wadqa walda weʼetu beʼsi ʼem-westa zentu ʻeḍ.
9. Baṣḥu malāʼekta samāy westa hagar wa-nabaru heyya.
10. ʼI-ḥoru sabʼ xaba weʼetu mak^{w}annen.

Lesson 6

6.1 The Personal Pronouns (Independent Form).

	Singular		Plural	
1st pers. common gender	*ʾána*	I	*néḥna*	we
2nd pers. masculine	*ʾánta*	you	*ʾantému*	you
2nd pers. feminine	*ʾánti*	you	*ʾantén*	you
3rd pers. masculine	*weʾétu*	he, it	*ʾemuntú*	they
3rd pers. feminine	*yeʾéti*	she, it	*ʾemāntú*	they

The form *weʾetomu* is also used for the 3rd pers. masc. *and* fem. plural. Readers unfamiliar with other Semitic languages should make special note of the gender distinction in the 2nd person; this feature is present in all the pronominal inflections in the language.

6.2 Non-verbal Sentences with a Nominal Predicate.

a. The subject is a personal pronoun: $\text{Noun}_{\text{pred.}} + \text{Pronoun}_{\text{subj.}}$

Beʾsi ʾana.	I am a man.
Beʾsit ʾanti.	You are a woman.
Maš̌agger weʾetu.	He is a fisherman.
Mak^{w}ānent ʾemuntu.	They are judges.
Nabiyāt neḥna.	We are prophets.
ʾIyarusālēm yeʾeti.	It is Jerusalem.

For special emphasis the pronoun may be duplicated at the head of the clause:

ʾAna beʾsi ʾana. I am a man.

Weʾetu is sometimes used as a neutralized copula in sentences of this type, regardless of the person, number, or gender of the real pronominal subject. One may thus find: *ʾAna mak^{w}annen weʾetu*, *ʾAnta mak^{w}annen weʾetu*, etc. or *ʾAna weʾetu mak^{w}annen*, etc. Such usages vary from text to text, but they are not rare constructions. They should be viewed as a replacement of the constructions given above by those of the following section, with the personal pronouns simply taking the place of the nominal subject.

b. If the subject is a noun, the distinction between subject and predicate can be made only on the basis of the semantics of the context. There are three possible forms for such predications:

$Noun_1$ + $Noun_2$	*Yoḥannes makʷannen.*
$Noun_1$ + $Noun_2$ + 3rd pers. pron.	*Yoḥannes makʷannen we'etu.*
$Noun_1$ + 3rd pers. pron. + $Noun_2$	*Yoḥannes we'etu makʷannen.*

These may all be translated as "John is a/the judge." Note especially the use of the 3rd pers. pronoun as a copula; there will usually be agreement in number and gender if the nouns denote human being, but, as noted above, there is a tendency for *we'etu* to be generalized for all purposes as a neutral copula.

c. If the subject is a demonstrative pronoun (note that the words given as demonstrative adjectives in the preceding lesson also function as pronouns), the most frequent word order is Dem. pron. + 3rd pers. pron. + Noun:

Zentu we'etu 'orit wa-nabiyāt.	This is the Law and the Prophets.
Zāti ye'eti walatta negušˇ.	This is the daughter of the king.
'Ellu 'emuntu weluda neguš.	These are the sons of the king.

6.3 The Plural Demonstratives.

these	masc.	*'ellú, 'ellontú*
	fem.	*'ellā́, 'ellāntú*
those	masc.	*'emuntú*
	fem.	*'emāntú*

Vocabulary 6

Nouns:

ḥayq (pl. *-āt*) shore (of sea or lake).

ʿed (pl. *ʿedaw*) coll. men, males; the menfolk (of a given community); also used as a plural of *be'si*.

'emm (pl. *-āt*) mother.

'ab (pl. *'abaw*) father, forefather, ancestor; *bēta 'ab* family.

met (pl. *'amtāt*) husband.

daqiq (coll.) children, offspring, progeny.

negešt (pl. *-āt*) queen.

Conjunction:

'allā but (after a preceding negative clause).

Proper Names:

Yoḥannes John.

'Egzi'abḥēr God (cannot, as a proper name, be used in the construct state).

'Amlāk the Lord (may, as an epithet, be used in construct; e.g. *'Amlāka samāy* the Lord of Heaven).

'Esrā'ēl Israel. *Daqiqa 'Esrā'ēl* the Children of Israel, the Israelites.

And the Independent Personal Pronouns given in the lesson.

Exercises

A. 1. Ṣaḥāfi 'ana.
2. 'Anest 'emāntu.
3. Mašaggerān neḥna.
4. 'Edawa hagar neḥna.
5. Mak^{w}annen 'anta.
6. Gabra neguš 'anta.
7. Be'sita nabiy 'anti.
8. 'Anesta mašaggerān 'anten.
9. Malā'ekta 'Egzi'abḥēr 'antemu.
10. Daqiqa 'Esrā'ēl 'emuntu.
11. 'Emma Yoḥannes ye'eti.
12. 'Aba negešt we'etu.
13. Negešta zāti hagar ye'eti.
14. 'Aba 'emuntu welud we'etu.
15. Ḥamara 'ellu mašaggerān ye'eti.
16. Daqiqa zentu gabr 'emuntu.
17. 'Aq^{w}ṣela zentu 'eḍ we'etu.
18. Meta zāti be'sit we'etu.

B. 1. 'Ellu 'emuntu sab'a zāti hagar.
2. 'Ellontu 'emuntu mak^{w}ānent.
3. 'Ellāntu 'emāntu 'anesta neguš.
4. 'Ellu 'emuntu liqāna ḥezb.
5. Ze-we'etu nabiya 'Egzi'abḥēr.
6. Zāti ye'eti 'emma 'ellāntu 'awāled.
7. 'Ellontu 'emuntu 'amtāta 'anest.
8. Zentu we'etu nagara 'Amlāk.
9. Ellu 'emuntu daqiqa mak^{w}annen.
10. Neḥna nabiyāta 'Egzi'abḥēr neḥna.
11. 'Antemu ṣaḥaft 'antemu.
12. Ze-we'etu gadām, wa-'ellu 'emuntu 'arāwita gadām.
13. 'Ellu sab' 'emuntu 'amtāta 'emāntu 'anest.
14. Ze-we'etu 'Amlāka samāy.
15. Zāti ye'eti fenota gadām.

C. 1. G^{w}ayyā 'ellā 'anest 'em-hagar.

2. 'I-g^{w}ayyu 'amtāta 'anest, 'allā nabaru westa hagar.

3. Bo'u daqiqa we'etu mak^{w}annen xaba neguš.

4. Gab'at 'emma zentu gabr 'em-ye'eti hagar.

5. Warada barad wa-zenām diba 'abyāta zāti hagar.

6. Baṣḥa zentu neguš mesla negešt xaba hagar.

7. 'I-nabaru weluda hagar heyya, 'allā roṣu westa ḥayq.

8. Gab'u 'emuntu sab' 'em-'adbār.

9. ʻArga 'em-westa ḥayq wa-bo'a westa hagar.

10. Baṣḥat 'aḥmāra 'emuntu mašaggerān xaba ḥayq.

Lesson 7

7.1 The Accusative Case. The accusative is the only case marked by a special ending and is used primarily as the direct object of a transitive verb. The ending is usually *-a* on both singular and plural nouns:

Ḥanaṣa bēta.	He built a house.
Ḥanaṣa ʾabyāta.	He built houses.

The following exceptions are to be noted:

(a) Final *-i* is replaced by *-ē*:

Reʾya beʾsē.	He saw a man.

(b) Final *-ā*, *-ē*, and *-o* undergo no change:

Rakaba marxo.	He found a key *(marxo)*.
Reʾya ʿāšā.	He saw a fish *(ʿāšā)*.
Našʾa ferē.	He took the fruit *(ferē)*.

(c) Personal names and place names are either left uninflected or take the ending *-há*:

Dāwit walada Salomonhā.	David begot Solomon.

Because a noun in construct already has an ending identical to that of the accusative case, there is no further change when such a noun is used as the direct object:

Rakaba bēta ṣaḥāfi.	He found the scribe's house.

7.2 Word Order. When there is no special emphasis or contrast desired, the normal order with a transitive verb is Verb + Subject + Object, as in

Takala beʾsi ʿeḍa.	The man planted a tree.

7.3 The Accusative of Goal. The accusative case is used also to express goal with verbs of motion:

Boʾa hagara.	He entered the city.
Ḥora ʾadbāra.	He went to the mountains.

All such accusatives, unlike the direct object, may be replaced by appropriate prepositional phrases *(westa hagar, westa ʾadbār)* without altering the meaning. Occasionally the accusative is used to indicate static position, as in

Nabara gadāma. He dwelt in the wilderness.

But this is rare, and a prepositional phrase *(ba-westa gadām)* is preferred.

7.4 The Accusative Forms of the Demonstratives.

zentú	acc. *zánta*		*ʾellāntú*	acc. *ʾellā́nta*
zātí	*zā́ta*		*weʾétu*	*weʾéta*
ze-	*za-*		*yeʾéti*	*yeʾéta*
ʾellontú	*ʾellónta*			

Zā-, *ʾellú*, and *ʾellā́* have no distinct accusative forms, nor do the personal pronouns *ʾemuntú* and *ʾemāntú* when used demonstratively as direct objects.

Vocabulary 7

Nouns:

ṣebāḥ (pl. *-āt*) m.f. (early) morning; the east.
mesēt (pl. *-āt*) evening, twilight.
wayn (pl. *ʾawyān*) m. vine; wine.
ʿaṣad (pl. *ʾaʿṣād*, *-āt*) m.f. any circumscribed area: courtyard, atrium; pen, stall; field, farm; village. *ʿaṣada wayn* vineyard.

Verbs:

reʾya to see.
ḥanaṣa to build, construct.
qatala to kill, murder.
rakaba to find, come upon; to acquire.
sadada to persecute; to drive out, banish, exile; to excommunicate; to divorce (a wife).
takala to plant; to fix in, implant.

Proper Names:

Kerestiyān (pl.) Christians. *bēta Kerestiyān* (pl. *bēta Kerestiyānāt*, *ʾabyāta Kerestiyānāt*) church; the Church.

Exercises

A. 1. Ḥanaṣu 'abyāta ba-westa hagar.
2. Qatalu negušа wa-negešta.
3. Takalu 'eḍawa heyya.
4. Re'yu 'adbāra.
5. Sadadu 'agberta 'em-westa bēt.
6. Qatalu Kerestiyāna ba-westa 'ellā 'ahgur.
7. 'I-rakabu 'aḥmāra mašaggerān.
8. Sadada liqāna ḥezb 'em-hagar.
9. Qatala zanta nabiya.
10. Takala 'aṣada wayn westa 'adbār.
11. Rakaba 'arwē ba-westa fenot.
12. Re'ya malā'ekta westa samāy.
13. Ḥanaṣa hagara ba-westa we'etu ḥayq.
14. 'I-rakaba 'edawa hagar.
15. Sadadu Kerestiyāna 'em-'abyāta Kerestiyānāt.

B. 1. Ba-ṣebāḥ ḥora 'aṣada mesla daqiqa mak^{w}annen.
2. Ba-mesēt gab'u 'em-heyya hagara.
3. Nabara heyya ba-ṣebāḥ wa-ba-mesēt.
4. Re'yu zenāma wa-barada wa-g^{w}ayyu.
5. Rakaba ṣaḥafta ba-westa bēta neguš.
6. G^{w}ayyat negešt bēta Kerestiyān ba-ṣebāḥ.
7. Sadada we'eta nabiya 'em-westa hagar.
8. Gab'a gadāma ba-mesēt.
9. Rakabu wayna westa we'etu bēt.
10. 'I-ḥanaṣu 'abyāta, 'allā nabaru ba-westa gadām mesla 'arāwit.
11. 'I-rakabu zāta ḥamara.
12. Roṣu 'amtāta 'anest ḥayqa.

Lesson 8

8.1 Interrogative Pronouns and Adjectives:

		accusative:
who?	*mannú*	*mánna*
what?	*ment*	*ménta*
which?	*ʾayy* (pl. *ʾayyāt*)	*ʾáyya* (pl. *ʾayyāta*)

These normally stand first in a clause unless governed by a preposition or in construct sequence with a preceding noun. Examples:

Mannu weʾetu zentu beʾsi?	Who is this man?
Manna qatalu?	Whom did they kill?
Ment weʾetu zentu?	What is this?
Menta rakaba?	What did he find?
ʾAyy hagar zāti?	Which city is this?
ʾAyya hagara ḥanaṣu?	Which city did they build?
Xaba mannu g^wayyu?	To whom did they flee?
Walda mannu ʾanta?	Whose son are you?
Baʾenta ment ḥora?	Why (lit. because of what) did he go?

There is also a rather rare specific plural for *mannu*, namely *ʾella mannú*:

ʾElla mannu ʾemuntu?	Who are they?

8.2 Interrogative Adverbs.

where?	*ʾaytē, ba-ʾaytē*	how?	*ʾefo*
whence?	*ʾem-ʾaytē*	why?	*la-ment, baʾenta ment*
when?	*māʾzē*		

These also usually stand first in a clause.

8.3 The Particles *-nu* and *-hu*. Any clause may be converted into question form by adding *-nu* (less frequently *-hu*) to the first word or phrase. Because these particles are in fact attached to the element of the sentence around which the interrogation centers, their use often requires a departure from normal word order:

ʾAnta-nu mak^{w}annen?	Are *you* a judge?
Zanta-nu reʾya?	Did he see *this*?
Neguš-nu maṣʾa?	Did the *king* come?

-*nu* is very frequently attached to the interrogative words (other than *mannu*) of the preceding paragraphs:

Menta-nu re'ya?	What did he see?
'Aytē-nu rakaba walda?	Where did he find the child?

8.4 The Remote Demonstratives. There is a second group of demonstrative pronouns/adjectives, much less frequent than the *we'etu/ ye'eti* group, used to indicate a more remote location or reference in relationship to the speaker and his audience. These correspond to English "that, that ... there, that ... yonder."

m.s. *zekú* (acc. *zék^{w}a*)
zektú (acc. *zékta*)
zek^{w}tú (acc. *zék^{w}ta*)

f.s. *'entekú* c.pl. *'ellekú*
'entāktî (acc. *'entâkta*) *'ellektú* (acc. *'elléкta*)
'ellek^{w}tú (acc. *'ellék^{w}ta*)

These demonstratives are sometimes employed with a slightly pejorative or disdainful nuance.

8.5 Accusative of Time. Words designating periods of time may be used adverbially in the accusative case to indicate the time when an action took place. Thus, *mesēta* = *ba-mesēt* in the evening, *ṣebāḥa* = *ba-ṣebāḥ* in the morning.

Vocabulary 8

Nouns:

lēlit (pl. *layāley*) m.f. night. *lēlita* = *ba-lēlit* at night, during the night.

Verbs:

kona to be, to become. Usually followed by a predicate noun or adjective in the accusative case: *kona kāhena* he was/became a priest. *Kona* may also be used impersonally: there/it was/ became. In this usage a following noun may be accusative (the predicate) or non-accusative (the subject): *kona lēlit(a)* it was night, it became night; *kona barad(a)* there was hail.

šēṭa to sell (to: *xaba, la-*).

gabra to act, work, function; to make, fashion, create, produce; to do, perform, enact, carry out.

Other:

la- (prep.) to, for (in the dative sense).

ba'enta (prep.) about, concerning; because of, on account of; for the sake of. *ba'enta ment* why? for what reason? *ba'enta-ze* because of this, thus, therefore.

Exercises

A. 1. Mannu we'etu zentu be'si? Mak^{w}annena zāti hagar we'etu.
2. Menta re'ya ba-westa 'adbār? Re'ya 'arāwita.
3. Mannu g^{w}ayya ba-lēlit? G^{w}ayyat negešt ba-lēlit.
4. 'Aytē g^{w}ayyat negešt? G^{w}ayyat gadāma.
5. 'Em-'ayy hagar g^{w}ayyat? G^{w}ayyat 'em-zāti hagar.
6. Ment we'etu zentu? Zentu we'etu ʻaṣada wayn.
7. Menta takalu zeyya? Takalu 'awyāna zeyya.
8. 'Ella mannu takalu 'ellu ʻeḍawa? Takalu ʻedawa hagar 'ellu ʻeḍawa.
9. 'Efo ḥora heyya? Ḥora heyya 'enta ye'eti fenot.
10. Mannu gabra zāta fenota? Gabru sab'a hagar zāta fenota.
11. Ba'enta mannu gabru zanta? Zanta gabru la-ḥezba hagar.
12. Mannu gabra zāta ḥamara? Zāta gabra we'etu mašagger.
13. Mā'zē ḥora hagara? Ḥora mesēta.
14. Mā'zē wadqa zeku ʻeḍ? Wadqa ba-lēlit.
15. La-mannu šēṭa zanta bēta? Šēṭa zanta bēta la-mak^{w}annen.
16. Ba'enta ment sadada Kerestiyāna?

B. 1. Mannu 'anta? 'Ana nabiya 'Egzi'abḥēr 'ana.
2. Xaba mannu šēṭa ḥamara? Šēṭa ḥamara xaba walda mak^{w}annen.
3. Manna sadadu 'em-hagar? Sadadu Kerestiyāna.
4. Menta-nu ḥanaṣu heyya? Ḥanaṣu bēta Kerestiyān.
5. Mannu kona nabiya? Kona Yoḥannes nabiya.
6. Kona walda ṣaḥāfi mak^{w}annena.
7. Konu ḥezba 'enteku hagar Kerestiyāna.
8. La-ment kona ṣaḥāfē?
9. Ba'enta-ze waḍ'u 'em-hagar wa-'i-gab'u.
10. Mannu gabra samāya? Gabra 'Egzi'abḥēr samāya.
11. Ment-nu warada 'em-samāy? Warada zenām.
12. 'Ayya bēta šēṭu? Zanta bēta šēṭu.

13. Menta-nu kona ba-ye'eti lēlit? Ba-ye'eti lēlit kona zenāma wa-barada.
14. 'Ayyāta 'ahgura ḥanaṣu? Ḥanaṣu 'elleku 'ahgura.
15. Manna sadadu 'em-bēta Kerestiyān? Sadadu 'ellonta nagašta.
16. Negeštāta-nu sadadu? 'I-sadadu negeštāta.
17. Ḥora-nu mesla ḥezb? Ḥora mesla ḥezb wa-mesla 'agbert.

Lesson 9

9.1 The Noun with Pronominal Suffixes. Pronominal possession is indicated by a series of suffixes attached directly to the noun. There are slight variations depending on whether the noun stem ends in a vowel or consonant.

(a) Singular nouns ending in a consonant (e.g. *hagar* city):

my city	*hagaréya*	accusative:	*hagaréya*
your (m.s.) city	*hagaréka*		*hagaráka*
your (f.s.) city	*hagaréki*		*hagaráki*
his city	*hagarú*		*hagaró*
her city	*hagarā́*		*hagarā́*
our city	*hagaréna*		*hagarána*
your (m.pl.) city	*hagarekému*		*hagarakému*
your (f.pl.) city	*hagarekén*		*hagarakén*
their (m.) city	*hagarómu*		*hagarómu*
their (f.) city	*hagarón*		*hagarón*

Note especially the *-u/-o* contrast in the 3rd pers. masc. sing. and the lack of a distinct accusative form in the 1st pers. sing. [In the traditional pronunciation the *-k-* of *-kemu* (and sometimes, of *-ken*) is doubled in all of the paradigms given in this lesson.]

(b) Singular nouns ending in *-i*, accusative *-ē* (e.g. *ṣaḥāfi*, *ṣaḥāfē* scribe):

my scribe	*ṣaḥāfíya*	accusative:	*ṣaḥāfíya*
your (m.s.) scribe	*ṣaḥāfíka*		*ṣaḥāfḗka*
your (f.s.) scribe	*ṣaḥāfíki*		*ṣaḥāfḗki*
his scribe	*ṣaḥāfihú*		*ṣaḥāfihú*
her scribe	*ṣaḥāfihā́*		*ṣaḥāfihā́*
our scribe	*ṣaḥāfína*		*ṣaḥāfína*
your (m.pl.) scribe	*ṣaḥāfikému*		*ṣaḥāfēkému*
your (f.pl.) scribe	*ṣaḥāfikén*		*ṣaḥāfēkén*
their (m.) scribe	*ṣaḥāfihómu*		*ṣaḥāfihómu*
their (f.) scribe	*ṣaḥāfihón*		*ṣaḥāfihón*

Note that the distinct accusative ending is retained only before the suffixes of the 2nd person.

(c) Singular nouns ending in a long vowel other than *-i* (e.g. *mendābē*, affliction):

my affliction	*mendābḗya*	accusative:	*mendābḗya*
your (m.s.) affliction	*mendābḗka* etc.		*mendābḗka* etc.

The suffixes are like those on *ṣaḥāfi* above, with no change whatever in the final stem vowel of the noun.

(d) Plural nouns. All plural nouns have a suffix *-i-* added to the stem before the pronominal suffixes. The resulting inflection is like that of the non-accusative forms of *ṣaḥāfi* above, except that the endings *-íya* and *-íki* usually appear as *-éya* and *-éki* respectively. There are no distinct accusative forms.

my cities	*ʾahguríya/ʾahguréya*
your (m.s.) cities	*ʾahguríka*
your (f.s.) cities	*ʾahguríki/ʾahguréki* etc.

(e) Collective nouns, like *daqiq*, are usually treated as singular (no *-i-*) before the pronominal suffixes; thus, *daqiqu*, not **daqiqihu*. Real plural forms, however, sporadically appear without the characteristic *-i-*, e.g. *liqānu* his elders (for *liqānihu*). Conversely, many singular nouns which superficially resemble plural forms may take the *-i-* of the plural; this is especially true of singular nouns with *-ā-* in the final stem syllable (notably *-ān*) and nouns ending in *-at* after a guttural consonant (and hence pronounced *-āt*; see p. 13).

(f) The four nouns *ʾab* (father), *ʾex*^{w} (brother), *ḥam* (father-in-law), and *ʾaf* (mouth) have extended forms in *-u-* (acc. *-ā-*) in the singular before the pronominal suffixes. Inflection is like that of *mendābē* above:

	ʾabuya...	*ʾexuya...*	*ḥamuya...*	*ʾafuya...*
acc.	*ʾabāya...*	*ʾex*^{w}*āya...*	*ḥamāya...*	*ʾafāya...*

The accusative forms are often replaced by the non-accusative.

(g) The noun *ʾed* (hand) appears in the singular with *-ē-* before suffixes: *ʾedēya*, *ʾedēka*, *ʾedēki*, *ʾedēhu*, *ʾedēhā* etc.

Vocabulary 9

Nouns:

ʾex^{w} (pl. *ʾaxaw*) brother. The acc. may be written *ʾex*^{w}*a* or *ʾexwa*.

ʾext (pl. *ʾaxāt*) sister.

medr (pl. *-āt*, *ʾamdār*) f.m. the earth; earth, ground, soil; land, district, country. *medra ṣebāḥ* eastern country. *ʾarwē medr* a snake.

beḥēr (pl. *baḥāwert*) m. region, province, district. *beḥēra ṣebāḥ* eastern region.

wangēl m.f. gospel.

mot m.f. death.

Verbs:

sakaba to lie, lie down.

mota to die.

sabaka to preach (dir. obj. in acc. or with *ba-*: *sabaka ba-wangēl* he preached the gospel).

ḥazana to be/become sad.

Other:

ʾemze (adv.) then, next, thereupon.

dexra (prep.) behind, in back of; *ba-dexra* idem; *ʾem-dexra* from behind, after (of time). *ʾem-dexra* (conj.) after. *dexra* (adv.) afterwards. *ʾemdexra-ze* afterwards.

Exercises

A. 1. gabreya	5. be’siteka	9. qālu	13. ‘aṣadomu
2. hagareya	6. be’siki	10. nagarātihu	14. ’a‘ṣādihomu
3. negušena	7. ’anestihomu	11. ṣaḥāfika	15. daqiqomu
4. bētena	8. liqānikemu	12. ṣaḥaftika	16. weludihomu

B. 1. bēta ’exuya	6. liqāna ḥezbena	11. zenāmāta beḥēru
2. ḥamara ’abuya	7. nagašta ’amdārihomu	12. nagara malā’ektihu
3. qālāta ’emmeya	8. ’ahgura medrekemu	13. ’amtāta ’awāledihā
4. mota ’exteya	9. baḥāwerta medromu	14. ’amdāra ṣebāḥ
5. ’agberta bētena	10. qālāta nabiyātihomu	15. ’arāwita medr

C. 1. Zentu we'etu 'exuka.

2. 'Aytē 'abuka?

3. Mannu we'etu mak^{w}anneneka?

4. 'Entākti ye'eti walatta 'exteya.

5. 'Ellu 'emuntu weluda 'ẹxuki.

6. Zentu we'etu qālāta 'abawina.

7. 'Aytē we'etu bēta 'abukemu?

8. Zentu we'etu 'arwē medr.

9. Yoḥannes mak^{w}annenomu we'etu.

10. Mannu we'etu ṣaḥāfika?

D. 1. Sakaba westa bēta 'exuhu.

2. Sabaka ba-wangēl westa 'emuntu baḥāwert.

3. Sakabu ʻedaw tāḥta ʻeḍaw.

4. Sabaku nagarāta wangēlu westa ye'eti hagar.

5. Ḥazanat ba'enta mota metā.

6. Ḥazana metā ba'enta motā.

7. Ḥazanā ba'enta mota 'amtātihon.

8. Wa-'emdexra mota metā gab'at xaba hagarā.

9. Wa-dexra mota metā.

10. Wa-'emze ḥorat gadāma lēlita wa-nabarat heyya.

11. Wa-'emdexra-ze waḍ'u 'em-heyya wa-ḥoru beḥēromu.

12. Mannu ḥanaṣa bētaka?

13. Qatalu ṣaḥaftina wa-'agbertina.

14. La-ment qatalu gabraka?

15. Menta gabra gabreka 'emdexra-ze?

16. 'Aytē rakabu ḥamaraka?

17. Mā'zē re'yu 'ex^{w}āka?

18. Mannu qatala 'ex^{w}āhu?

19. 'I-rakaba 'abāhu heyya.

20. Sabaka wangēlo heyya.

21. Šēṭa bēto la-ṣaḥāfi.

22. Manna sadada 'em-medreka?

23. Mannu g^{w}ayya medraka?

24. 'I-kona gabraka.

25. 'I-konu 'agbertina.

Lesson 10

10.1 Prepositions with Pronominal Suffixes. The pronominal object of a preposition is expressed by adding the suffixes of Lesson 9 to a presuffixal form of the preposition. This most commonly ends in -ē- and requires the forms of the suffixes after a vowel (cf. *ṣaḥāfi*):

ʾemenna:	*ʾemennēya, ʾemennēka, ʾemennēki,* etc.
diba:	*dibēya, dibēka, dibēki,* etc.
tāḥta:	*tāḥtēya, tāḥtēka, tāḥtēki,* etc.

and likewise for the prepositions *xaba/xabēya, mesla/meslēya, qedma/qedmēya* (before), *māʾkala/māʾkalēya* (among), *mangala/mangalēya* (toward), *dexra/dexrēya,* and *lāʿla/lāʿlēya* (upon). Occasionally one encounters one or another of these prepositions without the presuffixal -ē-; this is especially true of *māʾkala* before the 3rd person suffixes, where it may still be viewed as a simple noun: *ba-māʾkalomu* in their midst. Even more rarely, the simple prepositions may appear with final -ē, such as *xabē, dibē,* etc.

The three prepositions *westa, baʾenta,* and *kama* (like), differ from the preceding:

westa:	*westēteya, westēteka, westēteki, westētu,* etc., as though on a singular noun *westēt.*
baʾenta:	*baʾentiʾāya, baʾentiʾāka, baʾentiʾāki, baʾentiʾāhū* etc., on the stem *baʾentiʾa-.*
kama:	*kamāya, kamāka, kamāki, kamāhū* etc., on the stem *kamā-.*

Ba- and *la-* with suffixes will be given in a later lesson. *ʾEnta* and *ʾeska* (until) do not occur with suffixes.

10.2 The *waldu la-negus̆* Construction. Possession by a specific person may be expressed by the following very frequent construction, where the possessor is indicated first by the appropriate pronominal suffix of the third person and then introduced by the preposition *la-*:

waldu la-negus̆	the son of the king
bētā la-beʾsit	the house of the woman

faqādomu la-nabiyāt the wish of the prophets

The question naturally arises as to the difference between the simple construct *walda neguš* and the above construction. Although some study has been devoted to this problem, no rules can be given to account for every single example; this is hardly surprising in view of the heterogeneity of the material at our disposal. In essence, however,

(1) The *waldu la-negušs* construction is <u>*marked*</u> as definite and specific and can be used only when the second noun denotes a specific (as opposed to a generic) entity.

(2) The construct sequence *walda negušs* is <u>*unmarked*</u> in regard to definiteness and specificity and may be used in place of *waldu la-negušs* wherever the latter occurs.

Thus, *waldu la-negušs* can mean only "the king's son," but *walda negušs* may mean "a king's son, the king's son" or simply "a prince." Stylistically, *waldu la-negušs* is more flexible than the fixed and inseparable construct sequence; the elements may be transposed *(la-negušs waldu)* or separated (*Waldu 'anta la-'Egzi'abḥēr* You are the Son of God). It is probable that the construction originated as *la-negušs*... *waldu* ..., where *la-* served, not as a dative preposition, but as a marker of topicalization, and the suffix on the noun was actually resumptive (as for the king, ... his son...). It is by no means uncommon to find this word order, even with the initial *la-* omitted.

Although the *waldu la-negušs* construction is used extensively for personal possession, it is not restricted thereto, as our remarks would indicate. Note, for example,

hag^{w}lā la-hagar	the destruction of the city
'adyāmihu la-Yordānos	the districts of the Jordan.

Occasionally this construction is used between a preposition and a governed noun: *dibēhomu la-ḥezb* = *diba ḥezb*.

10.3 *K^{w}ell-*. The quantifier *k^{w}ell-*, corresponding to English "each, every, all," always requires a pronominal suffix. It may be used alone, as in

k^{w}ellena	all of us
k^{w}ellomu	all of them,

or in apposition to another pronominal element, as in

lakemu k^w*ellekemu*	to all of you
ḥoru k^w*ellomu*	they all went.

The 3rd pers. masc. singular form (k^w*ellu*, acc. k^w*ello*) is used independently in the sense "everything, everybody":

K^w*ellu delew.*	Everything is ready *(delew)*.
Wahabku lotu k^w*ello.*	I gave him everything.
ba-gaṣṣa k^w*ellu*	in the presence of everyone.

The 3rd person forms are used appositionally before a noun. When the noun is non-personal, whether singular or plural, the singular forms of k^w*ell-* are normal:

k^w*ellā hagar*	all the city, the whole city; each city
k^w*ellā ʾahgur*	all the cities
k^w*ellu baḥāwert*	all the districts.

Plural personal nouns may take either singular or plural forms of k^w*ell-*:

k^w*ellu*/k^w*ellomu nabiyāt*	all the prophets.

The demonstrative pronouns *ze-* and *zentu* regularly precede k^w*ell-*:

zentu k^w*ellu*	all this
ze-k^w*ellu beḥēr*	this whole district, all of this district

Vocabulary 10

Nouns:

ʿelat (pl. *-āt*) f.m. day; less specifically, time. k^w*ello ʿelata* every day, all day.

maʿālt (pl. *mawāʿel*) m.f. day, daytime. *maʿālta* during the day. The plural *mawāʿel* is commonly regarded as the plural of *ʿelat* as well and is more frequent than *ʿelatāt*. *Mawāʿel* frequently has the more general sense of "period of time, era."

ʾamir m.f. day. Used only in certain fixed expressions: *ʾem-/ʾeska weʾetu/yeʾeti ʾamir* from/until that day (past or future); *weʾeta/yeʾeta ʾamira* on that day; k^w*ello ʾamira* every day, all day.

Verbs:

qarba to draw near, approach *(xaba, westa, la-)*.

xalafa to pass; to pass by *('enta, 'enta xaba)*, pass through *('enta westa)*, pass among *('enta mā'kala)*, pass away from, leave *('em-, 'em-xaba)*; to perish.

bakaya to weep, mourn (over: *diba, lā'la, ba'enta*).

Prepositions:

mā'kala among, in the midst of. *ba-mā'kala* idem. *'em-mā'kala* from among.

'eska until, up to, as far as.

lā'la on, upon; (motion down) onto; over, above, about, concerning. Partially synonymous with *diba*, with which it is often interchangeable.

qedma before (spatial), in the presence of. *ba-qedma* idem. *'em-qedma* from before, from the presence of; before (of time), prior to. *qedma* (adv.) previously, beforehand.

Exercises

A. Translate the following. Replace the phrase governed by the preposition with the appropriate pronominal suffix.

1. mesla 'axawihu
2. 'emenna 'amdārihomu
3. diba wangēlena
4. ba'enta motomu
5. westa baḥāwertihomu
6. 'eska zāti 'elat
7. ba'enta 'axāteya
8. 'eska we'etu lēlit
9. westa beḥēra ṣebāḥ
10. diba zentu wayn
11. ba-mā'kala 'a'ṣādātihu
12. dexra metā
13. 'eska we'etu mesēt
14. 'emenna 'awāledihā

B. 1. Maṣ'u k^{w}ellomu 'aḥzāb xabēhu.
2. Re'ya k^{w}ello samāya ba-qedmēhu.
3. Šēṭa xabēna k^{w}ello 'a'ṣādihu.
4. Gabra zanta k^{w}ello ba'enti'akemu.
5. Maṣ'a xabēya k^{w}ello 'amira.
6. Nabaru heyya k^{w}ello lēlita.
7. Gab'ā k^{w}ellon westa 'abyātihon.
8. Rakabu k^{w}ellā 'aḥmārihomu.
9. Maṣ'u 'em-k^{w}ellu baḥāwerta medr.

10. Ḥanaṣu zā-k^{w}ellā hagara.

C. 1. hagaru la-negušena
2. qālātihu la-mak^{w}annenena
3. weludihā la-zāti be’sit
4. ‘elata motu la-metā
5. ’exuhu la-gabr
6. ’axawihu wa-’axātihu la-Yoḥannes
7. ṣaḥaftihu la-neguš
8. daqiqomu la-mašaggerān
9. mawā‘elihā la-ye’eti negešt
10. ’aḥmārihomu la-’ellontu sab’

D. 1. Ba-ṣebāḥa ye’eti ‘elat qarbu xaba hagarena.
2. Ma‘ālta wa-lēlita nabaru zeyya wa-’i-gab’u beḥēromu.
3. Qarbat ‘elata motu la-we’etu nabiy.
4. Wa-ba-mesēt xalafa ’em-xabēhomu.
5. Ba’enta ment bakaya zentu wald?
6. Sakabu heyya ’eska mesēt wa-’emze ḥoru bētomu.
7. ’Efo xalafa ’enta mā’kalomu la-’ellontu ḥezb?
8. Bakayat diba motomu la-weludihā.
9. ’Enta ’ayy fenot xalafu ’em-zeyya?
10. Sabaka ba-wangēl westa k^{w}ellu ’ahgura zeku beḥēr.
11. ’Enta westa ’ayyāt ’ahgur xalafa mal’aka mot?
12. Bakayu lā‘la motu la-negušomu.
13. We’eta ’amira šēṭa bēto wa-xalafa ’em-xabēna.
14. G^{w}ayyu k^{w}ellomu ḥezb ’em-qedmēhu.
15. Zanta k^{w}ello gabra ’em-qedma motā la-be’situ.

Lesson 11

11.1 Types of Verbs. There are three basic lexical types of verbs related to the main triliteral root system. We shall designate these types as G, D, and L according to the stem forms of the Perfect:

G verbs	simple root + stem vowel pattern, e.g. *nabara* he sat
D verbs	root + doubling (D) of the second radical + stem vowel pattern, e.g. *naṣṣara* he looked (root *nṣr*)
L verbs	root + lengthening (L) of the first stem vowel + stem vowel pattern, e.g. *bāraka* he blessed (root *brk*).

The designation G, for German Grundstamm (basic stem), has been adopted from elsewhere in Semitic grammar studies in order to promote some uniformity in grammatical terminology. For any given triliteral root, only one of the above basic types is normally in use. There is no general derivational relationship among the three types, but quite a number of verbs may appear optionally as either G or D with no difference in meaning.

Ethiopic also has a significant number of quadriliteral and quinquiliteral roots, the nature of which will be discussed in a later lesson. Verbs formed from quadriliteral roots have the pattern *CaCCaC-* in the Perfect of the basic stem, which we shall designate as Q:

Q verbs	simple root + stem vowel pattern, e.g. *targ^{w}ama* he translated (root *trg^{w}m*).

When the second radical of a quadriliteral root is a *w* or a *y*, there is a regular contraction of *aw* to *o* and *ay* to *ē*, producing such forms as *dēgana* (from **daygana* he pursued) and *moqeḥa* (from **mawqaḥa* he imprisoned). Because these verbs resemble L verbs in having a long vowel in the first stem syllable and follow essentially the same inflectional pattern as L verbs, we shall designate them as Q/L in the vocabularies and Glossary. This designation is useful because there is often no way of knowing whether such verbs are a result of this contraction or whether they may not be derived from other sources.

G verbs are the most numerous and present the greatest variety in inflection. Two types of G verbs may be distinguished on the basis of their perfect stems: (1) the type represented by *nabara*, with -*a*- between C_2 and C_3, and (2) the type represented by *gabra* (he made), with no vowel between C_2 and C_3. This distinction is formally rather trivial since it is maintained only in the 3rd person forms of the Perfect (see below), but it does show the remains of an older system in which verbs of the *nabara* type were primarily action verbs and those of the *gabra* type were primarily stative verbs. For various reasons this distinction has become blurred in Ethiopic, as evidenced by the fact that *gabra* itself is an action verb.

11.2 The Full Inflection of the Perfect. The inflectional suffixes of the Perfect are the same for all types of verbs. Deviations from the norm occur because of underlying differences in type (*nabara* versus *gabra*) and because of phonetic changes occasioned by the presence of gutturals (*ʾ ʿ h ḥ x*) or semivowels (*y w*) in the root. Verbs from roots whose first radical is a guttural or semivowel (hence roots I-gutt. and I-W/Y) conform to the regular pattern and will be used without further comment. The full inflection of the Perfect is as follows:

	G	G	D	L	Q
3 m.s. he	*nabara*	*gabra*	*naṣṣara*	*bāraka*	*targʷama*
3 f.s. she	*nabarat*	*gabrat*	*naṣṣarat*	*bārakat*	*targʷamat*
2 m.s. you	*nabarka*	*gabarka*	*naṣṣarka*	*bārakka*	*targʷamka*
2 f.s. you	*nabarki*	*gabarki*	*naṣṣarki*	*bārakki*	*targʷamki*
1 c.s. I	*nabarku*	*gabarku*	*naṣṣarku*	*bārakku*	*targʷamku*
3 m.pl. they	*nabaru*	*gabru*	*naṣṣaru*	*bāraku*	*targʷamu*
3 f.pl. they	*nabarā*	*gabrā*	*naṣṣarā*	*bārakā*	*targʷamā*
2 m.pl. you	*nabarkemu*	*gabarkemu*	*naṣṣarkemu*	*bārakkemu*	*targʷamkemu*
2 f.pl. you	*nabarkĕn*	*gabarkĕn*	*naṣṣarkĕn*	*bārakkĕn*	*targʷamkĕn*
1 c.pl. we	*nabarna*	*gabarna*	*naṣṣarna*	*bārakna*	*targʷamna*

When the final stem consonant is *q* or *g*, the *k* of the personal endings is assimilated: **ʿaragku* (I went up) > *ʿaraggu*, **wadaqku* (I fell) > *wadaqqu*. Although the resultant doubling is clear in transliteration, it is not represented in the Ethiopic alphabet, where the two examples just given would appear as *ʿa-ra-gu* and *wa-da-qu* respectively. These could not be confused with the 3rd pers. pl. forms *ʿargu* and *wadqu* because of the presence of a vowel after the second root consonant, but a form written, e.g., *xa-da-gu* may be read either as *xadagu* (they left) or *xadaggu* (I left). A similar reading problem arises in connection with stem final *k* and *n*: *sa-ba-ku = sabakku/sabaku, ḥa-za-na = ḥazana/ḥazanna.*

Vocabulary 11

Nouns:

ḥegg (pl. *ḥegag*) m.f. law; the Law (scriptural sense); *gabra ḥegga* to perform, carry out the law. *ba-ḥegg* legally, lawfully.

maṣḥaf (pl. *maṣāḥeft*) m.f. book, document; writing, inscription.

lesān (pl. *-āt*) m.f. tongue; language. *lesāna Yonānāwiyān* Greek. *lesāna ʿEbrāyesṭ* Hebrew. *lesāna ʾAfrenj* Latin. *lesāna ʿArabi* Arabic. *lesāna Geʿz* Geʿez.

badn (pl. *ʾabdent*) m. corpse.

Verbs:

naṣṣara to look, look at (acc. or *westa, xaba*)

bāraka to bless.

targʷama to translate (from ... into: *ʾemenna ... la-, xaba*)

ʿaqaba to guard, keep watch on; to take care of, preserve, keep safe; to observe, keep (e.g. laws).

qabara to bury, inter.

dēgana Q/L to pursue, chase (acc. or *dexra, ʾem-dexra*). Usually, but not always, in a hostile sense.

Proper Names:

Yonānāwiyān the Greeks.

ʾAfrenj the Romans.

ʿEbrāwiyān the Hebrews.

Geʿz, ʾAgʿāzi the Ethiopians; *beḥēra Geʿz, beḥēra ʾAgʿāzi* Ethiopia.

ʾItyopyā Ethiopia.

Exercises

A. 1. Nabarku heyya ʾeska weʾetu ʾamir.
2. Waradku westa ḥayq ba-mesēt.
3. ʿAraggu ʾadbāra ba-ṣebāḥ.
4. Wadaqqu diba medr wa-sakabku heyya.
5. Ḥanaṣku zanta bēta la-weludeya.

6. ’I-qatalku ’ellonta sab’a.
7. Rakabku badna ba-westa fenot.
8. ‘Aqabku ḥegagihu ma‘ālta wa-lēlita.
9. Bārakku ḥezba wa-’emze xalafku ’em-xabēhomu.
10. Takalku ’awyāna ba-westa ‘aṣadeya.

B. 1. Qarabna xabēhomu.
2. Gabarna zanta k^wello ba’enti’akemu.
3. Sakabna heyya ’eska ṣebāḥ.
4. Sabakna k^wellena westa k^wellu baḥāwerta zāti medr.
5. Ḥazanna diba qālātihu la-mal’ak.
6. Targ^{w}amna zanta maṣāḥefta ’em-lesāna ‘Arabi.
7. Xalafna ’em-mā’kalomu ’emdexra motu la-negušomu.
8. Qabarna badno la-’abuna heyya.
9. Dēganna dexrēhomu la-daqiq ḥayqa.
10. Naṣṣarna xaba samāyāt.

C. 1. ’Aytē sabakka wangēlo?
2. Ba’enta ment ḥazankemu k^wellekemu?
3. Xaba ’ayy hagar qarabkemu ye’eta ‘elata?
4. Manna bārakka wa-manna ’i-bārakka?
5. ’Ayya maṣḥafa targ^{w}amka ’em-lesāna ’Afrenj?
6. Ba’enta ment ’i-‘aqabkemu ḥegageya?
7. ’Aytē qabarkemu badno la-’exukemu?
8. Targ^{w}amku ’ellu k^wello maṣāḥefta ’em-lesāna Yonānāwiyān.
9. Zanta gabarka ba-ḥegg.
10. Gabra k^wello ḥegaga ’Egzi’abḥēr ’eska ‘elata motu.

D. 1. Targ^{w}ama zanta maṣāḥefta ’em-lesāna Yonānāwiyān la-lesāna Ge‘z.
2. Nabara ba-westa ’Ityopyā mesla ’Ag‘āzi.
3. Menta naṣṣarkemu?
4. Qabaru ’abdentihomu la-’axawihomu.
5. G^wayya westa beḥēra Ge‘z wa-nabaru meslēhomu.
6. Xalafna ’enta xaba bētu wa-naṣṣarna westētu.
7. Sadadu ’arāwita ’em-hagar wa-dēganu ’emdexrēhomu ’eska mesēt.
8. La-ment gabarki zanta?
9. Ba’enta ment ’i-bakayā diba motomu la-’amtātihon?
10. ’Efo ‘aqabken weludiken ba-ye’eti ‘elat?
11. ’Efo wadaqqa ’em-diba bēt?
12. Sabaka ba-wangēl ba-westa k^wellu beḥēra ’Ityopyā.

Lesson 12

12.1 The Perfect: Roots II-Guttural. Only G verbs require special attention when the second root consonant is a guttural (*ʾ ʿ h ḥ x*); D and L verbs follow the regular patterns of formation and inflection. There are two types of such G verbs: (1) those corresponding to the type *nabara* (e.g. *saʾala* to ask), which are regular in every respect, and (2) those corresponding to the type *gabra* (e.g. *keḥda* to deny), which have *-e-* for *-a-* throughout in the stem:

saʾala	*saʾalu*	*keḥda*	*keḥdu*
saʾalat	*saʾalā*	*keḥdat*	*keḥdā*
saʾalka	*saʾalkemu*	*keḥedka*	*keḥedkemu*
saʾalki	*saʾalkēn*	*keḥedki*	*keḥedkēn*
saʾalku	*saʾalna*	*keḥedku*	*keḥedna*

Some D verbs from roots II-guttural (e.g. *mahhara* to teach) have parallel G verbs (*mahara*) already in the early stages of the classical language. This probably indicates that the loss of doubling of guttural consonants, carried through completely in the modern traditional pronunciation, is almost as old as the textual tradition itself. But because the regular D forms of such verbs also occur, there is no reason to reject the doubling of gutturals in our normalization of the classical forms.

Vocabulary 12

Nouns:

hāymānot m.f. faith (esp. Christian)

xebest (pl. *xabāwez*) m. bread; piece or loaf of bread. The *-z* of the plural is the original third radical of the root; the *-s-* of the singular represents an assimilation to the following *-t*.

dam (pl. *-āt*) m.f. blood.

ʾed (pl. *ʾedaw*) f.m. hand.

Verbs:

ṣaḥafa to write.

saʾala to ask for (acc. dir. obj.; from someone: *ʾem-*, *xaba*).

weḥza to flow.

seḥta to err, get lost; to stray (from a path or doctrine).
keḥda to deny, repudiate; intrans.: to lack faith, be an unbeliever.
gaššaṣa to rebuke, reproach; to instruct (by reproach or admonition).

Conjunctions:

soba when. The clause following a *soba*-clause may optionally begin with a (to us) redundant *wa-*: *Soba re'ya waldo, wa-roṣa xabēhu.* When he saw his son, he ran to him. Omission of the extra *wa-* is equally common.

'ama when. Same comment as the preceding.

Exercises

A.
1. 'em-'edēhu la-nabiy
2. ba-damu la-waldeya
3. xebest wa-wayn
4. hāymānotomu la-'axawina
5. lesānomu la-malā'ekt
6. hāymānotomu la-Kerestiyān
7. 'edawihā la-'extu
8. damu la-badnu
9. maṣāḥeftihu la-ṣaḥāfi
10. hāymānotomu la-daqiqomu

B.
1. Keḥedku hāymānoto la-'abuya.
2. Sa'alku xebesta 'emennēhu.
3. Seḥta 'em-fenot wa-mota.
4. 'I-seḥetku 'em-fenot.
5. Ṣaḥafku qālātihu westa maṣḥaf.
6. Weḥza dam 'em-'edawihu.
7. Gaššaṣku 'axaweya.
8. Keḥdat 'exteya nagarāteya.
9. Gaššaṣat weludihā.
10. La-ment keḥedkemu nagaro?
11. 'Ayya maṣḥafa ṣaḥafka?
12. 'Em-'aytē weḥza zentu dam?

C.
1. Wa-soba re'yu damo la-neguš, wa-gʷayyu 'em-qedmēhu.
2. Wa-soba bo'u hagarana we'eta 'amira, qatalu kʷellomu ʻedawa.
3. Wa-soba rakabu Kerestiyāna, qatalu liqānihomu.
4. 'Ama mota be'sihā, xalafat 'em-heyya wa-gab'at xaba bēta 'abuhā.
5. Maṣ'u xabēna wa-sa'alu wayna wa-xebesta 'emennēna.
6. Ba'enta ment keḥedkemu wangēla?
7. Gaššaṣa nabiy ḥezbā la-hagar soba seḥtu 'em-ḥegga 'Egzi'abḥēr.
8. Ṣaḥafa zanta kʷello maṣāḥefta ba-lesāna 'Afrenj.
9. 'Ama xalafa 'em-zentu beḥēr, wa-šēṭa bēto wa-ḥamaro la-'exuya.
10. 'Efo gabra soba sa'alkemu maṣāḥefta 'emennēhu?
11. La-ment gaššaṣa makʷannen 'ellonta sab'a?
12. Sadadu zanta neguša 'em-bēta Kerestiyān soba keḥda nagara wangēl wa-seḥta 'em-fenota hāymānotena.
13. 'Em-'ayy lesān xaba 'ayy lesān targʷamka zanta maṣḥafa?

14. Zentu we'etu ḥegagihomu la-Daqiqa 'Esrā'ēl wa-maṣāḥeftihomu.
15. ʿAqabu hagaromu 'em-'elleku sab'.
16. Mannu ṣaḥafa zanta nagara ba'enta mawāʿelihu la-we'etu neguš?
17. Wa-soba mota 'abuhomu, qabaru badno ba-westa we'etu beḥēr.
18. Wa-soba qarbu xabēya, 'i-naṣṣarku xabēhomu.
19. Menta-nu sa'alna 'emennēki?
20. Ba'enta ment 'i-ʿaqabkemu hāymānotomu la-'abawikemu?

Lesson 13

13.1 The Perfect: Roots III-Guttural. The basic lexical forms of verbs from roots III-Gutt. fall into two groups:

(a) All G verbs are the same (i.e. no *nabara/gabra* distinction is made) and have no vowel between C_2 and C_3: *maṣʾa, waḍʾa, gabʾa, baṣḥa*.

(b) All D, L, and Q verbs have *-e-* between C_2 and C_3: *nasseḥa* D he repented, *moqeḥa* Q/L he imprisoned.

Both groups, however, are inflected the same way, with *-ā-* in the final stem syllable of the 1st and 2nd person forms, analogous to the stem alternation of *gabar-* with *gabr-*:

G	*maṣʾa*	*maṣʾu*	D	*nasseḥa*	*nasseḥu*	Q/L	*moqeḥa*	*moqeḥu*
	maṣʾat	*maṣʾā*		*nasseḥat*	*nasseḥā*		*moqeḥat*	*moqeḥā*
	maṣāʾka	*maṣāʾkemu*		*nassāḥka*	*nassāḥkemu*		*moqāḥka*	*moqāḥkemu*
	maṣāʾki	*maṣāʾkēn*		*nassāḥki*	*nassāḥkēn*		*moqāḥki*	*moqāḥkēn*
	maṣāʾku	*maṣāʾna*		*nassāḥku*	*nassāḥna*		*moqāḥku*	*moqāḥna*

13.2 The Perfect with Object Suffixes. The pronominal object of a transitive verb is regularly suffixed directly to the verb. The forms of the object suffixes of the 1st and 2nd persons are almost identical to the possessive suffixes on the noun:

me	*-ni*	us	*-na*
you (m.s.)	*-ka*	you (m.pl.)	*-kemu*
you (f.s.)	*-ki*	you (f.pl.)	*-ken*

The attachment of these suffixes is relatively uncomplicated, as may be seen from the following table. Note the changes that take place in the subject endings before the suffixes in certain cases: *-at* becomes *-ata-*, *-ki* becomes *-ke-*, *-ken* becomes *-kenā-* or *-kā-*, and *-na* becomes *-nā-*.

	No Suff.	me	you$^{m.s.}$	you$^{f.s.}$	us	you$^{m.pl.}$	you$^{f.pl.}$
He	*-a*	*-áni*	*-áka*	*-áki*	*-ána*	*-akému*	*-akén*
She	*-at*	*-atáni*	*-atáka*	*-atáki*	*-atána*	*-atakému*	*-atakén*
You$^{m.s.}$	*-ka*	*-káni*	-	-	*-kána*	-	-
You$^{f.s.}$	*-ki*	*-kéni*	-	-	*-kéna*	-	-
I	*-ku*	-	*-kúka*	*-kúki*	-	*-kukému*	*-kukén*
They$^{m.}$	*-u*	*-úni*	*-úka*	*-úki*	*-úna*	*-ukému*	*-ukén*
They$^{f.}$	*-ā*	*-ā́ni*	*-ā́ka*	*-ā́ki*	*-ā́na*	*-ākému*	*-ākén*
You$^{m.pl.}$	*-kému*	*-kemúni*	-	-	*-kemúna*	-	-
You$^{f.pl.}$	*-ken*	*-kenā́ni* *-kā́ni*	-	-	*-kenā́na* *-kā́na*	-	-
We	*-na*	-	*-nā́ka*	*-nā́ki*	-	*-nākému*	*-nākén*

Vocabulary 13

Nouns:

māy (pl. *-āt*) m. water; liquid.

berhān (pl. *-āt*) m. light (lit. and fig.)

xaṭi'at (pl. *xaṭāwe'*, *xaṭāye'*) m.f. sin(s).

Verbs:

naš'a to raise, lift, pick up; to take, receive, accept; to capture; to take as a wife. *naš'a mesla* to take (someone) along.

marḥa to lead, guide.

sam'a to hear; to hear of, hear about; to heed, obey, listen to (acc. or *la-*).

mal'a (1) trans.: to fill (2 acc.: something with something; or acc. of what fills + *lā'la*, *westa*, *ba-* of what is filled, e.g. *Mal'a māya westa newāy* He filled the vessel with water); (2) intrans. to be full, filled (of, with: acc. or *'em-*); to be fulfilled, completed; to abound, be abundant.

farha to be afraid; to fear (acc. or *'emenna*).

nasseḥa to repent (of: *'emenna*, *ba'enta*).

Other:

kama (1) prep. (w. suff. *kamā-*) like, as; *kama-ze* like this, in this way, thus. (2) conj. that (introduces noun clause after verbs of speaking and perception, e.g. *Samā'ku kama mota* I heard that he had died.).

'esma conj. (1) because, for, since; (2) that (like *kama* above).

Exercises

A. 1. Maṣā'ku xabēhomu.
2. Baṣāḥku heyya ba-mesēt.
3. Waḍā'ku 'em-mā'kalomu.
4. Gabā'ku beḥēreya.
5. Našā'ku xebesta meslēya.
6. Marāḥku ḥezba westa fenot.
7. Farāhku 'em-we'etu mak^{w}annen.
8. Nassāḥku 'em-xaṭi'ateya.
9. 'I-samā'ku qālātihu.
10. 'I-nassāḥku 'em-nagareya.
11. Ba'enta ment farāhkemu 'agbertihu?
12. Menta samā'ka lēlita?
13. Mā'zē-nu nassāḥki 'em-xaṭāwe'eki?
14. Manna marāḥka westa hagar?
15. Mā'zē baṣāḥkemu zeyya?
16. 'Em-'ayy beḥēr waḍā'ka?
17. Mal'at medr māya.
18. Mal'a samāy berhāna.
19. Mal'u 'aḥmārihomu māya.
20. Mal'a mal'ak berhāna westa bēt.

B. 1. Naš'ani meslēhu.
2. Naš'uni meslēhomu.
3. Marḥani xaba hāymānot.
4. 'Aytē marḥaka?
5. Mannu naš'aki be'sita?
6. Ba'enta ment 'i-sam'uka?
7. Mannu gaššaṣakemu?
8. Mā'zē dēganukemu?
9. Sadaduna 'em-'abyātina.
10. Rakabuni ba-westa ḥamareya.
11. Gabrana 'Egzi'abḥēr.
12. 'I-re'yatana 'emmena.
13. 'I-bārakani 'abuya.
14. Naṣṣaruna welud.
15. 'Aqabāni 'axāteya.
16. 'I-farhuna 'arāwit.

C. 1. Ba'enta ment 'i-qatalkani?
2. 'Efo rakabkemuna?
3. La-ment sadadkemuni 'em-bēteya?
4. 'I-bāraknāka.
5. 'I-dēgankukemu.
6. La-ment gaššaṣkemuna?
7. La-ment farāhkāni?
8. Samā'nāken.
9. 'I-samā'kemuna.
10. 'I-našā'kemuni.

D. 1. Wa-soba samā'na zanta nagara, nassāḥna 'em-k^{w}ello xaṭāwe'ina.
2. Wa-soba rakabuna, wa-qatalu daqiqana wa-naš'u 'anestina meslēhomu.
3. 'Ama qarbat 'elata motu la-'abuna, bārakana wa-'emze xalafa 'em-xabēna xaba 'abawihu.
4. Wa-soba naṣṣaru westa samāy, re'yu berhāna wa-sam'u qālomu la-malā'ekt.
5. Ḥazanna we'eta 'amira 'esma gabarna zanta xaṭi'ata.

6. Weḥza māy westa hagar wa-mal’a k^{w}ello fenāwēhā.
7. Zentu wangēl we’etu berhān la-k^{w}ellu ’amdār wa-la-k^{w}ellu baḥāwert.
8. Wa-’ama samā‘na kama baṣḥa nabiy xaba hagarena, maṣā’na wa-samā‘na la-nagarātihu.
9. Sadaduna ’em-bēta Kerestiyān ’esma keḫedna qālāta wangēl wa-seḥetna ’em-hāymānotomu.
10. Soba sa’alka xebesta ’em-xabēna, ’i-samā‘nāka wa-sadadnāka ’em-qedmēna.
11. Weḥza wayn kama māy ba-westa bētu la-zentu mak^{w}annen.
12. Mal’a we’etu dabr ‘eḍawa wa-’arāwita.
13. Soba re’yā kama motu ’amtātihon, wadqā diba medr wa-bakayā.
14. Soba samā‘na kama naš’ukemu, nassāḥna kama ’i-maṣā’na wa-’i-‘aqabnākemu ’emennēhomu.
15. Ba-ye’eti lēlit kona berhāna ba-westa samāy, wa-marḥana zentu berhān westa hagarena.

Lesson 14

14.1 The Perfect: Roots III-W/Y. G verbs from these roots exhibit both *nabara* and *gabra* types (examples below). When the final stem syllables *-aw-* and *-ay-* are closed (in the 1st and 2nd person forms), there is an optional contraction of *aw* to *o*, which is quite common, and of *ay* to *ē*, which is rare. These same contractions occur in D, L, and Q verbs, whose stem formations are otherwise regular.

	(to cross)	(to weep)	(to be devastated)	(to drink)
G	*ʿadawa*	*bakaya*	*badwa*	*satya*
	ʿadawat	*bakayat*	*badwat*	*satyat*
	ʿadawka/ʿadoka	*bakayka/(bakēka)*	*badawka/badoka*	*satayka/(satēka)*
	etc.	etc.	etc.	etc.

	(to send)	(to pray)		(to inform)
D	*fannawa*	*ṣallaya*	L/Q	*zēnawa*
	fannawat	*ṣallayat*		*zēnawat*
	fannawka/fannoka	*ṣallayka/(ṣallēka)*		*zēnawka/zēnoka*

A number of G verbs are both II-guttural and III-Y. If of the *nabara* type (e.g. *laḥaya* to be beautiful), they follow *bakaya* above. If of the *gabra* type (cf. *keḥda*), there is a regular replacement of *-ey-* by *-i-* throughout:

reʾya	*reʾyu*
reʾyat	*reʾyā*
reʾika (for **reʾeyka*)	*reʾikemu* (for **reʾeykemu*)
reʾiki (for **reʾeyki*)	*reʾiken* (for **reʾeyken*)
reʾiku (for **reʾeyku*)	*reʾina* (for **reʾeyna*)

The most frequent verbs of this type are *reʾya* to see, *reʿya* to graze, *ṭeʿya* to get well, and *weʿya* to burn.

Vocabulary 14

Nouns:

bāḥr (pl. *ʾabḥert*) f.m. sea, ocean.
ʾebn (pl. *ʾeban*, *ʾaʾbān*) m.f. stone(s). *ʾebna barad* hailstone(s).
ḍaḥāy/ḍaḥay (pl. *-āt*) m.f. sun. *Hagara Ḍaḥāy* Heliopolis (in Egypt).

warx (pl. *'awrāx*) m.f. moon, month.

Verbs:

'adawa to cross (acc. dir. obj. or acc. of goal or prep. phrase).
'atawa to go home; to depart (for home).
we'ya to be burned up, consumed by fire
wadaya to put, place, set.
fannawa to send.
hallawa to exist, be. *Hallawa* either predicates existence *per se* (there is, there was), or it may be followed by a prepositional phrase predicating existence in a state or place. It is rarely used with a predicate noun or adjective, which is the normal function of *kona*. *Hallawa* is unusual in having both past and present tense meaning in the Perfect. Examples: *Hallawat hagar*, There is/was a city. *Halloku westa hagar*, I am/was in the city. *Hallawa meslēna*, He is/was with us. The distinction between *hallawa* and *kona* is not always maintained: *kona* may be used for *hallawa* in its past tense meaning, but not vice versa. The masc. sing. 3rd pers. form is often found as *hallo*, with contraction of the sequence *-awa-* to *o*; this is very seldom found in other verbs III-W.

Exercises

A. 1. Fannoku gabreya xabēhu.
2. Mannu fannawaka xabēya?
3. Wadaya xebesta qedmēhu.
4. Wadayna maṣāḥeftina ba-westa bēt.
5. 'Adona zanta beḥēra 'eska bāḥr.
6. 'Adawu bāḥra ba-'aḥmārihomu.
7. Mā'zē 'adoka ye'eta fenota?
8. La-ment 'atokemu beḥērakemu?
9. G^{w}ayayna Hagara Ḍaḥāy.
10. Re'iku dama westa 'edawihu.
11. 'I-re'ikemu-nu berhāna ḍaḥāy?
12. Wadayku 'a'bāna westa fenot.
13. Re'ina warxa ba-westa samāy.
14. 'I-halloku meslēhu we'eta 'amira.
15. Nabarna heyya we'eta warxa.
16. We'ya bētu wa-motu weludihu.
17. 'Emdexra-ze 'atoku medreya.
18. Mā'zē 'adokemu zek^{w}a bāḥra?
19. 'Aytē g^{w}ayaykemu soba sadadakemu?
20. Waradu dibēhomu 'a'bāna barad.

B. 1. 'Aytē re'ikana?
2. Mesla mannu halloka?
3. 'Aytē wadayka maṣḥafeya?
4. Ba'enta-ze fannokuka xabēhomu.
5. Naš'a 'ebna wa-qatala 'ex^{w}āhu.
6. We'yu-nu 'a'ṣādātihomu?

7. Ba-we’etu ’awrāx ’i-waḍā’na ’em-hagar.
8. Ḥanaṣku zanta bēta ba-’a’bān.
9. ‘Adawu ’abḥerta wa-baḥāwerta.
10. Diba mannu bakaykemu?
11. Kona ’exuhu mak^{w}annenana.
12. Konu weludihu mašaggerāna.
13. Kona we’etu maṣḥaf wangēlo.
14. Hallawa heyya ‘eḍaw wa-’a’bān.
15. Hallawa māy ba-westa ’abyāta hagar.
16. Ḥanaṣu bēta Kerestiyān diba ḥayqa bāḥr.
17. Xalafa ’em-xabēna wa-’atawa.
18. ’Aytē hallokemu we’eta ‘elata?
19. ’I-re’ikukemu heyya.
20. ’Aytē re’ikenāna?

C. 1. Fannoku zanta nabiya xabēkemu ’esma ’i-‘aqabkemu ḥegageya wa-seḥetkemu.
2. Nabaru ba-westa Hagara Ḍaḥāy ’eska motu la-we’etu neguš, wa-’emze ’atawu medromu.
3. Wa-soba re’ina ye’eta ḥamara, waradna westa ḥayqa bāḥr.
4. Naṣṣarku xaba ’adbār wa-re’iku berhāna kama berhāna ḍaḥāy.
5. ’Ama hallona meslēkemu, ’i-samā‘kemuna.
6. ’I-kona warxa ba-ye’eti lēlit, wa-g^{w}ayayna gadāma mesla daqiqena wa-’anestina.
7. ’Esma farāhna ’emenna ’ellontu sab’, waḍā’na ’em-heyya wa-‘adona medra ’eska zāti hagar.
8. ‘Adoku k^{w}ello baḥāwerta medr wa-k^{w}ello ’abḥertihā.
9. ’I-fannokuka xaba zentu ḥezb ’allā xaba k^{w}ellomu ’aḥzāba medr.

Lesson 15

15.1 The Perfect: Roots II-W/Y. The Perfect of G verbs from roots II-W and II-Y is distinctive. From roots II-W, e.g. *qwm* (to stand), the stem of the Perfect has *-o-* throughout; from roots II-Y, e.g. *šym* (to appoint), the stem has *-ē-* throughout.

qoma	*qomu*	*šēma*	*šēmu*
qomat	*qomā*	*šēmat*	*šēmā*
qomka	*qomkemu*	*šēmka*	*šēmkemu*
qomki	*qomken*	*šēmki*	*šēmken*
qomku	*qomna*	*šēmku*	*šēmna*

A few verbs from roots which are also III-gutt. or III-Y/W retain the second root consonant as "strong" and are inflected like the ordinary G verbs III-gutt. or III-W/Y. For example,

šawʿa	he sacrificed	*ḥaywa*	he lived, recovered
šawʿat		*ḥaywat*	
šawāʿka		*ḥayawka/ḥayoka*	
šawāʿki etc.		*ḥayawki/ḥayoki* etc.	

Šawʿa may also be inflected like *qoma*.

D verbs from roots II-W/Y are regular and offer no special problems: *fawwasa* to heal, *ṭayyaqa* to examine. We have already mentioned the contractions in Q verbs II-W/Y (§ 11.1), analogous to *qoma* and *šēma* above.

15.2 The Perfect with Object Suffixes (cont.). The 3rd person object pronouns are

him	*-o/-hu*	them (m.)	*-omu/-homu*
her	*-ā/-hā*	them (f.)	*-on/-hon.*

Their attachment is not so simple as that of the object pronouns of the 1st and 2nd persons. A review of the forms given in §13.2 shows the following alterations of the subject suffixes before the object suffixes:

-a	remains	*-a-*	*-u*	remains	*-u-*
-at	becomes	*-ata-*	*-ā*	remains	*-ā-*
-ka	remains	*-ka-*	*-kemu*	remains	*-kemu-*
-ki	becomes	*-ke-*	*-ken*	becomes	*-kenā-* or *-kā-*
-ku	remains	*-ku-*	*-na*	becomes	*-nā-*

Taking the altered form as the basis for our rules, we have the following:

(1) If the stem ends in *-ā-*, attach *-hu*, *-hā*, *-homu*, *-hon*.

(2) If the stem ends in *-u-* or *-e-*, attach *-o*, *-ā*, *-omu*, *-on* after changing *-u-* to *-eww-* and *-e-* to *-eyy-*.

(3) If the stem ends in *-a-*, drop the *-a-* and add *-o*, *-ā*, *-omu*, *-on*.

The following table illustrates these rules; note the variants that are not covered by the rules:

	No Suff.	him	her	them$^{m.}$	them$^{f.}$
He	*-a*	*-ó*	*-ā́*	*-ómu*	*-ón*
She	*-at*	*-ató*	*-atā́*	*-atómu*	*-atón*
You$^{m.s.}$	*-ka*	*-kó*	*-kā́*	*-kómu*	*-kón*
		-kāhú	*-kāhā́*		
You$^{f.s.}$	*-ki*	*-kéyyo*	*-kéyyā*	*-keyyómu*	*-kéyyon*
I	*-ku*	*-kéwwo*	*-kéwwā*	*-kewwómu*	*-kéwwon*
They$^{m.}$	*-u*	*-éwwo*	*-éwwā*	*-ewwómu*	*-éwwon*
They$^{f.}$	*-ā*	*-āhú*	*-āhā́*	*-āhómu*	*-āhón*
You$^{m.pl.}$	*-kemu*	*-keméwwo*	*-keméwwā*	*-kemewwómu*	*-keméwwon*
You$^{f.pl.}$	*-ken*	*-kenāhú*	*-kenāhā́*	*-kenāhómu*	*-kenāhón*
		-kāhú	*-kāhā́*		
We	*-na*	*-nāhú*	*-nāhā́*	*-nāhómu*	*-nāhón.*

15.3 The *qatalo la-neguš* Construction. In addition to the use of the accusative alone to mark the direct object of a transitive verb one may also employ the construction *qatalo la-neguš* (he killed the king), in which the object is first expressed pronominally (he killed him) and then introduced nominally with the preposition *la-* and the non-accusative form. The relationship of this construction to the use of the simple accusative is similar to the relationship between *waldu la-neguš* and the simple construct (see § 10.2). Thus, *qatalo la-neguš* is normally employed only when the object is specific and definite; the simple accusative may be used to express any direct object regardless of its definiteness.

Vocabulary 15

Nouns:

mašwāʿt (pl. *-āt*, *mašāweʿ*) m. sacrifice; less frequently: altar.
kāhen (pl. *-āt*) priest. *liqa kāhenāt* chief priest.
ʾēpis qopos (pl. *-āt*) bishop. *liqa ʾēpis qoposāt* archbishop.
diyāqon (pl. *-āt*) deacon.
pāppās (pl. *-āt*) bishop, archbishop, metropolitan. *liqa pāppāsāt* patriarch (of the Church).
qasis (pl. *qasāwest*) presbyter, elder.
ṭāʿot (pl. *-āt*) m. heathen idol(s).

Verbs:

moʾa to conquer, defeat, subdue.
šēma to appoint (to an office), designate (dir. obj. + obj. compl.: *šēmani kāhena* he appointed me priest); to put, place, set (usually over: *diba, lāʿla, westa*)
qoma to arise, stand; to stand, take a position; to come to a halt, stop.
šawʿa to sacrifice, offer (acc. dir. obj.; to: *la-*).
ḥaywa to live, be alive; to revive, come back to life; to recover, get well.
ṣawweʿa to call, summon; to invite; to proclaim.

Note: The direct object of many verbs may have an appositional complement, usually rendered in English by "as." "He sacrificed a lamb as an offering" is simply "He sacrificed a lamb, an offering" in Ethiopic: *Šawʿa bagʿa mašwāʿta.* The complement stands in the accusative case.

Exercises

A. 1. qatalomu
2. bārakomu
3. wadayo
4. ʿadawā
5. fannawomu
6. našʾatomu
7. marḥatomu
8. samʿāhomu
9. farhewwo
10. ṣaḥafewwo
11. keḥdewwo
12. gaššaṣewwā
13. naṣṣarewwomu
14. targ^{w}amewwomu
15. ʿaqabewwon

B. 1. Re’yewwo la-gabr.
2. Ḥanaṣewwā la-zāti hagar.
3. Qatalewwomu la-ḥezbena.
4. Rakabewwo la-waldomu.
5. Sadadewwo la-we’etu nabiy.
6. Šēṭo la-bētu.
7. Gabrā la-zāti ḥamar.
8. Bārakomu la-weludihu.
9. Naṣṣarewwomu la-malā’ekt.
10. Targ^{w}amo la-zentu maṣḥaf.
11. Farhomu la-weludihu la-neguš.
12. ‘Aqabon la-’awāledihā la-ye’eti be’sit.
13. ‘Aqabo la-badnu la-’abuhu.
14. Dēganewwo la-’exuhu ’adbāra.
15. Gaššaṣomu la-ḥezb.
16. Naš’ā la-be’situ meslēhu.
17. Marḥewwo la-be’si westa hagar.
18. ‘Adawewwo la-zentu beḥēr.
19. Wadayon la-’edawihu dibēhā.
20. Fannawewwomu la-liqāwentihomu xabēya.

C. 1. Šēṭku bēteya.
2. Šēṭkewwo la-’exuya.
3. Bo’ku bēto.
4. Mā’zē bo’kemu heyya?
5. Roṣna xaba kāhen.
6. ’Aytē ḥorkemu?
7. Konku diyāqona.
8. Konna kāhenāta.
9. ’Emze kona liqa pāppāsāt.
10. Šēmana diyāqonāta.
11. ’I-šēmuni ’ēpis qoposa.
12. Šēmewwomu qasāwesta.
13. Re’ikewwomu la-weludikemu.
14. Qatalkemewwomu la-kāhenātina.
15. ’I-samā‘kemewwomu la-qālātihomu la-’amtātihon.
16. ’I-našā’nāhu la-ṭā‘otekemu.
17. ’I-našā’kewwo la-maṣāḥeftika.
18. ’I-našā’kewwā la-be’siteka.
19. ’I-‘adonāhu la-beḥērekemu.
20. ’I-keḥedkemewwo la-’Egzi’abḥēr.

D. 1. Šēmomu kāhenāta wa-diyāqonāta wa-qasāwesta ba-bēta Kerestiyān.
2. Ṣawwe‘omu la-’agbertihu, wa-’i-maṣ’u xabēhu.
3. Soba ṣawwā‘kewwomu, sam‘uni wa-roṣu xabēya.
4. Qomku ba-qedmēhu wa-samā‘ku la-qālātihu.
5. ’I-naš’o ’Egzi’abḥēr la-mašāwe‘ihomu.
6. Šaw‘omu la-weludihomu la-ṭā‘otātihomu.
7. Šēmo liqa pāppāsāt ’ēpis qoposa ba-westa zentu beḥēr.
8. La-ment ’i-maṣ’u soba ṣawwā‘nāhomu?
9. Šaw‘ewwomu la-mašāwe‘ihomu la-’Egzi’abḥēr ’Amlāka samāy wa-medr.
10. ’I-šawā‘ku mašwā‘teya la-ṭā‘ot.
11. Waḍ’u ’em-hagar wa-mo’ewwomu la-’ellontu sab’.
12. Mo’kewwomu wa-našā’kewwon la-’ahgurihomu.
13. Ḥaywat be’situ wa-’i-motat.
14. Wa-soba sam‘a we’etu be’si zanta, ḥaywa wa-qoma wa-ḥora bēto.

15. ’Efo ḥayoka wa-’i-motka?
16. Wa-ba-zentu nagar qoma ḍaḥāy ba-westa samāy wa-’i-ḥora.
17. Wadayo ’Egzi’abḥēr la-ḍaḥāy berhāna la-ma‘ālt wa-la-warx berhāna la-lēlit.
18. Naš’o kāhen la-mašwā‘teya wa-šaw‘o la-’Egzi’abḥēr.
19. Soba ṣawwe‘ani neguš, roṣku xabēhu wa-wadaqqu qedmēhu.
20. Qomna heyya ba-westa fenot wa-’i-bo’na hagaromu.

Lesson 16

16.1 Adjectives. There are two basic types of adjectives in Ethiopic: (1) those associated with (or derived from) verbs, and (2) those derived from nouns by the addition of the suffixes *-āwi* and *-āy*. The second type is infrequent and relatively unimportant (see Lesson 19). We shall confine ourselves here to those of the first type, and more specifically to those associated with stative G verbs and a small group of stative D verbs. The adjectives of this group correspond most closely to the simple adjective of English and are the most frequently used in Ethiopic. There are four main patterns:

qetul	e.g.	*kebur*	glorious, mighty	verb:	*kabra*
qatil		*ṭabib*	wise, prudent		*ṭabba*
qātel		*ṣādeq*	righteous, just		*ṣadqa*
qattāl		*naddāy*	poor, needy.		*nadya*

Of these, *qetul* is the most common, but we shall begin with *qātel* since these exhibit the inflectional endings most simply. This is a small group, but it does include the ordinal numbers (e.g. *šāles* third; see Lesson 23) and a few other frequent adjectives such as *bāʿel* (rich) and *xāṭeʾ* (sinful).

Most adjectives are inflected for number and gender by the addition of the endings *-t* (fem. sing.), *-ān* (masc. pl.), and *-āt* (fem. pl.) to the masc. sing. base:

	Singular	Plural
masculine	*ṣādeq*	*ṣādeqān*
feminine	*ṣādeqt*	*ṣādeqāt*

When the stem ends in *-t*, *-d*, *-ṭ*, the *-t* of the fem. sing. is assimilated and not represented in the script: *bāʿed* (other), fem. *bāʿedd* (from **bāʿedt*).

16.2 Attributive Adjectives. An attributive adjective normally follows the noun it modifies. Agreement in number and gender is in accordance with the principles given in Lesson 5.

personal	masc.	sing.	*negus ṣādeq*	a just king
		pl.	*nagašt ṣādeqān*	just kings

personal	fem. sing.	*negešt ṣādeqt*	a just queen
	pl.	*negeštāt ṣādeqāt*	just queens

non-personal	*hagar bāʿed* / *hagar bāʿedd*	a different city
	ʾahgur bāʿed/bāʿedd / *ʾahgur bāʿedān/bāʿedāt*	different cities

There is also agreement in case:

Rakaba kāleʾta fenota.	He found another road.
Gʷayyu hagara bāʿedda.	They fled to another city.

Descriptive adjectives normally follow the noun they modify and if placed first, gain a certain emphasis. There are other adjectives, however, which normally occur before the modified noun. These include

a. the demonstrative adjectives (already introduced in Lessons 5-6);

b. cardinal and ordinal numbers (see Lesson 23; *kāleʾ* in the present vocabulary belongs to this group);

c. *kʷell-* each, every, all (Lesson 10);

d. the quantifying adjectives *ʿabiy* (large) and *bezux* (many, much), although both of these occur frequently in post-nominal position.

Vocabulary 16

Nouns:

sem (pl. *ʾasmāt*) m. name; fame, reputation.

newāy (pl. *-āt*) m. vessel, utensil, instrument; property, possessions, wealth.

ḥawāreyā (pl. *-t*) apostle.

radʾ (pl. *ʾardāʾ*, *ʾardeʾt*) helper, assistant; disciple, follower.

Adjectives (and Stative Verbs): [Because stative verbs have exactly the same range of meanings as their corresponding adjectives, definitions will not be repeated. The verb may have the meaning either of "being" or "becoming": thus, *beʿla* he was rich, he became rich, he has become rich.]

kāleʾ (f. *-t*) other, another, second. As noun: associate, companion.

bāʻed (f. *-d*) other, different; strange, alien.
xāṭe' (f. *-t*) sinful, wicked. As noun: sinner.
rāteʻ (f. *-t*) just, righteous, truthful, sincere. Verb: *ratʻa*.
bāʻel (f. *-t*; pl. *'abʻelt*) rich, wealthy. Verb: *beʻla*.
ṣādeq (f. *-t*) righteous, just, true; faithful, truthful. Verb: *ṣadqa*.

Verbs:

samaya to name. Note the constructions:

Samayato Yoḥannes(hā). } She named him John.
Samayato sema Yoḥannes(hā).
Samayato semo la-wald Yoḥannes(hā). She named the child John.

Exercises

A.
1. mak^{w}annen bāʻel
2. be'sit bāʻelt
3. liqān 'abʻelt
4. nabiy ṣādeq
5. nabiyāt ṣādeqān
6. welud ṣādeqān
7. 'awāled rāteʻāt
8. ḥezb xāṭe'ān
9. rad' rāteʻ
10. 'ardā' ṣādeqān
11. kāle't fenot
12. kāle't ḥamar
13. kāle' ʻeḍ
14. kāle'ān nabiyāt
15. baḥāwert bāʻed
16. nabiyāt bāʻedān
17. kāle' newāy
18. ḥawāreyāt rāteʻān
19. ṣaḥaft xāṭe'ān
20. kāle' ʻaṣada wayn

B.
1. Waḍ'u 'ardā'ihu westa k^{w}ello baḥāwerta medr.
2. Weḥza māy 'em-we'etu newāy.
3. Malā'ku wayna westa kāle' newāy wa-wadaykewwo qedmēhu.
4. Zentu we'etu 'asmātihomu la-'arde'tihu.
5. Qatalewwo la-nabiy xāṭe' wa-sadadewwomu la-'ardā'ihu 'em-mā'kalomu.
6. Qoma neguš wa-ṣawweʻomu la-'agbertihu.
7. Xalafna 'em-xabēhomu wa-'atona 'enta kāle't fenot.
8. Maṣ'u xaba kāhen mesla kāle' mašwāʻt.
9. Fannawo la-zentu ḥawāreyā rāteʻ westa hagarena.
10. Sadadu ṣaḥāfē xāṭe'a 'em-bētomu.
11. Naš'u newāyeya wa-g^{w}ayyu hagara bāʻedda.
12. Samayani 'abuya sema Yoḥannes.
13. Rakabku kāle'ta ḥamara xaba ḥayqa bāḥr.

14. Naš’a ’a’bāna wa-šaw‘a dibēhomu mašwā‘ta la-’Egzi’abḥēr.
15. Wa-naš’o la-walda ’exuhu meslēhu, wa-ḥora wa-baṣḥa beḥēra bā‘eda.
16. Wa-’emze ‘adawu kāle’ta bāḥra wa-baṣḥu xaba hagaru.
17. Nasseḥa we’etu xāṭe’ ’em-xaṭi’atu wa-gab’a westa bēta Kerestiyān.
18. Rakabomu la-kāle’ānihu ba-westa bēta mak^{w}annen.
19. Motu sab’ xāṭe’ān wa-ḥaywu sab’ rāte‘ān wa-ṣādeqān.
20. Hallawu sab’ xāṭe’ān ba-westa k^{w}ellā medr ba-we’etu mawā‘el.
21. Manna šēmka ’ēpis qoposa lā‘lēhomu?
22. Wa-soba mota liqa pāppāsāt, maṣ’u ḥezb ’em-baḥāwert bā‘edān hagaro wa-bakayu diba motu la-we’etu be’si ṣādeq.
23. Ḥanaṣu kāle’ta hagara ba-westa ’adbār wa-waḍ’u heyya ’em-mā’kalēna.
24. Ba-we’etu warx ’i-nabaru ’ardā’ihu meslēhu, ’allā ḥoru wa-sabaku wangēlo westa kāle’ān baḥāwert.
25. Mannu we’etu semeka wa-mannu we’etu ’asmātihomu la-’axawika?
26. Zanta maṣḥafa targ^{w}ama ’em-lesāna ’Afrenj, wa-kāle’āna ’em-lesāna Yonānāwiyān.

Lesson 17

17.1 Adjectives: the Pattern *Qetul*. By far the most common pattern for adjectives is *qetul*, which, with the related patterns *qettul* (from D verbs) and *qutul* (from L verbs), has certain formal peculiarities:

(a) When the fem. sing. ending *-t* is added, the *-u-* of the final stem syllable is replaced by *-e-*:

masc.	*kebur*	fem.	*kebert*	mighty, glorious
	qeddus		*qeddest*	holy
	buruk		*burekt*	blessed

(b) When the base form ends in *-uy*, the sequence *-eyt* expected according to the foregoing rule is usually, but not always, contracted to *-it*:

masc.	*xeruy*	fem.	*xerit*	chosen, elect
	beluy		*belit*	old, worn out
	ʾekuy		*ʾekit*	bad, evil

(c) When the second root consonant is *-w-*, the pattern *qetul* is optionally replaced by *qetel*. It is probable that this represents an assimilatory change of the sequence *-ewu-* to *-ewwe-* (with *-ww-*), but since the evidence is ambiguous on this point, we have retained the transcription with the simple *-w-*. Both *qetul* and *qetel* are attested as the base form for most of these adjectives:

masc.	*mewut/mewet*	fem.	*mewett*	dead
	dewuy/dewey		*deweyt*	ill, sick

(d) A similar change occurs when the third radical consonant is *-w-*. Here writings with *-ew* (not *-uw*) are more consistent. The feminine singular *-ewt* contracts to *-ut*:

masc.	*ʿelew*	fem.	*ʿelut*	perverse, wicked

The feminine plural of all these adjectives may be based on the masculine stem (thus *keburāt*, *beluyāt*, *deweyāt*) or, much more rarely, on the feminine singular form (thus *kebertāt*, *belitāt*, *deweytāt*). Note the feminine forms for stems with final dentals:

masc.	*kebud*	fem.	*kebedd*	heavy
	šeṭuṭ		*šeṭeṭṭ*	torn.

17.2 Adjectives as Predicates. Clauses with adjectival predicates have the following basic patterns:

(a) pronoun subject: $\text{Adj.}_{\text{pred.}} + \text{Pron.}_{\text{subj.}}$

(b) noun subject: $\text{Adj.}_{\text{pred.}} \pm$ 3rd pers. pron. + $\text{Noun}_{\text{subj.}}$

Examples:

Dewey ʾana.	I am ill.
Ṣādeqān neḥna.	We are righteous.
ʾEkuy weʾetu.	He is evil.
ʾEkuy weʾetu makʷannen.	The judge is bad.
Qeddest yeʾeti hagar.	The city is holy.
Ṣādeqān ʾemuntu nagašt.	The kings are just.
Rāteʿān nabiyāt.	The prophets are righteous.

Agreement in number and gender is present to the same extent as with the attributive adjective. An adjectival predicate is negated with *ʾi-*:

ʾI-dewey ʾana.	I am not ill.

The various syntactic patterns given here and elsewhere represent the nucleus of a given predication, basically a predicate + subject order for all predications in the language. When emphasis is required, or when a new subject is introduced, this may be placed at the beginning of the clause (termed preposing, topicalizing):

Nagašt ṣādeqān ʾemuntu.	The kings are righteous.

This order produces ambiguity, since our example could also be translated "They are just kings," taking *ṣādeqān* as attributive. Such ambiguities are usually resolved from the context or by the use of various preposing particles suffixed to the first element. These particles will be introduced in a later lesson.

17.3 Adverbial Predicates. Any local adverb *(heyya, zeyya)* or prepositional phrase may serve as the predicate of a non-verbal clause: *ʾAna zeyya* I am here; *Meslēna ʾEgziʾabḥēr* God is with us; *ʾEm-manfas qeddus weʾetu* It is from the Holy Spirit. *Hallawa* is used in such predications only when explicit past tense is required; even then an ambiguity about tense remains.

Vocabulary 17

Nouns:

manfas (pl. *-āt, manāfest*) m.f. spirit; the Spirit of God; a spirit or demon (good or bad). *Manfas Qeddus* the Holy Spirit.
lebs (pl. *'albās*) m. clothing, clothes; a garment.
warēzā (pl. *warāzut*) a youth, young man.
te'mert (pl. *-āt, ta'āmer, -āt*) m.f. a sign, omen; miracle, wonder.

Adjectives:

'elew (f. *'elut*) crooked, perverse, evil; rebellious, heretical.
qeddus (f. *qeddest*) holy, sacred; as noun: saint, esp. in titles, e.g. *Qeddus Mārqos* Saint Mark.
be'ul (f. *be'elt*) rich, wealthy.
mewut/mewet (f. *mewett*; pl. *mewutān, mewetān, mutān*) dead.
beluy (f. *belit*) old, worn out, decrepit, obsolete. Verb: *balya*. *Ḥegg Belit* the Old Testament.
bezux (f. *bezext*) many, much, numerous, abundant. Verb: *bazxa*.
'ekuy (f. *'ekit*) evil, bad, wicked. Verb: *'akya*.
dewuy/dewey (f. *deweyt*) sick, ill. Verb: *dawaya*.
retu' (f. *rete't*) just, righteous; straight, level, even; correct, proper, orthodox. *hāymānot rete't* the orthodox faith.
ḥezun (f. *ḥezent*) sad.

Exercises

A. 1. ḥamar belit
2. bezux xaṭi'at
3. ḥawāreyā qeddus
4. newāy beluy
5. rad' 'ekuy
6. neguš 'elew
7. kāhen retu'
8. bezux mašāwe'
9. sem 'ekuy
10. wald dewuy
11. 'a'bān bezext
12. bezux dam
13. maṣḥaf beluy
14. 'elat 'ekit
15. wangēl qeddus

B. Pluralize the singular items in Exercise A.

C. 1. Zāti hagar 'ekit ye'eti.
2. 'Elewān 'emuntu 'ardā'ihu.
3. Qeddest ye'eti zāti hagar.
4. Be'ulān 'emuntu ḥezba zentu beḥēr.
5. Mewut metā.
6. La-ment ḥezun 'anta?

7. ʼEkit yeʼeti zā-beʼsit.
8. Ze-weʼetu ḥegg qeddus.
9. Bezuxān ʼemuntu xāṭeʼān zeyya.
10. ʼAna dewey ʼana. ʼAnti-nu deweyt ʼanti?
11. Zentu weʼetu maṣāḥefta Ḥegg Belit.
12. Hallawu manāfest ʼekuyān heyya.
13. Hāymānotena hāymānot reteʻt yeʼeti.
14. Dewey zentu warēzā.
15. Beluy ʼalbāsihu.
16. Ze-weʼetu teʼmert qeddus.
17. Ḥezunān ʼemuntu ḥezbomu.
18. Beluy weʼetu lebseya.

D. 1. Gabra Qeddus Mārqos bezuxa taʼāmera.
2. Seḥtu ʼem-hāymānot reteʻt.
3. ʼI-samāʻna la-nagaru ʼekuy.
4. Warada Manfas Qeddus lāʻlēhu.
5. Ḥanaṣu bezuxāna ʼabyāta.
6. Qatalna weʼeta nabiya ʻelewa.
7. ʼI-reʼikemu-nu taʼāmerātihu?
8. Sadadewwomu la-sabʼ ʼekuyān.
9. Ḥezun metā baʼentiʼahā.
10. Takalu bezuxāta ʻeḍawa heyya.
11. Našʼewwo la-newāyu la-beʼsi beʻul.
12. Šēṭkewwā la-ḥamareya belit.
13. Fannawo la-radʼu xaba beʼsit deweyt.
14. Qarbu xabēhu ḥezb bezuxān.
15. Gaššaṣa warāzuta ʼekuyāna baʼenta xaṭiʼatomu.
16. Naṣṣarkewwo la-maṣḥaf wa-reʼiku kama Ḥegg Belit weʼetu.
17. Mannu targ^{w}ama Ḥegga Belita la-lesāna Geʻz?
18. Zentu teʼmert ʼem-Manfas Qeddus weʼetu.
19. Našʼa ʼalbāsa wa-g^{w}ayya ʼem-bēt.
20. Konat ʼemmu beʼsita beʻelta.
21. Bazxa newāyu wa-beʻla ba-māʼkala zentu ḥezb.
22. Dawayat ʼextu wa-ʼi-ḥaywat ʼeska zāti ʻelat.

Lesson 18

18.1 Adjectives: The Pattern *Qatil*. A relatively small but important group of adjectives has the pattern *qatil* or the related pattern *qattil* (from D verbs). The feminine singular is formed by replacing the stem vowel -*i*- with -*ā*-; no -*t* is added:

masc.	*ʿabiy*	fem.	*ʿabāy*	great, large
	ḥaddis		*ḥaddās*	new

The feminine plural may be based on either stem: *ḥaddisāt* or *ḥaddāsāt*.

The variant pattern *qetil* occurs when the middle root consonant is a guttural. The feminine form is the same as the preceding.

masc.	*reḥib*	fem.	*raḥāb*	broad

Many adjectives *qatil* have a common (masc. and fem.) internal plural form *qatalt* in addition to the external plural forms:

sing.	*ʿabiy*	plural	*ʿabayt*	great
	balix		*balāxt*	sharp
	ṭabib		*ṭababt*	wise.

18.2 The Comparative. The comparative is expressed by adding a prepositional phrase with *ʾemenna* to the adjective:

ʾEkuy weʾetu ʾemenna negš. He is more evil than the king.

The comparison may be intensified by the adverb *fadfāda* (much, much more):

Ṭabib weʾetu fadfāda ʾem-ʾexuhu. He is much wiser than his brother.

All stative verbs may be similarly construed:

Bazxu weʾetu ḥezb ʾem-ḥezbena. That people became more numerous than our people.

The adverb *ṭeqqa* (very) is also frequently used to intensify an adjective; it may be placed before the adjective or after it: *Ṭeqqa dewey weʾetu* or *Dewey ṭeqqa weʾetu* He is very ill.

Vocabulary 18

Nouns:

ʿāmat or *ʿām* (pl. *ʿāmatāt*) f.m. year.

šegā (pl. *-t*) m. flesh, meat (human or animal), esp. of the flesh as opposed to the spirit; frequently = body as a whole.

ḥabl (pl. *ʾaḥbāl*) m.f. rope, cord.

ḥeywat m.f. life, lifetime. *ḥaywa ḥeywata ʾekuya* he led a wicked life.

Adjectives and Stative Verbs:

ḥaddis (f. *ḥaddās*; pl. *ḥaddast*) new. *Ḥegg Ḥaddis* New Testament.

ʿabiy (f. *ʿabāy*: pl. *ʿabayt*) big, large, important, great; *ba-ʿabiy qāl* in a loud voice. Verb: *ʿabya*.

ṭabib (f. *ṭabāb*: pl. *ṭababt*) wise, prudent; skilled, expert (e.g. of craftsmen). Verb: *ṭabba*.

lehiq (f. *leheqt*) grown up, adult; old, eldest. Verb: *lehqa* to grow up.

nawix (f. *nawāx*; pl. *nawāxt*) high, lofty; tall; long; distant, far off. Verb: *noxa*.

Adverbs:

fadfāda exceedingly, very much, greatly.

ṭeqqa very, extremely.

Exercises

A. 1. ʾēpis qopos ṭabib
2. sem ʿabiy
3. lebs ḥaddis
4. warēzā nawix
5. taʾāmer ʿabayt
6. manāfest ʾekuyāt
7. ʾardeʾt ṭabibān
8. newāy ḥaddās
9. ḥegag ḥaddast
10. kāhen ʿabiy
11. mašāweʿ ʿabayt
12. dabr nawix
13. fenot nawāx
14. baḥāwert nawāxt
15. bāḥr ʿabāy

B. 1. Nawix ʾana ʾem-ʾexuya.
2. Nawāx yeʾeti ʾem-k^{w}ellon ʾaxātihā.
3. Nawāxt ʾadbāra beḥērekemu ʾem-ʾadbāra beḥērena.
4. Zentu lebs ḥaddis weʾetu ʾem-lebseya.
5. Lehiq ʾanta ʾemennēya.
6. Ṭabib ʾanta fadfāda ʾemenna kāleʾānika.
7. ʿAbiy zentu bēt ʾem-k^{w}ellu ʾabyāta hagar.

8. Lehiq zentu ḥawāreyā ’em-kāle’ān ḥawāreyāt.
9. Nawix fadfāda ’em-zeyya we’etu beḥēromu.
10. Be‘ul ’abuka ’em-’abuya.

C. 1. Naš’u ḥabla nawixa wa-ḥoru ḥayqa bāḥr.
2. Ba-ye’eti ‘āmat mo’na we’eta ḥezba.
3. Šēma kāhen diyāqonāta ḥaddasta.
4. Ḥaywa ḥeywata nawixa wa-’ekuya.
5. Šawā‘na šegā ’arāwit mašwā‘ta la-’Amlākena.
6. Šēṭku xabēhu ḥamareya wa-’aḥbāleya ḥaddisa.
7. Ṣawwe‘omu kāhen ‘abiy la-ḥezba hagar.
8. Maṣ’u sab’ ṭabibān wa-‘abayt wa-’ab‘elt xaba negušena.
9. Ṣadaqqu ba-ḥeywateya ’em-’axaweya.
10. Wa-soba leheqqu, fannawani ’abuya xaba ’exuhu.
11. Ṭabbat ’emmu ’em-kāle’āt ’anesta hagar.
12. ‘Abya semu la-zentu nabiy ba-k^{w}ellu baḥāwerta medrena.
13. Be’situ la-mak^{w}annen ṭeqqa be‘elt ye’eti.
14. Soba baṣāḥna xaba we’etu dabr, re’ina kama ṭeqqa nawix we’etu, wa-’i-‘adonāhu.
15. Ba-‘āmata motu la-pāppāsena mo’una ’ellontu sab’ ‘elewān wa-naš’ewwā la-hagarena.
16. Soba naṣṣarku zanta maṣḥafa, re’iku kama ’em-Ḥegg Belit we’etu.
17. Dawaya waldu wa-’i-ḥaywa ’eska mesēta ye’eti ‘elat.
18. Ṭababt wa-rāte‘ān ’emuntu ’ardā’ihu.
19. ’Efo ṭababka ’em-k^{w}ellena?
20. Našā’ku ’ebana ‘abayta wa-ḥanaṣku bēta.

Lesson 19

19.1 Adjectives: The Pattern *Qattāl*. Adjectives of the type *qattāl* have no consistent feminine form in the singular. One may find *qattālt* (no stem change), *qattalt* (with *-a-* for *-ā-*), or the masculine form may be used for the feminine. In the Ethiopic script adjectives of this pattern are indistinguishable in the singular from the feminine singular of the type *qatil* (i.e. *qatāl*). The traditional pronunciation merges all these forms and regularly doubles the second root consonant in both types.

19.2 Adjectives in *-āwi* and *-āy*. These adjectives are lexically numerous but are rather infrequently used, being equivalent to preferred relative constructions or construct phrases. They are based on a variety of nouns and denote "of" or "pertaining to," often corresponding to English adjectives in -ly: *medrāwi* of the world, worldly; *samāyāwi* of heaven, celestial, divine. Their forms are as follows:

masc. sing.	*samāyāwi*	plural	*samāyāwiyān* (or *-eyān*)
fem. sing.	*samāyāwit*		*samāyāwiyāt* (or *-eyāt*).

Optional forms in *-āy* occur for most such adjectives; these have no peculiarities in inflection: *-āy*, *-āyt*, *-āyān*, *-āyāt*.

19.3 Adjectives: Miscellaneous Types. The adjectival patterns treated in the preceding three lessons include the vast majority of derived adjectives in the language. Occasionally, however, other patterns, usually nominal in origin, are employed. E.g.

qatl: *ʾabd* (f. *ʾabedd*; pl. *ʾabdān*, *ʾabdāt*) foolish, ignorant, imprudent; as a noun: a fool.
qetāl: *ḥeyāw* (f. *-t*; pl. *-ān*, *-āt*) alive, living.

These are unproductive types as adjectives and will be given without further comment in the vocabularies.

19.4 Qualification. An adjective may stand in construct with a following noun, which qualifies its meaning:

ʾekuya lebb	evil of heart
šannāya gaṣṣ	beautiful of aspect (or face)

nawixa qom tall of stature.

19.5 Substantivization. Any adjective may be used as a noun, equivalent to English "one who is ... (those who are ...)":

dewuy one who is sick, a sick person
dewuyān the sick, those who are sick

The feminine singular *qetelt* is especially common in the sense of "that which is ...":

ʾekit that which is evil, evil, wickedness
reteʿt that which is correct or proper.

Note that a combination of substantivization and qualification may lead to superficial ambiguities:

ʾekuyāna lebb those who are evil of heart
ʾekuyāna hagar the evil ones of the city.

Vocabulary 19

Nouns and Derived Adjectives:

ʿālam (pl. *-āt*) m.f. world, this world; the universe, all creation; eternity, all time present, past, and future. *la-ʿālam* forever. *ʿālamāwi* of the world, worldly.

madxen (pl. *-ān*) savior, redeemer.

ʾegziʾ (pl. *ʾagāʾezt*, *ʾagāʾest*) lord, master, leader, chief. *ʾEgziʾena* Our Lord. *ʾegzeʾt* lady, mistress. *ʾEgzeʾtena* Our Lady (Mary).

mendābē m.f. affliction, torment.

lebb (pl. *ʾalbāb*) m.f. heart; mind, intellect.

gaṣṣ (pl. *-āt*) face; aspect, appearance; type, sort.

Adjectives:

nawwāx (f. idem) = *nawix*.

šannāy (f. *-t*) beautiful, fine, excellent, good (both physical and moral senses). Verb: *šannaya* D.

naddāy (f. *-t*) poor, destitute; deficient (in: *ba-*). Verb: *nadya*

xēr (f. *-t*) good, excellent (used in all senses of English "good").

ḥeyāw (f. *-t*) alive, living. *ʾemma-ḥeyāw* Mother of the Living (i.e. Eve).

medrāwi (f. -*t*) of the world, worldly (as opposed to spiritual or heavenly).

berhānāwi (f. -*t*) of or pertaining to light, esp. in the heavenly or spiritual sense.

samāyāwi (f. -*t*) heavenly, divine, celestial.

manfasāwi (f. -*t*) of the spirit, spiritual.

šegāwi fleshly (not spiritual), carnal (of sins).

wangēlāwi (f. -*t*) gospel (as adj.); as noun: evangelist.

ṣenuʿ (f. *ṣeneʿt*) strong, powerful; firm, sure; lasting, enduring; hard, harsh, severe. Verb: *ṣanʿa*.

Exercises

A. 1. ḥāymānot ṣeneʿt
2. lebb ṣenuʿ
3. waṛēzā xēr
4. beʾsi naddāy
5. ḥabl ṣenuʿ
6. newāy medrāwi
7. malʾak berhānāwi
8. hagar samāyāwit
9. nagarāt manfasāwiyān
10. ḥeywat šegāwi
11. beʾsit šannāyt
12. mendābē ʿabiy
13. gaṣṣ ʾekuy
14. dabr nawwāx
15. wangēlāwi rāteʿ

B. 1. wangēlu la-ʾEgziʾena
2. mendābēhomu la-Kerestiyān
3. qālātihu la-madxenena
4. ḥeywatā la-ʾEgzeʾtena
5. ʾalbābihomu la-ʿabayt
6. maṣāḥeftihomu la-wangēlāwiyān
7. gaṣṣātihomu la-warāzut
8. ʾabyātihomu la-ʾagāʾestina
9. naddāyāna zentu ʿālam
10. gaṣṣu la-Manfas Qeddus
11. ʾasmātihomu la-xērān wa-la-ʾekuyān
12. ʾasmātihomu la-samāyāweyān
13. nagaromu la-ʿelewān wa-xāṭeʾān
14. qālātihomu la-ṭababt
15. ḥeywatomu la-qeddusān
16. mendābēhomu la-naddāyān wa-deweyān
17. newāyomu la-ʿabayt wa-ʾabʿelt
18. xērāna lebb
19. šannāyāna gaṣṣ
20. ṣenuʿāna lebb

C. 1. Ḥeyāwān ’emuntu wa-’i-mutān.
2. Ṣene‘t ye’eti hāymānotu.
3. Xēr lebbeka wa-šannāy gaṣṣeka.
4. Naddāya lebb we’etu wa-’i-ṭabib.
5. Ṣenu‘āt ’ahgurihomu wa-‘abiyāt ’em-’ahgurikemu.
6. Ḥezuna gaṣṣ we’etu.
7. Naddāyān ’ardā’ihu wa-’i-bezux newāyomu.
8. Ḥeyāw ’Egzi’ena wa-’i-mewut.
9. Zāti fenot ṭeqqa nawwāx ye’eti.
10. Be‘ul ’egzi’eya fadfāda ’em-’agā’eztikemu.
11. Ḥaywa zentu qeddus ḥeywata manfasāwita.
12. Ṭeqqa ḥezunān ’emuntu ’albābihomu la-weludihu.

D. 1. We’eta ’amira xalafa ’Egzi’ena ’em-zentu ‘ālam wa-‘arga xaba ’abuhu samāyāwi.
2. Ba-mawā‘ela mendābē g^{w}ayayna hagara bā‘edda wa-nabarna ḥeyya ’eska motu la-negušena ‘elew.
3. Soba lehqu weludihu, waḍ’u ’em-bēta ’abuhomu wa-ḥoru westa kāle’ beḥēr.
4. Lehqat zāti walatt wa-šannayat ’em-k^{w}ellon ’anesta hagar.
5. ’Ama samā‘na kama maṣ’a ’Egzi’ena, waḍā’na wa-rakabnāhu ba-westa fenot.
6. ’I-samā‘kemu-nu ta’āmerāta ’Egze’tena?
7. Ba-ye’eti ‘āmat nadyu ’ab‘elt wa-be‘lu naddāyān.
8. Ḥazanu fadfāda ba-lebbomu wa-nasseḥu kama gabru zanta xaṭi’ata.
9. Sabaku wangēlāwiyān ba-wangēlu la-madxenena ba-westa k^{w}ello baḥāwerta ‘ālam.
10. Qarbu naddāyān xabēna wa-sa’alu xebesta wa-šegā ’emennēna.
11. Ṭeqqa šannāy ’aq^{w}ṣela zentu ‘eḍ nawwāx ba-berhāna ḍaḥāy.
12. Xalafu ’awrāx wa-‘āmatāt, wa-’i-be‘lu wa-’i-šannayat ḥeywatomu.
13. Maṣ’a lā‘lēhomu mendābē ‘abiy wa-’i-ṣan‘u ba-hāymānot rete‘t.
14. Sadadomu bā‘el la-naddāyān ’em-qedma bētu.
15. We‘ya lebbu la-zentu qeddus ba-hāymānot ṣene‘t.

Lesson 20

20.1 *La-* with Pronominal Suffixes.

líta	to me	*lā́na*	to us
lā́ka	to you (m.s.)	*lakḗmu*	to you (m.pl.)
lā́ki	to you (f.s.)	*lakḗn*	to you (f.pl.)
lotū́	to him	*lṓmu*	to them (m.)
lātí	to her	*lon*	to them (f.)

The preposition *la-* corresponds in general to the dative (to, for) of English. It is used idiomatically with many verbs, however, as will be noted in the vocabularies when appropriate.

20.2 Object Suffixes in a Dative or Prepositional Sense. Object suffixes on a verb are often used to express various case ("prepositional") relationships other than the accusative direct object. For example, in

Wahabani xebesta = Wahaba lita xebesta He gave me bread,

the verbal suffix expresses the dative, or indirect, object, equivalently expressed by the preposition *la-*. In

Sa'alani xebesta = Sa'ala xebesta 'emennēya/xabēya
He asked me for bread,

it corresponds to the prepositional phrases *'emennēya* or *xabēya*. There are only a few categories of verbs where such constructions are frequent, and these are listed below. It should be noted, however, that because personal direct objects (= accusative) of all transitive verbs are usually definite and suffixally expressed by the *qatalo la-neguš* construction, even the large corpus of material at our disposal does not always allow us to distinguish the various types of suffixed objects with some verbs. In describing constructions into which verbs enter, we shall employ the following designations:

acc. dir. obj. means that the verb takes a direct object in the accusative case, which may, if definite and specific, be suffixed directly to the verb in the *qatalo la-neguš* construction.

dat. suff. means that the indirect object (always expressible with *la-*) may be attached suffixally by the *qatalo la-neguš* construction. E.g. *Wahabo la-ʾabuhu warqa* He gave the money to his father.

obj. suff. means that the object of a prepositional phrase (other than *la-*) may be suffixed to the verb, as in our example with *saʾala* above. A typical listing for *saʾala* would be *saʾala* to ask (someone: *ʾemenna*, *xaba*, or obj. suff.) for (something: acc. dir. obj.). We shall also use the designation "obj. suff." when the evidence is ambiguous as to what the precise case relationship is.

a. Verbs of speaking, addressing, and telling:

Nagaro zanta.	He told him this.
Nagaro la-negušʾesma ...	He told the king that ...

b. Verbs of asking. See the example with *saʾala* above.

c. Verbs of giving, surrendering. In addition to the example with *wahaba* above, note

Maṭṭawomu hagara.	He surrendered the city to them.

d. Occasionally, verbs of robbing and depriving:

Našʾani warqeya.	He took my gold away from me.
Saraqani warqeya.	He robbed me of my gold.

e. The verbs of motion *baṣḥa*, *maṣʾa*, and occasionally others, when used in the sense of "befall, happen to, occur to":

Baṣḥani mawāʿela mendābē.	Days of affliction befell me.
Maṣʾani kāleʾ xellinnā.	Another thought occurred to me.

Here the suffixes replace phrases with *lāʿla* and *diba*.

f. Object suffixes on stative and intransitive verbs have three functions:

(1) Equivalent to a comparative construction:

Bazxana weʾetu ḥezb.	That people became more numerous than we (or: too numerous for us).

(2) When the subject is a part of the body or some inalienable feature of the subject (soul, reputation, etc.), a

dative suffix is commonly placed on the verb as a reinforcement of the possessive pronoun:

Mararatani nafseya.	My soul became bitter.
Ḥaywo lebbu.	His heart (i.e. courage) revived.

For the nuance compare English "on" in "His eyes went bad on him."

(3) Elsewhere the sense is that of an appropriate prepositional phrase:

Bakayato. She wept for him *(dibēhu, ba'enti'ahu).*

On the other hand, it should be noted that there are many verbs, especially of "sending, bringing, conducting," where the dative suffix *cannot* be used. E.g.

la'aka to send a message/messenger. The person to whom something is sent requires a preposition *la-* or *xaba*; if a place, the acc. of goal may be used. The message or messenger is the real acc. dir. obj., if expressed:

La'akani xabēhu.	He sent me (as messenger) to him.
Zanta la'aka xaba neguš.	He sent this (as a message) to the king.

wasada to lead, conduct, bring, take. Like the preceding, the person to whom someone or something is taken is introduced by a preposition *(la-, xaba, westa)*, but may not be suffixed to the verb.

The restriction involved in these verbs is apparently connected with the traversal of space (to, toward, over to), and even though the preposition *la-* may be used in this sense, the object is felt to be different from those illustrated above.

20.3 Partitive Apposition. The pronominal suffixes (whether dative or accusative is immaterial) are often used when a part of the body (etc., cf. f,2 above) is the object of the transitive verb:

Sam'ewwo qālo.	They heard his voice.
Gasasato lebso.	She touched his clothing.
'Asarewwo 'edawihu.	They bound his hands.

Vocabulary 20

Nouns:

mesṭir (pl. *-āt*) m.f. mystery (both general and religious senses); frequent in reference to the eucharist.

sisāy m. sustenance, food.

zamad (pl. *'azmād*) m. family, kin, relatives, clan, tribe; kind, sort, species. No clear distinction is maintained between the meanings of the singular and plural forms.

Verbs:

nagara to say, tell (acc. of what is said; dat. suff. or *la-* of person addressed).

nababa to speak to, tell (same constructions as *nagara*).

wahaba to give (acc. dir. obj.; dat. suff. or *la-* of indirect object).

la'aka to send (a message or messenger; see Lesson for constructions).

wasada to lead, conduct, bring, take (see Lesson for constructions).

mahara G / *mahhara* D to teach (someone: suff. obj.; something: acc. dir. obj. or *ba-*, *ba'enta*).

maṭṭawa D to surrender, hand over (acc. dir. obj.; dat. suff. or *la-* of indir. obj.).

'ammara D to tell, show, indicate, make known (something: acc. dir. obj.; to someone: obj. suff.).

Conjunction:

za- that, the fact that (introduces a noun clause after verbs of speaking etc., like *kama* and *'esma*). *ba'enta za-* (conj.) because.

Exercises

A. 1. Wahabani lebso.
2. Šēṭkewwo ḥamareya.
3. Sa'alani sisāya.
4. Marḥuni fenota.
5. Maṣ'ana mendābē.
6. 'Ammarana 'edawihu.
7. Maṭṭonāhu hagarana.
8. Wahabewwo šegā.
9. Naš'uni 'aḥbāleya.
10. 'Ammarkukemu mesṭira.
11. Wahabnāhomu wayna.
12. 'Ammarakemu ta'āmera.
13. Maharato lesāna 'Afrenj.
14. Sa'alato newāya.
15. Šēmana qasāwesta.
16. Bazxana ḥezb.
17. Ṣan'ana mendābē.
18. Ḥazano lebbu.

19. 'Akyo semu. 20. Sa'alkewwo ḥeywata.

B. Convert the verbal suffixes of Ex. A into equivalent prepositional phrases.

C. 1. Nagarkewwomu kama maṣā'ku 'em-kāle't hagar.
2. Nababkemewwo-nu la-zentu warēzā 'esma xalafa zamadu?
3. Wasadewwo la-zentu Qeddus xaba mak^{w}ānenta ḥezb.
4. Mahharo 'abuhu hāymānota rete'ta.
5. Maṭṭawewwā la-hagaromu la-we'etu negus̆.
6. 'I-maṭṭawnāhu hagarana la-we'etu negus̆.
7. Sa'alewwo xebesta wa-wahabomu 'ebana.
8. Zentu we'etu mesṭir 'abiy wa-qeddus.
9. La'ako la-waldu xabēna mesla zentu maṣḥaf.
10. Mannu maharakemu ba-lesāna Ge'z?
11. Maharkomu-nu la-weludika ba'enta wangēlu la-'Egzi'ena?
12. Gas̆s̆aṣomu wa-nagaromu kama fannawo 'Egzi'abḥēr la-waldu westa 'ālam ba'enti'ana k^{w}ellena.
13. La'aka lotu wa-nagaro kama gab'a 'egzi'omu 'em-ḥayqa bāḥr.
14. La-ment nagarkani s̆annāya wa-gabarka 'ekuya lā'lēya?
15. Wahaba lana ḥeywata ḥaddāsa wa-s̆annāyta.
16. Waḍ'a 'em-zamad 'abiy wa-be'ul.
17. Ba'enta ment 'i-samā'kemuni qālāteya?
18. Wahabnāhu sisāya la-fenot wa-fannonāhu westa gadāmāta we'etu beḥēr.
19. Nas̆'o la-warēzā meslēhu 'esma zamadu we'etu.
20. Wasadato la-be'si ba-westa bētā wa-'aqabato heyya 'eska xalafat lēlit.
21. Maṣā'ku ba'enta za-ṣawwā'kani.

Lesson 21

21.1 Medio-passive Verbs: Gt. Most active transitive G, D, L, and Q verbs may be converted into a medio-passive form by prefixing the element *ta-* (in the Perfect). We shall designate these verbs as Gt, Dt, Lt, and Qt respectively:

G	*qatala*	he killed	Gt	*taqatla*	he was killed
D	*fannawa*	he sent	Dt	*tafannawa*	he was sent
L	*bāraka*	he blessed	Lt	*tabāraka*	he was blessed
Q	*targ^{w}ama*	he translated	Qt	*tatarg^{w}ama*	it was translated.

The forms of the Gt verb for the various root types are as follows:

Sound	*taqatla*	he was killed
I-gutt.	*taḥanṣa*	it was built
II-gutt.	*taṣeḥfa*	it was written
III-gutt.	*tasamʿa*	it was heard
I-W	*tawalda*	he was born
II-W	*tamawʾa*	he was defeated
II-Y	*tašayma*	he was appointed
III-W	*tawarwa*	he cast himself down
III-Y	*tasamya*	he was named

$TaC_1aC_2C_3a$ is the norm for all Gt verbs regardless of their G type (i.e. *nabara* versus *gabra*), but an alternate form *taqatala* for some verbs is not uncommon, especially those from roots I-gutt. The basic form *taqatla*, with no vowel between C_2 and C_3, requires that verbs from roots II-gutt. have the vocalism associated with the *gabra* type, namely *taṣeḥfa* (cf. *keḥda*). Inflection of the Perfect follows the same general patterns described for G verbs of the corresponding root types:

taqatla	*taṣeḥfa*	*tasamʿa*	*tamawʾa*	*tašayma*	*tawarwa*
taqatlat	*taṣeḥfat*	*tasamʿat*	*tamawʾat*	*tašaymat*	*tawarwat*
taqatalka	*taṣeḥefka*	*tasamāʿka*	*tamawāʾka*	*tašayamka*	*tawarawka*
etc.	etc.	etc.	etc.	etc.	etc.

Contracted forms like **tamoʾa* are occasionally attested with roots II-W and III-gutt., but the uncontracted forms are the normal ones.

For most of the transitive G verbs introduced thus far the

corresponding Gt verb is a simple passive:

tafarha	he was feared	*tasadda*	he was driven out
tagabra	it was done/made	*tasamʿa*	it was heard
taḥanṣa	it was built	*tašayṭa*	it was sold
tamarḥa	he was led	*tašawʿa*	it was sacrificed
tamawʾa	he was defeated	*taṣeḥfa*	it was written
tanagra	it was spoken	*tatakla*	it was planted
taqabra	he was buried	*tawadya*	he was placed
taqatla	he was killed	*tawehba*	it was given.
tasabka	it was preached		

The passive verb is usually employed when the writer (speaker) does not wish to specify the agent (active subject). An agent is sometimes added, however, with the prepositions *ba-*, *ba-xaba*, or *ʾem-xaba*, but unless a person is involved, *ba-* would usually be taken as indicating instrument, not agent.

Gt verbs may also have a reflexive or middle meaning which requires special attention:

taʿadawa (1) = *ʿadawa*; (2) to transgress (a law: *ʾem-*; against a person: *lāʿla*).

taʿaqaba (1) passive of *ʿaqaba*; (2) to guard one's self against (*ʾemenna* or obj. suff.)

tarakba to be found. As virtually equivalent to *kona* (cf. French se trouver, Hebrew *nimṣāʾ*) it may be followed by a predicate noun or adjective in the accusative: *tarakba ṣādeqa* he was found (to be) righteous.

tareʾya to appear, seem (to be). Same remarks as with *tarakba* above.

There are some Gt verbs which either have no corresponding G verb or whose meanings are not directly related to the G verb. Note especially the following:

tanabba to be read, recited.

taleʾka to serve, minister to (acc. dir. obj.).

tamʿeʿa to become angry, enraged. (No G verb).

taḥašya to rejoice. (No G verb)

There are two Gt verbs with formal peculiarities:

tanašʾa is the regular passive of *našʾa* and means "to be taken, etc." The form *tanše'a*, inflected as though from a Q root *tnš'*, is reflexive and means "to get up, arise; to rise (from the dead); to rise up against *(lāʿla)*."

tamʿeʿa (to become angry) has the same peculiarities as *tanše'a*, but because of the clustering of gutturals at the end of the stem it has developed two variant stem forms. All possible inflections are found:

(1) *tamʿeʿa*	(2) *tamʿa*	(3) *tamaʿaʿa*
tamʿeʿat	*tamʿat*	*tamaʿaʿat*
tamʿāʿka etc.	*tamāʿka* etc.	*tamaʿāʿka* etc.

When the corresponding G verb governs two accusatives *(šēma, samaya, mal'a)*, the second accusative is retained after the passive Gt verb:

Tašayma kāhena.	He was appointed priest.
Tasamya Yoḥanneshā.	He was named John.
Tamal'a māya.	It was filled with water.

Vocabulary 21

Nouns:

tazkār memorial service or holiday, commemoration; memory; memorandum, notation. *gabra tazkāra* to celebrate a commemoration. *ʿelata tazkār* day of commemoration.

dammanā (pl. *-t*) m.f. cloud(s).

gebr (pl. *-āt*, *gebar*) m.f. deed, act; work, task, business; religious service, liturgy; product, artifact, creation.

meʿrāf (pl. *-āt*) a quiet place, a resting place; one's final resting place; a measure of length, a stade; chapter of a book.

maqšaft (pl. *-āt*) m.f. punishment, beating, whipping; frequently in the sense of "divine punishment."

maqdas temple, sanctuary. *Bēta Maqdas* the Temple in Jerusalem.

Verbs:

walada to bear (a child); to beget children (by: *ba-xaba*). *tawalda* Gt to be born.

mēṭa to turn away, divert; to turn, direct (e.g. face; toward: *xaba*); to return something/someone to original place; to convert, transform (acc. dir. obj. + *westa*, *la-*). *tamayṭa* Gt passive;

to be converted (religious sense); to turn around, come back, return.

taḥašaya/taḥašya Gt to rejoice (in, at: *ba-*, *ba'enta*).

tam'e'a/tam'a Gt to become angry, enraged (at: *lā'la*, *diba*, *ba'enta*).

'amna to be true; to believe (acc. dir. obj. or *la-*, esp. with persons); to believe in *(ba-)*, have faith in. *ta'amana/ta'amna* Gt (1) to be believed; (2) to believe in, have faith in (*ba-* or acc.); (3) to confess (sins); (4) to be confident, secure.

Proper Names:

Bēta Leḥēm Bethlehem.

'Iyasus Kerestos Jesus Christ.

Exercises

A. Transform each of the following into the passive, omitting the agent (subject).

Example: Ḥanaṣu hagara —> Taḥanṣat hagar.

1. Farāhku we'eta nagara.
2. Gabra 'Amlāk zanta 'ālama.
3. Qabarewwo la-šegāhu mesla zamadu.
4. Sadadewwo la-madxenena.
5. Qatalewwo la-'egzi'omu.
6. Samā'na qāla mendābēhu.
7. Šēṭna k^wello 'aḥbālina.
8. Ṣaḥafu 'asmātihomu westētu.
9. Wahabewwo sisāya wa-lebsa.
10. Marḥewwo la-warēzā zeyya.

B. 1. Tafarāhku ba'enta semeya 'abiy.
2. La-mannu tagabrat zāti ḥamar?
3. Tamaw'u ḥezbena wa-tanaš'at hagarena.
4. Tamarāḥna westa fenot rete't.
5. Tašayaṭku ba-'edawihomu la-'ellontu sab'.
6. Taṣeḥfa zentu maṣḥafa ḥegag ba-mawā'ela 'abawina.
7. Tasadadna 'em-'abyātina wa-'em-xaba 'azmādina.
8. Mā'zē-nu tamawā'kemu wa-tanašā'kemu?
9. Mannu tašayma 'ēpis qoposa diba beḥēreka?
10. Ye'eta 'amira tataklat hāymānot ṣene't ba-lebbu.

C. 1. Soba ta'adona we'eta dabra wa-baṣāḥna hagaromu, nabarna heyya k^wellā 'āmata.
2. Tale'ekkewwo la-zentu qeddus 'eska 'elata motu.
3. 'I-'aqabkemu ḥegaga ḥezbena wa-'i-ta'aqabkemu 'emenna xāṭe'ān.
4. Ta'aqabat hagarena wa-'i-tanaš'at.

5. Tanše'at 'em-heyya wa-gab'at xaba zamadā.
6. 'I-samā‘kemu-nu za-tanše'a 'Egzi'ena 'em-mutān wa-za ḥeyāw we'etu?
7. Ba-ye'eti ‘elat tarakabku ‘elewa wa-tasadadku 'em-mā'kalomu.
8. Tare'ya gaṣṣu ḍaḥaya wa-lebsu berhāna samāyāwē.
9. Tanabba zentu k^{w}ellu maṣḥaf ba-bēta maqdas ye'eta 'amira.
10. Tasamayku sema Yoḥanneshā ba-sema 'ex^{w}a 'abuya.
11. Tamal'a samāy berhāna wa-tasam‘a qāla malā'ekt.
12. Qatalewwo ba'enta za-ta‘adawa 'em-ḥegagihomu.
13. Wa-'emdexra-ze tale'ka ba-bēta maqdas k^{w}ello mawā‘ela ḥeywatu.
14. Zāti ‘elat tazkāra motu la-Qeddus Mārqos.
15. Tamal'a samāy dammanāta wa-warada zenām wa-barad.

D. 1. Waladat walda la-be'sihā wa-samayato sema Mārqos.
2. Tawalda 'Iyasus Kerestos ba-Bēta Leḥēm.
3. 'Aytē tawaladkemu 'anta wa-'axawika?
4. Tanabba lana maṣḥaf ba'enta gebara qeddusān.
5. Semu la-zentu maṣḥaf Gebra Ḥawāreyāt we'etu, wa-'em-Ḥegg Ḥaddis we'etu.
6. Wa-'emdexra sabaka ba-wangēl westa 'entākti medr, tamayṭa xabēna.
7. Wa-soba xalafa we'etu mendābē, taḥašayna fadfāda.
8. Fannawa 'Egzi'abḥēr zanta maqšafta lā‘lēna ba'enta xaṭi'atena.
9. Wa-'ama zanta nagarana, mēṭna gaṣṣātina 'emennēhu wa-'i-naṣṣarnāhu.
10. Rakabna me‘rāfa šannāya wa-nabarna heyya 'eska ṣebāḥ.
11. Wadayo la-šegāhu la-'abuhu westa me‘rāfu.
12. Ba-'ayy me‘rāfa zentu maṣḥaf tarakba nagara gebarihu?
13. Ba-'ayy ‘elata warx wa-ba-'ayy warxa ‘āmat tagabra tazkāru?
14. La-ment baṣḥana zentu maqšaft?
15. Ba-zentu qāl tamayṭa westa 'arwē medr wa-wadqa diba medr.
16. 'Amanna ba-qālātihu wa-konna Kerestiyāna.
17. Soba zanta samā‘ku, tam‘ā‘ku ṭeqqa fadfāda wa-našā'ku 'ebna wa-qatalkewwo.
18. Ḥoru xabēhu wa-ta'amnu xaṭāwe'ihomu.
19. 'I-'amanna lotu wa-sadadnāhu 'em-xabēna.
20. Tam‘a lā‘la 'ardā'ihu wa-xalafa 'em-qedmēhomu.

Lesson 22

22.1 Medio-Passive Verbs: Dt, Lt, Qt. The relationship of D to Dt etc. is like that of G to Gt and requires little further comment. Note the following verbs derived from D, L, and Q verbs already introduced:

Dt	*tafannawa*	to be sent
	tagaššaṣa	to be reproached, instructed
	tamaṭṭawa	to be surrendered, handed over; to accept, receive
	taṣawwe'a	to be summoned, called
Lt	*tabāraka*	to be blessed
Qt	*tatarg^{w}ama*	to be translated

The Dt verb *tanasseḥa* is synonymous with D *nasseḥa* to repent. *Tamaṭṭawa* in the sense "to receive, accept" illustrates an interesting phenomenon: when a verb in its active form governs both a direct and an indirect object, it is sometimes possible to effect the passive transformation on either object. This is fully comparable to English, where the passive counterpart of "They gave me the book" is either (1) "The book was given to me" or (2) "I was given the book." Thus, *Maṭṭawewwo hagara* (They surrendered the city to him) becomes either (1) *Tamaṭṭawat lotu hagar* (The city was surrendered to him) or (2) *Tamaṭṭawa hagara* (He was surrendered the city = He received or accepted the city). The Dt of D *mahhara* is similar: (1) the thing taught may be the subject, as in *Tamahhara ḥegg* (The law was taught), or (2) the person taught may be the subject, as in *Tamahhara ḥegga* (He was taught the law = He learned the law). In their second meanings both *tamaṭṭawa* and *tamahhara* may be listed as active transitive verbs governing a direct object in the accusative.

Although we stated earlier that there is usually no derivational relationship between G and D verbs, this requires some modification as we move further into the full verbal system. There is a significant group of Dt verbs which are derived, not from a corresponding D verb, but directly from a G verb, or at least from nouns or adjectives associated with the G system. The derivational chain G → Dt exhibits no single semantic parameter, but there are a few sub-groups that may be isolated:

(1) Dt verbs from stative G verbs have the basic meaning "to regard one's self as, to show one's self off as." These verbs tend to be pejorative, but need not be, and usually imply hypocrisy, deceit, or deficiency on the part of the subject.

tadawwaya	to feign illness, pretend to be sick
taʿabbaya	to be boastful, arrogant
taṣaddaqa	to give the appearance (falsely) of being righteous
taṭabbaba	to "act smart"; to be crafty, cunning.

(2) Dt verbs may simply be denominatives from nouns or adjectives, sometimes related to G verbs, sometimes isolated. It is difficult to characterize this group other than to speak of lexically specialized forms:

tanabbaya	to prophesy (to: *la-*; against: *lāʿla*); denominative from *nabiy*.
taseʾʾela	to ask someone (obj. suff. or *ba-xaba*) about something (acc. dir. obj. or *baʾenta*).
tagabbara	to work, do work; to work something, especially in an agricultural sense: to work a field or the land; to transact business (with: *mesla*).

(3) Other Dt verbs are related to causative (CD) verbs and will be treated later.

Taʾammara is both the passive of *ʾammara* and denominatively related to *teʾmert* (sign, signal): to give a sign or signal.

Dt verbs from roots II-gutt. alternate between the patterns *tamahhara* and *tamehhera*, *tasaʾʾala* and *taseʾʾela* etc.

Vocabulary 22

Nouns:

dawē (pl. *-yāt*) f.m. sickness, illness; disease.

dengel (pl. *danāgel*) virgin; also applied to men: celibate, monk.

ʾanadā m. skin, hide, leather; *ḥabla ʾanadā* thong.

sebḥat (pl. *-āt*) m.f. praise, hymn of praise; glory, majesty. *lotu sebḥat* To Him be praise (a frequent parenthetical remark after divine names).

xasār (pl. *-āt*) m.f. wretchedness, poverty, ignominy.

Verbs:

fawwasa to cure, heal (acc. of person or disease; acc. of person + *ʾem-*). Dt *tafawwasa* to be cured, healed.
tanabbaya Dt to prophesy (to: *la-*; against: *lāʿla*).
wassaka D to add (to: *diba, lāʿla*); to increase, augment (acc. dir. obj.). Dt *tawassaka* to be added to (*westa, xaba*, or obj. suff.).
tafaššeḥa Dt to rejoice (in: *ba-, baʾenta, lāʿla, diba*).
bēzawa Q/L to redeem (acc. dir. obj.; with: *ba-*; from: *ʾem-*). Qt *tabēzawa* to be redeemed; to redeem for one's self.

Exercises

A. 1. Tamawā’na wa-tamaṭṭawat hagarena westa ’edawihomu.
2. Wa-soba tagaššaṣu, wa-tamehheru ba’enta hāymānota Kerestiyān.
3. ’I-tamahhara zentu ḥegg ba-mawāʿelihu.
4. Taṣawweʿu wa-tafannawu westa k^{w}ellu baḥāwerta ʿālam.
5. Tamayṭu xaba bēta ’abuhomu wa-tabāraku ba-xabēhu.
6. Taṣeḥfa nagarātihu westa bezux maṣāḥeft, wa-tatarg^{w}amu la-lesānāt bāʿedd.
7. Taṣawwāʿku xaba liqa pāppāsāt wa-tašayamku ’ēpis qoposa diba zentu beḥēr.
8. Tawadya mašwāʿtu heyya wa-tašoʿa xaba ’Egzi’abḥēr.
9. Wa-soba tanabbaya lana, xalafa ’emennēna wa-ʿarga westa samāyāt.
10. Bakayna wa-ḥazanna ba’enta za-tawassakana xasār wa-maqšaft.

B. 1. Maṣ’u bezuxān deweyān xabēhu wa-fawwasomu k^{w}ellomu ba-Manfas Qeddus.
2. Tafawwasna ’em-dawēyātina wa-tanassāḥna ’em-xaṭāwe’ina.
3. Qoma ba-qedmēhomu la-ḥezb xāṭe’ān wa-tanabbaya lāʿlēhomu mendābē wa-maqšafta.
4. Soba re’ina kama we’etu ṣādeq ḥeyāw we’etu, tafaššāḥna fadfāda wa-wahabna sebḥata la-’Egzi’abḥēr.
5. Maṣ’a madxenena westa ʿālam wa-tabēzawana ba-damu ’em-xaṭi’at.
6. Tawassako newāy wa-kona bāʿela ṭeqqa.
7. Wassaknāhomu diba ḥezbena wa-konna ḥezba ʿabiya wa-beʿula.
8. Wassaku xaṭi’ata xaba xaṭi’at wa-’i-samʿewwo qālo la-’abuhomu.
9. Tamehhera lesāna Yonānāwiyān ba-xaba ’emmu.
10. Ḥaywa we’etu warēzā ’em-dawēhu wa-tamayṭa bēto.

C. 1. Wa-waladat ye'eti be'sit dengel walda wa-samayato semo la-waldā 'Iyasus (lotu sebḥat) 'esma madxena 'ālam we'etu.

2. 'Em-'ayy lesān tatarg^{w}ama zentu maṣḥaf beluy?

3. Naš'a 'anadā wa-gabra 'emennēhu 'albāsa šannāya.

4. Zentu ḥabla 'anadā ṭeqqa ṣenu' we'etu.

5. Tawassaku 'elatāt xaba ḥeywatu, wa-ḥaywa ḥeywata nawāxa fadfāda ba-zentu 'ālam.

6. Bēzawa k^{w}ello 'ālama ba-šegāhu wa-ba-damu.

7. Tafaššeḥu diba motomu la-xāṭe'ān wa-'elewān.

8. Nabarna heyya ba-xasār wa-'i-tafaššāḥna ba-ye'eti ḥeywat naddāyt.

9. Tanabba lita zentu nagar wa-tafawwasku 'em-dawēya.

10. Naš'on la-k^{w}ellon danāgel 'anestihu.

11. Wassakka newāyaka medrāwē wa-'i-wassakka newāyaka manfasāwē.

12. 'I-tanabbayu wangēlāwiyān, 'allā sabaku.

13. Wahabu lana sisāya la-k^{w}ellā 'elat wa-tale'kuna 'eska tafawwasna 'em-dawēna.

14. Wa-tafawwasa we'etu dewuy 'esma 'amna ba-qālāteya wa-'i-mēṭa lebbo 'em-hāymānot rete't.

15. Wa-'ama ta'ammaru, roṣna k^{w}ellena 'em-bēt westa fenot.

16. Tase''elana ba'enta ḥeywatena zeyya.

17. Tagabbarna medra wa-našā'na sisāyana 'emennēhā.

18. Ta'ammara zentu nagar lakemu ba'enta za-ṣādeqān 'antemu.

19. Ta'abbayka wa-gabarka 'ekuya lā'la naddāyāna ḥezb.

20. 'I-kona ṭabiba, 'allā taṭabbaba ba-qedma kāle'ānihu wa-ta'abbaya ba-gebrātihu wa-ba-qālātihu.

21. Nabarna westa ye'eti medr šannāyt wa-tagabbarna mesla 'aḥzābihā.

22. Ba'enta ment tadawwayka qedma mak^{w}annen wa-'i-nagarkāhu nagaraka?

23. Taṭabbabu wa-'i-ṭabbu, taṣaddaqu wa-'i-ṣadqu, ta'abbayu wa-'i-'abyu.

24. Ba'enta ment tase''elkenāna ba-xaba liqa pāppāsāt?

Lesson 23

23.1 Cardinal Numbers.

	Masculine			Feminine		
one	*'aḥadú*	acc.	*'aḥadá*	*'aḥattí̂*	acc.	*'aḥattá*
two	*kel'ētú*		*kel'ētá*	*kel'ētí̂*		*kel'ētá*
three	*šalastú*		*-tá*	*šalās*		*šalāsa*
four	*'arbā'tú*		*-tá*	*'arbā'*		*'arbā'a*
five	*xamestú*		*-tá*	*xams*		*xamsa*
six	*sedestú*		*-tá*	*sessú*		*sessú*
seven	*sab'atú*		*-tá*	*sab'ú*		*sab'ú*
eight	*samāntú*		*-tá*	*samānī̂*		*samānī̂*
nine	*tes'atú*		*-tá*	*tes'ú*		*tes'ú*
ten	*'ašartú*		*-tá*	*'ašrú*		*'ašrú*

Common variant forms: masculine (7) *sabā'tú*, (8) *samānitu*, (9) *tas'atú*, *tasā'tú*; feminine (10) *'ašr*. Note that the masculine numbers in *-tú* have accusative *-tá* but that feminines in *-ú* have no distinct accusative form. The form *kel'ē̂* is used for both masculine and feminine "two."

Cardinal numbers normally precede the object counted. Other than "one," agreement in gender is not always present, even with personal nouns, and there is a tendency to generalize the numbers in *-tú* for all uses. Agreement in case is normal. The counted noun may be either singular or plural, with a preference for the former:

'aḥadu be'si	*'aḥatti be'sit*	*kel'ētu 'abyāt*
kel'ēti hagar	*kel'ē dammanā*	*šalastu warx*
xams 'elat	*sessu 'anest*	*sabā'tu sab'*

'aḥadu/'aḥatti frequently has the sense "a certain": *'aḥadu be'si* a certain man. Numbers rarely stand in construct; the partitive is expressed by *'em-*:

šalastu 'em-'ardā'ihu — three of his disciples

23.2 Ordinal Numbers.

From "three" onward the ordinal numbers are based on the same roots as the cardinals, with the pattern *qātel* (f. *qātelt*); the accusative is simply in *-a*.

third	*šāles*	f.	*šālest*	seventh	*sābeʿ*	f.	*sābeʿt*
fourth	*rābeʿ*		*rābeʿt*	eighth	*sāmen*		*sāment*
fifth	*xāmes*		*xāmest*	ninth	*tāseʿ*		*tāseʿt*
sixth	*sādes*		*sādest*	tenth	*ʿāšer*		*ʿāšert*

For "first" *qadāmi* (f. *qadāmit*) is used. "Second" may be expressed in several ways: *kāleʾ* (f. *-t*), usually, but not exclusively, when only two items are involved; *dāgem* (f. *-t*); *kāʿeb* (f. *-t*), which is rare; *bāʿed* (f. *bāʿedd*), but which has also the additional meaning "other, strange, foreign."

All of the ordinals except *kāleʾ* appear also with the adjectival suffixes *-āwi* and *-āy*. The ordinal adjectives normally precede their noun:

šāles ʾanqaṣ	the third gate
rābeʿāwi beʾsi	the fourth man
sābeʿāwit hagar	the seventh city.

Note that the feminine form for ordinals in *-āy* is *-it*: *šālesit beʾsit* the third woman. A further derivative from the ordinal stem is *ʿāšerāt*, a tenth, tithe.

There is a second series of ordinals based on the pattern *qatul* and used almost exclusively to designate days of the week or month or hours of the day:

ba-ʿašur ʿelat	on the tenth day (of the month)
šalus lēlit	the third night (of the week or of the particular time period in question)
rabuʿ la-warx	the fourth day of the month.

They also occur in place of the regular cardinals when days, hours, or months are counted:

Nabara heyya šalusa ʿelata/mawāʿela. He stayed there three days.

Note in particular that "second" is *sanuy* (f. *sanit*), based on a root not used in the other number series. When the context is clear, the nouns for day and hour are omitted: *ba-šalus* on the third (day), at the third (hour).

23.3 Cardinal Adverbs. From "three" to "ten" the pattern *qetl* in the accusative *(qetla)* denotes "three times, thrice," etc.

šelsa	*sedsa*	*tesʿa*
rebʿa	*sebʿa*	*ʿešra*
xemsa	*semna*	

These forms of the numbers are also used occasionally as feminine cardinals: *šels hagar* three cities. "Once" may be expressed by *'aḥatta* or *meʿra*; "twice" by *kāʿeba* or *dāgema*, both of which are frequent in the sense "again, a second time."

Exercises

A. 1. šalās hagar
2. šalastu nagašt
3. šalās negešt
4. šālest ḥamar
5. xamestu xabāwez
6. xamestu gabr
7. xams 'ext
8. sedestu mašaggerān
9. sessu be'sit
10. sedestu 'arāwita medr
11. 'arbāʿtu mak^{w}annen
12. 'arbāʿ ʿeḍ
13. 'arbāʿtu 'aq^{w}ṣel
14. sabʿatu qālāt
15. sabāʿtu warx
16. sabʿu ʿāmat
17. samāntu welud
18. samāni walatt
19. sāment ʿāmat
20. sābeʿ mal'ak
21. tesʿatu ṣaḥaft

B. 1. Šēṭkewwo šalasta ḥabla.
2. Gabarku kel'ēta newāya.
3. Mēṭna 'ellonta 'arbāʿta weluda xaba bētomu.
4. Ba-qadāmit ʿāmatu mo'a xamsa 'ahgura.
5. Ba-dāgem warx ʿadawu sedesta dabra.
6. We'eta warxa ḥanaṣu kel'ēta ʿabiya 'abyāta.
7. 'Ammarana xamesta mesṭira qeddusa.
8. Šēma tesʿata diyāqona wa-xamesta qasisa dibēhomu.
9. Maharewwo ba-ʿašartu lesānāt.
10. Wasadewwomu la-'ellontu šalastu sab' xaba neguš.
11. La'aka xabēya kel'ē malā'ekta.
12. Maṣ'a xabēna 'aḥadu 'em-zamadu.
13. Wahabomu sisāya la-samāni ʿelat.
14. Nabaru meslēna sedesta 'awrāxa.
15. Nabarna meslēhomu ʿašru ʿāmata.
16. 'I-nagarkukemu-nu zanta šelsa? La-ment 'i-samāʿkemuni?
17. Gab'a xaba bēteya rebʿa wa-'i-rakabani meʿra.
18. Tabēzawa 'azmādihu xemsa.
19. Zentu tanabba lomu dāgema.
20. 'I-tamʿeʿa kāʿeba.

C. 1. Ze-we'etu qadāmi ḥegg.

2. Wahaba lotu ‘āšerāta ’em-k^{w}ellu newāyu.
3. Ba-šalus tamaṭṭawat hagarena.
4. Ba-mesēta rabu‘ tafawwasku ’em-dawēya.
5. Ba-ṣebāḥa sadus ‘elat la-warx tamayṭu beḥēromu.
6. Ba-‘ašur taṣawwā‘na qedmēhu.
7. Nagarana nagara ba’enta sab‘u danāgel ṭababt.
8. Wa-’emze qarbat rābe‘āwit be’sit wa-sa’alatana sisāya.
9. Nabaru heyya ’eska tasu‘.
10. Wasadewwo la-we’etu ’arwē ba-xamestu ’aḥbāl ṣenu‘.
11. Tafannawu xamestu ’em-’ardā’ihu xabēkemu.
12. Tamaṭṭawā sessu ’em-’ahgurihomu la-neguša kāle’t medr.
13. Gabra kel’ē ’albāsa ’em-’anadā wa-wahabo lana.
14. ’I-naš’u ḥawāreyāt sisāya meslēhomu.
15. Ze-we’etu ’asmāta zentu xamestu maṣāḥeft mesla ’asmāta me‘rāfātihomu.
16. ’I-rakaba ba-westa zāti hagar ’aḥada be’sē rāte‘a wa-ṣādeqa.
17. Samayato la-šālesāwi waldā sema Yoḥanneshā.
18. Tale’ku ḳel’ētu ’em-weludihā ba-bēta maqdas.
19. Tanabba zentu ‘ašartu ḥegg qedmēna we’eta ’amira.
20. Ba-‘āšerāwit ‘āmat xalafa zentu xasār wa-maqšaft ’em-dibēna.

Lesson 24

24.1 Associative (Reciprocal) Verbs: Glt. For many G verbs there is a derived verb marked by the prefix *ta-* and a lengthening of the stem vowel *(-ā-)* between C_1 and C_2 and expressing reciprocity or mutual activity. Though relatively infrequent, these verbs are not rare, and it is probable that they could be formed at will for many verbs other than those for which we have actual attestations. Listed below are the most important Glt verbs from roots already introduced. For convenience they are divided into two groups: (1) those whose meanings are more or less predictable from the general notion of reciprocity or association, and (2) those whose meanings require special attention. Note further that these verbs are distinct from Lt verbs, which they resemble formally, since they are derivationally linked to G (or perhaps Gt) and not to lexical L verbs.

(1) *tabākaya* to weep together, mourn mutually
takāḥada to argue with, contradict (obj. suff.; concerning: *ba'enta*)
taqāraba to approach one another, come close together; frequent in the sexual sense: to have intercourse
tarāwaṣa to run as a group
tanāṣara to look at one another (note relationship to D verb)
taqātala to fight or kill one another; to fight (with: *mesla* or acc.)
tarā'aya to look at one another, see one another (*gaṣṣa ba-gaṣṣ* face to face)
tamā'e'a to get mad at one another
tasā'ala to find out by asking around
tasāme'a to hear and understand one another, each other's language.

(2) *tabāṣeḥa* to bring (someone: acc. dir. obj.) before a judge (a legal term)
tabāwe'a to intrude, slip in uninvited (into, among: acc.)
tagābe'a to gather, assemble (intrans.)
tarākaba to congregate; to join, associate with (*mesla* or acc.)
tanāgara to speak with (*mesla*, *xaba*, or acc.; about: *ba-*, *ba'enta*, or acc.); to speak (a language: *ba-*).

tanābaba = *tanāgara*

tašāyaṭa to buy (acc. dir. obj.)

tawālada to procreate; to increase or flourish by procreation.

taxālafa to wander to and fro

taqāwama to oppose, withstand, take a stand against (acc. dir. obj. or *mesla*, *lāʿla*, *qedma*); less commonly: to stand up for *(la-)*.

tafānawa to bid farewell to (obj. suff.); note relationship to D verb.

The verbs *tawālada* and *taxālafa* illustrate a further component in the semantic range of Glt verbs, namely that of repeated (iterative) action. Taking this in conjunction with the more usual associative/ reciprocal meaning, we may speak more generally of the Glt as representing a lexical pluralization of the base verb, with emphasis on involvement in an ongoing or repeated activity rather than on a single, punctual act.

There is no corresponding associative/reciprocal form for D or L verbs, although a few, like *tanāṣara* and *tafānawa* above, have Glt derivatives. There is, however, a Qlt form from Q verbs, with *-ā-* between the second and third radicals: *tasanāʾawa* (root: *snʾw*) to come to a mutual agreement, be in accord.

Vocabulary 24

Nouns:

teʾzāz (pl. *-āt*) f.m. order, command, edict; law, commandment. *bateʾzāza* at the command of.

kidān (pl. *-āt*) m.f. (1) pact, treaty, covenant; (2) will, testament. *Kidān Belit* Old Testament; *Kidān Ḥaddās* New Testament. *gabra/ šēma/takāyada kidāna xaba/mesla* to make a K. with. *Kidān* is also a technical term denoting benefit promised by God to those who celebrate the commemoration of a particular saint.

mesl (pl. *mesal*, *meslāt*, *ʾamsāl*) m. likeness, form, image; proverb. The form *ʾamsāl* is frequent as a singular (pl. *-āt*) with the same meanings. *ba-ʾamsāla* in the likeness of.

ʿaṣf (pl. *-āt*, *ʾaʿṣeft*) m. tunic, cloak, mantle.

sutāfē (rarely *sutāf*) m.f. sing. and coll., companion, associate, consort.

ṣab' (pl. *'aṣbā'*, *-t*) m.f. war, battle. *ḥora/waḍ'a ṣab'a* to go out to battle.

Verbs:

takāyada Glt (root *kyd* of *kidān* above) to make a treaty, pact, covenant (with: *mesla* or obj. suff.); to promise.

ṣab'a to make war, fight (with: acc.). Glt *taṣābe'a* to fight one another; to fight (acc. dir. obj. or *mesla*).

'oda trans : to go around, to surround; to avoid (a place); intrans.: to go around, circulate, tour.

rad'a to help (someone: obj. suff.). Gt *tarad'a* passive. Glt *tarāde'a* to render mutual aid, to help (acc. dir. obj. or *mesla*).

tasātafa Lt to associate with (acc. or *mesla*); to share (something: *ba-*) with someone (acc.).

tasanā'awa Qlt to come to an agreement, be in accord.

Other:

bakama prep. according to, in accordance with; conj. according as, as.

babaynāti- prep. among, between (used mainly with verbs denoting actions with are reciprocal; frequent with Glt verbs: *tanāṣaru babaynātihomu* they looked at one another; *tabākayu babaynātihomu* they wept together). It does not occur without pronominal suffixes.

Exercises

A. 1. Wa-soba re'yu bezuxa mewutāna, tabākayu fadfāda.
   2. Takāḥaduna 'ellontu 'elewān ba'enta hāymānot rete't.
   3. 'I-taqārabu 'eska tawalda waldomu.
   4. Wa-soba zanta sam'u, tarāwaṣu westa fenot.
   5. Tanāṣaru babaynātihomu wa-'i-taqārabu.
   6. Tamā'e'u fadfāda wa-taqātalu babaynātihomu.
   7. Tarā'ayna gaṣṣa ba-gaṣṣ wa-'i-tasāmā'na.
   8. Taṣābā'na meslēhomu me'ra ba-ye'eti 'āmat.
   9. Taqārabu wa-taqātalu wa-motu bezuxān 'emennēhomu.
   10. Soba tasā'alu 'esma mota negušomu, fannawu xabēya mal'aka mesla zentu maṣḥaf.

B. 1. Takāyadana 'Egzi'abḥēr.
   2. Gabra kidāna mesla ḥezbu.
   3. Šēmna kidāna xaba we'etu neguš.

4. Takāyadna kidāna mesla ’egzi’ena.
5. Ḥorna ṣab’a ye’eta ‘āmata wa-ṣabā’na bezuxa ’aḥzāba.
6. Wa-’emze waḍ’u k^{w}ellomu warāzuta hagar ṣab’a ba-te’zāza neguš.
7. ‘Oda hagaromu wa-’i-ṣab’omu.
8. Soba dawayku, rad’ani we’etu be’si xēr wa-ḥayoku ’em-dawēya.
9. Ta‘adawna ’em-ḥegagihu wa-’i-samā‘na te’zāzātihu.
10. Taqārabu ’emuntu kel’ētu warēzā wa-taqātalu.
11. Wa-’emze tasanā’awu ba’enta Kerestiyān wa-’i-taṣābe’u meslēhomu.
12. Tarāde’u babaynātihomu wa-konu be‘ulāna ṭeqqa.
13. Nabarku meslēhu wa-tarādā’kewwo ba’enta ‘elewāna zeku beḥēr.
14. Zanta gabarna bakama te’zāzeka.
15. Tasātafnāhomu ba-newāyena wa-ba-sisāyena.

C. 1. ’Em-mannu tašāyaṭka zanta maṣḥafa beluya?
2. Tašāyaṭkewwo ’em-be’si be‘ul.
3. Tabāṣeḥewwomu la-’ellontu sedestu sab’ xaba mak^{w}annen.
4. ’Efo tabāwe’ewwo xāṭe’ān wa-’ekuyān la-ḥezbena?
5. Tagābe’u sab’a zamadu wa-tasanā’awu ba’enta newāyu.
6. Tarākabku mesla zentu qeddus wa-tale’ekkewwo.
7. Tarākabu ḥezb wa-gabru tazkāra negušomu mewut.
8. Tanāgara meslēhā wa-tašāyaṭa we’eta maṣḥafa qeddusa ’emennēhā.
9. Wa-soba ta’ammara te’mert, tagābā’na la-ṣab’.
10. Waḍ’u wa-tawāladu wa-mal’u k^{w}ellā medra.
11. Tamayaṭna wa-tagābā’na westa bētu la-mak^{w}annen.
12. Wa-soba tabākayu, tafānawewwo la-waldomu.
13. Taqāwamu lā‘lēhomu wa-sadadewwomu ’em-mā’kalomu.
14. Wa-’emdexra tasaddu, taxālafu ’em-beḥēr la-beḥēr.
15. Taḥašyu ba-gebrātihu ‘abayt wa-tafaššeḥu ba-qālātihu ṭababt.
16. Soba zanta tanābabana, tam‘ā‘na wa-tabāṣāḥnāhu qedma kāhen ‘abiy.
17. Tabāwe’una wa-takalu ’ekita ba-mā’kalēna.
18. Ba’enta ment tasātafkemewwomu la-’ekuyān?

D. 1. ’Em-ment gabarka zanta ‘aṣfa?
2. Ba-’amsāla mannu gabra ’Egzi’abḥēr be’sē?
3. Ṭabib we’etu wa-šannāy ṭeqqa ’amsālihu.
4. Tare’ya lana ba-’amsāla mal’ak berhānāwi.
5. ‘Odna westa we’etu beḥēr bezuxa ’awrāxa.
6. Zentu maṣḥaf ba’enta ’aṣbā’ta ’abawina we’etu.

7. Zentu rad' kona sutāfēhu la-'Egzi'ena.
8. 'I-hallawa sutāfē 'Egzi'abḥēr; 'aḥadu we'etu.
9. 'Odo dammanā kama 'aṣf berhānāwi.
10. Takāyada 'Egzi'abḥēr mesla ḥezbu kel'ē kidānāta: 'aḥatti tasamyat Kidāna Belita wa-kāle't tasamyat Kidāna Ḥaddāsa.

Lesson 25

25.1 Relative Pronouns and Relative Clauses. The relative pronouns are

masc. sing.	*za-*	common plural	*ʾella*
fem. sing.	*ʾenta*		

Za- may replace *ʾenta* and *ʾella* unless the latter are used absolutely (see below). Note that *za-* is written proclitically: *beʾsi za-maṣʾa* the man who came.

a. Relative clauses where the relative pronoun is the subject of the clause offer no special problems:

beʾsi za-tašāyaṭa bēteya	the man who bought my house
beʾsit ʾenta waladat walda	the woman who gave birth to the child
nabiyāt ʾella tanabbayu heyya	the prophets who prophesied there

b. When the relative pronoun is the direct object of the verb in its clause, this may be indicated by a resumptive pronoun on the verb; this is not, however, necessary:

beʾsi za-reʾyewwo (or: *za-reʾyu*)	the man whom they saw

c. When the relative pronoun stands in a prepositional relationship (e.g. in which, of which, to which), a resumptive pronoun is normally employed:

hagar ʾenta semā ʾIyarusālēm	a city whose name is Jerusalem
beʾsi za-qatalewwo la-waldu	the man whose son they killed
medr za-nabaru westētā	the land in which they settled

If there is no possibility of ambiguity, a preposition may stand before the relative pronoun. This is most frequent with *ba-*, as in

mawāʿelihu ba-za ʾastarʾayomu kokab	the time at which the star appeared unto them

Very rarely the preposition is placed after the relative pronoun:

medr ʾenta xaba maṣāʾna	the land to which we have come

This is probably to be viewed as a secondary "filling out" of the construction employing *xaba* alone (see below).

d. The nominalization of relative clauses is very frequent:

za-mota	the one who died
ʾella ʾem-westa ṣaḥaft	those who were from among the scribes
ʾella nabaru heyya	those who had settled there

e. To be distinguished from the preceding is the construction in which the relative pronouns function absolutely and stand in what is essentially a construct relationship with a following noun:

za-lamṣ	a leper (lit. the one of leprosy)
ʾenta ʾOreyo	the wife of Uriah (she of Uriah)
ʾella sagal	diviners (those of divination)
ʾella ʾagānent	demoniacs (those of demons)

f. Closely related to this is the use of *za-* (seldom *ʾenta* or *ʾella*) before the names of materials from which something is made:

manbar za-warq	a golden throne (lit. a throne, one of gold)
qenāt za-ʾanadā	a leather belt

g. Deriving from this appositional use, the pronoun *za-* became quite generalized as a "preposition" expressing the genitive case relationship. Its frequency varies from text to text, but it appears most commonly where the construct is prohibited by an intervening adjective or suffix or when proper names are involved:

wangēl qeddus za-ʾEgziʾena	the holy gospel of our Lord
Bētaleḥēm za-Yehudā	Bethlehem of Judah
ʿaṣada wayn za-Hagripos	the Vineyard of Agrippa
Gālilā ʾenta ʾaḥzāb	Galilee of the gentiles

h. Any of the preceding attributive clauses and phrases may stand before as well as after the modified noun:

za-mota beʾsi	the man who died
ʾella maṣʾu sabʾ	the men who came
za-warq manbar	a golden throne

Note especially such expressions as

za-maṭana-ze hāymānot	such faith (lit. faith which is to the extent of this)
za-kama-ze šelṭān	such authority (lit. authority which is like this)

i. The relative pronoun is occasionally omitted, but this usage is common only in short non-verbal clauses following an indefinite antecedent:

beʾsi semu Yoḥannes a man whose name is/was John.

25.2 *ʾAma* and *xaba*. *ʾAma* has several different functions which should be noted:

(1) preposition: at the time of (e.g. *ʾama motu*, *ʾama weʾetu mendābē*); it frequently precedes a time word and is equivalent to "on": *ʾama ʿelata* on the day of. It may be combined with *ʾem-* (*ʾem-ʾama* from the time of), *la-* (*la-ʾama* at the time of), and *ʾeska* (*ʾeska ʾama* until the time of).

(2) conjunction: when, at the time when, followed by a verbal clause: *ʾem-ʾama* from when, from the time when/that.

(3) relative adverb: e.g. *weʾeta ʾamira ʾama reʾikewwo* on that day when I saw him. Note that it combines a relative and an adverbial function when used thus.

The word *xaba*, already introduced as a preposition, also functions as a relative adverb "where, the place where." E.g. *makān xaba nabarku* the place where I sat down. The noun of place is commonly omitted and *xaba* itself takes on the full meaning of "the place where." As such it may be preceded by other prepositions:

Tanšeʾat ʾem-xaba wadqat.	She got up from where she had fallen.
Waḍʾa ʾenta xaba maṣʾa.	He left the same way he came by.
Roṣu ʾeska xaba wadqa.	They ran to where he had fallen.

It may also be used as the direct object of a verb:

ʾI-rakaba xaba nabarna.	He did not find the place where we had settled.

Vocabulary 25

Nouns:

ḍamr m.f. wool

ṣag^{w}r hair (human or animal); fur, feathers, plumage.

warq m. gold, money.

berur (pl. *-āt*) m. silver.

xaṣin (pl. *xaṣāwent*) m. iron; sword, weapon; tool, implement.

bert m. copper.

gamal (pl. *-āt*, *'agmāl*) m.f. camel.

qenāt (pl. *-āt*, *qenāwet*) m. belt, cincture.

mā's/mā'ṡ (pl. *'am'est*, *'am'est*) m.f. skin, hide, leather (syn. of *'anadā*).

sayf (pl. *'asyāf*, *'asyeft*) m.f. sword.

makān (pl. *-āt*) m.f. place, locale.

Exercises

A. 1. sab' 'ella mo'u hagarana
2. 'ardā' 'ella hallawu meslēhu
3. mašagger za-šēṭa zāta ḥamara
4. be'si ṭabib za-gabra zanta sayfa
5. welud 'ella motu ba-dawē
6. 'anest 'ella ḥazanā dibēhu
7. ḥezb za-'adawo la-beḥērena
8. mal'ak za-marḥana 'em-gadām
9. maṣāḥeft za-we'yu we'eta 'amira
10. xāṭe'ān 'ella nasseḥu 'em-xaṭi'atomu
11. hagar 'enta naš'ewwā
12. nagar za-samā'nāhu
13. berhān za-mal'o westa samāy
14. neguš 'ekuy za-farhu 'em-qedmēhu
15. fenot 'enta seḥetna 'emennēhā
16. hāymānot za-keḥdewwā
17. ḍamr za-šēṭu lana
18. warq za-naš'uni 'em-bēteya
19. berur za-gabra zanta sayfa 'emennēhu
20. 'agmāl za-tašāyaṭna 'em-xabēhu
21. hagar 'enta semā Hagara Ḍaḥāy
22. be'si za-semu la-'abuhu Yoḥannes we'etu
23. be'sit 'enta qabarewwo la-badnu la-metā
24. be'sit 'enta fawwaso 'Iyasus la-waldā
25. nabiyāt 'ella tafannawu xabēna
26. dengel 'enta tawalda madxena 'ālam ba-xabēhā
27. warq wa-berur za-tawassaka la-newāyu
28. xaṣin wa-bert za-rakabna westa we'etu 'adbār
29. wald za-bēzawu ḥeywato ba-warq

30. ’Egzi’ena za-wahabo sebḥata bezuxa
31. qeddus za-našā’na šegāhu wa-qabarna westa zentu makān
32. ’anadā wa-ṣagʷra gamal za-tagabra lebsu ’emennēhu
33. za-maṣ’a xasār wa-mendābē
34. ’enta šēṭato zanta maṣḥafa be’sit
35. ’ella gabrā zanta ’albāsa ’anest.
36. ’ella tafawwasu ’em-dawēyātihomu ḥezb
37. ’ella ṣanʻu ba-hāymānot reteʻt Kerestiyān
38. ’ella taṣawweʻu wa-’ella ’i-taṣawweʻu
39. ’ella nabaru ba-mā’kala ḥezbena
40. za-tabāraka ’em-xaba ’Egzi’abḥēr

B. 1. newāy za-warq
2. ’albās za-ṣagʷra gamal
3. qenāt za-mā’s
4. dammanā za-berhān
5. ʻaṣf za-ḍamr
6. bēt za-’ebn
7. ḥamar ’enta ʻeḍ
8. sayf za-xaṣin
9. ’asyeft ’enta bert
10. mašwāʻt za-xebest wa-wayn

C. 1. kidān za-takāyada sutāfēhu meslēna
2. kidān za-tasanā’awu ba’enti’ahu babaynātihomu
3. ḥezb ’ella ʻodewwo
4. ḥezb ’ella taṣābe’una
5. xāṭe’ān ’ella tabāwe’una
6. te’zāz za-wadayo dibēna
7. te’zāz za-gabarna zanta bakamāhu
8. ’abyāt za-wassakna la-hagarena
9. neguš za-maṭṭawewwo lotu la-newāyomu
10. ḥezb ’ella tagaššaṣu wa-tamehheru reteʻta

D. 1. ’I-wadayku warqeya westa we’etu makān.
2. Rakabna zanta makāna ’ekuya fadfāda wa-’i-nabarna westētu.
3. ’Ama šalus la-warx xalafu ’em-xabēna.
4. Baṣāḥna zeyya ’ama kona ’abuna makʷannena beḥēr.
5. ’I-tanāgarana ’em-’ama gaššaṣnāhu ba’enta za-gabra.
6. ’Ama maṣā’kemu xaba makān xaba hallo, ’i-re’ikemewwo-nu?
7. Hallona meslēhu ’eska ’ama mota, wa-’emze gabā’na xaba ḥanaṣna bētana.
8. Tanše’a ’em-xaba nabara wa-dēgana dexrēna.
9. ’I-gabā’ku hagara ’enta xaba waḍā’ku.
10. Maṣ’a xaba qomna wa-tase’’elana ba’enta fenota bāḥr.

Lesson 26

26.1 Causative Verbs: CG, CD, CL, CQ. The second major class of derived verbs from each of the bases G, D, L, and Q is the causative, marked in the Perfect by the prefix *ʾa-*:

G	*gabʾa*	to come back	CG	*ʾagbeʾa*	to bring back
D	*šannaya*	to be beautiful	CD	*ʾašannaya*	to make beautiful
L	*māsana*	to perish	CL	*ʾamāsana*	to destroy
Q	*dangaḍa*	to be disturbed	CQ	*ʾadangaḍa*	to disturb

In this lesson we shall deal with the causative verbs from G verbal bases. These are the most numerous and varied of the four types. The basic form of the Perfect is $'aC_1C_2aC_3a$, subject to modification only with roots III-guttural and II-W/Y. As noted previously, the final stem vowel before C_3 = guttural is either zero (e.g. *maṣʾa*) or *e* (e.g. *nasseḥa*), depending on whether the preceding syllable was originally short (*ma-ṣe-ʾa* > *maṣʾa*) or long (*nas-se-ḥa, mo-qe-ḥa*); thus, in CG verbs we regularly have *e*: *ʾam-ṣe-ʾa, ʾag-be-ʾa* etc. Inflection follows the pattern already given for verbs III-guttural:

ʾagbeʾa, ʾagbeʾat, ʾagbāʾka, ʾagbāʾki, ʾagbāʾku, etc.

Causative verbs from roots II-W usually have a loss of the second radical; from *qoma* we have *ʾaqama, ʾaqamat, ʾaqamka, ʾaqamki, ʾaqamku* etc. If the root is III-gutt. in addition, *a* is replaced by *e*: *ʾabeʾa, ʾabeʾat, ʾabāʾka*, etc. (from *boʾa*). The CG form *ʾaqoma* is also attested, inflected like *qoma*. From roots II-Y the CG form *ʾakēda* (root *kyd*) is the normal one, without loss of the second radical.

26.2 The Meaning of CG Verbs. From stative G verbs the CG verb is primarily factitive, as in

G	*ʾakya*	to be bad	CG	*ʾaʾkaya*	to make (something) bad

Since all meanings of the simple G verb are at least theoretically incorporated into the CG verb, we shall not repeat here the full range of meanings for those verbs already introduced. Special attention should be given to the secondary, less predictable meanings that some of the verbs have acquired.

ʾaʾkaya to make (something) bad; to act badly (toward: *lāʿla*, *diba*)

ʾaʿbaya to make great, to increase, augment; to extol, exalt

ʾabʿala to make rich

ʾablaya to age, make old, render obsolete

ʾabzexa to multiply, make numerous; to produce a lot of, have a lot of

ʾadwaya to make ill

ʾafreha to frighten

ʾaḥyawa to restore to life; to heal, cure; to let live

ʾaḥzana to make sad; often used impersonally: *ʾi-ʾaḥzano* he was not saddened

ʾandaya to reduce to poverty

ʾanoxa/ʾanexa to extend, put forth (e.g. one's hand); to lengthen, make long(er); to raise high, elevate, exalt; *ʾanexa manfasa lāʿla* he was patient about.

ʾarteʿa to make right, correct, straight, stable

ʾaṣdaqa to make righteous, just; to declare just or innocent

ʾaṣneʿa to make firm, strong, etc.; to grasp firmly *(ba-)*; to learn by heart *(ba-lebbu)*

ʾaṭbaba to make wise

From other intransitive verbs the CG verb has the basic idea of causing, ordering, or permitting someone or something to perform a certain action. With verbs of motion the exact direction of the motion is often ambiguous, producing several translation values in English. For example, the CG verb *ʾaʾtawa* (from *ʾatawa* to go home) has the following possible meanings in English: to send someone home, to let someone go home, to order someone to go home; to bring someone/something home, to bring someone/something indoors. The context will usually make clear which of the various nuances of the causative force applies.

ʾaʿdawa to bring, lead, or take across

ʾaʿraga to bring, lead, or take up; to offer up (a sacrifice)

ʾaʿoda to lead or take around, usually in the sense of causing to travel about, circulate in a place *(westa)*

ʾabkaya to move to tears

ʾabṣeḥa to bring

ʾabeʾa	to bring, lead, or take in; to introduce, insert
ʾagbeʾa	to bring, lead, or take back; to turn back, deflect; to hand over, betray (acc. dir. obj.; to: *westa ʾeda*)
ʾag^{w}yaya	to put to flight
ʾalhaqa	to raise, rear (e.g. children, plants)
ʾamʿeʿa	to enrage (note the relationship to the Gt verb *tamʿeʿa*)
ʾamṣeʾa	to bring, offer; to cause to happen, bring about
ʾamota/ʾamata	to let die; to put to death; to have someone killed
ʾanbara	to set, place, deposit; to settle, cause to dwell
ʾaqraba	to cause to approach; to bring near, to offer
ʾaqama	to set up, establish; to confirm the truth of; to carry out the terms of; to cause to cease (e.g. rain)
ʾaroṣa	to cause to run (esp. of horses)
ʾasḥata	to lead astray; to lead into sin or error
ʾaskaba	to cause to lie down
ʾawʿaya	to burn something up; to burn, scorch
ʾawdaqa	to drop, let fall; to throw down, cast down; to fell, hew down.
ʾawḍeʾa	to bring, lead, or take forth; to expel; to put forth, produce
ʾawḥaza	to cause to flow (esp. tears)
ʾawrada	to bring, send, or lead down
ʾaxlafa	to cause to pass; to pass (time)

All of the verbs in the preceding lists are singly transitive, taking a direct object in the accusative. Causative verbs do not, as a rule, take dative pronominal suffixes.

When the negative *ʾi-* is prefixed to a causative form beginning with *ʾa-*, *ʾiʾa-* becomes *ʾiya-*. We shall transcribe this secondary *-y-* as *-ỷ-* to prevent confusion. E.g. *ʾi-ʾaʾmara* → *ʾi-ỷaʾmara* he did not know.

Vocabularly 26

Nouns:

ʾessāt m.f. fire.

nafs (pl. *-āt*) m.f. soul, spirit, breath, vital life-force; a person.

'arami coll. pagans, heathens, non-Christians. *'aramāwi* adj. idem.

manker (pl. *-āt*) miracle, marvel, wonder; also adjective (f. *-t*) marvelous, wondrous.

Verbs:

faṭara to create, produce; to devise, fabricate. Gt *tafaṭra* passive.

saḥaba to pull, drag, draw; to attract (to: *xaba*); to protract (*qāla, nagara*). Gt *taseḥba* passive.

sagada to bow down (to: *la-*, *qedma*).

ṭaf'a to go out (of a light or fire); to perish, vanish. CG *'aṭfe'a* to extinguish; to destroy, annihilate.

'a'mara CG to know, understand, comprehend, realize, learn. Gt *ta'amra* passive.

Exercises

A. 1. 'Aṣne'a k^wello maṣāḥefta Kidān Ḥaddās ba-lebbu.
2. 'Adwayo māya zāti hagar wa-mota.
3. 'Aḥzanana motā la-'egze'tena.
4. 'Afrehomu zentu mendābē wa-g^wayyu 'em-heyya.
5. 'Aḥyawa 'Iyasus mewutāna wa-fawwasa dewuyāna.
6. Dāgema 'aḥyawomu la-deweyān 'em-dawēhomu.
7. 'Aḥyawuna wa-'i-qataluna.
8. 'Abzexa gebara šannāyāta.
9. 'Anāxku 'edaweya wa-našā'kewwo la-we'etu maṣḥaf.
10. 'A'baya 'Egzi'abḥēr weludihu wa-newāyo ṭeqqa fadfāda.
11. La-ment 'a'kaykemu lā'lēya?
12. Mahharomu la-'ardā'ihu wa-'aṭbabomu.
13. 'Arte'a 'albāba 'elewāna wa-'aṣdaqa xāṭe'āna.
14. 'Anexa 'elatāta ḥeywateya diba medr.
15. 'Aṣne'a hāymānotomu.
16. 'Ab'ala naddāyāna wa-'andaya 'ab'elta.
17. 'I-ỳa'kayku diba kāle'āneya.
18. 'A'baya semo ba-k^wellu baḥāwerta 'ālam.
19. Manna 'aṣdaqqa ba-westa ye'eti hagar?
20. 'Anexa manfaso lā'la gebara weludihu wa-'i-gaššaṣomu.

B. 1. 'Axlafna samānta 'āmata heyya.
2. 'A'dokewwomu westa kāle' beḥēr.
3. 'A'ragewwo diba ḥamaromu.

4. ’Amṣe’a lita kel’ēta newāya.
5. ’Am‘e‘o nagaru la-mak^{w}annen.
6. ’A‘ragna ’arbā‘ta mašwā‘ta.
7. ’Aqraba lotu wayna wa-xebesta.
8. ’Awḥaza māya ’em-ye’eti ’ebn.
9. ’Agbā’kewwo xaba zamadu.
10. ’Abā’na ’asyeftihomu westa bēt.
11. Manna wa-menta ’abā’kemu lana?
12. ’Aqama zanta kidāna meslēna.
13. La-ment ’i-’aqamkemu qālāta kidānu?
14. ’Awḍā’na newāyo wa-’aw‘ayna bēto.
15. ’Askabāhomu la-weludihon tāḥta ‘eḍ.
16. ’Awdaqu ’asyāfihomu wa-roṣu ’em-qedmēna.
17. ’Awrada ’essāta dibēhomu.
18. ’Alhaqo be’si ’aramāwi.
19. ’Ag^{w}yayna sedesta ’emennēhomu.
20. ’I-ṭaf’a ’essāt we’eta lēlita.
21. Zentu we’etu makān za-’a‘odana westētu.
22. ’Ellontu ’ella ’amatewwomu la-liqānina.
23. Zentu we’etu makān xaba ’anbaru šegāhu.
24. ’Abe’a warqa westa bēteya wa-’anbaro qedmēya.
25. ’Amṣe’a lana tes‘ata gamala.

C. 1. Faṭara ’Egzi’abḥēr samāya wa-medra.
2. ’Abzexa sisāyana wa-’i-nadayna.
3. ’Efo ’aṭfā’kemu zāta ’essāta?
4. ’Awdaqa ‘eḍa wa-wadayo westa ’essāt.
5. ’Awdaqa bētomu dibēhomu wa-’amatomu.
6. Sagadu lotu wa-wahabewwo warqa wa-berura.
7. ’Abzexa ta’āmera wa-mankerāta wa-’amnu bezuxān ba-wangēlu.
8. Nabara ba-mā’kala ’arami wa-sagada la-ṭā‘otomu.
9. Mota ’abuhu wa-’alhaqo ’ex^{w}a ’abuhu, be’si xēr wa-ṭabib.
10. Tafaṭra zentu ‘ālam ba’enti’akemu wa-ba’enta daqiqekemu.
11. Saḥabana gaṣṣu šannāy wa-nagaru ṭabib.
12. Saḥabewwo westa hagar ’eska mal’a damu westa k^{w}ellu fenāwihā.
13. Saḥabku qāleya ’eska mesēt, wa-’emze xalafku ’em-xabēhomu.
14. Ṭaf’at ’essāt ba-maqdasa ṭā‘otomu.
15. Soba sam‘u nagaro, ’a’maru ’esma madxenomu we’etu.

16. ’A’marku ḥeggaka wa-tafaššāḥku ba-qālātihu.
17. ’Awḍe’u xaṣina wa-berta ’em-’adbāra beḥēromu wa-šēṭewwo la-sab’ bā‘edān.
18. Ba-samun ’a’marna kama maṭṭawa ’abuna nafso.
19. Taseḥebna xabēhu ba’enta mankerāt za-gabra.
20. ’Aṭfe’u ’ahgurihu wa-naš’u ḥezbo ’agberta.
21. ’Asḥatomu nagara we’etu nabiy ‘elew la-ḥezb, wa-’i-nabaru ṣenu‘āna ba-hāymānotomu.
22. ’Agbe’ewwo westa ’edawa liqāna ḥezb, wa-’emuntu ’amotewwo.
23. ’Aw‘aya berhāna ḍaḥāy gaṣṣātihomu.

Lesson 27

27.1 Causative Verbs: CG (continued). Causative verbs derived from transitive G verbs are theoretically doubly transitive: to cause (someone) to do (something). In practice, however, the first object is usually personal and suffixed to the verb, thus obscuring its "accusative" status: *ʾarʾayana maṣḥafa* he showed us a book (lit. he caused us to see a book). Even more frequently one of the two objects is omitted (usually the first) and the translation must be adjusted accordingly:

ʾAqtala weʾeta nabiya.	He had that prophet killed (lit. he caused someone unspecified to kill...)
ʾAsmeʿa teʾzazo.	He made known his decree. (lit. he caused someone unspecified to hear...).

Following are the CG verbs derived from transitive G verbs already introduced:

ʾaʾmana	to convert (in the religious sense)
ʾaʿdawa	to lead or take (someone: acc. dir. obj.) across (acc. dir. obj.)
ʾaʿqaba	to hand (someone/something: acc. dir. obj.) over to (someone: obj. suff. or *xaba*) for safekeeping
ʾagbara	to make or order (someone: acc. dir. obj.) do or make (something: acc. dir. obj.)
ʾaḥnaṣa	to have (acc. dir. obj.) built; to cause (someone: acc. dir. obj.) to build (acc. dir. obj.)
ʾakḥada	to contradict, not believe (acc. dir. obj.); to lead (someone: acc. dir. obj.) from the faith
ʾamoʾa/ʾameʾa	to make (someone: acc. dir. obj.) victorious (over: *lāʿla*, *ba-*)
ʾanbaba	to read, recite (acc. dir. obj.); to study, meditate.
ʾanšeʾa	to raise, cause to rise (from seated or lying position)
ʾanṣara	to look (usually with the preposition *mangala* toward)
ʾaqbara	to cause, allow, order (someone: acc. dir. obj.) to bury (someone: acc. dir. obj.)
ʾaqtala	to cause or order (someone: acc. dir. obj.) to kill (someone: acc. dir. obj.); to have (someone: acc. dir.

obj.) killed

ʾarʾaya to show (someone/something: acc. dir. obj.) to (someone: obj. suff.); to reveal, make manifest (acc. dir. obj.)

ʾarkaba to cause (someone: acc. dir. obj.) to find or acquire (something: acc. dir. obj.)

ʾasmeʿa to announce (acc. dir. obj.) to (obj. suff. or *la-*); to summon (acc. dir. obj.) as a witness

ʾasmaya to be well known, famous, outstanding

ʾaṣḥafa to cause (someone: acc. dir. obj.) to write (acc. dir. obj.)

ʾawlada to cause (someone: acc. dir. obj.) to bear a child; to beget a child (acc. dir. obj.)

27.2 Causative Verbs: CD, CL, CQ. Causative verbs from D, L, and Q bases are much less frequent than CG verbs. Note the following:

ʾaʾammara used like D *ʾammara*, but not in the Perfect, where it is replaced by *ʾaʾmara* C in the sense of the D verb.

ʾagabbara to make (someone: acc. dir. obj.) do (something: acc. dir. obj.)

ʾanasseḥa to lead (someone: acc. dir. obj.) to repentance

ʾašannaya to adorn, deck out, array

ʾabēzawa to have (someone: acc. dir. obj.) redeemed

27.3 General Remarks on the Verbal System. The basic lexical types G, D, L, and Q, with their medio-passive, reciprocal, and causative derivatives, form a group of isolated but parallel systems:

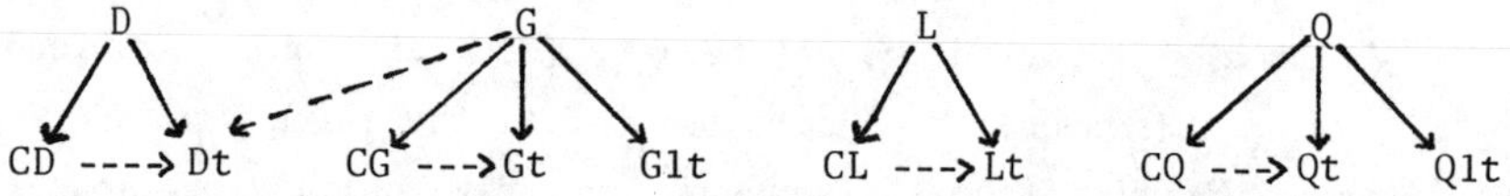

Occasionally there is no base verb, and a transitive-intransitive relationship exists between the causative and the medio-passive verbs, as indicated by the dotted lines above. Examples of this are

CG/Gt	*ʾaʾmara/taʾamra*	to know/be known
	ʾamʿeʿa/tamʿeʿa	to enrage/be enraged
CD/Dt	*ʾasaffawa/tasaffawa*	to give hope/have hope
CQ/Qt	*ʾamandaba/tamandaba*	to afflict/be afflicted

In a few instances there is a derivational relationship between two base types, especially G and D. As noted previously, this is sometimes only apparent and a result of partial mergings for phonetic reasons (e.g. *mahara/mahhara*). In other cases, however, the relationship is real but is not based on any productive derivational process within Ethiopic itself; such forms are either remnants of an earlier stage of the language or creations under the influence of other Semitic languages such as Aramaic and Arabic. It is also possible for any of the derived systems to be used to form denominative verbs; these stand outside of the derived system relationships proper because of their specialized meanings. The verb *ʾasmaya* (to be famous, outstanding) in our list above is a good example of this. The expected meaning of CG *ʾasmaya*, relative to G *samaya*, would be "to cause to name"; *ʾasmaya*, however, is denominative from the adjective *semuy* famous.

Vocabulary 27

Nouns:

ʾegr (pl. *ʾegar*, *ʾaʾgār*) f.m. foot. *westa/xaba ʾegara* at the feet of. *ba-ʾegr* on foot. *ʾegra ḍaḥāy* ray of sunlight.

ʾanqaṣ/ʾanqaḍ (pl. *ʾanāqeṣ*) m.f. gate (of city, temple, or other large structures).

tergʷāmē (pl. *tergʷāmeyāt*) m.f. translation, interpretation. *za-ba-tergʷāmēhu*, *ze-weʾetu tergʷāmēhu* the interpretation of which is.

ṭent beginning; *ʾem-ṭent* from the beginning.

nadd m. flame; *nadda ʾessāt* idem.

Verbs:

ʾaṭmaqa CG to baptize (acc. dir. obj.). Gt *taṭamqa* passive.

nadda to burn (subject is fire, flame, anger etc.). CG *ʾandada* to set afire, ignite. Glt *tanādada* to burn with a mutual passion.

ʾaʿrafa CG (1) intrans.: to rest, find rest, come to rest; to die; (2) trans.: to give rest (to: obj. suff.; from: *ʾemenna*).

ʾafqara CG to love (acc. dir. obj.). Gt *tafaqra* to be loved, beloved. Glt *tafāqara* to love one another; to love (someone: *mesla*).

ʾamandaba CQ to afflict, oppress (acc. dir. obj.). Qt *tamandaba* to be oppressed.

ʾasaffawa CD to promise (something: acc. dir. obj.) to (someone: obj.

suff. or *la-*). Dt *tasaffawa* to hope for, expect, look forward to (acc. dir. obj.).

Other:

mangala (presuffixal: *mangalē-*) prep. to, toward, in the direction of. *ba-mangala* idem. *la-mangala* idem. *'em-mangala* from the direction of; on the part of.

Proper Names:

'Abrehām Abraham; *Sālēm* Salem (cf. Gen. 14:18); *Malka Ṣēdēq* Melchizedek; *Nox* Noah; *'Adām* Adam; *Gebṣ* Egypt; *Sēm* Shem.

Exercises

A. 1. 'A'manomu wa-'aṭmaqomu ba-sema 'ab wa-wald wa-manfas qeddus.
2. 'A'dokewwomu 'adbāra wa-'anbarkewwomu zeyya xaba nabarku baṭent.
3. 'I-y̓afqarani, wa-'amandabani 'eska qarabku la-mot.
4. Wa-'emze 'a'rafani 'em-mendābēya wa-'aqama kidāna meslēya.
5. Xaba mannu 'a'qabkemu warqa wa-berura za-wahabku lakemu?
6. Qoma westa 'anqaṣa hagar wa-tase''elomu la-'ella xalafu ba'enta weludihu.
7. Sa'alkewwo 'aṣfa za-'a'qabkewwo xabēhu wa-'i-wahabo lita.
8. 'Agbarana zanta mak^{w}annen 'ekuy.
9. 'Agbarkewwomu šalāsa ḥamara la-neguš wa-sutāfēhu.
10. Wadaqna westa 'egarihu wa-sa'alnāhu ḥeywata.
11. 'Aḥnaṣa zāta hagara wa-'emze 'anbarana westētā.
12. 'Andada nadda 'essāt wa-wadaya k^{w}ello maṣāḥeftina westētu.
13. Ment-nu terg^{w}āmēhu la-zentu mesl?
14. Nagarana ba'enta 'amsāl za-'aṣḥafa ba-maṣḥaf.
15. Ḥoru ba-'egr 'em-Gebṣ 'eska 'Iyarusālēm.

B. 1. Mannu 'akḥadakemu wa-'agabbarakemu zanta gebra 'ekuya?
2. 'Anṣaru mangala hagar wa-re'yu 'abiya nadda 'essāt za-'arga 'emennēhā westa samāy.
3. 'Anše'ewwomu la-dewuyān wa-'amṣe'ewwomu xabēhu 'anqaṣa bēta maqdas.
4. 'A'rafku westa we'etu makān wa-'emze ḥorku kā'eba westa fenot mangala bāḥr.
5. 'Anbabu zanta k^{w}ello maṣḥafa šelsa ba-ye'eti lēlit.

6. 'Anasseḥo wa-ta'amna xaṭāwe'ihu wa-taṭamqa ba-māy.
7. 'Ašannayewwā la-be'sit wa-wasadewwā xaba neguš.
8. 'Asaffawomu ḥeywata za-la-'ālam.
9. Soba tamandabu ba'enta hāymānotomu, la'aku liqomu la-neguš.
10. 'Ame'ana 'Egzi'abḥēr lā'la 'aḥzāba zentu medr.
11. 'A'maru kama 'odna hagaromu soba sam'u te'merta za-ta'ammarna.
12. 'I-takāyadkemu-nu kidāna meslēna? La-ment waḍā'kemu wa-taṣābā'kemu mesla warāzuta ḥezbena?
13. Tafaqra zentu wald šannāy ba-xaba k^{w}ellomu sab'a hagar.
14. Tasātafa 'em-ṭent mesla 'ekuyāna lebb.
15. Samā'na nagaro 'em-ṭent wa-'i-'amanna botu wa-'akḥadnāhu.

C. 1. 'Aytē 'aqbara neguš 'abdentihomu la-'ella taqatlu sab'?
2. Ba-zāti te'mert 'ar'ayana mesṭira qeddusa za-Ḥegg Ḥaddās.
3. Zentu we'etu 'asmātihomu la-'ella 'asmayu ba-we'etu ṣab'.
4. Mannu nagašt 'ella taṣābe'omu 'Abrehām?
5. 'Arkabo 'Egzi'abḥēr la-'Abrehām bezuxa newāya westa Gebṣ.
6. Radā'nāhu la-zentu naddāy wa-wahabnāhu sisāya wa-lebsa.
7. 'Awḍe'omu mak^{w}annen la-'emuntu sab' wa-'aqtalomu qedma k^{w}ellu ḥezb.
8. 'Awlada bezuxa weluda wa-'awāleda, wa-bazxa zamadu 'em-kāle'ān 'azmād za-we'etu makān.
9. Fannawo Nox la-Sēm waldu mesla šegā 'abuna 'Adām, wa-'anbaro ba-mā'kala medr 'enta ye'eti westa 'Iyarusālēm.
10. Naš'o Sēm la-Malka Ṣēdēq 'em-bēta 'abuhu, wa-marḥomu mal'aka 'Egzi'abḥēr 'eska basḥu Sālēmhā; wa-tašayma Malka Ṣēdēq kāhena, wa-naš'a 'a'bāna wa-'a'raga dibēhomu mašwā'ta ba-xebest wa-wayn za-warada lotu 'em-samāy kama te'merta mesṭira Ḥegg Ḥaddās.
11. Wa-'amṣe'u malā'ekt sisāya la-Malka Ṣēdēq, wa-kona lebsu 'anadā wa-qenātu za-mā's; wa-nabara heyya wa-tale'ka qedma šegā 'abuna 'Adām xaba taḥanṣa me'rāfu.
12. Wa-'ama tamayṭa 'Abrehām 'em-ṣab', 'em-dexra mo'a nagašta, xalafa 'enta xaba hagara Sālēm (ze-we'etu 'Iyarusālēm bakama terg^{w}āmēhomu la-ṭabibānina), wa-'aqraba lotu Malka Ṣēdēq (za-tasamya kāhena wa-neguša Sālēm westa Ḥegg Belit) xebesta wa-wayna, wa-'Abrehām wahabo 'āšerāta 'em-k^{w}ellu newāyu.

Lesson 28

28.1 *Ba-* with Pronominal Suffixes.

bêya	in me	*bêna*	in us
bêka	in you (m.s.)	*bekému*	in you (m.pl.)
bêki	in you (f.s.)	*bekén*	in you (f.pl.)
bo, botû	in him	*bómu*	in them (m.)
bā, bātî	in her	*bon, bontû, botón*	in them (f.)

In these forms the preposition may have its plain meaning (by, with, in) or one of the special meanings treated in the following paragraphs. [The Tradition has *-tt-* in the 3rd person forms.]

28.2 *Ba-* Indicating Possession. The full paradigm of *ba-* given above functions pseudoverbally to indicate possession. The object possessed appears regularly, but not consistently, in the accusative case like a direct object:

Beya warqa.	I have gold.
Bomu xebesta.	They have bread.
Bekemu hāymānota.	You have faith.

If the possessor is a noun, it must be used appositionally with the 3rd person suffix on the preposition:

Be'si botu kel'ēta weluda.	A man has/had two sons.
Be'sit bāti kel'ēta 'amtāta.	A woman has/had two husbands.

The negative is formed by prefixing *'al-*: *'albeya, 'albeka, 'albeki, 'albo(tu)*, etc.:

'Albena māya.	We have no water.
'Albomu hāymānota.	They have no faith.

Clauses with the *ba-* of possession have no specific tense value, which is gained from the general context of the utterance. Tense is made explicit by using the verb *kona* with pronominal suffixes in the dative sense:

'I-kono walda.	He had no son.
soba kono 'ašru 'āmat	when he was ten years old

The thing possessed may be in the accusative (as the object of an impersonal verb phrase) or the non-accusative (as the subject of *kona*), as our examples show.

28.3 *Bo(tu)* Indicating Existence. The 3rd pers. masc. sing. form *bo* or *botu* (negative *ʾalbo, ʾalbotu*) is used to predicate existence. The following noun may be accusative or non-accusative:

Bo māy/māya.	There is water.
ʾAlbo xebest(a).	There is no bread.

28.4 *Bo za-* as the Equivalent of an Indefinite Pronoun. The *bo* of existence is especially frequent in combination with the relative pronoun *za-* (the plural *ʾella* is rare in this particular construction), a combination best translated in English by the indefinite pronouns "someone, something, no one, nothing." Study the following examples carefully, noting the ambiguity of *za-* as either the subject or object (in some sense) of its clause:

ʾemma bo za-xadaga beʾsito	if (*ʾemma*) someone divorces his wife
ʾalbo za-rakaba heyya	he found nothing (or no one) there
ʾalbo za-rakaba warqeya	no one found my gold
ʾalbo za-balʿu	none of them ate, or they ate nothing
ʾalbo za-samʿa qalo	he heard no one's voice, or no one heard his voice.

Such ambiguities may be cleared up by resumptive pronouns or by different object constructions, but they are frequent and should be anticipated.

The positive forms are used to express a correlated distributive idea:

Bo za-boʾa hagara wa-bo za-g^wayya.	One (or some) entered the city and the other (or some) fled.
Bo za-qatalu wa-bo za-ʾi-qatalu.	Some they killed and some they did not kill.

28.5 *ʾAlbo ... za-ʾenbala*: Only. The preposition (or conjunction) *ʾenbala* or *za-ʾenbala* is frequently correlated with *ʾalbo* in both possessive and existential uses; it is best translated by English "only":

ʾAlbena zeyya zaʾenbala xams xebest.	We have here only five loaves.
ʾAlbo za-reʾya zaʾenbala beʾsitu.	He saw only his wife.

'Albo za-wahaba lana za'enbala māy. — He gave us only water.

There is a vacillation between viewing *za'enbala* as a preposition followed by the non-accusative and as a conjunction (with ellipsis) followed by the case required in the preceding clause. Our examples could just as well have the accusatives *xamsa xebesta* (object of *'albena*), *be'sito* (object of *re'ya*), and *māya* (object of *wahaba*). This is comparable to the confusion in English between "but" as a preposition (He saw no one but me) and as a conjunction (No one was there but I).

Vocabulary 28

Nouns:

šā'n (pl. *'aš'en, 'aš'ān, 'ašā'en*) shoe, sandal.
totān (pl. *-āt*) thong, lace; *totāna šā'n* shoelace, sandal-thong.
'aṣq (pl. *'a'ṣuq, -āt*) m.f. branch; palm branch.
'Ayx the Deluge.

Verbs:

wagara G (or *waggara* D) to throw, cast (acc. dir. obj.); to stone (someone: obj. suff.) ± *ba-'ebn/'eban*. Gt *tawagra* = Dt *tawaggara* to be stoned. Glt *tawāgara* to throw stones at one another.

ganaza to prepare (a body) for burial. Gt *taganza* passive. CG *'agnaza* causative.

bataka to break (trans.). Gt *tabatka* to break (intrans.).

tarfa/tarafa to be left over, remain, survive. CG *'atrafa* to leave (as a remainder).

xašaša to seek, look for; to demand, require (from: *ba-xaba, 'emenna*); to study, pursue diligently. Gt *taxašša* passive and reflexive (to seek for one's self). Glt *taxāšaša* to inquire collectively, discuss with one another (something: obj. suff.).

xadaga (1) to leave, abandon, desert; to divorce (a wife); (2) to forgive (acc. dir. obj. of debt or sin; *la-* of person forgiven); (3) to neglect, ignore; (4) to renounce, give up; (5) to let, allow; (6) intrans.: to stop, cease, desist. Gt *taxadga* passive of all transitive meanings. Glt *taxādaga* to divorce (someone: *mesla*).

Other:

'enbala/za'enbala prep. (with pron. suff. -ē-) without, except for, excepting.

Proper Names:

Barnābas Barnabas; *Pēṭros* Peter; *Romē* Rome; *'Eskenderyā* Alexandria (in Egypt).

Exercises

A. 1. Beya ʻabiya sayfa za-xaṣin.
2. Bena sedesta gamala.
3. Beka-nu berura?
4. 'Albeya berura; beya berta.
5. Botu qenāta šannāya za-warq wa-za-mā's.
6. Bo maqšafta wa-xasāra ba-zentu makān.
7. Bo bezuxa tazkārāta ba-zentu warx.
8. 'Albo totānāta la-'ašā'enina.
9. 'Albo ʻaṣqa diba we'etu ʻeḍ.
10. 'Albomu meʻrāfa westa zentu ʻālam.
11. Konana samāni ʻāmat za-mendābē wa-maqšaft.
12. 'I-kona dammanāt westa samāy.
13. Gabra gebara šannāya wa-kono sem ʻabiy.
14. Kono ʻašru wa-xams ʻāmat.
15. 'I-kono la-'Amlākena sutāfē.
16. Kono la-Yoḥannes 'albāsa za-ṣag^{w}ra gamal.
17. 'I-konomu 'ašā'en la-'egarihomu.
18. Bomu 'albāsa ḍamr.
19. Bāti meta 'em-beḥēr bāʻed.
20. Beka ʻabiya sema ba'enta za-ṭabib 'anta.

B. 1. ḥeywat za-la-ʻālam
2. sayf za-bo qatalkewwo
3. 'aʻṣuq za-bataku 'em-ʻeḍ
4. ʻaṣq za-wadqa diba bētena
5. q^{w}aṣl wa-ʻaṣq za-wagaru westa 'essāt
6. totān za-tabatka 'em-šā'nu
7. 'Ayx za-mal'a māyu westa k^{w}ellu medr
8. 'abuna za-ganazna badno

9. badn za-ganazewwo ba-'albās šannāyt
10. warāzut 'ella tarfu 'em-zentu ṣab'
11. za-tarfu maṣāḥefta 'abawina
12. za-wagaro wa-qatalo nabiy
13. 'ašā'en za-'anadā xēr
14. sab' 'ella 'atrafa ba-mā'kala hagar
15. wald za-xašašewwo wa-'i-rakabewwo

C. 1. Bo za-wagarewwo ba-'eban wa-bo za-'i-wagarewwo.
2. Tawaggara zentu qeddus ba-xaba sab' ʿelewān za-hagar.
3. Tamāʿeʿu 'ellontu warāzut babaynātihomu wa-tawāgaru ba-'ebn.
4. Bo za-bataku 'aʿṣuqa 'em-ʿeḍaw wa-wadayewwo qedmēhu ba-westa fenot.
5. Wa-'emdexra ganazewwo la-badnu, qabarewwo mesla 'abawihu.
6. Wa-soba tabatka sayfu ba-'edawihu, wa-g^{w}ayya 'em-ṣab'.
7. 'Albo za-xašašu za'enbala weludihomu.
8. 'Albo za-tarfu za'enbala 'ellontu sedestu sab'.
9. La-ment xadaggana westa zeku makān?
10. Xadagā la-be'situ wa-naš'a kāle'ta be'sita.
11. Xadaga lakemu 'Egzi'abḥēr xaṭāwe'ikemu.
12. Xadaggemu ḥegageya wa-seḥetkemu 'em-fenot za-'ar'aykukemu.
13. Taxašašna meʿrāfa wa-'albo za-rakabna za'enbala maqšafta wa-xasāra.
14. Tabākayna 'esma taxadagna wa-'i-konana sisāya wa-māya.
15. Bo za-'amnu ba-qālu wa-bo za-'akḥadewwo.
16. Bo za-tamayṭa westa 'Iyarusālēm wa-bo za-nabara westa Bābilon.
17. Soba samʿa neguš zanta, 'agnazo la-badnu la-zentu qeddus wa-'aqbaro ba-westa makān xaba taqabru ʿabayta ḥezb.
18. Ze-we'etu za-tarfa 'em-maṣāḥefta we'etu ṭabib.
19. 'I-xadaga lita xaṭi'ateya 'esma 'i-nassāḥku.
20. Fannawa 'Egzi'abḥēr 'Ayxa lāʿla medr ba'enta xaṭāweʿa sab'.
21. 'Emdexra 'Ayx 'albo za-tarfu za'enbala Nox wa-zamadu.
22. Wa-soba re'ya Mārqos za-basḫa lāʿla ḥawāreyāt mendābē wa-maqšaft wa-xasār, xadagomu ba-ye'eti hagar wa-gab'a ba-hagara 'Iyarusālēm. Wa-soba tamayṭu ḥawāreyāt xaba 'Iyarusālēm, wa-tanāgaru ba'enta 'aḥzāb 'ella tamayṭu westa hāymānot wa-ba'enta ta'āmerāt wa-mankerāt za-gabra 'Egzi'abḥēr ba-'edawihomu, ḥazana fadfāda wa-nasseḥa ba'enta za-xadagomu.

23. ’Emdexra motu la-Barnābas ḥora Mārqos xaba Pēṭros hagara Romē wa-kona lotu rad’a, wa-ba-heyya ṣaḥafa wangēlo za-targ^{w}ama lotu Pēṭros (westa lesāna ’Afrenj), za-sabaka botu westa hagara Romē. Wa-’emdexra-ze ḥora ba-te’zāza ’Egzi’ena ’Iyasus Kerestos (lotu sebḥat) wa-ba-te’zāzomu la-ḥawāreyāt westa hagara ’Eskenderyā, wa-sabaka westētā ba-wangēl qeddus.

Lesson 29

29.1 Interrogatives with *za-*. A frequent variation on the plain use of the interrogatives is achieved with the use of *za-*. For example,

Mannu gabra zanta? Who did this?

becomes

Mannu za-gabra zanta?

where the relative clause is the second member of a non-verbal construction. It is not uncommon to find the pronominal element *we'etu* inserted:

Mannu we'etu za-gabra zanta?

On the surface this would appear to mean "Who is *(we'etu)* the-one-who *(za-)* ...?" but in view of the uses cited in the following paragraphs, it is clear that we are dealing with a more emphatic construction corresponding to the cleft sentence pattern of English (e.g. It was there that I saw him). Thus, the *we'etu* is to be regarded as the real grammatical subject: It *(we'etu)* is who *(mannu)* who *(za-)* did this?

This transformation is frequent with interrogative adverbs as well as pronouns:

'Efo za-'i-sam'u la-qālu?	Why did they not heed his words?
Ba'aytē za-rakabka maṣḥafa?	Where did you find the book?

Although these are emphatic constructions, the translations "It was where ...?" "It was how ...?" are too ungainly in English; more idiomatic would be "Where was it that ...?" "Why was it that ...?"

29.2 Indefinite Pronouns. The attachment of the suffixes *-hi* and *-ni* to *mannu* or *ment* produces the equivalent of the English indefinite pronouns "anyone (no one), anything (nothing)." These generally occur in negative sentences:

'I-re'yu manna-hi.	They saw no one.
'I-gabra menta-hi.	He did nothing.

A more emphatic negation is achieved by prefixing *wa-'i-* to the pronoun:

ʾI-reʾyu wa-ʾi-manna-hi.	They saw no one at all.
ʾI-nagara zanta wa-ʾi-la-mannu-hi.	He told this to no one at all.

It is not uncommon to find a combination (not always strictly logical) of these forms with the construction *ʾalbo za-* of the preceding lesson:

ʾAlbo za-reʾyu wa-ʾi-manna-hi zaʾenbala ʾIyasus.	They saw no one at all but Jesus.

29.3 *ʾAkko.* The transformation noted above in connection with the interrogatives is applied freely to negative clauses in order to emphasize the element of the clause negated. The negative *ʾakko* is used for this construction:

ʾAkko heyya za-reʾyani.	It was not there that he saw me.

Any element of a basic sentence may be emphasized in this way. For example,

ʾI-ḥanaṣa zentu beʾsi bēto heyya.	This man did not build his house there.

may be transformed as follows:

ʾAkko heyya za-ḥanaṣa zentu beʾsi bēto.
ʾAkko bētu za-ḥanaṣa zentu beʾsi heyya.
ʾAkko zentu beʾsi za-ḥanaṣa bēta heyya.

The positive counterpart of this construction is rare and is recognizable only from the *za-* prefixed to the verbal phrase:

ʾEllu-kē za-yārakk^{w}esewwo la-ḥezb.	It is these things that defile people.
Ba-ṣagā za-našāʾkemu.	It was free of charge that you received.

The negative *ʾakko* is used also to negate phrases in general, often when there is an ellipsis:

ʾAmlāka ḥeyāwān weʾetu, wa-ʾakko ʾamlāka mewutān.	He is the God of the living and not the God of the dead.
Wa-bāḥtu faqādaka yekun, wa-ʾakko faqādeya.	But let it be what you want and not what I want.

kama za-šelṭāna-bo wa-ʾakko kama ṣaḥaftomu	like one who has authority, and not like their own scribes

A contrasting clause following an *ʾakko za-* construction is usually introduced by the conjunction *ʾallā*. In this usage *ʾakko za-* (it is not that ...) may occur with the verb alone:

ʾAkko za-motat, ʾallā tenawwem.	She hasn't really died; she only sleeps.

Note finally that *ʾakko-hu* and *ʾakko-nu*, like *ʾalbo-nu*, may be used to convert a statement into a question expecting a positive answer:

ʾAkko-hu šannāya zarʿa zarāʿka westa garāht?	Did you not sow good seed in the field?

Vocabulary 29

Nouns:

maʿʿat m.f. wrath.
ṣebur/ḍebur clay, mud. CG *ʾaṣbara ṣebura* to work clay.
zēnā (pl. *-t*) m.f. news, report; narrative, story, account; pronouncement.
gizē (pl. *-yāt*) m.f. time: (1) the specific time of or for an event; (2) time in a more general durative sense. Very frequent in set phrases: *weʾeta gizē, yeʾeta gizē* at that time; *(ba-)gizē ṣebāḥ/mesēt* etc. in the morning/evening etc.; *ba-gizēhu* at its/the proper time; *ba-gizēhā* immediately, straightway; *ba-kʷellu gizē* always. *Gizē* is also equivalent to a conjunction before verbal clauses: when, whenever; e.g. *gizē ṣawwāʿkani* when you summoned me. The same is true for the compounds *ba-gizē*, *ʾem-gizē*, and *ʾeska gizē*.
moqeḥ (pl. *mawāqeḥt*) bonds, fetters, chains. *ʾasara/wadaya westa moqeḥ* to cast into bonds. *bēta moqeḥ* prison. See verb below.

Verbs:

ḥatata to investigate, examine, scrutinize (acc. dir. obj.); legal sense: to question, interrogate. Gt *taḥatata* passive.
nagša to become king, ruler; to rule (over: *la-*, *lāʿla*, *diba*). CG *ʾangaša* to make (someone: acc. dir. obj.) king (over: *la-*, *lāʿla*).

hadʾa to quiet down, become quiet, tranquil. CG *ʾahdeʾa* to pacify, calm down, make tranquil. Adj. *heduʾ* quiet, tranquil, placid.

kašata to reveal, uncover, lay bare; to open (esp. the mouth, lips, eyes; a book); to reveal, make manifest (mysteries etc.). Gt *takašta* passive.

moqeḥa Q to put into chains, bonds; to put into prison. Qt *tamoqeḥa* to be bound in chains, to be cast into prison. CQ *ʾamoqeḥa* to have someone cast into prison.

Other:

heyyanta (with pron. suff. -ē-) prep. in the place of, instead of.

bāḥtu adv. but, however. May occur first in the clause, especially as *wa-bāḥtu*, or be placed after the first main element of the clause, especially if this is some element preposed for emphasis.

Exercises

A. 1. Mannu za-faṭarana ʼem-ṣebura medr?
2. Mannu za-ʼamṣeʼa lakemu zanta zēnā?
3. ʼEfo za-ʼaʼmarkemu kama tafawwasku ʼem-dawēya?
4. ʼEfo za-kašata lakemu ʼEgziʼabḥēr zanta ʻabiya mesṭira?
5. Māʼzē za-ṭafʼat zāti ʼessāt?
6. ʼAytē za-moqeḥewwo la-malʼaku la-negušena?
7. Ment za-ʼaḥzanakemu kama-ze?
8. Menta nagaru soba hadʼa bāḥr?
9. Baʼenta ment za-sagadkemu la-ṭāʻot?
10. Mannu za-nagša heyyantēhu?
11. Soba hadʼat maʻʻatu, nasseḥa baʼenta za-gabra.
12. ʼI-kašatku menta-hi la-ʼellontu sabʼ.
13. Wassaka ṣebura diba ṣebur wa-gabra šalasta newāyāta šannāyāta ṭeqqa.
14. ʼAnexa manfaso lāʻlēhomu wa-ʼi-nagaromu menta-hi.
15. ʼAṣneʻomu lebbomu ba-qālātihu wa-ʼi-g^{w}ayya mannu-hi.
16. Mannu za-saḥabewwo westa fenot wa-ʼamatewwo heyya?
17. ʼAnexani nagaru nafseya, wa-wahabku sebḥata la-ʼEgziʼeya.
18. Dengel yeʼeti za-waladato la-madxenena ba-xaba Manfas Qeddus.
19. ʼAkko zeyya za-tanabbaya ʼallā ba-ʼIyarusālēm.
20. ʼI-y̓aʼmaru menta-ni ʼesma ʼi-baṣḥomu zēnā.

B. 1. ʼAkko ʼarami za-ʼalhaqewwo ʼallā Kerestiyān.

2. ’Akko ba-sema ’Egzi’abḥēr za-gabra zanta, ’allā ba-manāfest ’ekuyān.
3. ’I-warada zenām ba-gizēhu.
4. Wa-ba-gizēhā tafawwasat ’em-dawēhā.
5. Tawehba lana zentu wangēl la-k^{w}ellu gizē.
6. Ba-gizē tafaṭra medr ’i-hallawa ḍaḥāy wa-warx westa samāy.
7. ’Akko zentu be’si za-wadayu westa moqeḥ ’allā kāle’ānihu.
8. Meslēkemu ’ana ba-k^{w}ellu gizē.
9. ’I-’afreha qālu wa-’i-manna-hi za’enbalēya.
10. ’Akko ba-gizē mesēt za-baṣḥa xabēna, ’allā ba-gizē ṣebāḥ.
11. Taṣaddaqu wa-taṭabbabu, wa-bāḥtu ’i-samā‘nāhomu wa-’akḥadnāhomu.
12. ’Andayo ’Egzi’abḥēr wa-’adwayo, wa-’aṭfe’o la-zamadu ’em-gaṣṣa medr; wa-’emdexra-ze bāḥtu ’ab‘alo dāgema wa-’aḥyawo, wa-’abzexa zamado ’em-za-kona ba-ṭent, wa-’a‘bayo semo ba-k^{w}ellu medr.
13. ’I-nagara zanta wa-’i-la-mannu-hi za’^{e}nbala la-kāhen.
14. ’Albo ta’āmera wa-mankerāta za’enbala ’em-xaba ’Egzi’abḥēr.
15. ’Akko-hu tadawwayka soba ṣawwā‘kuka?
16. Bo za-’aṣbara ṣebura wa-bo za-gabra newāyāta ’em-warq wa-berur.
17. Ta’amra zēnāhu la-zentu qeddus westa k^{w}ellu medr.
18. ’I-ta‘abbayku ba’enta ment-ni ba-k^{w}ellu ḥeywateya.
19. ’A’kaya diba ’axawihu wa-’amoqeḥomu westa bēta moqeḥ, wa-nabaru heyya šalasta warxa.
20. Taṣawwe‘a zentu nabiy xaba neguš ba’enta za-dawayat walattu ṭeqqa fadfāda.

C. 1. Wa-soba ḥatatewwomu mak^{w}ānent, ’a’tawewwomu.
2. Wa-’ama sabaka ba-wangēl westa Romē, tamoqeḥa.
3. Tawassakat hagaromu xaba ’ahgura neguša Gebṣ.
4. Mannu za-’angašaka dibēna?
5. Ze-we’etu za-takašta ba-mawā‘elihu la-zentu nabiy maṣḥaf.
6. ’Ahdā’ka nafseya ba-qāleka ṭabib.
7. ’Akko zeyya za-’a‘dokewwomu ’allā heyya.
8. ’A‘rago diba dabr nawwāx wa-’ar’ayo k^{w}ello medra qedmēhu.
9. ’Akko ba’enta-ze za-tafannoku lakemu, ’allā ba’enta maṣḥaf za-rakabkemu westa bēta maqdas.
10. Taḥatatna wa-tarakabna naddāyāna hāymānot.
11. ’Abe’o westa bētu wa-’ar’ayo walatto za-motat.

12. ʼAgbeʼomu la-ḥezb ʼem-hagara Bābilon, wa-bāḥtu bo za-nabaru heyya mesla ʼanestihomu ʼaramāweyāt.
13. ʼAkko zeyya za-ʼanbaromu, ʼallā ba-kāleʼt hagar.
14. ʼAʻodomu la-ḥezb ba-westa gadām bezuxa ʻāmata.
15. Ḥatatu k^wello newāyana wa-bāḥtu ʼi-rakabu warqana.
16. ʼAlbena sisāya zaʼenbala xebesta za-ʼaqrabkana ba-ṣebāḥ.
17. ʼAlbo za-ʼameʼana lāʻlēkemu ʼenbala ʼEgziʼabḥēr ʼAmlākena.
18. Mannu za-bēzawakemu wa-ʼaqama zanta kidāna za-la-ʻālam meslēkemu?

Lesson 30

30.1 The Infinitive: Form. The base forms of the infinitives of the various types of verbs are as follows:

G	*qatil*	D	*qattelo*	L	*qātelo*	Q	*targ^{w}emo*
Gt	*taqatelo*	Dt	*taqattelo*	Lt	*taqātelo*	Qt	*tatarg^{w}emo*
CG	*ʾaqtelo*	CD	*ʾaqattelo*	CL	*ʾaqātelo*	CQ	*ʾatarg^{w}emo*

A simple rule-of-thumb for the formation of the infinitive of all verb types other than G verbs is to replace the final stem vowel of the Perfect (using *taqatala* for Gt verbs) with *-e-* and to add the ending *-o*. When pronominal suffixes are added to any infinitive in *-o* (to be illustrated below), *-o* is replaced by *-ot-*.

Infinitives of G verbs have the base *qatil*, which is subject to a few variations with the various root types. With roots II-gutt. we have *qetil*: *mehir* to teach, *seḥit* to err. The *-i-* of the second syllable may optionally be replaced by *-e-* with roots II-W/Y and III-W/Y. The following list illustrates these possibilities:

nabir	to sit	*seḥit*	to err	*warid*	to descend
gabir	to do	*maṣiʾ*	to come	*qawim*, *qawem*	to stand
ʿarig	to ascend	*baṣiḥ*	to arrive	*šayiṭ*, *šayeṭ*	to sell
xašiš	to seek	*mehir*	to teach	*bakiy*, *bakey*	to weep
seʾil	to ask	*reʾiy*, *reʾey*	to see		

As with other verb types, the addition of a pronominal suffix requires a stem in *-ot-*: Thus, *gabirot-*, *mehirot-*, *qawimot-*, *qawemot-*, *reʾeyot-* etc.

30.2 The Infinitive: Uses. The most frequent use of the infinitive is as a complement in the accusative to such verbs as

kehla	to be able	*rasʿa*	to forget (to do)
seʾna	to be unable	*farha*	to be afraid (to do)
kalʾa	to prevent (from doing)	*xadaga*	to stop (doing)
ʾabaya	to refuse (to do)		

Examples:

ʾI-kehelna bawiʾa.	We were not able to enter.
Seʾnu ḥawira.	They could not go.
Kalʾani waḍiʾa.	He prevented me from leaving.

ʾAbayku g^wayeya.	I refused to flee.
Rasāʿku gabiʾa.	I forgot to return.
Farha nabira heyya.	He was afraid to remain there.
Xadagu maṣiʾa xabēna.	They stopped coming to us.

There is a second group of verbs frequently used with an infinitive and which are best translated in English as adverbs:

qadama to do first or beforehand *ʾabzexa* to do a lot, frequently
ʾafṭana to do quickly or soon *g^wandaya* to do late, tardily
xabra to do jointly, together
dagama to do again, continue to do

Most of these verbs also admit of a coordinated construction with the second verb, with or without the conjunction *wa-*:

Qadamku baṣiḥa (or *baṣāḥku*).	I arrived first, I arrived beforehand.
Xabarna tagabbero (or *tagabbarna*).	We worked together.
Dagama maṣiʾa (or *maṣʾa*).	He came again.
ʾAbzexu taqātelo (or *taqātalu*).	They fought together a lot.
G^wandayku baṣiḥa (or *baṣāḥku*).	I arrived late.

The infinitive of a transitive verb usually stands in construct with its noun object:

Seʾna qatila waldu.	He was unable to kill his son.
Xabru ḥaniṣa hagar.	They built the city together.

The accusative is occasionally used, however, and is in fact required if the object is separated from the infinitive:

Zanta beʾsē ʾi-kehla qatila. He was unable to kill this man.

Pronominal objects are expressed by the suffixes as they appear on a noun in the accusative: *qatiloteya* to kill me, *qatilotaka* to kill you, *qatiloto* to kill him, etc. The counterpart of the *qatalo la-negus̆* construction may also be employed for noun objects: *qatiloto la-zentu beʾsi* to kill this man. Occasionally suffixes that properly belong to the infinitive are transferred to the main verb:

ʾAbayu qatiloto → *ʾAbayewwo qatila* They refused to kill him.

The infinitives of both transitive and intransitive verbs may be used as gerunds and take subjective genitive pronominal suffixes in whatever case is required by the context; e.g. *qatiloteka* your killing, *bakeyotu* his weeping, etc. The addition of a direct object in the accusative (e.g. *qatiloteya zanta be'sē* my killing this man) is possible, but this is not a frequent construction.

Some infinitives have been adopted as ordinary nouns. Note, for example, *weḥiz* current, flow, *'amin* faith, belief, *'a'mero* knowledge, *'i-ya'mero* ignorance.

Vocabulary 30

Verbs:

kehla (rarely *kahala*) to be able; to prevail against (obj. suff. or *mesla*). Gt *takehla* (1) = *kehla*, especially when used, by attraction, with a following infinitive of a Gt verb; (2) impersonal: to be possible (+ inf.). CG *'akhala* to enable, make able.

se'na to be unable. Gt *tase'na* to be impossible (+ inf.). Both *takehla* and *tase'na* may take personal obj. suff. in the dative sense: *tase'nani ḥawira* it was impossible for me to go.

kal'a to prevent; to withhold (acc. dir. obj.; from: *'em-*). Gt *takal'a* passive; to abstain (from: *'em-*).

'abaya to refuse, be unwilling; to refuse, say no to; to spurn, disobey.

dagama to do (something) again (+ inf. or with second verb coordinated).

qadama to go before, precede (obj. suff. or *la-*, *'em-*); to do beforehand, first (+ inf. or coordinated verb). CG *'aqdama* (1) = *qadama* in coordinated usage; (2) to put or place first; (3) to happen, exist, be first/previous/beforehand. Gt *taqadma* to occur, take place first/beforehand. Glt *taqādama* to go/come out to meet.

faṭana to be swift, quick. CG *'afṭana* to hurry, hasten; with inf. or coordinated verb: to hurry to do, to do quickly. *feṭun* adj. swift, quick.

xabra/xabara (1) to be connected or associated (with: *mesla*); (2) to join, associate (with: *mesla*); to conspire (against: *lā'la*); to be in accord with, agree with (*mesla*, *ba-*; subject usually words, thing, stories); to share something (acc. dir. obj.) with (*mesla*); with infinitive or coordinated verb: to do jointly, together. CG *'axbara* to associate (someone: acc. dir. obj.) with *(mesla)*; to make a conspiracy; to be in agreement, accord. Gt *taxabra* to be associated (with: *mesla*).

g^{w}andaya Q to last, remain; to delay, tarry, be slow in coming; with inf.: to be tardy or late in doing, to be too long in doing. CG *'ag^{w}andaya* to put off, delay, defer (e.g. salvation, prayer); to put off a person (obj. suff.). Qlt *tag^{w}anādaya* to delay in doing (*lā'la, lā'la* + inf.; inf. alone).

Exercises

A. 1. 'Abaya kašita semu.
2. Kal'uni nagiša heyyanta 'abuya.
3. Kalā'nāhomu ḥatita maṣāḥeftina.
4. Se'enku batika zentu 'aṣq.
5. 'Abayku xadiga weludeya heyya.
6. 'I-kehelku rakiba be'siteya.
7. 'Abayna sagida la-ṭā'ot.
8. 'Abayu ṣabi'a 'axawihomu.
9. 'I-kehlu 'awida hagarena.
10. Se'enna radi'a 'emuntu sab'.
11. La-ment 'abaykemu radi'oteya?
12. Kal'uni mayeṭoto xaba zamadu.
13. Se'nu 'aminoto.
14. 'I-kehla mawi'otana.
15. 'Efo za-'i-kehla šayimotakemu qasāwesta?
16. 'Abayu wehiba lana sisāya.
17. 'Abayku moqeḥoto la-zentu qeddus.
18. 'I-kehla nagirotana wa-'i-menta-ni.
19. Se'nat walidoto la-waldā wa-motat.
20. Mannu za-kal'aka nabibotomu?
21. Kalā'nāhomu seḥiboto 'em-westa bētu.
22. La-ment 'abayka šawi'a la-'Egzi'abḥēr?
23. La-ment 'abayat mehirotaki ba-lesāna 'Afrenj?
24. Dawaya wa-'i-kehla qawima ba-'egarihu.
25. Kal'ana le'ika zēnā xabēka.
26. 'I-kehelku 'ahde'o ma''ateya.
27. Se'nu faṭira wa-'i-menta-ni 'em-ṣebur.
28. 'Abaya 'atrefo 'aḥadu be'si.

29. Za’enbala ’albās šannāyt ’i-kehelna ganizoto la-badnu.
30. ’I-kehelna kali’otomu wagiroto la-we’etu nabiy.
31. ’Abayu taṭameqo ba-xaba Yoḥannes.
32. Se’nu ’a‘refo heyya.
33. Se’enna ’aṭfe’oto la-nadda ’essāt.
34. Kehlu tasaffewo ḥeywat za-la-‘ālam.
35. ’Abaya ḥawira mangala we’etu dabr.
36. Se’newwā fawweso.
37. ’Abayomu ’a’tewo.
38. Dagamu tabāṣeḥoto xabēhu.
39. ’I-kehelna takāḥedotomu.
40. ’Abaya tarākebo meslēhomu.
41. Kal’omu la-ḥezb tagābe’o.
42. Mannu za-kehla taqāwemo za-kama-ze be’sē?
43. Se’nu tašāyeṭo sisāya.
44. Kehlu ’a’meno bezuxāna.
45. ’Abayani ’ar’eyo maṣḥafu.
46. ’Abaya ’aṭmeqotana.

B. 1. Faṭanana weḥiz heyya wa-’i-takehlana ‘adiwa.
2. ‘Abiy ’a’merotu ’em-’a’merotena fadfāda.
3. Warada zenām wa-’i-kehlat ’essāt nadida.
4. Dagamu ’amandebotomu la-Kerestiyān.
5. ’Emdexra ta’amna xaṭi’ato, takehla taṭameqo.
6. Qadama ‘ariga westa dabr, wa-dexra ‘argu ’ardā’ihu.
7. ’Akhalana te’zāzu gabi’a hagarana.
8. We’eta gizē tase’nomu g^{w}ayeya.
9. Tase’nana qariba xaba ’anāqeṣa hagar.
10. ’Aqdamu nagaru zanta nabiyāt ba-mawā‘ela ’abawina.
11. Qadama bawi’a, wa-bo’na ’em-dexrēhu.
12. Soba xalafa māya ’Ayx, qadama takala Nox ‘aṣada wayn.
13. ’Abayu te’zāzātihu wa-dagamu seḥita ’em-fenot rete‘t.
14. Tanāgarana ba’enta tamayeṭotomu la-’aḥzāb westa ’amina ’Egzi’ena.
15. ’I-g^{w}andaya motu.
16. G^{w}andaya gabru gabi’a hagara.
17. Xabru lā‘lēya la-qatiloteya, wa-bāḥtu kehelku g^{w}ayeya ’emennēhomu.
18. Xabarna k^{w}ellena ḥaniṣa ’abyāta ḥaddisa.

19. Xabra nagaru mesla zēnā za-samā'na 'em-mal'aka neguš.

20. La-ment 'axbarkemu zanta ṭā'ota 'ekuya mesla 'Egzi'abḥēr wa-bētu?

Lesson 31

31.1 The Perfective Active Participle. From every verb there is formed a perfective active participle which is inflected for person, number, and gender. The basic stem may be derived, for all practical purposes, from that of the infinitive (to which it is identical in G verbs) by changing *-e-* to *-i-* in the final stem syllable (between C_2 and C_3):

G	*qatil-*	D	*qattil-*	L	*qātil-*	Q	*targ^{w}im-*
Gt	*taqatil-*	Dt	*taqattil-*	Lt	*taqātil-*	Qt	*tatarg^{w}im-*
CG	*ʾaqtil-*	CD	*ʾaqattil-*	CL	*ʾaqātil-*	CQ	*ʾatarg^{w}im-*

There is the same optional variation between *-e-* and *-i-* in G verbs as was found in the infinitive with various unsound root types.

The perfective active participle is inflected like a noun in the accusative:

qatilo	he, having killed	*qatilomu*	they (m.), having killed
qatilā	she, having killed	*qatilon*	they (f.), having killed
qatilaka	you (m.s.), "	*qatilakemu*	you (m.pl.), "
qatilaki	you (f.s.), "	*qatilaken*	you (f.pl.), "
qatileya	I, having killed	*qatilana*	we, having killed

We have designated this form as an active participle because of its meaning with transitive active verbs; if the verbal stem is passive, however, this form has a correspondingly passive meaning: Gt *taqatilo* he, having been killed.

The perfective active participle is used to express the fact that an act has been completed prior to the time of the main verb. It is thus always subordinate in value, corresponding to English temporal clauses with "when, after" or participial phrases (Having arrived, I ...; Having sat down, he ...) or to absolute constructions (The sun having set, ...). It is most frequently used in Ethiopic before the main verb but is not restricted to that position:

Nabireya tanāgarku meslēhomu. Having sat down, I spoke with them.

A noun subject is added appositionally to the appropriate 3rd person form. In English we tend to view an expressed noun as the subject of the following main verb; in Ethiopic, however, the noun subject clearly belongs to the subordinate pharse:

Nabiro 'Iyasus, nagaromu ... Having sat down, Jesus said to them ...

Suffixed object pronouns cannot be added to this form (see § 48.4). An object noun may be expressed with the simple accusative or with *la-* alone:

Qatileya be'sē (or: *la-be'si*), *g^{w}ayayku.*	Having slain the man, I fled.

While the use of the Perfective Active Participle as a preposed complement to the subject is the most frequent use, it may stand as a complement to any other element in the clause or to the entire clause (as an absolute):

Rakabuni nabireya heyya.	They found me seated (lit. I having sat down) there.
Rakabu bēto wadiqo.	They found his house in ruins (lit. it having collapsed).
Tamawi'ā hagarena, g^{w}ayayna.	After our city was defeated, we fled.

It must be emphasized that in spite of the English translation values the Perfective Active Participle describes a completed prior event, punctually conceived, and only incidentally does it describe a concomitant state. Thus "having sat down" implies "seated, sitting" as possible translation values, but only because of the particular verb used; our second example above could not be translated "They found his house collapsing."

The Perfective Active Participle is not negated. An equivalent negative expression must employ a subordinate clause with *soba* or *'enza* (see next lesson) plus the Perfect, e.g. *wa-'enza 'i-rakaba māya, xalafa* and having found no water, he continued on his way.

Vocabulary 31

Nouns:

lāhm (pl. *'alhemt*) m.f. bull, cow. *'aṣada 'alhemt* stockyard.

ṣenf (pl. *ṣenaf*, *'aṣnāf*) m. edge, margin, hem; shore, bank; end, limit. *'aṣnāfa medr* the ends of the earth.

ṣāmā/ḍāmā (pl. *-t*) m.f. labor, toil, work; device, artifice.

kesād/kešād (pl. *-āt*, *kesāwed*, *kasāwed*) m.f. neck.

salām m.f. safety; peace. *ba-salām* safely; in peace. *gabra salāma mesla* to make peace with. *Salām laka* Greetings! *Lā'lēhu salām* May peace be upon him!

nafās (pl. *-āt*) m.f. wind.

Verbs:

'asara to tie up, bind (acc. dir. obj.); to tie (something: acc.) to (something: *ba-*, *westa*). Gt *ta'asra* passive.

fatḥa to untie, loosen, open (acc. dir. obj.); to let loose, set free (acc. dir. obj.); to forgive (sins: acc. dir. obj.); to pass judgment (on behalf of: *la-*). Gt *tafatḥa* passive. CG *'afteḥa* to bring to judgment. Glt *tafāteḥa* to engage in a legal case (with: acc. or *mesla*).

'axaza to seize, grasp, hold (acc. dir. obj. or *ba-*); to take captive; to possess, control, occupy. Gt *ta'exza* (sic!) passive. CG *'a'xaza* to order (someone) held. Glt *ta'āxaza* to be involved in a battle or similar activity (with: acc. or *mesla*).

matara to cut, cut off (both lit. and fig.). Gt *tamatra* passive. D *mattara* = G. Dt *tamattara* = Gt.

Other:

ṣemma, *ṣemmita*, *ba-ṣemmit* adv. secretly, in secret, in private.

Exercises

A. 1. Tašāyiṭo lāhma, wasado xaba 'aṣadu.
2. Baṣiḥomu ṣenfa bāḥr, 'i-kehlu 'adiwoto ba'enta nafās 'abiy.
3. Ba-'ayy ṣāmā za-kehlu qatiloto?
4. Kawino nafās, 'i-kehelna ḥawira westa bāḥr.
5. Kawino mesēta, nabarna heyya wa-'i-ḥorna 'eska ṣebāḥ.
6. Gabirana salāma meslēhomu, 'i-ṣabā'nāhomu.
7. 'Asiromu ḥabla westa kesādu, wasadewwo 'enta fenot kama lāhm.
8. Hadi'o nafās, takehlomu 'ariga westa ḥamaromu.
9. Xadigo 'abāhu wa-'emmo, xabra mesla we'etu be'si qeddus.
10. Wagiromu xaṣāwentihomu diba medr, 'abayu waḍi'a ṣab'a.
11. Tabatiko 'aṣq za-nabara dibēhu, wadqa diba medr wa-taqatla.
12. Tase'nani nabira heyya ba-salām 'esma 'i-'afqaruni ḥezb wa-'amandabuni.

13. Fannawomu la-malā'ektihu westa 'aṣnāfa medr meslà zentu zēnā.
14. 'Afṭino tanše'o, dēganomu.
15. Ḥanaṣu lomu bēta Kerestiyān westa makāna 'aṣada 'alhemt xaba ṣenfa bāḥr.
16. Soba rakabnāhomu ta'asiromu, matarna 'aḥbālihomu wa-fatāḥnāhomu.
17. Ta'exizo, tawadya westa bēta moqeḥ.
18. Maṣi'omu ṣemmita ba-lēlit, xabarna meslēhomu lā'la we'etu neguš 'ekuy.
19. Tafawwisā 'em-dawēhā, tafaššeḥat fadfāda wa-'amnat ba-wangēl za-sabaka botu.
20. Tanaši'on 'anest 'em-'amtātihon, bakayā wa-'abayā tagabbero.

B. 1. Nabireya ba-mā'kalomu, tanābabku meslēhomu 'eska ṣebāḥ.
2. Maṣi'aka xabēhomu, ment za-tasāyaṭka 'emennēhomu?
3. Zanta sami'omu, tanāṣaru babaynātihomu wa-'i-kehlu nabiba wa-'i-menta-ni.
4. 'Aṣni'o lebbo, taqāwamomu wa-mo'omu.
5. Waḍi'omu westa medr, tawāladu wa-mal'ewwā.
6. Tamā'i'omu, tanše'u wa-taqātalu babaynātihomu.
7. Ṭafi'on 'ahgurina, taxālafna heyya wa-zeyya ba-k^{w}ellu medr.
8. Taqāribomu, waladat lotu walda šannāya.
9. Sami'ana la-qālātihu, takāḥadnāhu wa-'awḍā'nāhu 'em-xabēna.
10. Tabāwi'o westa mā'kalomu, 'asḥatomu 'em-hāymānot rete't.
11. Tasadido 'exuya 'em-makānu, tasātafkewwo ba-bēteya wa-ba-newāyeya.
12. Tasanā'iwana, takāyadna kidāna babaynātina.
13. Faṭiro be'sē ba-'amsālu, samayo sema 'Adāmhā.
14. Taqatilo sutāfēhu, 'i-kehla nagiša lā'la ḥezbu.
15. 'Exizomu 'asyeftihomu ba-'edawihomu, 'afṭanu wa-waḍ'u ṣab'a.
16. Tafatiḥo mawāqeḥihu, tanše'a wa-g^{w}ayya 'em-xaba 'ella 'axazewwo.
17. Taqādimomu warāzut, ta'āxazu meslēhomu ba-ṣab' 'eska mesēt.
18. Tabāṣiḥeya we'eta be'sē ba-qedma mak^{w}annen, tafātāḥku meslēhu ba'enta newāy 'ekuy za-šēṭani.

Lesson 32

32.1 The Imperfect: G Verbs from Sound Roots. All verbs have five inflected stems: Perfect, Perfective Participle, Imperfect, Subjunctive, and Imperative. The lexical base types (G, D, L, and Q) and a few of the derived verbal types (e.g. CG) have, in addition, verbal nouns and adjectives of a fairly regular and predictable formation which should be learned as part of the verbal system itself. In this and the following lessons we shall take up these remaining forms of the verb, beginning with the G verbs from sound roots.

The Imperfect stem of the G verb has the pattern $-C_1aC_2C_2eC_3-$; inflection is by means of prefixes and suffixes:

yenabber	he will sit	*yenabberu*	they (m.) will sit
tenabber	she will sit	*yenabberā*	they (f.) will sit
tenabber	you (m.s.) will sit	*tenabberu*	you (m.pl.) will sit
tenabberi	you (f.s.) will sit	*tenabberā*	you (f.pl.) will sit
ʾenabber	I shall sit	*nenabber*	we shall sit

When the negative *ʾi-* is prefixed to the 1st person singular form, the ʾ becomes *y* (which we write as *ẏ*: *ʾi-ẏenabber* I shall not sit), a form easily confused with the 3rd person masculine singular. Cf. remarks at end of § 26.2.

When the second and third root consonants are identical, the Imperfect forms ending in a vowel show an optional shortening; thus, from *nababa* (to speak)

yenabbu = *yenabbebu*   *tenabbu* = *tenabbebu*.

Object suffixes are attached to Imperfect forms ending in a vowel just as to the corresponding vowel of the Perfect:

to *-i*: *-íni/-éni* *-éyyo* *-éyyā* etc.
to *-u*: *-úni* *-úka* *-úki* *-éwwo* *-éwwā* etc.
to *-ā*: *-ā́ni* *-ā́ka* *-ā́ki* *-āhú* *-āhā́* etc.

Stems ending in a consonant take the same suffixes as the 3rd person masculine singular of the Perfect, including the "linking" vowel -a-:

yeqattel: *yeqattelā́ni* *yeqattelā́ka* *yeqattelā́ki* *yeqattelṓ* etc.

32.2 Independent Uses of the Imperfect.

(1) Simple future: *yenabber* he will sit.

(2) Durative (no specific tense): he was (is, will be) sitting.

(3) Habitual (no specific tense): he used to sit, he would (regularly) sit, he sits (as a matter of habit), he will sit (ditto).

(4) General present: *yaʿabbi* he is great (from *ʿabya*). While this is really a subdivision of the durative/habitual use, it merits special mention because of its high frequency in relative clauses, which are used instead of the corresponding simple adjective with many verbs:

Yemaṣṣeʾ za-yaʿabbi ʾemennēya.	One who is greater than I shall come.
ʾessāt za-yenadded	a burning flame

Tense for the habitual and durative uses must be gained from the context in most instances. It may be made explicit through the use of various construction, especially with the verb *kona* and the expression *wa-kona soba* (and while):

Kona yenabber heyya.	He was sitting there.
	He used to sit there.
Wa-kona soba yenabber heyya...	And while he was sitting there...

32.3 Dependent Uses of the Imperfect. The most frequent dependent use of the Imperfect is with the conjunction *ʾenza* (when, while)

(1) as complement to the subject:

Nabara ʾenza yenabbeb.	He sat speaking.

(2) as complement to an object:

Rakabewwo la-beʾsi ʾenza yenabber heyya.	They found the man sitting there.

(3) as circumstantial to the entire predication:

Wa-ʾenza yebakki ʾĒremeyās la-ḥezb, ʾawḍeʾewwo.	And as Jeremiah wept for the people, they led him away.

The *ʾenza* may be omitted from the subject and object complement constructions:

Nabara yenabbeb.	He sat speaking.
Reʾya beʾsē yeqarreb.	He saw a man approaching.

The Imperfect in these uses is always durative, indicating an extended action or situation during which or along with which the action of the main verb occurs. Because *ʾenza* often immediately precedes the verb of its clause, the transposition of other elements of the dependent clause for emphasis may place them before *ʾenza*:

Rakabo westa maqāber ʾenza yenabber. He found him dwelling among the tombs.

Vocabulary 32

Nouns:

xoxt (pl. *-āt*, *xawāxew*) m.f. door, doorway.
maskot (pl. *masākew*) m.f. window.
ʾaragāy (f. *-t*, *ʾaragit*; pl. *ʾaʾrug*) old person. *ʾaragāwi* (f. *-t*; pl. *ʾaragāweyān*) idem.

Verbs:

zakara to remember, to mention. Gt *tazakra* passive.
kabra to be glorious, magnificent, great, famous, illustrious. CG *ʾakbara* to make or regard as glorious etc. *kebur* (f. *kebert*) glorious etc.
rak^{w}sa to be unclean, impure, polluted, contaminated; bad (in general). CG *ʾark^{w}asa* to pollute, contaminate, defile. *rekus* (f. *rek^{w}est*) unclean etc.
falasa to separate, go away, depart, emigrate; to secede, split off (from: *ʾemenna*); *falasa xaba* to go over to the side of; *falasa ʾem-zentu ʿālam* to die. CG *ʾaflasa* to send away, deport, exile, remove. Glt *tafālasa* to wander as exiles from one place to another; to pass (from one generation to another).
ʾarxawa CG to open. Gt *tarexwa* passive and middle. *rexew* adj. open.

Other:

wa-kona soba and when (followed by Perfect or Imperfect); and while (foll. by Imperfect).

Exercises

A. 1. ʾEgabber salāma mesla ḥezba zāti hagar.
2. ʾEqarreb xabēka ba-mesēt.
3. Yenadded zentu ʾessāt k^{w}ello gizē.
4. ʾAlbo za-yetarref ʾemdexra weʾetu mendābē.

5. Mannu za-yenaggeš heyyantēka?
6. 'Albo za-yeṭabbeb za'enbala hāymānot.
7. Mannu yeṣaddeq ba-qedma 'Egzi'abḥēr?
8. Konu yenabberu westa ṣenfa bāḥr.
9. Terakkebu 'alhemtikemu xaba 'aṣadeya.
10. Ba-'ayy ṣāmā neqattel zanta ṣādeqa?
11. Nesaddedomu la-Kerestiyān 'em-mā'kalēna.
12. 'Etakkel 'awyāneya zeyya xaba 'albo nafās.
13. Nesabbek wangēlo 'eska 'aṣnāfa medr.
14. Neqabbero mesla 'abawihu.
15. Konu yesaggedu la-ṭā'ot za-'ebn wa-za-'eḍ.
16. We'eta gizē 'ekaššet lakemu nagaro.
17. Tematter-nu 'a'ṣuqa 'em-'eḍ?
18. Mannu yezakker semeya 'emdexra motku?
19. Yekabber semeka 'em-sema 'exuka.
20. 'Efo nefalles 'em-zāti medr šannāyt?
21. Westa 'ayy makān tenabberā?
22. 'Aytē za-terakkebi waldaki?
23. La-mannu tenaggereyyo zanta zēnā?
24. Yeqatteluna 'ellontu sab'.

B. Translate the following relative clauses with English nominal or adjectival expressions. E.g. *za-yegabber mankerāta* a worker of miracles.

1. za-yegabber newāya 'em-bert
2. 'ella yetarrefu 'emdexra ṣab'
3. 'ella yenabberu westa zāti hagar
4. za-yegabber 'albāsa wa-qanāweta 'em-mā's
5. be'si za-yenabbeb fadfāda
6. 'ella yeqattelu ba-sayf
7. 'ella qadamuna
8. za-yesaddedana
9. 'ella yesaggedu la-ṭā'ot rekus
10. za-yegabber 'asyefta 'em-xaṣin
11. za-yegabber ṣāmāhu la-'egzi'u
12. za-yesabbek ba-wangēl
13. 'ella yegannezu 'abdenta
14. mal'ak za-yefaṭṭen

C. 1. 'Arxawa xoxta wa-waḍ'a 'em-bēt.

2. Soba tarexwa xoxt, re'ina 'aragāyta 'enza tenabber westa bēt mesla walda waldā.

3. Rakibana xoxta rexewa, bo'na westa bēt.

4. 'Enza tenabber be'situ xaba maskot, re'yato 'enza yeqarreb westa fenot.

5. Tarexiwomu masākew, bo'a 'abiy nafās wa-'aṭfe'a berhānāta.

6. 'Akko qālātihu za-'akbaro 'allā gebarihu.

7. 'Esma se'enna 'awḍe'o manāfest rekusān 'em-we'etu makān, xadagnāhu.

8. 'Akko sisayomu za-'ark^{w}asomu 'allā qālātihomu.

9. Nagarani zentu qeddus kama ba-šalus yefalles 'em-zentu 'ālam.

10. Tezakkeru-nu zanta nagara 'emdexra xadaggukemu?

11. Wa-tazakra ta'āmer za-gabra 'eska zāti 'elat.

12. 'I-tarākabu mesla 'ella yesaggedu la-ṭā'ot.

13. Rakabnāhu 'enza yebattek 'a'ṣuqa 'em-'eḍawina.

14. Falasna xaba kāle' 'egzi' wa-xabarna meslēhu lā'la 'egzi'ena qadāmi.

15. Tasadidomu 'em-hagaromu, tafālasu 'em-beḥēr westa beḥēr.

16. 'Enza nezakker ḥeywatana šannāya heyya, tabākayna.

17. Rakaba we'eta 'aragāwē yenabber xaba xoxta bētu.

18. Tedaggemu-nu tegabberu za-kama-ze gebra 'ekuya?

Lesson 33

33.1 The Subjunctive: G Verbs from Sound Roots. The stem of the Subjunctive is -$C_1C_2eC_3$- or -$C_1C_2aC_3$-, where the vowel *e* or *a* is lexically determined and not predictable. As may be seen from the following list, there is a correlation between verbs of the *nabara* type and subjunctives with -*e*-, and between those of the *gabra* type and subjunctives with -*a*-. There are many exceptions, however, and some verbs have both forms.

bataka	subj.:	*yebtek*	*qadama*	subj.:	*yeqdem*
dagama		*yedgem*	*qarba*		*yeqrab*
falasa		*yefles*	*qatala*		*yeqtel*
faṭara		*yefṭer*	*rakaba*		*yerkab/yerkeb*
gabra		*yegbar*	*rak^{w}sa*		*yerk^{w}as/yerk^{w}es*
ganaza		*yegnez*	*sabaka*		*yesbek*
kabra		*yekbar*	*sadada*		*yesded*
kašata		*yekšet*	*sakaba*		*yeskab/yeskeb*
nababa		*yenbeb*	*sagada*		*yesged*
nabara		*yenbar*	*ṣadqa*		*yeṣdaq/yeṣdeq*
nadda		*yended/yendad*	*takala*		*yetkel*
nagara		*yenger*	*tarfa*		*yetraf/yetref*
nagša		*yengeš/yengaš*	*ṭabba*		*yeṭbab/yeṭbeb*
qabara		*yeqber/yeqbar*	*zakara*		*yezker*

The inflection of the Subjunctive is exactly like that of the Imperfect:

yeqtel teqtel teqtel teqteli 'eqtel; yeqtelu yeqtelā teqtelu etc.

Suffixes are added as to the Imperfect, with the exception of those of the 2nd person when added to a stem ending in a consonant. They are added directly to the Subjunctive stem without an intervening -*a*-: *yeqtêlka, yeqtêlki; yeqtelkêmu, yeqtelkên.* [The Tradition has the stem stressed in *yeqtêlo, yeqtêlā, yeqtêlon.*]

33.2 The Uses of the Subjunctive.

a. Independent. The Subjunctive as the verb of a main clause has an injunctive (cohortative, jussive) force:

ʾEnger.	Let me speak.
Terkabewwo.	May you find him.
ʾI-neskab.	Let us not lie down.

The positive form may optionally be preceded by *la-*:

La-yeqrab.	Let him approach.

The 2nd person forms with the negative *ʾi-* are equivalent to the negative imperative:

ʾI-tenbar zeyya.	Don't sit here.
ʾI-teqtelo.	Don't kill him.

b. Dependent. The Subjunctive, with or without the conjunction *kama*, expresses purpose or result when subordinated to another verb:

Qarbu kama yesgedu lotu. They approached in order to bow down to him.

Quite a number of frequent verbs function virtually as auxiliary verbs with a following Subjunctive; e.g. *faqada* (to want, wish), *ʾaxaza* (to begin), *waṭana* (to begin), *makara* (to decide to), *xadaga* (to let, allow). An English infinitive construction is often the best translation value:

Faqada kama yenbar heyya.	He wanted to remain there.
Faqada kama ʾenbar heyya.	He wanted me to remain there.
ʾAxazu yesbeku.	They began to preach.
Waṭanna neqrab.	We began to approach.
Makara kama yeqtelani.	He decided to kill me.

After *xadaga* there is often an anticipation of the subject of the subordinate clause:

Xadago la-beʾsi kama yenbar.	He allowed the man to remain.

Kama ʾi- may be translated by "lest":

G^{w}*ayayku (ʾeg*^{w}*ayyi) kama ʾi-yerkabuni.*	I fled (shall flee) lest they find me. (or: so that they would/will not find me.

Infinitival complements are also found with some of these verbs, but their use with the subjunctive is more frequent. Infinitives with prefixed *la-* may also be used to express purpose; this too is much less frequent than the subjunctive (± *kama*).

Other frequent uses of the Subjunctive are the following:

(a) After the conjunctions *(za)ʾenbala* and *ʾem-qedma*, both meaning "before":

Nagaromu zaʾenbala yeflesu.	He spoke to them before they left.
ʾI-hallona ʾem-qedma yefṭerana.	We did not exist before he created us.

(b) After the impersonal verb *dalawa* (imperfect: *yedallew-*) to be fitting, suitable, proper:

ʾI-yedallewani kama ʾeqrab lotu.	It is not proper that I approach him (or: I am not worthy to...).

(c) After the predicatively used adjective *maftew* "it is necessary":

Maftew kama neqbero.	It is necessary that we bury him.

Vocabulary 33

Nouns:

ʾeg^{w}āl (pl. *-āt*) coll. or sing., the young of any animal or fowl, including humans. *ʾeg^{w}āla ʾemma-ḥeyāw* man, mankind.

derhem (pl. *-āt*, *darāhem*) drachma, denarius; gold or silver coin.

x^{w}elq^{w}/x^{w}alq^{w} (pl. *x^{w}elaq^{w}*) m. number, amount. *ʾalbo x^{w}elq^{w}a N* there is no limit to N, N is boundless, innumerable.

Verbs:

faqada (yefqed) to want, wish, desire, require (acc. dir. obj.); for use with Subj., see Lesson. Gt *tafaqda* passive.

makara (yemker) to plan, propose, decide on (acc. dir. obj. or subjunctive); to take counsel (with: *mesla*); to test, choose by testing. CG *ʾamkara* to advise, give counsel to (obj. suff.). Glt *tamākara* to take counsel together (with: *mesla*); to deliberate and decide to (+ subjunctive).

dalawa to weigh (acc. dir. obj.; out to: obj. suff.); to be useful, suitable, proper, correct (see Lesson). Gt *tadalwa* to be weighed.

waṭana to begin (acc. dir. obj. or + Subj. or Infinitive). Gt *tawaṭna* passive.

ʾazzaza D to order, command (obj. suff. + subjunctive). Dt *taʾazzaza* passive; to obey (someone: *la-*).

Other:

maftew it is necessary, fitting, proper, obligatory (see Lesson for construction).

Exercises

A. 1. Neqtel 'alhemtihomu.
2. La-yegbar za-yefaqqed.
3. 'I-tetkelu 'awyāna heyya.
4. Nesdedomu westa 'aṣnāfa beḥērena.
5. 'I-tenbebu qāla 'ekuya.
6. Faqadku kama 'edgem nabiba.
7. Faqadu kama yenbaru meslēna.
8. Faqadat kama tefles 'em-heyya.
9. 'I-faqada yengeš lā'lēna.
10. 'I-teqtelu sab'a.
11. 'I-faqadna nesged la-ṭā'ot.
12. 'I-faqadu daqiq kama yeskabu.
13. Maftew kama negnezo la-badnu.
14. Maftew kama tesbek wangēlo.
15. 'I-terk^{w}esu westa 'albābikemu.
16. Xašašu kama yeqtelewwo.
17. G^{w}ayayna 'emqedma yerkabuna.
18. 'I-yedallewani kama 'enbar meslēka.
19. 'I-yedallewomu kama yeqdemuna.
20. Tefaqqedu-nu tekšetu lana 'asmātikemu?
21. Zanta gabra kama yeṭbab.
22. 'Efaqqed kama tezkerani 'emdexra waḍā'ku.
23. 'I-faqadu yeqrabu xaba taqabra.
24. La-tended 'essāta hāymānotekemu la-'ālam.
25. 'Ayte za-hallo 'Egzi'abḥēr za'enbala yefṭer 'ālama?
26. Mā'zē-nu waṭanka tesbek ba-wangēl?
27. 'I-yedallewo la-zentu be'si kama yeqrab xaba zentu makān.
28. 'I-tedgemu gabira zanta.
29. La-yekbar semeka westa k^{w}ellā medr.
30. Baṣḥa xabēna kama yengerana zēnāhu la-we'etu nabiy wa-mankerātihu.

B. 1. Tarakbu ’enza yenabberu mesla ’abuhomu.

2. Taqārabna kama negbar salāma.

3. ’I-tarākabna meslēhomu kama ’i-nerk^{w}as.

4. Soba tanāgaru meslēna, ’i-faqadna nengeromu wa-’i-menta-ni.

5. ’Anbaba lana zanta maṣḥafa kama nezker gebarihomu la-qeddusān.

6. Makara yenbar zeyya meslēna.

7. Dalawa warqa wa-berura wa-’anbaro ba-qedmēya.

8. Sami‘omu zanta, waṭanu taqātelo.

9. ’Azzazana kama negbar lotu ‘abāya ḥamara.

10. ’Azzazkewwomu kama yeqbaru mutānihomu.

11. Maṣ’a madxenena westa ‘ālam ba’enta ’eg^{w}āla ’emma-ḥeyāw.

12. ’I-yetraf wa-’i-’aḥadu ’emennēhomu.

13. Tašāyaṭku zanta maṣḥafa ’emennēhā ba-šalastu derhem.

14. ’Albo x^{w}elq^{w}a ’ekuyān westa zentu makān.

15. ’Amkarkewwo kama yekšet lomu zanta nagara.

16. Maftew kama tezkeru nagareya.

17. La-ment ’i-ta’azzazkemu lita soba ’a’markemu te’zāzeya?

18. Maftew k^{w}ello gizē la-ta’azzezo la-’egzi’eka.

19. Wehibo lita darāhema warq, tašāyaṭku sisāya wa-lebsa la-zamadeya.

20. Ṭeqqa bezux we’etu x^{w}elq^{w}a darāhem za-tarakbu westa bētu.

21. ’Amṣe’a lana ’eg^{w}āla lāhm.

22. Tamākaru kama yeflesu ’em-zeyya mesla ’azmādihomu.

23. Zentu qeddus we’etu xamestu ’em-x^{w}elq^{w}omu la-liqāna pāpāsāt.

24. Maftew kama negbar bakama ’azzazuna.

Lesson 34

34.1 The Imperative: G Verbs from Sound Roots. The Imperative may be formed directly from the stem of the Subjunctive by inserting *-e-* between C_1 and C_2:

Subjunctive:	*yenbar*	Imperative:	*nebar*	sit!
	yeqtel		*qetel*	kill!

The Imperative is inflected for number and gender, taking the same endings as the 2nd person forms of the Subjunctive and Imperfect:

masc. sing.	*nebar*	masc. pl.	*nebaru*
fem. sing.	*nebari*	fem. pl.	*nebarā*

Object suffixes of the 1st and 3rd persons are added as to the Subjunctive and Imperfect: e.g.

qeteláni, qetélo, qetélā; qetelúni, qeteléwwo, qeteléwwā etc.

[The Tradition deletes the stem vowel in *qetláni*, *qetlána*.]

34.2 The Agent Noun *qatāli*. From most active G verbs there may be made the form *qatāli* (fem. *qatālit*; pl. *qatāleyān/qatāleyāt* or common *qatalt*), an agent noun denoting one who performs, usually habitually or professionally, the action denoted by the verb:

faṭāri	one who creates, a creator
ṣaḥāfi	one who writes, a scribe, writer.

The form is usually treated as a noun and may stand in construct with a following noun, the equivalent of the direct object in the corresponding verbal construction:

faṭārē medr	the creator of the world
ṣaḥāfē zentu maṣḥaf	the writer of this book.

Occasionally, as a result of the verbal force of the form, the accusative is used:

sa'āli ḥeywata	one who asks for life.

With many verbs the *qatāli* form is little used, the relative phrase *(za-yeqattel)* being preferred. Listed below are the more frequent nouns *qatāli* from sound roots introduced up to this point. If the common plural form *qatalt* is attested, it is noted.

faqādi one who actively seeks something (e.g. mercy, evil, revenge); a specialized meaning (with the pl. *faqadd* < **faqadt*) is "necromancer."

faṭāri creator (always refers to God).

gabāri (pl. *gabart*) maker, fashioner, craftsman; the word shares many of the idioms associated with the verb *gabra*.

makāri counselor, advisor.

nabāri (pl. *nabart*) a household servant; rarely: a resident.

nagāši (pl. *nagašt*) king, ruler. Note that the plural form of *negus̆* is borrowed from this synonymous word.

qatāli (pl. *qatalt*) murderer, killer.

sabāki preacher.

sadādi persecutor; also: exorcist.

tarāfi survivor.

A *qatāli* form may stand in apposition to another noun and function as an adjective. Attested mainly as adjectives are

nabābi garrulous, talkative, boastful; more rarely: capable of speech, rational.

nadādi burning, blazing (limited to such items as fire, wrath, lust).

The word *qadāmi* deserves special note. We have already met the word as the ordinal "first." Its more general adjectival notions are "first, previous, prior, antecedent"; as a noun (usually plural): "those who came before, the ancients, men of old; those who go first, nobles, princes." *Qadāmi* is also a noun meaning "beginning, the first or best of anything." *Qadāmi*, *qadāmihu*, and *qadāmē* (the acc.) are used adverbially: "at first, in the beginning, previously, in the first instance."

A number of active verbs have a noun (or adjective) of the pattern *qattāl*, which we met in connection with stative verbs (*nawwāx*, *naddāy*, etc.). The meaning of this form is similar to that of *qatāli*, but its occurrence is much rarer. Among the sound roots introduced thus far only the word

gabbār (coll.) workers, laborers; *liqa gabbār* foreman

deserves mention.

Vocabulary 34

Nouns and Adjectives:

ṭerāz (pl. *-āt*) fragment or fascicle of a book.
nakir (f. *nakār*; pl. *nakart*) adj. strange, alien, foreign; other, different; marvelous, wonderful.
Kerestiyānāwi (f. *-t*) a Christian; adj. Christian.

Verbs:

šamra (yešmar) to take delight, be pleased (with, in: *ba-*). CG *ʾašmara* to please, delight, give pleasure to (obj. suff. or *la-*).
ḍansa (yeḍnes, yeḍnas) to become pregnant (by: *ʾem-*); to conceive (a child: acc. dir. obj.). Gt *taḍansa* to be conceived.
zabaṭa (yezbeṭ) to beat, whip, (sometimes) kill (acc. dir. obj.; the part of the body may be specified with *diba*, *westa*, or *lāʿla*). Gt *tazabṭa* passive. Glt *tazābaṭa* reciprocal. *zabāṭi* ruffian, fighter.
gadafa (yegdef) to throw, cast; esp. to throw away, discard; to lose by waste or neglect. Gt *tagadfa* passive.
ḍēwawa Q/L to take captive, lead away captive, deport, exile. Qt *taḍēwawa* passive.

Other:

qadimu adv. first, at first, previously, before this; *ʾem-qadimu* idem. Also used as a noun in a few fixed expressions: *mawāʿela qadimu* days of old; *za-qadimu* things of old.

Exercises

A. 1. Nebar zeyya meslēya wa-ʾi-tenbeb.
2. Segedu la-ʾamsāleya kama ʾi-y̓eqtelkemu.
3. Gedef zanta lebsa beluya westa ʾessāt.
4. Nebeb, gabreya, wa-ʾana ʾegabber za-saʾalka.
5. Qedemani ʾanta, ʾesma ʾi-yedallewani kama ʾana ʾeqdemka.
6. ʾI-tefles ʾemennēya xabēhu; nebar meslēya.
7. Genezewwo la-badnu ba-ʾalbās šannāyt wa-qeberewwo xaba ʾammarkukemu.
8. Kešet lita za-nagaraka.
9. Zekeri qāleya wa-ʾi-tengeri wa-ʾi-la-mannu-hi.

10. Negeruni x^welq^{w}a sab' qatalt 'ella maṣ'u lā'lēkemu.
11. Negeruna za-temakkeru 'antemu kama tegbaru.
12. 'I-tezbeṭo, 'esma be'si rāte' wa-xēr we'etu.
13. 'I-tegdef maṣāḥefta za-botu qāla 'Egzi'abḥēr.
14. Sededu qatalta wa-zabāṭeyāna 'em-mā'kalēkemu.

B. 1. qatāli ṣenu'
2. šalastu tarāfeyan
3. sadādē Kerestiyān
4. maṣāḥefta qadamt
5. liqāna gabbār
6. gabārē bert
7. makāri ṭabib
8. 'aragāy nabābi
9. nagāši ṣādeq
10. sabāki nabābi
11. 'arwē nabābi
12. sadādē manāfest 'ekuyān
13. warēzā zabāṭi
14. ma''at nadādit
15. gabarta salām
16. faṭārē samāy
17. faṭārina
18. qadāmē warāzutikemu
19. qadāmihu la-'ālam
20. te'zāzāta qadamta hagar
21. faqādē newāy 'ālamāwi
22. gabārē ḥegg
23. nabarta bētu
24. qatalt 'elewān
25. gabbāra neguš

C. 1. Zabaṭewwo 'eska wadqa 'em-maskot wa-mota.
2. 'Azzaza zanta ṣāmā lā'lēna ba'enta xaṭi'atena.
3. 'I-faqadat kama teḍnas.
4. We'eta 'amira teḍannes dengel.
5. Zentu we'etu waldeya za-šamarku bo.
6. 'Ašmarana fadfāda nagaru ṭabib wa-xēr.
7. Nabarna xaba ḥayqa bāḥr 'enza nešammer ba-nafās wa-berhāna ḍaḥāy.
8. Zabaṭkewwo la-'arwē diba kesādu wa-'amatkewwo.
9. Ḍēwawewwomu la-ḥezb westa hagara Bābilon, wa-meslēhomu 'Ēremeyās nabiy.
10. Matarewwo 'edēhu la-zabāṭi wa-sadadewwo.
11. La-ment kama-ze tegaddef ḥeywataka?
12. Naš'ani ba-kesādeya wa-'axaza yezbeṭani.
13. Seḥibomu la-be'si westa ṣenfa bāḥr, wagarewwo westētu.
14. Wa-soba re'ya 'abuhā 'esma ḍansat walattu, tam'e'a fadfāda wa-tase''elā mannu za-gabra zanta.
15. Xalafa be'si Kerestiyānāwi qedmēhu, wa-meslēhu maṣḥaf 'abiy wa-nakir.

16. Tagābe'u k^{w}ellomu tarāfeyān ba-'aḥadu makān, wa-tamākaru ba'enta za-yegabberu.
17. Nakir we'etu gaṣṣu la-zentu 'aragāy; 'em-beḥēr bā'ed we'etu.
18. 'Aflasomu la-ḥezbena wa-ḍēwawomu westa medr nakār wa-nawāx.
19. 'Arxiwā xoxta bētā, gadafat k^{w}ello newāyā westa fenot.
20. Šēṭu 'eg^{w}ālomu la-kāhenāt, 'ella šo'ewwomu mašwā'ta la-ṭā'ot.
21. 'Ark^{w}asu manāfesta mewutān zanta makāna.
22. Rakabku ṭerāza, wa-dibēhu qālāt nakart za-'i-kehelku 'anbebo.
23. Wadiqā westa 'egarihu la-mak^{w}annen, sa'alato ḥeywata waldā.
24. 'Andadu nabartihu bēto, wa-naši'omu warqo g^{w}ayyu.
25. Soba bo'a we'etu sabāki westa 'anqaṣa hagar, tabatka totāna šā'nu, wa-xašaša gabārē 'ašā'en kama yegbar lotu kāle'a.
26. Nagirana zēnā 'em-ṭent, tanšā'na wa-xašašna makāna hedu'a kama neskab 'eska ṣebāḥ.
27. Zentu we'etu qadāmihu la-nagar za-'anbabku westa we'etu maṣḥaf.
28. Tanše'u gabbār lā'la liqomu wa-qatalewwo ba-xaṣāwentihomu.
29. Wa-'enza we'etu qeddus ba-'aḥatti 'elat yenabber westa 'anqaṣa hagar, xalafat qedmēhu 'aḥatti be'sit 'aragāyt Kerestiyānāwit, wa-meslēhā 'aḥadu ṭerāz 'em-maṣḥafa Pāwlos ḥawāreyā. Wa-naš'ā la-ye'eti ṭerāz, wa-soba 'anbabā, rakaba westētā qāla nakira wa-'a'mero mankera. Tašāyaṭā la-ṭerāz 'emennēhā ba-'aḥadu derhema warq wa-'azzazā kama terkab za-tarfa 'em-zentu maṣḥaf. Ḥorat wa-'amṣe'at lotu šalāsa ṭerāzāta kāle'āta, wa-wahabā 'arbā'ta derhema warq. Wa-'emze fannawato xaba bēta Kerestiyān. Heyya xašaša k^{w}ello maṣḥafa xaba 'aḥadu 'em-kāhenāt, wa-wahabo maṣḥafa, wa-'anbabo wa-'aṣne'o ba-lebbu, wa-'amna ba-'Egzi'ena 'Iyasus Kerestos (lotu sebḥat).

Lesson 35

35.1 The Verbal Adjective *Qetul*. In our previous discussion of the adjective we noted that the pattern *qetul* is the one most frequently used in deriving adjectives from stative G verbs. Adjectives of the same pattern are derived also from transitive active G verbs and from many intransitive active ones as well. The underlying voice of the form depends entirely on that of the verb from which it is derived:

(a)	Active transitive:	*qetul* is passive, corresponding to the English passive perfect participle.
(b)	Active intransitive:	*qetul* is resultative, i.e. an adjective describing the state resulting from the action of the verb. It is often equivalent to a perfect active participle: *nebur* having sat/having settled = seated, sitting, situated, residing, resident.
(c)	Stative verbs:	*qetul* is a simple adjective, as already discussed.

As with all verbal adjectives in Ethiopic, the frequency of these forms is somewhat low because of the preference for relative clauses with finite verbs. The following are the verbal adjectives *qetul* from roots learned thus far:

(a) Transitive active verbs:

betuk	broken	*qebur*	buried
feṭur	created	*qetul*	slain
gebur	worked (of various materials); done, made, finished	*sedud*	expelled, exiled, excommunicated
genuz	prepared for burial	*tekul*	planted; implanted, fixed
kešut	uncovered, bare; open (esp. of the eyes)	*zebuṭ*	beaten
		zekur	mentioned, remembered
geduf	thrown, cast; thrown away, discarded; lost, rejected (of persons)		

And, relative to the C verbs *ʾaṭmaqa* and *ʾafqara*:

ṭemuq	baptized
fequr	beloved

(b) Intransitive active verbs:

ḍenest	pregnant (fem. only)
felus	exiled, in exile
nebur	sitting, seated, situated; residing; as noun: resident
nedud	burning, flaming (e.g. *lebb, maʿʿat*)
neguš	king (only as a noun)
qerub	nearby, near, adjacent (to: *la-, xaba*); at hand, nigh (of time); *(ba-)qeruba* prep. near (suffixes may be added as to an acc. noun)
segud	prostrate (in a position of worship or adoration)
sekub	lying down
šemur	pleasing (to: *la-, ba-xaba, ba-qedma*), nice, pleasant
teruf	excellent, outstanding. The fem. form *tereft* (or the plural *terufāt*) is used as a noun: virtue, excellence, perfection.

(c) Stative verbs. These have already been given in the Vocabularies as adjectives.

Adjectives of the pattern *qetul* are frequently used as adverbs, with prefixed *ba-* or in the accusative case:

ba-feṭun = *feṭuna* swiftly, quickly, soon
kešuta openly, publicly.

35.2 Further Remarks on Complements.

(a) Adjectives as subject or object complements may be introduced by *ʾenza*: *ʾEnza dewey nabarku westa bēteya.* I remained at home (while) ill.

(b) Less commonly, a full non-verbal clause may be used circumstantially with *ʾenza*: *Reʾiku beʾse ʾenza yebus ʾedēhu.* I saw a man with a withered hand (lit. his hand being withered).

(c) Subject or object complements may also be expressed by the adjective alone with a personal pronominal suffix:

Ḥora ḥezunu.	He went away sad.
Ḥorku ḥezuneya.	I went away sad.
Rakabewwo ḥeyāwo.	They found him alive.
Rakabomu ḥeyāwānihomu.	He found them alive.

The case and suffix of the adjective depend on the status of the word to which they stand in apposition:

'I-tewaḍḍe' ḥeyāweka.	You will not go forth alive (nom.).
'I-yenašše'uka ḥeyāwaka.	They will not take you alive (acc.).

Vocabulary 35

Nouns:

nag^{w}*adg*^{w}*ād* (pl. *-āt*) thunder.
mabraq (pl. *mabāreqt*) m. lightning.
'asḥatyā m.f. ice, hail, snow, frost.

Verbs:

māsana L to be ruined, destroyed; to perish; to become corrupt, rotten. CL *'amāsana* to corrupt, destroy, wipe out. Lt *tamāsana* passive of CL.
dakma (yedkem/yedkam) to be tired, weary, feeble, infirm. CG *'adkama* causative. *dekum* (f. *dekemt*) tired, weary, weak, feeble, ill.
ḍarfa/ḍarafa (yeḍref) to blaspheme (against: *lāʿla, la-*, acc.). *ḍeruf* blasphemous, wicked, impious. *ḍarāfi* (pl. *-yān*) blasphemer.
q^{w}*arra/q*^{w}*arara* to be cold, cool; to cool (of anger). CG *'aq*^{w}*rara* caus. *q*^{w}*arir* (f. *q*^{w}*arār*) cold, cool.
masala (yemsal) to resemble, be like (acc. dir. obj.); to seem, appear as (obj. suff. of person; acc. of predicate noun or adjective, or *kama*; e.g. *Yemasselani fenot retuʿa* The road seems straight to me; *Yemasselani kama warx* It looks like the moon to me); impersonal: it seems (obj. suffix of person + *kama/za-* with perf. or imperf.). CG *'amsala* to regard as, hold as equivalent to (two accusatives, or acc. + *kama*).

Exercises

A. 1. mabraq feṭun
2. be'si ḍeruf
3. 'aragāy dekum
4. ḥezb felusān

5. waldeya fequr
6. welud ṭemuqān
7. ’albās geduf
8. ’ašā’en gedufān
9. warēzā qetul
10. totān betuk
11. be’si zebuṭ
12. badn qebur
13. šegā genuz
14. xaṣin gebur
15. gaṣṣ kešut
16. ‘elew sedud
17. sem zekur
18. be’sit ḍenest
19. hagar nebert diba dabr
20. ’aragāyt sekebt diba medr
21. qāl šemur la-’ella sam‘ewwo
22. kāhen ṣādeq wa-teruf
23. beḥēr qerub la-bāḥr
24. māy q^{w}arir kama ’asḥatyā
25. qāl ‘abiy kama nag^{w}adg^{w}ād
26. sayf tekelt ba-’egru
27. sem zekert westa zentu maṣḥaf
28. ḥezb segudān qedma ṭā‘otomu.
29. ṭerāz geduf westa fenot
30. ‘eḍ qerebt la-bētena
31. gamal feṭent wa-ṣene‘t
32. naddāy zebuṭ
33. ’aragit Kerestiyānāwit
34. zēnā nakir wa-ḍeruf
35. newāy beluy wa-geduf

B. Replace the adjectives in 1-18 above with the appropriate relative clause. E.g. *mabraq feṭun* = *mabraq za-yefaṭṭen*; *be’si zebuṭ* = *be’si za-tazabṭa*.

C. 1. Dekum ’ana wa-’efaqqed ’enbar.
2. Ḍeruf ’anta wa-rekus we’etu qāleka.
3. Temasselani ḍarāfē wa-gabārē ’ekit.
4. ’Amsalna ḍarāfeyāna kama qatalt.
5. ’Amsalewwomu la-qeddusānihomu qadamt kama malā’ekt ’em-xaba ’Egzi’abḥēr.
6. Zentu beḥēr yemasselani šemura fadfāda.
7. ’Adkamana zentu mendābē wa-faqadna nefles westa kāle’ makān.
8. Maṣ’a nafās q^{w}arir mesla bezux zenām wa-’asḥatyā wa-’aṭfe’a ’essāta za-’andadu.
9. Soba q^{w}ararat ma‘‘atu, ṣawwe‘ani wa-wahabani za-sa’alku.
10. Masalomu gaṣṣu gaṣṣa mal’aka berhān.
11. Masalo kama re’ya be’sē ’aragāya ’enza yeqarreb westa fenot.
12. Rakaba ‘abiya sayfa ’enza tekul westa ‘eḍ ṣenu‘.
13. Roṣu feṭuna xabēna wa-’anše’una ’em-xaba wadaqna.
14. Nabaru ’ardā’ihu mesla šegāhu genuz wa-’i-yaqbarewwo.
15. ’I-teḍref lā‘la ’Egzi’abḥēr kama ’i-yeqtelka ba-mabraqu.
16. Masalomu be’sē xēra wa-terufa, wa-bāḥtu kona ’ekuya wa-‘elewa

ba-lebbu.

17. 'Afrehomu mabraq wa-nag^{w}adg^{w}ād wa-gab'u 'abyātihomu.
18. Māsanā 'ahgurihomu wa-taḍēwawu ḥezbomu.
19. Bekemu-nu bezuxāna 'alhemta?
20. 'Albo ṣenfa la-xaṭi'atomu wa-'albo x^{w}elq^{w}a gebarihomu 'ekuyāt.
21. 'Amāsanu 'abyāta wa-'a'ṣādāta za-ḥanaṣna ba-ṣāmā 'abiy wa-ṣenu'.
22. 'Asarewwo wa-wagarewwo ḍerufo westa bēta moqeḥ.
23. Rakabewwomu la-falāseyān neburānihomu heyya ba-salām.
24. Tafatḥu mawāqeḥina wa-waḍā'na feṭuna 'em-heyya.
25. Tamatrat ḥeywatu la-we'etu ḍarāfi ba-mabraq za-tafannawa 'em-samāy.
26. 'I-kehlu bawi'a bēta Kerestiyān 'esma 'i-ṭemuqān 'emuntu.
27. Zanta nagara kešuta, wa-bāḥtu kāle'a nagara ṣemmita.
28. 'Em-qadimu koṅu yenabberu sab' manfasāweyān westa 'ellontu 'adbār, wa-bāḥtu 'em-dexra motu liqānihomu, falasu westa baḥāwert bā'edān.

Lesson 36

36.1 The Verbal Noun. There is associated with nearly every G verb a noun denoting the action or quality defined by the verbal root. Neither the form nor the meaning of these nouns is completely predictable. The form may be any one (or more) of a dozen patterns, but there are only seven of relatively high frequency *(qetlat, qetl, qetal, qetāl, qatal, qatāl, qatl)*. The meanings may range from abstract (e.g. *ṭebab* wisdom) to concrete (e.g. *takl* a plant, shoot). In general, however, the range of possibilities, both in form and meaning, is small and it is convenient to learn these nouns for a given verb when the verb is first met. Below are the verbal nouns of the G verbs from sound roots which have been introduced up to this point.

(a) The pattern *qetlat*. This is the most common type and could apparently be formed at will from any active verbal root. With many verbs, however, it is obviously of secondary importance in comparison to another more frequent pattern. The forms *qetlat* listed below are the main verbal noun for the roots in question, or at least, are as frequent as any of the others that may be attested. Note that in some instances the verbal noun of the G type occurs where the verb itself is attested only as CG or Gt.

betkat	breaking, fracture, rupture
ḍerfat	blasphemy
felsat	wandering, travel; exile; death; assumption (into heaven). *Felsata Bābilon* the Babylonian Exile.
feṭrat	the act of creation; what is created, creatures; nature, character; kind, species.
gebrat	fashion, way in which something is made and appears; form, shape
genzat	preparation for burial
nebrat	sitting down; session; position; condition, state; manner or mode of life; dwelling (act or place)
neddat	flame, burning
qetlat	killing, murder
rekbat	finding; acquisition
sebkat	preaching, proclamation; a preaching mission

seddat exile, expulsion; persecution

segdat prostration, act of adoration

šemrat favor, approval, consent; *ba-šemrata* with the consent/approval of

šeṭqat cutting, splitting; a cut, split

ṭemqat baptism

zebṭat beating, whipping

Plurals, when attested, are uniformly in *-āt*.

(b) The pattern *qetl*.

ḍens pregnancy; also (rarely) foetus

feqr love

gebr already given in Voc. 21. In addition to the meanings given there, *gebr* is also employed rather curiously as an adverb "necessarily, out of necessity"; *ba-gebr* idem.

kebr glory, honor; splendor, magnificence

mekr plan; counsel, advice; consideration, deliberation; prudence, wisdom; opinion, point of view (e.g. *ba-mekreya* in my opinion)

negš reign, rule

rekʷs uncleanness, pollution; anything unclean, any vile thing

qʷerr cold, coldness

ṣedq justice; *gabra ṣedqa* to do justice; *ʾi-kona ṣedqa* + inf.: it is not right to ...; righteousness, virtue; truth, the truth. *ba-ṣedq* correctly, rightly, justly.

zekr mention, memory; commemoration

Plurals, when attested, are uniformly at *-āt*.

(c) The pattern *qetal*:

ṭebab wisdom

(d) The pattern *qetāl*:

nebāb speech, what one says, manner of speaking

terāf remainder, residue; overflow, abundance. *Terāfāta Nagašt* the OT book of Chronicles (lit. the remainder or overflow from Kings)

dekām weariness, infirmity, weakness

Plurals, when attested, are uniformly in *-āt*.

(e) The pattern *qatal*:

nagar already given in Voc. 5
qabar burial, funeral
taraf synonym of *terāf* above

(f) The pattern *qatāl*:

faqād (pl. *-āt*) m.f. desire, wish, will; *ba-faqādu* of his own accord; *mašwā ʿta faqād* voluntary offering; *za'enbala faqād* involuntarily.
nafās already given in Voc. 30

(g) The pattern *qatl* tends to be used more for the formation of concrete nouns than for verbal nouns in the narrower sense. Nouns like *nafs*, *nadd*, *bēt (*bayt)*, *gabr*, *wald*, etc., although clearly associated with G verbs, are simply derived nouns and do not have the meaning required for verbal nouns. On the other hand,

qatl killing, murder; also: fighting, battle (*gabra qatla mesla* to fight a battle with)
takl (pl. *-āt*; *'atkelt*) a plant, tree; *ʿaṣada 'atkelt* orchard, grove; also fig. in such expressions as *takla ṣedq* and *takla hāymānot*

do qualify, though in both instances concrete meanings exist side by side with the abstract. Indeed, the fact that all the patterns introduced here are sometimes used for derived nouns that are not felt to be verbal nouns means that the meaning of no noun can be taken for granted on the basis of its form alone and should always be checked in the lexicon.

All verbal nouns tend to be variable in gender (m.f.) and, as indicated, are pluralized with *-āt* with very few exceptions.

36.2 The Cognate Accusative. Verbal nouns, in general, are construed as ordinary nouns and offer no special translation problems. There is one usage, however, that requires special attention: the verbal noun may be used as the object of its cognate verb in order to add emphasis or specification. When so used, it does not affect the ordinary constructions of the verb in question, being added more or less as an adverbial phrase:

Zabaṭewwo zebṭata ʿeṣuba.	They beat him severely (lit. a severe beating).
Ganazewwo la-badnu genzata šannāya.	They prepared his corpse splendidly for burial (lit. a splendid preparation).

Vocabulary 36

Nouns:

geʿz (pl. *-āt*) mode of life, manner; nature, quality, essential nature (both of persons and things).

ṣalot (pl. *-āt*) prayer(s).

ʾaṣbāʿt (pl. *ʾaṣābeʿ*) f.m. finger, toe.

ʾezn (pl. *ʾezan, ʾaʾzān*) f. ear.

ʿayn (pl. *ʾaʿyent*) f. eye. *sabʾa ʿayn* spies, scouts.

Verbs:

ṣalma/ṣalama (yeṣlam/yeṣlem) to grow dark, be black; of eyes: to grow blind; *ṣalma gaṣṣu* he became angry. CG *ʾaṣlama* causative. *ṣelum* dark, obscured, blinded. *ṣalim* (f. *ṣalām*) black. *ṣelmat* m.f. darkness; the days of the month after the 15th are known as *mawāʿela ṣelmat* (days of wane); dating may use the formula *ʾama X-u la-ṣelmata Y* on the X-day (using qatul as the number) of the second half of the month Y.

šaṭaqa (yešṭeq) to cut, split. Gt *tašaṭqa* passive. *šeṭuq* cut, split. *šeṭqat* cutting, splitting, a cut, split.

xadara to reside, dwell, inhabit (usually with a prepositional phrase, but sometimes with the acc. of place); *xadara lāʿla* to reside in, possess (said of demons or spirits in a person). CG *ʾaxdara* causative. Gt *taxadra* to be inhabited. Glt *taxādara* to live together, cohabit (with: *mesla*).

ʿaṣaba/ʿaṣba (yeʿṣeb/yeʿṣab) to be hard, harsh, difficult (for: obj. suff.); to be necessary. *ʿeṣub* harsh, difficult, onerous; difficult (to do: *la-* + inf.). *ba-ʿeṣub* with difficulty.

Exercises

A. 1. rekbata warq
2. qetlata sabʾa ʿayn
3. neddata maʿʿateya
4. gebrata ʾanāqeṣihā
5. nebratu la-neguš
6. genzata badnu

7. feṭrata ḍaḥāy wa-warx
8. felsata zentu ḥezb
9. ḍerfatu la-zeku ʼarami
10. felsata Bābilon
11. nebrata makāreyān
12. nebratomu ba-westa gadām
13. ṣelmata lēlit
14. šeṭqata ʼalbāsihu
15. gebrata zentu newāy za-bert
16. berhān wa-ṣelmat
17. nebratu wa-geʻzu
18. geʻzātihomu la-ṣādeqān
19. betkata ḥabl

B. 1. ʼAytē za-xadarkemu ba-mawāʻela felsatekemu?
2. Tasadda ʼem-xabēhomu baʼenta ḍerfatu ʼekuy.
3. Wa-ʼemze mēṭo la-weʼetu qeddus ʼem-seddatu.
4. Hadʼat medrena ʼem-qetlat wa-ʼem-maqšaft ba-gizē negšu.
5. Menta gabra ʼEgziʼabḥēr ʼemdexra feṭrata ʼabuna ʼAdām?
6. Nenabber zeyya ʼeska yeq^{w}arrer neddata maʻʻat za-westa lebbu.
7. Ganazewwo genzata šannāya wa-qabarewwo ba-ʻabiy kebr.
8. Nagarā la-negešt baʼenta nebratu la-weʼetu neguš wa-baʼenta kebra bētu wa-k^{w}ellu geʻzu.
9. Soba tasamʻa qāla betkata ʼaʻṣuq, wa-roṣna feṭuna ʼem-tāḥta ʻeḍaw.
10. Tareʼyana gebrata ʼalbāsihu nakira ṭeqqa.
11. Tanāgara meslēna baʼenta rekbata maṣḥaf beluy westa bēta maqdas.
12. Baʼenta ment matarewwo ʼaṣābeʻihu la-zentu beʼsi?
13. ʼI-kehelna taxādero meslēhomu baʼenta rek^{w}somu.
14. Soba samʻa ṣalotātihomu la-Kerestiyān, tamʻeʻa fadfāda wa-ʼazzazomu la-ʼagbertihu kama yezbeṭewwomu wa-yeqtelewwomu.
15. Wa-ʼemdexra nagarana mekro, xabarna meslēhu.

C. 1. ba-šemrata ʼegziʼomu
2. segdatomu la-ṭāʻot
3. sebkata wangēl za-madxenena
4. ṭemqata ʼeg^{w}ālihomu
5. rekbata darāhema berur
6. ḍensā la-walattu
7. gebrāt ʼekuyāt za-xadart
8. qabar kebur
9. baʼenta kebra nagašt
10. feqru la-waldu
11. bakama faqādu la-ʼabuhu
12. ʼatkelt betukān ʼem-xaba barad
13. ṭebab tereft
14. kešuta ʼezan wa-feṭuna ʼaʼmero

D. 1. Za-ʼayy-nu beʼsi zentu ḍens?
2. Šannāyāt ʼaʻyentihā wa-šemurāt qālātihā.
3. Ṣalim gaṣṣu kama ṣelmata dammanāta zenām.
4. Geʻza ḥeywat reteʻt feqr weʼetu.
5. Motu westa gadām ʼem-q^{w}erra lēlit wa-ʼem-neddata ḍaḥāy ba-maʻālt.

6. Ment we'etu mekreka ba'enta ṭebaba qadamt?
7. 'I-'amanna nebābo.
8. Zanta gabarna la-zekru la-'abuna za-mota 'ama xamusu la-ṣelmata zentu warx.
9. Wa-kona samāy ṣeluma, wa-tasam'a qāla nag^{w}adg^{w}ād wa-nafās, wa-tare'ya berhāna mabrạq.
10. Tašaṭqa 'aṣbā'tu wa-weḥza bezux dam 'em-'edēhu.
11. Kal'una xadira ba-mā'kalomu wa-sadaduna zeyya.
12. Zentu we'etu terāfa nagara we'etu nabiy.
13. 'I-gabarku zanta ba-gebr 'allā ba-faqādeya.
14. Ba'enta gebru 'ekuy wadqa 'em-kebru wa-kona kā'eba be'sē naddāya.
15. Takala takla ṣenu'a za-hāymānot westa 'albābihomu.
16. Zāti ṣāmā 'eṣebt ye'eti; 'i-nefaqqed kama negbarā ba'enta dekāmena.
17. 'Aṣbatomu nebratomu heyya, wa-falasu westa kāle' beḥēr.
18. 'Eṣub la-ḥaniṣ za'enbala 'a'bān.
19. Naš'ani meslēhu soba ḥora westa sebkat.
20. 'Eṣubāt qālātihu la-'a'mero.
21. Xadara manfas rekus lā'lēhu, wa-'i-faqada wa-'i-mannu-hi kama yeqrab xabēhu.
22. G^{w}ayyu mesla tarafa newāyomu.
23. 'Ama kašata 'a'yentihu, 'i-re'ya menta-ni westa ṣelmat za-'odato.

Lesson 37

37.1 Nouns of Place: the Pattern *meqtāl*. There are two principal types of nouns with prefixed *m-* derived from G verbs. The most consistently predictable in terms of meaning is *meqtāl* (i.e. $meC_1C_2\bar{a}C_3$), which usually denotes the place where the action of the verb is customarily performed:

mendād furnace, oven, fireplace

mesgād a place where one worships, a shrine, mosque

meskāb a bed, couch; a place to lie down

meṭmāq a place for baptizing, baptistry; also: a pool in general

menbār a place where something is put; residence, where one lives; base, foundation (of a pillar etc.)

meqrāb neighborhood, vicinity

Occasionally, however, words of this pattern develop specialized meanings which must be learned separately:

megbār action, practice, behavior, custom(s); what one does, business

menbāb a paragraph or section (pericope) of a text, as divided for public reading

merkāb acquisition; pay, stipend for performing one's office

The gender of these nouns is variable (m.f.); plurals, when attested, are uniformly in *-āt*.

37.2 Nouns of the Pattern *maqtal(t)*. The second type of noun with prefixed *m-* is *maqtal* (i.e. $maC_1C_2aC_3$). Nouns of this formation cover a wide range of meanings (nouns of place, of instrument, of action) and should not be guessed at. We have already encountered *manfas*, *malʾak*, *mabraq*, and *makān* (from *kona*); note also:

magnaz materials used in preparing a body for burial

manbar (pl. *manābert*) m.f. throne, seat, chair

marxo (for **marxaw*; pl. *marāxut*) m.f. key

matkal (pl. *matākel*) stake, peg

For some verbs the form *maqtalt* (with final *-t*) is used, often along with *maqtal*, with the same range of meanings (cf. *mašwāʿt* from *šawʿa*;

maqšaft from *qašafa*):

maqbart (pl. *maqāber*, *-āt*) m. grave, tomb, sepulcher. The plural is also used as a singular.

manbart state, condition, mode of life (synonym of *nebrat*)

The pattern *maqtel* (and *maqtelt*) has two distinct functions: (1) an agent noun for CG verbs, to be discussed in a later lesson; (2) a derived noun from G verbs, similar in meaning (and sometimes a variant of) *maqtal*. Note

matkel = *matkal* above

mangešt (pl. *-āt*) m.f. kingdom; kingship, majesty. *mangešta samāyāt* the Kingdom of Heaven; *zamada/weluda mangešt* the royal family.

Vocabulary 37

Verbs:

nafsa to blow (subject: the wind). CG *ʾanfasa* to breathe something out (e.g. fire); to rest, take a breather, find relief (from: *ʾemenna*); to give rest or relief to.

baraqa (yebreq) to lightning, flash like lightning. CG *ʾabraqa* to make lightning.

qašafa (yeqšef) to beat, whip; to afflict, punish (with: *ba-*). Gt *taqašfa* passive. *qešuf* beaten, whipped, afflicted. *qešfat* punishment, affliction.

saqala (yesqel) to suspend, hang up (acc. dir. obj. + *ba-*, *westa*, *diba*, *lāʿla*); to crucify. Gt *tasaqla* passive; to depend (on: *ba-*, *xaba*); to adhere, cling (to: *westa*). *sequl* hanging, suspended, crucified; dependent (on: *ba-*, *westa*). *seqlat* crucifixion. *masqal* (pl. *masāqel*) m. cross.

Nouns:

reʾs (pl. *ʾarʾest*) m.f. head; top, summit; chief, leader; frequent with suffix as reflexive or intensive pronoun: *qatala reʾso* he killed himself; *qatalkewwo reʾseya* I myself killed him.

gannat (pl. *-āt*) f. garden; the Garden of Eden.

šerāy (pl. *-āt*) medicine, herbs, etc.; incantations, spells, magic. *za-/ʾella šerāy*, *sabʾa šerāy* dealers in magic and spells.

gānēn (pl. *ʾagānent*) demon, evil spirit. *za-gānēn* (pl. *ʾella 'agānent*) one possessed by an evil spirit.

Exercises

A. 1. matkal za-xaṣin
2. marxo bēteya
3. manbaru la-'Egzi'abḥēr
4. manbar kebur
5. 'ahgura mangeštu
6. mangešta samāyāt
7. marāxuta mangešta samāyāt
8. matākela 'eḍ
9. magnaz šannāy
10. maqābera nabiy
11. manbarta qadamta mangešt
12. mendād za-'essāt
13. mesgāda 'aramāwiyān
14. menbāra bētu
15. meqrābomu la-xāṭe'ān
16. rek^{w}sa megbārihomu
17. menbāba maṣḥaf qadāmi
18. masqal za-'eḍ
19. 'eḍa masqal
20. berhāna mabraq
21. manfas rekus
22. makān hedu'
23. manbar šannāy za-warq
24. manāberta mak^{w}ānent
25. mangeštāta medr
26. rekbata newāyu

B. 1. Wadaya ṭerāza maṣḥaf westa mendād.
2. Re'sa zentu dabr manbaru la-'Egzi'abḥēr we'etu.
3. Qatalato la-we'etu be'si 'ekuy ba-matkal za-'eḍ.
4. Nenbar qeruba la-mendād, 'esma waṭana nafās q^{w}arir nafisa.
5. 'Emdexra 'anfasna 'em-ṣāmāna, dāgema 'axazna gabira.
6. Taqašfu 'ellontu ḥezb xāṭe'ān ba-'essāt wa-'a'bān za-waradu lā'lēhomu 'em-samāy.
7. Ba'enta ment 'i-kehla warida 'em-diba masqal?
8. Sakaba diba meskābu wa-tadawwaya.
9. Xadaru 'abawina qadamt westa gannat šannāy fadfāda, wa-bāḥtu ta'adawu lā'la 'Egzi'abḥēr, wa-we'etu 'azzazomu la-malā'ektihu kama yesdedewwomu la-'abawina 'em-westa gannat xaba makān za-ṣelmat.
10. Tagābe'u xaba meṭmāq za-qerub la-bēta neguš.
11. Zentu 'eḍ we'etu 'em-masqal za-tasaqla 'Iyasus dibēhu.
12. Sequl ḥeywateya ba-te'zāza negušeka.
13. Soba baṣḥa we'eta makāna, re'ya k^{w}ellomu Kerestiyāna sequlāna diba masāqel ba-te'zāza we'etu neguš 'elew.
14. 'Emdexra seqlatu la-madxenena, g^{w}ayyu 'ardā'ihu kama 'i-yerkabewwomu sab'a hagar wa-yeqšefewwomu.
15. 'Amṣe'u lotu šerāya nakira 'em-'aṣnāfa medr, wa-bāḥtu 'i-kehlu

fawwesoto ’em-dawēhu ‘eṣub.

16. ’Awḍe’u ḥawāreyāt ’agānenta ba-sema ’Egzi’ena ’Iyasus Kerestos (lotu sebḥat).

17. Ṣawwe‘omu la-sadadd wa-’azzazomu kama yesdedewwo la-gānēn za-xadara lā‘la waldu, wa-bāḥtu ’i-kehlu sadidoto.

18. K^{w}ello ’amira ’anbabu lana ’aḥada menbāba ’em-maṣḥaf ba’enta ḥeywata qeddusān.

19. Sam‘a ’Egzi’abḥēr la-ṣalota nabiyu, wa-’asme‘a qāla nag^{w}adg^{w}ādu wa-’abraqa mabāreqtihu ba-westa samāy ṣalim.

20. Ṣawwe‘omu la-’ar’esta ḥezb xabēhu wa-tase’’elomu ba’enta za-kona ba-lēlit, wa-se’nu nagiroto wa-’i-menta-ni.

C. 1. naddāy qešuf wa-sedud
2. bezuxān ’ella-’agānent
3. ’ezn metert ’em-re’su
4. be’si metura ’ed
5. ḍarāfi metura lesān
6. ’atkelt nawixān wa-ṣenu‘ān
7. ba-šemrata liqa pāppāsāt
8. ṭebaba ṭabibān
9. maqbart kešut
10. metrata re’su
11. menbāra masqal
12. za’enbala faqād
13. mangala re’sa dabr
14. ‘eḍ tekul westa mā’kala gannat
15. ge‘za ’Ag‘āzi
16. merkāba gabbār
17. tāḥta meskābu
18. matkal betuk
19. ‘abiy mangešt
20. negš nawwāx
21. felsatā la-nafsu westa samāy
22. ’ebn ṣalām
23. maṣḥaf šeṭuq wa-geduf
24. ’a‘yent ṣelumāt
25. ’asmāta ’arāwita gannat
26. x^{w}elq^{w}a ’agānent

D. 1. Maftew kama ’eqšefka.
2. ’Amāsanu ‘aṣada ’atkelt.
3. ’Amkarkewwomu kama yeflesu.
4. ‘Araggu westa re’sa dabr.
5. Maṣ’ani dekām wa-se’enku ḥawira ba-’egr.
6. ’I-kona ṣedqa la-ḍēwewotomu.
7. ’Ammarana fenota ba-’aṣbā‘tu.
8. ’Akko zentu šerāy za-fawwaso.
9. Ṣalmā ’a‘yentihu wa-’i-kehla re’eya.
10. Xašašewwo kama yesqelewwo.
11. Tabatka ḥablu wa-wadqa westa māy.
12. ‘Eṣub we’etu la-’awḍe’otomu la-’agānent.
13. ’Enza dekum ‘arga westa dabr ba-‘eṣub.
14. Šamarna ba-q^{w}erra māya meṭmaq.
15. Nebābu za-’ark^{w}aso.

Lesson 38

38.1 G Verbs from roots I-Guttural: Remaining Forms.

(a) Imperfect, Subjunctive, and Imperative. Because of the guttural in first root position, the prefix of the Imperfect is uniformly with *-a-* instead of *-e-*. The Subjunctive and Imperative are without peculiarities.

Perfect	Imperfect	Subjunctive	Imperative
ʾamna	*yaʾammen*	*yeʾman*	*ʾeman*
ʾasara	*yaʾasser*	*yeʾser*	*ʾeser*
ʿaqaba	*yaʿaqqeb*	*yeʿqab*	*ʿeqab*
ʿarga	*yaʿarreg*	*yeʿreg/yeʿrag*	*ʿereg/ʿerag*
ʿaṣaba/ aṣba	*yaʿaṣṣeb*	*yeʿṣeb/yeʿṣab*	---
ḥanaṣa	*yaḥanneṣ*	*yeḥneṣ*	*ḥeneṣ*
ḥatata	*yaḥattet*	*yeḥtet*	*ḥetet*
ḥazana	*yaḥazzen*	*yeḥzan/yeḥzen*	*ḥezan/ḥezen*
xabra	*yaxabber*	*yexbar*	*xebar*
xadaga	*yaxaddeg*	*yexdeg*	*xedeg*
xadara	*yaxadder*	*yexder*	*xeder*
xalafa	*yaxallef*	*yexlef*	*xelef*
xašaša	*yaxašseš*	*yexšeš*	*xešeš*

(b) The verbal adjective *qetul*:

ʾemun faithful; trustworthy, true. *ʾemuna* adv. truly, in truth.

ʾesur bound, tied, captive; restricted.

ʿequb (1) under guard, in custody; (2) set aside, reserved (for: *la-*); (3) cautious, guarded. The feminine form *ʿeqebt* (pl. *ʿequbāt*) is used for "concubine, harem-woman."

ʿeṣub Vocabulary 36.

ḥenuṣ built, constructed.

xebur joined, associated. *xebura* adv. together, jointly, at one and the same time.

xedug left, abandoned, deserted; divorced.

xedur residing, dwelling.

xeluf crossing, passing.

The noun *xebest* is the fem. form of **xebuz* (baked), from the G verb *xabaza (yexbez)* to bake.

(c) The agent noun *qatāli*:

ʾamāni one who believes; adj. faithful.

ʿaqābi (pl. *ʿaqabt*) guard; note the compounds: *ʿaqābē ʾanqaṣ* door-keeper; *ʿaqābē (ʿaṣada) wayn* vintner, one in charge of the wine; *ʿaqābē reʾs/šegā* bodyguard; *ʿaqābē nabib* speaker, spokesman; *ʿaqābē gannat* gardener; *ʿaqābē šerāy* doctor, physician.

ḥanāṣi architect, builder.

xabāzi baker.

xadāri (pl. *xadart*) guest, sojourner.

xalāfi (pl. *xalaft*) passer-by, one passing; adj. transitory, transient. The fem. form *xalāfit* is used collectively: those passing by.

(d) The verbal nouns:

ʾesrat binding, tying, constricting.

ʾemnat faith, belief.

ʾamān truth; adj. (read ? *ʾammān*) true, faithful. *ʾamān, ʾamāna, ba-ʾamān* adv. truly, in truth.

ʿeqbat guarding; observing, conserving, keeping; watch, vigil.

ʿergat ascent, ascension; assumption into heaven; elevation (of the host).

ʿeṣab/ʿaṣāb harshness, difficulty; need, want.

ḥenṣ/ḥenṣat/ḥenṣā building, construction (both act and product).

ḥatatā investigation, interrogation.

ḥazan sadness, grief.

xebrat union, joining, association; consensus, accord.

xedgat remission (of sins, debts).

xedgāt/xedāgāt divorce; *maṣḥafa xedgāt* divorce document.

xedrat residing, dwelling.

xašašā (pl. -*t*) wish, desire.

(e) Nouns of the pattern *maqtal(t)*. Note the -*ā*- of the first syllable before the guttural.

māʾman adj. believing, faithful; true, trustworthy. The forms *meʾman* and *māʾmen* (fem. -*t*) are also frequent.

mā'sar (pl. *ma'āser*, -*t*) m.f. bond, fetter (of any sort); a vow. Synonymous forms are *mā'ser* and *mā'sart*.

mā'qab (pl. *ma'āqeb*, -*t*) guard, guard-station.

mā'reg (pl. *ma'āreg*, -*āt*) m.f. place of ascent, ascent; grade, degree, level, class; stairs, ladder.

māḥtat m. testimony, testifier, witness.

māxbar m.f. congregation, gathering; crowd, tumult; council; colleagues, associates; monastery, convent.

māxdar (pl. *maxāder*) dwelling-place, residence; room, cell.

(f) Nouns of the pattern *meqtāl*

mexlāf a place for crossing or passing through.

me'rāg (pl. -*āt*) place of ascent.

Vocabulary 38

Nouns:

mahāymen (f. -*t*) adj./noun faithful (in the religious sense); a believer.

Verbs:

'araba/'arba (ye'rab/ye'reb) to set (of heavenly bodies). CG *'a'raba* to cause to set. *'arab* west; Arabic. *'arb* Friday; *'elata 'arb*, *'arb 'elat* idem. *'erbat* setting. *'arabi* western; Arabian. *'arabāwi* idem. *me'rāb* the west; *me'rāba ḍaḥāy* idem.

xafara/xafra (yexfar) to be ashamed (of: *ba'enta*; to do something: inf. or verbal noun or subjunctive; before, in the presence of: *gaṣṣa*, *'emenna*); to fear, revere (someone: *gaṣṣa*, *'emenna*). Gt *taxafra* to be ashamed, put to shame. *xafrat* (pl. -*āt*) shame, impropriety, turpitude.

ḥamma/ḥamama (yeḥmam/yeḥmem) to be ill, suffer illness, pain or distress. CG *'aḥmama* to afflict with illness, pain, distress. G1t *taḥāmama* to hate one another. *ḥemum* ill, afflicted, distressed. *ḥemām* (pl. -*āt*) illness, pain, disease, affliction.

xaḍaba (yexḍeb) to wash, wash away. Gt *taxaḍba* to wash one's self (a part of the body may be added as acc. dir. obj.). *xeḍub* washed. *xeḍbat* washing, ablution. *mexḍāb* (pl. -*āt*) bath, bathing place.

ḥawwaṣa D to inspect, look at (acc. dir. obj.); to look in on, visit; to look after (both good and bad senses). Dt *taḥawwaṣa* passive.

Other:

ʿādi adv. still, yet, again, moreover, still more. With pron. suff. = to still be, as in *ʾenza ʿādina zeyya* while we are still here; *ʿādiya ḥeyāw* I am still alive. With following time-word: more, as in *ʿādi xamus* five days more.

sānit (ʿelat) the next day. *sānitā* idem. *ba-sānitā* on the next day (or night).

Exercises

A. 1. Xedeguni kama ʾexbar meslēkemu.
2. Xašašu kama yexlefu ʾenta māʾkala medrena.
3. ʾAzzazomu la-ʿaqabt kama yeʾserewwo.
4. Baʾenta ʾemnateka ʾi-y̓axaddegaka.
5. ʾI-teḥzani, walatteya, ʾesma ʾi-mota meteki ba-ṣabʾ.
6. La-yeḥtetu maṣāḥefta ḥegagihomu, wa-ʾemdexra ḥatatāhomu la-yengeruna menta rakabu westētomu.
7. Tagābeʾu k^wellomu ʾaḥzāba medr kama yeḥneṣu ʿabiya bēta la-nagāšihomu.
8. ʾEm-ʾayy ʿaqābē wayn tašāyaṭka zanta wayna? Xēr fadfāda weʾetu.
9. Reʾeyo neguš kama g^wayyu ʿaqabta šegāhu, wadqa diba sayfu wa-qatala reʾso.
10. ʾAbuhu ʿaqābē šerāy semuy weʾetu.
11. Maftew kama teʿqabu k^wello ḥegaga za-wahabkukemu.
12. Farāhna kama ʾi-yeʿṣabana ṣāmā.
13. ʾEmanu botu wa-terakkebu ḥeywata za-la-ʿālam.
14. ʾAlbena meʿrāfa xaba naxadder mesla daqiqena.
15. Taseʾʾelkewwo la-xalāfi baʾenta fenota bāḥr.
16. Xadart ba-māʾkalēkemu neḥna, wa-bāḥtu n̈aʿaqqeb ḥegagikemu ba-ʾamān.
17. Zentu menbāb weʾetu baʾenta ʿergatu la-nabiy westa samāy.
18. Wahabā maṣḥafa xedgāt wa-sadadā ʾem-westa bētu.
19. Baʾenta ment zentu ḥazan, waldeya?
20. Māsanu xelufānihomu westa bāḥr ba-ʾaḥmārihomu.
21. ʾI-texbaru gabira mesla xedurāna zentu makān.
22. Tagabbaru xebura ba-ḥenṣāhā la-zāti hagar kebert.
23. ʾAmāni ʾemun ʾanta, wa-baʾenta za-ʾamanka zaʾenbala yengeruka baʾenta taʾāmereya wa-mankerāteya, gabarku makāna ʿequba laka

re’seka westa bēta ’abuya za-ba-samāyāt.

24. Ṣādeqān ’emuntu wa-ṣenu‘ān ba-‘eqbata ḥegg.

25. ’Asiromu ‘aqābē ’anqaṣ wa-bawi’omu bēta neguš ba-ṣemmit, qatalewwomu la-‘aqabta re’su la-neguš wa-sadadewwomu la-zamada mangešt westa fenot.

B. 1. Kerestiyān mahāymenān
2. ‘aqābē nabib ṭabib wa-teruf
3. zamad ‘Arabi kebur
4. baḥāwerta me‘rāb
5. ‘aqābē gannat ’emun
6. be’si dewuy wa-ḥemum
7. lebs xeḍub ba-māy
8. xašašāhomu la-ḥezbu
9. ḥanāṣi ṭabib
10. hagar ḥeneṣt ba-ṣenfa bāḥr
11. ’anestihu wa-‘equbātihu
12. warēzā ’esura ’egarihu wa-’edawihu
13. re’sa xabāzeyān
14. ’aragāy ḥezun
15. be’sit xedegt
16. ba-‘elata ‘arb
17. ’emqedma ‘erbata ḍaḥāy
18. nafās ‘arabāwi
19. ba-lesāna ‘Arabi
20. xafratu la-negušomu
21. ḥemām ‘eṣub la-fawweso
22. xeḍbata kāhenāt
23. xafratena ba’enta za-gabarna
24. ba-‘ādi šalus

C. 1. Ba’enta ment ’i-ta’ammenā beya?
2. Ta’asserewwo ba-’aḥbāl ṣenu‘.
3. Sa’alnāhu xedgata xaṭāwe’ina.
4. Ṣawwe‘a ḥanāṣē wa-nagaro mekro la-ḥenṣata bēt ḥaddis.
5. Fatḥa ma’āserihomu la-’esurān.
6. ’Aqoma bezuxa ma‘āqebta westa ’amdār za-mo’a.
7. Taqādamnāhomu westa me‘rāga hagar, wa-’i-xadagnāhomu kama yeqrabu xaba ’anāqeṣa hagar.
8. Faqadku xalifa ’enta mā’kala māxbaromu, wa-’i-wahabuni mexlāfa.
9. Samā‘na māḥtatakemu lā‘la zentu be’si, wa-bāḥtu ’i-rakabna xaṭi’ata botu.
10. ’Albo za-’i-yaxaffer ba-ye’eti ‘elat.
11. La-ment ’aḥmamkana zanta ḥemāma ‘eṣuba?
12. Taxaḍabku ’edawiya wa-gaṣṣeya ba-māy q^warir za-zentu meṭmāq.
13. ’Enza ‘ādikemu meslēna, ’enaggerakemu ba’enta mangešta samāyāt.
14. Gab’a hagara wa-ḥawwaṣa bēta Kerestiyān za-ḥanaṣu westa ṣenfa bāḥr.
15. Tamākaru kama yeqtelewwo soba warada xaba mexḍāb.
16. Ba-sānitā xalafa ’em-zentu ‘ālam wa-bo’a westa māxbara qeddusān.

17. Ba'enta ment kalā'kani ḥawweṣotomu la-dewuyān wa-ḥemumān?
18. ʿĀdi sadus wa-'axallef 'em-xabēkemu.
19. Re'ya ʿabiya māʿrega 'enza menbāru diba medr wa-re'su westa samāy.
20. 'Atawu beḥēromu 'emqedma yeʿrab ḍaḥāy.

Lesson 39

39.1 G Verbs from Roots II-Guttural: The Remaining Forms.

(a) Imperfect, Subjunctive, and Imperative. All verbs of this root type have the same patterns for these stems, uniformly with *-a-* in the Subjunctive and Imperative. Note the vowel assimilation in the Imperfect *(*aGGe > eGGe)* and Imperative *(*eGa > aGa)*.

Perfect	Imperfect	Subjunctive	Imperative
la'aka	*yele''ek*	*yel'ak*	*la'ak*

Regular verbs of this type already introduced are

be'la	*lehqa*	*se'na*	*seḥta*	*ṣaḥafa*
keḥda	*mahara*	*sa'ala*	*saḥaba*	

The verbs *'axaza* (also I-gutt.) and *kehla* have irregularities:

'axaza	*ye'exxez*	*ye'xaz*	*'axaz*
		ya'axaz	
kehla	*yekel*	*yekhal*	*kahal*

A number of Imperfects of this root type have *-ē-* instead of *-e-* in the first stem syllable, especially *yerē''i* for *yere''i* (he sees). The reason for this phenomenon is not clear. It is optional.

(b) Verbal adjectives *qetul*:

be'ul Voc. 17
ṣeḥuf written
seḥut erring, led into error
se'un impotent, powerless
le'uk sent; frequent as noun: apostle, messenger
mehur learned, expert (in: acc. or *ba-* or construct)
'exuz captive, held; possessed by (e.g. *'exuza 'agānent*); joined, continuous

(c) The agent noun *qatāli*:

ṣaḥāfi Voc. 5
kaḥādi infidel, non-believer; rebel
kahāli powerful, strong, capable; *kahālē* k^{w}*ellu* omnipotent; *kahāli la-* + inf./verbal noun: capable of (doing).
'axāzi owner, possessor; master, lord.

(d) Verbal nouns:

ṣeḥfat writing (act or product)
seʾlat request, prayer, petition
seḥtat error, sin; *zaʾenbala seḥtat* without error
kāḥd lack of faith, impiety, heresy; disobedience, rebellion; *zaʾenbala kāḥd* without doubt, without fear of contradiction
keḥdat denial, apostacy, rebellion
lehqāt old age
lāʾk (pl. *-ān*) servant
ʾaxaz/ʾāxz m. fist

The derivatives of *beʿla* are a little confusing. The adjective *bāʿel* (f. *-t*) was introduced in Voc. 16. The plural *ʾabʿelt* probably belongs to the noun *bāʿl* (same written form as *bāʿel*) owner, possessor. A second adjective *beʿul* was given in Voc. 17. There are two additional nouns of identical appearance:

baʿāl (pl. *-āt*) m.f. feast, festival; *gabra baʿāla* to hold/celebrate a festival; *baʿāl tekelt* a fixed festival; *baʿāl ʾi-tekelt* a movable festival.
baʿʿāl (f. *-t*) owner, possessor, master (a synonym of *bāʿl* and sharing its plural *ʾabʿelt*).

Then finally there is the simple verbal noun *beʿl* riches, wealth.

(e) Nouns with prefixed *m-*:

maṣḥaf Voc. 11
malheqt (coll.) elders, seniors (either as a synonym of *liqān/liqāwent* or in reference to persons older in age, e.g. *ʾaxawihu malheqt* his older brothers). The plural forms *malheqāt*, *malāheqt*, *-āt* also occur.
malʾekt (pl. *-āt*) epistle, letter; legate, legation; ministry, service, office, function.

39.2 The Verb *behla* to say. The Perfect of this verb has been replaced by a unique prefixed conjugational form:

yebē	he said	*yebēlu*	they (m.) said
tebē	she said	*yebēlā*	they (f.) said
tebē	you (m.) said	*tebēlu*	you (m.pl.) said

tebēli	you (f.) said	*tebēlā*	you (f.pl.) said
ʾebē	I said	*nebē*	we said

The loss of the final *-l* apparently results from an old misdivision when a dative suffix was attached: *yebēlana* → *yebē lana* he said to us. The *-l-* is always "restored" when a dative suffix is added to any of the above forms ending in *-ē*. These forms are very frequent, being used regularly to introduce direct speech.

The Imperfect, Subjunctive, and Imperative are also irregular, with uniform loss of *-h-*:

Imperfect: *yebel* Subjunctive: *yebal* Imperative: *bal*

Inflection is normal. The appropriate form of the Imperfect with *ʾenza* may be used after any verb of speaking to introduce direct speech:

wa-yebēlo ʾenza yebel	and he said to him (he-saying):
wa-saʾalkewwo ʾenza ʾebel	and I asked him (I-saying):
wa-nagarewwo ʾenza yebelu	and they spoke to him (they-saying):

Note the derived verbs, regular in formation:

Gt *tabehla* to be spoken, said; to be spoken of, named, mentioned

Glt *tabāhala* to speak (debate, discuss, argue) with one another (*mesla, babaynāti-*, acc.).

But CG *ʾabala* to cause to say, without *-h-*.

Vocabulary 39

Nouns:

māʿbal/māʿbel (pl. *-āt*) m.f. wave, flood.
ferē (pl. *-yāt, fereyāt*) m. fruit (lit. and fig.), blossom, bud; *gabra/wahaba ferē* to produce fruit.

Verbs:

neʾsa (yenʾas) to be small, little (in size or importance); to be young. CG *ʾanʾasa* causative. *neʾus* (f. *neʾest*) small, little, young. *naʾās* a young girl (fem. of an unattested **neʾis*). *neʾs* childhood, infancy. *nestit* a little, a small amount; used in construct (e.g. *nestita xebest*) or appositionally like an adjective (e.g. *hagar nestit* a small village). *nestita* adv. a little, for a little while; *baba-nestit* little by little.

reḥqa (yerḥaq) to be distant, remote, far off (both spatial and temporal). CG *ʾarḥaqa* to remove, put at a distance; to delay. Glt *tarāḥaqa* to separate (mutually) (from: *ʾemenna, mesla*, obj. suff.). *reḥuq* far away, remote, distant; *reḥuqa maʿʿat* slow to anger. *reḥuqa* = *ba-reḥuq* adv. at a distance. *ʾem-reḥuq* from afar. *reḥqat* a period of time or interval of space.

meḥra/maḥara (yemḥar) to have mercy, pity (on: *la-* or obj. suff.). CG *ʾamḥara* to move to pity. Gt *tameḥra* to be shown pity/mercy. *meḥrat* (pl. *-āt*) mercy, pity; *gabra meḥrata la-/mesla/lāʿla* to have pity on, show mercy toward. *maḥāri* (one who is) merciful.

ṭeʿma/ṭaʿama (yeṭʿam/yeṭʿem) to taste, to experience (e.g. death); to be tasty, delicious. CG *ʾaṭʿama* to give (something: acc. dir. obj.) to (someone: *la-* or obj. suff.) to taste; to make sweet, pleasant. *ṭeʿum* tasty, delicious, sweet, pleasant. *ṭāʿm* (pl. *-āt*) m.f. taste, flavor; sweet taste, pleasant taste.

lehqa This verb also has the meanings "to grow old" and (rarely) "to grow, increase in size or quantity" in addition to the sense "to grow up, reach puberty."

sawwara D to hide, cover over, conceal, protect. Dt *tasawwara* reflexive and passive.

Other:

nāhu an emphasizing particle, usually rendered as "behold." It calls attention to the immediacy (spatial or temporal) of what follows. If used alone with a following noun, it may be taken as a full predication: "Here, now, is X."

neʿ- an Imperative base: come! Forms are m.s. *naʿā*, f.s. *neʿi*, m.pl. *neʿu*, f.pl. *naʿā*.

ʾo- vocative particle: O! Usually prefixed, as in *ʾo-negš* O king!, but with *ʾEgziʾ* it is regularly suffixed: *ʾEgziʾo* O Lord! It may also express wonder or grief.

Exercises

A. 1. Xabirakemu meslēya tebeʿʿelu.

2. K^{w}ellomu sabʾ yelehhequ wa-yaxallefu westa meʿrāfomu.

3. Yeseḥḥetu ʾenza yekeḥḥedu ʾamāna wangēlu.

4. Naxaššeš kama nel’akka xabēhu mesla se’latena.
5. ’Emehheraka k^{w}ello maṣāḥefta za-Ḥegg Belit wa-Ḥegg Ḥaddis.
6. La-ment tese’’enu ḥatitoto la-zentu be’si?
7. Nenbar zeyya ’enza nedakkem wa-nese’’en ḥawira.
8. ’Anta teṣeḥḥef zanta k^{w}ello diba maṣḥaf.
9. Re’ināhomu ’enza yeseḥḥebewwo westa fenāwē hagar.
10. Bawi’ana heyya ne’exxezo wa-na’assero ’egarihu wa-’edawihu.
11. ’I-yekelu taqāwemo ba-qedma ’Amlak kahālē k^{w}ellu.
12. ’I-yekel ’ana takāḥedotaka ba’enta ’amāna qālātihu.
13. Ba-sānitā nekel taqārebo wa-tanābebo babaynātina.
14. ’Albo za-tekelu gabira wa-’i-menta-ni za’enbala qawim wa-tarā’eyo babaynātikemu.
15. Tawālidakemu tekelu mali’a westa k^{w}ellā medr.
16. ’I-tese’’enu-nu tabāṣeḥoto?
17. Maharani ba-lesāna Yonānāwiyān.
18. ’I-temharomu la-daqiqeka ’ekita.
19. Faqadat kama teb‘al.
20. Zanta maftew kama tegbar ’emqedma telhaq wa-tedkam.
21. ’I-tekḥadewwo la-’Egzi’ena, ’esma ’i-hallawa ḥeywat za-la-‘ālam za’enbalēhu.
22. Sa’alo sisaya wa-’albāsa; ’i-tes’alo warqa.
23. Nexlef ’em-zeyya ’emqedma ya’axazu yezbeṭuna.
24. Ṣaḥafu lana mal’ekta nawixa ba’enta xelfatekemu westa bāḥr.
25. ’Egzi’abḥēr ’Amlāk we’etu za-ye’exxez k^{w}ello ba-’edawihu.
26. Wa-ba-gizēhā sawwara dammanā gaṣṣa ḍaḥāy wa-mal’a ṣelmat westa medr.
27. Tasawwarku ’emennēhomu wa-’i-kehlu rakiboteya.

B.
1. ’aragāy mehura ḥegg
2. ’aragit dekemt wa-se’ent
3. warēzā ’exuza gānēn
4. sab’ ’exuzān westa bēta moqeḥ
5. maṣḥaf ṣeḥuf ba-ṣeḥfat šannāy
6. ’axāzē ‘ālam
7. nagāši ’axāzi
8. keḥdata seḥutān
9. ba-lehqātihu la-’abuna
10. be‘la we’etu neguš kebur
11. Mal’ekta Pāwlos xaba sab’a Romē
12. kāḥdomu la ’ellontu ‘elewān
13. qetlata kaḥādeyān
14. ba‘‘āla ḥamar
15. Ba‘āla Masqal
16. malāheqta ’Esrā’ēl
17. lā’k ’emun
18. takl ne’us
19. beḥēr reḥuq

20. 'axāteya malāheqt
21. ḥamar ne'est
22. 'asmātihomu la-lā'kānihu
23. $nag^{w}adg^{w}$ād reḥuq
24. mal'ekta zentu kāhen ṣādeq
25. za'enbala meḥrat
26. 'egzi' kahāli la-radi'otana
27. 'egzi' maḥāri
28. nestita māy q^{w}arir
29. be'si ṭe'uma nebāb
30. mā'bala māy
31. ferē šannāy
32. ferē ṭe'um
33. nestita ferē
34. ṭā'ma mot
35. ṭā'ma zentu ferē
36. mā'bala zenām
37. 'em-ne'su 'eska lehqātu
38. ḥeywat za'enbala seḥtat
39. 'axaz ṣenu'

C. 1. Wa-yebēlomu 'enza yebel: "La-ment tekeḫḫeduni?"
2. Wa-nagarkewwo 'enza 'ebel: "Ne'us 'ana wa-'i-kahāli la-gabira zentu.
3. Ze-we'etu madxen za-tabehla westa maṣḥafa qadamt.
4. Balewwo 'esma 'i-nekel sagida lotu.
5. Wa-tafāniwomu, tarāḥaqu wa-'atawu beḥēromu.
6. 'I-ỷarḥaqa 'Egzi'abḥēr 'elata ma''atu.
7. 'Em-ne'su 'i-gabra 'ekita wa-ḥora westa fenot rete't.
8. Qomu ba-reḥuq 'enza 'i-yefaqqedu yeqrabu.
9. Reḥuq fadfāda beḥēru la-zentu nakir.
10. Tene''esi 'em-'axawiki, wa-bāḥtu teṭabbebi 'emennēhomu.
11. Maṣ'a mā'bala zenām wa-'aṭfe'a nadda 'essāt za-'andadu.
12. 'I-yegabber 'eḍ šannāy ferē 'ekuya.
13. Maḥarnāhomu la-naddāyān wa-wahabnāhomu sisāya.
14. Meḥrana wa-marḥana xaba bētu.
15. Nāhu berhān warada 'em-samāy wa-marḥomu fenota.
16. Ne'i xabēya, walatteya, wa-'i-terḥaqi 'emennēya.
17. Maḥarana 'o-neguš wa-'i-teqtelana.
18. 'Awidomu lotu kaḥādeyān, 'asaru ḥabla westa kešādu.
19. Za-ya'ammen ba-zentu nagar 'i-yeṭe''em mota.
20. Wa-'i-yekel wa-'i-mannu-hi sawwerotaka 'em-zentu mendābē wa-xasār.

Lesson 40

40.1 G Verbs from Roots III-Guttural: The Remaining Forms.

(a) Imperfect, Subjunctive, and Imperative. All verbs from this root type have the same stem patterns in these forms:

Perfect	Imperfect	Subjunctive	Imperative
maṣʾa	*yemaṣṣeʾ*	*yemṣāʾ*	*meṣāʾ*

The addition of any vowel (subject suffix or object suffix) to the Subjunctive or Imperative is normally accompanied by a stem change (-*ā*- to -*e*-):

yemṣāʾ	*yemṣeʾu*	*meṣāʾ*	*meṣeʾu*	*yemṣāʾ*
temṣāʾ	*yemṣeʾā*	*meṣeʾi*	*meṣeʾā*	*yemṣeʾani*
temṣāʾ	*temṣeʾu*			*yemṣāʾka*
temṣeʾi	*temṣeʾā*			*yemṣāʾki*
ʾemṣāʾ	*nemṣāʾ*			*yemṣeʾo*
				yemṣeʾā etc.

One also encounters forms with the -*ā*- retained, as in *yemṣāʾu* (for *yemṣeʾu*). The G verbs from roots III-guttural introduced up to this point are

maṣʾa	*našʾa*	*malʾa*	*ratʿa*	*radʾa*	*kalʾa*
gabʾa	*marḥa*	*farha*	*ṣanʿa*	*ṭafʾa*	*fatḥa*
baṣḥa	*samʿa*	*bazxa*	*ṣabʾa*	*hadʾa*	

(b) The verbal adjectives *qetul*:

meluʾ full (of: *ʾem*- or acc.); abundant, copious; filling (acc.)

semuʿ famous, illustrious; notorious

fetuḥ open; forgiven (person or sin)

retuʿ, *bezux*, *ṣenuʿ*, and *heduʾ* have already been introduced.

(c) The agent noun *qatāli*:

marāḥi leader (cf. *marḥ* below)

samāʿi hearing, listening to; obedient; as noun (pl. *samāʿt*) witness, martyr

gabāʾi (pl. *gabāʾt*) mercenary, hired worker. The relationship of this word to the verb *gabʾa* is not entirely clear.

farāhi fearful, reverent. *farrāh* fearful, timid.

fatāḥi (pl. *fatāḥt*) judge

ṣanāʿi (pl. *ṣanāʿt*) strong, firm; fortified

ṣabāʾi warrior, soldier; the fem. form *ṣabāʾit* f.m. is used as a collective term for "army, troops"

radāʾi helper, assistant

(d) Verbal nouns:

meṣʾat arrival, advent, coming

marḥ (pl. *ʾamreḥt*) leader

melʾ what fills (e.g. *melʾa ʾed* a handful). *ba-melʾu* (or with other suff.) in toto, completely

semʿ (pl. *-āt*) m.f. rumor, report; testimony; martyrdom, martyrs

bezx multitude, large number or amount

gebʾat return; conversion (to: *westa*)

ferhat (pl. *-āt*) fear, dread, awe; fearfulness, timidity

feth̩ judgment (act or fact)

retʿ justice, what is right, true etc.; truth

ṣenʿ/ṣenʿat hardness, firmness; strength, power, force; *ṣenʿa samāy* the firmament of the sky

ṭefʾat extinction, destruction, loss

hedʾat peace, tranquillity

kelʾat prohibition, prevention

radʾēt help, assistance; helper, assistant

(e) Nouns with prefixed *m-*:

memṣāʾ place of origin

megbāʾ refuge, place to return to

meṣnāʿ (pl. *-āt*) firm base; firmament (of heaven)

mabzext major part, majority; most of

Vocabulary 40

Nouns:

ṣagā (pl. *-t*) m.f. grace, favor, kindness; gift, payment, reward, *ba-ṣagā* gratis, as a gift.

hagarit town, city (a less common and more restricted word than *hagar*).

Verbs:

xab'a (yexbā') to hide, conceal (acc. dir. obj.). Gt *taxab'a* reflexive and passive. *xebu'* hidden, concealed; secret, arcane; *ba-xebu'* secretly, in secret. *mexbā'* (pl. *-āt*) hiding place, hidden place; receptacle.

ṣanḥa (yeṣnāḥ) to wait, await, expect (acc. dir. obj.); to be imminent (to: dat. suff. or *la-*); to lie in wait for. CG *'aṣneḥa* to set traps or snares for; to set in ambush; to promise (i.e. cause to expect); to prepare (something: acc.) for *(la-)*. *ṣenuḥ* waiting, expectant; put aside, reserved.

šar'a (yešrā') to put into order, arrange; to establish, set up, ordain. Gt *tašar'a* passive. *šeru'* arranged, ordered, established, ordained. *šer'at* (pl. *-āt*) order, arrangement, disposition; decree, edict, command; law, statute; treaty, pact, testament; custom, habit, any fixed pattern.

faṣṣama D to complete, finish, end; to fulfill, accomplish; with a following inf.: to finish doing something. Dt *tafaṣṣama* passive.

Exercises

A. 1. Menta tegabberu soba yebaṣṣeḥakemu 'elata mendābē?
2. Waḍā'na feṭuna 'emqedma yemṣe'u qatalt.
3. 'I-faqadu kama yegbe'u westa 'Iyarusālēm.
4. Nešā' 'exʷāka meslēka.
5. 'I-tefrāh, waldeya; 'ana 'eradde'aka.
6. Baṣḥu heyya 'enza yemarreḥewwomu malā'ekta 'Amlāk.
7. 'I-ỷesamme' la-ṣalotātikemu wa-'i-ỷenašše' mašwā'takemu.
8. Seme'u la-qālātihu 'esma mahāymen rāte' wa-ṣādeq we'etu.
9. Yemaṣṣe'u 'ella yeṣanne'ukemu wa-yenašše'u 'ahgurikemu.
10. Mannu za-yekalle'ana gabi'a beḥērana?
11. We'eta 'amira yahadde' medr 'em-mendābē wa-qatl.
12. Mele'u darāhema westa 'edawihu wa-xedegu yegbā' bēto.
13. 'Azzazomu la-'aqabtihu kama yeṣbā' meslēhu lā'la kaḥādeyān.
14. Ye'eta 'elata yefatteḥana kʷellana.
15. 'Enza 'efatteḥ maskota re'ikewwo la-'exuya yemaṣṣe' westa fenot.
16. Ba-mesēta we'etu 'elat gabra 'abiya ba'āla wa-ṣawwe'omu la-kʷellomu ḥezb xabēhu.

17. Nekel tamehiro bezux ’em-ge‘zu wa-nebratu la-zentu qeddus.
18. Wa-’emdexra-ze ‘ādi yemaṣṣe’akemu mā‘bala māy wa-yeṭaffe’ā nafsātikemu kama nadda ’essāt.
19. ‘Eqabi ’essāta kama ’i-teṭfā’.
20. Yebazzexu ’ellontu sab’ ’emennēkemu; ’i-tekelu taṣābe’o meslēhomu.

B. 1. ’eska meṣ’atu la-waldeya fequr
2. marḥ ṭabib wa-’amāni
3. meṭmāq melu’ māya
4. mabzexta zentu māxbara mahāymenān
5. ‘aqābē šerāy semu‘
6. sem‘ ’ekuy
7. ba’enta sem‘a Qeddus Mārqos
8. welud samā‘eyān
9. bezxa ṣalotātikemu
10. moqeḥ fetuḥ
11. berhān melu’ samāya
12. samā‘t qetulān
13. hagar ṣanā‘it
14. xaṭāwe’ feteḥt
15. ’amreḥt ’ekuyān
16. mabzexta x^{w}elq^{w}omu
17. ba-‘elata fetḥekemu
18. ṣen‘a hāymānoteka
19. hed’ata me‘rāfomu
20. marāḥi maḥāri
21. ṣen‘a ’āxzu
22. ba-qedma ṣabā’ita ’Egzi’abḥēr
23. sem‘ātāta Kerestiyān
24. za’enbala kel’at
25. wald ne’us wa-farrāh
26. fetḥa ‘elewān wa-kaḥādeyān
27. ṭef’ata ’ahgurihomu
28. ferhata lebb
29. be’si farāhē ’Egzi’abḥēr
30. ṣabā’eyān ṣenu‘āna lebb

C. 1. ’Emenna ’ayy makān ’anta? Ment we’etu memṣā’eka?
2. Falāseyān neḥna wa-’albena megbā’a.
3. Mannu za-gabra meṣnā‘a samāy?
4. ’Egzi’abḥēr fatāḥina we’etu wa-radā’ina ba-k^{w}ellu gebarina.
5. Gabarka xaṭi’ataka ba-xebu’, wa-’ana bāḥtu ’eqaššefaka kešuta.
6. Ba-ṣagāhu la-’Egzi’abḥēr za-baṣāḥkemu zanta makāna hedu’a ba-salām.
7. ’Aṣneḥuni kama ye’xazuni wa-yeqteluni.
8. Neṣanneḥ zeyya ’eska ya‘arreb ḍaḥāy.
9. Yeṣanneḥ lakemu k^{w}ellekemu ‘elata mendābē.
10. ’Albo xaba naxabbe’ warqana.
11. Sami‘omu zanta, g^{w}ayyu wa-taxab’u.
12. ’Aytē za-taxabā’ka soba konu yaxaššešuka?
13. ’I-teṣneḥani, ’esma ’i-y̓egabbe’ xabēka.
14. Wa-soba faṣṣama mal’ekto, xadagomu wa-gab’a samāya.

15. Ḥaniṣana hagarita ne’esta, naxadder bāti ba-salām.
16. Šar‘omu fenāwēhomu la-ḍaḥāy wa-warx.
17. Soba šar‘a ṣabā’tihu qedmēna, farāhna wa-g^{w}ayayna.
18. Ṣaḥafa lomu šer‘ata māxbaromu za-bakamāhā yegabberu k^{w}ello gebrātihomu.
19. ’Azzazomu la-ṣabā’tihu ba’enta šer‘atomu ba-ṣab’.
20. Ba’enta ment tekeḥḥedu šer‘atāteya wa-te’zāzāteya?
21. Šar‘u ’ellontu ṭabibān šer‘ata ’awrāx wa-šer‘ata ‘āmatāt.
22. Lakemu wa-la-daqiqekemu tašar‘a zentu ḥegg za-la-‘ālam.
23. Šannāy we’etu, ’esma wahabana rad’ēta.
24. Ḥaywa k^{w}ello ḥeywato ba-ṣedq wa-ba-reṭ‘.

Lesson 41

41.1 G Verbs from Roots I-W: The Remaining Forms.

(a) Imperfect, Subjunctive, and Imperative. Many of these verbs have a shorter form of the root, without the initial *w-*, in the Subjunctive and Imperative, and often in the verbal noun (see below). The short form is usually associated with the stem vowel *-a-*, but there are exceptions; some verbs have two or even three Subjunctive forms. Note also the irregular Imperfect of the verb *wahaba*.

Perfect	Imperfect	Subjunctive	Imperative	Verbal Noun
warada	*yewarred*	*yerad*	*rad*	*redat*
wadqa	*yewaddeq*	*yedaq*	*daq*	*deqat*
wahaba	*yehub*	*yahab*	*hab*	*habt*
wasada	*yewassed*	*yesad*	*sad*	
		yesed	*sed*	
		yewsed		
walada	*yewalled*	*yelad*	*lad*	*ledat*
waḍ'a	*yewaḍḍe'*	*yeḍā'*	*ḍā'*	*ḍa'at*
wagara	*yewagger*	*yegar*	*gar/ger*	
		yewger	*weger*	
waṭana	*yewaṭṭen*	*yeṭan*		*ṭent*
		yewṭen	*weṭen*	
weḥza	*yeweḥḥez*	*yaḥaz*		*weḥiz/weḥzat*
		yewḥaz		

Unlike other verbs III-gutt. (cf. *yemṣā'* in Lesson 40) the subjunctive and imperative forms *yeḍā'* and *ḍā'* retain the *-ā-* in inflection; thus *teḍā'i*, *yeḍā'u*, *yeḍā'ā* etc.; *ḍā'*, *ḍā'i*, *ḍā'u*, *ḍā'ā*.

(b) The verbal adjectives *qetul*:

weduq fallen, lying fallen

welud (1) pl. of *wald*; (2) syn. of *wald* in the singular

weḍu' departing, emerging; many secondary meanings: lacking (in: *'em-*), alien (to: *'em-*), etc.

(c) Verbal Nouns:

redat descent

deqat ruin, fall, collapse

habt a gift

ledat birth

ḍaʾat exit, departure; *ʾem-X ḍaʾatu* he is from X, a native of X

wagr (pl. *ʾawger*, *-āt*) heap, mound, hill

weḥiz (pl. *-āt*, *waḥāyezt*) river, stream; flow, torrent

weḥzat flow, flowing

(d) The agent noun *qatāli*:

walādi (f. *-t*) parent

wahābi one who gives, donor; adj. generous

(e) Nouns with prefixed *m-*:

murād (for **mewrād*) place of descent, downward slope

mulād place of birth, native land

muḍāʾ place of exit; source

muḥāza māy aqueduct, canal

mogart sling

Note also the derived noun *tewled(d)* (pl. *-āt*) a generation; progeny, offspring.

Vocabulary 41

Nouns:

ʿawd (pl. *ʾaʿwād*) environs, neighborhood, vicinity; area in general; a court of law; a circuit, period of time. *ʿawda* prep. around, surrounding (suffixes added as to an acc. noun).

dābēlā (pl. *-t*) male of any animal, especially ram, he-goat.

ḥarrā coll. army, troops, soldiers.

Verbs:

waraqa (yewreq) to spit. *merāq* (an irregular formation) spittle, saliva.

ʾawtara CG to continue, persevere in, be assiduous in (acc. dir. obj. or inf.); to direct (hand, eyes) to *(xaba, lāʿla, la-)*. *watra* adv. always, perpetually, continuously, assiduously.

warasa (yeras) to inherit. CG *ʾawrasa* to make someone an heir. Gt *tawarsa* to gain by inheritance (acc. dir. obj.). Glt *tawārasa* to inherit (jointly or singly), gain possession of. *warāsi*

heir. *rest* (pl. -*āt*) inheritance. *mawārest* (pl. of unattested
moras) heirs.

saᶜama (yesᶜam) to kiss. Gt *taseᶜma* passive. Glt *tasāᶜama* to kiss
one another. *seᶜmat* a kiss.

rassaya D to put, place, set; to impute (something: acc. dir. obj.)
to (someone: *lāᶜla, la-*); to make/regard something (acc. dir.
obj.) as/into something (acc. dir. obj. or *kama, westa, la-*);

Exercises

A. 1. 'I-yewarred zenām ba-gizēhu.

2. Yewaddeq zentu bēt wa-'i-yaḥannesewwo dāgema.

3. 'Ehubakemu warqa wa-berura.

4. Tewassed zanta dābēlā xaba ᶜaṣadeya.

5. 'Ewadde' 'em-hagar ba-ṣebāḥ.

6. Nāhu 'anti tewalledi walda.

7. 'Ewaggero westa mendād.

8. Tehubuni-nu xebesta?

9. 'I-terad xaba ḥayq.

10. Nebari zeyya kama 'i-tedaqi.

11. Sa'alnāhu kama yahabana māya.

12. Maftew kama nesado xaba makᵂannen.

13. Garo heyya wa-'i-tahabo wa-'i-menta-ni 'em-sisāy.

14. La-nerkabomu 'emqedma yewṭenu yeṣbe'u.

15. Faqadat tegbā' bētā 'emqedma telad waldā.

16. Ta'azzaza la-walādeyānihu wa-naš'a lotu be'sita.

17. Ṭeqqa 'ekuy we'etu zentu tewledd.

18. Sadewwo xabēya kama 'engero.

19. Nahabkemu 'albāsa.

20. Zāti medr mele'ta 'awger ye'eti.

21. Wagara 'ebna ba-mogartu wa-qatala 'exᵂāhu.

22. 'I-konomu māxdara 'emdexra deqata bētomu.

23. Mannu wahabaka za-kama-ze habta kebura?

24. Rakabat metā weduqa mewuta westa fenot.

25. Wadaya ferē wa-xebesta westa mexbā'.

26. Rakabewwo westa murāda dabr.

27. Ḥanaṣu muḥāza māy nawwāxa 'em-'adbār 'eska hagar.

B. 1. Mannu yewarres newāyaka?

2. Qomu ḥarrāhu ‘awdo.
3. Taseḥba kama dābēlā.
4. Waraqa merāqa diba medr.
5. ’Albotu warāsē.
6. Rassayomu kama ‘aqabta re’su.
7. Qarba xabēhu wa-sa‘amo.
8. Tawārasu ’axawihu newāya ’abuhomu.
9. Qatalewwo za’enbala yeras resto.
10. ‘Abiy wa-kebur restekemu.
11. Rassayo la-’exuhu liqa ḥarrā.
12. Rassayewwā la-hagarena gadāma.
13. Tewarres zāti tewledd ’ekita ’abawihomu.
14. Radu westa meṭmāq wa-šemaru ba-māy q^{w}arir.
15. Mota ’emdexra deqata mangeštu.
16. ’I-tenbeb soba yewasseduka heyya.
17. Faqada yegbā’ xaba mulādu.
18. Qatalu ‘ašarta dābēlāta la-ba‘ālomu.
19. Qomku diba wagr ne’us wa-naṣṣarku mangala me‘rāb.
20. Matarewwo re’so wa-saqalewwo diba matkal ba-qedma k^{w}ellu ḥezb.
21. Ḍansat wa-waladat lotu warāsē.
22. Taqārabu wa-tasā‘amu wa-tanāgaru.
23. ’I-tewreq zeyya ’esma makān qeddus we’etu.
24. Nezbeṭo wa-neqtelo, wa-neḥna newarres heyyantēhu.
25. Xāṭe’ān ’emuntu ’ella ‘awdeka.
26. Ḍēwiwo zanta ḥezba rassayomu ’agberta wa-lā’kāna la-qadamta hagar.
27. La-ment rassayka ’ekita lā‘lēna?
28. ’Awtara gabira megbāra terufa k^{w}ello ḥeywato.
29. Kona yehub me‘rāfa la-dekumān.
30. Māsanat k^{w}ellā tewleddāta medr ba-’Ayx za’enbala Nox wa-zamadu.
31. Maṣ’a xabēhomu ba-’amsāla ’aragāy ṣeluma ‘ayn.
32. Soba ya‘aṣṣebaka ṣāmā, temaṣṣe’ xabēya kama ’ahabka rad’ēta.

Lesson 42

42.1 G Verbs from Roots II-W/Y: The Remaining Forms.

(a) Imperfect, Subjunctive, and Imperative.

Root Type	Perfect	Imperfect	Subjunctive	Imperative
II-W	*roṣa*	*yerawweṣ*	*yeruṣ*	*ruṣ*
II-Y	*šēma*	*yešayyem*	*yešim*	*šim*

The above forms are typical for nearly all verbs of these two root types. A few verbs II-W exhibit alternate forms with *-o-* in the Subjunctive and Imperative:

ḥora	*yaḥawwer*	*yeḥor/yeḥur*	*ḥor/ḥur*
ṣora	*yeṣawwer*	*yeṣor/yeṣur*	*ṣor/ṣur*

The two verbs *boʾa* and *moʾa* have *-ā-* in the Subjunctive and Imperative:

boʾa	*yebawweʾ*	*yebāʾ*	*bāʾ*
moʾa	*yemawweʾ*	*yemāʾ/yemuʾ*	*māʾ*

The *-ā-* is usually retained throughout inflection (i.e. it is not replaced with *-e-*): *yebāʾ*, *tebāʾ*, *tebāʾ*, *tebāʾi*, *ʾebāʾ*; *yebāʾu*, *yebāʾā* etc.

The verbs of these two root types which have been introduced thus far are *ḥora*, *boʾa*, *moʾa*, *mota*, *roṣa*, *kona*, *qoma*, *šawʿa (yešuʿ)*, *noxa*, *ʿoda*; *šēṭa*, *šēma*, *mēṭa*.

(b) Verbal adjectives *qetul*:

šeyum appointed, set, placed.

mewut, *nawix*, and *nawwāx* have already been introduced.

(c) Verbal nouns:

ḥurat (pl. *-āt*) going, manner of going; departure, journey; way of life, manners, customs.

ḥewār (pl. *-āt*) porch, ambulatory.

baʾat (pl. *-āt*) entry, entrance, entering; cave, lair, den, cell.

muʾat victory (for self); defeat (for another).

qom m. stature, height.

qumat nature, state, condition.

nux m. length (of time, space); height.

ʿudat circle, circuit, orbit.

šēṭ price, value.

šimat (pl. *-āt*) m.f. ordination; office, position.

miṭat a turning (to or from); a return; change, mutation.

(d) The agent noun *qatāli*:

mawāʾi victorious.

rawāṣi running, swift.

mawāti mortal.

qawāmi standing, stable; as noun: patron, protector.

šawāʿi (pl. *šawāʿt*) sacrificer, priest.

ʿawādi messenger, herald; preacher.

šayāṭi (pl. *šayaṭṭ*) seller, merchant.

Note also *qawwām* tall, erect. The noun *ḥawāreyā* (i.e. *ḥawāri* + *-ā*) has already been introduced. A further noun of unusual formation is *māwetā* a dead person, corpse; *ʾegʷāla māwetā* an orphan.

(e) Nouns of the pattern *meqtāl*:

meḥwār (pl. *-āt*) the distance one may travel in a given time (e.g. *meḥwāra šalus* a journey of three days, the distance covered in a three-day journey); course, orbit.

mebwāʾ/mubāʾ (pl. *-āt*) place for entering; act of entering.

merwāṣ distance run, course; a race, race-course.

meqwām (pl. *-āt*) location, place where one stops or stands; *meqwāma māy* pool.

mešwāʿ (pl. *-āt*) altar.

mešyāṭ (pl. *-āt*) marketplace, forum.

The noun *mubāʾ* is patterned after *muḍāʾ* (exit); *baʾat*, given above, is patterned after *ḍaʾat*. Contrarily, the retention of *-ā-* in the inflection of *yeḍāʾ/ḍāʾ*, noted in §41.1(a), is due to the influence of *yebāʾ*, where the length of the stem vowel is a fixed characteristic of the root type and not secondarily due to the final guttural (and hence changeable to *-e-*).

(f) Nouns corresponding to the pattern *maqtal(t)*:

mabāʾ (pl. *-āt*) m.f. offering.

makān already introduced.

mašwāʿt already introduced.

masāyemt (pl. of unattested **masyam*) container(s), basket(s).

Vocabulary 42

Nouns:

kokab (pl. *kawākebt*) m. star. *kokaba ṣebāḥ/mesēt* morning/evening star.

faras (pl. *ʾafrās*) m.f. horse. *sabʾa ʾafrās* horsemen.

Verbs:

ṣoma (yeṣum) to fast. *ṣewum* adj. fasting. *ṣom* (pl. *ʾaṣwām, -āt*) a fast, fasting.

noma (yenum) to sleep. CG *ʾanoma/ʾanama* to put to sleep. *newām* m. sleep.

ṣora (yeṣor/yeṣur) to carry, bear (lit. and fig.). CG *ʾaṣora/ʾaṣara* causative. Gt *taṣawra* passive. *ṣewur* bearing, burdened (with: acc.). *ṣor* (pl. *ʾaṣwār*) burden. *ṣawwār* carrier(s), porter(s). *ṣawāri* (f. *-t*; pl. *ṣawart*) one who carries, bears (e.g. *ṭebab, zēnā*).

ʿoqa (yeʿuq) to beware of, take care for, be cautious of (*lāʿla, la-,* acc.); esp. common in the imperative with a neg. subjunctive: take care not to, be careful not to (*ʿuq kama ʾi-...*). CG *ʾaʿoqa* to make known, show (acc. dir. obj.; to: dat. suff.). Gt *taʿawqa* to be noticed, perceived, recognized; to be made known, revealed. *ʿewuq* familiar, well-known.

ʾawšeʾa CG to respond, answer; to take up a discourse. Glt *tawāšeʾa* to speak against, contradict; dispute, argue (with: dat. suff. or *la-*). *šāʾšāʾ* eloquence, refined manner of speaking.

k^wannana D to judge, condemn, punish (acc. dir. obj.); to rule, have power (over: acc. or *ba-*). CD *ʾak^wannana* to put someone (suff. obj.) in charge of (acc. or *lāʿla*). Dt *tak^wannana* passive. Glt *tak^wānana* to become reconciled (with: *mesla*).

Other:

ʾafʾa/ʾafʾā adv. (to the) outside; *ʾafʾa ʾem-* (to/on the) outside of.

sobēhā adv. immediately, thereupon, then.

Exercises

A. 1. ’Aytē-nu taḥawweri?
2. Re’yewwo la-farasu yerawweṣ mangala weḥiz.
3. Teqawwemu qeruba ’anqaṣ ’eska ’ebaṣṣeḥ.
4. Mannu za-yemayyeṭ zanta mendābē ’emennēna?
5. ’Axazewwo ’enza yebawwe’ bēta Kerestiyān.
6. ’Efaqqed ’eḥur meslēka.
7. Kunu ṭabibāna kama qadamtina.
8. Ruṣi xabēhu wa-sa’aleyyo rad’ēta.
9. Ba-sema ’Egzi’abḥēr za-temawwe’u zanta ḥezba.
10. Zanta ’efaqqed kama tegbar lita ’emqedma ’emut.
11. ’Aqomkuka zeyya kama te‘qab ḥezbeya watra.
12. Zanta gabiro yenawwex mawā‘elihu diba medr.
13. Ḥuru westa gadām wa-ṣeneḥuni heyya.
14. Ne’exxezomu ’enza yebawwe’u yešu‘u mašwā‘tihomu.
15. Bā’ xabēna ba-lēlit kama ’i-ya’axazuka.
16. ’Efaqqed kama tekun rad’eya.
17. Wa-sobēhā ’aroṣu ’afrāsihomu westa mā’kala ṣab’.
18. Miṭewwo la-zentu be’si xaba zamadu.
19. We’eta ’amira yemawwetu mabzexta mahāymenān ba’enti’aya.
20. ’Ellu yekawwenu ’ar’estikemu.
21. Maftew kama nequm zeyya wa-neṣneḥo.
22. Kun ṣādeqa kama yenux mawā‘elika westa zentu ‘ālam.
23. Nebā’ bēta maqdas wa-nahabo la-kāhen mašwā‘tana.
24. La-nemā’omu la-kaḥādeyān wa-neqtelomu.
25. Yedallewana kama nemiṭ ’a‘yentina ’em-gaṣṣa kebru.

B. 1. ’afrāsa ḥarrā
2. ṣom nawix
3. ḥewāra zāti ḥenṣā
4. mabā’ ne’us wa-naddāy
5. newāya mešyāṭ
6. ba’ata ’arwē
7. mu’ata ’Abrehām
8. nuxa mawā‘elihu
9. mešwā‘āta ṭā‘otātihomu
10. kāhen šeyum la-‘ālam
11. qumata negšu
12. warēzā nawixa qom
13. ḥewāra bēta neguš
14. dābēlāta mašwā‘t
15. ’a‘wāda hagar
16. ḥuratu la-madxenena
17. nuxa zentu ḥabl
18. ’em-ṭenta šimatu
19. miṭatu ’em-xaṭi’at
20. faras rawāṣi
21. ‘udata ḍaḥāy westa samāy
22. qasāwest šeyumān lā‘lēna

23. šeṭ ‘abiy
24. diba mešwā‘a bēta maqdas
25. šimateya kebert
26. ba’atu la-zentu qeddus westa gadām
27. ’emdexra mu’ateya dibēhomu
28. qumata māxbarena
29. miṭatena xaba hāymānot rete‘t
30. ’aṣwām wa-ba‘ālāt
31. ḥuratu wa-ge‘zu wa-nebratu la-neguš
32. šēṭa newāyeka
33. mubā’a ba’atu
34. ṭā‘ot qawwām
35. mesyāṭāta hagar
36. sab’ mawāteyān
37. kāhenāt wa-šawā‘t
38. qāla ‘awādihu
39. ’abyāta šayaṭṭ
40. mangešt qawāmi
41. merwāṣa kawākebt
42. meḥwāra sadus

C. 1. Wa-soba k^{w}annanewwo, ’awḍe’ewwo ’af’a ’em-hagar wa-’amatewwo.
2. Zentu makān ṭeqqa ‘ewuq we’etu ba-k^{w}ellā medr.
3. Wa-’emdexra.newām nawwāx tafawwasa ’em-ḥemāmu.
4. Wa-’awše’a ’enza yebel: ’Ana ’i-y̓ekaššet lakemu za-tefaqqedu.
5. La-ment ’aṣorkani zanta ‘abiya ṣora, wa-’ana ne’us wa-dekum?
6. ’Ellontu ’emuntu ṣabā’t ’em-ḥarrāhu la-mak^{w}annen za-’ak^{w}annano neguš lā‘lēna.
7. Ṣawarta ḥegg wa-‘aqabta hāymānot rete‘t neḥna
8. Sekab wa-num kama ’i-tekun dekuma ba-ṣebāḥ.
9. ‘Uqu kama ’i-yesme‘ukemu ’enza tenaggeru qālāta za-kama-ze.
10. ’I-nekel ḥayewa ba-salām ’enza ṣewurāna xaṭi’at.
11. Soba ’a‘oqana mekro, taxabarna meslēhu kama nerde’o.
12. ’I-kehla tak^{w}āneno mesla ’axawihu malāheqt.
13. Rakabewwo la-qeddus yenawwem westa ba’atu.
14. Šamrat ba-ṭebabu wa-ba-šā’šā’a nebābu.
15. Waradu malā’ekt ’em-westa samāy ’enza yeṣawweru ’essāta ba-’edawihomu.
16. ’Anomo ’Egzi’abḥēr kama yegbar be’sita ’em-šegāhu.
17. Tak^{w}anninomu tawagru westa bēta moqeḥ.
18. ‘Uqi kama ’i-teqrabi xabēhu za’enbala te’zāzu.
19. Nawwāxa qom wa-šannāya gaṣṣ we’etu.
20. Ṣor zanta warqa ba-xebu’ wa-‘uq kama ’i-yerkabo wa-’i-mannu-hi.
21. ’I-yekelu ṣewumānihomu la-’axlefo zentu xasār.
22. Wa-soba ta‘awqa mekru, tamayaṭku lā‘lēhu wa-qatalkewwo.
23. ’Azzazomu la-ṣawwārihu yeṣuru newāya bētu wa-yegarewwo ’af’a ’em-hagar.

Lesson 43

43.1 G Verbs from Roots III-W/Y: The Remaining Forms.

(a) Imperfect, Subjunctive, and Imperative. These forms show the normal triliteral patterns *yeqattel*, *yeqtel/yeqtal*, *qetel/qetal*; stem-final *-ey* and *-ew* are usually replaced by *-i* and *-u* respectively when no ending beginning with a vowel is added; hence e.g. *yebakki*, *yebakkeyu*, *yesammi*, *yesammeyo* etc. Note especially the verbs *re'ya*, *we'ya*, and *wadaya*, which combine the peculiarities of several root types.

Root Type	Perfect	Imperfect	Subjunctive	Imperative
III-Y	*bakaya*	*yebakki*	*yebki*	*beki*
	samaya	*yesammi*	*yesmi*	*semi*
	balya	*yeballi*	*yebli*	---
	nadya	*yenaddi*	*yendi*	---
	'akya	*ya'akki*	*ye'kay*	---
	ʿabya	*yaʿabbi*	*yeʿbay*	---
	'abaya	*ya'abbi*	*ye'bay*	*'ebay*
	re'ya	*yere''i*	*yer'ay*	*re'i*
		yerē''i		*ra'ay*
	weʿya	*yeweʿʿi*	*yaʿay*	---
	wadaya	*yewaddi*	*yeday*	*day*
	g^wayya	*yeg^{w}ayyi*	*yeg^{w}yay*	*g^weyay*
			yeg^{w}yi	*g^weyi*
	dawaya	*yedawwi*	*yedway*	---
III-W	*'atawa*	*ya'attu*	*ye'tu/ye'taw*	*'etu/'etaw*
	ʿadawa	*yaʿaddu*	*yeʿdu/yeʿdaw*	*ʿedu/ʿedaw*

(b) Verbal adjectives *qetul*:

weʿuy hot, burning.
semuy named, called; famous, illustrious.

(c) Agent nouns *qatāli*:

balāyi old, wearing out (adj.).
g^wayāy(i) fugitive.
ra'āyi (pl. *-yān*, *-eyān*; *ra'ayt*) observer, seer; *ra'āyē xebu'āt* soothsayer; *ra'āyē kokab* astrologer.

The final -*i* of this form is often "absorbed" by the root final -*y*. Thus, a form written *ba-lā-y* is either *balāy(i)* or *ballāy* (form *qattāl*). But because the latter form is so rare, such writings are taken as *qatāli* when the full writing of such a form (e.g. *ba-lā-yi*) is attested elsewhere. Some ambiguity must remain, however, with infrequent words.

(d) Verbal nouns:

bekay m. weeping, lamentation.
nedēt/nedyat poverty.
ʾetwat/ʾetot return (home); return, yield (of crops).
ʾekay (pl. -*āt*) evil, wickedness.
ʿebay (pl. -*āt*) greatness, size; magnificence, majesty.
gʷeyyā flight.
rāʾy (pl. -*āt*) vision, revelation; appearance, form, aspect.
reʾyat appearance, aspect, form.
wāʿy fire, heat, burning.
weʿyat burning, conflagration.

(e) Nouns with prefixed *m*-:

meʾtāw home, place to which one returns; act of returning.
megʷyāy refuge, asylum.
māʿdot (pl. *maʿādew*) the opposite side (of river, mountains, etc.); *māʿdota* prep. across, to the opposite side of, beyond.
mudāy (pl. -*āt*) a container of any sort; basket, hamper.

Vocabulary 43

Nouns:

ʿazaqt (pl. -*āt*, *ʿazaqāt*) f.m. well, cistern.
ʾaraft (pl. *ʾarafāt*) m.f. wall, partition.
ṭeqm wall, city wall, fortification wall. *ʾarafta ṭeqm* fortification walls. *ʾahgura ṭeqm* fortified cities.

Verbs:

safaya (yesfi) to sew. Gt *tasafya* pass. *safāyi* sewer, tailor, cobbler. *masfē* awl.
karaya (yekri) to dig (e.g. a well), dig in (the ground), dig through (a wall). Gt *takarya* pass. *karāyi (karayt)* in *karāyē maqāber*

grave-digger.

ḥalaya (yeḥli) to sing, make music; to sing about (acc. dir. obj.). *ḥalāyi* (f. *-t*) (pl. *ḥalayt*) singer. *māḥlēt* (pl. *-āt, maḥāley*) song, singing, music.

ṭeʿya (yeṭʿay) to be healthy, well. CG *ʾaṭʿaya* to make healthy, well, cause to recover. *ṭeʿuy* (f. *ṭeʿit*) well, healthy (of person or place). *ṭeʿinnā* good health.

ʾabeḥa CG (root *bwḥ*) to allow, permit (obj. suff. of person plus subjunctive of verb). Gt *tabawḥa* passive; to have power over (*lāʿla, ba-*). *bewuḥ la-* it is permitted for (someone; + subjunctive). *mabāḥt* power, authority, permission.

ʾazlafa CG to continue (doing), persevere in (doing), followed by acc. verbal noun or acc. inf. *zelufa, la-zelufu* adv. continuously, continually, perpetually, forever. *zalfa* adv. idem; always, regularly, frequently, often. *ʾi ... zalfa* adv. never. *zazalf* adj. perpetual. *la-zalāfu, la-zelāfu* = *la-zelufu*.

Exercises

A. 1. Dayo westa ʿazaqt wa-xedego heyya ʾeska yemawwet.
2. Menta tesammeyewwā la-zāti hagar?
3. ʾI-šannāy ʾalbās za-yeballi.
4. ʾI-teʾbay ʾaʿbeyo sema negušeka.
5. Mannu za-yenaddi ba-lebbu ʾenza yaʾammen ba-ʾEgziʾena?
6. ʾAlbo meḥrata za-taʿabbi ʾem-meḥratu.
7. Weʾeta gizē terēʾʾeyu taʾāmera wa-mankerāta.
8. ʾI-taʿay maʿʿateka lāʿlēna.
9. ʾEnza neqarreb reʾina hagaromu ʾenza teweʿʿi ba-reḥuq
10. Mannu za-yegaddef newāyo ʾemqedma yebli?
11. ʾAzzazana kama neday zanta dābēlā westa ʿaṣadu.
12. Faqadu yeg^{w}yayu wa-bāḥtu ʾi-kehlu.
13. ʾEbayu ʾarʾeyoto maṣāḥeftikemu.
14. Yedawwi waldeya wa-ʾefarreh kama ʾi-yemut.
15. ʾAzzazana kama neʿdaw zanta weḥiza wa-naʾaxaz zāta medra.
16. Semeyo la-waldeka sema Yoḥannes.
17. Mannu weʾetu zentu beʾsi za-yaʾabbi bawiʾa bētana?
18. ʾI-teḥur westa fenot kama ʾi-yerʾayuka wa-yeqteluka.
19. Sekab wa-num kama ʾi-tedway wa-temut.
20. ʾAytē-nu tefaqqed ʾedayo la-zentu newāy?

21. ʻEqab newāyaka watra kama ʼi-tendi.
22. Maftew kama neg^{w}yi ʼemqedma yerʼayuna.
23. ʼEtewu beḥērakemu wa-ʼi-tegbeʼu zeyya.
24. ʻEdewu medra mangala meʻrāb ʼeska tebaṣṣeḥu xaba māxdaromu.
25. ʼAmṣeʼa ʼašāʼenihu xaba safāyi kama yesfeyomu ba-masfēhu.

B. 1. ʻeḍ ḥeyāw
2. safāyi ṭabib
3. māḥlēt šemert
4. warēzā ṭeʻuy
5. ḍaḥāy weʻuy
6. mabāḥt za-kama-ze
7. sem semuy
8. ḥalāyi ṭabib
9. ṣagā za-zalf
10. faras dewuy
11. ʼašāʼen balāyi
12. māʻdota bāḥr
13. weʻyata hagaromu
14. karāyē maqāber
15. fenot weʻuy
16. makān ṭeʻuy
17. rāʼya lēlit
18. g^{w}ayāyi dekum
19. ʻebayu la-ʼAmlāk
20. meg^{w}yāy ṣenuʻ
21. ba-ṭeʻinnā wa-ba-salām
22. wāʻya ḍaḥāy
23. rāʼy nakir
24. tarāfi ḥeyāw
25. masfēhu la-safāyi
26. radʼētena wa-meg^{w}yāyena
27. qāla ḥalayt
28. māʻdota gadām
29. mak^{w}annen semuy
30. karāyeyāna ʻazaqt
31. masfē za-xaṣin
32. lebs balāyi
33. maḥāley ṭeʻumāt
34. ba-mabāḥtu la-mak^{w}annen
35. wāʻya maʻālt
36. ṭeʻinnāhomu la-daqiqomu
37. g^{w}eyyāhomu la-walādeyānihu
38. ʻebaya beʻlu
39. reʼyata gaṣṣu
40. ʻabiy mudāya ferē

C. 1. Šaṭaqa ʼaṣābeʻihu ʼenza yesaffi ba-masfē.
2. ʼI-kehla ʻariga ʼem-ʻazaqt za-wadqa westētu.
3. ʼEnza naxallef ʼenta xaba bēta Kerestiyān samāʻna qāla kāhen yeḥalli sebḥāta ʼEgziʼena.
4. Rakabnāhu ʼenza yeqawwem xaba ʼarafta bētu.
5. Nabiromu heyya karayu ʻazaqāta wa-ḥanaṣu ṭeqma.
6. Maharana maḥāleya ḥezbeka.
7. ʼI-bewuḥ lakemu tebāʼu zeyya.
8. ʼAqomomu diba ṭeqma hagar kama yeʻqabewwā.
9. Wa-nawimo šalusa, ṭeʻya ʼem-dawēhu.
10. ʼAbeḥomu yeʻdawu westa beḥēru.
11. ʼI-tekelu ʼexiza ʼahgura ṭeqm za-ḥanaṣu heyya.

12. Mannu za-wahabaka za-kama-ze mabāḥta?
13. 'Azlafu gabira 'ekit wa-'abayu sami'a lita.
14. Nenabber zeyya la-zelufu wa-'i-naxaddegaka zalfa.
15. Soba sam'omu 'enza yekarreyu 'arafta bētu qoma wa-g^{w}ayya.
16. Wa-soba tasafya 'aš̄ā'enihu, wadayomu diba 'egarihu wa-xalafa.
17. Bewuḥ lana kama nahabkemu zanta mal'ekta.
18. Kona yemaṣṣe' xabēna zalfa mesla zēnā ba'enta 'azmādina.
19. 'I-tequm 'emqedma teṭ'ay.
20. Qadāmihu 'i-kehla ḥaleya wa-'i-menta-ni, 'allā 'emdexra rā'y za-re'ya ba-newāmu kona ḥalāyē ṭabiba wa-šannāya.
21. Maftew kama 'erkab safāyē 'albās kama yesfi 'aṣfeya.
22. 'Akko ba-šerāy za-teṭe''i 'allā ba-hāymānot.

Lesson 44

44.1 Gt Verbs: Imperfect, Subjunctive, and Imperative.

Root Type	Perfect	Imperfect	Subjunctive	Imperative
Sound	*taqatla*	*yetqattal*	*yetqatal*	*taqatal*
I-gutt.	*taḥanṣa*	*yetḥannaṣ*	*yetḥanaṣ*	*taḥanaṣ*
II-gutt.	*tabehla*	*yetbahhal*	*yetbahal*	*tabahal*
III-gutt.	*tafatḥa*	*yetfattāḥ*	*yetfatāḥ*	*tafatāḥ*
I-W	*tawalda*	*yetwallad*	*yetwalad*	*tawalad*
II-W	*tamawʾa*	*yetmawwāʾ*	*yetmawāʾ*	*tamawāʾ*
II-Y	*tamayṭa*	*yetmayyaṭ*	*yetmayaṭ*	*tamayaṭ*
III-W	*tarexwa*	*yetraxxaw*	*yetraxaw*	*taraxaw*
III-Y	*takarya*	*yetkarray*	*yetkaray*	*takaray*

These forms are all regular within the rules set out in the preceding lessons. The imperfect and subjunctive differ only in the doubling of the middle radical, which is, of course, not indicated in the script. Forms with *-ā-* before C_3=guttural are inflected like the corresponding forms of *yemṣāʾ*, with the replacement *ā* —> *e* before endings beginning with a vowel. The final *-aw* of roots III-W may also appear as *-o* when nothing is added: *yetraxxo*, *yetraxo*, *taraxo*.

When C_1 is a dental or sibilant *(t, ṭ, ḍ, d, s, š, ṣ, z)*, the *-t-* of the prefix is assimilated completely: *yettakkal*, *yeṭṭammaq*, *yeddallaw*, *yeḍḍarraf*, *yessammay*, *yeššaṭṭaq*, *yeṣṣawwar*, *yezzakkar*. While this is clear in transliteration, these forms are a great source of difficulty for beginners reading from the Ethiopic script, where the doubling is not indicated. The only outward difference between the imperfects G and Gt is the *-a-* in the final stem syllable: *ye-ša-ye-m* = *yešayyem*; *ye-ša-ya-m* = *yeššayyam* or *yeššayam*. The imperfect and subjunctive forms of *tanšeʾa* (to arise) are normal: *yetnaššāʾ*, *yetnašāʾ*, but the imperative is *tanšeʾ*.

44.2 Glt Verbs: Imperfect, Subjunctive, and Imperative.

Root Type	Perfect	Imperfect	Subjunctive	Imperative
Sound	*taqāraba*	*yetqār(r)ab*	*yetqārab*	*taqārab*
I-Gutt.	*taxālafa*	*yetxāl(l)af*	*yetxālaf*	*taxālaf*
II-Gutt.	*takāḥada*	*yetkāḥ(ḥ)ad*	*yetkāḥad*	*takāḥad*
III-Gutt.	*tagābeʾa*	*yetgāb(b)āʾ*	*yetgābāʾ*	*tagābāʾ*

I-W	*tawālada*	*yetwāl(l)ad*	*yetwālad*	*tawālad*
II-W	*taqāwama*	*yetqāw(w)am*	*yetqāwam*	*taqāwam*
II-Y	*takāyada*	*yetkāy(y)ad*	*yetkāyad*	*takāyad*
III-W	*tafānawa*	*yetfān(n)aw*	*yetfānaw*	*tafānaw*
III-Y	*tarā'aya*	*yetrā'(')ay*	*yetrā'ay*	*tarā'ay*

The assimilations involving C_1 noted in the preceding paragraph also apply here. E.g. **yetšāyaṭ* > *yeššāyaṭ* he will buy, **yetsā'alu* > *yessā'alu* they will ask around. The optional doubling indicated in the Imperfect is found in the tradition but is not followed in our transliterations.

44.3 *Hallawa* with the Subjunctive and Imperfect. *Hallawa* is used impersonally with an object (dative) suffix followed by the Subjunctive to express intention or obligation. Thus *hallawomu yeḥuru* may be translated variously as "they intend to go, they ought to go, they are to go, they should go." Less commonly *hallawa* may be inflected with a personal subject: *halloku 'eḥur* I am/was to go. *Hallawa* may also be used with a following imperfect: *hallawa yenabber*, a construction with a wide variety of translation possibilities. It may be past or present durative (he is/was sitting) or it may express the immediate future (he is about to sit, he is going to sit). It has occasionally the intention/obligation nuance of the subjunctive construction above. Only the context can determine its appropriate value.

Exercises

1. Yetfaqqar Kerestos 'esma maḥāri we'etu; yetfarrāh 'esma 'Egzi' we'etu.
2. Ba-ye'eti 'elat yekawwenu xāṭe'ān kama za-'i-yetfaṭṭar.
3. Hallawa 'Egzi'abḥēr za'enbala yetfaṭar 'ālam.
4. Yetfatteḥā 'a'yentihomu wa-yere''eyu kebro la-'Amlāk.
5. Mā'zē netfattāḥ 'em-ma'āserina?
6. Yehubakemu za-yetfaqqad.
7. Zentu ṣagā yetfaqqad fadfāda 'em-k^{w}ellu newāy medrāwi.
8. Zentu we'etu 'asmāta ba'ālāt za-yetgabbaru ba-māxbarekemu.
9. Maftew neḥur 'emqedma yetgabar sisāyena.
10. 'Aqabewwo la-badnu 'enza yetgannaz.
11. Yetgaddafu 'abdentihomu la-'arāwita gadām.

12. Ba’enta xaṭi’ateka tetgaddaf ’em-mā’kalēna.
13. Soba yetḥannaṣ ṭeqma hagarekemu, ’i-yemawwe’akemu wa-’i-mannu-hi.
14. Samā‘nāhomu ’enza yetḥaššayu ba’enta mu’atomu.
15. ’I-tetḥašay ’emqedma yetgabar gebreka.
16. Hallawana k^{w}ellena netḥatat ba-xaba ’Egzi’abḥēr.
17. Tetḥattat ba’enta k^{w}ellu za-gabarka.
18. Zentu we’etu ge‘zomu la-’abawina za-yedallewana kama netmarāḥ ba-megbārātihomu.
19. La-ment netmawwā’ ba-xaba kaḥādeyān?
20. Re’ina samāyāta ’enza yetmalle’u malā’ekta berhānāwiyāna.
21. Soba tesamme‘ zanta, tetma‘‘ā‘ fadfāda.
22. ’I-tetma‘ā‘ dibēya ’esma ’akko ’ana za-gabarku zanta.
23. Sayf ’i-yetmayyaṭ ’em-lā‘lēkemu ’eska yemawwetu k^{w}ellomu xāṭe’ān.
24. Mā’zē-nu tetmayyaṭu ’em-xaṭi’atekemu westa fenota ṣedq?
25. Ye’eta ‘elata ’i-tetmaḥḥaru ba-xaba fatāḥtikemu.
26. Zentu we’etu semu la-’Egzi’abḥēr za-’i-yetnaggar.
27. Zāti ṣalot tetnabbab ’emqedma yetnabab menbāba wangēl.
28. Tanše’i wa-ḥuri bētaki wa-’ana ’aḥawwer meslēki.
29. Tetnaššā’ wa-teg^{w}ayyi Gebṣa ’esma yaxaššešuka kama yeqteluka.
30. ’Anta tetnaššā’ westa samāy ’enza taḥayyu.
31. Maṣ’u wa-naš’ewwo la-badnu ṣemmita ’emqedma yetqabar.
32. Soba re’ya k^{w}ellomu ṣabā’tihu ’enza yetqattalu, farha wa-g^{w}ayya.
33. Yedallewakemu kama tetqašafu ba’enta zentu gebr.
34. We’eta ’amira tessaddadu wa-tetqattalu ba’enti’aya.
35. Wa-yessabbak zentu wangēl xaba ’aṣnāfa medr.
36. ’Efaqqed ’essamā‘ ’emqedma ’essadad ’em-medreya.
37. Menta yessammay semu la-waldeka?
38. Yessamay zentu wald ba-sema ’abuhu.
39. ’Axaššeš safāyē kama yessafay šā’neya.
40. Yessaqqal salāma ‘ālam ba-faqādu la-’Egzi’abḥēr.
41. Ba-zentu makān yessaqqal madxenena ba-masqala ‘eḍ ’enza yeššawwā‘ ba’enta ’eg^{w}āla ’emma-ḥeyāw.
42. ’Antemu teššayyaṭu kama ’alhemt westa ’edawa ’ella yemawwe’ukemu.
43. Yeṣṣaḥḥafu watra xaṭāwe’ikemu westa maṣḥafa fetḥ.
44. Tettakkal hāymānot westa ’albābikemu kama ‘eḍ ṣenu‘ wa-qawwām za-’i-yekel nafās ’awdeqoto.
45. La-yetwadayu ’ellu maṣāḥeft westa mexbā’.
46. Zentu yetwahhab lakemu ba-ṣagā.

47. Taxabā' feṭuna kama 'i-tetrakab.
48. Mota 'emqedma yeššayam kāhena.
49. Wa-nabara heyya 'enza yetla''ak watra ba-qedma 'Egzi'abḥēr.
50. Fannokuka 'af'a 'em-beḥēr kama tet'aqab 'em-k^wellu mendābē.
51. Zentu ḥeggeya za-yet'aqqab ma'ālta wa-lēlita.
52. Ba-ṣebāḥ yessaḥḥab qedma mak^wannen.
53. Rakabomu la-weludihu 'enza yet'addawu 'emenna te'zāzāta 'Egzi'abḥēr.
54. 'Etxaššaš wa-'i-yetrakkab.
55. Yetkaray 'azaqt ba-zentu makān kama yekunana māy.
56. Yessammā' qāla bekāy ba-k^wellā hagar.
57. Hallawana netxabā'.
58. Hallawo yet'awaq ba'enta gebrātihu.
59. Gebar šannāya kama tetfaqar ba-xaba k^wellomu sab'.
60. Radu westa meṭmāq wa-taṭamaqu ba-sema 'ab wa-wald wa-manfas qeddus.

Lesson 45

45.1 CG Verbs: The Remaining Forms. With the exception of verbs from roots II-W/Y, all CG verbs have the same underlying pattern in the Imperfect, Subjunctive, and Imperative stems. Note how closely these resemble the forms of the corresponding G verbs, the main difference lying in the long *-ā-* of the prefix and the stable vowel *(-e-)* of the Subjunctive and Imperative. Stem-final *-ew* and *-ey* are treated as elsewhere.

Root Type	Perfect	Imperfect	Subjunctive	Imperative
Sound	*ʾanbara*	*yānabber*	*yānber*	*ʾanber*
I-gutt.	*ʾaḥzana*	*yāḥazzen*	*yāḥzen*	*ʾaḥzen*
II-gutt.	*ʾabʿala*	*yābeʿʿel*	*yābʿel*	*ʾabʿel*
III-gutt.	*ʾamṣeʾa*	*yāmaṣṣeʾ*	*yāmṣeʾ*	*ʾamṣeʾ*
I-W	*ʾawrada*	*yāwarred*	*yāwred*	*ʾawred*
II-W	*ʾaqoma*	*yāqawwem*	*yāqum*	*ʾaqum*
	ʾaqama		*yāqem*	*ʾaqem*
II-Y	*ʾakēda*	*yākayyed*	*yākid*	*ʾakid*
			yāked (rare)	*ʾaked*
III-W	*ʾaḥyawa*	*yāḥayyew-*	*yāḥyew-*	*ʾaḥyew-*
III-Y	*ʾabkaya*	*yābakkey-*	*yābkey-*	*ʾabkey-*

The long *-ā-* in the closed syllable of the prefix is exceptional. It arises presumably from the loss of *ʾ* in these forms, e.g. **yaʾanber* > *yānber*.

There are no verbal nouns derived regularly from CG verbs other than the ordinary infinitive (see Lesson 30), Occasionally one encounters derived nouns of the pattern *ʾaqtalā*, e.g.

ʾarʾayā image, form, likeness, appearance; type, standard, norm, pattern; copy, transcription.

This is in imitation of a pattern properly belonging to the D or Q system, which will be taken up in a later lesson.

Quite a number of CG verbs have an agent noun (or adjective) of the patterns *maqtel* (fem. *-t*) or *maqtali* (fem. *-t*). These are equivalent forms. The following are the most frequent from verbs introduced thus far:

māʾmer (1) knowing, skilled; (2) a soothsayer.

mabkey mourner (professional)

mafreh fear-inspiring, dreadful

māḥmem grievous, afflicting with grief or pain

māḥyew/māḥyawi life-giving, salvific

māḥzen/māḥzani saddening, provoking sadness. The noun *māḥzan* (cause of sadness) is used interchangeably with *māḥzen*.

mamker (pl. *mamākert*) counselor, advisor

masmer/masmari pleasing (to: *xaba, la-*)

maṭmeq baptizer; esp. in *Yoḥannes Maṭmeq* John the Baptist.

As noted earlier, some CG verbs have verbal nouns and adjectives proper to G verbs (e.g. *feqr, fequr, meʿrāf*). Note, in addition,

ʿeraft (pl. *-āt*) f.m. rest, peace, quiet; often a euphemism for death.

The pattern *ʾaqtāli* (cf. *qatāli*) is also sometimes employed as an agent noun, but the form is not a productive one for CG verbs.

Vocabulary 45

ʾankara CG to wonder, be astonished, marvel (at: acc. or *ʾemenna, baʾenta, ba-*, or a clause introduced by *ʾefo, kama*, or *ʾesma*): to find (something: acc.) strange. Gt *tanakra* to be admired, wondered at; to seem/be strange. Glt *tanākara* to be alien to (obj. suff.); to renounce, repudiate (obj. suff.). *nakir* (see Voc. 34). *manker* (see Voc. 26).

dexna (yedxan) to escape safely (from: *ʾemenna*); to be safe, unharmed; to be saved (in the religious sense). CG *ʾadxana* to save, keep safe, rescue; to save (rel. sense). *dexun* safe, unharmed; saved (rel. sense); immune to, free of *(ʾemenna)*. *dāxen* adj. safe, whole, sound, unharmed. *dāxn* safety, well-being, security. *dāxnā/dexnā* idem. *madxen* = *madxani* savior, redeemer. *madxanit* m.f. salvation, safety, redemption.

Exercises

1. Ba-'ayy nagar 'ā'ammenakemu?
2. 'I-tābzexu nagira.
3. Tālehheq zāta ʿeḍa 'eska tenawwex.
4. Xaba qāla ṭabibān 'aqreb 'eznaka.

5. Sami‘omu ḥezb zanta ’ankaru fadfāda.
6. ’Efo nā’ammer kama maṣ’at zāti ‘elat?
7. Yādakkemo zentu ṣāmā.
8. ’I-tām‘e‘o la-’egzi’eka kama ’i-yezbeṭka.
9. ’Aq^{w}rer ma‘‘ataka ’emqedma tenbeb.
10. Ba-ye’eti ‘elat ’i-yedexxen wa-’i-’aḥadu-ni ’em-fetḥa ’Amlāk.
11. Yā’attewukemu ḥeyāwānikemu.
12. Maṣ’a gānēn lā‘lēhu ’enza yādawweyo.
13. Yāmeḥḥeruni ’ellu ’aḥzāb.
14. Yāqattelewwo la-ṣādeq, wa-la-xāṭe’ yefatteḥu ma’āserihu.
15. ’Adxenana ’Egzi’o ’esma netmawwā’ ’em-xaba kaḥādeyān.
16. Zanta ’ā’exxezakemu westa lebbekemu la-zelufu.
17. Wa-ba-we’etu gizē ’āfallesakemu ’em-hagarekemu feqert.
18. K^{w}ellu mamker yāmakker mekra.
19. Yaḥayyewu ’ella yāqawwemu qāla kidāneya.
20. ’Antemu tānakkeru ba’enta za-’egabber qedmēkemu.
21. Nā‘beyo la-sema ’Amlākena.
22. ’I-y̓āfaqqer mašwā‘ta za-tešawwe‘u lita.
23. Ba’enta ment tāmasseluni nabiya.
24. Warada te’mert ’em-samāy ’enza yārē’’eyo mesṭira Ḥegg Ḥaddis.
25. Dāxen-nu ’anta, ’o-’abuna?
26. Yā‘abbeyaka ’emenna k^{w}ellomu nagašta medr.
27. ’I-tāfrehomu la-ḥezb ba-qālāt za-kama-ze.
28. ’Amṣe’ewwomu lita kama ’er’ayomu.
29. Nā‘reg mašwā‘ta la-’Egzi’abḥēr kama yāmu’ana ba-’ella yeṣabbe’u lā‘lēna.
30. Zeyya tekelu nabira ba-salām wa-dāxn.
31. Mannu za-yā‘addewana zanta gadāma?
32. Yāfaṭṭenu yegabberu salāma meslēna.
33. ’I-tān’esu ṭebaba maṣāḥefta qadamt.
34. ’I-tārḥequ ḥeggeya ’em-xabēkemu.
35. Tanākarewwo la-ḥeggena wa-la-ge‘zena.
36. Xaba mannu tā‘aqqeb newāyaka?
37. Yāg^{w}ayyi sab’a ’afrāsihomu ba-ferhat ‘abiy.
38. ’Anta-nu tānabbeb lana zanta mal’ekta?
39. Yārakkebakemu zentu maṣḥaf be‘la manfasāwē.
40. Ze-we’etu maṣḥaf ba’enta madxanita ‘ālam.
41. ’I-tā‘reb ḍaḥāya ba-zāti ‘elat ’enza teṣawwem.

42. ʼĀgabber la-reʼseya manbara za-warq.
43. ʼAzzazomu kama yānberu šegāhu heyya.
44. La-ment tārakk^{w}esu bēteya qeddusa?
45. Nāṣuromu ʼaṣwārina.
46. ʼAʻregewwomu westa ʼarafta ṭeqm za-hagar.
47. Qoma westa ḥamar ʼenza yāhaddeʼ māʻbalāta bāḥr ba-qālu.
48. ʼArteʻu fenāwikemu wa-megbārikemu kama ʼi-temutu.
49. ʼI-tānded ʼessāta ʼeska yeq^{w}arrer lēlit.
50. ʼI-yātarref zentu neguš ʼekuy ʼaḥada ʼem-ḥezbena.
51. ʼAʻrefi zeyya ʼeska yāgabbeʼomu la-weludiki.
52. Baʼenta ment kama-ze tāḥammemā la-nafseya ʼEgziʼo?
53. Tānaddeyaka zāti ḥeywat zaʼenbala kelʼat.
54. Yārexxu ʼEgziʼabḥēr masākewa samāy wa-yāwarred zenāma.
55. La-ment tanākarkemewwā la-ṭebaba ʼabawikemu?
56. Tāʻawwedo la-ʻawādika westa k^{w}ellu baḥāwert.
57. Westa zentu makān tāḥanneṣ lita bēta ḥaddisa.
58. Wa-ʼemdexra zentu mendābē ʼanta tānaffes ʼem-xasāra ʻālam.
59. ʼI-tāsḥetomu la-ḥezbeya ʼem-ʻeqbata ḥeggeya.
60. ʼAṭʻemana nestita ferē.
61. Yeʼeta ʼamira nāʻawweqaka kidāna ḥaddisa.
62. Wa-ba-gizēhā yāḥayyewomu la-k^{w}ellomu mewutān xebura.
63. Faqadu kama yāngešewwo lāʻlēhomu.
64. Tāsammi hagareka westa k^{w}ellā medr.
65. Rakabewwo ʼenza yāṭammeqomu la-k^{w}ellomu ḥezb.
66. ʼAbʻelana ba-newāy manfasāwi, ʼo-ʼEgziʼena.
67. ʼI-tāḥzeno la-ʼabuka ba-ḥeywatu.
68. Soba tewaddeq ʼanta, nāhu ʼana ʼānaššeʼaka.
69. La-yāšmerka mekreya za-ʼenaggeraka ʼo-neguš.
70. ʼI-tāwʻi bēteya.
71. ʼI-tābkeyana ba-zēnāka ḥezun ʼo-ʼaragāy.
72. ʼAmutani ʼesma ʼi-yʼefaqqed ʼeḥyaw.
73. Weʼeta gizē tānaṣṣeru mangala bēteya wa-tebakkeyu.
74. Wa-tāṣeḥḥefo zanta teʼzāza diba ʼebn ʻabiy.
75. Tāwaḍḍeʼewwo ʼafʼa ʼem-bētu wa-tewaggerewwo ba-ʼebn.
76. ʼI-tābleyu ʼašāʼenikemu, ʼesma ʼi-yekawwenukemu kāleʼān.
77. ʼAkber ʼabāka wa-ʼemmaka k^{w}ello mawāʻela ḥeywatomu.
78. ʼĀnawwemo bezuxa ʻāmata kama ʼi-yerʼay deqata hagar wa-felsata ḥezb.

79. ’Āṣallem gaṣṣa ḍaḥāy wa-yefarreh k^wellu lebb.
80. ’I-yāwwared zenāma ba-gizēhu.
81. Fannawa ’agbertihu yābṣeḥuna hagara.
82. ’Egzi’abḥēr yākehhelana ba-k^wellu za-nefaqqed.
83. Yānux ’Egzi’abḥēr mawā‘elikemu diba medr.
84. ’Aṣne‘u ’albābikemu wa-’i-tefrehu.
85. Soba yenaggeruka, ’anta ’i-tāwašše’.
86. ’Abe’ewwomu zeyya wa-’anberewwomu qedmēya.
87. Yākeḥḥedo nagareka ’emenna faṭārihu.
88. ’Allā ’āqaddem ’emaṣṣe’ xabēkemu.
89. Yebēlomu kama yāṣneḥu lotu ḥamara.
90. Zanta xasāra yāxallef ’em-dibēna wa-naxadder ba-salām la-zelufu.

B. 1. gaṣṣ mafreh
2. zebṭat ‘abiy wa-māḥmem
3. manfas qeddus māḥyawi
4. zēnā māḥzen
5. mamker ṭabib
6. ḥeywat mašmert la-’Egzi’abḥēr
7. motu la-Yoḥannes Maṭmeq
8. nebāb māḥzani
9. g^weyyā mamākertihu
10. mak^wannen mā’mera ḥegg
11. maṭmequ la-’Iyasus
12. wangēl māḥyew
13. maḥāleya mabkeyān
14. ḥemām māḥzen
15. mā’mera ta’āmer
16. ’ar’ayā gaṣṣu
17. Kunomu ’ar’ayā.
18. ’ar’ayā maṣḥafa nabiyāt

Lesson 46

46.1 D Verbs: Imperfect, Subjunctive, and Imperative. The inflected forms of D verbs exhibit such regularity regardless of root type that an extended exposition is unnecessary.

Root Type	Perfect	Imperfect	Subjunctive	Imperative
Sound	*faṣṣama*	*yefēṣṣem*	*yefaṣṣem*	*faṣṣem*
I-Gutt.	*'azzaza*	*ye'ēzzez*	*ya'azzez*	*'azzez*
II-Gutt.	*mahhara*	*yemēhher*	*yemahher*	*mahher*
			yemehher	*mehher*
III-Gutt.	*nasseḥa*	*yenēsseḥ*	*yenasseḥ*	*nasseḥ*
I-W	*wassaka*	*yewēssek*	*yewassek*	*wassek*
II-W	*fawwasa*	*yefēwwes*	*yefawwes*	*fawwes*
II-Y	*ṭayyaqa*	*yeṭēyyeq*	*yeṭayyeq*	*ṭayyeq*
III-W	*fannawa*	*yefēnnew-*	*yefannew-*	*fannew-*
III-Y	*rassaya*	*yerēssey-*	*yerassey-*	*rassey-*

As elsewhere, stems in *-ew-* and *-ey-* become *-u* and *-i* respectively when no further ending or suffix is added. The inflection of all of the above forms is the same as that of the corresponding G verbal forms, including the addition of object suffixes.

46.2 The Names of the Months. The traditional Ethiopian calendar consists of twelve months of thirty days plus a thirteenth month of five days (or six in leap years). New Year's Day falls on September 11 of our calendar and the months are ordered as follows:

Maskaram	Sept. 11 - Oct. 10	*Miyāzyā*	Apr. 9 - May 8
Ṭeqemt	Oct. 11 - Nov. 9	*Genbot*	May 9 - June 7
Xedār	Nov. 10 - Dec. 9	*Šenē/Senē*	June 8 - July 7
Tāxšāš	Dec. 10 - Jan. 8	*Ḥamlē*	July 8 - Aug. 6
Ṭerr	Jan. 9 - Feb. 7	*Naḥāsē*	Aug. 7 - Sept. 5
Yakātit	Feb. 8 - Mar. 9	*Pāg^{w}emēn*	Sept. 6 - Sept. 10
Maggābit	Mar. 10 - Apr. 8		

The dates given are one day after those of Dillmann *(Lexicon passim)*, who allows for the beginning of a day at the sunset of the previous day. Aside from *Pāg^{w}emēn*, which is from Greek *epagómenai*, the origin of the month names is quite obscure; in many instances they represent nominal forms not proper to the classical language.

46.3 The Numbers Above Ten.

(a) 11-19. The gender distinctions noted with the units are preserved in the teens. Thus,

masculine:	*ʿašartu wa-ʾaḥadu*	feminine:	*ʿašru wa-ʾaḥatti*	11
	ʿašartu wa-kelʾētu		*ʿašru wa-kelʾē*	12
	ʿašartu wa-šalastu		*ʿašru wa-šalās*	13

When days of the month are enumerated (ordinal or cardinal), the forms *ʿašur wa-sanuy*, *ʿašur wa-šalus*, etc. are used.

(b) 20-90. The tens are based on the corresponding units with the ending *-ā*, excepting 20, where the base of 10 is used:

20	*ʿešrā*	50	*xamsā*	80	*samānyā*
30	*šalāsā*	60	*sessā*	90	*tasʿā, tesʿā*
40	*ʾarbeʿā*	70	*sabʿā*		

These are unmodified for case or gender. Units are simply added, but the normal gender distinctions are retained:

21 *ʿešrā wa-ʾaḥadu/ʾaḥatti*

22 *ʿešrā wa-kelʾētu/kelʾē* etc.

(c) 100 is *meʾt* (pl. *ʾamʾāt*). 1000 is normally expressed as 10 hundred: *ʿašartu meʾt*, 2000 as 20 hundred, *ʿešrā meʾt*, etc.

(d) Ordinals above ten may be expressed by cardinals. There are, however, separate ordinal forms of the tens: *ʿešrāwi* 20th, *šalāsāwi* 30th, etc.

In Ethiopic texts the numbers are frequently represented by figures (see above, page 7); these must, of course, be read with the appropriate cardinal or ordinal form.

Vocabulary 46

ṭayyaqa D to examine, observe closely, scrutinize, investigate, explore; to ascertain by examining. CD *ʾaṭayyaqa* to inform (someone: obj. suff.) of (something: acc. dir. obj.). Dt *taṭayyaqa* to seek certainty, try to make sure; also passive: to be ascertained, found out for sure.

ṣallaya D to pray (to: *xaba*, *qedma*; for: *baʾenta*, *lāʿla*, *diba*), to pray for (something: acc. dir. obj.).

bagʿ (f. *bageʿt*; pl. *ʾabāgeʿ*) sheep, lamb.

Exercises

A. 1. La-mannu nerēsseyo nagāšē lā‘lēna?

2. ’Enza yenēsseḥu qarbu wa-sagadu lotu.

3. ’I-maftew kama nemaṭṭewā la-hagar westa ’edawihu la-zentu kaḥādi.

4. Tegabberu k^wello za-’e’ēzzezakemu.

5. Mannu za-ye’ēmmerana fenota?

6. Mannu yek^{w}ēnnen mak^{w}ānenta?

7. ’Ana ’ehēllu meslēkemu la-zelufu.

8. Ṣawwe‘ lita safāyē. Tabatka qenāteya.

9. Hallo watra yeḥēwweṣomu la-mahāymenān ’ella bēta Kerestiyān.

10. Naṣṣer ge‘za ṣādeq kama tā’mer ṣedqa.

11. Ṭayyequ maṣāḥefta ṭabibān qadamt.

12. ’Emenna mannu tetmahharu šā’šā’a?

13. Rasseyu mašwā‘ta diba mešwā‘ wa-ḥuru ’af’a ’em-zentu makān.

14. ’Enza yegēššeṣana yebēlana bezuxa ba’enta qadamtina.

15. Nebar zeyya ’eska tefēṣṣem gebraka.

16. Nefēwwesā la-nafseka ba-’emnat wa-ba-feqr, wa-’akko ba-šerāy.

17. Wehibaka liṭa warqa šēṭ, ’emēṭṭewaka za-tašāyaṭka.

18. Teṭēyyequ ’albābikemu wa-bāḥtu ’i-terakkebu ṣedqa.

19. ’Axazku ’enasseḥ ba’enta xaṭi’ateya.

20. ’Azzazo kama yefannewo la-waldu westa gadām.

21. La-ment tefaqqedu tefannewuni ’enza ’ana ’edawwi wa-’edakkem?

22. ’Efo neṭēyyeq ’amāna ba’enta zentu rā’y za-re’ika?

23. Nešā’ zanta marxo wa-sawwero ’em-’a‘yenta sab’.

24. Mehherana māḥlēta ḥaddisa.

25. ’I-yefaqqed kama ’emahherka wa-’i-menta-ni.

26. Ba-ye’eti ‘elat yesēwwer ḍaḥāy berhāno wa-yehēllu ṣelmat ba-k^wellā medr.

27. La-ment terēssi ’aṣwāra za-kama-ze dibēna?

28. ’I-tefēṣṣem mawā‘ela šimateka ba-salām.

29. Soba yebaṣṣeḥani ‘elata moteya, ḥawweṣ ’anta be’siteya wa-waldeya kama ’i-yeššayaṭu kama ’agbert.

30. La-neṣalli xaba ’Egzi’ena ba’enta dewuyānina.

31. Naṣṣeru westa samāy wa-ṭayyequ ‘udata ḍaḥāy wa-merwāṣa kawākebt kama tā’meru kebro la-’Egzi’abḥēr wa-ṭebabo.

32. ’I-nefaqqed kama ’anta tehallu meslēna ba-we’etu gizē.

33. ’I-tegaššeṣani ’allā gaššeṣo la-’exuya.

34. Rakabkewwomu ’enza yeṣēlleyu wa-yebakkeyu diba mutānihomu.

B. 1. ‘ašartu wa-kel’ētu rad’

2. ‘ašru wa-kel’ē hagar

3. ‘ešrā ‘azaqt

4. tas‘ā wa-tes‘u bag‘

5. šalāsā wa-samāntu šayaṭṭ

6. ‘ašartu wa-šalastu warēzā

7. ‘ašartu me’t malā’ekt

8. me’t wa-sab‘ā faras

9. samānyā me’t ṣabā’t

10. xamsā wa-xamestu xebest

11. ba-‘ašur wa-samun la-warx

12. ’ama ‘ašur wa-xamus la-warxa Genbot

13. ba-‘ešrā wa-rabu‘ la-Maggābit

14. ’ama tasu‘u la-ṣelmata Miyāzyā

15. ’ama sanuy la-warxa Ṭeqemt

Lesson 47

47.1 D Verbs: Verbal Adjectives. These are normally of the pattern *qettul*, with an occasional *qattil* (e.g. *ḥaddis*) or *qattāl* (e.g. *šannāy*):

ʾezzuz commanded, ordered (of person or thing). Note the expressions

ʾezzuz (weʾetu) kama + Subj. It has been commanded that ...

ba-kama ʾezzuz (ba-xaba) as has been commanded (by) ...

ʿebbuy arrogant, insolent, haughty (cf. Dt *taʿabbaya*).

fennew sent.

fešsuḥ happy, joyous, rejoicing (cf. Dt *tafašseḥa*).

feṣṣum done, accomplished, completed, fulfilled, consummated; perfect, whole, complete.

geššuṣ (well-)instructed, learned.

k^wennun judged, condemned, subject to punishment.

meṭṭew handed over, delivered.

nessuḥ repentant.

ressuy prepared, made ready; equipped (with: *ba-*).

sewwur hidden, covered, concealed.

ṣewwuʿ summoned, invited.

šennuy adorned, decked out, lovely.

ṭeyyuq perceptive; accurate; certain, sure; as adv. *ṭeyyuqa* accurately, carefully, precisely, exactly.

47.2 D Verbs: Agent Nouns. These are of two types: *qattāli* (quite rare) and *maqattel*. For D verbs occurring thus far only the following are of any importance:

mafawwes physician.

magaššeṣ teacher, instructor.

mak^{w}annen (see Voc. 5).

nassāḥi (one who is) penitent.

mašanney the best (of), the best part (of)

mamehher (f. *-t*) teacher.

Mamehher is traditionally read *mamher*. The noun *mašagger* also belongs to this group, although the related verb is either CG *ʾašgara* or CD *ʾašaggara* to cast nets, fish, to capture by trapping. Note also Gt *tašagra* to be captured, ensnared (used in quite a wide sense), and *mašgart* (pl. *mašāger*) snare, net, trap.

47.3 D Verbs: Verbal Nouns. There are about nine noun patterns regularly used to form verbal nouns from D verbs. These fall into four groups according to the stem:

(a) *qettel, qettelā, qettelāt, qettelennā*:

feššeḥā joy, happiness (cf. *feššuḥ* above).

nesseḥā repentance, regret, penitence.

ṣewweʿā call, summons, invitation.

qeddesāt holiness, sanctity, sacredness; frequent in construct phrases: e.g. *hagara qeddesāt* holy city.

qeddesennā = *qeddesāt*.

šenn beauty (if reduced from a form **šenni*).

(b) *qettāl, qettālē, qettalē* (with short *-a-*):

fennā (from **fennāw*?) a less frequent synonym of *fenot*; also used in the expression *fennā sark* early evening. The noun *fenot*, because of its relationship with the D verb *fannawa*, should probably be read as *fennot* (*pace* the Tradition); the plural forms *fennāw* and *fennāwē* (sic) are also felt to be the plurals of *fennā*.

feṣṣāmē consummation, end, completion, perfection.

ḥewwāṣē visit, visitation, attention.

neṣṣārē a look, glance, viewing; sight (ability to see).

qeddāsē sanctification, consecration; the sacred service or liturgy.

ṣewwāʿē = *ṣewweʿā* above.

k^wennanē (pl. *-yāt*) judgment, condemnation, punishment.

(c) *qattalā* (cf. *qatalā* from G verbs: *xašašā, ḥatatā*).

ʾabbasā sin (see Voc. below).

dammanā cloud (see Voc. below).

(d) *qattel* (properly the infinitive base without the terminal *-o*):

fawwes cure, healing (often fig.); medicine, medication

Because such pairs as *qetl/qettel* and *qetlāt/qettelāt* are indistinguishable in Ethiopic script, only the underlying verb (G or D) can determine the proper form. Even then one cannot be certain, since languages are not always consistent. When there is reasonable doubt, we have listed both possibilities in the Lexicon, but for the sake of simplicity one form has been used in the transliteration of the texts. It should be noted too that the ending *-ennā*, although frequently associated with verbal nouns of D verbs, is used also to derive nouns from G verbs and from miscellaneous (frequently quadriliteral) bases: E.g. *Kerestennā* Christianity; *dengelennā* virginity; *yawhennā* gentleness (cf. G *yawha* to be gentle); *rəš'ennā* old age (cf. G *raš'a* to grow old); *lehqennā* old age (G *lehqa*).

The same is true of the ending *-ān*, sometimes associated with D verbs, as in *šelṭān* power, authority (D *šallaṭa* to exercise power), but more frequently associated with G verbs, as in *be'dān* change, *beḍ'ān* beatification, *berhān* light, *ge'zān* manumission, *res'ān* forgetfulness, *'erqān* nakedness, *felṭān* splitting, dividing, and others.

47.4 D Verbs: Nouns with Prefixed *M-*. These appear to be the same pattern used for G derivatives *(meqtāl)*; the Tradition, however, reads *meqettāl* and we vocalize accordingly:

mek^{w}*ennān*	place of judgment, court, tribunal; judicial district, hence, more generally, province, prefecture.
mesewwār	hidden place, hiding place.
meṣellāy	place to pray, chapel.
mešennāy	= *mašanney* above.

Vocabulary 47

qaddasa D to sanctify, make or regard as holy (acc. dir. obj.); to perform sacred offices. Dt *taqaddasa* passive.

ḥaddasa D to renew, renovate, restore. Dt *taḥaddasa* passive.

dammana D to become clouded (esp. of face, fig.); to be obscured by clouds. *demmun* clouded, obscured by clouds.

'abbasa D to commit a crime or sin (against: *lā'la*, *la-*). *'abbāsi* = *ma'abbes* sinner, criminal. *'abbasā* (pl. *-t*) sin, crime.

Exercises

A. 1. ṣewwe'ā la-nesseḥā
2. fesṣāmēhu la-ḥenṣāhomu
3. qeddāsē bētu la-'Egzi'abḥēr
4. fesšeḥā za-la-'ālam za'enbala ḥazan
5. 'eska fennā sark za-zāti 'elat
6. ba-fesšeḥā 'abiy wa-ba-māḥlēt fesšuḥ
7. nesseḥā k^{w}ellu māxbarena

8. nesseḥāka wa-xedgata xaṭi’ateka
9. qeddesennā zentu makān
10. ba-‘elata k^wennanēkemu
11. fawwesu la-dewuy
12. fawwesomu la-’ekuyāna lebb ’em-’abbasāhomu
13. feṣṣāmē ḥenṣata hagara qeddesātihu
14. ḥewwāṣēhu la-’Egzi’abḥēr xaba ṣādeqān wa-rāte‘ān

B. 1. mak^{w}annen ‘ebbuy
2. manbar ressuy la-kebru
3. mal’ekt feṣṣum
4. ’ardā’ geššuṣān
5. xalāfi ṣewwu‘ la-bawi’
6. makān šennuy la-‘abiy ba‘āl
7. mašanneya warāzutihomu
8. mexḍāb sewwur ’em-xalāfeyān
9. be’si ḥemmum wa-nassāḥi
10. mafawwes ṭabib ba-megbāru
11. lā’k fennew westa hagar
12. mamehher maḥāri
13. hagarit meṭṭew la-mawā’ihā
14. be’sit feššeḥt wa-šennit
15. bēt ressuy la-nebratekemu
16. xāṭe’ān k^wennunān wa-’i-nessuḥān
17. nassāḥi fetuḥ
18. marāḥi geššuṣ wa-semuy
19. samā‘i feṣṣum
20. magaššeṣ ’ekuy
21. šenna gaṣṣu

C. 1. La-ment tāzallefu ’abbeso lā‘lēya wa-ta‘adewo ’em-ḥegageya?
2. Ba-zentu qāl waṭana samāy dammeno wa-ne’sa berhāna ḍaḥāy.
3. Wasadewwomu westa mek^{w}ennān, wa-tarakibomu ma’abbesāna tak^{w}annanu k^wennanē ‘abiya wa-‘eṣuba.
4. Ḥaddasu hagaromu wa-ḥanaṣu ṭeqma ṣenu‘a ‘awdā.
5. Faṣṣimana ḥenṣata bēta maqdas, qaddasnāhu ba-‘abiy feššeḥā.
6. ’Albo mesewwār za-yesēwwer re’so bo.
7. La-yetqatal za-ye’ēbbes lā‘la te’zāzāta ’Egzi’abḥēr.
8. ’Abeḥewwo kama yefannu ’axāhu xaba mak^{w}annen.
9. Yahabka ’Egzi’ena salāma wa-ṭe‘innā kama tebṣāḥ westa feṣṣāmē ḥeywateka ba-feššeḥā.
10. Teḥēddesu ba‘ālāta za-xadaggemu, wa-tedaggemu ’anbebo maṣāḥefta qeddusāt k^wello ’amira.
11. Kun nessuḥa wa-’i-tekun k^wennuna.
12. Kuni feṣṣemt ba-k^wellu za-tegabberi.
13. Kawino geššuṣa wa-mā’mera ḥegg, ’axaza mehherotomu la-’aḥzāba hagaru.
14. ’I-yābawweḥomu la-fennewān kama yebā’u xabēhu.
15. ’Enza yesabbek nesseḥā wa-xedgata xaṭi’at, ṣawwe‘omu la-ḥezb.

Lesson 48

48.1 Dt Verbs: Imperfect, Subjunctive, and Imperative. These follow the corresponding forms of the D verb except for the *-a-* in the final stem syllable.

Root Type	Perfect	Imperfect	Subjunctive	Imperative
Sound	*tafaṣṣama*	*yetfēṣṣam*	*yetfaṣṣam*	*tafaṣṣam*
I-Gutt.	*taʾazzaza*	*yetʾēzzaz*	*yetʾazzaz*	*taʾazzaz*
II-Gutt.	*tamahhara* *tamehhera*	*yetmēhhar*	*yetmahhar*	*tamahhar*
III-Gutt.	*tanasseḥa*	*yetnēssāḥ*	*yetnassāḥ*	*tanassāḥ*
I-W	*tawassaka*	*yetwēssak*	*yetwassak*	*tawassak*
II-W	*tafawwasa*	*yetfēwwas*	*yetfawwas*	*tafawwas*
II-Y	*taṭayyaqa*	*yeṭṭēyyaq*	*yeṭṭayyaq*	*taṭayyaq*
III-W	*tafannawa*	*yetfēnnaw*	*yetfannaw*	*tafannaw*
III-Y	*tarassaya*	*yetrēssay*	*yetrassay*	*tarassay*

48.2 Dt Verbs: Verbal Nouns. While no verbal adjective or agent noun is derive regularly from Dt verbs, there are two verbal nouns of relatively high frequency: *teqtelt* and *taqtāl*:

teʾzāz (altered from the pattern *taqtāl*; Voc. 24).

tafṣāmēt (with added *-ēt*) consummation, end, completion, perfection.

tagšāṣ (pl. *-āt*) rebuke, reproach; instruction, education.

tersit equipment of any sort: clothing, ornaments, furnishings, trappings.

tawsāk (pl. *-āt*) addition, supplement, any added part.

temhert (pl. *-āt*) what is taught, doctrine, teaching; study, learning.

teʿbit arrogance, insolence, haughtiness.

tefšeḥt (pl. *-āt*) joy, happiness.

tasfā (for **tasfāw*) hope, expectation (of, for: *xaba*, *diba*, *la-*).

tagbār product, creation; work, labor; commerce, business.

The noun *tewledd* (for **-dt*) appears to belong to this pattern, although no related Dt verb exists; the same is true for the partly synonymous *tezmedd* (for **-dt*).

48.3 CD Verbs. The stem forms follow those of D verbs and present no unusual features. There are no regularly derived verbal nouns or adjectives.

Perfect	Imperfect	Subjunctive	Imperative
'akʷannana	*yākʷēnnen*	*yākʷannen*	*'akʷannen*
'as̆annaya	*yās̆ẹnney-*	*yās̆anney-*	*'as̆anney-*
'asaffawa	*yāsēffew-*	*yāsaffew-*	*'asaffew-*

48.4 Independent Personal Pronouns. There are three series of independent pronouns in addition to the subject forms given in Lesson 6.

(a) Subject:			(b) Direct Obj.:		
	laliya	*lalina*		*kiyāya*	*kiyāna*
	lalika	*lalikemu*		*kiyāka*	*kiyākemu*
	laliki	*laliken*		*kiyāki*	*kiyāken*
	lalihu	*lalihomu*		*kiyāhu*	*kiyāhomu*
	lalihā	*lalihon*		*kiyāhā*	*kiyāhon*

(c) Possessive:

Masc. sing. reference	Fem. sing. reference	Plural reference
zi'aya	*'enti'aya*	*'elli'aya*
zi'aka	*'enti'aka*	*'elli'aka*
zi'aki	*'enti'aki*	*'elli'aki*
zi'ahu etc.	*'enti'ahu* etc.	*'elli'ahu* etc.

The subject forms are the least frequent and are employed only when a strong emphasis or contrast is required. They are usually appositional to other pronominal markers (e.g. verb subjects, other independent pronouns) and correspond to the English intensive pronouns:

Re'ikewwo laliya.	I myself saw him.
We'etu lalihu 'Egzi'ena we'etu.	He himself is our Savior.

Very rarely, they may be used to modify a noun: *lalihu qāleka* your very word.

The direct object forms are employed either for emphasis, as in

Kiyāka re'ina, 'akko kiyāhu.	We saw you, not him.

or to express the direct object of the perfective active participle (*qatilo* form):

Kiyāhu qatilo gʷayya.	Having slain him, he fled.

Both *lalihu* and *kiyāhu* (or other third person forms) are used occasionally without reference to case to emphasize a noun:

be'si kiyāhu/lalihu	the man himself, the very man.

The possessive forms are quite frequent. Most important to note is their pronominal (not adjectival) status (mine, yours, his, hers, etc.); a noun must stand in the construct before them, as in

bēta zi'aya	my house, the/a house of mine
be'sita 'enti'aya	my wife, a wife of mine
'agberta 'elli'aya	(the) servants of mine, my servants,

unless they are used predicatively as true pronouns:

Zentu bēt zi'aya we'etu.	This house is mine.

They are frequently preceded by *za-*, which may be taken as a relative

maṣḥaf za-zi'aya	the book which is mine, my book

or a nominalized relative:

Yekawwenana za-zi'ahu.	We shall possess that which is his.

Vocabulary 48

tarassaya Dt to put on (something: acc. dir. obj.) as a garment, to don (acc. dir. obj. or *ba-*); to get ready, prepare oneself (for: *ba-*).

tagabbara Dt to labor, toil, work (intrans.); to produce (something: acc. dir. obj.) by labor (literal or figurative); to work the ground, to farm (acc. of *medr* or *garāht*, field).

Lesson 49

49.1 L, CL, and Lt Verbs: The Remaining Forms.

	Perfect	Imperfect	Subjunctive	Imperative
L	*māsana*	*yemāsen*	*yemāsen*	*māsen*
Lt	*tamāsana*	*yetmāsan*	*yetmāsan*	*tamāsan*
CL	*ʾamāsana*	*yāmāsen*	*yāmāsen*	*ʾamāsen*

[The Tradition has a doubled second radical in all Imperfect forms: *yemāssen* etc.]

The verbal adjective is of the pattern *qutul*: *musun* (f. *musent*).

The agent noun, if it exists, is usually of the pattern *qātāli*: *māsāni*; *maqātel* is also a possible pattern.

Verbal nouns are limited to just a few types, *qutālē*, *qutelā*, and *qātāl* being the most frequent. Listed below, for reference, are the attested forms for the more important L verbs that will be encountered in the readings.

	Perfect	Verbal Adj.	Verbal Noun	Agent Noun
to perish	*māsana*	*musun*	*musenā*	*māsāni*
to mourn	*lāḥawa*	*luḥew/leḥew*	(*lāḥ*)	---
to rescue	*bāleḥa*	---	---	*bālāḥi*
to console	*nāzaza*	---	*nuzāzē*	*nāzāzi*
to associate	*tasātafa*	*sutuf*	*sutāfē*	---
to establish	*šārara*	*šurur/šerur*	*šurārē*	*šārāri*
to labor	*ṣāmawa*	---	*ṣāmā*	---
to bless	*bāraka*	*buruk*	*burākē*	---
to show mercy	*tašāhala*	---	(*šāhl*)	---
to vex	*šāqaya*	---	(*šeqāy*)	---

Verbal nouns and adjectives proper to the G verbal system sometimes exist for roots whose actual verbal forms are L. The following deserve mention:

barakat (pl. *-āt*) blessing, prosperity.
lāḥ mourning, grieving (apparently from **laḥw*).
šāhl mercy, clemency.
mašqē goad; weaver's comb.
mašarrat foundation.

As noted previously, Quadriliteral verbs II-W/Y undergo a contraction (*ay>ē, aw>o*) which brings them into the pattern of the L verbs listed above. The remaining forms for these verbs are as follows.

	Perfect	Imperfect	Subjunctive	Imperative
L	*dēgana*	*yedēgen*	*yedēgen*	*dēgen*
Lt	*tadēgana*	*yeddēgan*	*yeddēgan*	*tadēgan*
CL	*'adēgana*	*yādēgen*	*yādēgen*	*'adēgen*
L	*moqeḥa*	*yemoqeḥ*	*yemoqeḥ*	*moqeḥ*
Lt	*tamoqeḥa*	*yetmoqāḥ*	*yetmoqāḥ*	*tamoqāḥ*
CL	*'amoqeḥa*	*yāmoqeḥ*	*yāmoqeḥ*	*'amoqeḥ*

Verbal nouns and adjectives follow those of L verbs or Q verbs; the following is a representative selection:

	Perfect	Verbal Adj.	Verbal Noun	Agent Noun
to err	*gēgaya*	*giguy*	*gēgāy*	---
to pursue	*dēgana*	---	---	*dēgāni*
to tell	*zēnawa*	---	*zēnā*	*zēnāwi, mazēnew*
to nourish	*sēsaya*	---	*sisāy, sisit*	*masēsey*
to take captive	*ḍēwawa*	*ḍēwew/ḍiwew*	*ḍēwā(wē)*	---
to imprison	*moqeḥa*	*muquḥ*	*muqāḥē*	---
to shepherd	*tanolawa*	---	---	*nolāwi.*

49.2 CGt, CDt, CLt, and CGlt Verbs. Each of the basic lexical types G, D, and L possesses a derived form characterized (in the Perfect) by the prefix *'asta-*:

	Perfect	Imperfect	Subjunctive	Imperative
CGt	*'astaq(a)tala*	*yāstaqattel*	*yāstaqtel*	*'astaqtel*
CDt	*'astaqattala*	*yāstaqēttel*	*yāstaqattel*	*'astaqattel*
CLt/CGlt	*'astaqātala*	*yāstaqātel*	*yāstaqātel*	*'astaqātel*

	Infinitive	Perf.Act.Part.	Agent Noun	Verbal Noun
CGt	*'astaqtelo(t)*	*'astaqtil-*	*mastaqatel* *mastaqtel*	*('esteqtāl)*
CDt	*'astaqattelo(t)*	*'astaqattil-*	*mastaqattel*	
CLt/CGlt	*'astaqātelo(t)*	*'astaqātil-*	*mastaqātel*	*('estequtāl)*

Formally these verbs may be viewed as either (1) causatives of the corresponding *-t* verbs, as in

Glt *tagābe'a* to gather (intrans.) → CGlt *'astagābe'a* to gather (trans.),

or (2) reflexives of the corresponding causative, as in

CG *'ar'aya* to show ⟶ CGt *'astar'aya* to show one's self, to appear.

In actual practice, however, the meanings of these verbs must be learned as they occur. The exact sequence of derivation for a given root is usually not entirely clear, either because some of the bases involved are unattested or no longer in use, or because a particular verb was created *de novo* by a sophisticated translator for a given passage.

In addition to *'astar'aya* and *'astagābe'a*, the following verbs are relatively frequent and should be made a part of one's permanent vocabulary:

CGt *'astabqʷe'a* to beseech, implore, entreat (someone: o.s. or *ba-xaba/'em-xaba*; for something: a.d.o.); to intercede (for: *ba'enta*).

CGt *'astamḥara* to show mercy to, have pity on (a.d.o. or *la-/diba*); to seek mercy (for one's self or someone else: *la-*).

CGlt *'astawādaya* to accuse, bring charges against (someone: a.d.o.); cf. *wedēt* charge, accusation.

CGlt *'astaḥāmama* to study diligently, pursue eagerly, give close attention to (a.d.o. or *ba'enta/xaba/ba-*).

CGlt *'astawāsaba* to marry off (a son or daughter: a.d.o.; to: *mesla*, o.s.); cf. CG *'awsaba* to marry (someone: a.d.o.); *sabsāb* marriage, wedding.

Lesson 50

50.1 Quadriliteral Verbs: The Remaining Forms.

	Perfect	Imperfect	Subjunctive	Imperative
Q	*dangaḍa*	*yedanaggeḍ*	*yedangeḍ*	*dangeḍ*
Qt	*tamandaba*	*yetmanaddeb*	*yetmandab*	*tamandab*
CQ	*ʾamandaba*	*yāmanaddeb*	*yāmandeb*	*ʾamandeb*
Q1t	*tamanādaba*	*yetmanādab*	*yetmanādab*	*tamanādab*

The verbal adjective is of the pattern *denguḍ*. The verbal noun is usually of the pattern *dengāḍē*, **dengeḍā*, or **dengeḍennā*. Derived verbs such as CQt *ʾastamandaba* and CQ1t *ʾastamanādaba* also exist.

Verbs from roots II-W/Y (Q/L) were given in the preceding lesson. Occasionally, a Q1t form is attested which shows the original second radical, e.g. *tazēyānawa* to inform one another.

Although the vast majority of verbal roots in Ethiopic are triliteral, quadriliteral roots are not rare, even in ordinary, non-ornate prose. One frequent root type has the pattern $C_1C_2C_1C_2$ and appears to be formed by a reduplication of a biconsonantal root C_1C_2. But since these "short" roots cannot otherwise be isolated, the quadriliteral form must be taken as primitive in the language. Examples:

lamlama to grow green, blossom	*gʷadgʷada* to knock
qaṭqaṭa to grind, crush	*gēgaya* to err, go astray, sin (cf. 49.1)
badbada to die (of disease)	
fadfada to be numerous, excessive	*sēsaya* to nourish, sustain (cf. 49.1)

Note, too, nouns of the same pattern: *lēlit* (**layleyt*: pl. *layāley*) and *kabkāb* wedding.

A second type of quadriliteral verb is a specifically Ethiopic creation, resulting from the verbalization of nouns *maqtal*, *maqtel*, and *meqtāl*. The underlying triliteral root has, in some instances, fallen into disuse and can be identified only through cognates in other Semitic languages. Examples of this type are

moqeḥa to imprison (*moqeḥ* fetter, bond; original root *wqḥ*)
ʾamāxbara to convene a council (*māxbar* council).

The verbalization of other nominal forms is also possible, as in

Qt *ta'amlaka* to become divine; cf. *'Amlāk*.

Qt *tamathata* to appear as a spectre (*methat*, root *mth*).

Based on nouns of foreign origin are, *inter alia*,

CQ *'amasṭara* to deal in mysteries (*mesṭir*, perhaps ultimately from Greek).

Q *mank^{w}asa* to become a monk (*manakos*, from Greek *monakhos*).

CQ *'asanbata* to observe the sabbath (*sanbat*, ultimately from Hebrew).

Q *maṣwata* to practice charity (*meṣwāt*, ultimately from Hebrew).

But most quadriliteral roots have no obvious derivational source and must be taken as primary in the Ethiopic lexicon, although they may have triliteral origins at some earlier stage of Semitic. Quadriliteral nouns without associated verbs are not uncommon: e.g.

tak^{w}lā (for **tak^{w}lāw*; pl. *tak^{w}ālut*; root *tk^{w}lw*) wolf
kokab (for **kawkab*; pl. *kawākeb*; root *kwkb*) star
dengel (pl. *danāgel* ; root *dngl*) virgin.

50.2 Quinquiliteral Verbs.

Perfect	Imperfect	Subjunctive	Imperative	Infinitive
'adlaqlaqa	*yādlaqalleq*	*yādlaqleq*	*'adlaqleq*	*'adlaqleqo(t)*

Note that the initial segment of these forms is like that of the causatives. Verbal roots with five radicals are very rare and almost always involve some sort of root reduplication, e.g.

'asqoqawa to mourn, lament; verbal noun: *saqoqāw* (imperf. *yāsqoqu*)

'adlaqlaqa to shake, quake (trans. and intrans.); verbal noun: *deleqleq*

'aqyāḥyeḥa to grow reddish (cf. *qayeḥ* red).

50.3 N Verbs. A special type of quinquiliteral verb is marked by a prefixed -*n*- and a quadriliteral root, usually of the type $C_1C_2C_1C_2$:

	Perfect	Imperfect	Subjunctive	Imperative
N	*'anqalqala*	*yānqalaqqel*	*yānqalqel*	*'anqalqel*
Nt	*tanqalqala*	*yenqalaqqal*	*yenqalqal*	*tanqalqal*

Nt Imperfect and Subjunctive forms are very rare; those given above are normative, without the -*t*- (presumably **yentq*- > *yenq*-). Because these verbs do not have clear counterparts elsewhere in Semitic, there is some ambiguity about their analysis. When the root is also attested without the initial -*n*-, as in

Q $g^{w}adg^{w}ada$ to knock (at a door) N $ʾang^{w}adg^{w}ada$ to thunder,

or, when a corresponding noun exists without the -*n*-, as in

N *ʾanṣafṣafa* to ooze; *ṣafṣāf* juice,

the analysis as an N verb is probably justified. With many of these verbs, however, no cognate without the -*n*- is attested, and an analysis as an ordinary quinqiliteral is possible. These verbs, as a semantic class, almost always refer to a process involving the constant repetition of a single action, e.g.

ʾangargara to roll, spin; *nagargār* spinning; a type of epilepsy.
$ʾang^{w}arg^{w}ara$ to be angry; to murmur, mutter, grumble.
ʾanqalqala to move, shake, quake; *naqalqāl* motion, quaking.
ʾansosawa to walk, stroll (imperf. *yānsosu*, not **yānsawassu*).
ʾanṣafṣafa to ooze, drip; *naṣafṣāf*, *ṣafṣāf* drops, juice.
ʾanbalbala to flame, blaze; *nabalbāl* flame.

The verbal noun of the type *naqalqāl* is fairly consistent for N verbs.

50.4 A Special Adjective Type: *Qataltil*. A rare type of adjective is derived by reduplicating -C_2C_3 of a triliteral root, with with the resulting pattern *qataltil*. These are more or less limited to adjectives of color and taste, with a few others, and usually correspond to English adjectives in -ish:

ṣaʿadʿid whitish, rather like white: cf. *ṣāʿdā* white.
maʿārʿir sweetish; cf. *maʿār* honey.
damanmin rather cloudy, gloomy; cf. *dammanā* cloud.

Lesson 51

51.1 Conditional Sentences.

a. Real conditions. The protasis is introduced with *ʾemma* or *laʾemma* if; the apodosis may be introduced with *wa-*, but is more commonly unmarked. The verb forms used depend to some extent on the tense desired, but there is a predominance of the Perfect in the protasis and the Imperfect in the apodosis when the sentence states a present general or future condition:

ʾEmma nabarka zeyya, (wa-)yerakkebuka.	If you remain here, they will find you.

If the conditional sentence describes a situation in the past, the verbs of both the protasis and the apodosis are in the Perfect:

ʾEmma rexebku, wahabuni xebesta. If I was hungry, they gave me bread.

In present and future conditions the Imperfect may also appear in the protasis. *ʾEmma* may be replaced by *ʾemma-hi/ʾemma-ni* (even if) or *ʾemma-sa* (but if, if however, if really). The apodosis may have an imperative or injunctive (subjunctive) verb if the meaning requires it:

ʾEmma rakabka beʾsē rexuba, habo mableʿa.	If you find a hungry man, give him food.

Note the expression *ʾemma ʾakko* (lit. if not), also spelled *ʾemmāʾkko* (± *-sa*), which may usually be translated "otherwise, if such is not the case."

b. Contrary-to-fact Conditions. The protasis is introduced with *soba*, and each verb of the apodosis is preceded by the conditional particle *ʾem-*:

Soba rakabkewwo, ʾem-ʾaxazkewwo wa-ʾem-qatalkewwo.	If I had found him, I would have seized him and killed him.

The Perfect is required in the apodosis; the Perfect is used in the protasis for past conditions, the Imperfect for present conditions. The interrogative particles *-hu* and *-nu* appear rather frequently in the protases of both types of conditional sentences. These usually have no translation value, but they may indicate the presence of an indirect quotation (cf. English if = whether).

51.2 Optative Sentences. The particle *ʾem-* mentioned above may be used with the Perfect in an independent clause to express the optative:

ʾEm-nassāḥku! Would that I had repented!

Soba may be used in the same way. Interrogative sentences have a similar nuance if used rhetorically:

Mannu yeradde'ani! Who will help me = Would that someone would help me!

51.3 The Syllogistic Construction *Za ... ʾefo ...* This rather rare construction expresses the condition "If X is true, how much more so is Y true." The *ʾefo* of the second clause is usually followed by *fadfāda* or *ʾenka* (see below) or both. The following two examples from the Gospel of Matthew illustrate how this basic pattern may be obscured by intervening adverbial or adjectival clauses or by ellipsis:

6:30 *Za-šāʿra gadām za-yom hallo wa-gēsama westa ʾessāt yetwadday, ʾEgziʾabḥēr za-kama-ze yālabbeso, ʾefo ʾenka fadfāda kiyākemu, ḥeṣuṣāna hāymānot.*

O you who lack faith, if God thus clothes the wild vegetation, which exists today but tomorrow is thrown into the fire, how much more so (will he clothe) you.

7:11 *Za-ʾantemu ʾenka ʾenza ʾekuyān, ʾantemu tāʾammeru šannāya habta wehiba la-weludikemu, ʾefo fadfāda ʾabukemu za-ba-samāyāt yehub šannāya la-ʾella yeseʾʾelewwo.*

If you, though evil, know enough to give a good gift to your children, how much more so will your heavenly Father give what is good to those who ask Him (for it).

51.4 The Sentence Particles. A special set of particles, mostly enclitic, is used in the more sophisticated translations to provide the same logical connectives and focussing particles found in the Greek original. The more important of these are listed below with a brief characterization of their function. Details concerning their employment can be acquired only from a parallel reading of the Ethiopic and Greek texts, a practice that should be adopted by every serious student.

a. *-sa* but, however, on the other hand. This particle most frequently corresponds to Greek *dé*; it is usually added to the first word or word-group of a clause to mark a contrast with the preceding statement. This contrast may be vivid or may be merely the introduction of a new subject or topic. *-sa* in this usage usually co-occurs with the conjunction *wa-*. *-sa* may also be used for Greek *mén*, marking the first of two contrasting statements.

The traditional pronunciation of this particle is *-ssá*, with the regular introduction of *-e-* after a word-final consonant. Thus, what we write morphologically as *ʾanta-sa* or *samāyāt-sa* are pronounced *ʾantassá*, *samāyātessá*. The pronoun *ʾana* is the only word that alters its form before this particle: *ʾana* + *sa* —> *ʾane-sa*.

b. *-hi/-ni* even ..., the ... in question, that very ... These two particles are of equal weight, so to speak, and are used interchangeably. They mark a stronger emphasis than *-sa*; they may be used alone or be correlated with a similar particle in the preceding or following clause. The special meaning of *-hi/-ni* with interrogative pronouns has already been noted in § 29.2.

c. *-kē* therefore. This particle marks a statement as being a logical result of the preceding statement. It corresponds frequently to Greek *gár*. It may optionally be followed by *ʾenka* (see below).

d. *ʾengā* is an inferential particle suggesting a conclusion from what precedes, often with a nuance of doubt or skepticism. It is most frequent in, but not limited to, questions, where it may usually be translated "then, so, therefore."

e. *ʾenka* is very similar to *ʾengā* above, but is more frequent and less restricted in usage. Ordinarily it is postpositive to some sentence element and may therefore serve a double function as emphasizer and logical connective. It is especially common after *-kē*, but may also occur with its own enclitics, e.g. *ʾenka-sa*, *ʾenka-sa-kē*. In a negative statement, *ʾenka* is equivalent to "(no) longer, (no) more."

f. *-ma*. This emphatic particle is very rare and is restricted to use on personal pronouns, interrogative pronouns and adverbs, and a few miscellaneous adverbial expressions. E.g. *mannu-ma*, *ʾaytē-nu-ma*, *māʾzē-nu-ma*, *weʾetu-ma*. Its great rarity precludes any clear identification of its meaning other than its emphasizing function. Note the compound *mima* "either, or, whether," sometimes coordinated with a following *-nu*. E.g. Matt. 21:25:

(Whence came John's baptizing?) *'Em-samāy-nu wa-mima 'em-sab'-nu?* From heaven or from man?

51.5 The Repeated Prepositions *ba-ba*, *la-la*, and *za-za*. The repetition of these prepositions is used to express a distributive notion, translated in various ways. The following examples from the Gospel of Matthew illustrate this usage and also the fact that there is no single formulaic relationship to the underlying Greek.

4.24 *'amṣe'u xabēhu k^wello deweyāna wa-k^wello ḥemumāna za-la-la zi'ahu ḥemāmomu* they brought to him all the sick, those afflicted with various diseases (πάντας τοὺς κακῶς ἔχοντας ποικίλαις νόσοις καὶ βασάνοις συνεχομένους)

18:22 *'ādi 'eska sab'ā ba-ba seb'* even up to seventy times seven (ἕως ἑβδομηκοντάκις ἑπτά)

20:2 *takāhala mesla gabā't ba-ba dinār la-'elat* he agreed with the workers on one dinar each for the day (ἐκ δηναρίου τὴν ἡμέραν)

20:10 *naš'u ba-ba dinār 'emuntu-hi* and they too received a dinar each (ἀνὰ δηνάριον)

21:41 *'ella yehubewwo ferēhu ba-ba gizēhu* who will give him its fruit at each season thereof (ἐν τοῖς καιροῖς αὐτῶν)

24:7 *yemaṣṣe' raxāb wa-bedbed wa-hakak ba-ba baḥāwertihu* there will be famine, pestilence, and disorder in various places (κατὰ τόπους)

25:15 *la-la 'aḥadu bakama yekelu* to each according as they are able (ἑκάστῳ κατὰ τὴν ἰδίαν δύναμιν)

25:32 *yefalleṭomu za-za zi'ahomu* he will separate them from one another (ἀφορίσει αὐτοὺς ἀπ' ἀλλήλων)

26:22 *'axazu yebalu ba-ba 'aḥadu* they began to say individually (εἷς ἕκαστος)

Note also such lexical items as *ba-ba nestit* (little by little) and *ba-ba 'ebrētomu* (each in his own turn).

51.6 A Special Use of the Third Person Singular Pronominal Suffixes. The pronominal suffixes of the 3rd pers. sing. (*-hu*, *-u*; *-hā*, *-ā*) are sometimes used with the force of a definite article or weak demonstrative. Thus, it is sometimes necessary to translate, e.g. *be'sihu* as "that man, the man in question" rather than "his man." This usage is especially frequent on nouns denoting points or periods of time (e.g. *ba-'elatu* on the day in question) and appears in such fixed expressions as *'amēhā*, *qadāmihu*, *sobēhā*, *(ba-)gizēhu*, and *(ba-) sānitā*.

51.7 The Periphrastic Passive. The 3rd pers. plural of an active verb with a direct object is often used as a periphrasis for the passive. E.g.

yesaddeduka = you will be persecuted.

This usage is easily identifiable by the absence of a specific subject in a given context or by the logical impossibility of taking the 3rd pers. subject literally, as in

be'sit 'enta daḥarewwā a woman who has been divorced.

Deserving of special note are mixed constructions, such as those with *hallawa* plus the subjunctive, where the logical subject appears as a suffix on *hallawa*:

wa-kamāhu la-walda 'eg^wāla 'emma-ḥeyāw-ni hallawo yāḥmemewwo
and thus too is the Son of Man to be afflicted.

hallawo ... yāgbe'ewwo westa 'eda sab'
he is to be betrayed into the hand of man.

51.8 Attributive Adjectives in Construct Phrases. It is possible to use a noun and adjective in a construct relationship (either order) to express the equivalent of a noun plus a modifying adjective:

'amreḥta 'ewurān = blind guides
ḥassāweyāna nabiyāt = false prophets.

This construction is very rare in the texts that follow.

Texts in Transliteration

The following texts have been transliterated in accordance with the understanding of the grammar developed in the preceding lessons. Needless to say, the ambiguities mentioned in the Introduction remain, but the reader should by now be aware of the problems involved. The glosses are added on the assumption that the lesson vocabularies have been mastered.

I. Lives of the Saints

These are the same selections given by A. Dillmann, *Chrestomathia Aethiopica* (Leipzig, 1866), pp. 16-39, where the text in the Ethiopic alphabet may be found. A few emendations have been made, mainly those suggested by Dillmann himself or a subsequent editor. The selections are taken from the *Synaxarion*,[1] a large collection of hagiographic material compiled from various early sources, mostly in Greek, and divided into daily readings, with the life of a given saint assigned to the day commemorating his death. The Ethiopic version of this work is based on an Arabic intermediary, as betrayed by the presence of numerous Arabicisms in the text. We have not commented upon these because a knowledge of Arabic is not presupposed on the part of the reader.

---

1. For the full work see I. Guidi and S. Grébaut, *Le synaxaire éthiopien. Patrologia Orientalis* I, VII, XV, and XXVI, and A. E. W. Budge, *The Book of Saints of the Ethiopic Church* (Cambridge, 1928).

A. Melchizedek[1]

Ba-zāti ʻelat (ʼama šalus la-Pāgʷemēn) tazkāra motu la-Malka Ṣēdēq. Wa-zentu-sa Malka Ṣēdēq walda Qāynān[2] walda waldu la-Sēm. Wa-soba kono ʻašartu wa-xamestu ʻāmat ʼem-ʼama tawalda, ʼazzazo ʼEgziʼabḥēr la-Nox kama yefannewo la-Sēm waldu mesla šegā ʼabuna ʼAdām, wa-yānbero ba-māʼkala medr ʼenta yeʼeti Qarānyo. Wa-ʼammaro kama yemaṣṣeʼ madxena ʻālam, wa-yeššawwāʻ westētu, wa-yetbēzawo la-ʼAdām ba-damu.

Wa-našʼo Sēm la-Malka Ṣēdēq ʼem-bēta ʼabuhu ba-xebuʼ, wa-baṣḥu heyya ʼenza yemarreḥomu malʼaka ʼEgziʼabḥēr. Wa-tašayma Malka Ṣēdēq kāhena, wa-našʼa ʻašarta wa-kelʼēta ʼaʼbāna, wa-ʼaʻraga dibēhomu mašwāʻta ba-xebest wa-wayn za-warada lotu ʼem-samāy ʼenza yāreʼʼi mesṭira Ḥegg Ḥaddis.

Wa-sisāya-ni yāmaṣṣeʼu lotu malāʼekt. Wa-kona lebsu ʼanadā, wa-qenātu za-māʼs. Wa-nabara ʼenza yetlaʼʼak qedma šegā ʼabuna ʼAdām. Wa-ʼama tamayṭa ʼAbrehām ʼem-ṣabʼ, mawiʼo nagašta, ʼaqraba lotu xebesta wa-wayna, wa-weʼetu-ni wahabo ʻāšerāta ʼem-kʷellu newāyu. Wa-tasamya kāhena wa-neguša Salēm.

Salām[3] la-Malka Ṣēdēq ʼamsālu wa-sutāfu
la-za-maṣʼa qāl ba-dammanā dengel ʻaṣfu.
Ṭabibān gebro bakama ṣaḥafu,
la-šegā ʼAdām xaba taḥanṣa meʻrāfu
zentu kāhen yenabber la-zelufu.

---

1. This selection concerns Melchizedek, the priest of Salem mentioned in Gen. 14, Psalm 110, and the Epistle to the Hebrews. For the understanding of the passage it is sufficient to note that Melchizedek was taken by the early Church as the archetypal priest and prefiguration of Christ. He is presented here as attendant over the body of Our Father Adam, which, according to legend, lies buried in *Qarānyo*, i.e. Gk. *Kraníou (tópos)*, the Place of the Skull, Golgotha, Calvary, where Christ was crucified.

2. Cf. Gen. 11:13 in LXX: *Kainan*, listed as a grandson of Shem, the son of Noah.

3. "Peace (be) unto Melchizedek, the likeness and companion of the Word which came in the Virgin Cloud, its Mantle. As the sages wrote of his deeds, this priest dwells forever where the final resting place of Adam's body was built."

B. St. Mark the Evangelist

Ba-zāti ʻelat (ʼama šalāsā la-Miyāzyā) kona semʻa Qeddus Mārqos wangēlāwi, liqa pāppāsāt za-hagara ʼEskenderyā. Wa-zentu qeddus[1] kona semu la-ʼabuhu ʼArsew Pāwlos[2] ʼem-beḥēra Xams ʼAhgur;[3] wa-semā la-ʼemmu Māryām, wa-yeʼeti zekert westa maṣḥafa Gebra Ḥawāreyāt.[4] Wa-kona semu la-zentu ḥawāreyā qadāmi Yoḥannes, bakama maṣḥafa Gebra Ḥawāreyāt, ʼesma ḥawāreyāt konu yeṣēlleyu westa bēta Māryām ʼemmu la-Yoḥannes za-tasamya Mārqos ḥawāreyā. Wa-zāti beʼsit konat bāʻelta, wa-maharato la-waldā Mārqos ba-lesāna Yonānāwiyān wa-ba-lesāna ʼAfrenj wa-ba-lesāna ʻEbrāyesṭ.

Wa-soba lehqa, našʼo Barnābas meslēhu westa sebkat soba ḥora mesla Pāwlos. Wa-soba reʼya za-baṣḥa lāʻlēhomu mendābē wa-maqšaft wa-xasār, xadagomu ba-hagara Penfelyā[5] wa-gabʼa ba-hagara ʼIyarusālēm. Wa-soba tamayṭu ḥawāreyāt xaba ʼIyarusālēm, wa-tanāgaru ba-tamayeṭ(ot)omu la-ʼaḥzāb westa ʼamina ʼEgziʼena ʼIyasus Kerestos (lotu sebḥat), wa-zakama gabra ʼEgziʼabḥēr ba-ʼedawihomu taʼāmerāta wa-mankerāta, ḥazana wa-nasseḥa baʼenta za-ḥora ʼemennēhomu. Wa-ʼemze xašaša kama yeḥur meslēhomu, wa-ʼi-faqada Pāwlos ḥawāreyā kama yenšeʼo,[6] ʼesma weʼetu xadagomu; ʼallā našʼo Barnābas meslēhu, ʼesma weʼetu zamadu.

Wa-ʼemdexra ʻeraftu la-Barnābas, ḥora xaba Pēṭros hagara Romē wa-kona lotu radʼa, wa-ba-heyya ṣaḥafa wangēlo za-targʷama lotu Pēṭros, za-sabaka botu westa hagara Romē. Wa-ʼemdexra-ze ḥora ba-teʼzāza ʼEgziʼena ʼIyasus Kerestos (lotu sebḥat) wa-ba-teʼzāzomu la-ḥawāreyāt westa hagara ʼEskenderyā, wa-sabaka westētā ba-sebkata wangēl qeddus. Wa-ʻādi sabaka ba-westa hagara ʼAfrāqyā[7] wa-Barqā[8]

---

1. This type of preposing is frequent in some texts: "As for this saint, the name of his father was...." Cf. remarks in §10.2.

2. *ʼArsew Pāwlos*: an error for *ʼAresṭu-pāwlos*, a rendering of Gk. *Aristobulos*.

3. *Xams ʼAhgur*: presumably the Pentapolis on the Dead Sea. The Pentapolis mentioned below is a district of Cyrene in Africa.

4. Cf. Acts 12:12.

5. Pamphylia, on the coast of Asia Minor. Cf. Acts 13:13.

6. Cf. Acts 15:38ff.

7. Africa, the province.

8. Barce, a city of the Pentapolis in Cyrene (Libya).

wa-Xams 'Ahgur.

Wa-soba bo'a westa hagara 'Eskenderyā, wa-tabatka totāna 'ašā'enihu 'em-'egarihu. Wa-kona xaba 'anqaṣa hagar 'aḥadu be'si safāyi, wa-wahabo Qeddus 'ašā'enihu kama yesfi lotu. Wa-'enza we'etu yesaffi ba-masfē, tašaṭqa 'aṣābe'ihu, wa-weḥza dam 'emennēhu, wa-yebē ba-lesāna Yonānāwiyan, "'Istāwos,"[9] za-ba-terg^{w}āmēhu "'Aḥadu 'Egzi'abḥēr." Wa-yebēlo Qeddus Mārqos, "Bo-nu tā'ammero la-'Egzi'abḥēr?" Wa-yebēlo, "'Albo, 'allā nesammi semo bāḥtito,[10] wa-'i-nā'ammero." Wa-'axaza yengero Qeddus Mārqos 'em-ṭent za-faṭara[11] 'Egzi'abḥēr samāya wa-medra, wa-zakama kona ta'adewotu la-'abuna 'Adām, wa-meṣ'ato la-māya 'Ayx, wa-zakama 'asaffawo 'Egzi'abḥēr la-Musē, wa-'awḍe'omu la-daqiqa 'Esrā'ēl 'em-Gebṣ wa-wahabomu ḥegga, wa-zakama ḍēwawomu la-daqiqa 'Esrā'ēl xaba hagara Bābilon, wa-'agbe'omu xaba hagara 'Iyarusālēm, wa-zakama tasabbe'a[12] 'Egzi'ena 'Iyasus Kerestos (lotu sebḥat), zakama[13] tanabbayu nabiyāt ba'enta meṣ'atu.

Wa-'emze waraqa merāqa westa ṣebur, wa-gabra diba[14] 'edawihu za-we'etu safāy, wa-tafawwasa sobēhā.[15] Wa-kona semu la-safāy 'Anyānos. Wa-wasado la-Qeddus Mārqos xaba bētu, wa-'abṣeḥa lotu waldo wa-zamado, wa-gaššaṣomu la-k^{w}ellomu Mārqos ḥawāreyā, wa-

---

9. An oath, taken here to be Gk. *heîs theós* one god.

10. *bāḥtit-* alone, sole, only; used appositionally, always with a pronominal suffix, e.g. *'ana bāḥtiteya* I alone; *rakabkewwo bāḥtito* I found him alone (or: him only). *'enta bāḥtit-* by oneself, alone; e.g. *nabara 'enta bāḥtitu* he sat by himself.

11. Here begins a rather inelegant series of clauses and phrases as the object of *yengero*.

12. Dt *tasabbe'a* to become man, be incarnate. A denominative verb from *sab'*. The verbal noun is *tesbe't* incarnation.

13. *bakama* would perhaps be better here than *zakama*.

14. *gabra diba*: if the text is correct, this is probably to be taken as "applied (it) to." This verbal phrase also has the meaning "to deal with, dispose of, do with," as in *Menta 'egabber diba zentu newāy*? What shall I do with this vessel? *diba 'edawa* also means "through the agency of."

15. One expects *la-* instead of *za-* before *we'etu*. *sobēhā* adv. immediately, straightway.

maharomu, wa-'aṭmaqomu ṭemqata Kerestennā[16] ba-sema 'ab wa-wald wa-manfas qeddus.

Wa-soba bazxu mahāymenān 'ella 'amnu ba-'Egzi'ena 'Iyasus Kerestos (lotu sebḥat), wa-sam'u sab'a hagar zēnāhu la-Qeddus Mārqos, wa-tagābe'u, wa-faqadu kama yeqtelewwo. Wa-šēmo Qeddus Mārqos la-'Anyānos 'ēpis-qoposa wa-la-daqiqu qasāwesta wa-diyāqonāta. Wa-waḍ'a xaba hagara Barqā wa-xaba Xams 'Ahgur, wa-sabaka westētomu, wa-'aṣne'omu westa hāymānot rete't. Wa-nabara xabēhomu kel'ēta 'āmata, wa-šēma lomu 'ēpis-qoposāta wa-qasāwesta wa-diyāqonāta.

Wa-'emze tamayṭa xaba hagara 'Eskenderyā, wa-rakabomu la-mahāymenān ba-za-tawassaku wa-ḥanaṣu lomu[17] bēta Kerestiyān, za-'eweqt westa makāna 'aṣada 'alhemt xaba ṣenfa bāḥr. Wa-konu kaḥādeyān yaxaššešewwo la-Qeddus Mārqos ba-k^{w}ellu ṣāmā kama yeqtelewwo; wa-kona we'etu ba-k^{w}ellu gizē yeḥēwweṣo la-Xams 'Ahgur wa-yetmayyaṭ wa-yebawwe' westa hagara 'Eskenderyā ba-xebu'. Wa-ba-'aḥatti 'elat tamayṭa 'em-Xams 'Ahgur, wa-bo'a westa bēta Kerestiyān ba-Ba'āla Tenšā'ē,[18] 'ama 'ešrā wa-tasu' la-warxa Maggābit. Wa-k^{w}ellomu 'aḥzāb ya'awwedewwo, wa-bo'u kaḥādeyān westa bēta Kerestiyān, wa-rassayu 'aḥbāla westa kesādu la-Qeddus Mārqos, wa-saḥabewwo westa k^{w}ellu hagar, wa-'emuntu 'enza yebelu: "'Ādi nesḥabo la-dābēlā westa 'aṣada lāhm," Wa-mal'a damu la-Qeddus westa k^{w}ellu fenota hagar wa-'awdā wa-'aṣnāfihā.

Wa-soba kona lēlita, 'astar'aya[19] 'Egzi'ena 'Iyasus Kerestos (lotu sebḥat) ba-'ar'ayā za-kona botu mesla ḥawāreyāt, wa-wahabo salāma, wa-'aṣne'o, wa-takāyado, wa-yebēlo: "Nāhu 'anta konka

---

16. *Kerestennā* Christianity. Here virtually an adjective: "Christian baptism."

17. The *za- ... lomu* clause modifies *bēta Kerestiyān*.

18. *Ba'āla Tenšā'ē* the Feast of the Resurrection (Easter). Note the formation of *tenšā'ē*, a verbal noun of the (secondarily) quadriliteral verb *tanše'a*.

19. *'astar'aya* CGt to appear (unto: o.s. or *la-*). Translate the phrase beginning with *ba-'ar'ayā* as "in the form *('ar'ayā)* he had (when he was) with the apostles." Less likely: "in a vision in which he was with the apostles" (but apparently taken so by Dillmann s.v. *'ar'ayā* in his Glossary).

ʿerruya[20] mesla ḥawāreyāt ʾaxawika." Wa-tafaššeḥat nafsu wa-taḥašyat. Wa-ba-sānitā kāʿeba rassayu ʾaḥbāla westa kesādu wa-saḥabewwo westa k^wellā hagar. Ba-tafṣāmēta maʿālt maṭṭawa nafso. Wa-kaḥādeyān-sa ʾandadu ʾessāta ʿabiya, wa-wagaru šegāhu la-Qeddus westētu. Wa-ba-šemratu la-ʾEgziʾena ʾIyasus Kerestos (lotu sebḥat) kona ṣelmat wa-nafās q^warir; ḍaḥāy-ni sawwara berhāno, wa-kona mabraq wa-nag^wadg^{w}ād wa-zenām wa-ʾasḥatyā, ʾeska g^wayyu kaḥādeyān. Wa-maṣʾu sabʾ mahāymenān, wa-našʾu šegāhu la-Qeddus Mārqos ʾenza ṭeʿuy weʾetu wa-ʾi-baṣḥo wa-ʾi-ment-ni ʾem-musenā,[21] wa-ganazewwo ba-šannāy ʾalbās, wa-ʾanbarewwo westa makān xebuʾ.

Salām la-Mārqos la-Māryām ʾeg^{w}ālā,[22]
za-saḥabewwo ba-ʾaḥbāl westa ʿaṣada semʿ kama dābēlā;
ʾama ʾawʿeyoto faqadu la-ʾessāt ba-nabalbālā,[23]
la-zenām wa-ʾasḥatyā yāṭaffeʾo māʿbalā,
wa-mabraq-ni la-šegāhu kallalā.[24]

C. Dionysius, Patriarch of Alexandria

Ba-zāti ʿelat (ʾama ʿašur wa-šalus la-Maggābit) ʾaʿrafa ʾab qeddus Deyonāsyos[1] liqa pāppāsāt za-hagara ʾEskenderyā, wa-weʾetu

---

20. D *ʿarraya* (more rarely G *ʿaraya, yeʿri*) to be level, smooth; to be equal (to: *la-, mesla, kama*); to make equal, level; to share (acc. dir. obj.) equally. CD *ʾaʿarraya* to make (something: acc. dir. obj.) equal (to: *mesla*). Dt *taʿarraya* pass. of CD. *ʿerruy* (fem. *ʿerrit*) equal (to: *la-, mesla*), the same (as); *ʿerruya* = *ba-ʿerruy* equally, to the same extent. *ʿerreyennā/ʿerrinnā* vn. equality.

21. *musenā* corruption (physical or moral). *musun* corrupt, corrupted. The *ʾem-* is partitive: "nothing of corruption." Note the use of the negated perfect with *ʾenza*; cf. the remarks in §31.1.

22. Note the inverted order of the phrases *ʾeg^{w}ālā la-Māryām*, *nabalbālā la-ʾessāt*, *māʿbalā la-zenām*, *kallalā la-šegāhu*.

23. Q *ʾanbalbala* to flame. *nabalbāl* flame.

24. D *kallala* to crown (someone: acc. dir. obj.); fig. to surround like a crown. Dt *takallala* to be crowned (with: acc., e.g. *takallala kebra* he was crowned with glory; or *ba-*). *kellul* crowned (with: *ba-*). *kellālē* vn. crowning, coronation. *ʾaklil* (pl. *-āt*) crown, diadem (lit. and fig.)

1. Dionysius, Patriarch of Alexandria from c247-c265, a

'em x^{w}elqomu la-'abaw liqāna pāppāsāt ʿašartu wa-'arbāʿtu. La-zentu 'ab qeddus konu 'abawihu 'aramāweyāna wa-kaḥādeyāna; wa-we'etu tamehra temherta bezuxāta,'esma 'abuhu kona 'em-zamad kebur, wa-xallaya[2] lotu 'em-ne'su wa-maharo k^{w}ello ṭebaba wa-temherta, 'eska kona mamehhera la-ṭabibān 'aramāweyān.

'Enza we'etu yenabber ba-'aḥatti ʿelat, wa-nāhu 'aḥatti be'sit 'aragāyt Kerestiyānāwit xalafat qedmēhu, wa-meslēha 'aḥatti ṭerâz 'em-maṣḥafa Mal'ektu la-Pāwlos ḥawāreyā. Wa-tebēlo: "Tašāyaṭ 'emennēya." Wa-naš'ā la-ye'eti ṭerāz, wa-soba 'anbabā, rakaba westētā qāla nakira wa-'a'mero[3] madmema.[4] Wa-yebēlā: "Ba-mi-maṭan tešayyeṭā?"[5] Wa-tebēlo: "Ba-'aḥadu derhema warq." Wa-yebēlā: "Ḥuri wa-ḥeteti 'emma[6] terakkebi za-tarfa 'em-zentu maṣḥaf, wa-'amṣe'i lita." Wa-ḥorat wa-'amṣe'at lotu šalāsa ṭerāzāta kāle'āta, wa-wahabā 'arbāʿta derhema warq. Wa-soba 'anbabomu, rakabo la-maṣḥaf ḥeṣuṣa,[7]

---

disciple of Origen.

2. D *xallaya* to think, ponder, meditate (about: acc. dir. obj. or *ba'enta*); to think up, devise (acc. dir. obj.); to decide (to do: *kama* + subj.); to take thought of or notice of, to take care of, look after (someone: obj. suff. or *ba'enta*, *la-*). CD *'axallaya* to cause (someone: obj. suff.) to think about or decide to do. Dt *taxallaya* to be thought of, conceived. *xellinnā* mind, thought, intellect; product of thought, idea; process of thought, thinking, cogitation; proposal, advice, opinion.

3. The text has *'a'maro*. *'a'mero madmema* astonishing knowledge.

4. C *'admama* (rare) to astonish, stupify. Gt *tadamma* = Dt *tadammama* to be astonished, amazed, stupified. *madmem* marvelous, astonishing; n. miracle, marvel.

5. One expects *tešayyeteyyā* since he is addressing a woman. *Ba-mi-maṭan* for how much?

6. *'emma, la'emma* conj. if, whether.

7. G *ḥaṣṣa/ḥaṣaṣa (yeḥṣeṣ)* to decrease (in quantity), become inferior (in quality), be deficient; to be subtracted. CG *'aḥṣaṣa* to diminish, make less, worse, inferior; to be deficient (in doing: inf.; in: acc. or *'emenna*); to subtract, cause a loss of (acc. dir. obj., with obj. suff. of person so affected). *ḥeṣuṣ* minor, less, small, inferior, deficient, lacking. *ḥeṣaṣ/ḥeṣṣat* vn. decrease, diminution,

wa-yebēlā: "Ḥuri wa-xešeši 'em-zentu maṣḥaf za-tarfa." Wa-tebēlo: "'Ane-sa rakabku 'ellonta ba-westa maṣḥaf; wa-la'emma faqadka maṣḥafa Pāwlos ḥawāreyā feṣṣuma, xešeš 'em-xaba sab'a zāti bēta Kerestiyān." Wa-yebēlā: "La'emma xašaškewwo 'emennēhomu, yehubuni-hu kiyāhu?" Wa-tebēlo: "'Ewwa."[8] Wa-ḥora wa-xašaša maṣḥafa Pāwlos xaba 'aḥadu 'em-kāhenāt, wa-wahabo kiyāhu. Wa-'anbabo wa-'aṣne'o ba-lebbu, wa-kona yānabbebā gahhāda[9] za'enbala maṣḥaf, wa-'amna ba-'Egzi'ena 'Iyasus Kerestos (lotu sebḥat).

Wa-'emze ḥora xaba Qeddus Demēṭros[10] liqa pāppāsāt, wa-sa'alo kama yāṭmeqo ṭemqata Kerestennā. Wa-maharo kʷello za-faqada, wa-'aṭmaqo. Wa-kona feṣṣuma ba-'a'mero ḥegga bēta Kerestiyān; wa-rassayo 'Abbā[11] Demēṭros mamehhera ba-weluda bēta Kerestiyān. Wa-soba tašayma 'Abbā Yārōkelā[12] liqa pāppāsāt, rassayo la-zentu 'Abbā heyyantēhu ba-westa hagara 'Eskenderyā kama yegbar fetḥa mā'kala mahāymenān, wa-'abeḥo kʷello gebra peppesennā[13] kama yemaggeb.[14] Wa-soba 'a'rafa 'Abbā Yārōkelā, tasanā'awu kʷellomu 'aḥzāb, wa-šēmewwo la-zentu 'ab qeddus 'Abbā Diyonāsyos liqa pāppāsāt lā'la hagara 'Eskenderyā. Wa-'aqaba mar'ēto[15] ba-šannāy ta'aqebo.

---

deficiency, lack.

8. *'ewwa* yes.

9. C *'aghada* to make public, show openly, make manifest; to act or speak openly. Gt *tagehda* passive. *gehud* (f. *gehedd*) clear, manifest, open, obvious. *gahhād* adj. idem; *gahhāda* adv. openly, manifestly, publicly. *gehdat* vn. openness.

10. *Demēṭros* Demetrius, patriarch of Alexandria c.189-c.231.

11. *'Abbā* an honorific title applied to venerated men of any station in religious life.

12. *Yārōkelā* Heraclas, Patriarch of Alexandria c.231-c.247.

13. *peppesennā* the office of *pāppās* (bishop): episcopacy, see.

14. D *maggaba* to administrate, be in charge of (acc. dir. obj.); to surround and protect (with: *ba-*). CD *'amaggaba* to place (someone: acc. dir. obj.) in charge of (acc. dir. obj. or *lā'la*, *diba*, *ba-*). Dt *tamaggaba* to be placed in charge of. *meggeb/megb* office, post, duty, ministry. *maggābi* (pl. *-eyān*, *maggabt*) administrator, guardian; a general designation for various types of rulers: prefect, proconsul, satrap, governor.

15. *re'ya* G (imperf. *yere''i*, *yerē''i*; subj. *yer'ay*; imptv.

Wa-baṣḥa mendābē ʻabiy wa-ḥazan ba-mawāʻela šimatu, ʼesma weʼetu tašayma ba-mawāʻela mangeštu la-Fileppos,[16] wa-kona yāfaqqeromu Fileppos la-Kerestiyān, wa-soba tanšeʼa lāʻlēhu Dākēwos[17] wa-taṣābeʼo wa-moʼo wa-qatalo la-Fileppos, wa-nagša heyyantēhu. Wa-ʼamandabomu la-mahāymenān mendābē ʻabiya, wa-qatalomu la-samāʻtāt bezuxān ʼemenna liqāna pāppāsāt wa-ʼēpis qoposāt wa-kāleʼān ʼem-meʼmanān. Wa-g^{w}ayyu ʼemennēhu bezuxān sabʼ baʼenta dengāḍē[18] wa-ferhat, wa-boʼu westa gadāmāt, wa-motu bezuxān ʼemennēhomu ba-heyya. Wa-ʼaxazewwo ḥarrāhu la-zentu ʼab, wa-ʼaxsarewwo.[19]

Wa-ʼemze ṭafʼa weʼetu kaḥādi, wa-nagša heyyantēhu Gerlāwos.[20] Wa-hadʼa mendābē ʼem-weluda ṭemqat ba-mawāʻelihu la-zentu neguš. Wa-soba mota, wa-nagša heyyantēhu Wālāryos,[21] ʼanšeʼa kāʻeba mendābē lāʻla bēta Kerestiyān. Wa-ʼaxazewwo mak^{w}ānentihu la-zentu ʼab qeddus, wa-moqeḥewwo wa-k^{w}annanewwo k^{w}ennanē ʻabiya ʻeṣuba fadfāda. Wa-ʼemze xašašu ʼemennēhu kama yesged la-ṭāʻot, wa-ʼawšeʼomu wa-yebēlomu: "Neḥna-sa ʼi-nesagged la-ṭāʻotāt rekusān zaʼenbala la-ʼEgziʼabḥēr ʼAb wa-Waldu ʼIyasus Kerestos (lotu sebḥat) wa-la-Manfas Qeddus." Wa-tameʻʻa lāʻlēhu neguš fadfāda, wa-qatala ba-qedmēhu bezuxāna sabʼa kama yāfreho, wa-qeddus-sa ʼi-farha ʼemennēhu. Wa-sadado, wa-nabara

---

raʻay) to pasture, tend (herds, flocks); to graze (subject: flocks). Gt *tareʻya* to graze, be tended. *marʻēt* (pl. *-āt*, *marāʻey*) cattle, flock, herd; pasture. *marʻay* idem. *merʻāy* a pasture.

16. *Fileppos* Philip (the Arab), emperor of Rome 244-249.

17. *Dākēwos* Decius, emperor of Rome 249-251, known primarily for his systematic persecution of the Christians.

18. Q *dangaḍa* to be astonished, stupified, amazed, disturbed in mind, terrified. CQ *ʼadangaḍa* to astonish etc. *denguḍ* va. astonished etc. *dengāḍē* vn. astonishment etc. *madangeḍ* adj. astonishing etc.

19. C *ʼaxsara* (text has *xasara*, an error). G *xasra (yexsar)* to be in bad straits, wretched, miserable; to suffer loss, be reduced to poverty; to be dishonored, vilified, despised. CG *ʼaxsara* to cause/inflict/afflict (with) any of the preceding states (with acc. dir. obj. of person). *xesur* wretched, impoverished, afflicted, vile, despised. *xasār* (Vocab. 22).

20. *Gerlāwos* Gallus, successor of Decius; ruled 251-253.

21. *Wālāryos* Valerianus, successor of Gallus; ruled 253-260.

westa seddat bezuxa mawā'ela. Wa-'emdexra-ze mēṭo 'em-seddat wa-yebēlo: "Samā'ku ba'enti'aka kama 'anta teqēddes ba-xebu' ba-bāḥtiteka." Wa-'awše'a qeddus wa-yebēlo: "Neḥna-sa 'i-naxaddeg ṣalotātina wa-qeddāseyātina 'i-ba-ma'ālt wa-'i-ba-lēlit." Wa-'emze tamayṭa qeddus xaba ḥezb 'ella meslēhu wa-yebēlomu: "Ḥuru wa-qaddesu. La'emma konku reḥuqa 'emennēkemu ba-šegā, 'ane-sa 'ehēllu meslēkemu ba-Manfas Qeddus." Wa-tame''a mak^{w}annen, wa-mēṭo westa seddat.

Wa-tanše'a lā'la zentu kaḥādi te'yent[22] 'em-sab'a barbār,[23] wa-farha 'emennēhomu, wa-qatalewwo; wa-maṭṭawa la-waldu mangešto. Wa-kona waldu ṭabiba wa-mā'mera fadfāda, wa-fatḥomu la-k^{w}ellomu mahāymenān 'ella moqeḥomu 'abuhu, wa-mēṭomu la-'ella westa seddat. Wa-ṣaḥafa lomu maṣḥafa mal'ekt xaba liqa pāppāsāt wa-yebēlomu: "'I-tefrehu-'a[24] wa-'i-tedangeḍu-'a. 'Arxewu-'a 'abyāta Kerestiyānā-tikemu[25] wa-yāxtewu[26] wa-'i-yebaṣṣeḥ lā'lēkemu wa-'i-ment-ni 'em-'ekuy-'a. Wa-ḥaywa zentu 'ab za-tarfa 'em-mawā'elihu ba-hed'at wa-ba-salām.

Wa-'astar'aya ba-mawā'elihu la-zentu gaṣṣāt[27] bezuxāt ba'enta hāymānot. 'Em-we'etu 'esma[28] sab' 'astar'ayu ba-beḥēra 'Arabyā; seḥtu wa-yebēlu ba-'ekaya megbāromu 'esma nafs temawwet mesla šegā wa-'emze tetnaššā' meslēhu ba-'elata tenšā'ē. Wa-'astagābe'a[29]

---

22. *te'yent* (pl. *-āt, ta'ayen*) army, host; camp, encampment; tent(s); gathering, congregation, assembly. Technically the verbal noun of *ta'ayyana*, originally to dig wells *('a'yent)* in locating a camp; hence: to set up camp, to camp; with *lā'la*: to besiege.

23. *sab'a barbār* barbarians, plunderers, robbers.

24. The suffix *-'a* is attached to indicate quoted material. It may, as here, be joined to the first few words of a quotation and to the last, or, more rarely, to every single word of the text.

25. Note the illogical position of the suffix *-kemu*.

26. G *xatawa* to burn, be alight. CG *'axtawa* to light (a lamp); to burn, emit light. *maxtot* (pl. *maxātew*) lamp.

27. *gaṣṣ* is used here almost in the sense of "heresy," i.e. alternate "aspects or forms" of the faith.

28. *'Em-we'etu 'esma*: an idiom: "An example of this is that..."

29. CGlt *'astagābe'a* to gather, assemble (trans.); *'astagābe'a māxbara lā'la* to convene an ecclesiastical council against.

lā'lēhomu māxbara, wa-'awgazomu[30] wa-mataromu. Wa-kāle'ān kā'eba konu ba-ge'za 'Argēnes[31] wa-Sabalyos.

Wa-soba lehqa zentu 'ab, 'astar'aya Pāwlos Sāmisāṭi,[32] liqa pāppāsāt za-hagara 'Anṣokiyā,[33] za-keḥdo la-wald. Wa-'astagābe'a lā'lēhu māxbara, wa-'awgazo wa-mataro. 'I-baṣḥa meslēhomu zentu 'ab ba'enta reš'ennāhu[34] wa-fannawa mal'ekta 'enta mele't 'em-k^{w}ellu ṭebab wa-ṣagā, wa-kašata westētā hāymānota rete'ta. Wa-soba baṣḥa xaba reš'ennā šannāy, falasa xaba 'Egzi'abḥēr za-'afqaro 'emdexra nabara diba manbara Mārqos[35] wangēlāwi 'ašarta wa-samānta 'āmata.

Salām la-Deyonāsyos mamehhera ṭabibān k^{w}ellu,
'em-seḥtat za-mēṭo la-Pāwlos mal'ekta qālu.
Dexra[36] rakabo mendābē wa-seddat ba-mawā'elu,
falasa yom[37] hagarita berhān za-lā'lu[38]
mesla qeddusān xebura yahallu.

---

30. C *'awgaza* to excommunicate, anathematize, curse. Glt *tawāgaza* to alienate oneself from (acc. dir. obj.). *weguz* excommunicated, cursed. *wegzat/gezat* vn. excommunication.

31. *ba-ge'za 'Argēnes wa-Sabalyos*: "in accord with the thinking of Origen (184-254) and Sabellius (fl. 220)."

32. *Pāwlos Sāmisāṭi* Paul of Samosata, heretical bishop of Antioch 260-268.

33. *'Anṣokiyā* Antioch.

34. G *raš'a (yeršā')* to grow old. CG *'arše'a* caus. *reš'* = *reš'ennā* = *reš'ān* old age.

35. *manbara Mārqos*, a designation of the See of Alexandria, founded traditionally by St. Mark.

36. *dexra* is most simply taken here as a conjunction, = *'emdexra*.

37. *yom* adv. today, on this day; (here) on this day of the year.

38. *lā'lu* adv. above; freq. in the adj. phrase *za-lā'lu* upper, esp. (as here) in the sense "celestial, heavenly." *'em-X wa-lā'lu 'emennēhu* from X onward (in enumerations). *ba-lā'lu* above, on high. *'em-lā'lu* from above, from on high.

D. Macarius the Elder[1]

'Ama 'ešrā wa-sabu' la-Maggābit 'a'rafa 'ab qeddus wa-beṣu',[2] māxtota gadām, 'aba k^{w}ellomu manakosāt[3] za-gadāma 'Asqēṭes,[4] 'Abbā Maqāres za-ya'abbi. Zentu qeddus kona 'em-sab'a hagara Sasuwir[5] 'em-dawala[6] Manuf[7] 'em-dabuba[8] Gebṣ. Wa-konu 'abawihu xērāna wa-ṣādeqāna, wa-semu la-'abuhu 'Abrehām, wa-semā la-'emmu Sārā, wa-ye'eti kama Sārā wa-'Ēlesābēṭ taḥawwer ba-te'zāza 'Egzi'abḥēr ba-teḥḥetennā.[9] Wa-kona 'abuhu kāhena wa-kebura, wa-yetla''ak westa bēta maqdas watra ba-fariha 'Egzi'abḥēr ba-neṣḥennā[10] wa-qeddesennā, wa-bāraka 'Egzi'abḥēr lā'lēhomu wa-'ab'alomu ba-k^{w}ellu megbāromu. Wa-konu yehubewwomu meṣwāta[11] k^{w}ello 'amira la-naddāyān, wa-yemeḥḥerewwomu

---

1. Macarius the Elder (the Great), c. 300 - c. 391, a disciple of St. Anthony and one of the most famous of the desert fathers.

2. *beṣu'/beḍu'* fortunate, blessed; vowed, dedicated. G *baḍ'a (yebḍā')* to vow. CG *'abḍe'a* to make or declare blessed; to obtain a vow; to become happy, blessed. *beḍ'at* a vow. *beḍu'āwi* beatific, blessed. *beḍ'ān* beatification, blessedness.

3. *manakos* (pl. *-āt*) monk, nun. Q *mank^{w}asa* to become a monk, live a monastic life. *manakosāyt* nun. *menk^{w}esennā* monasticism.

4. *'Asqēṭes* Scetis, Scete: the Lower Egyptian center of monasticism, in the Western Delta.

5. *Sasuwir* a town of Lower Egypt.

6. *dawal* (pl. *'adwāl*) region, district, territory.

7. *Manuf* Memphis.

8. *dabub* the north.

9. *teḥḥetennā* humility, humbleness. Dt *tateḥḥeta* to humble one's self, be submissive, to act or be inferior, lowly. *teḥḥut* humble, modest, obedient; lowly, ignoble. The root is also attested in the G system as G *teḥta* to be humble, CG *'atḥata* to make humble, to subject. Note the preposition *tāḥta*, which is also an adverb "below, from below," and the noun *matḥett* (form *maqtelt*) lower or inferior part, most frequently used in the accusative as a preposition = *tāḥta*.

10. *neṣḥennā* purity, chastity, innocence. G *naṣḥa (yenṣāḥ)* to be pure, clean. CG *'anṣeḥa* to purify, cleanse; to regard as pure. *neṣuḥ* pure, clean; innocent, uncorrupted, sincere. *neṣḥ* purification, etc. *manṣeḥi* one who purifies.

la-k^{w}ellomu sabʼ, wa-yetgādalu[12] watra ba-ṣom wa-ṣalot; wa-ʼi-kona lomu wald. Wa-ʼastarʼaya lotu ʼAbrehām ba-rāʼy ʼem-xaba ʼEgziʼabḥēr, wa-ʼaṭayyaqo kama ʼEgziʼabḥēr hallo kama yahabo walda za-yekawwen zekru westa k^{w}ellu ʼaṣnāfa medr wa-yewalled weluda manfasāweyāna. Wa-wahabo ʼEgziʼabḥēr zanta qeddusa Maqāres-hā, za-ba-terg^{w}āmēhu la-semu qeddus beṣuʻ.

Wa-kona ṣagā ʼEgziʼabḥēr lāʻlēhu ʼem-neʼsu wa-yetʼēzzaz la-ʼabawihu. Wa-soba lehqa ba-ʼakālu,[13] faqadu ʼabawihu kama yāstawāsebewwo[14] lotu beʼsita, wa-kona ʼi-yefaqqed zanta gebra, wa-ʼagabbarewwo kama yegbar faqādomu, wa-taʼazzaza lomu, wa-ʼastawāsabewwo zaʼenbala faqādu. Wa-soba boʼa westa ṣerḥu,[15] rassaya reʼso kama za-yedawwi, wa-nabara bezuxa ʻelatāta kama-ze. Wa-ʼemdexra-ze xašaša ʼabuhu wa-yebēlo, "Xedegani ʼeḥur xaba gadām kama ʼeṭʻay nestita ʼem-zentu dawē." Wa-kona k^{w}ello ʼamira yeseʼʼelo la-ʼEgziʼabḥēr ba-gizē ṣalotu kama yemreḥo westa gabira šemratu.

Wa-ʼemdexra-ze ḥora xaba gadāma ʼAsqēṭes. Wa-soba kona westa gadām, reʼya rāʼya zakama Kirubēl[16] za-sedestu kenafihu[17], ʼaxaza ba-ʼedēhu wa-ʼaʻrago malʻelta[18] reʼsa dabr, wa-ʼarʼayo k^{w}ello gadāma,

---

11. *meṣwāt* act of charity, benefaction. Q *maṣwata* to give alms, practice charity. Qt *tamaṣwata* to receive alms.

12. Glt *tagādala* to struggle, contend (esp. in religious sense of struggling against temptation). *gadl* (pl. *-āt*) a struggle, contest (esp. of saints and martyrs); title of works about the lives of saints and ascetics. *mastagādel* a contender, "soldier of Christ."

13. *ʼakāl* (pl. *-āt*) body, limbs, stature; substance, hypostasis, person. *lehqa ba-ʼakālu* he reached maturity.

14. CG *ʼawsaba* to marry (subj. man; obj. woman). CGlt *ʼastawāsaba* to give someone (a.d.o.) in marriage, to marry off. *sabsāb* marriage.

15. *ṣerḥ* (pl. *ʼaṣrāḥ*, *ʼaṣreḥt*) room, chamber, house; bedroom.

16. *kirubēl* a cherub, the cherubim. *kirub* idem. *kirubāwi* cherubic.

17. *kenf* (pl. *kenaf*, *ʼaknāf*) wing.

18. *malʻelt* upper part or surface of anything; usually *malʻelta* prep. above. G *laʻala* to be high, superior. CG *ʼalʻala* = CD *ʼalaʻʻala* to raise up, elevate, exalt. Dt *talaʻʻala/taleʻʻela* pass. of CD; to be higher (than: *ʼemenna*). *leʻul/leʻʻul* high, lofty,

mešrāqā wa-meʿrābā wa-nuxā wa-gedmā,[19] wa-yebēlo: "Nāhu wahabaka ʾEgziʾabḥēr zanta gadāma resta laka wa-la-weludeka." Wa-soba tamayṭa ʾem-westa gadām, wa-rakabā la-yeʾeti walatt ʾenza tedawwi. Wa-ʾemze ʾaʿrafat ʾenza hallawat ba-dengelennā, wa-ʾaʾkʷato[20] la-ʾEgziʾena ʾIyasus Kerestos (lotu sebḥat) bezuxa. Wa-ʾemdexra xedāṭ[21] mawāʿel kāʿeba ʾaʿrafu ʾabawihu, wa-wahaba kʷello newāya za-xadagewwo la-naddāyān wa-la-meskinān[22] wa-la-ṣennusān.[23] Wa-sabʾa Sāsuwir-sa hagaru soba reʾyu ṣedqo wa-neṣḥennāhu la-qeddus ʾAbbā Maqāres, šēmewwo qasisa lāʿlēhomu, wa-ḥanaṣu lotu makāna ba-ʾafʾa hagar, wa-konu sabʾa hagar yaḥawweru xabēhu wa-yetmēṭṭawu mesṭirāta qeddesāt ʾemennēhu.

Wa-hallawat ʾaḥatti walatt ba-yeʾeti hagar dengel, wa-zammawat[24] mesla ʾaḥadu warēzā, wa-ḍansat, wa-yebēlā weʾetu warēzā, "Soba taseʾʾelaki ʾabuki mannu za-ʾamāsana dengelennāki, baliyo ʾesma weʾetu qasis bāḥtāwi[25] ʾamāsana dengelennāya."[26] Wa-soba ʾaʾmara

---

superior, exalted.

19. *mešrāq* (pl. *-āt*) the east. G *šaraqa (yešreq)* to rise, shine (of the sun). CG *ʾašraqa* to cause or order to rise (i.e. the sun). *šarq (ʾašrāq)* rising (of heavenly bodies); the east; the new moon, the calends. *šerqat* vn. rising, appearance. *šaraqāwi* eastern. *gedm* (pl. *gedam*) width, breadth.

20. CG *ʾaʾkʷata* to praise. Gt *taʾakʷta* pass. *ʾekut* praised, lauded. *ʾaʾkʷāti* one who renders praise or thanks. *ʾaʾkʷatēt* vn. praise, glory, thanksgiving.

21. *xedāṭ* n. a little, a small amount; adj. (pl. *-āt*) few.

22. *meskin* a pauper, poor person. *meskinat* poverty.

23. *ṣennus* poor, indigent, wretched. Dt *taṣannasa* to be impoverished, reduced to poverty. *taṣnās* vn. poverty, wretchedness; lack, deficiency.

24. D *zammawa* to commit adultery; to have illicit intercourse (with: *mesla* or a.d.o.). CD *ʾazammawa* caus. *zemmut* n. adultery, harlotry. *zammā* whore, adulterer, fornicator. *zammāwi* idem. These terms are applied to both males and females.

25. *bāḥtāwi* anchorite, one who lives in solitude. Qt *tabāḥtawa* to take up a life of solitude. *beḥtew* adj. alone, solitary. *beḥtewennā* anchoritism.

26. Note the use of *ʾesma* to introduce direct quotation, as

'abuhā kama ye'eti ḍansat, wa-tase''elā 'abuhā, wa-yebēlā, "Mannu za-gabra beki zanta xafrata?" Wa-'awše'ato wa-tebēlo, "'Aḥatta ʻelata ḥorku xaba we'etu bāḥtāwi qasis za-semu Maqāres. Naš'ani ba-xayl[27] wa-sakaba meslēya, wa-ḍanasku 'emennēhu." Wa-soba samʻu 'abawihā zanta nagara, wa-tameʻʻu fadfāda, wa-ḥoru xaba qeddus Maqāres, meslēhomu bezux sab'. Wa-'awḍe'ewwo la-qeddus 'em-ba'atu, wa-we'etu 'i-ya'mara menta za-kona, wa-zabaṭewwo zebṭata ʻabiya wa-māḥmema, 'eska qarba la-mawit. Wa-kona qeddus yessē''alomu 'enza yebelomu, "Ment ye'eti xaṭi'ateya 'esma 'antemu-ni tezabbeṭuni za'enbala meḥrat?" Wa-'emze 'asaru westa kesādu ḥabla, wa-dibēhu saqalu galʻāta[28] za-'aṣlamewwomu ba-feḥm,[29] wa-konu yeseḥḥebewwo lafē[30] wa-lafē kama 'abd[31] wa-yekēlleḥu[32] 'enza yebelu, "Zentu za-'amāsana dengelennāhā la-walattena."

Wa-ba-we'etu gizē 'astar'ayu malā'ekt ba-'amsāla sab', wa-yebēlewwomu la-'ellu 'ekuyān, "Ment za-gabra zentu mastagādel?" Wa-nagarewwomu za-gabra[33] lāʻla ye'eti. Wa-yebēlewwomu 'emuntu malā'ekt, "Zentu nagar ḥassat[34] we'etu, 'esma neḥna nā'ammero la-zentu be'si

---

indicated by the 1st pers. suffix on *dengelennāya*.

27. *xayl* (pl. *-āt*) strength, power, might; army, troops; *ba-xayl* by force. G *xēla* to become well, strong. D *xayyala* to be strong, etc.; to prevail over, be superior to (a.d.o.). CD *'axayyala* to make strong, etc. Dt *taxayyala* to be strengthened, strong; to prevail, dominate; to act with force (good or bad sense) against. *xeyyul* adj. strong, etc. *xayyāl* idem.

28. *galʻ* (pl. *-āt, 'agleʻt*) a pot.

29. *feḥm* (pl. *'afḥām*) carbon, coal.

30. *lafē wa-lafē* adv. this way and that, back and forth. *mangala lafē wa-lafē* idem. *māʻdota lafē* adv. on the other side, opposite.

31. *'abd* (pl. *-ān*) a fool; adj. foolish, stupid, unskilled; mad, insane. G *'abda (ye'bad)* to be mad, rage. CG *'a'bada* caus. CGt *'astā'bada* to regard as or treat as a fool; to despise, ridicule.

32. D *kalleḥa* to cry out, shout. *kellāḥ* a cry, shout.

33. "They told them what he had done to that (girl)."

34. *ḥassat* a lie, falsehood. D *ḥassawa* to lie, be deceitful, false. CD *'aḥassawa* to accuse of falsehood. Dt *taḥassawa* to be accused of falsehood, found out a liar. *ḥessew* false, deceitful.

'em-ne'su 'eska zāti ʿelat, wa-we'etu xēr wa-ṣādeq." Wa-qarbu 'emuntu malā'ekt xabēhu, wa-fatḥewwo 'em-mā'saru, wa-gadafu 'em-*lāʿlēhu* 'agleʿta. Wa-yebēlewwomu 'emuntu 'ekuyān, "'I-naxaddego yeḥur 'eska yehubana za-yetḥabbayo."[35] Wa-maṣ'a 'aḥadu be'si za-kona yešayyeṭ gebra 'edawihu,[36] wa-taḥabayo 'emennēhomu kama yahabā la-ye'eti walatt sisāyā 'eska 'ama tewalled. Wa-sadadewwo, wa-ḥora xaba ba'atu, wa-kona yegēššeṣā la-nafsu, wa-yebel, "'Ō-Maqāres, ye'zē nāhu kona laka be'sit wa-daqiq. Yedallewaka kama tetgabbar lēlita wa-maʿālta ba'enta sisāyeka wa-sisāyomu la-weludeka wa-la-be'siteka." Wa-kona watra yegabber 'asfarēdāta[37] wa-yehubo la-we'etu be'si 'ex^{w} fequr za-kona yetla''ako, wa-yešayyeṭomu wa-yehubā la-ye'eti be'sit sisāyā. Wa-nabara 'enza yegabber kama-ze 'eska qarba gizē walidotā la-ye'eti be'sit.

Wa-soba qarba ʿelata walidotā, wa-ʿaṣabā fadfāda, wa-nabarat westa ʿabiy mendābē 'arbeʿā maʿālta wa-'arbeʿā lēlita, wa-'alṣaqat[38] la-mawit, wa-'i-waladat. Wa-tebēlā 'emmā, "Ment za-kona 'emennēki[39] 'esma nāhu ye'zē temawweti?" Wa-tebēlā la-'emmā, "'Ewwa 'ane-sa 'i-yedallewani *walid*, 'esma zammawku 'ana mesla 'egalē[40] warēzā, wa-tanāgarku ba-nagara ḥassat lāʿla gabra 'Egzi'abḥēr, qasis qeddus 'Abbā Maqāres bāḥtāwi." Wa-soba samʿu 'abawihā zanta, ḥazanu fadfāda, wa-tagābe'u k^{w}ellomu mesla sab'a hagar, wa-tamākaru kama yeḥuru xaba qeddus wa-yes'alewwo kama yexdeg lomu 'abbasāhomu[41] za-gabru lāʿlēhu.

ḥassāwi a liar.

35. Gt *taḥabaya* to assume responsibility for (obj. suff.), stand as a guarantor for (someone: obj. suff.) to (a third party: *'emenna*).

36. I.e. his handicrafts.

37. *'asfarēdā* (pl. *-t*) basket.

38. CG *'alṣaqa* to be near, approach; with *la-* + inf.: to be about to. Glt *talāṣaqa* to stick together, be connected. CGlt *'astalāṣaqa* to glue together, join, connect. *leṣuq* joined, adhering; connected, continuous.

39. I.e. "What have you done so that ...?" Lit.: "What has come about through you ...?"

40. *'egalē* indef. pron./adj. a certain, a certain person, such-and-such (a person).

41. D *'abbasa* to sin, commit a crime. *'ebbus* wicked, criminal.

Wa-soba sam'a qeddus 'Abbā Maqāres kama sab'a hagar yefaqqedu yebṣeḥu xabēhu wa-yāstasreyu[42] 'emennēhu, wa-tazakkara we'eta rā'ya za-re'ya ba-gadām, qaddasa q^{w}erbāna, wa-tamaṭṭawu mesṭirāta qeddesāt.

Wa-'astar'aya lotu we'etu kirubēl za-sedestu kenafihu, wa-'axazo ba-'edēhu wa-marḥo 'eska 'abṣeḥo gadāma 'Asqēṭes, za-ba-terg^{w}āmēhu "Madālewa[43] 'albāb." Wa-yebēlo qeddus 'Abbā Maqāres la-we'etu kirubēl, "Ō-'egzi'eya, wassen[44] lita makāna za-'axadder westētu." Wa-'awše'a kirubēl wa-yebēlo, "'Ane-sa 'i-y̌ewēssen laka makāna, kama 'i-teḍā' 'em-makān za-'ewēssen laka wa-'i-tet'adaw te'zāza 'Egzi'abḥēr. Nāhu zentu gadām k^{w}ellantāhu[45] laka, wa-xaba za-faqadka ḥur wa-nebar botu." Wa-xadara qeddus Maqāres westa wessāṭē[46] gadām, makāna dabromu[47] la-qeddusān Rōmāweyān Maksimos[48] wa-Damātēwos. Wa-soba baṣḥa xabēhu, xadaru ba-qerub 'emennēhu; wa-'emdexra 'eraftomu 'azzazo mal'aka 'Egzi'abḥēr kama yeḥur wa-yexder westa makān za-we'etu dabra *zi'ahomu*. Wa-yebēlo mal'ak 'esma, "Zentu makān yessammay ba-semomu la-weludeka Maksimos wa-Damātēwos." Wa-we'etu 'eska zāti 'elat yessammay Dabra Bermos,[49] za-ba-terg^{w}āmēhu "Dabra Rom."

Wa-qeddus-sa 'Abbā Maqāres gabra lotu ba'ata ba-westētu, wa-nabara, wa-tagādala tagādelo 'abiya ba-ṣom wa-ba-ṣalot wa-sagid wa-tegāh[50] za'enbala ḍer'at.[51] Wa-konu yāstare''eyu lotu sayṭānāt[52]

'abbāsi sinner, criminal. *'abbasā* sin, crime, guilt. *ma'abbes* = *'abbāsi*.

42. G *saraya (yesray, yesri)* to forgive, excuse, pardon. Gt *tasarya* pass. CGt *'astasraya* to seek pardon (from: *'emenna*).

43. *madālew* scales, balance. The phrase *madālewa 'albāb* is an interpretation of the Coptic form of the name of Scete, *ši-hēt*.

44. D *wassana* to delimit, mark off, define. Dt *tawassana* pass. *wassan* boundary, limit.

45. *k^{w}ellantā-* (with pron. suff.) all of, the whole of.

46. *wessāṭē* interior, middle.

47. *dabr* also has the meaning "monastery."

48. *Maksimos wa-Damātēwos* Maximus and Dometius, semi-legendary brother saints associated with St. Macarius.

49. *Bermos* The Monastery of Baramus in the Wadi Natrun, with which Maximus and Dometius are traditionally associated.

50. G *tagha* to be wakeful, watchful, vigilant, attentive.

gahhāda wa-yeṣabbe'ewwo ba-lēlit. Wa-'emdexra šalastu ma'ālt 'enza yetgādal wa-yeṣāmu wa-yāmanaddebewwo sayṭānāt wa-'i-rakaba[53] 'erafta, xallaya wa-yebē ba-lebbu, "'Enza halloku westa 'ālam,[54] samā'ku zēnāhu la-qeddus 'Abbā 'Enṭonyos.[55] 'Etnaššā' wa-'aḥawwer xabēhu kama yemharani wa-yemreḥani fenota menk^{w}esennā, wa-yahabani 'a'mero wa-lebbunnā[56] kama 'elabbu mekromu la-sayṭānāt rekusān." Wa-tanše'a wa-ṣallaya, wa-ḥora westa gadām mangala mešrāq 'eska baṣḥa xaba 'aragāwi qeddus 'Abbā 'Enṭonyos. Wa-soba re'yo 'em-reḥuq, wa-yebēlo, "Zentu *'Esrā'ēlāwi* za-'albo ṣelḥut."[57] Wa-tawakfo[58] wa-ta'āmexo[59] ba-'abiy feššeḥā wa-kašata lotu xellinnāhu ba-feššeḥā kama wald mesla

---

teguh wakeful, etc. *tegāh* vigilance, etc. Note that not sleeping was considered an important ascetic accomplishment.

51. CG *'aḍre'a* (intrans.) to cease, stop, be at rest; (trans.) to bring to a stop. Gt *taḍar'a* = CG intrans. *ḍeru'* inert, at rest, brought to a stop. *ḍer'at* cessation, rest; *za'enbala ḍer'at* without ceasing, without interruptions.

52. *sayṭān* (pl. *-āt*) Satan; a devil, demon, adversary.

53. *wa-'i-rakaba.* Note the use of the negative perfect after *'enza* as the counterpart of the perfective active participle, which is not negated: "and not having found."

54. *'ālam* here and frequently in the sense of "the world outside the religious community, the secular world."

55. *'Enṭonyos* St. Anthony, the leading light of the early desert community.

56. D *labbawa* to comprehend, understand; to be intelligent; to be aware, conscious (of: *'emenna*). CD *'alabbawa* caus. Dt *talabbawa* to be comprehended, understood. *lebbew* intelligent, comprehending. *labbāwi* idem. *lebbāwē* mind, intellect. *lebbunnā* idem; skill, cleverness.

57. Q *ṣalḥawa* to act treacherously. *ṣelḥew* treacherous, guileful. *ṣelḥut* treachery, guile, malice.

58. Gt *tawakfa* = Dt *tawakkafa* to accept, receive, take unto one's self; also passive of same. *wekuf/wekkuf* accepted, acceptable, agreeable, pleasant.

59. D *'ammexa* to greet. Glt *ta'āmexa* to greet one another, to kiss (in greeting). *'ammexā* a greeting, kiss; a gift offered out of respect.

’abuhu.

Wa-’aragāwi-sa qeddus ’Abbā ’Enṭonyos ta’āmexa re’so la-qeddus ’Abbā Maqāres, "’Ō-waldeya Maqāres, ’anta tessammay beṣu‘a bakama terg^{w}āmē semeka ba-lesāna Yonānāweyān, ’esma ’Egzi’abḥēr ’Amlākeya kašata lita gebraka wa-meṣ’ataka xabēya, wa-ba’enta-ze konku ’eṣanneḥ meṣ’ataka." Wa-’aragāwi-sa qeddus ’Abbā ’Enṭonyos maharo la-qeddus ’Abbā Maqāres k^{w}ello fenota menk^{w}esennā qeddest, wa-’aṣne‘o ba-nagar bezux za-yedallu la-gabira ṣedq, wa-kašata lotu ṣabi’otomu la-sayṭānāt. Wa-yebēlo kā‘eba, "’Emuntu hallawomu kama yeṣbe’uka ba-xebu’ ba-xellinnā kantu[60] wa-ba-megbārāt gahhāda ’eska la-mawit, kama tekun ’anta feṣṣuma soba yeṣabbe’uka, wa-ta‘aggaš ’eska la-mawit."[61] Wa-sa’alo qeddus ’Abbā Maqāres la-’Abbā ’Enṭonyos, wa-yebēlo, "Xedegani ’enbar ba-xabēka." Wa-yebēlo qeddus ’Abbā ’Enṭonyos, "Ḥur xaba makān za-wassana laka ’Egzi’abḥēr, wa-ta‘aggaš westētu." Wa-’emdexra nabara xaba ’aragāwi ’Abbā ’Enṭonyos xedāṭa mawā‘ela ’enza yetmahhar ’emennēhu šer‘ata menk^{w}esennā wa-šer‘ata ṣedq, tanše’a wa-tamayṭa xaba makānu ’enza yetfēššāḥ wa-yetḥaššay ba-šer‘atāt wa-ba-temhertāt māḥyawit za-tamehra ’emenna ’ab qeddus ’Abbā ’Enṭonyos.

Wa-kā‘eba ’Abbā Maqāres beṣu‘ tarākaba mesla ’Abbā Sarābyon[62] ’ēpis-qopos, wa-yebēlo, "K^{w}ello mawā‘ela za-nabarku xaba ’abuya ’Abbā ’Enṭonyos ’i-re’ikewwo ’enza yenawwem gemurā."[63]

Wa-nabara qeddus Maqāres westa makānu bezuxa mawā‘ela ’enza

---

60. *kantu* n. vanity, emptiness; frequently in construct phrases, as here: *xellinnā kantu* vain thoughts. *ba-kantu* = *kanto* adv. in vain; fortuitously, without purpose, without reward or result.

61. The syntax here is strange. Understand *hallawaka* before *kama tekun*. *tet‘aggaš* would be better than *ta‘aggaš*. Dt *ta‘aggaša* to be patient, persevere; to practice restraint, abstinence. CDt *’asta‘aggaša* caus. of Dt; to bear patiently. *ta‘aggāši* patient, persevering. *te‘gešt* temperance, continence, patience, tolerance. *masta‘ageš* temperant, patient, long-suffering.

62. *Sarābyon* Serapion, Bishop of Thmuis in Lower Egypt.

63. CG *’agmara* to perfect, finish, consummate; to include completely, to comprehend. Gt *tagamra* pass. *gemurā* adv. always, altogether, completely; common with negative: (not) at all. *la-gemurā* adv. forever, always.

yetgādal wa-yeḍḍammad[64] westa fenota menk^{w}esennā, wa-kona watra kirubēl yeḥēwweṣo gahhāda. Wa-ba-'aḥatti 'elat sam'a qāla 'em-samāy za-yebelo, "'O-Maqāres, ba'enta za-samā'ka qāleya wa-te'zāzeya, wa-maṣā'ka xabēya, wa-xadarka westa zentu makān, nāhu 'ana 'āstagābe' westa zentu makān 'aḥzāba za-'i-yetx^{w}ēllaq^w[65] 'em-k^{w}ellu tezmedd[66] wa-'em-k^{w}ellu baḥāwert wa-'em-k^{w}ellu lesānāt, wa-yetla''akuni wa-yebāreku semeya ba-megbārātihomu šannāyt. Tawakafomu wa-mereḥomu westa fenota ṣedq." Wa-soba sam'a qeddus 'Abbā Maqāres zanta, taxayyala wa-ṣan'a lebbu. Wa-'enza yeqawwem ba-gizē ṣalot ba-lēlit, wa-kašata lotu 'Egzi'abḥēr 'ezanihu, wa-sam'omu la-sayṭānāt 'enza yetmākaru babaynātihomu, wa-yebēlu, "La'emma xadagnāhu la-zentu be'si yexder westa zāti gadām, yerēsseyewwā la-zāti 'ahgura samāyāweyān, 'esma 'emuntu yetwēkkalu[67] ba-ḥeywat za-la-'ālam, wa-yesaddeduna 'em-zentu 'ālam ba-ḥemāma k^{w}ennanē ṣalotātihomu. Ne'u ye'zē netgābā' lā'lēhu. Yogi[68] nekel nesdedo 'em-zentu makān."

Wa-soba sam'a qeddus Maqāres zanta, ṣan'a lebbu, wa-taxayyala lā'la sayṭānāt, wa-kona yebāreko la-'Egzi'abḥēr za-kašata lotu 'ezanihu 'eska sam'a megbāromu la-sayṭānāt wa-'a'mara dekāmomu. Wa-'emdexra-ze tagābe'u lā'lēhu sayṭānāt, wa-ṣab'ewwo ṣab'a 'abiya, wa-'andadu 'essāta lā'la xoxta ba'atu, wa-konu yenašše'u 'em-we'etu[69] 'essāt wa-yewaddeyu westa ba'atu, wa-konat ye'eti 'essāt teṭaffe' ba-ṣalotu la-'Abbā Maqāres. Wa-soba tamaw'u 'em-zentu, wadayu westa

---

64. G *ḍamada* to join, bind together, yoke. Gt *taḍamda* pass.; to dedicate one's self to, pursue assiduously, submit one's self to, minister to. *ḍemud* joined, connected; zealous, assiduous; as n. devoté, disciple, servant. *ḍemd* yoke, pair. *ḍammād* sectarian, zealot, devoté. *maḍmad* rope, thong.

65. D *x*^{w}*allaq*^{w}*a* to count, number, reckon. Dt *tax*^{w}*allaq*^{w}*a* pass. *x*^{w}*elluq*(^{w}) counted, numbered, reckoned. *x*^{w}*elq*^{w}/*x*^{w}*alq*^{w} (pl. *x*^{w}*elaq*^{w}) number, sum. *x*^{w}*ellāq*^{w}*ē* vn. numbering, counting.

66. Gt *tazamda* to be related. *tezmedd* family, tribe, race, species.

67. Dt *tawakkala* to trust or have faith (in: *ba-*, *diba*, or obj. suff.). *wekkul* trusting, confiding, dependent. *tewkelt* vn. trust, faith, confidence.

68. *yogi* adv. perhaps, by chance, perchance.

69. Partitive use: "they would take some of that fire..."

lebbu xellinnā zemmut wa-tekkāza[70] lebb wa-*ḥemāma* wa-*te'bita* wa-feqra kebra zentu 'ālam: ferhata wa-temkeḥta,[71] hakēta[72] wa-ḍerfata, wa-xaṭi'a[73] hāymānot, wa-qabiṣa[74] tasfā 'emenna 'Egzi'abḥēr, wa-za-yefadaffed[75] 'em-zentu kʷellu, ṣab'ewwo lotu bakama nagaro qeddus 'Abbā 'Enṭonyos.

Wa-soba nabara nawixa mawā'ela wa-sayṭānāt yeṣabbe'ewwo ba-zentu megbārāt ḥešumāt,[76] tanše'a kā'eba wa-ḥora xạba qeddus 'Enṭonyos. Wa-soba re'yo 'Enṭonyos 'em-reḥuq, nagaromu la-'ardā'ihu, wa-yebē, "Zentu 'Esrā'ēlāwi ba-'amān za-'albo ṣelḥut westa lebbu. Terē''eyewwo-nu, 'o-weludeya, la-zentu be'si? Hallawo kama yekun batra[77] ṣedq retu'a wa-nawixa la-bezuxān 'aḥzāb, wa-yekawwenu lotu ferēyāta ṭe'umāta 'em-'afuhu la-'Egzi'abḥēr Ṣabā'ot." Wa-soba sam'a qeddus 'Abbā Maqāres, sagada lotu diba medr, wa-'anše'o 'Abbā 'Enṭonyos feṭuna, wa-ta'āmexo wa-sa'amo, 'esma we'etu re'ya gaṣṣo

---

70. D *takkaza* to be sad, distressed, troubled in mind, to be concerned. CD *'atakkaza* caus. *tekkuz* sad, etc. *tekkāz* (pl. *-āt*) sadness, grief, care, concern; business, task.

71. Dt *tamakkeḥa* to boast. *mekkeḥ* = *temkeḥt* boasting. *makkāḥ* boastful.

72. Gt *tahakaya* to be idle, lazy, negligent, remiss; to cease, stop, be inactive. CG *'ahkaya* caus. *hakkāy* lazy, idle. *hakēt* laziness, idleness, negligence.

73. G *xaṭ'a* to lack, not have, not find; (rarely) to sin. CG *'axṭe'a* to deprive (someone: a.d.o. or obj. suff.) of (a.d.o.), to cause to lack; to cause to sin. Gt *taxaṭ'a* to withdraw, go away; to be absent, lacking. *xeṭu'* not having, deprived.

74. G *qabaṣa (yeqbaṣ, yeqbeṣ)* to be discouraged, be in distress. *qabaṣa tasfā 'emenna* to lose hope, to despair; to abandon, give up on. CG *'aqbaṣa* to cause to despair. *qebuṣ* discouraged, despairing. *qebṣat* despair.

75. Q *fadfada* to increase, become numerous, abundant; to surpass, be superior. *wa-za-yefadaffed 'em-zentu* and what's more. CQ *'afadfada* caus.; to surpass (someone in: two acc.).

76. G *ḥašama* to be bad, foul, evil. CG *'aḥšama* to act wickedly; to make foul, evil; to harm, damage. *ḥešum* bad, foul, evil, harmful. *ḥešam* (pl. *-āt*) wickedness, evil; crime, harm.

77. *batr* (pl. *'abter*) staff, branch.

welluṭa[78] kama gaṣṣa za-yedawwi ba'enta bezux ṣab' za-yeṣabbe'ewwo sayṭānāt. Wa-'emdexra ṣallayu, nabaru xebura, wa-'awše'a qeddus 'Enṭonyos ba-feššeḥā wa-yebēlo, "Dāxen-nu[79] halloka, 'o-waldeya Maqāres?" 'Awše'a qeddus Maqāres wa-yebēlo, "Nāhu 'abdaraka[80] 'Egzi'abḥēr wa-kašata laka k^{w}ello 'emennēya." Wa-sobēhā maharo wa-'aṣne'o wa-yebēlo, "Ṣenā' wa-'i-tefrāh, 'esma kama-ze maftew lana kama net'aggašo la-zentu makkarā k^{w}ello za-yāmaṣṣe'u lā'lēna ṣalā'tena.[81] Wa-ba'enta-ze yedallewana kama nekun mamehherāna la-'aḥzāb bezuxān 'ella yāfaqqeru ṭebaba manfasāwita, 'enta ye'eti $menk^{w}$esennā." Wa-yebēlo, "O-waldeya Maqāres, tazakkar we'eta qāla za-nagaraka 'Egzi' enza taḥawwer teqdāḥ[82] māya." Wa-soba sam'a qeddus 'Abbā Maqāres zanta, 'ankara fadfāda, wa-'a'mara kama megbārātihu wa-xebu'ātihu takašta lotu la-qeddus 'Enṭonyos ba-manfas qeddus.

Wa-nabara xaba 'aragāwi 'Abbā 'Enṭonyos bezuxa mawā'ela 'enza yetbārak 'emennēhu wa-yetmēhhar te'zāzātihu, wa-xašaša 'emennēhu kama yālbeso[83] 'askēmā qeddusa. Wa-ṣallaya lā'lēhu, wa-'albaso 'albāsa

---

78. D *wallaṭa* to change, alter, transform. Dt *tawallaṭa* pass. *welluṭ* changed, transformed, different. *wellāṭē* change, alteration, transformation. *tawlāṭ* change; exchange, price.

79. A relatively infrequent use of *hallawa* with an adjectival predicate.

80. CG *'abdara* to prefer, choose, select, favor; with foll. inf.: to do something eagerly, willingly, with undivided attention. Gt *tabadra* pass. G *badara* to hurry, precede, arrive first. Glt *tabādara* to compete with (in running), to race. *badr* contest, running.

81. G *ṣal'a (yeṣlā')* to hate, be hostile toward. Gt *taṣal'a* pass. and reflex. Glt *taṣāle'a* to act hostilely toward one another. *ṣelu'* hated, hateful. *ṣel'/ṣal'* hatred, enmity. *ṣalā'i* (pl. *ṣalā't*) enemy, hater.

82. G *qadḥa (yeqdāḥ)* to draw water. Gt *taqadḥa* pass. *qadāḥi* drawer of water; cup-bearer. *maqdeḥt* water-jar.

83. G *labsa (yelbas)* to dress (intrans.); to don (a garment: a.d.o.). CG *'albasa* to clothe, dress (trans.), with acc. of person and acc. of garment. Gt *talabsa* pass. and reflex. *lebus* dressed, clothed. *lebs* (pl. *'albās*) garment. *lebsat* vn. dressing, clothing,

kiyāhu,[84] wa-ba'enta-ze tasamya rad'u la-qeddus 'Enṭonyos. Wa-'emze yebēlo 'aragāwi 'Abbā 'Enṭonyos ba-xebu' kama "Tethakkay kama temṣā' xabēya zeyya. 'Ana 'emdexra mawā'el 'aḥawwer xaba 'Egzi'abḥēr." Wa-soba sam'a 'Abbā Maqāres zanta nagara, tanše'a wa-sagada lotu, wa-sa'alo kama yenbar ba-xabēhu wa-yerasseyo delewa[85] yenšā' barakato manfasāwita. Wa-yebēlo, "Nebar ba-xabēya." Wa-nabara ba-xabēhu. Wa-yebēlo 'Enṭonyos, "Wa-'emdexra xedāṭ mawā'el yā'arrefaka 'Egzi'abḥēr 'em-zentu ṣab'a xellinnā 'ekuy, wa-'emdexra-ze yeṣabbe'uka sayṭānāt gahhāda. Ṣenā' wa-ta'aqab wa-'i-tāḥzeno la-we'etu kirubēl za-rassayo 'Egzi'abḥēr meslēka la-rad'ēteka yahallu[86] meslēka 'eska tafṣāmēta mawā'elika, wa-ya'aqqebaka bakama 'azzaza 'Egzi'abḥēr 'Amlākeka." Wa-wahabo 'Abbā 'Enṭonyos batra zi'ahu, wa-ta'āmexo 'ammexā qeddesāt, wa-'a'rafa wa-taqabra šegāhu ba-makān xebu' za-'i-yā'ammer mannu-hi makāno.

Wa-tamayṭa qeddus 'Abbā Maqāres xaba gadāma 'Asqēṭes, wa-nabara westa makānu, wa-tasam'a zēnāhu westa k^{w}ellu 'aṣnāfa medr. Wa-gabra 'Egzi'abḥēr diba 'edawihu ta'āmerāta 'abayta, wa-'emennēhu 'esma[87] neguša 'Anṣokiyā[88] fannawā la-walattu xabēhu za-yeṣṣē''an[89] dibēhā

---

donning. *malbas(t)* (pl. *malābes*) garment, tunic.

84. An unusual use of *kiyāhu*, either "those same garments" or "his own garments." The latter seems more likely in view of the following clause.

85. *delew* (f. *delut*) adj. worthy (to do: subjunctive), deserving; proper; weighed. *delwat* weight, worthiness, propriety. CG *'adlawa* to please, satisfy (someone: a.d.o. or *la-*); to adulate, fawn over, flatter. *madlew* hypocrite, fawner, an unjust official or judge. Dt *tadallawa* to prepare one's self, get ready; to live in luxury. *tadlā* preparation; propriety, appropriateness, worthiness; luxury, affluence. CDt *'astadallawa* to prepare, make ready (trans.). CGlt *'astadālawa* idem. *barakat* (pl. *-āt*) blessing.

86. *yahallu* = *kama yahallu* and governs only what follows.

87. Cf. Note 28 in the preceding selection.

88. *'Anṣokiyā* Antioch.

89. Dt *taṣe''ena* to mount, ride on (an animal or vehicle); also, as here, of a demon possessing a person. D *ṣa''ana* to load (an animal or vehicle). *ṣe''un* laden; riding, mounted. *mastaṣe''en* horseman.

manfas rekus; wa-baṣḥat xabēhu ba-'amsāla warēzā, wa-'a'mara kama ye'eti walatt, wa-fawwasā wa-fannawā xaba 'abuhā wa-'emmā. Wa-soba wahabewwo warqa bezuxa, 'i-naš'a wa-'i-menta-ni 'emennēhomu.

Wa-hallo 'aḥadu manakos westa hagara 'Awsim;[90] seḥta wa-yebē: "Albo tenšā'ē mutān." Wa-'asḥatomu la-bezuxān sab', wa-ba'enta 'aminotomu botu konu yetwēkkafu qālo. Wa-ḥora 'ēpis-qopos za-hagara 'Awsim xaba 'Abbā Maqāres, wa-nagaro kama 'asḥatomu we'etu la-ḥezba zi'ahu, wa-sa'alo se'lata bezuxa[91] kama yetrāde'o. Wa-tanše'a 'Abbā Maqāres, wa-ḥora mesla 'ēpis-qopos xaba hagara 'Awsim, wa-re'yo la-we'etu bāḥtāwi za-westētu manfas rekus. Wa-soba tanāgara meslēhu ba'enta tenšā'ē mutān, wa-'awše'a we'etu bāḥtāwi wa-yebēlo: "'Ane-sa 'i-ya'ammen kama mewutān yetnašše'u, la'emma 'i-yanšā'ka lita be'sē 'emenna maqāber." Wa-ṣallaya qeddus 'Abbā Maqāres, wa-sa'ala xaba 'Egzi'abḥēr, wa-sobēhā tanše'a we'etu 'aḥadu be'si 'emenna mewutān (wa-kona be'sihu 'em-*kaḥādeyān* qadamt). Wa-'amna we'etu bāḥtāwi, wa-tamayṭa 'em-seḥtatu, wa-kamāhu[92] k^{w}ellomu ḥezb 'ella 'asḥatomu tamayṭu. Wa-sa'alo we'etu be'si za-'anše'o 'em-mewutān la-qeddus 'Abbā Maqāres kama yāṭmeqo ṭemqata Kerestennā. Wa-'aṭmaqo wa-'albaso 'albāsa menk^{w}esennā, wa-nabara xabēhu sabā'ta 'āmata, wa-'a'rafa.

Wa-'emdexra-ze tanše'a qeddus 'Abbā Maqāres, wa-sa'ala[93] westa gadām kama yā'mer la'emma hallo westa gadām sab' 'em-qedmēhu. Wa-re'eyo kel'ē 'edawa 'eruqāna,[94] farha 'emennēhomu, 'esma masalo kama 'emuntu sayṭānāt, wa-ṣallaya ba-qedmēhomu 'elbāltaribon[95] (za-we'etu:

---

90. *'Awsim* Letopolis, just north of Memphis.

91. Cognate accusative: "he asked him repeatedly (or earnestly)."

92. *kamāhu* adv. likewise, in the same way.

93. *sa'ala* is rather curious here, unless in the sense "to make inquiry, to investigate." A variant text has *bo'a*. The *'em-qedmēhu* of the following clause is to be taken in the sense of "superior to him" (in spiritual perfection).

94. G *'arqa/'araqa* to be naked, empty; to be orphaned. CG *'a'raqa* to strip bare; to empty out. Gt *ta'arqa* to be stripped, denuded, emptied. *'eruq* naked, empty. *'erāq* (appositional pron. suff. obligatory) naked, empty, alone. *'erqān* nakedness; shame (the sexual parts).

95. A corruption, through Arabic, of Greek *ho patēr humōn*, the

'Abuna za-ba-samāyāt). Wa-kiyāhu-ni ṣawwe'ewwo ba-semu wa-yebēlewwo: "'I-tefrāh 'o-Maqāres." Wa-'a'mara kama 'emuntu qeddusān gadāmāweyān. Wa-tase''elewwo ba'enta sab'a ʿālam wa-megbāromu, wa-yebēlomu: "'Egzi'abḥēr ba-meḥratu yexēlli diba k^{w}ellomu." Wa-'emze tase''elomu la'emma kona yāq^{w}arreromu q^{w}erra keramt[96] wa-yālehhebomu[97] ḥarura[98] ḍaḥāy ba-gizē ḥagāy.[99] Wa-'awše'ewwo wa-yebēlewwo: "'Egzi'abḥēr rad'ana maṭana[100] zentu 'arbeʿā ʿāmat, wa-nabarna westa gadām. 'I-y̓aq^{w}rarana keramt wa-'i-y̓alhabana ḥagāy." Wa-yebēlomu qeddus 'Abbā Maqāres: "'Efo 'ekawwen kamākemu?" Wa-yebēlewwo: "Nebar westa ba'ateka, wa-beki lāʿla xaṭi'ateka, wa-'anta tekawwen kamāna." Wa-tabāraka 'emennēhomu, wa-tamayṭa xaba makānu.

Wa-soba bazxu manakosāt, wa-karayu lomu ʿazaqta, wa-ḥanaṣu lomu. Wa-soba warada westētā qeddus kama yetxaḍab, 'anxalewwā[101] sayṭānāt lāʿlēhu kama yeqtelewwo. Wa-maṣ'u manakosāt, wa-'awḍe'ewwo 'emennēhā. Wa-soba faqada 'Egzi'abḥēr ʿerafto, fannawa lotu kirubēl-hā za-kona yeḥēwweṣo, wa-yebēlo: "Tadallaw, 'esma neḥna nemaṣṣe' xabēka wa-nenašše'aka." Wa-'ar'ayo la-'Abbā 'Enṭonyos wa-la-māxbara qeddusān wa-k^{w}ellomu xaylāta samāyāweyāna, 'eska 'ama maṭṭawa nafso. Wa-kona k^{w}ellu mawāʿela ḥeywatu tesʿā wa-sabāʿta ʿāmata. Wa-kona semʿa ba-zentu[102] Babnudā rad'u, kama we'etu re'ya *nafso* la-qeddus

---

first words of the Lord's Prayer, as the following parenthesis explains.

96. *keramt* winter; rainy season; year. G *karma/karama* to spend the winter; to belong to the previous year. *karāmi* of or pertaining to the previous year.

97. G *lahaba* to flame, burn. CG *'alhaba* to burn, ignite (trans.). *lāhb* flame, heat.

98. G *ḥarra/ḥarara (yeḥrar, yeḥrer)* to burn (intrans.), be afire. CG *'aḥrara* to burn (trans.). *ḥarur* heat, fervor, passion, ardor.

99. *ḥagāy* summer.

100. *maṭana* prep. during, for the extent of.

101. G *nexla (yenxal)* to collapse, fall into ruin, be destroyed. CG *'anxala* to knock down, destroy, devastate, topple.

102. *ba-zentu* apparently refers to the following account. Translate: "His disciple Babnuda was a witness to the following, namely that ..."

'Abbā Maqāres ta'arreg xaba samāy, wa-sam'omu la-sayṭānāt 'enza yekēlleḥu wa-yebelu ba-dexrēhu: "Mo'kana, 'O-Maqāri, mo'kana." Wa-yebēlomu qeddus 'Abbā Maqāres: "'Ādiya 'eska ye'zē."[103] Wa-soba bo'a qeddus westa gannat, kalleḥu ba-qāl le''ul 'enza yebelu: "Mo'kana, 'O-Maqāri." Wa-yebēlomu qeddus 'Abbā Maqāres: "Yetbārak semu za-'adxanani 'em-'edēkemu."

Wa-kona qeddus 'ama ḥeyāw,[104] 'azzazomu la-weludu kama yexbe'u šegāhu. Wa-maṣ'u sab' 'em-hagaru Susāwir, wa-wahabu newāya la-rad'u Yoḥannes za-kona yegēššeṣo k^{w}ello gizē yebelo: "Ta'aqab 'em-'afqero newāy." Wa-marḥomu we'etu, wa-'ar'ayomu šegāhu la-qeddus 'Abbā Maqāres, wa-naš'ewwo wa-wasadewwo xaba hagaromu, wa-nabara ba-heyya me'ta wa-sessā 'āmata 'eska mawā'ela mangešta 'Arab. Wa-rad'u-sa Yoḥannes kona zelgusa[105] ba'enta 'afqerotu newāya. Wa-'emdexra-ze ḥoru weludu manakosāt xaba hagaru Susāwir, wa-faqadu kama yenše'u šegāhu, wa-tanše'u lā'lēhomu sab'a hagar mesla mak^{w}annen, wa-kal'ewwomu. Wa-ba-ye'eti lēlit 'astar'ayo qeddus 'Abbā Maqāres la-mak^{w}annen wa-yebēlo: "Xedegani 'eḥur mesla weludeya." Wa-ba-ṣebāḥ ṣawwe'omu mak^{w}annen la-manakosāt, wa-'azzazomu kama yeṣuru šegāhu. Wa-ṣorewwo sobēhā, wa-'anbarewwo westa bēta Kerestiyān ba-zemmārē[106] wa-ba-māḥlēt bezux 'ama 'ašur wa-tasu' la-Naḥasē, wa-kona 'emennēhu ta'āmerāt wa-mankerāt 'abayt.

Salām la-Maqāres za-'abiy kebru,
'esma 'aqaba mar'ēto la-'Enṭonyos ba-batru.
'Emenna[107] 'aḥadu 'aḥadu 'enbala yāxṣeru

---

103. "I am still here." (i.e. in spite of your torments and temptations). *ye'zē(-ni)* adv. now.

104. *wa-kona ... 'ama ḥeyāw* and while he was still alive. Cf. *wa-kona soba*.

105. Q *zalgasa* to be afflicted with a dreadful disease (leprosy, elephantiasis). *zelgus* leprous (or sim.). *zelgāsē* leprosy, elephantiasis.

106. D *zammara* (1) to make music; to play instruments, sing; (2) to state or proclaim authoritatively, to bear witness to. CG *'azmara* = D (2). *zemmur* authority, witness. *zemmārē* psalm, hymn. *mazammer* psalmist, church singer. *mazmur* (pl. *-āt*) psalm, the psalter; chorus of singers. *mezmār* authority, witness.

107. The third and fourth lines are difficult. I would

soba ʻerruya daqiqu wa-megbārāta ṣedq gabru,
madālewa ʼalbāb tasamyat ʼeska yom dabru.

E. Salāmā[1]

Ba-zāti ʻelat (ʼama ʻešrā wa-sadus la-Ḥamlē) ʼaʻrafa ʼAbbā Salāmā, kašātē berhān, pāppās za-ʼItyopyā, wa-kama-ze weʼetu zēnāhu. Maṣʼa ʼaḥadu beʼsi ʼem-beḥēra Ṣerʻ[2] za-semu Mērobopyos,[3] liqa ṭababt, ʼenza yefaqqed yerʼayā la-beḥēra ʼItyopyā, wa-meslēhu kelʼētu daqiq ʼem-ʼazmādihu, semu la-ʼaḥadu Ferēmnāṭos[4] wa-kāleʼu ʼAdseyos,[5] wa-bo ʼella yesammeyewwo Sidrākos. Wa-baṣḥa ba-ḥamar ḥayqa beḥēra ʼAgʻāzi, wa-reʼya k^wello šannāyāta za-fetwata[6] lebbu. Wa-ʼenza yefaqqed yetmayaṭ beḥēro, tanšeʼu lāʻlēhu ḍarr,[7] wa-qatalewwo mesla k^ellomu

---

suggest "Because his children and righteous deeds amounted to the same thing (for him), without one detracting from the other, his monastery was named 'The Balance of Hearts (i.e. desires, aspirations)' (and is called thus) up to this very day." For the sense, see note 43 above and the frequent mention of "his spiritual children" in accounts of Macarius' life. The main language problem is the idiom *gabra ʻerruya*, for which I can find no exact parallel, although the suggested translation is quite in keeping with other intransitive uses of *gabra*. G *xaṣara (yexṣer)* to be short. CG *ʼaxṣara* to shorten, curtail. *xeṣur* short, shortened. *xaṣir* (f. *xaṣār*) idem.

1. *ʼAbbā Salāmā*, i.e. Frumentius, the traditional founder of Ethiopic Christianity in the fourth century.

2. *Ṣerʻ* Greece, the Greeks. *ba-Ṣerʻ* in Greek. *Ṣerʻāwi* adj. Greek.

3. *Mērobopyos* Meropius.

4. *Ferēmnāṭos* Frumentius.

5. *ʼAdseyos* Aedesius.

6. G *fatawa* to desire strongly (often, but not necessarily, in bad sense: to lust for, be greedy for). CG *ʼaftawa* caus.; to please, satisfy. *fetew* desired, desirable, pleasing, pleasant. *fetwat* vn. desire, lust, craving; the thing desired, pleasure. *fetwatāwi* libidinous, given to excessive desires.

7. *ḍarr* (pl. *ʼaḍrār*) enemy, adversary. *ḍarrāwi* adj. enemy, hostile. CG *ʼaḍrara* to be hostile. Glt *taḍārara* to act hostile

'ella meslēhu, wa-tarafu 'ellu kel'ētu daqiq ne'usān. Wa-ḍēwawewwomu sab'a hagar, wa-maharewwomu gebra taqātelo,[8] wa-wasadewwomu 'ammexā la-negušа 'Aksum[9] za-semu 'Ella-'alādā, wa-šēmo neguš la-'Adseyos maggābē bēta qaṭin[10] wa-la-Ferēmnāṭos 'aqābē ḥegg wa-ṣaḥāfē 'Aksum.

Wa-'emdexra xedāṭ mawā'el 'a'rafa neguš, wa-xadaga 'eg^wāla ne'usa mesla 'emmu, wa-nagšu 'Ella-'Azg^wāg^wā. Wa-nabaru 'Adseyos wa-Ferēmnāṭos 'enza yaḥaḍḍenewwo[11] la-ḥeḍān wa-yemēhherewwo hāymānota Kerestos (lotu sebḥat) ba-ba-nestit nestita. Wa-ḥanaṣu lotu meṣellāya, wa-'astagābe'u xabēhu daqiqa 'enza yemēhherewwomu mazmura wa-māḥlēta. Wa-soba 'abṣeḥa zeku ḥeḍān 'aqma[12] werzāwē, sa'alewwo kama yefannewomu hagaromu. Wa-'Adseyos ḥora Ṭiros[13] beḥēra kama yer'ay walādeyānihu. Wa-Ferēmnāṭos-ni baṣḥa 'Eskenderyā xaba liqa pāppāsāt 'Abbā 'Atnātyos,[14] wa-rakabo ba-ḥaddis šimatu, wa-zēnawo k^wello za-baṣḥa lā'lēhu wa-ba'enta hāymānotomu la-beḥēra 'Ag'āzi, wa-zakama 'amnu ba-Kerestos (lotu sebḥat), 'enza 'albomu pāppāsāt wa-qasāwest.

Wa-'emze šēmo 'Abbā 'Atnātyos la-Ferēmnāṭos kama yekun pāppāsa la-beḥēra 'Ag'āzi za-'Ityopyā, wa-fannawo mesla 'abiy kebr. Wa-baṣiḥo beḥēra 'Ag'āzi 'ama mangeštomu la-'Abrehā[15] wa-'Aṣbeḥa, sabaka

---

toward, be an enemy of.

8. I.e. arts of warfare.

9. *'Aksum* Aksum (Axum), center of the Axumite Kingdom, known from the first century onward in Classical, inscriptional, and Arabic sources.

10. *qaṭin* servants, domestics (collective).

11. G *ḥaḍana (yeḥḍen)* to nurse, nourish, foster, cultivate; to take care of (one's young). Gt *taḥaḍna* pass. *ḥeḍn* (pl. *ḥeḍan*) bosom, embrace. *ḥeḍnat* vn. nourishing, nursing. *ḥeḍān* (pl. *-āt*) infant, very young child. *māḥḍan* (pl. *-āt*, *maḥāḍen*) womb.

12. *'aqm* measure, degree, extent; moderation; end, completion, maturation. *ba-'aqm* moderately. *'aqma werzāwē* maturity, manhood. D *'aqqama* to define, set limits to. *'eqqum* limited, defined, determined. *'eqqāmē* determination, definition.

13. *Ṭiros* Tyre.

14. *'Atnātyos* Athanasius the Great, Bishop of Alexandria 328-373.

15. *'Abrehā* and *'Aṣbeḥa*. Apparently an anachronistic

ba-salāma Kerestos (lotu sebḥat) westa k^w^ellu 'adyāmihā,[16] wa-ba'entaze tasamya 'Abbā Salāmā. Wa-'emdexra 'a'manomu la-sab'a 'Ityopyā, 'a'rafa ba-salām.

"Salām" ba-qāla sebḥat 'ebelo
'enza 'ā'abbeyo wa-'ālē''elo
la-Salāmā, xoxt za-meḥrat wa-tašāhelo.[17]
'Ašraqa za-'Ityopyā la-berhāna Kerestos ṣadālo,[18]
'enza lā'lēhu ṣelmat wa-qobār[19] hallo.

F. Yārēd[1]

Ba-zāti 'elat ('ama 'ašur wa-'eḥud la-Genbot) 'a'rafa Yārēd māḥlētāy,[2] 'amsālihomu la-Surāfēl.[3] Wa-zentu Yārēd 'em-'azmādihu we'etu la-'Abbā Gēdēwon 'em-kāhenāta 'Aksum, 'enta ye'eti qadāmit 'em-'ella taḥanṣā 'abyāta Kerestiyānāt ba-hagara 'Ityopyā, wa-tasabka bāti hāymānota Kerestos, wa-taqaddasat ba-sema 'Egze'tena Māryām. Wa-zentu 'Abbā Gēdēwon soba waṭana yemharo mazmura Dāwit la-beḍu' Yārēd, se'na 'aqiboto 'eska bezux mawā'el.[4] Wa-'emze soba zabaṭo wa-'aḥmamo, wa-g^w^ayya westa gadām wa-'aṣlala[5] tāḥta 'om.[6] Wa-re'ya

---

reference to 'Ella 'Aṣbeḥa and 'Abreha of the 6th century. The latter is famous for his expedition against Mecca in 570.

16. *'adyām* (pl. only) area, region, environs, neighborhood, adjacent district.

17. Glt *tašāhala* to show mercy (to: a.d.o.); to forgive. *šāhl* mercy, kindness. *mastašāhel* merciful, lenient; seeking mercy or forgiveness.

18. G *ṣadala* to shine, be splendid. CG *'aṣdala* to shine, emit light, gleam. *ṣedul* shining, splendid. *ṣadāl* splendor, light, gleam.

19. *qobār* (pl. *-āt*) blackness, darkness.

1. *Yārēd* Yared, the patron saint of Ethiopic church music.

2. *māḥlētāy* musician, singer.

3. *surāfēl* seraph, seraphim.

4. *'eska bezux mawā'el* for very long.

5. CG *'aṣlala* to furnish shade; to seek the shade; to sit, live, dwell. D *ṣallala* to shade, cover. Dt *taṣallala* to be shaded, dark. *ṣalalo* lampblack, soot. *ṣellālot/ṣelālot* shade, shadow(s), darkness. *meṣlāl/meṣellāl* a shady place, arbor, pavilion. *maṣallat* tabernacle, tent. *Ba'āla Maṣallat* Feast of Tabernacles.

ʿeḍē[7] ʾenza yaʿarreg malʿelta ʿom, wa-baṣiḥo xaba manfaqā[8] yewaddeq westa medr; bezuxa gizē yegabber kamāhu, wa-ʾem-ʿeṣub ʿarga malʿelta ʿom. Wa-soba reʾya Yārēd tegāho la-ʿeḍē, nasseḥa ba-nafsu, wa-tamayṭa xaba mamehheru wa-yebē: "Seray lita, ʾo-ʾAbbā, wa-rasseyani za-faqadka." Wa-tawakfo mamehheru manfasāwi. Wa-soba saʾala xaba ʾEgziʾabḥēr ba-bekāy, tarexwa lebbunnāhu, wa-tamehra ba-ʾaḥatti ʿelat maṣāḥefta beluya wa-ḥaddisa.[9]

Wa-ʾemze tašayma diyāqona. Wa-ba-weʾetu mawāʿel ʾalbo māxlaqta[10] qenē[11] ba-leʿʿul zēmā[12] zaʾenbala ba-laḥosās.[13] Wa-soba faqada ʾEgziʾabḥēr kama yāqem lotu tazkāra,[14] wa-fannawa lotu šalasta ʾaʿwāfa ʾem-gannata ʾĒdōm,[15] wa-tanāgarewwo ba-lesāna sabʾ, wa-mašaṭewwo[16] meslēhomu westa ʾIyarusālēm samāyāwit, wa-ba-heyya

---

6. *ʿom* (pl. *ʾaʿwām, -āt*) tree, trees, dense grove, woods.

7. *ʿeḍē* (pl. *-yāt, ʿeḍayāt*) worm, caterpiller. G *ʿaḍaya/ʿaḍya* to putrify, get wormy.

8. G *nafaqa* to divide, separate. L *nāfaqa* to divide (usually in half, into two parts or factions); to be hesitant, doubtful, skeptical. Lt *tanāfaqa* to divide (intrans.), break up into factions. Gt *tanafqa* idem. *nefuq* divided, split. *nufuq* hesitant, doubtful. *nafq* compartment, box. *nefq* half, one of two parts. *nufāqē* division, dissension, skepticism. *manfaq* half, one of two parts; faction, sect, splinter-group; the half-way point (as here).

9. I.e. the Old and New Testaments.

10. G *xalqa (yexlaq, yexleq)* to come to an end, be finished, consummated; to perish, disappear. CG *ʾaxlaqa* caus. *xelqat* end, consummation, completion, death. *māxlaqt* end, completion; consummation, climax, death; performance, execution (as here).

11. *qenē* church singing, church music.

12. *zēmā* melody, tune, song. *leʿʿul zēmā* a type of singing, perhaps falsetto or possibly referring to an obligatto upper melody.

13. *laḥosas* whispering; the reference here is to a style of singing.

14. *ʾaqama tazkāra* to establish a commemoration (for) = to guarantee someone a permanent place among the saints of the church for whom there are fixed commemoration days.

15. *ʾĒdom* Eden.

16. G *mašaṭa (yemšeṭ)* to snatch, snatch away, seize and carry

tamehra māḥlētomu la-ʻešrā wa-ʼarbāʻtu kāhenāta samāy. Wa-soba tamayṭa xaba hellāwēhu,[17] boʼa westa bēta Kerestiyān qeddest za-Gabaza ʼAksum[18] ba-gizē šalastu saʻāt, wa-kalleḥa ba-leʻʻul qāl ʼenza yebel: "Hālē luyā la-ʼAb, hālē luyā la-Wald, hālēluyā wa-la-Manfas Qeddus. Qadāmihā la-Ṣeyon[19] samāya šārara,[20] wa-ba-dāgem ʼarʼayo la-Musē zakama yegabber gebrā la-dabtarā."[21] Wa-samayā la-zāti māḥlēta ʼaryām.[22] Wa-soba samʻu demḍa[23] qālu, roṣu neguš-ni wa-negešt-ni mesla pāppās wa-kāhenāt wa-ʻabayta neguš, wa-waʻalu[24] ʼenza yesammeʻewwo. Wa-šarʻa māḥlēta la-la-zamanu[25] ʼem-ʻāmat ʼeska ʻāmat za-ḥagāy wa-za-keramt, za-maṣaw[26] wa-za-ṣadāy,[27] la-baʻālāt wa-la-sanābet,[28] za-malāʼekt wa-za-nabiyāt, za-samāʻtāt wa-za-ṣādeqān, ba-šalastu zēmā za-weʼetu geʻz[29] wa-ʻezl wa-ʼarārāy, wa-ʼi-yaʻaddu

---

off by force. CG *ʼamšaṭa* to flee, escape. Gt *tamašṭa* pass. and reflex. of G. *mešuṭ* seized, snatched. *mašāṭi* (pl. *mašaṭṭ*) rapacious, violent. *mamšaṭ* handle, lever.

17. *hellāwē* vn. being, essence, nature, substance. *tamayṭa xaba hellāwēhu* he returned to his normal state.

18. *Gabaza ʼAksum* Guardian of Aksum, epithet of the Mother Church at Aksum.

19. *Ṣeyon* Zion. *Musē* Moses.

20. L *šārara* to found, establish. Lt *tašārara* pass. *šerur/šurur* founded, established. *šurārē* founding, foundation. *šārāri* founder. *mašarrat* (pl. *-āt*) foundation, firmament, bottom. CQ *ʼamašrata* to found. Qt *tamašrata* pass. of CQ. "He founded the heavens as the first Zion (lit. the beginning of Zion)."

21. *dabtarā* (pl. *dabāter*) tent, tabernacle.

22. *ʼaryām* (pl. only) highest heaven, the heavenly heights. *māḥlēta ʼaryām* is a technical musical term.

23. G *damḍa (yedmeḍ, yedmaḍ)* to sound. CG *ʼadmaḍa* caus. *demḍ* sound, noise.

24. G *waʻala/weʻla (yaʻal)* to pass the day, remain. *waʻāli* attendant, servant.

25. "each at its proper time." See §51.5.

26. *maṣaw/maḍaw* spring (season).

27. *ṣadāy* autumn.

28. *sanbat* (pl. *-āt*, *sanābet*) sabbath; Sunday *(sanbata Kerestiyān)*; week. CQ *ʼasanbata* to observe the sabbath or Sunday.

’em-šalastu zēmāhu ’emma-hi nebāba sab’ ’aw[30] neqāwa[31] ‘of wa-’ensesā.[32]

Wa-ba-’aḥatti ‘elat ’enza yezēmmer Yārēd, qawimo tāḥta[33] neguš Gabra-Masqal, wa-neguš-ni ’enza yāḍamme’[34] qālo, takla batra xaṣin westa mekyāda[35] ’egarihu, ’enza yeweḥḥez ’emennēhu dam bezux wa-’i-ta‘awqo la-Yārēd ’eska faṣṣama māḥlēta. Wa-soba re’ya neguš, dangaḍa wa-malxa[36] batro ’em-’egru, wa-yebēlo: "Sa’alani za-tefaqqed ‘asba[37] zentu dameka za-take‘wa."[38] Wa-yebēlo Yārēd: "Maḥal[39] lita kama ’i-te’bayani." Wa-soba maḥala lotu, yebēlo Yārēd: "Fannawani kama ’emank^{w}es." Wa-sami‘o neguš, takkaza ṭeqqa mesla k^{w}ellu mak^{w}ānentihu, wa-kama yekle’o-hi farha maḥalā. Wa-bawi’o Yārēd westa bēta

---

29. *ge‘z*, *‘ezl*, and *’arāray* are the three modes of singing *(zēmā)*. *Ge‘z* is the ordinary mode; *‘ezl* is reserved for fast-days, funerals, and the Lenten season; *’arāray* is used for feast-days and other happy occasions.

30. "Nothing surpasses his three modes of singing, whether it be the speech of man or *(’aw)* the cry of birds and animals."

31. *neqāw* animal sounds. G *naqawa* = D *naqqawa* to emit its appropriate sound (subj. may be bird or animal).

32. *’ensesā* animals, beasts, cattle. *’ensesāwi* adj. animal, bestial. Qt *ta’ansasa* to become like a brute animal.

33. *tāḥta* here adv. below. Yared is standing on a platform, with the king below him.

34. CG *’aḍme’a* to listen to, to hear.

35. G *kēda (yekid)* to tread, trample (on: a.d.o.); to thresh (by treading). CG *’akēda* to make tread; to thresh. Gt *takayda* pass. of G. *mekyād* sole of the foot, footprint; base; threshing floor. *makayyad/makyad* idem; also footstool.

36. G *malxa (yemlāx)* to tear out, uproot, draw out. Gt *tamalxa* pass. *melux* uprooted, torn out.

37. G *‘asaba* to hire (for wages). *‘asb* wages, hire, pay reward. *‘assāb* hireling, mercenary.

38. G *ka‘awa (yek‘aw)* to pour out, spew out (trans.). Gt *take‘wa* idem intrans.

39. G *maḥala (yemḥal)* to swear (an oath). CG *’amḥala* to beswear, adjure. Glt *tamāḥala* to take a mutual oath, to conspire. *maḥalā* oath, treaty.

Kerestiyān, qoma qedma tābota[40] Ṣeyon, wa-soba yebē "qeddest wa-beḍe‘t, sebbeḥt wa-burekt, kebert wa-le‘‘elt"[41] ’eska tafṣāmētu, tala‘‘ala ’em-medr maṭana ’emmat.[42]

Wa-’em-heyya ḥora xaba gadāma Samēn,[43] wa-nabara ba-heyya ba-ṣom wa-ba-ṣalot, wa-’aṣāmawa[44] šegāhu fadfāda, wa-faṣṣama gadlo ba-heyya. Wa-wahabo ’Egzi’abḥēr kidāna la-za-yeṣēwwe‘ semo wa-yegabber tazkāro.[45] Wa-’emze ’a‘rafa ba-salām, wa-maqāberihu-sa ’i-ta‘awqa ’eska yom.

Salām la-Yārēd[46] sebḥata malā’ekt la-ḥawwāṣē,
’enta[47] ’a‘raga ’em-lebbu xellinnā manfas rawāṣē.
La-temherta maṣḥaf gab’a ’em-xaba kona nafāṣē[48]
ba-bezux ṣāmā za-’albo ḥuṣāṣē,[49]
mal‘elta gʷenda[50] ‘om naṣṣiro ’enza ya‘arreg ‘eḍē.

---

40. *tābot* (pl. *-āt*) ark (of Noah, of the Covenant).

41. A phrase from the liturgy.

42. *’emmat* (pl. *-āt*) cubit; forearm.

43. *Samēn* a mountainous region of Ethiopia. *samēn* is otherwise "south."

44. L *ṣāmawa (yeṣāmu)* to labor, toil. CL *’aṣāmawa* to inflict harsh labor on; to mortify (the flesh, as an ascetic practice). Cf. the noun *ṣāmā*.

45. *kidān* is used here in the special sense of a promise given by God to a particular saint that those who hereafter commemorate him or invoke his name will incur special favor thereby.

46. "Peace be to Yared, observer of the glory of the angels, from whose heart the spirit caused swift thought to ascend (i.e. made him forgetful); he returned from where he had fled (lit. was fugitive) to the study of scripture with much labor, without letting up, after watching a caterpiller climbing up the trunk of a tree." The separation of *ḥawwāṣē* from *sebḥata malā’ekt* is an extreme example of poetic license. The exact meaning of *manfas* is not clear; it probably is nothing more than "(his) nature, disposition."

47. *’enta* poetic for *za-* (relative).

48. G *nafaṣa (yenfeṣ)* to flee, escape. CG *’anfaṣa* to put to flight. *nafāṣi* fugitive. *nafāṣit* remnant, what survives (a disaster).

49. *ḥuṣāṣē* = *ḥeṣaṣ*.

50. *gʷend* (pl. *-āt*, *’agʷnād*) trunk of a tree; a restraining

G. Takla Hāymānot[1]

'Ama zāti 'elat ('ešrā wa-rabu' la-Naḥasē) 'a'rafa mamehhera 'ālam 'abuna Takla Hāymānot. Wa-la-zentu qeddus kona sema 'abuhu Ṣagā Za-'ab, wa-sema 'emmu 'Egzi' Xarayā.[2] Wa-kona Ṣagā Za-'ab 'em-zamada kāhenāt 'ella 'abrehewwā[3] la-'Ityopyā ba-hāymānotomu. Wa-be'situ-ni 'Egzi' Xarayā konat makāna,[4] wa-nabaru ba-zentu 'enza yaḥazzenu wa-yetēkkezu wa-yeṣēlleyu xaba 'Egzi'abḥēr kama yahabomu weluda. Wa-'enza hallawu ba-zentu nagar, 'anše'o Sayṭān la-Motalāmē[5] šeyuma[6] Dāmot,[5] wa-malaka[7] kʷello 'adyāma Šēwā 'eska bāḥra Žemmā. Wa-nabaru kʷellomu makʷānenta hagar 'enza yehubewwo lotu be'sitomu

---

device, a stock.

1. *Takla Hāymānot*, the famous Ethiopic saint associated with the end of the Zagwē Dynasty and the beginning of the Solomonic Dynasty c. 1270. He was the founder of Dabra Libānos, the most important monastery in Ethiopia.

2. G *xaraya/xarya (yexray)* to choose, select. Gt *taxarya* pass. *xeruy* chosen, selected; pleasing, acceptable; an arbiter, mediator; *xeruyān* the Elect (i.e. those who will be saved at the last day). *xeryat* choice, selection.

3. G *barha (yebrāh)* to shine, be bright, be light (cf. *berhān*). CG *'abreha* to illuminate, cause to shine; to emit light. *beruh* bright, shining; cheerful, happy.

4. G *makana (yemken)* to be sterile, childless. D *makkana* = CG *'amkana* to orphan. *makān* (f. of unattested **makin*) sterile, childless. *meknat* childlessness.

5. *Motalāmē* a personal name. *Dāmot* a province, NW of Shoa province. *Šēwā* Shoa province. *bāḥra Žemmā* a tributary of the Blue Nile.

6. *šeyum* as a noun: appointee, official, governor, prefect.

7. G *malaka (yemlek)* to take possession of, occupy, rule. Gt *tamalka* pass. *meluk* occupied, possessed, subject. *malāki* owner, ruler, heir. *melkennā* dominion, power, authority. A second set of forms from the same root, but deriving their meanings from *'Amlāk* God should be noted: C *'amlaka* to worship God, to worship as a god (a.d.o. or *la-*). Gt *tamalka* to be made lord or divine. *meluk* pious. *'amlākāwi* divine. *malakot* lordship, deity, divinity. *malakotāwi* divine. *mamlaki* one who worships God or gods.

ba-ba-'ebrētomu;[8] wa-'em-ze za-māhraka-hi[9] soba yerakkeb 'anesta lāḥeyāta,[10] yerēsseyon 'equbātihu.

Wa-ba-we'etu mawā'el baṣḥa hagara Ṣelāleś, wa-qatala k^{w}ello Kerestiyāna. Wa-Ṣagā Za-'ab-sa g^{w}ayya 'em-ferhata qatl, wa-la-be'situ-sa 'Egzi' Xarayā ḏēwawewwā ḥarrāhu, wa-'abṣeḥewwā xabēhu. Wa-soba re'yā, 'ankara šennā, wa-tafaššeḥo lebbu, wa-wahabā sarg^{w}a[11] bezuxa, wa-'astadālawa šer'ata kabkāb,[12] wa-fannawa xaba mak^{w}ānentihu wa-šeyumānihu kama yetgābe'u la-kabkāb. Wa-soba sam'at zanta 'Egzi' Xarayā, gabrat ṣalota xaba 'Egzi'abḥēr kama yādxenā 'em-tedmerta[13] 'arami. Wa-sobēhā maṣ'a Mikā'ēl liqa malā'ekt, wa-ṣorā ba-kenfu berhānāwi 'em-medra Dāmot ba-gizē šalās sa'āt, wa-'abseḥā medr Zorarē ba-gizē tes'u sa'āt, wa-'abe'ā westa bēta Kerestiyān. Wa-soba waḍ'a metā Ṣagā Za-'ab 'em-bēta maqdas mesla mā'ṭant,[14] naṣṣarā qawimā 'enza sergutā ye'eti.[15] 'Ankara ba-lebbu wa-yebē: "Ment-nu zāti be'sit wa-mannu 'amṣe'ā zeyya?" Wa-'emdexra feṣṣāmē ṣalot, soba ḥatatā, 'a'mara kama ye'eti be'situ. Wa-ye'eti-ni nagarato k^{w}ello za-gabra lāti 'Egzi'abḥēr 'em-ṭentu 'eska tafṣāmētu.

Wa-ba-'aḥatti lēlit 'astar'ayomu mal'aka 'Egzi'abḥēr, wa-

---

8. Glt *tabāraya* to follow successively, to do by turns. *'ebrēt* alternation, successive turn(s); round or tour of duty or office. *ba-'ebrēta* during the administration of. *ba-ba-'ebrētomu* each in his own turn.

9. Q *māhraka* to take captive, take as booty. *mehrekā* booty, spoils. *wa-'em-ze za-māhraka-hi* and even from those whom he took captive.

10. *lāḥey* (f. *lāḥeyt*) beautiful.

11. CQ *'asargawa* to adorn, deck out, beautify. Qt *tasargawa* pass. and reflex. *sergew* (f. *sergut*) adorned, beautified. *sarg^{w}* adornment, beautification. *sergāwē* idem.

12. *kabkāb* wedding, wedding feast.

13. D *dammara* to insert, mix in, join together, unite. Dt *tadammara* pass.; to be married. *demmur* mixed, united, joined. *demmārē* union, joining, uniting. *tedmert* union, marriage.

14. G *'aṭana (ye'ṭen)* to burn incense. *'eṭān* incense. *mā'ṭant* (pl. *ma'āṭen*) censer, thurible.

15. A combination of two constructions: *'enza sergut ye'eti* and *('enza) sergutā*.

zēnawomu kama yewalledu walda za-yebaṣṣeḥ semu‘āta ṣedqu westa k^{w}ellu ’aṣnāfa ‘ālam. Wa-’emdexra xedāṭ mawā‘el taḍansa zentu qeddus, wa-tawalda ’ama ‘ešrā wa-sanuy la-Tāxšāš, wa-kona ‘abiya tefšeḥta westa bēta ’abuhu wa-’emmu wa-xaba k^{w}ellomu ’azmādihu. Wa-ba-‘elata ’abe’ewwo Kerestennā[16] samayewwo semo Feššeḥā Ṣeyon. Wa-lehqa ba-Manfas Qeddus wa-ba-xayla ṭebab. Wa-nabara ’enza yegabber ta’āmera wa-mankera za-’albo x^{w}elq^{w}a ’eska yānakkeru ’emennēhu k^{w}ellomu ’ella re’yu wa-sam‘u. Wa-’emze wasadewwo xaba pāppās ’Abbā Gērellos[17] kama yešimo šimata diqunā,[18] ’enza ba-we’etu mawā‘el ’Abbā Benyāmi liqa pāppāsāt za-La’eskenderyā ’ama mangešta Zag^{w}ē ba-’emnat.[19] Wa-soba ’abṣeḥewwo xaba pāppās, tanabbaya lotu ’enza yebel ’esma "Zentu wald yekawwen newāya xeruya." Wa-naši’o šimata diqunā, tamayṭa westa beḥēru.

Wa-soba lehqa wa-kona warēzā, wafara[20] gadāma kama yen‘aw[21] ’arāwita. Wa-gizē qatr[22] ’astar’ayo ’Egzi’ena nabiro ba-kenfa Mikā’ēl ba-’amsāla warēzā šannāy lāḥeya gaṣṣu. Wa-yebēlo: "’I-tefrāh, ’o-fequreya. ’Em-ye’zē-sa ’i-tekawwen na‘āwē ’arāwit, ’allā tāšagger nafsāta xāṭe’ān bezuxāta. Wa-yekun semeka Takla Hāymānot, ’esma ’ana xaraykuka ’em-karša[23] ’emmeka, wa-qaddaskuka kama ’Ēremeyās nabiy wa-kama Yoḥannes Maṭmeq. Wa-nāhu ṣaggokuka[24] šelṭāna[25] kama tefawwes

16. "to bring someone to Christianity" = to baptize, christen. Note *ba-‘elata* used as a conjunction.

17. *Gērellos* Cyrillus.

18. *diqunā* diaconate. *La’eskenderyā* = *’Eskenderyā*.

19. The rulers of the Zag^{w}ē Dynasty (c. 1137 - c. 1270) were eventually converted to Christianity. The phrase *ba-’emnat* refers to that latter phase of the dynasty.

20. G *wafara (yewfer, yufar)* to go out into the country. *wafr* the countryside, fields, farmland. *mufār* farmland, pasture.

21. G *na‘awa (yen‘aw)* to hunt; to catch birds. *na‘āwi* hunter. *na‘awē/nā‘wē* hunting

22. *qatr* noon, midday.

23. *karš* (pl. *-āt*) belly, stomach.

24. D *ṣaggawa* to show grace or favor (to: obj. suff. or *la-*); to bestow gifts. Dt *taṣaggawa* to be shown grace or favor. *ṣaggāwi/ ṣagāwi* liberal, generous.

25. D *šallaṭa* to have power, authority. CD *’ašallaṭa* = CG

deweyāna wa-tesded manāfesta rekusāna ʼem-westa k^{w}ellu makān." Wazanta behilo tasawwara ʼemennēhu.

Wa-ʼemze ʼatawa westa māxdaru, wa-zarawa[26] k^{w}ello newāyo la-naddāyān wa-la-meskinān, wa-našʼa merg^{w}eza,[27] wa-xadaga bēto rexewa, wa-waḍʼa ba-lēlit ʼenza yebel: "Menta yebaqq^{w}eʻo[28] la-sabʼ laʼemma k^{w}ello ʻālama rabḥa[29] wa-nafso hag^{w}ala.[30] Wa-ʼemze našʼa šimata kehnat, wa-waṭana yesbek hāymānota wangēl ba-k^{w}ellu medra Śēwā, wa-ʼaṭmaqa ba-ʼaḥatti ʻelat maṭana 10,000 nafs. Wa-saʻara[31] k^{w}ello meḥrāmāta[32] ṭāʻot, wa-gazama[33] ʼaʻwāmātihomu ʼeska g^{w}ayyu Sayṭānāt

---

ʼaslaṭa to give power to. Dt *tašallaṭa* = Gt *tašalṭa* to acquire power, authority; to rule. *šeluṭ/šelluṭ* powerful, in power. *šelṭān* (pl. *-āt*) power, authority. CQ *ʼašalṭana* to delegate power to.

26. G *zarawa (yezru)* to scatter, disperse, distribute. Gt *tazarwa* pass. *zerew* scattered, dispersed. *zerwat* dispersion. *zarāwi* (one) who scatters, disperses; prodigal, extravagant.

27. *merg^{w}ez* staff. Qt *tamarg^{w}aza* to lean upon.

28. G *baq^{w}ʻa (yebq^{w}āʻ)* to be useful, of benefit, profitable, suitable, appropriate (to a person: obj. suff. or *la-*); *beq^{w}eʻani* Please. CGt *ʼastabq^{w}eʻa* to plead, beseech, pray (with, to: obj. suff.). *bāq^{w}eʻ* useful, beneficial. *baq^{w}āʻi* = *bāq^{w}eʻ*; also benefactor. *baq^{w}ʻēt* use, usefulness.

29. G *rabḥa (yerbāḥ)* to gain (as) profit; to be profitable. CG *ʼarbeḥa* to make profitable, to make (someone) profit. *rebāḥ/rabāḥ* profit, interest, gain.

30. G *hag^{w}la/hag^{w}ala* to perish, die; to lose, suffer a loss. CG *ʼahg^{w}ala* to destroy. Gt *tahag^{w}la* to perish, die, be destroyed. *hegul* lost, destroyed. *hag^{w}l* destruction, end. *māhg^{w}el* = *māhg^{w}ali* destroyer; adj. destructive.

31. G^1 *saʻara (yesʻar)* to destroy, violate, annul, dissolve, bring to an end. G^2 *seʻra* = Gt *taseʻra* pass. of G^1. *seʻrat* destruction, violation, annulment; dismissal, removal (from office).

32. G *ḥarama* to set aside as sacred, to dedicate (something, someone) to a deity; to regard as taboo. D *ḥarrama* to anathematize. CG *ʼaḥrama* = G; also: to make or declare as taboo. Dt *taḥarrama* to be taboo, prohibited; to abstain from for reasons of taboo; to be superstitious. *ḥerum* sacred, forbidden, taboo, anathematized; abstinent. *ḥermat* (pl. *-āt*) anything sacred, ritual, ceremony. *meḥrām*

'ella yaxadderu bomu. Wa-ba-medra Dāmot-hi 'a'mana bezuxāna māreyāna[34] wa-masaggelāna,[35] wa-bezuxa 'elata taqāwamo la-Motalāmē 'elew ba'enta hāymānot rete't 'eska 'a'mano ba-Kerestos. Wa-'a'manomu la-bezuxān 'ella meslēhu. Wa-'astar'aya 'amēhā[36] lebsa menk^w^esennā ba-medra Śēwā. Wa-nabara 'enza yeḍḍammad ba-ṣom wa-ba-ṣalot za-'albo x^w^elq^w^a 'eska 'aqne'omu[37] la-manakosāt bā'edān.

Wa-'emze ḥora medra 'Amḥarā taṣe''ino ba-saragalā[38] 'Ēleyās, wa-baṣḥa xaba 'Abbā Ba-ṣalota Mikā'ēl mastagādel manakos, wa-nabara xabēhu bezuxa mawā'ela 'enza yetqannay[39] lotu kama gabr wa-yeḍḍammad la-ṣalotu. Wa-'emze tamayṭa medra Śēwā, wa-tarākabo la-Marqos walda 'exwa 'abuhu. Wa-nabaru xebura ba-gadāma Wagadā, wa-tagābe'u xaba qeddus maṭana 'aša̲rtu wa-sedestu 'arde't, wa-'albasomu 'albāsa menk^w^esennā.

Wa-'em-heyya ḥora medra Gerāryā, wa-gabra ṣomā'ta[40] mā'kala

---

(pl. *-āt*) sacred precinct, temple. *teḥremt* abstinence, devotion.

33. G *gazama (yegzem)* to cut down (a tree), to fell; to cut, hew (wood). Gt *tagazma* pass.

34. *māri* (pl. *māreyān, māreyāt, mārayt*) heathen priest, soothsayer. Dt *tamarraya* = Glt *tamāraya* to divine, practice divination, soothsaying.

35. C *'asgala* to divine, practice augury. CGt *'astasagala* idem; to consult diviners. *sagal* divination. *masaggel* (pl. *-ān*) diviner, magician, soothsayer.

36. *'amēhā* adv. then, at that time.

37. G *qan'a (yeqnā')* to be zealous, eager; to envy, be jealous of (person: *la-*; thing: *'emenna*); to emulate, imitate (a.d.o.). CG *'aqne'a* to incite to zeal or imitation. Glt *taqāne'a* to be jealous of one another. CGlt *'astaqāne'a* to cause to be mutually envious. *qan'* = *qen'at* jealousy; zeal; emulation; intense hate or love. *qanā'i* (one who is) jealous, zealous, envious.

38. *saragalā* (pl. *-t*) cart, wagon, chariot. The reference here is to the chariot which took Elijah to heaven (2 Kings 2).

39. G *qanaya (yeqni)* to reduce to servitude, to subject, rule; to force to work. CG *'aqnaya* idem. Gt *taqanya* pass. of G; to serve, minister to (a person); to work (e.g. a field). *qenuy* subject, servant, slave. *qenē* servitude; service, ministry; task, office, function. *qenyat* domination, dominion, subjection.

ṣolā‘t,[41] wa-’i-yewaḍḍe’ ’em-heyya lēlita wa-ma‘ālta, wa-’i-yeṭe‘‘em menta-ni za’enbala qʷaṣl bāḥtitā, wa-setēhu[42]-ni māy. Wa-maṣ’u xabēhu bezuxān ‘ed wa-’anest, wa-konu manakosāta wa-maballatāta,[43] wa-yaxadderu westa ’aḥatti bēt, wa-’i-yet’āmaru babaynātihomu be’si mesla be’sit, wa-ba-gizē ṣalot wa-qʷerbān[44] yeqawwemu xebura, ’esma Sayṭān ta’asra ba-mawā‘elihu.

Wa-’emze nadaqa[45] westa ṣolā‘tu ba-’amsāla meḍnegā‘,[46] wa-takala westētu xaṣāwenta balixāta[47] ’enta dexrēhu ba-yamānu[48] wa-ba-ḍagāmu[49] kama ’i-yāsmek[50] botu; wa-qoma westētu sabā‘ta ‘āmata ’eska tasabra[51] ’agadā[52] ’egru. Wa-nabara ’enza ’i-yeṭe‘‘em menta-ni ’em-ferēyāt wa-’i-qʷaṣla wa-’i-māya maṭana ’arbā‘tu ‘āmat. Wa-’emze maṣ’a xabēhu ’Egzi’ena ’Iyasus Kerestos (lotu sebḥat), wa-meslēhu ’Egze’tena Māryām wa-‘as̆artu wa-kel’ētu ḥawāreyāt wa-ṣādeqān wa-

---

40. *ṣomā‘t* (pl. *-āt*) monk's cell.

41. *ṣolā‘* (pl. *-āt, -t*) rock(s).

42. G *satya (yestay)* to drink. CG *’astaya* to cause to drink, to give a drink to. Gt *tasatya* pass. *setē* = *setāy* = *mastē* a drink (the act or what is drunk). *satāy(i)* a drinker; one who is fond of drinking. *mestāy* a place for drinking, a watering place.

43. *maballat* (pl. *-āt*) widow, widowhood; nun.

44. *qʷerbān* (pl. *-āt*) offering, sacrifice; spec. the communion (eucharist).

45. G *nadaqa* to build, erect. Gt *tanadqa* pass. *nedq* building, structure, wall. *nadāqi* builder.

46. *meḍnegā‘* a railing, railed enclosure; a place where one leans or reclines.

47. G *balxa* to be sharp. CG *’ablexa* to sharpen. *belx* sharp edge or point. *balix* sharp.

48. *yamān* the right side or hand. *yemn* idem; *yemna* adv. on/to the right. *yemuna* adv. rightly, correctly.

49. *ḍagām* the left side or hand. *ḍegm* idem.

50. CG *’asmaka* to lean; to prop up, cause to lean. *masmak(t)* prop, support. *mesmāk* idem.

51. G *sabara (yesber)* to break (into pieces). Gt *tasabra* pass.; to be overcome by disaster. *sebur* broken. *sebr* fragment, piece. *sebār* idem. *sebrat* vn. breaking, fracturing.

52. *’agadā* large bone of the leg; tibia; shin-bone.

samā'tāt wa-Mikā'ēl wa-Gabre'ēl, wa-yebēlo: "O-fequreya, 'anta-hi tamasalkani[53] ba-ḥemāmeya, wa-'ana-hi 'ā'ērreyaka ba-mangešteya. Nāhu tafaṣṣama k^{w}ellu dekāmeka ba-ze 'ālam, wa-*konka* wekkufa ba-xabēya. 'Em-ye'zē-sa na'ā kama teras ḥeywata za-la-'ālam." Wa-'emze wahabo kidāna la-za yeṣēwwe' semo wa-la-za yegabber tazkāro. Wa-'emze ḥamma nestita ba-ḥemāma bedbed,[54] wa-'a'rafa ba-reš'ān ṭelul[55] 'enza mawā'elihu tes'ā wa-tes'ata 'āmata wa-'ašarta 'awrāxa wa-'ašarta 'elata. Wa-ganazewwo ba-kebr wa-ba-sebḥat, wa-qabarewwo westa maqāber.

Salām 'ebel 'enbala 'armemo[56] ba-ṣewwā'ē[57]
kiyāka 'aba kiyāka radā'ē Takla Hāymānot mawā'ē.
'Enza texēlli tasfā tenšā'ē,
'aṣnā'ka ba-qawim 'a'gāra kel'ē
wa-'em-setē māy 'aḥramka g^{w}er'ē.[58]

---

53. Gt *tamasla* = Dt *tamassala* (1) to become or be made like/similar (to: a.d.o. or *la-*, *ba-*, *kama*); (2) to imitate; (3) to transform one's self, change (into: a.d.o. or *ba-*, *la-*, *kama*, *ba-'amsāla*); (4) to be represented (by a likeness).

54. *bedbed* plague, fatal illness. Q *badbada* to die.

55. G *ṭalla* to be moist. CG *'aṭlala* to moisten, bedew. *ṭelul* moist, rich, fat, prosperous. *ṭall* dew. *maṭlali* moistening, refreshing.

56. CG *'armama* to be silent; to make silent. Gt *taramma* to be passed over in silence. CGlt *'astarāmama* to make silent, quiet down, make tranquil. *marmem* silent. *'armāmi* silent, not speaking.

57. The verbal noun is used here with acc. attributes: "in calling you 'Father,' (in calling) you 'Helper, Takla Hāymanot, the Conqueror."

58. *g^{w}er'ē* (pl. *g^{w}arā'it*) throat, neck. Qt *tag^{w}ar'aya* to strangle (hang) one's self.

II. The Book of Baruch

The text transcribed here is essentially that of August Dillmann, *Chrestomathia aethiopica* (Leipzig 1866; reprinted Berlin 1950), pp. 1-15. I have made a few emendations in various passages, basing my reading on the Greek text as edited by James Rendel Harris, *The Rest of the Words of Baruch* (London 1889), but I have made no effort to reconstruct an "original" text. My aim is solely to present a readable version of this interesting work.

The numbering of the verses is simply serial and follows the divisions of the Ethiopic text. The Roman numeral headings and the Arabic numerals in parentheses are chapter and verse according to the Greek text of Harris. The correspondence is only approximate where the two texts diverge.

Tarafa nagar za-Bārok za-'i-kona xebu'a
za-'ama yeḍḍēwawu Bābilon[1]

I

1 (1) Wa-kona soba ḍēwawomu la-daqiqa 'Esrā'ēl negušа Kalādēwon,[2]
nababo 'Egzi'abḥēr la-'Ēremeyās wa-yebēlo: "'Ēremeyās xeruyeya,
tanše' wa-ḍā' 'em-zāti hagar, 'anta wa-Bārok, 'esma halloku 'āmāsenā
'em-bezxa[3] xaṭi'atomu la-'ella yenabberu westētā; (2) 'esma ṣaloteka-
ni kama 'amd[4] ṣenu' ba-mā'kala hagar wa-kama qeṣr[5] za-'admās[6] 'awdā.
(3) Wa-ye'zē-ni tanše'u wa-ḥoru wa-ḍā'u za'enbala yemṣā' xayla

---

1. The two *za-* clauses of this title have the appearance of being added rather loosely to a shorter original title (cf. the Greek). Dillmann (*Chrest.*, p. viii) translates: Reliqua verborum Baruchi, haud apocrypha, quae ad tempus quo in Babylonia captivi erant pertinent.

2. *Kalādēwon* the Chaldeans.

3. *'em-* here and *ba-* in vs. 4 (similar phrase) are used somewhat loosely in the sense "because of."

4. *'amd* (pl. *'a'mād*) column, pillar.

5. *qeṣr/qaṣr* (pl. *'aqṣār*) wall, enclosure, fortification-wall. G *qaṣara* to enclose or fortify with a wall.

6. *'admās* the hardest substance, from Gk. *adamas*.

Kalādēwon wa-ye'udā la-hagar."

2 (4) Wa-nababa 'Ēremeyās 'enza yebel: "'Āstabaqq^{w}e'aka 'Egzi'eya, 'azzezo la-gabreka kama yetnāgar qedmēka." Wa-yebēlo 'Egzi'abḥēr: "Nebeb xeruyeya 'Ēremeyās."

3 (5) Wa-nababa 'Ēremeyās wa-yebē: "'Egzi'o, za-k^{w}ello te'exxez, temēṭṭu-nu zāta hagara xerita westa 'edēhomu la-Kalādēwon, kama yezzaxxar[7] neguš mesla ḥezabihu wa-yebal: 'Taxayyalku qeddesta[8] hagara za-'Amlāk'? (6) Ḥāsa,[9] 'Egzi'o. 'Emma-sa faqādeka[10] we'etu, ba-'edēka tāmāsenā."

4 (7) Wa-yebēlo 'Egzi' la-'Ēremeyās: "'Esma xeruyeya 'anta, tanše' wa-ḏā'u, 'anta wa-Bārok, 'esma halloku 'āmāsenā ba-xaṭi'atomu la-'ella yenabberu westētā; (8) wa-'i-neguš wa-'i-xayla zi'ahu 'i-yekel bawi'a westa hagar la'emma 'ana 'i-qadamku wa-'i-ỷarxawku 'anāqeṣihā. (9) Tanše' ye'zē-ni, wa-ḥor xaba Bārok, wa-zēnewo zanta nagara. (10) Wa-tanši'akemu soba kona sedestu sa'āt za-lēlit, ne'u westa qeṣra hagar, wa-'ana 'ārē''eyakemu. Wa-la'emma 'ana 'i-qadamku 'amāsenotā la-hagar, 'i-yekelu bawi'otā."

II

5 (11) Wa-zanta behilo 'Egzi' xalafa 'em-xaba 'Ēremeyās. (1) Wa-'Ēremeyās sobēhā šaṭaṭa[11] 'albāsihu, wa-wadaya ḥamada[12] diba re'su, wa-bo'a westa bēta maqdas.

6 (2) Wa-re'iyo Bārok la-'Ēremeyās 'enza melu' marēta[13] diba re'su wa-'albāsihu-ni šeṭuṭ, ṣarxa[14] ba-'abiy qāl 'enza yebel: "'Abuya 'Ēremeyās, menta konka, wa-'ayya xaṭi'ata gabru ḥezb?"

---

7. Dt *tazaxxara/tazexxera* to boast; to brawl. *zexxur* boastful, arrogant; quarrelsome. *tezxert* vn. boasting, insolence; strife, brawling.

8. Reading *qeddesta* for *westa/we'eta*. Cf. Gk.

9. *ḥāsa* exclam. Heaven forbid! Let it not be so!

10. Reading *faqādeka* for *faqadka*; cf. the Gk. If *faqadka* is retained, the following *we'etu* should be deleted.

11. G *šaṭaṭa (yešṭeṭ)* to tear (apart), rend. Gt *tašaṭṭa* pass. *šeṭuṭ* torn, rent. *šeṭṭat* vn. tearing, rending; the part torn off, tatter, fragment.

12. *ḥamad* ash(es). G *ḥamda* = Gt *taḥamda* to be burned to ashes.

13. *marēt* dirt, dust. *marētāwi* adj.

14. G *ṣarxa (yeṣrāx)* to cry out. *ṣerāx* a cry, shout.

7 (3) 'Esma soba ye'ēbbesu ḥezb, yaḥazzen 'Ēremeyās wa-yewaddi ḥamada diba re'su, wa-yeṣēlli ba'enta ḥezb 'eska yetxaddag lomu 'abbasāhomu la-ḥezb.

8 (4) Wa-tase''elo Bārok 'enza yebel: "'Abuya 'Ēremeyās, menta konka wa-menta konu ḥezb?"

9 (5) Wa-yebēlo 'Ēremeyās: "'Eqab kama 'i-nešṭeṭ 'albāsina,[15] 'allā nešṭeṭ 'albābina; wa-'i-neday māya westa me'qālāt,[16] 'allā[17] nebki retu'a 'eska nemalle'omu 'anbe'a,[18] 'esma 'em-ye'zē 'i-yemeḥḥerewwo la-ze ḥezb."

10 (6) Wa-yebē Bārok: "'Abuya 'Ēremeyās, menta konka?" (7) Wa-yebēlo 'Ēremeyās: "'Esma 'Amlāk yemēṭṭewā la-hagar westa 'edēhu la-neguša Kalādēwon, 'esma yeḍēwewomu la-ḥezb ba-'ekit."[19]

11 (8) Wa-sami'o zanta k^{w}ello Bārok šaṭaṭa 'albāsihu wa-yebē: "'Abuya 'Ēremeyās, menta la'aku laka?"

12 (9) Wa-yebēlo 'Ēremeyās: "Ṣenāḥ meslēya 'eska sedestu sa'at za-lēlit kama tā'mer za-'amān nagar."

13 (10) Wa-nabaru bēta maqdas 'enza yebakkeyu.

III

14 (1) Wa-soba kona sedestu sa'at za-lēlit, za-yebēlo[20] 'Egzi' la-'Ēremeyās kama yeḍā' mesla Bārok, wa-baṣḥu westa qeṣra hagar, wa-nabaru 'enza yeṣanneḥu.

15 (2) Wa-kona qāla qarn,[21] wa-waḍ'u malā'ekt 'em-samāy, wa-ba-'edawihomu yeṣawweru berhānatā 'essāt, wa-qomu westa qeṣra hagar.

16 (3) Wa-sobēhā 'Ēremeyās wa-Bārok bakayu 'enza yebelu 'esma: "Ye'zē 'a'marna kama 'amān nagar."

17 (4) Wa-'astabq^{w}e'omu 'Ēremeyās la-malā'ekt 'enza yebel:

---

15. Cf. Joel 2:13.

16. *me'qāl* (pl. *-āt*) basin, reservoir. CG *'a'qala* to collect water in a basin or reservoir.

17. Reading *'allā* for *kama*. Cf. Gk.

18. *'anbe'* (pl. *'anābe'*) tear(s). CG *'anbe'a* to weep.

19. *ba-'ekit* badly, direly, in dire circumstances.

20. Note the lack of resumption in the relative clause.

21. *qarn* (pl. *'aqrent*) horn (of animal); horn blown in battle etc.; tip, end. Glt *taqārana* to oppose, resist. *taqārāni* adj. contrary, resisting, opposing. *mastaqāren* idem.

"’Āstabaqqʷe‘akemu, kʷello[22] ’i-tāhgʷelu hagara ’eska ’ese’’elo la-’Egzi’abḥēr ’aḥatta nagara." Wa-nababomu ’Egzi’ la-malā’ekt ’enza yebel: "’I-tāhgʷelu hagara ’eska ’etnāgar mesla ’Ēremeyās xeruyeya."

18 Wa-sobēhā tanāgara ’Ēremeyās ’enza yebel: "’Āstabaqqʷe‘aka ’Egzi’eya, ’azzez lita kama ’etnāgar meslēka." (5) Wa-yebēlo: "Nebeb xeruyeya ’Ēremeyās za-tefaqqed."

19 (6) Wa-yebēlo ’Ēremeyās: "Nāhu ye’zē ’a’marna, ’Egzi’eya, kama temēṭṭewā la-hagar westa ’eda ṣalā’tā, wa-yenašše’ā ḥezb za-’em-Bābilon. (7) Wa-menta tefaqqed kama ’egbar qeddesta qenēna, ba-xebu’ za-netqannay?[23] Wa-menta tefaqqed ’egbar dibēhomu?"

20 (8) Wa-yebēlo ’Egzi’: "Neše’omu wa-maṭṭewā la-medr wa-la-bēta maqdas ’enza tebel: 'Wa-’anti-ni medr, seme‘i qāla faṭāriki za-faṭaraki ba-xayla māyāt, za-xatamaki[24] ba-7-māxtamt. Tamaṭṭawi šennaki, wa-‘eqabi newāya qenēki ’eska meṣ’atu la-fequr."

21 (9) Wa-nababa ’Ēremeyās wa-yebē: "’Āstabaqqʷe‘aka ’Egzi’eya, ’ar’eyani za-’egabber la-’Abēmēlēk ’Ityopyāwi, za-we’etu bezuxa ‘aqabomu la-ḥezb wa-la-gabreka-ni ’Ēremeyās fadfāda ’em-kʷellu sab’a hagar, wa-we’etu ’awḍe’ani ’em-westa ‘azaqta ‘am‘am.[25] Wa-’i-yefaqqed lotu yer’ay[26] musenāhā wa-hagʷlā la-hagar, kama ’i-yeḥzan."

22 (10) Wa-yebēlo ’Egzi’ la-’Ēremeyās: "Fannewo westa ‘aṣada wayn za-Hagrippās[27] ba-fenot za-dabr, wa-’ana ’ekaddeno[28] ’eska

---

22. *kʷello* adv. altogether, completely; with negative: (not) at all. Here it seems to mean "(not) just yet."

23. In spite of the awkwardness, no obvious changes can be made. The phrase *ba-xebu’* has no counterpart in the Greek and stands in an ambiguous position in the Ethiopic. *qeddest qenē* refers to the vessels of the Temple service.

24. G *xatama (yextem)* to seal, close and seal. Gt *taxatma* pass. *xetum* sealed, signed and sealed. *xatāmi* an. one who seals, signer. *māxtam(t)* a seal.

25. *‘am‘am* mud, slime.

26. An unusual construction with *faqada*: "I do not want him to see ..."

27. *Hagrippās* Agrippa (anachronistically).

28. G *kadana (yekden)* to cover, protect; to pardon (sins). Gt *takadna* pass. *kedun* covered, protected. *kedān* (pl. *-āt*) covering; esp. tunic, garment. *kednat* vn. protection. *kadāni* an. protector.

'āgabbe'omu la-ḥezb westa hagar. (11) Wa-'anta 'Ēremeyās ḥor mesla ḥezb 'eska tebaṣṣeḥu medra Bābilon, wa-nebar tetnēbbay lomu 'eska 'āgabbe'omu westa hagaromu. (12) Wa-la-Bārok-hi xedego heyya westa 'Iyarusālēm."

23 (13) Wa-nagaro 'Egzi' zanta kʷello la-'Ēremeyās, wa-xalafa 'em-xaba 'Ēremeyās westa samāy.

24 (14) Wa-'Ēremeyās wa-Bārok bo'u westa bēta maqdas, wa-kʷello newāya za-qenēhomu maṭṭawewwā la-medr bakama 'azzazomu 'Egzi'. Wa-sobēhā šarabato[29] medr. Wa-nabaru kel'ēhomu wa-bakayu.

25 (15) Wa-ba-sānitā ṣabiḥo[30] fannawo 'Ēremeyās la-'Abēmēlēk 'enza yebel: "Nešā' karabo,[31] wa-ḥor 'enta fenota dabr westa 'aṣada wayn za-Hagrippās, wa-'amṣe' nestita balasa[32] la-deweyān ḥezb, 'esma[33] tefšeḥta 'Egzi' hallo westa re'seka wa-sebḥatu." Wa-ḥora we'etu-ni bakama 'azzazo.

IV

26 (1) Wa-ba-sānitā ṣabiḥo xayla Kalādēwon 'odewwā la-hagar. Wa-nafxa[34] ba-qarn 'abiy mal'ak, wa-yebē we'etu: "Bā'u xayla Kalādēwon. Nāhu yetraxxaw lakemu 'anāqeṣ."

27 (2) Wa-sobēhā bo'a neguš mesla sarāwitu,[35] wa-ḍēwawu kʷello ḥezba.

28 (3) Wa-sobēhā 'Ēremeyās naš'a marāxuta za-bēta maqdas, wa-waḍ'a 'af'ā 'em-hagar, wa-wagaro la-zentu marāxut qedma ḍaḥāy 'enza yebel: "Laka 'ebelaka ḍaḥāy. Nešā' marāxuta za-bēta 'Amlāk, wa-'eqabomu 'eska mawā'el za-yessē''alaka 'Egzi'abḥēr ba'enti'ahu, (4) 'esma lana 'i-kona delwata[36] la-'aqibotu, 'esma tarakabna neḥna-sa

---

29. G *šaraba* to drink in, absorb.

30. G *ṣabḥa (yeṣbāḥ)* to grow light, to dawn; *ṣabiḥo* at dawn. Glt *taṣābeḥa* to greet early in the day.

31. *karabo* basket.

32. *balas/balasā* (pl. *-t*, *'ablās*) fig(s) (tree or fruit).

33. Ignore *'esma* and translate the clause as a blessing.

34. G *nafxa (yenfāx)* to blow, breathe; to blow into, inflate; *nafxa ba-qarn* to blow a horn. Gt *tanafxa* to be inflated, to swell. *nefxat* vn. inflation, blowing.

35. *sarwē* (pl. *sarāwit*) troops, army, cohorts; a military leader.

36. Reading *delwata* for *delwata ledatena*. A dittography seems

'enza naḥaḍḍenā la-xaṭi'atena."

29 (5) Wa-'enza yebakki 'Ēremeyās la-ḥezb, 'awḍe'ewwo 'enza yātēkkelewwo,[37] wa-nad'ewwo[38] mesla ḥezb 'eska Bābilon.

30 (6) Wa-Bārok-sa naš'a ḥamada wa-wadaya westa re'su, wa-nabara, wa-'asqoqawa[39] zanta saqoqāwa, wa-yebē: "Ba'enta ment māsanat 'Iyarusālēm, 'allā[40] ba'enta xaṭi'atu la-fequr ḥezb? Wa-tawehbat ba-'eda ṣalā'ihā[41] ba'enta xaṭi'atena wa-za-ḥezb. (7) 'Allā, kama 'i-yezzaxxaru xāṭe'ān wa-'i-yebalu 'Kehelna naši'otā la-hagara 'Amlāk ba-xaylena,' -- 'i-kona ba-ṣen'ekemu za-kehelkemewwā 'allā ba-xaṭi'atena tawehbat lakemu. (8) Wa-'Amlākena yemeḥḥerana wa-yāgabbe'ana westa hagarena, wa-lakemu-sa ḥeywat 'albo. (9) Beḍu'ān 'emuntu 'abawina 'Abrehām wa-Yesḥaq wa-Yā'qob, 'esma waḍ'u 'em-ze 'ālam wa-'i-re'yu musenāhā la-zāti hagar."

31 (10) Wa-'emdexra zanta tanāgara, waḍ'a 'enza yebakki, wa-yebē: "'Aḥazzen ba'enti'aki, 'Iyarusālēm." Wa-waḍ'a 'em-hagar, wa-xadara westa maqāber, wa-yemaṣṣe'u malā'ekt wa-yezēnewewwo ba'enta k^wellu.

V

32 (1) Wa-'Abēmēlēk-ni 'amse'a balasa gizē qatr 'em-xaba la'ako 'Ēremeyās, wa-rakaba 'eḍa ṣefeqta,[42] wa-nabara, wa-'aṣlala, kama yā'ref nestita. Wa-'asmaka re'so diba mudāya balas, wa-noma sessā

---

likely.

37. CD *'atakkala* to push, shove, hit.

38. G *nad'a* to drive (as cattle). Gt *tanad'a* pass. *nadā'i* one who drives, expels.

39. Q *'asqoqawa* to lament, sing a dirge. *saqoqāw* dirge, lamentation. *masqoqew* an. mourner; adj. lamenting, mourning.

40. *'allā*, normally used after a negative clause, will occur frequently in contexts where rhetorical questions imply a negative statement of some sort. Here it should be rendered as "unless, except."

41. G *ṣal'a (yeṣlā')* to hate, be hostile toward (a.d.o.). *ṣalā'i* (pl. *ṣalā't*) enemy, hater, detractor.

42. *ṣefuq* dense, thick, crowded; frequent. CG *'aṣfaqa* to make dense; to do something frequently (+ inf.). Gt *taṣafqa* to be dense, crowded.

wa-sedesta ʿāmata, wa-ʾi-naqha[43] ʾem-newāmu.

33 (2) Wa-ʾemdexra-ze mawāʿel tanše'a, wa-naqha ʾem-newāmu, wa-yebē: "ʿĀdi[44] soba nomku nestita, ʾesma ʿādi yekabbedani[45] reʾseya, wa-ʾi-ṭeʿiku[46] newāma."

34 (3) Wa-kašata zekʷa mudāya balas, wa-rakaba zekʷa balasa ḥaddisāna wa-yānṣafaṣṣef[47] ḥalibon.[48]

35 (4) Wa-faqada yenum dāgema, ʾesma yekabbedo reʾsu wa-ʾi-ṭeʿya deqqāsa,[49] wa-yebē: (5) "ʾEfarreh kama ʾi-y̓enum wa-ʾi-y̓egʷandi, kama ʾi-yeḥisani[50] ʾabuya ʾĒremeyās, ʾesma ṣehiqo[51] fannawani ba-nagh.[52] (6) Wa-yeʾzēni ʾetnaššāʾ wa-ʾaḥawwer, ʾesma moqa-sa[53] wāʿy

---

43. G *naqha (yenqāh)* to wake up, be awake, be alert. CG *ʾanqeha* to awaken, revive. *nequh* awake, watchful, alert. *neqhat* vn. watchfulness, alertness.

44. The exact force of *ʿādi soba ... ʾesma ʿādi* here is not clear. Either "Although I have slept a little (for my head is still heavy), I have not benefited from the sleep" or "Although I have slept a little, my head is still heavy and I...."

45. G *kabda* to be heavy, serious. CG *ʾakbada* to make heavy; to be burdensome. *kebud* heavy. *kebad* vn. heaviness. *kabd* the liver; the stomach.

46. Dillmann (*Chrest.*, p. 5) has a misprint here. Note the variants *ṭeʿeyku*, *ṭaʿayku*.

47. N *ʾanṣafṣafa* to ooze, drip; trans.: to exude in drops. *naṣafṣāf* juice, drops. *ṣafṣāf* idem.

48. *ḥalib* milk, juice. G *ḥalaba (yeḥleb)* to milk.

49. D *daqqasa* to sleep. *deqqās* vn. sleep.

50. G *ḥēsa (yeḥis)* to scold, reprove. Gt *taḥaysa* pass. *ḥis* vn. reproach, scolding.

51. G *ṣehqa (yeṣhaq)* to desire; to be eager for, pursue diligently; to take care of. CG *ʾaṣhaqa* caus. *ṣehuq* desirous, eager, concerned. *ṣāhq* vn. desire, eagerness, concern. *ṣehiqo* here is equivalent to an adverb "deliberately, with concern."

52. G *nagha* to dawn, grow light. CG *ʾangeha* to do something early in the day. *nagh* early morning.

53. G *moqa (yemuq)* to grow hot; to become intense (of the heat). CG *ʾamoqa* caus. CGlt *ʾastamāwaqa* to cause to become hot. *moq* heat. *muqat* heat. *mewuq* hot.

wa-'albo soba yaxaddeg ba-k^wellahi."[54]

36 (7) Wa-tanše'a, wa-naš'a mudāya balasu, wa-bo'a westa hagara 'Iyarusālēm, wa-'i-ya'mara hagara wa-'i-bēto, wa-yebē: (8) "Buruk 'anta 'Egzi'o," 'esma 'abiy dengāḍē warada lā'lēhu.

37 Wa-yebē: "'Akko-nu zāti ye'eti hagara 'Iyarusālēm? (9) Yogi 'egēgi[55] 'esma 'enta fenota dabr maṣā'ku. Wa-'emma 'akko,[56] (10) 'esma yekabbedani re'seya wa-'i-ṭe'iku newāma, wa-yezanagge'ani[57] lebbeya. (11) Wa-'efo 'ezēnu zanta nagara ba-xaba 'Ēremeyās, zakama tabā'adatani[58] hagar?"

38 (12) Wa-xašaša k^wello te'merta za-hallo westa hagar kama yā'mer la'emma-nu[59] 'Iyarusālēm ye'eti.

39 (13) Wa-gab'a kā'eba westa hagar, wa-xašaša la'emma-bo za-yā'ammero, wa-xaṭ'a.

40 (14) Wa-yebē: "Buruk 'anta 'Egzi'o, 'esma 'abiy dengāḍē wadqa lā'lēya." (15) Wa-waḍ'a kā'eba 'em-hagar reḥuqa, wa-nabara 'enza yaḥazzen wa-'enza xaba yaḥawwer 'i-yā'ammer.

41 (16) Wa-'anbara zek^wa mudāya balas, wa-yebē: "'Enabber zeyya 'eska yā'attet[60] 'Egzi'abḥēr zanta heyyata[61] 'em-lā'lēya.

---

54. *k^wellahi/k^wellehi* adv. everywhere, wherever. *ba-k^wellahi* idem. This is an awkward clause: "for the heat has grown intense and is not (lit. never) lacking anywhere."

55. Q *gēgaya* to err, go astray, get lost; to sin, commit error. N *'angēgaya* to wander back and forth, hither and yon. *giguy* lost, erring; sinful, wicked. *gēgāy* vn. error, sin, crime, guilt.

56. *'emma 'akko* otherwise.

57. Q *zange'a* to be insane, mad, crazy. *zengu'* mad, raving; stupid, inept.

58. G *ba'ada* to change, alter. Gt *taba'ada* = Glt *tabā'ada* to move away, emigrate; to be changed, altered, alien, unfamiliar. *be'ud* different, alien, strange. *bā'dennā* change, difference.

59. Note the -*nu* in an indirect question. *la'emma-nu* whether.

60. G *'atata* to go away, be removed. CG *'a'tata* to remove, take away. Gt *ta'atata* = Dt *ta'attata* = G or pass. of CG. *'etut* remote, distant.

61. *heyyat* negligence, forgetfulness, amnesia. CG *'ahyaya* to cause to forget, to induce amnesia. Dt *tahayyaya* to neglect, skip, be unconcerned about.

42 (17) Wa-'emdexra-ze nabiro re'ya be'sē lehiqa ya'attu 'em-ḥaql,[62] wa-yebēlo 'Abēmēlēk: "Laka 'ebelaka 'anta lehiq. 'Ayy ye'eti zāti hagar?" Wa-yebēlo 'aragāy: "'Iyarusālēm ye'eti."

43 (18) Wa-yebēlo 'Abēmēlēk: "'Aytē hallo 'Ēremeyās kāhen wa-Bārok Lēwāwi[63] wa-kʷellu ḥezba-ze hagar? -- 'esma 'albo za-rakabku."

44 (19) Wa-yebēlo 'aragāy: "'Akko-nu 'em-zāti hagar 'anta, wa-ye'zē-ni-ma[64] tezzēkkaro la-'Ēremeyās (20) kama tessa''al ba'enti'ahu? Zanta kʷello mawā'ela nabiraka, (21) 'Ēremeyās-sa-kē westa Bābilon hallo mesla ḥezb, 'esma taḍēwawa wa-tawehba westa 'edēhu la-Nābukadanaṣor[65] negušа Fāres, wa-ḥora heyya kama yetnabbay lomu."

45 (22) Wa-'amēhā sam'a 'Abēmēlēk 'em-xaba we'etu 'aragāy, wa-yebēlo 'Abēmēlēk: (23) "Soba 'akko be'si lehiq 'anta, 'em[66]-ṣa'alkuka[67] wa-'em-šaḥaqqu[68] lā'lēka, 'allā 'i-yekawwen kama yāstaḥaqqeru[69] sab'a wa-be'sē lehiqa. Wa-soba 'akko za-kama-ze, 'em-'ebē zangā'ka.

46 Wa-ba'enta-sa za-tebē, 'Ḥezb taḍēwawu westa Bābilon,' (24) 'asrāba[70] samāy ṭeqqa la'emma warada dibēhomu 'i-kona gizēhu kama

---

62. *ḥaql* (pl. *'aḥqul*, *'aḥqāl*, *'aḥqelt*) field; any vast and empty tract. *ḥaqqāl* farmer.

63. *Lēwāwi* Levite.

64. *-ma* see above, §51.4f.

65. *Nābukadanaṣor* Nebuchadnezzar, king of Babylon (*Fāres*, lit. Persia).

66. *'em-* the conditional particle. See §51.1.

67. G *ṣa'ala* / D *ṣa''ala* to curse, revile. Dt *taṣe''ela/taṣa''ala* pass. *ṣe'ul/ṣe''ul* despised. *ṣe'lat* vn. cursing, reviling. *ṣa'āli* an. curser, railer.

68. G *šaḥaqa/šeḥqa (yešḥaq)* to ridicule (a.d.o. or *lā'la*). CG *'ašḥaqa* caus. *šāḥq/šaḥaq* ridicule. *mešḥāq* comedy theater.

69. CGt *'astāḥqara/'astaḥaqara* to revile, ridicule. *ḥequr* vile, despicable. The form here, if subjunctive, is CDt.

70. *'asrāb* (pl. only) cataracts, downpours. The meaning here is surely "Sooner would the cataracts of heaven descend upon them out of season than that they should go to Babylon," but this is a paraphrase of the actual Ethiopic: "Even if the cataracts of heaven descended upon them, it would not be the proper time for them to go

yeḥoru westa Bābilon. Wa-'anta-sa tebē, 'Taḏēwawu westa Bābilon.'

47 (25) Wa-'ane-sa, bakama fannawani 'abuya 'Ēremeyās, ḥorku westa 'aṣada wayn za-Hagrippās ba'enta xedāṯ balas, kama nahab la-deweyān 'ella westa ḥezb.

48 Ḥorku wa-baṣāḥku heyya, wa-našā'ku za-'azzazani, wa-tamayaṭku, wa-'enza 'aḥawwer (26) rakabku 'eḏa, wa-nabarku tāḥtēhā kama 'āṣlel, 'esma gizē qatr we'etu. Wa-'em-heyya[71] 'asmakku westa mudāya balas, wa-nomku, wa-naqiheya masalani za-g^{w}andayku, wa-kašatku zanta mudāya balas, wa-rakabku 'enza yānṣafaṣṣef ḥalib bakama našā'kewwomu xariyeya.[72] Wa-nawā[73] tebal 'anta-sa: 'Taḏēwawu ḥezb westa Bābilon,' (27) wa-nawā re'i kama 'i-ṣamhayaya[74] balasu-ni."

49 (28) Wa-kašata lotu mudāya balas, wa-'ar'ayo, (29) wa-naṣṣara 'aragāy kama ḥaddis we'etu balas, wa-yānṣafaṣṣef ḥalibu.

50 (30) Wa-sobēhā 'ankara we'etu 'aragāy, wa-yebēlo la-'Abēmēlēk: "Ṣādeq 'anta, waldeya, 'esma 'i-faqada 'Amlāk yār'ika musenāhā la-hagar, wa-'amṣe'a 'Amlāk nuzāzē[75] lā'lēka, wa-'ahyayaka. Nāhu yom sessā wa-sedestu 'āmat kona 'em-'ama taḏēwawu ḥezb westa Bābilon.

51 (31) Wa-'emma tefattu tā'mer wa-teṭayyeq, waldeya, naṣṣer wa-re'i westa garāweh.[76] kama šarṣa[77] 'azre'tihā,[78] wa-la-balas-ni kama 'i-kona gizēhu." Wa-'a'mara kama 'i-kona zamanu la-ze-k^{w}ellu.

52 (32) Sobēhā 'Abēmēlēk yebē ba-'abiy qāl: "'Ebārekaka 'Egzi'o, 'Amlākiya, 'Amlāka samāy wa-medr, 'eraftomu la-nafs ṣādeqān

---

to Babylon."

71. *'em-heyya* is temporal here: "and then, next."

72. "Just as I selectively picked them."

73. *nawā* = *nāhu*. The two *nawā*'s are coordinated here: "on the one hand ... on the other ..."

74. Q *ṣamhayaya* to wither, dry up.

75. L *nāzaza* to console. Lt *tanāzaza* pass. *nāzāzi* an. consoler. *nuzāzē* vn. consolation.

76. *garāht* (pl. *garāweh*) field, arable land.

77. G *šaraṣa/šarṣa (yešreṣ/yešraṣ)* to sprout. CG *'asraṣa* caus. *šarṣ* vn. sprout, sprouting.

78. *zar'* (pl. *'azre't*) seed (lit. and fig.); progeny. G *zar'a* to sow, scatter (seed). Gt *tazar'a* pass. The root ZR' is also found as ZR'.

ba-k^{w}ellu baḥāwert."

53 (33) Wa-yebēlo la-’aragāy: "’Ayy we’etu zentu warx?" Wa-yebēlo: "‘Ašuru wa-sanuyu la-warxa Nēsān,[79] za-we’etu Miyāzyā."

54 (34) Wa-’emdexra zentu wahabo ’Abēmēlēk la-zentu ’aragāy ’em-diba zentu ’ablās, wa-yebēlo: "’Amlāk yemrāḥka ’enta lā‘lu hagara ’Iyarusālēm."

VI

55 (1) Wa-tanše’a ’Abēmēlēk, wa-waḍ’a ’af’ā ’em-hagar, wa-ṣallaya xaba ’Egzi’abḥēr. Wa-nāhu maṣ’a mal’ak wa-marḥo xaba Bārok, wa-rakabo westa maqāber ’enza yenabber.

56 (2) Wa-soba ta’āmexu wa-tabākayu babaynātihomu, wa-tasā‘amu, wa-re’ya balasa westa mudāyu, wa-’al‘ala ’a‘yentihu westa samāy, wa-ṣallaya ’enza yebel:[80] "‘Abiy we’etu ’Amlāk, za-yehubomu ‘asbomu la-ṣādeqānihu. (3) Tadallawi, nafseya, wa-tafaššeḥi,’enza tenaggeri la-badneki, la-bēteki qeddus za-šegā: 'Wa-lāḥeki[81] yetmayyaṭ westa berhān.' Wa-’emdexra-ze yemaṣṣe’ me’man, wa-yāgabbe’aki westa badneki. (4) Ḥawweṣi westa zazi’aki dengelennā hāymānot, wa-’emani taḥayyewi. (5) Ḥawweṣi westa-ze balas; nawā sessā wa-sedestu ‘āmat ’em-’ama taqašmu, wa-’i-māsanu wa-’i-ṣē’u,[82] ’allā ḥalibomu yānṣafaṣṣefu ’eska ye’zē. (6) Kama-ze yetgabbar dibēki, šegāya, ’esma ‘aqabki te’zāzaki ’em-xaba mal’aka ṣedq. (7) Za-‘aqaba mudāya

---

79. *Nēsān* the Hebrew month Nisan.

80. The prayer in this verse is difficult in a few places. On the basis of the Greek variants I suggest *’enza tenaggeri la-badneki la-bēteki qeddus za-šegā* (saying to your body, to your holy house of flesh) for *’enza tenaggeri la-badn za-šegā la-bēt qeddus* (to the body of flesh, to the holy house). This change is not essential, however. In the lines that follow, it is not clear whether they are addressed by Baruch to his soul or by his soul to its body. I take only one clause for the latter and the remainder for the former. The correction of *šegāya* to *šegāki* toward the end of the verse, as suggested by E. Littmann (apud Dillmann, *Chrest.*, p. 291) is both unnecessary and contrary to the Greek. A change of the following *’esma* to *’emma* would, however, suit the meaning better.

81. *lāḥ* mourning, grief. L *lāḥawa* to mourn, grieve. *leḥew/luḥew* grieving.

82. G *ṣē’a* to rot. *ṣeyu’* rotten. *ṣi’at* rottenness, decay.

balas we'etu kā'eba ya'aqqebaki ba-xayla zi'ahu."

57 (8) Wa-kama-ze behilo Bārok, 'awše'a 'Abēmēlēk wa-yebēlo: "Tanše' kā'eba. Neṣalli kama yār'eyana 'Egzi' qālāta za-neṣeḥḥef la-'Ēremeyās westa Bābilon kednata[83] za-kadanani dibēya."

58 (9) Wa-ṣallaya Bārok wa-yebē: "Xayleya 'Amlāk 'Egzi' we'etu, wa-berhān za-yewaḍḍe' 'em-'afuhu. 'Ābadder 'āstabaqq^{w}e'aka, wa-'eganni[84] la-xiruteka.[85] 'Abiy semeka, wa-'albo za-yekel 'a'meroto. (10) 'Aḍme' ṣalota gabreka kama 'emmura yekun ba-lebbeya faqādaka la-gabir, wa-'efannu la-kāhena zi'aka 'Ēremeyās westa Bābilon."

59 (11) Wa-'enza zanta yeṣēlli, maṣ'a mal'ak wa-yebēlo: (12) "Bārok, makārē berhān, 'i-taxalli kama tefannu 'anta xaba 'Ēremeyās. Gēsa-ma[86] ba-sa'ata berhān yemaṣṣe' xabēka nesr.[87] Wa-'anta lalika ḥawweṣ ba'enta 'Ēremeyās, (13) wa-ṣaḥaf westa maṣḥaf, wa-balomu kama-ze la-weluda 'Esrā'ēl: 'Za-yekawwen 'engedā[88] ba-westētekemu yetfalaṭ[89] 'enta bāḥtitu 'eska 'ašur wa-xamus 'elat; wa-'emdexra-ze 'ābawwe'akemu westa hagar -- yebē 'Egzi'; (14) za-'i-tafalṭa ba-'ašur wa-xamus 'em-Bābilon, -- yebā' 'Ēremeyās westa hagar, wa-yezlefomu la-sab'a Bābilon -- yebē 'Egzi'.'"[90]

---

83. Although *ṣaḥafa* may take as a direct object the substance of what is written, this is already contained in the *za-* of the relative clause. *Ba'enta* should probably be inserted before *kednata*.

84. G *ganaya (yegnay)* to bow down; to submit, be submissive; to render humble thanks. CG *'agnaya* to subject. Glt *tagānaya* to confess one's sins, to seek pardon. *genāy* humble thanks.

85. *xirut* excellence, goodness, virtue.

86. *gēsa-m, gēsa-ma* adv. tomorrow. G *gēsa (yegis)* to rise/go/come in the morning. The suffix *-ma* seems to have been misunderstood as part of the root; *gēsam* is also used as a noun: the morrow.

87. *nesr* (pl. *'ansert*) eagle, vulture.

88. *'engedā* (pl. *'anāged*) stranger, guest. Qt *ta'angada* to be a stranger or guest.

89. G *falaṭa (yefleṭ)* to separate, divide, segregate, put into a separate group or category; to distinguish, discern. CG *'aflaṭa* to speak distinctly, to make a distinction. Gt *tafalṭa* pass. Glt *tafālaṭa* to separate from one another. *feluṭ* separate, distinct. *felṭat* vn. separation, division, distinction.

90. The meaning of the end of this verse is not immediately

60 (15) Zanta behilo mal'ak xalafa 'em-xaba Bārok. (16) Wa-Bārok fannawo 'eska marḥeb,[91] wa-'amṣe'a kertāsa[92] wa-māya ḥemmat,[93] wa-ṣaḥafa 'enza yebel: (See the end of this selection for the Letter.)

VII

61 (1) Wa-tanše'a Bārok wa-waḍ'a, ṣeḥifo kama-ze, 'em-maqāber.

62 (2) Wa-yebēlo nesr: "Bāḥaka[94] Bārok, maggābē hāymānot." (3) Wa-yebēlo Bārok: "'Esma xeruy 'anta 'em-k^{w}ellu 'a'wāfa samāy, tetnāgar. 'Em-berhāna 'a'yentika 'emmur 'anta; (4) wa-ye'zē-ni 'ar'eyani menta tegabber ba-zeyya."

63 (5) Wa-yebēlo nesr: "Tafannoku zeyya kama k^{w}ello qāla zatefaqqed tel'akani kiyāya."

64 (6) Wa-yebēlo Bārok: "Tekel-nu 'ellānta nagara 'abṣeḥo xaba 'Ēremeyās westa Bābilon?" (7) Wa-yebēlo nesr: "Ba'enta-ze tafannawku."

65 (8) Wa-naš'a Bārok maṣḥafa wa-10 wa-5 balasa 'em-zeku mudāya balas za-'amṣe'a 'Abēmēlēk, wa-'asara westa kesādu la-nesr.

66. Wa-yebēlo: (9) "Laka 'ebel nesr, negušomu la-k^{w}ellomu 'a'wāf. Ḥor ba-salām wa-ba-ḥeywat. Zēnā 'amṣe' lana. (10) Wa-'itetmasalo la-q^{w}ā'[95] za-fannawo Nox, wa-'abaya gabi'a dāgema xabēhu; 'allā tamasalā la-regb[96] za-šelsa 'agbe'at qāla la-Nox. (11) Kamāhu 'anta-ni nešā' zanta qālāta šannāya la-'Ēremeyās wa-la-'ella hallawu meslēhu 'Esrā'ēl, kama šannāya yekunka; wa-nešā' zanta tefšeḥta

---

clear in the Ethiopic or the Greek ("The one who does not separate himself from Babylon is not to enter the city, O Jeremiah. I am finding fault with them so that they will not be accepted back by the Babylonians.") See verse 90 below for the situation alluded to here.

91. G *reḥba (yerḥab)* to be wide, spacious, ample. CG *'arḥaba* caus. *reḥub* wide, spacious. *reḥib* (f. *raḥāb*) idem. *reḥb* width, breadth. *rāḥb* = *reḥbat* idem. *marḥeb* (pl. *marāḥebt*) a wide place, street, forum, marketplace.

92. *kertās* parchment, paper.

93. *ḥemmat* soot. *māya ḥemmat* ink.

94. *bāḥ/bāḥa* (with or without pron. suff.) exclam. Greetings! *bāḥa behla* to greet.

95. *q^{w}ā'* (pl. *-āt*) raven, crow.

96. *regb ('argāb)* dove.

la-ḥezb xeruyāna ʾAmlāk.

67 (12) Wa-ʾemma-ni ʿoduka ʾaʿwāf k^wellu, wa-k^wellomu ṣalāʾeyānihā la-ṣedq, ʾenza yefaqqedu yeqteluka, tabādar, wa-ʾEgziʾ yahabka xayla; wa-ʾi-tetmayaṭ ʾi-la-yamān wa-ʾi-la-ḍagām, ʾallā kama ḥaṣ[97] za-yaḥawwer retuʿa ḥor ba-xayla ʾAmlāk."

68 (13) Wa-zanta behilo Bārok, sarara[98] nesr mesla maṣḥaf, wa-ḥora westa Bābilon. Wa-ʾaʿrafa diba ʿamd za-ʾafʾā ʾem-hagar ba-makān za-gadām, wa-ṣanḥa heyya ʾeska yaxallef ʾĒremeyās wa-bāʿedān ḥezb.

69 (14) Wa-xalafu ʾenta heyya kama yeqberu beʾsē za-mota, ʾesma saʾalo ʾĒremeyās la-Nābukadanaṣor ʾenza yebel: "Habani medra xaba ʾeqabber ʾem-ḥezbeya." Wa-wahabo.

70 (15) Wa-ʾenza yaḥawweru wa-yebakkeyu lāʿla za-mota, basḥu qedma zeku nesr. Wa-ṣarxa nesr ba-ʿabiy qāl wa-yebē: "Laka ʾebelaka ʾĒremeyās xeruya ʾAmlāk. Ḥur wa-ʾastagābeʾomu la-k^wellomu ḥezb, wa-yemṣeʾu zeyya kama yesmeʿu šannāya zēnā za-ʾamṣāʾku."

71 (16) Wa-samiʿo zanta, sabbeḥo[99] la-ʾEgziʾabḥēr, wa-sobēhā ʾastagābeʾa k^wello ḥezba wa-ʾanestiyāhomu wa-daqiqomu, wa-basḥu xaba hallo nesr.

72 (17) Wa-warada zeku nesr xaba badn, wa-kēdo, wa-ḥaywa. Wa-zanta gabra kama yeʾmanu; (18) wa-ʾankara k^wellu ḥezb baʾenta za-kona.

73 Wa-yebēlu: "Yogi zentu weʾetu ʾAmlāk za-ʾastarʾayomu la-ʾabawina ba-gadām mesla Musē; wa-tamasla ba-ʾamsāla nesr, wa-ʾastarʾaya lana kama ʾenta nesr ʿabiy."

74 (19) Wa-yebēlo nesr la-ʾĒremeyās ʾenza yebel: "Naʿā wa-semāʿ zanta maṣḥafa, wa-ʾanbeb la-ḥezb." Wa-ʾanbaba lomu.

75 (20) Wa-soba samʿu ḥezb, bakayu k^wellomu xebura, wa-wadayu ḥamada westa reʾsomu, wa-yebēlewwo la-ʾĒremeyās: (21) "ʾAdxenana. Menta negbar kama negbāʾ westa hagarena?"

76 (22) Wa-tanšeʾa ʾĒremeyās wa-yebēlomu: "K^wello za-samāʿkemu westa maṣḥaf, kamāhu gebaru, wa-yāgabbeʾakemu westa hagarekemu."

77 (23) Wa-ṣaḥafa ʾĒremeyās maṣḥafa la-Bārok, kama-ze ʾenza

---

97. *ḥaṣ* (pl. *ʾaḥṣā, -t*) arrow.

98. G *sarara (yesrer)* to fly. *serur* flying, in flight. *serrat* flight, flying. *sarāri* = *serur*

99. D *sabbeḥa* to praise, laud, glorify. Dt *tasabbeḥa* pass. *sebbuḥ* praised, glorified. *sebbāḥē* praise, glorification, hymn. *sebḥat/sebbeḥāt* praise.

yebel: "Waldeya fequr, 'i-tethakay ṣalota 'enza teganni la-'Amlāk ba'enti'ana, kama yemreḥana westa fenotena, 'eska newaḍḍe' ba-te'zāza zentu neguš xāṭe'.

78 "Wa-'anta-sa ṣedqa rakabka ba-qedma 'Amlāk, za-'i-xadagaka temṣā' meslēna, kama 'i-ter'ay 'ekuya za-yetgabbar dibēhomu la-ḥezb ba-Bābilon.

79 (24) "Bakama 'ab za-bo weluda 'aḥada, wa-we'etu tawehba kama yetk^{w}annan, wa-'ella hallawu xaba 'abuhu, 'ella yenāzezewwo, yekaddenu gaṣṣomu kama 'i-yer'ayewwo la-'abuhu yaxasser ba-ḥazan, kama-ze kiyāka tašāhalaka 'Amlāk, wa-'i-xadagaka temṣā' Bābilon kama 'i-ter'ay mendābē ḥezb.

80 "Esma 'em-'ama baṣāḥna westa zentu hagar, 'i-ya'rafna 'eska yom 'em-ḥazan, sessā wa-sedestu 'āmat yom. (25) 'Enza naxaššeš nerkab[100] 'em-ḥezb sequlān 'em-xaba Nābukadanaṣor neguš, 'enza yebakkeyu wa-yebelu: 'Tašāhalana 'amlāk Sor.'[101] (26) Wa-soba samā'ku zanta nagara, ḥazanku wa-bakayku, soba yeṣēwwe'u kāle'a 'amlāka sequlān, wa-yebelu 'Tašāhalana.' Wa-kā'eba 'ezzēkkar 'ana ba'āla za-gabarna ba-'Iyarusālēm za'enbala neḍḍēwaw; (27) wa-tazakkireya 'egabbe' westa bēteya 'enza 'eṣṣē''ar[102] wa-'ebakki.

81 (28) "Wa-ye'zē-ni 'astabq^{w}e'u la-'Amlākena ba-xaba hallawkemu, 'anta wa-'Abēmēlēk, ba'enta ḥezb, kama yesme'u qāleya wa-nagara 'afuya, kama yeḍā'u 'emenna Fāres.

82 (29) "Wa-ye'zē-ni 'ebelaka, k^{w}ello mawā'ela za-nabarna zeyya 'axazuna 'enza yebelu: 'Negeruna māḥlēta ḥaddisa 'em-maḥāleyihā la-Ṣeyon, maḥāleya za-'amlākekemu.' Wa-nebēlomu: ''Efo naḥalli lakemu

---

100. The Ethiopic "While we were seeking to find" does not make too much sense. The Greek has "Often, on going out, I would find some of the people being crucified by Nebuchadnezzar the king..."

101. *Sor* = Gk. *Sar*, presumably from Heb. *zār*, a designation for any foreign deity. The Greek of the following is also clearer than the Ethiopic: "On hearing this, I would grieve on two accounts: not only because they were being crucified, but also because they were calling on an alien god."

102. G *ṣe'ra* to be grieved, pained, afflicted. CG *'aṣ'ara* = CD *'aṣa''ara* to inflict grief or pain upon. Dt *taṣe''era* pass. of CD. *ṣe'ur/ṣe''ur* grieved, pained, afflicted. *ṣa'r* pain, torment, grief, affliction.

'enza hallona westa medra nakir?"

83 (30) Kama-ze ṣeḥifo 'Ēremeyās, 'asara maṣḥafo westa kesāda nesr wa-yebēlo: "Ḥur ba-salām, wa-'Egzi' yaḥawweṣ lā'lēka."

84 (31) Wa-ḥora nesr, wa-sarara, wa-'abṣeḥa maṣḥafa xaba Bārok. Wa-naši'o Bārok 'anbaba maṣḥafa, wa-bakaya soba sam'a ḥemāmomu la-ḥezb wa-mendābēhomu.

85 (32) Wa-'Ēremeyās-sa naš'a we'eta balasa wa-wahabomu la-deweyān, la-'ella westa ḥezb. Wa-nabara 'enza yemēhheromu kama 'i-yegbaru megbāromu la-ḥezba Bābilon.

VIII

86 (1) Wa-soba baṣḥa 'elat ba-za yāwaḍḍe'omu 'Amlāk la-ḥezb 'em-Bābilon, wa-yebēlo 'Egzi' la-'Ēremeyās: (2) "Tanše' 'anta wa-ḥezbeka, wa-ne'u westa Yordānos, wa-balomu la-ḥezb: 'Yefaqqed 'Egzi' yekden megbāra za-ḥezba Bābilon; wa-la-tabā't[103] za-'awsaba 'anesta Bābilon ba-dibēkemu, wa-'anest-ni 'ella 'awsabā 'emennēhomu -- neftenomu.'[104] (3) Wa-'ella sam'uka-sa, 'āgabbe'omu westa 'Iyarusālēm; wa-la-'ella 'i-sam'uka 'i-texdegomu yebā'u westētā."

87 (4) Wa-'Ēremeyās kama-ze 'anbaba lomu zanta k^{w}ello, wa-'amṣe'omu westa Yordānos kama yeftenomu.

88 Wa-'enza yenaggeromu zanta nagara za-yebēlo 'Egzi', nāfaqu 'ella 'awsabu, wa-'i-faqadu kama yesme'ewwo la-'Ēremeyās. Wa-bo 'ella yebēlewwo: "'I-naxaddeg 'anestiyāna[105] la-'ālam; nenašše'on meslēna westa hagarena." (5) Wa-xalafu 'em-Yordānos, wa-baṣḥu westa 'Iyarusālēm.

89 Wa-qomu 'Ēremeyās wa-Bārok wa-'Abēmēlēk 'enza yebelu: "K^{w}ellu be'si za-'awsaba 'em-Bābilon 'i-yebawwe' westa hagarena." (6) Wa-yebēlu 'ella 'awsabu 'anesta la-biṣomu:[106] "Tanše'u, negbā'

---

103. G *tab'a* to be brave, manly. *teb'* = *teb'at* bravery, courage, virtue. *tabā't* (pl. *'atbu'*) n. a male. *tabbā'* = *tabā'i* (pl. *tabā't*) adj. male, strong. *tabā'tāwi* (or *-āy*) adj. male, masculine.

104. G *fatana (yeften)* to investigate, explore; to examine, test. CG *'aftana* to hand over for examination. Gt *tafatna* pass. of G. *fetun* investigated, examined, tested. *fatāni* examiner, tester.

105. *'anestiyā* (coll.) the women, womenfolk.

106. *biṣ* (pl. *'abyāṣ*) friend, comrade, companion; neighbor; a single individual. D *bayyaṣa* to separate, distinguish, discern. Glt *tabāyaṣa* to become companions.

westa Bābilon." Wa-xalafu wa-gab'u.

90 (7) Wa-soba re'yewwomu sab'a Bābilon, waḍ'u kama yetqabbalewwomu;[107] wa-'i-xadagewwomu kama yebā'u westa Bābilon, 'enza yebelu: "'Antemu qedma kiyāna ṣalā'kemuna, wa-ba-xebu' waḍā'kemu 'em-xabēna; wa-ba'enta zentu 'i-tebawwe'u westa hagarena, 'esma tamāḥalna ba-sema 'amlākena kama kiyākemu wa-'awāledikemu 'i-netwēkkaf, 'esma ba-xebu' xalafkemu 'emennēna."

91 (8) Wa-sami'omu kama-ze gab'u westa 'Iyarusālēm, wa-ḥanaṣu lomu 'ahgura westa 'adyāmihā la-'Iyarusālēm, wa-samayewwā la-zeku hagar Samāreyā. (9) Wa-fannawa xabēhomu 'Ēremeyās 'enza yebel: "Nasseḥu wa-nawā yemaṣṣe' mal'aka ṣedq wa-yāgabbe'akemu westa makānekemu za-nawwāx."[108]

IX

92 (1) Wa-nabaru 'enza yetfēššeḥu wa-yešawwe'u sabu'a 'elata ba'enta ḥezb.

93 (2) Wa-'ama 'ašur 'elat 'em-za tagabra zentu, 'a'raga 'Ēremeyās mašwā'ta bāḥtitu.

94 (3) Wa-ṣallaya 'Ēremeyās 'enza yebel: "Qeddus qeddus qeddus 'anta, ma'azā[109] ṭe'um la-sab', wa-berhān za-ba-'amān za-tābarreh lita 'eska 'ana 'ebaṣṣeh qedmēka. 'Āstabaqq^{w}e'aka ba'enta ḥezbeka, wa-'ese''elaka ba'enta qāla ma'ar'ir[110] za-Surāfēl, (4) wa-ba'enta ma'azā 'eṭān za-Kirubēl; (5) wa-'ese''elaka 'ewwa[111] māḥlētāy Mikā'ēl (mal'aka ṣedq we'etu), za-yārexxu 'anāqeṣa ṣedq 'eska yebawwe'ewwon. (6) 'Āstabaqq^{w}e'aka 'Egzi' la-k^{w}ellu, wa-'Egzi' za-k^{w}ello ye'exxez, wa-k^{w}ello faṭara za-yāstare''i, wa-za-'i-tawalda, za-k^{w}ello faṣṣama, wa-k^{w}ellu feṭrat xebu' hallo xabēhu, za'enbala

---

107. The *'i-* is probably to be omitted, but could be justified for the second meaning of Dt *taqabbala* to go out to meet; to welcome, accept, receive.

108. The *za-* with the adjective is unusual. The phrase seems to mean no more than "your lofty place."

109. G *me'za* to smell good, be fragrant. CG *'am'aza* to scent, perfume. Dt *tame''eza* to be scented, fragrant. *me'uz* fragrant, sweet. *ma'azā* (pl. *-t*) fragrance, pleasant scent.

110. *ma'ār* honey. *ma'ar'ir* adj. sweet. CQ *'amā'rara* to sweeten.

111. *'ewwa* here adv. "even, indeed, surely."

yetgabaru ba-xebu'."

95 (7) Wa-zanta ṣallaya. Wa-faṣṣimo ṣaloto, qoma 'Ēremeyās westa bēta maqdas, wa-meslēhu Bārok wa-'Abēmēlēk; wa-kona 'Ēremeyās kama 'aḥadu be'si za-waḍ'a nafsu 'em-lā'lēhu.

96 (8) Wa-sobēhā wadqu Bārok wa-'Abēmēlēk, wa-'awyawu[112] ba-'abiy qāl, wa-yebēlu: "Way lana. 'Abuna 'Ēremeyās kāhena 'Amlāk xalafa 'emennēna."

97 (9) Wa-sami'omu kama-ze ḥezb, roṣu xabēhu, wa-rakabewwo la-'Ēremeyās weduqa wa-meweta. Wa-bakayu wa-šaṭaṭu 'albāsihomu, wa-wadayu ḥamada diba re'somu, wa-bakayu bekāya marira.[113]

98 (10) Wa-'emdexra 'astadālawu ba-za yeqabberewwo, maṣ'a qāl za-yebel: "'I-tegnezewwo. Ḥeyāw we'etu, wa-nafsu tegabbe' diba šegāhu dāgema."

99 (12) Wa-sami'omu zanta qāla, 'i-ganazewwo, 'allā nabaru 'enza ya'aqqebewwo 'awdo šalusa mawā'ela, 'eska tegabbe' nafsu westa šegāhu.

100 (13) Wa-kona qāl ba-mā'kala k^{w}ellomu wa-yebē: "Sabbeḥewwo ba-'aḥadu qāl, sabbeḥewwo la-'Amlāk; wa-k^{w}ellekemu sabbeḥu la-masiḥ[114] walda 'Amlāk, za-yānaqqehakemu wa-yek^{w}ēnnenakemu, 'Iyasus walda Amlāk, berhān la-k^{w}ellu 'ālam, wa-māxtot za-'i-yeṭaffe', wa-ḥeywat za-hāymānot.

101 (14) "Wa-yekawwen 'emdexra-ze mawā'el šalās me't wa-šalās sanbatāt za-mawā'el la-meṣ'atu westa medr. 'Eḍa ḥeywat, za-hallo westa gannat wa-'i-tatakla, yerēsseyomu la-k^{w}ellu 'eḍ za-['ī-]yāwaḍḍe' ferē wa-yebusāna[115] kama yemṣe'u xabēhu, wa-yerēsseyomu kama yegbaru ferē wa-yešraṣu, wa-ferēhomu yenabber mesla malā'ekt.

102 (15) "Wa-ba'enta takla 'eḍaw, kama yelamlemu[116] wa-yenuxu,

---

112. Q *'awyawa* to wail in mourning. *'awyāt* vn. wailing.

113. G *marra/marara (yemrar, yemrer)* to be bitter (lit. and fig.). CG *'amrara* to be bitter; to make bitter, exacerbate, aggravate; to behave bitterly or sharply. *marir* (f. *marār*) adj. bitter. *merar* (pl. *-āt*) = *merrat* vn. bitterness.

114. *masiḥ* the Anointed, the Messiah.

115. G *yabsa (yeybas)* to be dry, arid. CG *'aybasa* caus. *yebus* dry, arid. *yabs* dry land, the dry ground.

116. Q *lamlama* to bloom, grow green; to be tender. *lemlāmē* verdure, tenderness.

nahab ṣabbāḥta[117] la-'Iyor[118] kama 'i-yeybas šerawihomu[119] kama takl za-'i-'axaza šerwu medra.

103 "Wa-za-ḥebra[120] qayeḥ[121] yāṣa'addu[122] kama ḍamr, (16) wa-māy za-ṭe'um marira yekawwen, wa-marir ṭe'uma yekawwen ba-'abiy ḥašēt; (17) wa-tefšeḥtāta 'Amlāk la-dasayāt[123] kama yefrayu[124] ferē ba-nagara 'afuhu [la-]walda zi'ahu.

104 (18) "Wa-we'etu lalihu yebawwe' westa 'ālam, wa-yaxarri lotu ḥawāreyāta 'ašarta wa-kel'ēta kama yetra'ay lomu za-'ana re'iku sergewa,[125] za-yetfēnno 'em-xaba 'abuhu, za-yemaṣṣe' westa 'ālam wa-westa Dabra Zayt[126] yekayyed, wa-yāṣaggeb[127] nafsa rexebta."[128]

---

117. D *ṣabbeḥa* to exact/collect taxes or tribute. CD *'aṣabbeḥa* caus. *ṣabbāḥt* tribute, taxes. *maṣabbeḥ* tax-collector. *maṣabbeḥi* idem. *meṣebbāḥ* tax office.

118. *'iyor, 'ayar* (pl. *-āt*) the air, atmosphere (from Gk. *aēr*).

119. *šerw* (pl. *-āt, šeraw, 'ašrāw*) root; nerve, muscle, tendon. G *šarawa* = D *šarrawa* to eradicate, extirpate. Gt *tašarwa* = Dt *tašarrawa* pass. *šerrāwē* eradication, extirpation.

120. *ḥebr* (pl. *-āt, ḥebar*) color. *ḥebur* many-colored, variegated. CG *'aḥbara* to clean, polish.

121. G *qēḥa* to grow red. *qayeḥ/qayiḥ* (f. *qayāḥ*) red. *qiḥat* red(ness). Q *'aqyāḥyeḥa* to make/become reddish.

122. Q *ṣā'dawa* to be white. CQ *'aṣā'dawa* caus. *ṣe'dew* adj. white. *ṣā'dā/ṣa'adā* (pl. *ṣa'ādew*) adj. white. *ṣe'dāwē* whiteness. *ṣa'ad'id* adj. whitish.

123. *dasēt* (pl. *dasayāt*) island. The phrase *la-dasayāt* is the predicate of this clause; the translation is less awkward with a verb supplied: "The joys of the Lord (will extend) to the islands."

124. G *faraya/farya (yefray)* to bear fruit, be fruitful. CG *'afraya* caus.; also = G. *mafrey* an. as adj. fruitful.

125. *sergewa* in the accusative is probably to be taken as a predicate complement: "so that the one whom I saw adorned might appear unto them."

126. *Dabra Zayt* the Mount of Olives.

127. G *ṣagba* to be sated, filled, satisfied; to be sick of something. CG *'aṣgaba* to satiate, satisfy. *ṣegub* sated, full, satisfied. *ṣegāb* satiety, abundance.

128. G *rexba (yerxab)* to be hungry. CG *'arxaba* caus. *rexub*

105 (19) Wa-kama-ze nagara 'Ēremeyās ba'enta walda 'Amlāk, kama yemaṣṣe' westa ʻālam.

106 (20) Wa-soba samʻu zanta ḥezb, tameʻʻu ba'enta zentu, wa-yebēlu: "Zentu we'etu nagarāt za-'Isāyeyās[129] walda 'Amoṣ, za-yebel: 'Re'iku 'Amlāka walda 'Amlāk.' (21) Ye'zē-ni tanše'u, negbar dibēhu bakama gabarna diba 'Isāyeyās." Wa-yebēlu manfaqomu: "'Albo. Dā'emu[130] ba-'ebn newaggero."

107 Wa-ṣarxu lomu Bārok wa-'Abēmēlēk 'enza yebelu: "Ba-zāti mot 'i-teqtelewwo."

108 (22) Wa-ḥazanu Bārok wa-'Abēmēlēk ba'enta 'Ēremeyās, wa-ʻādi 'i-xadagewwo yezēnewomu xebu'āta za-re'ya.

109 (23) Wa-yebēlomu 'Ēremeyās: "'Armemu. 'I-tebkeyu, 'esma 'i-yekelu qatiloteya 'eska 'ezēnewakemu k^{w}ello za-re'iku. (24) Wa-ye'zē-ni 'amṣe'u lita 'aḥatta 'ebna." Wa-'amṣe'u lotu 'ebna 'aḥatta.

110 (25) Wa-'aqamā wa-yebē: "Berhān za-la-ʻālam, rassi zāta 'ebna re'yata sab' tekun." Wa-sobēhā kona 'ebn ba-re'yata 'Ēremeyās za-yemasselo.

111 (27) Wa-'axazu yewaggerewwo la-'ebn 'enza yemasselomu 'Ēremeyās-hā.

112 (28) Wa-'Ēremeyās zēnawomu la-Bārok wa-la-'Abēmēlēk k^{w}ello za-re'ya xebu'āta, (29) wa-'emdexra-ze faṣṣimo nagirotomu, ḥora wa-qoma mā'kala ḥezb, faqido kama yefaṣṣem meggebo.

113 (30) Wa-sobēhā ṣarxa lomu zeku 'ebn wa-yebē: "'O-'abdān daqiqa 'Esrā'ēl, ba'enta ment tewēggeruni 'enza tāmasseluni 'Ēremeyās-hā? Wa-'Ēremeyās nawā mā'kalēkemu yeqawwem."

114 (31) Wa-soba re'yewwo, roṣu mesla bezux 'ebn, wa-faṣṣamu ʻalewo,[131] (32) wa-qabarewwo. Wa-naš'u we'eta 'ebna, wa-'anbaru

---

hungry, starving. *raxab/raxāb* hunger, famine.

129. *'Isāyeyās* Isaiah the Prophet.

130. *dā'emu* adv. again, further, rather.

131. *faṣṣamu ʻalewo* is difficult; probably: "They put an end to his apostacy," taking *ʻalewo* as an infinitive (*qatil* form) without the usual suffix *-ot-*. G *ʻalawa (yeʻlu)* to pervert; to act perversely, to transgress (laws etc.); to be rebellious, evil, refractory, apostate, heretical. CG *'aʻlawa* caus.; to translate (from one language into another); to copy or transcribe. *ʻelwat* disaster; perversity, heresy, apostacy; copy, transcription. *ʻalāwi* wicked,

westa maqāberihu, wa-rassayewwo kama ʼenta maʻṣo,[132] wa-ṣaḥafu westētu ʼenza yebelu: "Nawā zentu weʼetu radʼu la-ʼĒremeyās."

Addendum: The Letter from Baruch to Jeremiah

The text of this letter is corrupt and was relegated by Dillmann (*Chrestomathia*, p. 8) to the foot of the page. When read in the light of the Greek version, however, it does appear to be almost coherent, if one allows for a few minor emendations.

60a (17) Baʼenta: Bārok gabra ʼAmlāk yeṣeḥḥef maṣḥafa la-ʼĒremeyās westa ḍēwā Bābilon. Feššeḥā wa-ḥašēt. ʼEsma ʼAmlāk ʼi-yaxaddegana neḍāʼ ḥezunānina baʼenta ṣeʻlat wa-musenā. (18) Baʼenta-ze ʼastamḥara ʼEgziʼ diba ʼanbeʻena, wa-tazakkara šerʻata za-ʼaqdama mesla ʼabawina ʼAbrehām Yesḥaq wa-Yāʻqob.

60b (19) Wa-fannawa malʼako xabēya, wa-nagarani ʼellānta nagara za-laʼakku xabēka. (20) ʼEllā ʼemāntu nagar za-gabra ʼEgziʼ ʼAmlāka ʼEsrāʼēl, za-ʼawḍeʼana ʼem-medra Gebṣ za-ʼessāt: (21) ʼEsma ʼi-ʻaqabkemu k^{w}ello ṣedqātihu, ʼallā ʼalʻalkemu lebbakemu wa-ʼagzafkemu kesādakemu qedmēhu, wa-maṭṭawakemu westa ʼetona Bābilon, (22) ʼesma ʼi-samāʻkemu qāleya -- yebē ʼEgziʼabḥēr ʼem-ʼafa ʼĒremeyās q^{w}elʻēhu.

60c La-ʼella samʻu ʼāwaḍḍeʼomu ʼem-Bābilon, wa-ʼi-yekawwenu nagda ʼem-ʼIyarusālēm ba-Bābilon.

60d (23) Wa-ʼemma-sa tefattu tāʼmeromu, fetenomu ba-māya Yordānos, wa-za-ʼi-yesammeʻ yetʼammar. Zentu teʼmert: za-yaʻabbi māxtam.

60a To wit (?): Baruch, the servant of God, writes a letter to Jeremiah in the Babylonian exile. Joy and happiness! For God will not allow us to depart (from this life) grieving about the revilement and destruction (of the city). Therefore, God has taken pity on our tears and has remembered the covenant which he established previously with our fathers Abraham, Isaac, and Jacob.

60b He sent his angel to me and told me these words which I

---

perverse; infidel, heretical.

132. G *ʻaṣawa (yeʻṣew)* to close, shut, lock, bolt. Gt *taʻaṣwa* pass. *ʻeṣew* locked, closed, bolted. *ʻaṣāwi* doorkeeper. *māʻṣo* (pl. *maʻāṣut*) door, gate; lock, bolt.

have sent to you (herewith). These are those words which the Lord God of Israel made, who led us out of the fiery land of Egypt: "Because you did not keep all his righteous (acts), but became haughty and refractory, he has handed you over to the furnace of Babylon, for you did not heed my voice" -- thus said the Lord through Jeremiah, his servant.

60c Those who have heeded I shall bring forth from Babylon, and they will not be exiles from Jerusalem in Babylon.

60d If you wish to know them, test them in the water of the Jordan, and let him who does not heed become known. This is the sign: the great seal (i.e. baptism).

III. The Gospel of Matthew

The text transliterated here is that of the Ethiopic New Testament distributed by the British (and American) Bible Society: *Wangēl Qeddus za-ʾEgziʾena wa-Madxenena ʾIyasus Kerestos wa-maṣāheftihomu la-ḥawāreyātu qeddusān* (Leipzig, 1899; reprinted 1949). This Gospel was selected for inclusion here both because it is available in Ethiopic script at a modest price and because its familiarity eliminates the need for excessive glossing. Reference to an English translation or to the Greek original will help clear up syntactic points not discussed in the notes. It is assumed that the reader is familiar with the personal and place names which occur.

Wangēl qeddus za-'Egzi'ena wa-madxanina 'Iyasus Kerestos,
za-we'etu besrāta Māttēwos ḥawāreyā

Chapter I

Maṣḥafa ledatu la-'Iyasus Kerestos walda Dāwit walda 'Abrehām

(18) Wa-la-'Iyasus Kerestos kama-ze we'etu ledatu. Wa-tafexrat 'emmu Māryām la-Yosēf, wa-za'enbala yetqārabu tarakbat 'enza-bā westa māḥḍanā 'em-manfas qeddus. (19) Wa-Yosēf-sa faxāriha, 'esma ṣādeq we'etu, 'i-faqada yekšetā, wa-makara ṣemmita yexdegā. (20) Wa-'enza zanta yexēlli, nāhu 'astar'ayo mal'aka 'Egzi'abḥēr ba-ḥelm 'enza yebel:

Yosēf walda Dāwit, 'i-tefrāh naši'otā la-Māryām fexerteka, 'esma za-'em-lā'lēhā yetwallad 'em-manfas qeddus we'etu. (21) Wa-tewalled walda, wa-teṣawwe' semo 'Iyasus-hā, 'esma we'etu yādexxen ḥezbo 'em-xaṭāwe'ihomu. (22) Wa-ze-k^{w}ellu kona kama yetfaṣṣam za-tabehla 'em-xaba 'Egzi'abḥēr ba-nabiy 'enza yebel:

Nāhu dengel teḍannes wa-tewalled walda, wa-yeṣēwwe'u semo 'Amānu'ēl, za-we'etu ba-terg^{w}āmēhu: meslēna 'Egzi'abḥēr.

(23) Wa-tanši'o Yosēf 'em-newāmu, gabra bakama 'azzazo mal'aka 'Egzi'abḥēr. Wa-naš'a la-Māryām fexertu, wa-'i-ya'marā 'eska waladat walda za-bak^{w}rā. Wa-ṣawwe'a semo 'Iyasus-hā.

Chapter II

1. Ba'enta sab'a sagal

(1) Wa-tawalido 'Iyasus ba-Bētaleḥēm za-Yehudā ba-mawā'ela Hērodes neguš, nāhu masaggelān 'em-beḥēra ṣebāḥ baṣḥu westa 'Iyarusālēm 'enza

---

I Title: *besrāt/besserāt* good news, gospel.

18. G *faxara (yefxar)* to espouse, become engaged to (obj.: woman). Gt *tafaxara/tafexra* pass. *fexert* fiancée. *faxāri* fiancé. *bā westa māḥḍanā* she has in her womb = she is pregnant.

20. *ḥelm* (pl. *'aḥlām*) dream. G *ḥalama* to dream. Dt *taḥallama* to dream dreams, see visions.

23. *bak^{w}r* firstborn. The usual construction of this word, with a pronominal suffix, indicates that it is a noun and not an adjective: "a son who was her firstborn." Gt *tabak^{w}ra* to be the firstborn; to give birth for the first time. *bek^{w}rennā* status of firstborn.

yebelu: (2)

> 'Aytē hallo za-tawalda negūša 'Ayhud? 'Esma re'ina kokaba zi'ahu ba-mešrāq wa-maṣā'na kama nesged lotu.

(3) Wa-sami‘o Hērodes neguš, dangaḍa wa-tahawka, wa-k^{w}ellā 'Iyarusālēm meslēhu. (4) Wa-'astagābi'o la-k^{w}ellomu līqāna kāhenāt wa-ṣaḥafta ḥezb, tase''elomu ba-'aytē yetwallad Kerestos. (5) Wa-yebēlewwo:

> Ba-Bētaleḥēm za-Yehudā, 'esma kamāhu ṣeḥuf ba-nabiy: (6)
>
> > Wa-'anti-ni Bētaleḥem, medra Yehudā, 'i-taḥaṣṣeṣi 'emenna masāfenta Yehudā, 'esma 'emennēki yewaḍḍe' neguš mak^{w}annen za-yerē‘‘eyomu la-ḥezbeya 'Esrā'ēl.

(7) Wa-'emze ṣawwe‘omu Hērodes la-masaggelān ṣemmita, wa-taṭayyaqa 'em-xabēhomu mawā‘elihu ba-za 'astar'ayomu kokab. (8) Wa-fannawomu Bētaleḥēm-hā wa-yebēlomu:

> Ḥawirakemu, tasa''alu ṭeyyuqa ba'enta ḥeḍān. Wa-'emkama rakabkemewwo, zēnewuni kama 'emṣā' 'ana-hi wa-'esged lotu.

(9) Wa-sami‘omu 'em-xaba neguš, ḥoru. Wa-nāhu kokab za-re'yu za-'em-ṣebāḥ yemarreḥomu 'eska soba baṣiḥo qoma mal‘elta xaba hallo ḥeḍān. (10) Wa-re'eyomu kokaba, tafaššeḥu feššeḥā ‘abiya. (11) Wa-bawi'omu westa bēt, re'yewwo la-ḥeḍān mesla Māryām 'emmu. Wa-wadqu wa-sagadu lotu, wa-'arxawu mazāgebtihomu, wa-'abe'u lotu 'ammexā: warqa wa-sexina wa-karbē. (12) Wa-nagaromu ba-ḥelm kama 'i-yegbe'u xaba Hērodes, wa-'enta kāle' fenot gab'u wa-'atawu beḥēromu.

2. Ba'enta 'ella taqatlu ḥeḍānāt

(13) Wa-'emdexra xalafu, nāhu mal'aka 'Egzi'abḥēr 'astar'ayo ba-ḥelm

---

II 3. G *hoka (yehuk)* to move, agitate, disturb. Gt *tahawka* pass. *hawk* motion, movement, agitation, disturbance; mob, crowd, tumult. *hukat* idem.

6. G *safana (yesfen)* to become strong, powerful; to exercise control, rule (over: *diba, lā‘la, la-*, or a.d.o.). *safāni* ruler, controller, governor. *masfen* (pl. *masāfent*) ruler, governor, prefect, high official, judge; *masfena me't* centurion. *mesfenā* the office or status of a *masfen*.

8. *'emkama* conj. as soon as.

11. G *zagaba (yezgeb)* to store up, accumulate, hoard; to store away, hide. Gt *tazagba* pass. *mazgab* (pl. *mazāgebt*) treasure, wealth; store-room, magazine. *sexin* frankincense. *karbē* myrrh.

la-Yosēf 'enza yebel:

Tanše' wa-nešā' ḥeḏāna wa-'emmo, wa-g^{w}eyay westa Gebṣ, wa-hallu heyya 'eska 'ama 'enaggèraka, 'esma hallawo la-Hērodes yexšešo la-ḥeḏān kama yeqtelo.

(14) Wa-tanši'o, naš'a ḥeḏāna wa-'emmo ba-lēlit, wa-ḥora westa Gebṣ. (15) Wa-nabara heyya 'eska 'ama motu la-Hērodes, kama yetfaṣṣam za-tabehla 'em-xaba 'Egzi'abḥēr ba-nabiy 'enza yebel:

'Em-Gebṣ ṣawwā'kewwo la-waldeya.

(16) Wa-soba re'ya Hērodes kama tasālaqu lā'lēhu sab'a sagal, tam'e'a ṭeqqa, wa-fannawa wa-qatala k^{w}ello ḥeḏānāta za-Bētaleḥēm wa-za-westa k^{w}ellu 'adyāmihā za-kel'ē 'āmat wa-za-yene''es-hi, bakama mawā'el za-taṭayyaqa 'em-xaba 'ella sagal. (17) 'Amēhā tafaṣṣama za-tabehla ba-'Ēremeyās nabiy 'enza yebel:

(18) Qāl ba-Rāmā tasam'a, bekāy wa-saqoqāw bezux; Rāḥēl 'enza tebakki ba'enta weludā, wa-ta'abbi tanāzezo, 'esma 'i-konewwā weludā.

(19) Wa-mawito Hērodes, nāhu mal'aka 'Egzi'abḥēr 'astar'ayo ba-ḥelm la-Yosēf ba-Gebṣ (20) 'enza yebel:

Tanši'aka, nešā' ḥeḏāna wa-'emmo, wa-ḥur westa medra 'Esrā'ēl, 'esma motu 'ella yaxaššešewwā la-nafsa ze-ḥeḏān.

(21) Wa-tanši'o, naš'a ḥeḏāna wa-'emmo, wa-bo'a medra 'Esrā'ēl. (22) Wa-sami'o kama 'Arkēlā'os yenaggeš la-Yehudā heyyanta 'abuhu Hērodes, farha ḥawira heyya. Wa-'astar'ayo ba-ḥelm, wa-tageḥša westa Galilā. (23) Wa-baṣiḥo, xadara westa beḥēr 'enta semā Nāzerēt, kama yetfaṣṣam za-tabehla ba-nabiy, kama Nāzerāwi yessammay waldeya.

Chapter III

3. Ba'enta Yoḥannes zakama sabaka mangešta samāyāt

(1) Wa-ba-we'etu mawā'el basḥa Yoḥannes Maṭmeq 'enza yesabbek ba-gadāma Yehudā, (2) 'enza yebel:

Nasseḥu, 'esma qarbat mangešta samāyāt. (3) 'Esma zentu we'etu za-tabehla ba-'Isāyeyās nabiy 'enza yebel:

Qāla za-yeṣarrex ba-gadām; 'astadālewu fenoto la-

---

16. Glt *tasālaqa* to joke, sport, play; to mock, make fun of *(lā'la)*. *selāq* sport, play; mockery. *mastasāleq* mocker, scorner.

22. CG *'agḥaša* to take aside, to divert; to remove, take away. Gt *tageḥša* to depart, withdraw.

’Egzi’abḥēr, wa-retu‘a gebaru maṣyāḥto.

(4) Wa-we’etu Yoḥannes lebsu za-yelabbes za-ṣag^{w}ra gamal, wa-qenātu za-’adim westa ḥaq^{w}ēhu, wa-sisāyu ’anbaṭā wa-ma‘āra gadām. (5) Wa-tewaḍḍe’ xabēhu k^{w}ellā ’Iyarusālēm wa-k^{w}ellā Yehudā wa-k^{w}ellu ’adyāmihu la-Yordānos, (6) wa-yeṭṭammaqu ’em-xabēhu westa Yordānos falag ’enza yet’ammanu xaṭāwe’ihomu. (7) Wa-soba re’ya bezuxāna Farisāweyāna wa-Saduqāweyāna ’enza yemaṣṣe’u westa ṭemqatu ṣemmita, wa-yebēlomu:

> Tewledda ’arāwita medr. Mannu ’ammarakemu teg^{w}yayu ’em-’enta temaṣṣe’ ma‘‘at? (8) Gebaru-kē ’enka šannāya ferē za-yedallewakemu la-nesseḥā. (9) Wa-’i-yemsalkemu ba-behila: ’Aba bena ’Abrehām-hā. ’Ebelakemu kama yekel ’Egzi’abḥēr ’em-’ellāntu ’a’bān ’anše’o weluda la-’Abrehām. (10) ’Esma nāhu wadde’a māḥḍē westa g^{w}enda ‘eḍaw yenabber. K^{w}ellu-ke ‘eḍ za-’i-yefarri ferē šannāya yetgazzam wa-westa ’essāt yetwadday. (11) ’Ane-sa-kē ’āṭammeqakemu ba-māy la-nesseḥā; wa-za-’emdexrēya-sa yemaṣṣe’ yeṣanne‘ ’emennēya, za-’i-yedallewani ’eṣur ’ašā’eno. We’etu-sa yāṭammeqakemu ba-manfas qeddus wa-ba-’essāt. (12) Za-maš‘ē westa ’edēhu, wa-yānaṣṣeḥ ‘awdo, wa-yāstagābe’ šernāyo westa mazgabu wa-ḥašaro-sa yāwe‘‘i ba-’essāt za-’i-yeṭaffe’.

(13) ’Amēhā maṣ’a ’Iyasus ’em-Galilā westa Yordānos xaba Yoḥannes kama yeṭṭamaq ’emennēhu. (14) Wa-Yoḥannes yekalle’o ’enza yebel:

> ’Ana ’efaqqed ’em-xabēka ’eṭṭamaq, wa-’anta-nu temaṣṣe’ xabēya?

(15) Wa-’awše’a ’Iyasus wa-yebēlo:

> Xedeg ye’zē-sa, ’esma kama-ze yedallewana nefaṣṣem k^{w}ello ṣedqa.

III 3. G *ṣēḥa (yeṣiḥ)* to make level, to pave (a road). Gt *taṣēḥa* pass. *ṣeyuḥ* level, even, paved; easy. *maṣyāḥt* highway.

4. *’adim* leather. *ḥaq*^{w}*ē* (pl. *-yāt*) loins. *’anbaṭā* (pl. *’anābeṭ*) locust(s). *ma‘ār* honey.

6. *falag* (pl. *’aflāg*) river.

7. *-kē ’enka* see §51.4.

10. D *wadde’a* to finish, complete; used as an auxiliary verb in the sense of "already": *wadde’a yenabber* is already seated, positioned, resting. Dt *tawadde’a* pass. *māḥḍē/māḥṣē* axe.

12. G *ša‘aya* to winnow. *maš‘ē* winnowing-fork. *‘awd* here: threshing-floor. *šernāy/sernāy* wheat. *ḥašar* chaff, piece of straw.

Wa-’emze xadago. (16) Wa-taṭamiqo ’Iyasus, sobēhā waḍ’a ’em-māy, wa-nāhu tarexwa lotu samāy, wa-re’ya manfasa ’Egzi’abḥēr ’enza yewarred kama regb, wa-nabara lā‘lēhu. (17) Wa-nāhu maṣ’a qāl ’em-samāy za-yebel:

> Ze-we’etu waldeya za-’āfaqqer, za-botu šamarku.

Chapter IV

(1) Wa-’emze ’Iyasus ’a‘rago manfas gadāma yetmakkar ’em-xaba Diyābelos. (2) Wa-ṣawimo mawā‘ela ’arbe‘ā wa-’arbe‘ā layāleya, wa-’emdexra-ze rexba. (3) Wa-qarba za-yāmēkkero wa-yebēlo:

> ’Emma waldu-sa ’anta la-’Egzi’abḥēr, bal kama ’ellu ’a’bān xebesta yekunā.

(4) Wa-’awše’a ’Iyasus wa-yebē:

> Ṣeḥuf kama ’akko ba-xebest kema za-yaḥayyu sab’, ’allā ba-k^{w}ellu qāl za-yewaḍḍe’ ’em-’afuhu la-’Egzi’abḥēr.

(5) Wa-’emze naš’o Diyābelos westa qeddest hagar, wa-’aqamo westa tadbāba bēta maqdas, (6) wa-yebēlo:

> ’Emma-sa ’amān waldu ’anta la-’Egzi’abḥēr, wa-tawaraw tāḥta. ’Esma ṣeḥuf kama la-malā’ektihu ye’ēzzezomu ba’enti’aka kama ye‘qabuka ba-k^{w}ellu fenoteka, wa-ba-’edaw yānašše’uka kama ’i-tet‘aqaf ba-’ebn ’eg̣raka.

(7) Wa-’awše’a ’Iyasus wa-yebēlo:

> Kā‘eba ṣeḥuf: ’I-tāmakkero la-’Egzi’abḥēr ’Amlākeka.

(8) Wa-’emze ‘ādi naš’o Diyābelos westa dabr nawwāx ṭeqqa, wa-’ar’ayo k^{w}ello mangeštāta ‘ālam wa-kebromu. (9) Wa-yebēlo:

> Zanta k^{w}ello ’ehubaka la’emma sagadka lita wa-’ammāxkani.

(10) Wa-’emze yebēlo ’Iyasus:

> Ḥur ’emdexrēya Sayṭān. Ṣeḥuf we’etu: La-’Egzi’abḥēr ’Amlākeka tesged, wa-kiyāhu bāḥtito tāmlek.

IV 1. Dt *tamakkara* to be tested, tempted, tried. CD *’amakkara* to test, try, tempt, examine. *mekkur* tempted, tried. *makkarā* (pl. *-t*) examination, testing, trying, temptation.

5. *tadbāb* roof, top, summit, pinnacle.

6. *warwa (yewru)* to throw, cast. Gt *tawarwa* pass. and reflex. CG *’a‘qafa* to impede, present an obstacle to (o.s.). Gt *ta‘aqfa* to be hindered, impeded; to stumble, knock against. *‘eqeft* (pl. *-āt*) impediment, obstacle, hindrance, *mā‘qaf/mā‘qef* idem.

(11) Wa-'emze xadago Diyābelos, wa-nāhu malā'ekt maṣ'u yetla'akewwo. (12) Wa-sami'o 'Iyasus kama Yoḥannes ta'exza, tageḥša westa Galilā. (13) Wa-xadagā la-Nāzerēt. Wa-maṣi'o, xadara Qefernāhom, 'enta mangala bāḥr westa 'adbāra Zābulon wa-Neftālēm, (14) kama yetfaṣṣam za-tabehla ba-'Isāyeyās nabiy 'enza yebel:

Medra Zābulon wa-medra Neftālēm, fenota bāḥr mā'dota Yordānos, Galilā 'enta 'aḥzāb. (16) Ḥezb za-yenabber westa ṣelmat re'ya berhāna 'abiya; wa-la-'ella-hi yenabberu westa ṣelmat wa-ṣelālota mot berhān šaraqa lomu.

4. Ba'enta temhert qadāmi za-mahara 'Egzi'ena Kerestos

(17) 'Em-'amēhā 'axaza 'Iyasus yesbek wa-yebal:

Tanasseḥu, 'esma qarbat mangešta samāyāt.

(18) Wa-'enza yānsosu mangala bāḥra Galilā, re'ya kel'ēta 'axawa, Sem'on-hā, za-tasamya Pēṭros, wa-'Endreyās-hā 'exwāhu, 'enza yewaddeyu marbabta westa bāḥr, 'esma mašaggerān 'emuntu. (19) Wa-yebēlomu 'Iyasus:

Ne'u, telewuni dexrēya, wa-'erēsseyakemu tekunu mašaggerāna sab'.

(20) Wa-ba-gizēhā xadagu mašāgerihomu wa-talawewwo. (21) Wa-'adiwo 'em-heyya, re'ya kāle'āna kel'ēta 'axawa, Yā'qob-ha walda Zabdēwos wa-Yoḥannes-hā 'exwāhu, westa ḥamar mesla Zabdēwos 'abuhomu yešarre'u mašāgerihomu, wa-ṣawwe'omu. (22) Wa-ba-gizēhā xadigomu ḥamara wa-'abāhomu, talawewwo. (23) Wa-'ansosawa 'Iyasus westa k^{w}ellu Galilā

---

17. *'em-'amēhā* from that time onward.

18. Q *'ansosawa* to walk, stroll. G *rababa* to expand, extend, spread out (trans.). Gt *tarabba* pass. and intrans. *rebbat* expansion, extension. *marbabt* net.

19. G *talawa (yetlu)* to follow, accompany (a.d.o. or *la-*). CG *'atlawa* caus. Glt *tatālawa* recipr. *telwat/telot* vn. following; dowry. *talāwi* follower; disciple, pupil; sectarian; successor. *matlew* adj. following. *matlew/matlo* that which follows, succession; rest, remainder. *matlewa* adv. then, immediately thereafter, in succession.

20. *mašgart* (pl. *mašāger*) net, fishing-gear. CG *'ašgara* to hunt, trap, snare, fish. Gt *tašagra* pass. *šagarāt* guards (of jail or prison). *'ašgāri* hunter, fisherman.

’enza yemēhher ba-mek^{w}rābātihomu wa-yesabbek wangēla mangešt wa-yefēwwes k^{w}ello dawē wa-k^{w}ello ḥemāma za-westa ḥezb. (24) Wa-waḍ’a semu‘ātu westa k^{w}ellā Soreyā, wa-’amṣe’u xabēhu k^{w}ello deweyāna wa-k^{w}ello ḥemumāna za-la-la zi’ahu ḥemāmomu, wa-ṣe‘‘urāna wa-’ella-hi ’agānent wa-warxāweyāna wa-’ella-hi nagargār wa-maḍāg^{w}e‘āna; wa-yāḥayyewomu. (25) Wa-talawewwo bezuxān ’aḥzāb ’em-Galilā wa-’em-‘Ašru ’Ahgur wa-’em-’Iyarusālēm wa-’em-Yehudā wa-’em-mā‘dota Yordānos.

Chapter V

5. Ba’enta beḍu‘ān

(1) Wa-re’eyo ’aḥzāba, ‘arga westa dabr. Wa-nabiro, qarbu xabēhu ’ardā’ihu. (2) Wa-kašata ’afāhu, wa-maharomu ’enza yebel:

> (3) Beḍu‘ān naddāyān ba-manfas, ’esma lomu ye’eti mangešta samāyāt. (4) Beḍu‘ān ’ella yelāḥewu ye’zē, ’esma ’emuntu yetfēššeḥu. (5) Beḍu‘ān yawwāhān, ’esma ’emuntu yewarresewwā la-medr. (6) Beḍu‘ān ’ella yerexxebu wa-yeṣamme’u la-ṣedq, ’esma ’emuntu yeṣaggebu. (7) Beḍu‘ān maḥāreyān, ’esma ’emuntu yetmaḥḥaru. (8) Beḍu‘ān neṣuḥāna lebb, ’esma ’emuntu yerē’’eyewwo la-’Egzi’abḥēr. (9) Beḍu‘ān gabāreyāna salām, ’esma ’emuntu weluda ’Egzi’abḥēr yessammayu. (10) Beḍu‘ān ’ella yessaddadu ba’enta ṣedq, ’esma lomu ye’eti mangešta samāyāt. (11) Beḍu‘ān ’antemu soba yesaddedukemu wa-yezanagg^{w}egukemu wa-yenabb(eb)u k^{w}ello ’ekaya lā‘lēkemu, ’enza yeḥēssewu ba-’enti’aya. (12) Tafaššeḥu wa-taḥašayu, ’esma ‘asbekemu bezux we’etu ba-samāyāt, ’esma kama-ze sadadewwomu

---

23. *mek^{w}rāb* (pl. *-āt*) temple, shrine, synagogue.

24. *la-la* see §51.5. *warxāwi* lunatic. *nagargār* a type of epilepsy; rolling, spinning. Q *’angargara* to roll, spin (trans. and intrans.). *maḍāg^{w}e‘* a paralytic. CLt *’astaḍāg^{w}e‘a* to place on a bed or litter. *ḍeg‘/ḍegā‘* pillow, mattress.

V 5. *yawwāh* mild, gentle, modest, submissive; innocent, simple. G *yawha* = D *yawweha* to be gentle etc.; to please, charm; to persuade, entice. *yawhat* mildness etc. *yawwāhat* idem. *yawhennā* idem.

6. G *ṣam’a (yeṣmā’)* to be thirsty (for: *la-*). CG *’aṣme’a* caus. *ṣemu’* thirsty. *ṣem’* thirst.

11. Q *zang^{w}ag^{w}a* to ridicule, hold in scorn. *zeng^{w}āg^{w}ē* scorn, ridicule.

la-nabiyāt ’ella ’em-qedmēkemu. (13) ’Antemu we’etu ṣēw la-medr. Wa-’emma-sa ṣēw lasḥa, ba-ment-nu yetqēssam? ’Albo-kē ’enka la-za-yebaqq^{w}e‘ za’enbala la-gadif ’af’a wa-yekayyedo sab’. (14) ’Antemu we’etu berhānu la-‘ālam. ’I-tekel hagar taxabe’o ’enta mal‘elta dabr tenabber. (15) Wa-’i-yāxattewu māxtota kama yānberewwā tāḥta kafar, ’allā diba taqwāmā, wa-tābarreh la-k^{w}ellomu ’ella westa bēt. (16) Kamāhu yebrāh berhānekemu ba-qedma sab’, kama yer’ayu megbārikemu šannāya wa-yesabbeḥewwo la-’abukemu za-ba-samāyāt. (17) ’I-yemsalkemu za-maṣā’ku ’es‘ar ’orita wa-nabiyāta. ’I-maṣā’ku ’es‘aromu ’allā ’efaṣṣemomu. (18) ’Amān ’ebelakemu: ’eska yaxallef samāy wa-medr, yawṭā ’enta ’aḥatti qerḍatā ’i-taxallef ’em-’orit ’eska soba k^{w}ellu yetgabbar. (19) Za-kē fatḥa ’aḥatta ’em-’ellā te’zāzāt ’enta taḥaṣṣeṣ, wa-yemēhher kama-ze la-sab’, ḥeṣuṣa yessammay ba-mangešta samāyāt. Wa-za-sa yemēhher wa-yegabber we’etu ‘abiya yessammay ba-mangešta samāyāt. (20) Nāhu ’ebelakemu kama ’emma ’i-fadfada ṣedqekemu fadfāda ’em-ṣaḥaft wa-’em-Farisāweyān, ’i-tebawwe’u westa mangešta samāyāt. (21) Samā‘kemu kama tabehla la-qadamt: ’i-teqtel nafsa, wa-za-sa qatala rasḥa we’etu la-k^{w}ennanē. (22) Wa-’ane-sa ’ebelakemu: k^{w}ellu za-yāme‘‘e‘ ’exwāhu rasḥa we’etu la-k^{w}ennanē; wa-za-hi yebē ’exwāhu za-ḍarq rasḥa we’etu la-‘awd; wa-za-hi yebē ’abd

---

13. *ṣēw* salt. G *lasḥa (yelsāḥ)* to be unseasoned, insipid, tasteless, fatuous. *lesuḥ* insipid etc. D *qassama* to season, make tasty. Dt *taqassama* pass. *qessum* well-seasoned, tasty. *maqsem* (pl. *maqāsem*) (highly) seasoned food.

15. *kafar* (pl. *’akfār*) a container for measuring, a bushel.

18. G *qaraḍa/qaraṣa* to incise, sculpt. Gt *taqarṣa* pass. *qerḍat/qerṣat/q^{w}erṣat* the stroke of a letter; stroke, mark, incision. *yawṭā ’enta ’aḥatti qerḍatā* "the letter iota, whose stroke is (but) one." *’orit* the Mosaic Law, the Pentateuch.

21. G *rasḥa* to be subject or liable (to: *la-*), to be in danger of; to be a defendant; to be unclean, dirty. CG *’arseḥa* to condemn; to make dirty, pollute, contaminate. *resuḥ* dirty, etc.; the accused, defendant. *resḥat* (pl. *-āt*) dirt, filth, pollution; crime, guilt.

22. *ḍarq* (pl. *’aḍreqt*) a patch, tatter. *za-ḍarq* adj. patched, threadbare; here an interpretation of Gk *raka*, an obscure term of

rasḥa we’etu la-Gahānnama ’essāt. (23) Wa-’emkama-kē tābawwe’ ’ammexāka westa meswā‘, wa-ba-heyya tazakkarka kama-bo ’exuka za-yaḥayyesaka, (24) xedeg heyya mabā’aka qedma meswā‘, wa-ḥur, qedma tak^{w}ānan mesla ’exuka, wa-’emze gabi’aka ’abe’ ’ammexāka. (25) Kun ṭabiba la-‘edeweka feṭuna, ’enza halloka meslēhu westa fenot, kama ’i-yemaṭṭuka ‘edeweka la-mak^{w}annen, wa-mak^{w}annen la-lā’ku, wa-westa moqeḥ tetwaday. (26) ’Amān ’ebelaka: ’i-tewaḍḍe’ ’em-heyya ’eska soba tefaddi ṭeyyuqa k^{w}ello. (27) Samā‘kemu kama tabehla: ’I-tezammew. (28) Wa-’ane-sa ’ebelakemu: k^{w}ellu za-yerē’’i be’sita wa-yefattewā wadde’a zammawa bāti ba-lebbu. (29) ’Emma ‘ayneka ’enta yamān tāseḥḥetaka, melexā wa-’awḍe’ā ’em-lā‘lēka, ’esma yexēyyesaka kama yethag^{w}al ’aḥadu ’emenna ’abāleka ’em-k^{w}ellu šegāka yetwaday westa Gahānnam. (30) Wa-’emma ’enta yamān ’edēka tāseḥḥetaka, meterā wa-’awḍe’ā ’em-lā‘lēka, ’esma yexēyyesaka yethag^{w}al ’aḥadu ’emenna ’abāleka ’em-k^{w}ellantāhu šegāka westa Gahānnam yetwaday. (31) Wa-tabehla: za-xadaga be’sito yahabā maṣḥafa xedgātihā. (32) Wa-’ane-sa ’ebelakemu kama k^{w}ellu za-yaxaddeg be’sito za’enbala tezammu yerēsseyā tezammu. (33) Wa-za-hi xedegta ’awsaba zammawa. Wa-kā‘eba samā‘kemu kama tabehla la-qadamt: ’I-temḥalu ba-ḥassat; ’agbe’u bāḥtu la-’Egzi’abḥēr maḥalākemu. (34) Wa-’ane-sa ’ebelakemu: ’I-temḥalu gemurā: wa-’i-samāya, ’esma manbaru la-’Egzi’abḥēr we’etu; (35) wa-’i-medra, ’esma makayyada ’egarihu ye’eti; wa-’i-ba-’Iyarusālēm, ’esma hagaru ye’eti la-neguš ‘abiy. (36)

---

abuse.

25. *‘edew* (pl. *-ān*) enemy.

26. G *fadaya (yefdi)* to pay back, to pay a debt. Gt *tafadya* to exact payment or punishment; to receive payment or punishment, to be paid back. *fedā* repayment, retribution; punishment, revenge. *fadāy(i)* one who pays back. *mafdē* money; reward, payment.

29. D *xayyasa* to be better, more outstanding. Often impersonal: *yexēyyesani kama* + subj.: it is better for me that ... CD *’axayyasa* to make better, more pleasing. *xisan* excellence. *’abāl* (pl. *-āt*) limb or member of the body; body, person, self. Note the *’em-* of the comparative prefixed directly to the clause beginning with *k^{w}ellu šegāka*.

Wa-'i-ba-re'seka temḥal, 'esma 'i-tekel 'aḥatta še'erta re'seka ṣa'adā rasseyo wa-'i-'aṣlemo. (37) Yekun bāḥtu nagarekemu 'emma-hi 'ewwa 'ewwa wa-'emma-hi 'albo 'albo. (38) Wa-fadfāda-sa 'em-'ellu 'em-'ekuy we'etu. (39) Samā'kemu kama tabehla: 'Ayn bēzā 'ayn, wa-senn bēzā senn. Wa-'ane-sa 'ebelakemu: 'I-tetqāwamewwo la-'ekuy; wa-la-za-hi ṣaf'aka 'enta yamān maltāḥtaka miṭ lotu kāle'tā-hi. (40) Wa-la-za-hi yefaqqed yet'aggalka wa-malbasaka yenšā', xedeg lotu wa-lebsaka-ni. (41) Wa-la-za-hi 'abbaṭaka me'rāfa 'aḥada, ḥur meslēhu kel'ēta. (42) La-za yese''elaka hab wa-la-za yefaqqed 'em-xabēka yetlaqqāḥ 'i-tekle'o. (43) Samā'kemu kama tabehla: 'Afqer biṣaka, wa-ṣelā' ṣalā'ēka. (44) Wa-'ane-sa 'ebelakemu: 'Afqeru ṣalā'takemu, bārekewwomu la-'ella yeraggemukemu, šannāya gebaru la-'ella yeṣalle'ukemu, wa-ṣalleyu ba'enta 'ella yesaddedukemu, (45) kama tekunu weluda la-'abukemu za-ba-samāyāt. 'Esma ḍaḥāya yāšarreq lā'la 'ekuyān wa-xērān, wa-yāzannem zenāma

---

36. G *šeʿra* to grow, be green. *šāʿr* (pl. *'ašʿert*) herbage, vegetation, grass. *šeʿur* grassy, covered with vegetation. *šeʿert* (pl. *'ašʿert*) hair (of head or body).

37. *'emma-hi* ... *'emma-hi* either ... or.

39. *bēzā* prep. in exchange for; n. price of redemption. *senn* (pl. *senan, 'asnān*) tooth. Dt *tasannana* = Glt *tasānana* to enter into litigation with, to contend with. *tasnān* lawsuit, litigation, controversy. G *ṣafʿa (yeṣfāʿ)* to strike, slap, box. Gt *taṣafʿa* pass. *ṣefʿat* a blow, slap. *maltāḥt* (pl. *malāteḥ*) jaw, cheek.

40. Dt *taʿaggala* to cheat, defraud; to oppress, treat unjustly, rob. *teʿgelt* fraud, defrauding, robbing; injury, damage.

41. D *ʿabbaṭa* to compel, force, coerce.

42. Dt *talaqqeḥa* to borrow. D *laqqeḥa* to lend. *leqqāḥ* a loan.

44. G *ragama (yergem)* to curse, execrate. Gt *taragma* pass. Glt *tarāgama* pass. *regum* cursed, execrated. *ragāmi* curser, execrator. *margam* (pl. *-āt*) curse, execration.

45. G *zanma* to rain. CG *'aznama* to bring rain, cause it to rain. D *ʿammaḍa* to sin, act unjustly or wickedly; to harm, injure. *ʿammāḍi* unjust, wicked, criminal. *ʿammaḍā* injustice, wickedness.

lāʿla ṣādeqān wa-ʿammāḍeyān. (46) Wa-'emma-sa tāfaqqeru za-yāfaqqerakemu, menta ʿasba bekemu? 'Akko-hu maṣabbeḥāweyān-hi kamāhu yegabberu? (47) Wa-'emma ta'āmāxkemu 'axawikemu kema, menta 'enka fadfāda tegabberu? 'Akko-nu 'aḥzāb-ni kiyāhu-sa yegabberu? (48) Kunu-kē 'antemu-sa feṣṣumāna kama 'abukemu samāyāwi feṣṣum we'etu.

Chapter VI

(1) Wa-bāḥtu ʿuqu meṣwātakemu 'i-tegbaru la-ʿayna sab' kama tāstar'eyu lomu. Wa-'emma-'akko-sa, ʿasba 'albekemu ba-xaba 'abukemu za-ba-samāyāt. (2) Soba-kē tegabber meṣwāta, 'i-tenfāx qarna qedmēka, kama madlewān yegabberu ba-makʷārebt wa-ba-'askʷāt, kama yet'akʷatu 'em-xaba sab'. 'Amān 'ebelakemu, hagʷlu ʿesētomu. (3) Wa-'anta-sa, soba tegabber meṣwāta, 'i-tā'mer ḍagāmeka za-tegabber yamāneka, (4) kama ba-xebu' yekun meṣwāteka. Wa-'abuka za-yerē''i za-ba-xebu' yefaddeyaka kešuta. (5) Wa-soba-hi teṣēlleyu, 'i-tekunu kama madlewān, 'esma yāfaqqeru ba-makʷārebt wa-westa ma'āzena marāḥebt qawima wa-ṣalleyo, kama yāstar'eyu la-sab'. 'Amān 'ebelakemu, hagʷlu ʿesētomu. (6) Wa-'anta-sa soba teṣēlli, bā' bētaka wa-ʿeṣu xoxtaka, wa-ṣalli la-'abuka la-za-ba-xebu', wa-'abuka za-yerē''i ba-xebu' yaʿasseyaka kešuta. (7) Wa-'enza teṣēlleyu, 'i-tezangeʿu kama 'aḥzāb, 'esma yemasselomu ba-'abzexo nebābomu za-yesammeʿomu. (8) 'I-tetmasalewwomu-kē, 'esma yā'ammer 'abukemu śamāyāwi za-tefaqqedu za'enbala tes'alewwo. (9) Kama-ze-kē ṣalleyu 'antemu-sa:

'Abuna za-ba-samāyāt, yetqaddas semeka. (10) Temṣā' mangešteka. Yekun faqādaka bakama ba-samay wa-ba-medr-ni. (11) Sisāyana za-la-la ʿelatena habana yom. (12) Wa-xedeg lana 'abbasāna kama neḥna-ni naxaddeg la-za-'abbasa lana. (13) Wa-'i-tābe'ana westa mansut, 'allā 'adxenana wa-bāleḥana 'em-kʷellu 'ekuy;

---

maʿammeḍ = *ʿammāḍi*.

VI 2. *sakʷat/sakot ('askʷāt)* street, quarter. G *ʿasaya* to repay. Gt *taʿasya* to be repaid, accept repayment. *ʿesēt* payment, reward.

5. *mā'zen(t), mā'zan(t)* (pl. *ma'āzen*) corner.

13. *mansut (manāsew)* temptation, danger; calamity, divine punishment. CQ *'amansawa* to lead to destruction/temptation. Qt

’esma zi’aka ye’eti mangešt, xayl, wa-sebḥāt la-ʿālama ʿālam. ’Amēn.

(14) ’Esma ’emma xadaggemu la-sab’ ’abbasāhomu, yaxaddeg lakemu-ni ’abukemu samāyāwi ’abbasākemu. (15) Wa-’emma-sa ’i-xadaggemu la-sab’ ’abbasāhomu, ’abukemu-ni ’i-yaxaddeg ’abbasākemu. (16) Wa-soba teṣawwemu, ’i-tekunu kama madlewān; ’i-teṣamahayyu. (17) ’Esma yāmāsenu gaṣṣomu kama yāstar’eyu la-sab’ kama ṣomu. ’Amān ’ebelakemu, sallaṭu ʿesētomu. Wa-’anta-sa, soba teṣawwem, qebā’ re’saka, wa-gaṣṣaka taxaḍab, (18) kama ’i-tāstar’i la-sab’ kama ṣomka, za’enbala la-’abuka za-ba-xebu’. Wa-’abuka za-yerē’’i za-ba-xebu’ yaʿasseyaka kešuta. (19) ’I-tezgebu lakemu mazāgebta westa medr, xaba ḍāḍē wa-q^wenq^{w}enē yāmāseno, wa-xaba saraqt yekarreyu wa-yesarrequ. (20) Zegebu lakemu mazāgebta westa samāyāt, xaba ’i-yāmāseno ḍāḍē wa-’i-q^wenq^{w}enē, wa-xaba saraqt ’i-yekarreyu wa-’i-yesarrequ. (21) ’Esma xaba hallo mazgabeka, heyya yehēllu lebbeka-ni. (22) Māxtotu la-šegāka we’etu ʿayneka. Wa-’emkama ʿayneka sefuḥ we’etu, k^wellu

---

tamansawa pass. *mensew* liable to temptation/punishment. *mensāwē* = *mansut*. L *bāleḥa* to rescue, save, liberate. Lt *tabāleḥa* pass. *bāləḥi* liberator, protector.

17. G *salaṭa* (1) to be whole, perfect; (2) to accept/bring back (something) whole/complete/in its entirety; to pay back; (3) to consummate, finish up/off. D *sallaṭa* = G(2) and G(3); also: to be effective, to accomplish results. Gt *tasalṭa* = Dt *tasallaṭa* to be finished, consummated, completed. *sellāṭē* completion. G *qab’a (yeqbā’)* to smear, anoint. Gt *taqab’a* pass. and reflex. *qebu’* smeared, anointed. *qeb’* (olive)oil, ointment, butter. *qeb’at* anointing.

19. *ḍāḍē* moth, worm. *q^wenq^{w}enē* moth, worm.

20. *sarāqi* (pl. *saraqt*) thief. G *saraqa (yesreq)* to steal. CG *’asraqa* caus. Gt *tasarqa* pass. *serq/sarq* stolen object; theft.

22. G *safḥa (yesfāḥ)* trans.: to expand, extend, spread out; intrans.: idem. Gt *tasafḥa* = intrans. G. *sefuḥ* spread out, extended; wide, spacious, ample; open, sincere, guileless; generous. *sefḥ* expansion, extension; width, expanse; sincerity; warp (of a loom). *sefḥat* extension, width, capacity. *masfeḥ* hammer, mallet; anvil. G *ḍoga* to be savage, perverse, evil, malignant. *ḍewug* = *ḍawwāg* perverse, evil, malignant, wild, savage. *ḍug* perverseness etc.

šegāka beruh we'etu. Wa-'emma-sa 'ayneka ḍawwāg we'etu, k^{w}ellu šegāka ṣelmata yekawwen. (23) Wa-'emma-sa berhān za-lā'lēka ṣelmat we'etu, ṣelmateka 'efo? (24) 'Albo za-yekel la-kel'ē 'agā'ezt taqaneyo. Wa-'emma-'akko, 'aḥada yeṣalle' wa-kāle'o yāfaqqer. Wa-'emma-'akko, la-'aḥadu yet'ēzzaz wa-la-kāle'u 'i-yet'ēzzaz. 'I-tekelu-kē la-'Egzi'abḥēr taqaneyo wa-la-newāy. (25) Wa-ba'enta-ze 'ebelakemu: 'I-tetakkezu la-nafsekemu za-teballe'u wa-la-nafestekemu za-telabbesu. 'Akko-hu nafs ta'abbi 'em-sisit, wa-nafest 'em-lebs? (26) Naṣṣeru 'a'wāfa samāy kama 'i-yezarre'u wa-'i-ya'arreru wa-'i-yāstagābe'u westa 'abyāt, wa-'abukemu samāyāwi yesēseyomu. 'Akko-nu 'antemu fadfāda texēyyesewwomu? (27) Mannu 'emennēkemu ba-takkezo za-yekel wasseko 'em-diba qomu 'emmata 'aḥatta? (28) Wa-ba'enta 'arāz-ni menta-nu texēlleyu? Re'eyu ṣegēyāta gadām kama yelehhequ, 'i-yeṣāmewu wa-'i-yefattelu. (29) 'Ebelakemu kama Salomon ṭeqqa ba-k^{w}ellu kebru 'i-labsa kama 'aḥadu 'em-'ellu. (30) Za-šā'ra gadām, za-yom hallo wa-gēsama westa 'essāt yetwadday, 'Egzi'abḥēr za-kama-ze yālabbeso, 'efo 'enka fadfāda kiyākemu, ḥeṣuṣāna hāymānot? (31) 'I-tetakkezu-kē 'enka 'enza tebelu: Menta neballe' wa-menta nesatti wa-menta netkaddan? (32) 'Esma zanta-sa k^{w}ello 'aḥzāb yaxaššešewwo, wa-lakemu-sa yā'ammer 'abukemu samāyāwi kama tefaqqedu zanta k^{w}ello. (33) 'Antemu-sa xeššu maqdema mangešta zi'ahu wa-ṣedqo, wa-zentu k^{w}ellu yetwēssakakemu. (34) 'I-tetakkezu-kē la-gēsam, 'esma gēsam-sa texēlli la-re'sā. Ya'akkelā la-'elat 'ekayā.

Chapter VII

(1) 'I-tek^{w}annenu kama 'i-tetk^{w}annanu. (2) 'Esma ba-k^{w}ennanē za-

---

26. G *'arara* to harvest. *mā'rar* harvest.

28. D *'arraza* to prepare or furnish clothing. *'arāz/'arrāz* (pl. *-āt*) clothing, vestments. G *ṣagaya* to flower. *ṣeguy* flowering, decorated with flowers. *ṣegē* (pl. *-yāt*) flower. G *fatala (yeftel)* to twist, spin. Gt *tafatla* pass. *fetul* spun, twisted. *fatl* (pl. *'aftāl, 'aftelt*) thread, cord. *fetlo* twisted work.

30. *za-...'efo* ... see §51.3.

33. *maqdema* is here an adv.: beforehand, first.

34. G *'akala (ye'kal, ye'kel)* to be sufficient for, to satisfy (o.s. or *la-*); to be approximately. CG *'a'kala* = Gt *ta'akla* to be satisfied, have enough. *'ekul* sufficient, enough.

k^{w}annankemu tetk^{w}ēnnanu ’antemu, wa-ba-masfart za-safarkemu yesafferu lakemu. (3) Mẹnta-nu tere’’i ḥašara za-westa ‘ayna ’exuka, wa-šarwē za-westa ‘ayneka ’i-tebēyyen? (4) Wa-’efo tebelo la-’exuka: "Xedeg ’āwḍe’ ḥašara ’em-westa ‘ayneka," wa-nāhu šarwē westa ‘ayneka? (5) Madlew, ’awḍe’ qedma šarwē ’em-westa ‘ayneka, wa-’emze terē’’i la-’awḍe’o ḥašara za-westa ‘ayna ’exuka. (6) ’I-tahabu qeddesta la-kalabāt, wa-’i-tedayu bāḥreyakemu qedma ’aḥrew, kama ’i-yekidewwomu ba-’egarihomu wa-tamayeṭomu yenḍexukemu. (7) Sa’alu wa-yetwahhabakemu. Xeššu wa-terakkebu. G^{w}adg^{w}edu wa-yetraxxawakemu. (8) ’Esma k^{w}ellu za-yese’’el yenašše’, wa-za-hi yaxaššeš yerakkeb, wa-la-za-hi g^{w}adg^{w}ada yetraxxawo. (9) Mannu we’etu ’emennēkemu be’si za-yese’’elo waldu xebesta, bo-nu ’ebna yehubo? (10) Wa-’emma-hi ‘āšā sa’alo, ’arwē medr-nu yehubo? (11) Za-’antemu ’enka ’enza ’ekuyān, ’antemu tā’ammeru šannāya habta wehiba la-weludekemu, ’efo fadfāda ’abukemu za-ba-samāyāt yehub šannāya la-’ella yese’’elewwo? (12) K^{w}ello-kē za-tefaqqedu yegbaru lakemu sab’, kamāhu gebaru lomu ’antemu-ni, ’esma zentu we’etu ’orit-ni wa-nabiyāt. (13) Bā’u ’enta ṣabāb ’anqaṣ, ’esma raḥāb ’anqaṣ wa-sefeḥt fenot ’enta tewassed westa hag^{w}l, wa-bezuxān ’emuntu ’ella yebawwe’u westētā. (14) Ṭeqqa ṣabāb ’anqaṣ wa-ṣe‘eqt fenot ’enta tewassed westa ḥeywat, wa-wexudān ’emunto ’ella

---

VII 2. G *safara* to measure (out). Gt *tasafra* pass. Glt *tasāfara* to mete out, distribute. *sefur* measured. *masfart* (pl. *masāfer*) a measure, specific amount.

3. *šarwē* (pl. *šarāwit*) beam, timber. D *bayyana* to discern, distinguish, make out. CD *’abayyana* to make clear, evident.

6. *kalb* (pl. *kalabāt*, *’aklebt*, *’aklāb*) dog. *bāḥrey* (pl. *-āt*) pearl. *ḥarāweyā* (pl. *’aḥrew*) pig, sow, swine. G *naḍxa (yenḍāx)* to strike, beat, knock down, trample, Gt *tanaḍxa* pass.

7. Q *g^{w}adg^{w}ada* to knock (on a door).

10. *‘āšā* (pl. *-t*) fish.

13. G *ṣabba/ṣababa (yeṣbeb)* to be (too) narrow; to narrow, confine. CG *’aṣbaba* caus. *ṣabib* (f. *ṣabāb*) narrow, confined. *ṣebbat* narrowness. *maṣbeb* a narrow place, narrow pass.

14. CG *’aṣ‘aqa* to press in on, to confine. *ṣe‘uq* narrow, confined. *ṣā‘q* confinement, press; need. *maṣ‘eq* adj. pressing, confining. G *wexda* to be few, small. *wexud* few, small, scanty. *wexdat* paucity, scantiness.

yerakkebewwā. (15) Taʿaqabu ʾem-ḥassāweyān nabiyāt, ʾella yemaṣṣeʾu xabēkemu ba-ʾalbāsa ʾabāgeʿ, wa-ʾenta wesṭomu-sa tak^{w}lāt mašaṭṭ ʾemuntu. (16) Wa-ʾem-ferēhomu tāʾammerewwomu. Yeqaššemu-hu ʾem-ʾašwāk ʾaskāla, wa-ʾem-ʾamēkalā balasa? (17) Kamāhu-kē k^{w}ellu ʿeḍ šannāy ferē šannāya yefarri, wa-ʾekuy-sa ʿeḍ ferē ʾekuya yefarri. (18) ʾI-yekel ʿeḍ šannāy ferē ʾekuya fareya, wa-ʾi-ʿeḍ ʾekuy ferē šannāya fareya. (19) K^{w}ellu ʿeḍ za-ʾi-yefarri ferē šannāya yegazzemewwo, wa-westa ʾessāt yewaddeyewwo. (20) Wa-ʾem-ferēhomu ʾenka tāʾammerewwomu. (21) ʾAkko k^{w}ellu za-yebelani "ʾEgziʾo, ʾEgziʾo" za-yebawweʾ westa mangešta samāyāt, zaʾenbala za-yegabber faqādo la-ʾabuya za-ba-samāyāt. (22) Bezuxān yebeluni ba-yeʾeti ʿelat:

> ʾEgziʾo, ʾEgziʾo, ʾakko-nu ba-semeka tanabbayna wa-ba-semeka ʾagānenta ʾawḍāʾna wa-ba-semeka xaylāta bezuxa gabarna?

(23) Wa-yeʾeta sobē ʾāʾammenomu:

> Gemurā ʾi-yāʾammerakemu. Raḥaqu ʾemennēya k^{w}ellekemu ʾella tegabberu ʿammaḍā.

(24) K^{w}ellu-kē za-yesammeʿ zanta nagareya wa-yegabbero yemassel beʾsē ṭabiba za-ḥanaṣa bēto diba k^{w}ak^{w}ḥ. (25) Wa-warada zenām, wa-maṣʾu waḥāyezt, wa-nafxu nafāsāt, wa-gafʿewwo la-weʾetu bēt, wa-ʾi-wadqa, ʾesma diba k^{w}ak^{w}ḥ tašārara. (26) Wa-k^{w}ellu za-yesammeʿ zanta nagareya wa-ʾi-yegabbero yemassel beʾsē ʾabda za-ḥanaṣa bēto diba xoṣā. (27) Wa-warada zenām, wa-maṣʾu waḥāyezt, wa-nafxu nafāsāt, wa-gafʿewwo la-weʾetu bēt, wa-wadqa, wa-kona deqatu ʿabiya.

---

15. *tak^{w}lā* (pl. *-t*) wolf.

16. G *qašama (yeqšem)* to pick (fruit), gather, collect, harvest. Gt *taqašma* pass. *qašm* harvest, picking; the crops harvested (pl. *ʾaqšām*). *qašāmi/qaššām* a fruit/berry/grape-picker. *šok* (pl. *ʾašwāk*) thorn; sting. *ʾaskāl* (pl. *-āt*) grape(s). *ʾamēkalā* a thorny plant.

23. *sobē* is used nominally here: *yeʾeta sobē* at that time, on that occasion. *ʾaʾmana* in the sense: to profess, confirm as a fact, assert.

24. *k^{w}ak^{w}ḥ* rock(s), stone(s).

25. G *gafʿa (yegfāʿ)* to harm, injure, oppress. Gt *tagafʿa* pass. *gefuʿ* injured, harmed; violent. *gefʿ* harm, injury; violence; oppression. *gafāʿi* oppressor, tyrant.

26. *xoṣā* sand.

(28) Wa-soba faṣṣama 'Iyasus zanta nagára, tadammu 'aḥzāb ba-mehherotu, (29) 'esma yemēhheromu kama za-šelṭāna-bo, wa-'akko kama ṣaḥaftomu.

Chapter VIII

6. Ba'enta za-lamṣ

(1) Wa-'enza yewarred 'em-dabr, talawewwo sab' bezuxān. (2) Wa-nāhu maṣ'a za-lamṣ, wa-sagada lotu 'enza yebel:

'Egzi'o, 'emma-sa faqadka, tekel 'anṣeḥoteya.

(3) Wa-safiḥo 'edēhu, gasaso wa-yebēlo:

'Efaqqed. Neṣāḥ.

Wa-naṣḥa 'em-lamṣu ba-gizēhā. (4) Wa-yebēlo 'Iyasus:

ʻUq 'i-tenger wa-'i-la-mannu-hi, wa-bāḥtu ḥur wa-'ar'i re'saka la-kāhen, wa-'abe' mabā'aka, bakama 'azzaza Musē, la-semʻ lomu.

7. Ba'enta walda masfen

(5) Wa-bawi'o Qefernāhom, maṣ'a xabēhu ḥabē me't, (6) wa-yebēlo:

'Egzi'o, dewey waldeya, wa-yesakkeb westa bēt maḍāg^{w}eʻ ṭeqqa ṣeʻur.

(7) Wa-yebēlo 'Iyasus:

Naya, 'emaṣṣe' 'ana wa-'efēwweso.

(8) Wa-'awše'a ḥabē me't wa-yebē:

'Egzi'o, 'i-yedallewani kama 'anta tebā' tāḥta ṭafareya. Dā'emu bal qāla, wa-yaḥayyu waldeya, (9) 'esma 'ana-hi be'si mak^{w}annen 'ana, wa-beya ḥarrā 'ella 'ek^{w}ēnnen, wa-'ebelo la-ze: "Ḥur," wa-yaḥawwer, wa-la-kāle'u-ni: "Naʻā," wa-yemaṣṣe', wa-la-

---

VIII 2. *lamṣ* leprosy. *za-lamṣ* a leper.

3. G *gasasa (yegses)* to touch. Gt *tagassa* pass. *gessat* a touch, touching.

5. *ḥabi* (pl. *ḥabayt*) prefect, governor, procurator. *ḥabē me't* centurion.

7. *naya* = *na-* + pron. suff.; this particle is used to prepose or topicalize a pronominal element: *naya* = "as for me, I for my part" or similarly.

8. G *ṭafara* to roof over, to put up a ceiling. *ṭafar* roof, ceiling. *dā'emu* adv. just, merely, only; furthermore, moreover; rather, but, on the contrary.

gabreya-ni: "Gebar zanta," wa-yegabber.

(10) Wa-sami'o 'Iyasus, 'ankara wa-yebēlomu la-'ella yetallewewwo: 'Amān 'ebelakemu 'i-rakabku za-maṭana-ze hāymānota ba-westa k^{w}ellu 'Esrā'ēl. (11) Wa-bāḥtu 'ebelakemu: bezuxān yemaṣṣe'u 'em-mešrāq wa-'em-me'rāb, wa-yeraffequ mesla 'Abrehām wa-Yesḥaq wa-Yā'qob ba-mangešta samāyāt, (12) wa-la-weluda mangešt-sa yāwaḍḍe'ewwomu westa ṣanāfi ṣelmat. Heyya hallo bekāy wa-ḥaqeya senan.

(13) Wa-yebēlo 'Iyasus la-we'etu ḥabē me't:

Ḥur-kē, wa-bakama ta'amanka yekunka.

Wa-ḥaywa waldu ba-ye'eti sa'āt. Wa-gabi'o masfen westa bētu, rakabo la-q^{w}el'ēhu ḥayewo.

8. Ba'enta ḥamāta Pēṭros

(14) Wa-bawi'o 'Iyasus bēto la-Pēṭros, rakabā la-ḥamāta Pēṭros 'enza tesakkeb tefaḍḍen. (15) Wa-gasasā 'edēhā, wa-xadagā faḍantā, wa-tanše'at wa-tale'katomu.

9. Ba'enta 'ella ḥaywu 'em-bezux dawē

(16) Wa-mesēta kawino, 'amṣe'u xabēhu bezuxāna 'ella 'agānent, wa-'awḍe'omu ba-qālu, wa-fawwasa k^{w}ello deweyāna, (17) kama yetfaṣṣam qāla 'Isāyeyās nabiy za-yebē:

We'etu naš'a dawēna, wa-ṣora ḥemāmana.

(18) Wa-soba re'ya 'Iyasus sab'a bezuxāna za-talawewwo, 'azzaza yeḥuru mā'dota.

---

11. G *rafaqa (yerfeq)* to recline at a meal. CG *'arfaqa* caus. *merfāq* a place to recline; a meal, party, symposium. *marfaq* threshhold.

12. *ṣanāfi* adj. exterior, extreme, outer. G *ḥaqaya* to grind/gnash the teeth. CG *'aḥqaya* caus.

13. *q^{w}el'ē* (f. *-t*; pl. *-yāt*) servant, domestic.

14. *ḥam* (w. suff. *ḥamū-*, acc. *ḥamā-*; pl. *'aḥmāw*) father-in-law, son-in-law. *ḥamāt* mother-in-law, daughter-in-law. Glt *taḥāmawa* to acquire an in-law. *tāḥmā* in-law relationship. G *faḍana* to have a fever. *faḍant* fever.

10. Ba’enta za-kal’o ’i-yetlewo

(19) Wa-maṣ’a xabēhu ’aḥadu ṣaḥāfi wa-yebēlo:

Liq, ’etluka-nu xaba ḥorka?

(20) Wa-yebēlo ’Iyasus:

Q^{w}anāṣel-ni gebaba bomu, wa-’a‘wāfa samāy-ni xaba yāṣallelu, wa-walda ’eg^{w}āla ’emma-ḥeyāw-sa ’albotu xaba yāsammek re’so.

(21) Wa-yebēlo kāle’ ’em-’ardā’ihu:

’Egzi’o, ’abeḥani ’eqdem ḥawira wa-’eqbaro la-’abuya.

(22) Wa-yebēlo ’Iyasus:

Telewani, wa-xedegomu la-mewutān yeqbaru mewutānihomu.

11. Ba’enta za-gaššaṣa bāḥra

(23) Wa-‘arga westa ḥamar, wa-talawewwo ’ardā’ihu. (24) Wa-nāhu ‘abiy deleqleq kona ba-westa bāḥr ’eska soba ḥamar yessēwwar ’emenna mogad, wa-we’etu-sa yenawwem. (25) Wa-qarbu ’ardā’ihu, wa-’anqehewwo wa-yebēlewwo:

’Egzi’o, ’adxenana, ’esma nemawwet.

(26) Wa-yebēlomu:

La-ment farrāhān ’antemu, ḥeṣuṣāna hāymānot?

Wa-tanši’o, gaššaṣomu la-nafāsāt-ni wa-la-bāḥr, wa-kona zāḥna ‘abiya.

(27) Wa-’ankaru sab’ wa-yebēlu:

Mannu ’engā we’etu zentu za-yet’ēzzazu lotu bāḥr-ni wa-nafāsāt-ni?

12. Ba’enta ’ella ’agānent

(28) Wa-baṣiḥo mā‘dota beḥēra Gērgēsēnon, taqabbalewwo kel’ētu ’ella ’agānent ’em-maqāberāt waḍi’omu, ’ekuyān ṭeqqa ’eska soba ’i-yekel mannu-hi xalifa ’enta ye’eti fenot. (29) Wa-nāhu ṣarxu ’enza yebelu:

---

20. *q^{w}enṣel* (pl. *q^{w}anāṣel*) fox, wolf. *gebb* (pl. *gebab*, *’agbāb*) hole, cave, lair.

24. CQ *’adlaqaqa* to shake, quake, tremble; also caus. of same. *deleqleq* violent motion, storm, tempest; earthquake. *mogad* (pl. *mawāged*) wave.

26. G *zeḥna* to be tranquil, calm. CG *’azḥana* caus. *zeḥun* calm, tranquil. *zāḥn* calm, tranquillity.

27. *’engā* part. in questions; *mannu ’engā* Who, then, ...?

Menta bena meslēka 'Iyasus walda 'Egzi'abḥēr? Maṣā'ka zeyya tešāqeyana za'enbala yebṣāḥ gizēhu?

(30) Wa-botu heyya mar'aya 'aḥrew bezux yetra''ay reḥuqa 'emennēhomu,

(31) wa-'astabq^{w}e'ewwo 'agānent wa-yebēlewwo:

'Emma-sa tāwaḍḍe'ana, fannewana diba mar'aya 'aḥrew.

(32) Wa-yebēlomu: Ḥuru. Wa-waḍi'omu, ḥoru wa-bo'u westa 'aḥrew, wa-roṣu k^{w}ellu mar'aya 'aḥrew, wa-ṣadfu westa bāḥr wa-motu westa māy. (33) Wa-g^{w}ayyu nolot wa-'atawu hagara, wa-zēnawu k^{w}ello wa-za-ba'enta 'ella 'agānent-hi. (34) Wa-nāhu waḍ'u k^{w}ellu hagar yetqabbalewwo la-'Iyasus, wa-soba re'yewwo, 'astabq^{w}e'ewwo yexlef 'em-dawalomu.

Chapter IX

13. Ba'enta maḍāg^{w}e'

(1) Wa-'arigo westa ḥamar, 'adawa wa-baṣḥa hagaro. (2) Wa-'amṣe'u xabēhu deweya maḍāg^{w}e'a 'enza yeṣawwerewwo ba-'arāt, wa-re'eyo 'Iyasus hāymānotomu, yebēlo la-we'etu maḍāg^{w}e':

Ta'aman, waldeya. Yetxaddagu xaṭāwe'ika.

(3) Wa-nāhu 'ella 'em-westa ṣaḥaft yebēlu babaynātihomu:

Yeḍarref zentu-sa.

(4) Wa-'a'maromu 'Iyasus xellinnāhomu, wa-yebēlomu:

La-ment texēlleyu 'ekuya ba-'albābikemu? (5) Ment yeqallel: 'em-behila "yetxaddagu laka xaṭāwe'ika" wa-'em-behila "tanše' wa-ḥur"? (6) Wa-kama tā'meru kama bewuḥ lotu la-walda 'eg^{w}āla

---

29. L *šāqaya* to afflict, vex, torment. Lt *tašāqaya* pass. *šeqāy* vexation, torment. *mašqē* goad; weaver's comb.

32. G *ṣadfa* to rush/plunge headlong. CG *'aṣdafa* caus. *ṣadf ('aṣdāf)* precipitous place, precipice, abyss.

33. *nolāwi* (pl. *nolot*) shepherd, herdsman. Qt *tanolawa* to function as a shepherd, to tend flocks.

IX 2. *'arāt* (pl. *-āt*) bed. The imptv. of *ta'amna* also has the meaning: "Take heart."

5. G *qalala* to be light, easy, swift, slight. CG *'aqlala* to lighten, diminish a burden; to make swift, agile; to scorn, disdain, make light of. CD *'aqallala* to consider light, to lighten. CGlt *'astaqālala* to lighten; to scorn, disdain, despise, revile. *qalil* (f. *qalāl*) light, etc. *maqlali* one who lightens of alleviates. *'em* ... *'em* whether ... or.

’emma-ḥeyāw ba-diba medr yexdeg xaṭi’ata --
wa-’emze yebēlo la-we’etu maḍāgʷeʻ:

Tanše’ wa-nešā’ ʻarātaka, wa-ḥur bētaka.

(7) Wa-tanši’o, ḥora bēto. (8) Wa-re’eyomu ’aḥzāb, ’ankaru wa-’a’kʷatewwo la-’Egzi’abḥēr za-wahaba za-kama-ze šelṭāna la-sab’.

14. Ba’enta Māttēwos

(9) Wa-xalifo ’Iyasus ’em-heyya, rakaba be’sē ’enza yenabber westa meṣebbāḥ, za-semu Māttēwos, wa-yebēlo: "Telewani." Wa-tanši’o, talawo. (10) Wa-’enza yeraffeq westa bēt, nāhu maṣ’u bezuxān maṣabbeḥān wa-xāṭe’ān wa-rafaqu mesla ’Iyasus wa-’ardā’ihu. (11) Wa-re’eyomu Farisāweyān, yebēlewwomu la-’ardā’ihu:

La-ment mesla maṣabbeḥān wa-xāṭe’ān yeballeʻ liqekemu?

(12) Wa-samiʻo ’Iyasus, yebēlomu:

’I-yefaqqedewwo ṭeʻuyān la-ʻaqābē šerāy, za-enbala ’ella yaḥammu. (13) Ḥuru wa-’a’meru ment we’etu za-yebē:

Meḥrata ’efaqqed wa-’akko mašwāʻta,
’esma ’i-maṣā’ku ’eṣawweʻ ṣādeqāna ’alla xāṭe’āna la-nesseḥā.

(14) Wa-’emze maṣ’u xabēhu ’ardā’ihu la-Yoḥannes ’enza yebelu:

La-ment neḥna wa-Farisāweyān neṣawwem bezuxa, wa-’ardā’ika-sa ’i-yeṣawwemu?

(15) Wa-yebēlomu ’Iyasus:

Ba-’aytē yekelu daqiqu la-mar’ʻāwi lāḥewo ’amṭāna hallo marʻāwi meslēhomu? Wa-bāḥtu yemaṣṣe’ mawāʻel ’ama yetnaššā’ marʻāwi ’emennēhomu, wa-’amēhā yeṣawwemu. (16) Wa-’albo za-yeṭaqqeb dergeḥā lebsa westa šeṭṭata lebs beluy, ’esma yānaṭṭeʻo ḥeyāwo la-lebs, wa-fadfāda yekawwen šeṭṭatu. (17) Wa-’i-yewaddeyu wayna ḥaddisa westa zeqqāt beluy; wa-’emma ’akko-sa, yenaqqeʻu zeqqāt, wa-waynu-hi yetkaʻʻaw, wa-zeqqāt-ni yethaggʷalu. Wa-

---

15. *marʻā* wedding, marriage. *marʻāwi* groom, son-in-law. *marʻāt* (pl. *marāʻew*) bride, daughter-in-law. Qt *tamarʻawa* to get married (to a woman: o.s.). *’amṭāna* conj. as long as.

16. G *ṭaqaba* to sew, attach by sewing. *ṭeqbat* sewing, stitch. *dergeḥā* a patch. CG *’anṭeʻa* to tear off/apart.

17. *zeqq* (pl. *-āt*) wineskin. G *naqʻa* trans. and intrans.: to split, burst, rupture. CG *’anqeʻa* = G trans. *nequʻ* split, ruptured, cracked. *naqʻ* (pl. *’anqeʻt*) fountain, source, spring. *neqʻat* split,

bāḥtu la-wayn ḥaddis westa zeqqāt ḥaddis yewaddeyewwo, wa-yetʿaqqabu kel'ēhomu.

15. Ba'enta walatta maggābē mek^{w}rāb

(18) Wa-'enza zanta yenaggeromu, nāhu maṣ'a 'aḥadu mak^{w}annen wa-sagada lotu 'enza yebel:

Walatteya ye'zē motat, wa-bāḥtu naʿā 'anber 'edēka lāʿlēhā, wa-taḥayyu.

(19) Wa-tanše'a 'Iyasus, wa-talawo, wa-'ardā'ihu-ni.

16. Ba'enta 'enta yeweḥḥezā dam

(20) Wa-nāhu be'sit, 'enta dam yeweḥḥezā 'em-ʿašartu wa-kel'ētu ʿāmat, maṣ'at 'enta dexrēhu, (21) wa-gasasat ṣenfa lebsu, wa-tebē ba-lebbā:

'Emkama gasasku lebso 'aḥayyu.

(22) Wa-tamayṭa 'Iyasus, wa-re'yā, wa-yebē:

Ta'amani, walatteya, hāymānoteki 'aḥyawataki.

Wa-ḥaywat be'sit 'em-we'etu saʿāt. (23) Wa-maṣi'o 'Iyasus bētȯ la-we'etu mak^{w}annen, re'ya mabkeyāna wa-sab'a 'enza yethawwaku. (24) Wa-yebēlomu:

Tagaḥašu, 'esma 'akko za-motat ḥeḍān, 'allā tenawwem.

(25) Wa-šaḥaqewwo. Wa-soba waḍ'u sab', bo'a wa-'axazā 'edēhā, wa-tanše'at ḥeḍān.

17. Ba'enta kel'ē ʿewurān

(26) Wa-waḍ'a semuʿātu westa k^{w}ellā ye'eti medr. (27) Wa-xalifo 'Iyasus 'em-heyya, talawewwo kel'ētu ʿewurān 'enza yeṣarrexu wa-yebelu:

Tašāhalana, walda Dāwit.

(28) Wa-bawi'o bēta, maṣ'u xabēhu 'emuntu ʿewurān, wa-yebēlomu 'Iyasus:

Ta'ammenu-hu kama 'ekel zanta gabira?

Wa-yebēlewwo: 'Ewwa, 'Egzi'o. (29) Wa-gasasomu 'aʿyentihomu 'enza yebel:

---

crack, fissure. *manqeʿt* thigh.

27. G *ʿora* to be blind. CG *'aʿora* to blind. Dt *taʿawwara* to neglect, overlook, let pass unnoticed; to despise. *ʿewur* blind. *ʿurat* blindness.

Bakama hāymānotekemu yekunkemu.

(30) Wa-sobēhā takašta ’a‘yentihomu. Wa-gaššaṣomu ’Iyasus ’enza yebel:

‘Uqu ’albo za-yā’ammer.

(31) Wa-waḍi’omu, nagaru westa k^{w}ellu we’etu beḥēr.

18. Ba’enta ṣemum za-gānēn

(32) Wa-’emza waḍ’u ’emuntu, nāhu ’amṣe’u xabēhu za-gānēn ṣemuma.
(33) Wa-waḍi’o gānēnu, nababa we’etu ṣemum, wa-’ankaru sab’ ’enza yebelu:

Gemurā ’i-ỷastar’aya za-kama-ze ba-westa ’Esrā’ēl.

(34) Wa-yebēlu Farisāweyān:

Ba-mal’akomu la-’agānent yāwaḍḍe’omu la-’agānent.

(35) Wa-’ansosawa ’Iyasus westa k^{w}ellu ’ahgur wa-baḥāwert ’enza yemēhher ba-mek^{w}rābātihomu wa-yesabbek wangēla mangešt wa-yefēwwes k^{w}ello dawē wa-k^{w}ello ḥemāma za-westa ḥezb. (36) Wa-re’eyo bezuxāna sab’a, maḥaromu, ’esma seruḥān ’emuntu wa-gedufān kama ’abāge‘ za-’albo nolāwē. (37) Wa-yebēlomu la-’ardā’ihu:

Mā’raru-sa bezux, wa-gabbāru xedāṭān. (38) ’Astabq^{w}e‘ewwo ’enka la-bā‘la mā’rar kama yefannu gabbāra la-mā’raru.

Chapter X

19. Ba’enta za-’azzazomu la-ḥawāreyāt

(1) Wa-ṣawwe‘omu la-‘ašartu wa-kel’ētu ’ardā’ihu, wa-wahabomu šelṭāna diba manāfest rekusān kama yāwaḍḍe’ewwomu wa-yefawwesu k^{w}ello dawē wa-ḥemāma. (2) Wa-la-‘ašartu wa-kel’ētu ḥawāreyāt kama-ze ’asmātihomu: qadāmi Sem‘on za-tasamya Pēṭros, wa-’Endreyās ’exuhu; (3) Yā‘qob walda Zabdēwos wa-Yoḥannes ’exuhu; Fileppos wa-Bartalomēwos; Tomās wa-Māttēwos maṣabbeḥāwi; wa-Yā‘qob walda ’Elfeyos wa-Lebdeyos za-

---

32. G *ṣamma* to be deaf and dumb. CG *’aṣmama* to make deaf, dumb. Gt *taṣamama* to be made deaf, to feign deafness. *ṣemum* deaf and/or dumb.

36. G *sarḥa (yesrāḥ)* to labor to the point of exhaustion, to be afflicted with difficult tasks or duties. CG *’asreḥa* to tire, exhaust; to cause or impose labor/misery. *seruḥ* vexed, exhausted. *serāḥ* (pl. *-āt*) labor, bother, exhaustion, affliction. *gedufān* in the sense of "cast out, rejected."

tasamya Tādēwos; (4) wa-Sem'on Qananāwi, wa-Yehudā 'Asqorotāwi, za-we'etu 'agbe'o. (5) 'Ellonta 'ašarta wa-kel'ēta fannawomu 'Iyasus, wa-'azzazomu 'enza yebel:

Westa fenota 'aḥzāb 'i-teḥuru, wa-westa hagara Sāmer 'i-tebā'u.

(6) Wa-ḥuru bāḥtu xaba 'abāge' za-tahag^{w}la za-bēta 'Esrā'ēl. (7) Wa-ḥawirakemu, sebeku 'enza tebelu:

Qarbat mangešta samāyāt.

(8) Dewuyāna fawwesu, mutāna 'anše'u, 'ella lamṣ 'anṣeḥu, 'agānenta 'awḍe'u. Ba-ṣagā za-našā'kemu, ba-ṣagā habu. (9) 'I-tāṭreyu lakemu warqa wa-berura wa-'i-ṣariqa westa qenāwetikemu, (10) wa-'i-ṣefnata la-fenot wa-'i-kel'ēta kedānāta wa-'i-'ašā'ena wa-'i-batra, 'esma yedallewo sisāyu la-za-yetqannay. (11) Wa-westa 'enta bo'kemu hagar, wa-'emma-ni 'a'ṣādāt, tasā'alu mannu za-yedallewo ba-westētā, wa-heyya xederu 'eska 'ama tewaḍḍe'u. (12) Wa-bawi'akemu westa bēt, ta'āmexewwā. (13) Wa-'emma yedallewā la-ye'eti bēt, yemṣā' salāmekemu lā'lēhā; wa-'emma-sa 'i-yedallewā, yegbā' salāmekemu lā'lēkemu. (14) Wa-la-za-sa 'i-tawakfakemu wa-'i-sam'akemu nagarakemu, waḍi'akemu 'af'a 'em-ye'eti bēt we-'em-ye'eti hagar, negefu ṣabala 'egarikemu. (15) 'Amān 'ebelakemu kama yešexxetā medra Sadom wa-Gamorā 'ama 'elata dayn fadfāda 'em-ye'eti hagar. (16) Wa-nāhu 'ana 'efēnnewakemu kama 'abāge' mā'kala tak^{w}lāt. Kunu 'enka ṭabibāna kama 'arwē medr wa-yawwāhāna kama regb. (17) Wa-ta'aqabu 'em-sab' 'esma yāgabbe'ukemu westa 'a'wād, wa-yeqaššefukemu ba-

---

X 4. *'agbe'a* in the sense "hand over, betray."

9. CG *'aṭraya* to acquire, possess. Gt *taṭarya* pass. *ṭerit* possession, property, wealth. *ṣariq* copper, small coin. *ṣariqat* thin disk, a cake.

10. *ṣefnat* pack, wallet.

14. G *nagafa (yengef)* to knock off, shake off, dispel. CG *'angafa* idem. Gt *tanagfa* pass.; to lose leaves. *neguf* deciduous. *ṣabal* dust. *ṣebul* dust.

15. G *šaxata/šexta* to be at east, at rest, comfortable, well-off. D *šaxxata* to put at ease, allow to rest. CD *'ašaxxata* = D. Dt *tašexxeta* pass. of D. *šexut* relaxed, at rest, at ease. *šāxt* tranquillity, relaxation, rest. D *dayyana* to judge, condemn, punish. Dt *tadayyana* = Gt *tadayna* pass. *dayn* judgment, punishment, condemnation, esp. of the Last Judgment.

mek^{w}rābātihomu, (18) wa-yewassedukemu xaba masāfent wa-nagašt ba’enti’aya la-sem‘ lomu wa-la-’aḥzāb. (19) Wa-soba yāgabbe’ukemu, ’i-taxalleyu ’efo menta tetnāgaru, ’esma yetwahhabakemu ba-ye’eti sa‘āt za-tetnāgaru. (20) ’Esma ’i-konkemu ’antemu ’ella tetnāgaru, ’allā manfasu la-’abukemu we’etu yetnāgar ba-lā‘lēkemu. (21) Wa-yāgabbe’ ’exew ’exwāhu la-mot, wa-’ab-ni weludo, wa-yetnašše’u welud lā‘la ’azmādihomu, wa-yeqattelewwomu. (22) Wa-tekawwenu ṣelu’āna ba-xaba k^{w}ellu sab’ ba’enta semeya. Wa-za-sa ’azlafa te‘gešto we’etu yedexxen. (23) Wa-soba yesaddedukemu ba-westa zāti hagar, g^{w}eyyu westa kāle’tā. ’Amān ’ebelakemu: ’i-yetfēṣṣamā ’ahgura ’Esrā’ēl ’eska soba yemaṣṣe’ walda ’eg^{w}āla ’emma-ḥeyāw. (24) ’Albo rad’ za-ya‘abbi ’em-liqu wa-’i-gabr-ni za-ya‘abbi ’em-’egzi’u. (25) Maṭanu la-rad’ yekun kama liqu, wa-la-gabr-ni kama ’egzi’u. Za-la-bā‘la bēt ba-Be‘ēl Zēbul yebēlewwo, ’efo fadfāda la-sab’a bētu. (26) ’I-tefrehewwomu-kē ’enka ’esma ’albo kedun za-’i-yetkaššat, wa-xebu’ za-’i-yet‘awwaq. (27) Za-nagarkukemu ba-ṣelmat negerewwo ba-berhān, wa-za-ni westa ’eznekemu nagarkukemu sebekewwo ba-diba ’anḥest. (28) Wa-’i-tefrehewwomu la-’ella yeqattelu šegā, wa-nafsakemu-sa ’i-yekelu qatila. Wa-bāḥtu ferehewwo la-za-yekel nafsa wa-šegā xebura ’ahg^{w}elo ba-westa Gahānnam. (29) ’Akko-nu kel’ētu ’a‘wāf yeššayyaṭā ba-ṣariqa ’asāreyon? Wa-’aḥatti ’emennēhon ’i-tewaddeq westa medr za’enbala yā’mer ’abukemu. (30) Wa-lakemu-sa še‘erta re’sekemu-ni k^{w}ellon x^{w}eluqāt ’emāntu. (31) ’I-tefrehu-kē. ’Em-bezux ’a‘wāf texēyyesu ’antemu. (32) K^{w}ellu ’enka za-ya’ammen beya ba-qedma sab’ ’a’ammeno ’ana-hi ba-qedma ’abuya za-ba-samāyāt. (33) Wa-la-za-sa keḥdani ba-qedma sab’ ’ekeḥḥedo ’ana-hi ba-qedma ’abuya za-ba-samāyāt. (34) ’I-yemsalkemu za-maṣā’ku salāma ’eday westa medr. ’I-maṣā’ku ’eday salāma ’allā maṭbāḥta. (35) Wa-maṣā’ku ’efleṭ be’sē ’em-’abuhu, wa-walatta-ni ’em-’emmā, wa-mar‘āta-ni ’em-ḥamātā. (36) Wa-ḍarru la-sab’ sab’a bētu. (37) Za-yāfaqqer ’abāhu wa-’emmo ’emmenēya ’i-yedallu lita. Wa-za-yāfaqqer waldo wa-walatto ’emennēya ’i-yedallu

---

27. *nāḥs* (pl. *’anḥest*) roof, rooftop.

29. *’asāreyon* a small coin; Gk. *assarion*.

34. G *ṭabḥa* to make an incision; to sacrifice. Gt *taṭabḥa* pass. *ṭebḥ* sacrifice, sacrificial victim. *ṭebḥat* sacrifice. *maṭbāḥt* (pl. *maṭābeḥ*) knife, sword.

lita. (38) Wa-za-'i-naš'a masqalo wa-za-'i-talawa dexrēya 'i-yedallu lita. (39) Za-rakabā la-nafsu yegaddefā, wa-za-sa gadafā la-nafsu ba'enti'aya yerakkebā. (40) Za-kiyākemu tawakfa kiyāya tawakfa, wa-za-kiyāya tawakfa tawakfo la-za-fannawani. (41) Za-tawakfa nabiya ba-sema nabiy 'asba nabiy yenašše', wa-za-tawakfa ṣādeqa ba-sema ṣādeq 'asba ṣādeq yenašše'. (42) Wa-za-'astaya 'aḥada 'em-'ellu ne'usān ṣewā'a māy q^warir bāḥtito ba-sema rad', 'amān 'ebelakemu: 'I-yāhagg^{w}el 'asbo.

Chapter XI

20. Ba'enta 'ella tafannawu 'em-xaba Yoḥannes

(1) Wa-kona 'emza sallaṭa 'Iyasus 'azzezotomu la-'ašartu wa-kel'ētu 'ardā'ihu, xalafa 'em-heyya kama yemhar wa-yesbek westa 'ahgurihomu. (2) Wa-sami'o Yoḥannes megbārihu la-Kerestos ba-bēta moqeḥ, fannawa xabēhu kel'ēta 'em-'ardā'ihu. (3) Wa-yebēlo:

'Anta-nu za-yemaṣṣe'? Wa-bo-nu kāle'a za-nessēffo?

(4) Wa-'awše'a 'Iyasus, wa-yebēlomu:

Ḥawirakemu, zēnewewwo la-Yoḥannes za-tesamme'u wa-za-terē''eyu. (5) 'Ewurān yerē''eyu; ḥankāsān yaḥawweru; 'ella lamṣ yenaṣṣeḥu; wa-ṣemumān yesamme'u; mutān yetnašše'u; wa-naddāyān yezzēnawu. (6) Wa-beḍu' we'etu za-'i-ta'aqfa beya.

(7) Wa-soba xalafu 'ellu, 'axaza 'Iyasus yebalomu la-'aḥzāb ba'enta Yoḥannes:

Menta waḍā'kemu gadāma ter'ayu? Ber'a-nu za-yetḥawwas 'em-nafās? (8) Wa-menta-nu-ma waḍā'kemu ter'ayu? Be'sē-nu za-ressuy ba-qaṭant 'albās? Nāhu 'ella-sa qaṭanta yelabbesu westa 'abyāta nagašt hallawu. (9) Wa-menta-nu-ma waḍā'kemu ter'ayu?

---

42. *ṣewā'* (pl. *-āt*) cup.

XI 5. Q *ḥankasa* to limp, be lame. *ḥankās* lame, crippled. *ḥenkāsē* lameness.

7. *ber'* (pl. *'abrā'*) reed; arm of a candelabrum. CG *'aḥosa* to move, shake, agitate. Gt *taḥosa* idem intrans. or pass.; *za-yetḥawwas* reptiles, "creeping things." *ḥusat* motion, movement. *ḥewās* (pl. *-āt*) a (physical) sense. *ḥawisā* exclam. of wonder or admiration.

8. *qaṭin* (f. *qaṭān*, pl. *qaṭant*) fine, delicate; n. fine clothes. *qeṭnat* fineness, delicacy.

Nabiya-nu? 'Ewwa 'ebelakemu, wa-fadfāda 'em-nabiy. (10) 'Esma zentu we'etu za-ba'enti'ahu taṣeḥfa:

Nāhu 'ana 'efēnnu mal'akeya qedma gaṣṣeka, za-yeṣayyeḥ fenotaka ba-qedmēka.

(11) 'Amān 'ebelakemu: 'I-tanše'a 'em-tewledda 'anest za-ya'abbi 'em-Yoḥannes Maṭmeq, wa-ba-mangešta samāyāt-sa za-yene''es ya'abbi 'emennēhu. (12) Wa-'em-mawā'ela Yoḥannes Maṭmeq 'eska ye'zē tetgaffā' mangešta samāyāt, wa-gefu'ān yethayyadewwā. (13) 'Esma k^wellomu nabiyāt wa-'orit 'eska Yoḥannes tanabbayu, (14) wa-'emma-sa tefaqqedu tetwakkafewwo, we'etu 'Ēleyās za-hallawo yemṣā'. (15) Za-bo 'a'zāna sami'a la-yesmā'. (16) Ba-mannu 'āstamāselā la-zāti tewledd? Temassel daqiqa 'ella yenabberu westa mešyāṭ wa-yeṣēwwe'u biṣomu wa-yebelewwomu:

(17) 'Anzarna lakemu, wa-'i-zafankemu; 'asqoqawna lakemu, wa-'i-bakaykemu.

(18) 'Esma maṣ'a Yoḥannes 'enza 'i-yeballe' wa-'i-yesatti, wa-yebēlewwo:

Gānēna botu.

(19) Wa-maṣ'a walda 'eg^wāla 'emma-ḥeyāw 'enza yeballe' wa-yesatti, wa-yebēlewwo:

Nawā be'si balā'i wa-satāyē wayn, 'arka maṣabbeḥān wa-xāṭe'ān. Wa-ṣadqat ṭebab 'em-daqiqā.

(20) Wa-'emze 'axaza 'Iyasus yeḥison la-'ahgur 'ella ba-westēton gabra xayla bezuxa, 'esma 'i-nasseḥu. (21) Wa-yebēlon:

'Alē laki K^warāzi. 'Alē laki Bēta-Sāyedā. 'Esma soba-sa ba-

---

12. G *hēda (yehid)* to take by force, violence. Gt *tahayda* pass. and reflex. *hayd* violence, taking by force; booty, prey. *hayādi* a violent person, plunderer.

17. Q *'anzara* to pipe, play a musical instrument. *'enzir* a musical instrument of any sort. *ma'anzer* musician, piper, flute-player. G *zafana* to dance. *zafan* n. dancing. *zafāni* (f. *-t*) dancer. *mezfān* a place for dancing.

19. Glt *ta'āraka* to become friends (with). *'ark* (f. *'arekt*; pl. *'a'rekt*, *'arkān*, *'arkāt*) friend.

21. *'alē la-* Woe unto .... *šaqq* (pl. *-āt*, *'ašqāq*) sack, sack-cloth.

Ṭiros wa-ba-Sidonā tagabra xayl za-tagabra ba-westēteken, 'em-wadde'a ba-šaqq wa-ba-ḥamad 'em-nasseḥu. (22) Wa-bāḥtu 'ebelaken: Ṭiros wa-Sidonā šexutāta yekawwenā 'ama 'elata dayn 'emennēken. (23) Wa-'anti-ni Qefernāhom, la'emma 'eska samāy tetlē''ali, 'eska Gahānnam tewarredi. (24) 'Esma soba ba-Sadom-hu tagabra xayl za-tagabra ba-westēteki, 'em-hallawat 'eska yom. (25) Wa-bāḥtu 'ebelakemu kama medra Sadom šexetta tekawwen ba-'elata dayn 'emennēki.

(26) Ba-we'etu mawā'el 'awše'a 'Iyasus wa-yebē:

'Esēbbeḥaka 'Abā 'Egzi'a samāy wa-medr, 'esma xabā'ka zanta 'em-ṭabibān wa-'em-mā'merān, wa-kašatkon la-ḥeḍānāt. (27) 'Ewwa, 'Abā, 'esma kama-ze kona šemrateka ba-qedmēka. (28) K^{W}ellu tawehbani 'em-xaba 'abuya, wa-'albo za-yā'ammero la-wald za'enbala 'ab, wa-la-'ab-ni 'albo za-yā'ammero za'enbala wald, wa-la-za-faqada wald yekšet lotu. (29) Ne'u xabēya k^{W}ellekemu seruḥān wa-ṣewurān, wa-'ana 'ā'arrefakemu. (30) Neše'u 'ar'uteya dibēkemu, wa-'a'meru 'emennēya kama yawwāh 'ana wa-teḥḥut lebbeya, wa-terakkebu 'erafta la-nafsekemu, 'esma 'ar'uteya šannāy, wa-ṣoreya qalil we'etu.

Chapter XII

(1) Ba-we'etu mawā'el xalafa 'Iyasus ba-sanbat 'enta mangala garāweh, wa-'ardā'ihu-sa rexbu, wa-'axazu yemḥawu šawita wa-yeble'u. (2) Wa-re'eyomu Farisāweyān, yebēlewwo:

Nāhu 'ardā'ika yegabberu za-'i-yekawwen gabira ba-sanbat.

(3) Wa-yebēlomu:

'I-y̌anbabkemu-nu za-gabra Dāwit 'ama rexba, we'etu-ni wa-'ella meslēhu, zakama bo'a bēto la-'Egzi'abḥēr, wa-xabāweza q^{W}erbān bal'a, za-'i-yekawweno la-bali' wa-'i-la-'ella meslēhu, za'enbala la-kāhenāt la-bāḥtitomu? (6) Wa-'i-y̌anbabkemu-nu westa 'orit kama ba-sanbatāt kāhenāt ba-bēta maqdas sanbata yārakk^{W}esu, wa-'i-yekawwenomu gēgāya? (6) 'Ebelakemu kama za-ya'abbi 'em-bēta maqdas hallo zeyya. (7) Soba-sa tā'ammeru ment we'etu "Meḥrata 'efaqqed wa-'akko mašwā'ta," 'em-'i-

---

30. *'ar'ut* a yoke.

XII 1. G *maḥawa (yemḥaw)* to pluck. Gt *tameḥwa* pass. G *šawaya* to ripen (of grain). *šawit* ear of grain.

k^{w}annankemewwomu la-’ella ’i-ye’ēbbesu. (8) ’Esma ’egzi’ we’etu la-sanbat walda ’eg^{w}āla ’emma-ḥeyāw.

21. Ba’enta za-yabsat ’edēhu

(9) Wa-faliso ’em-heyya, ḥora westa mek^{w}rābomu. (10) Wa-nāhu be’si za-’edēhu yabsat. Wa-tase’’elewwo ’enza yebelu:

Yekawwen-nu ba-sanbat fawweso?

kama yāstawādeyewwo. (11) Wa-yebēlomu:

Mannu ’em-westētekemu be’si za-bo ’aḥatta bag‘a, wa-’emma wadqat ba-sanbat westa gebb, ’akko-nu ye’exxezā wa-yānaššeʼā? (12) ’Efo ’enka fadfāda yexēyyes sab’ ’em-bag‘. Yekawwen-kē ba-sanbatāt gabira šannāy.

(13) Wa-’emze yebēlo la-we’etu be’si: Sefāḥ ’edēka. Wa-safḥa ’edēhu, wa-ḥaywat sobēhā, wa-gab’at kama kāle’tā. (14) Wa-waḍi’omu Farisāweyān, tamākaru ba’enti’ahu kama yeqtelewwo. (15) Wa-’a’miro ’Iyasus, tageḥša ’em-heyya. Wa-talawewwo bezuxān sab’, wa-’aḥyawomu la-k^{w}ellomu. (16) Wa-gaššaṣomu kama ’i-yāghedewwo, (17) kama yetfaṣṣam za-tabehla ba-’Isāyeyās nabiy ’enza yebel:

Nāhu waldeya za-xarayku, fequreya za-šamrat nafseya. ’Ānabber manfaseya lā‘lēhu, wa-k^{w}ennanē la-’aḥzāb yenagger. (19) ’I-yedammeḍ wa-’i-yeṣarrex, wa-’albo za-yesamme‘ ba-ṣegg^{w} qālo. (20) Ber‘a qeṭquṭa ’i-yesabber, wa-šu‘a za-yeṭayyes ’i-yāṭaffe’ ’eska yāgabbe’ fetḥa la-mawi’, (21) wa-ba-sema zi’ahu ’aḥzāb yet’ammanu.

22. Ba’enta za-gānēn ‘ewur wa-ṣemum

(22) Wa-’emze ’amṣe’u lotu za-gānēn ‘ewura wa-ṣemuma, wa-fawwaso ’eska we’etu ‘ewur wa-ṣemum wa-bahhām nababa-hi wa-re’ya-hi. (23) Wa-yeddammamu k^{w}ellomu ’aḥzāb, wa-yebēlu:

’Akko-nu ze-we’etu walda Dāwit?

---

10. CGlt *’astawādaya* to bring charges against, to accuse.

19. *ṣegg^{w}* (pl. *ṣeg^{w}ag^{w}*) street, market-place.

20. Q *qaṭqaṭa* to grind; to break. *qeṭquṭ* ground, broken. *qeṭqāṭē* vn. grinding, breaking. *šu‘/su‘* flax, tinder. G *ṭēsa (yeṭis)* to smoke. CG *’aṭēsa* caus. *ṭis* smoke.

22. G *behma (yebham)* to be mute. *bahhām* mute. *behmat* muteness.

(24) Wa-Farisāweyān-sa sami'omu yebēlu:

Zentu-sa 'i-yāwaḍḍe' 'agānenta za'enbala ba-Be'ēl Zēbul, mak^{w}annenomu la-'agānent.

(25) Wa-'a'miro 'Iyasus xellinnāhomu, yebēlomu:

K^{w}ellu mangešt 'enta tetnāfaq babaynātihā temāsen, wa-k^{w}ellu hagar wa-'emma-hi bēt 'enta tetnāfaq babaynātihā 'i-teqawwem. (26) Wa-'emma-sa Sayṭān Sayṭāna yāwaḍḍe', babaynātihu tanāfaqa. 'Efo 'enka teqawwem mangeštu? (27) Wa-'emma-sa 'ana ba-Be'ēl Zēbul 'āwaḍḍe'omu la-'agānent, weludekemu ba-ment yāwaḍḍe'omu? Ba'enta-ze 'emuntu fatāḥta yekawwenukemu. (28) Wa-'emma-sa 'ana ba-manfasa 'Egzi'abḥēr 'āwaḍḍe' 'agānenta, 'engā baṣḥat lā'lēkemu mangešta 'Egzi'abḥēr. (29) Wa-'efo yekel mannu-hi bawi'a bēta xayyāl wa-newāyo hayeda za'enbala 'emma 'i-qadama 'asiroto la-xayyāl? Wa-'emze bēto yebarabber. (30) Za-'i-kona meslēya 'edeweya we'etu, wa-za-'i-yāstagābe' meslēya yezarrewani. (31) Ba'enta-ze 'ebelakemu: K^{w}ellu xaṭi'at wa-ḍerfat yetxaddag la-sab', wa-za-sa la-manfas qeddus ḍarafa 'i-yetxaddag lotu. (32) Wa-za-yebē qāla lā'la walda 'eg^{w}āla 'emma-ḥeyāw yetxaddag lotu, wa-za-sa yebē lā'la manfas qeddus 'i-yetxaddag lotu 'i-ba-ze 'ālam wa-'i-ba-za-yemaṣṣe'. (33) 'Emma 'akko gebaru 'eḍa šannāya wa-ferēhu-ni šannāya, wa-'emma 'akko gebaru 'eḍa 'ekuya wa-ferēhu-ni 'ekuya, 'esma 'em-ferēhu 'eḍ yet'awwaq. (34) Tewledda 'arāwita medr, ba-'aytē tekelu šannāya tanāgero 'enza 'ekuyān 'antemu? 'Esma 'em-tarafa lebb yenabbeb 'af. (35) Xēr be'si 'em-šannāy mazgaba lebbu yāwaḍḍe' šannāya, wa-ma'ammeḍ be'si 'em-mazgaba 'ammaḍā yāwaḍḍe' 'ammaḍā. (36) 'Ane-sa 'ebelakemu: K^{w}ellu nebāb ḍeru' za-yenabbeb sab' yāgabbe'u ba'enti'ahu qāla ba-'elata dayn, (37) 'esma 'em-qālātika teṣaddeq wa-'em-qālātika tetk^{w}ēnnan.

23. Ba'enta 'ella sa'alu te'merta

(38) Wa-'emze 'awše'ewwo sab' 'em-ṣaḥaft wa-'em-Farisāweyān 'enza yebelu:

Liq, nefaqqed 'em-xabēka te'merta ner'ay.

(39) Wa-'awši'o, yebēlomu:

Tewledd 'ammāḍit wa-zammāwit te'merta taxaššeš, wa-te'mert 'i-yetwahhabā za'enbala te'merta Yonās nabiy. (40) 'Esma kama

Yonās nabara westa karša ʻanbari šalusa ʻelata wa-šalusa lēlita, kamāhu yenabber walda ʼegʷāla ʼemma-ḥeyāw westa lebbā la-medr šalusa ʻelata wa-šalusa lēlita. (41) Sabʼa Nanawē yetnaššeʼu ʼama kʷennanē mesla-zā tewledd wa-yetfāteḥewwā, ʼesma nasseḥu ba-sebkata Yonās. Wa-nāhu za-yaʻabbi ʼem-Yonās zeyya. (42) Negešta ʼazēb tetnaššāʼ ʼama ʻelata dayn mesla-zā tewledd wa-tetfāteḥā, ʼesma maṣʼat ʼem-ʼaṣnāfa medr tesmāʻ ṭebabo la-Salomon. Wa-nāhu za-yaʻabbi ʼem-Salomon zeyya. (43) Wa-ʼemkama waḍʼa manfas rekus ʼem-sabʼ, yaʻawwed ʼenta badw ʼenza yaxaššeš ʻerafta, wa-yaxaṭṭeʼ. (44) Wa-ʼemze yebel: ʼEgabbeʼ westa bēteya ʼem-xaba waḍāʼku. Wa-maṣiʼo, yerakkebo ʼenza yāstarakkeb ʼedewa wa-meruga. (45) Wa-ʼemze yaḥawwer wa-yāmaṣṣeʼ meslēhu sabʻata kāleʼāna manāfesta ʼella yaʼakkeyu ʼemennēhu, wa-bawiʼomu yaxadderu heyya, wa-yekawwen daxāritu la-weʼetu beʼsi za-yaʼakki ʼem-qadāmitu. Kamāhu yekawwenā la-zāti tewledd ʼekit.

(46) Wa-ʼenza yenaggeromu la-ʼaḥzāb, nāhu ʼemmu wa-ʼaxawihu yeqawwemu ʼafʼa ʼenza yefaqqedu yetnāgarewwo. (47) Wa-bo ʼem-ʼardāʼihu za-yebēlo:

Nāhu ʼemmeka wa-ʼaxawika ʼafʼa yeqawwemu wa-yaxaššešu yetnāgaruka.

(48) Wa-ʼawšeʼa wa-yebē la-za-nagaro:

Mannu yeʼeti ʼemmeya? Wa-ʼella mannu ʼemuntu ʼaxaweya?

(49) Wa-safḥa ʼedēhu xaba ʼardāʼihu wa-yebē:

Nāhu ʼemmeya wa-ʼaxaweya. (50) ʼEsma za-gabra faqādo la-ʼabuya za-ba-samāyāt weʼetu ʼexuya wa-ʼexteya wa-ʼemmeya-ni weʼetu.

---

40. *ʻanbari* whale.

42. *ʼazēb* the south.

43. *badw/badā* desert, wasteland, uncultivated area. G *badwa* to be desert, etc. CG *ʼabdawa* caus.

44. CGt *ʼastarkaba* to be at leisure (for); to be ready, opportune, convenient; to be busy with, involved in. G *ʼadawa* to sweep. *ʼedew* swept. *ʼedāw* sweepings. G *maraga* to plaster. *merug* plastered. *marg* plaster.

45. *dax(x)ārit* end. *qadāmit* beginning.

Chapter XIII

24. Ba’enta messālē

(1) Wa-ba-ye’eti ‘elat waḍi’o ’Iyasus ’em-bēt, nabara mangala bāḥr. (2) Wa-tagābe’u xabēhu sab’ bezux ’eska soba ya‘arreg westa ḥamar wa-yenabber, wa-k^{w}ellu sab’ westa ḥayq yeqawwemu. (3) Wa-nagaromu bezuxa ba-messālē ’enza yebel:

Nāhu waḍ’a za-yezarre‘ yezrā‘. (4) Wa-’enza yezarre‘, bo za-wadqa westa fenot, wa-maṣ’u ’a‘wāfa samāy wa-bal‘ewwo. (5) Wa-bo za-wadqa diba k^{w}ak^{w}ḥ, xaba ’albo marēta bezuxa; wa-we’eta gizē šaraṣa, ’esma ’albo ‘emaqa la-marētu. (6) Wa-šariqo ḍaḥāy, maṣlawa; wa-’esma ’albo šerwa, yabsa. (7) Wa-bo za-wadqa westa šok, wa-baq^{w}ala šok wa-xanaqo. (8) Wa-bo za-wadqa westa medr šannāyt, wa-wahaba ferē, bo za-me’ta wa-bo za-sessā wa-bo za-šalāsā. (9) Za-bo ’ezana sami‘a yesmā‘.

(10) Wa-qaribomu ’ardā’ihu, yebēlewwo:

Ba’enta ment ba-’amsāl tetnāgaromu?

(11) Wa-’awše’a wa-yebēlomu:

’Esma lakemu tawehba ’a’mero sewwurātihā la-mangešta samāyāt, wa-lomu-sa ’i-tawehba. (12) ’Esma la-za-bo yetwahhabo wa-yefadaffed, wa-la-za-sa ’albo ’ella-hi-bo yahayyedewwo. (13) Wa-ba’enta zentu ba-’amsāl ’etnāgaromu, ’esma ’enza yerē’’eyu ’i-yerē’’eyu, wa-’enza yesamme‘u ’i-yesamme‘u wa-’i-yelēbbewu. (14) Wa-yetfēṣṣam lā‘lēhomu tenbita ’Isāyeyās za-yebē:

Sami‘a tesamme‘u wa-’i-telēbbewu; wa-naṣṣero tenēṣṣeru wa-’i-terē’’eyu. (15) ’Esma gazfa lebbu la-ze ḥezb, wa-

---

XIII 3. *messālē* (pl. *-yāt, -eyāt*) parable, proverb, similitude.

5. G *‘amaqa (ye‘meq, ye‘maq)* to be deep. CG *’a‘maqa* to make deep, to penetrate deeply. *‘emuq* deep. *‘emaq* depth. *mā‘meq* (pl. *ma‘āmeq*) the deep, abyss.

6. Q *maṣlawa* to wilt, wither. CQ *’amaṣlawa* caus. Qt *tamaṣlawa* to become withered; to wrinkle the face. *meṣlew* wilted, withered, wrinkled.

7. G *baq^{w}ala/baq^{w}la* to sprout, grow. CG *’abq^{w}ala* caus. *baq^{w}l* (pl. *-āt*) plant, herb, vegetation. *baqalt* date-palm. G *xanaqa (yexneq)* to choke, throttle. Gt *taxanqa* pass. and reflex.

15. G *gazfa (yegzef)* to be dense, stupid, dull, stout. *gezaf/*

ba-'ezanihomu denqewa sam'u, wa-kadanu 'a'yentihomu, kama 'i-yer'ayu ba-'a'yentihomu, wa-ba-'ezanihomu 'i-yesme'u, wa-ba-lebbomu 'i-yelabbewu, wa-'i-yetmayaṭu, wa-'i-yeššāhalomu.

(16) Wa-lakemu-sa beḍu'āt 'a'yentikemu, 'esma yerē''eyā; wa-'ezanikemu, 'esma yesamme'ā. (17) 'Amān 'ebelakemu kama bezuxān nabiyāt wa-ṣādeqān fatawu yer'ayu za-terē''eyu, wa-'i-re'yu; wa-yesme'u za-tesamme'u, wa-'i-sam'u. (18) 'Antemu-kē seme'u messālēhu la-za-yezarre'. (19) K^wellu za-yesamme' nagara mangešta samāyāt wa-'i-yelēbbu, yemaṣṣe' 'ekuy wa-yemaššeṭ za-tazar'a westa lebbu. We'etu-kē za-tazar'a westa fenot. (20) Wa-za-sa westa k^wak^{w}ḥ tazar'a we'etu-ze za-nagara yesamme' wa-sobēhā ba-feššeḥā yetwēkkafo. (21) Wa-bāḥtu 'albo šerwa lā'lēhu; la-gizēhā dā'emu we'etu, wa-kawino-sa mendābē wa-seddat ba'enta-ze nagar, ba-gizēhā ya'allu. (22) Wa-za-sa westa šok tazar'a ze-we'etu za-nagara yesamme', wa-tekkāza ze-'ālam wa-sefṭata be'l taxanneqo la-nagar, wa-za'enbala ferē yekawwen. (23) Wa-za-sa westa medr šannāyt tazar'a ze-we'etu za-nagara yesamme' wa-yelēbbu, wa-yefarri wa-yegabber bo za-me'ta wa-bo za-sessā wa-bo za-šalāsā.

(24) Kāle'ta messālē 'amṣe'a lomu 'enza yebel:

Temassel mangešta samāyāt be'sē za-zar'a šannāya zar'a westa garāhtu. (25) Wa-'enza yenawwemu sab'u, maṣ'a ṣalā'ihu wa-zar'a kerdāda mā'kala šernāy, wa-xalafa. (26) Wa-soba baq^{w}ala šā'ru wa-faraya ferē, 'amēhā 'astar'aya kerdād-ni. (27) Wa-qaribomu 'arde'tihu la-bā'la garāht, yebēlewwo:

'Egzi'o, 'akko-hu šannāya zar'a zarā'ka westa garāhteka?

'Em-'aytē 'enka lotu kerdād?

(28) Wa-yebēlomu:

---

gezf density, dullness, stupidity. Q *danqawa* to be hard of hearing. *denqew* hard of hearing; slow-witted, dense.

21. *la-gizēhā dā'emu we'etu* it is only for a time (i.e. temporary).

22. CG *'asfaṭa* to persuade, entice, seduce, deceive. Gt *tasafṭa* pass. *sefṭat* seduction, lure, enticement. *safāṭi* seducer, deceiver.

25. *kerdād* weed(s).

Be'si ḍarrāwi gabra zanta.

Wa-'agbertihu-sa yebēlewwo:

Tefaqqed-nu 'enka neḥur wa-ne'reyon?

(29) Wa-yebēlomu:

'Albo, kama 'enza ta'arreyu kerdāda 'i-temḥawu meslēhomu šernāya-ni. (30) Xedegu yelhaqu xebura 'eska mā'rar, wa-ba-gizē mā'rar 'ebelomu la-'aḍadd:

'Ereyu qedma kerdāda wa-'eserewwomu kalāsesta la-andedotomu, wa-šernāyo-sa 'astagābe'u westa mazāgebteya.

(31) Kāle'ta messālē 'amṣe'a lomu 'enza yebel:

Temassel mangešta samāyāt xeṭṭata senāp̣ē 'enta naš'a be'si wa-zar'a westa garāhtu. (32) Wa-ye'eti tene''es 'em-kʷellu 'azre't. Wa-soba lehqat, ta'abbi 'em-kʷellu 'aḥmāl wa-tekawwen 'eḍa 'abiya 'eska yemaṣṣe'u 'a'wāfa samāy wa-yaxadderu westa 'a'ṣuqihā.

(33) Kāle'ta messālē nagaromu:

Temassel mangešta samāyāt beḥu'a za-naš'at be'sit wa-xab'ato westa ḥariḍ za-šalastu mašāles, wa-'abḥe'a kʷello.

(34) Zanta kʷello tanāgara 'Iyasus ba-messālē la-'aḥzāb, wa-za'enbala messālē 'i-tanāgaromu, (35) kama yetfaṣṣam za-tabehla ba-nabiy 'enza yebel:

'Ekaššet ba-messālē 'afuya, wa-'enagger za-xebu' za-'em-tekāt.

(36) Wa-'emze xadigo 'aḥzāba, bo'a westa bēt, wa-qarbu xabēhu

---

28. G *'araya (ye'ri)* to pick, gather, pluck up/out.

30. G *'aḍada* to harvest. Gt *ta'aḍda* pass. *'aḍādi* harvester. *mā'ḍad* sickle. *kelsest* (pl. *kalāsest*) bundle, sheaf.

31. *xeṭṭat* grain, seed. *senāp̣ē* mustard.

32. *ḥaml* (pl. *'aḥmāl*) vegetation, shrub(s).

33. G *beḥ'a* to ferment (intrans.). CG *'abḥe'a* to ferment (trans.). Gt *tabeḥ'a* = G. *beḥu'* fermented; leaven, yeast. *beḥ'at* fermentation. G *ḥaraḍa (yeḥreḍ)* to grind (flour). Gt *taḥarḍa* pass. *ḥariḍ* flour, dough. *māḥraḍ* mill, mill-stone. *mašlest* (pl. *mašāles*) a kind of measure.

35. *tekāt* antiquity, yore. *za-tekāt* ancient, old, primeval, pristine. *'em-tekāt* from of old, hitherto, once, formerly. CG *'atkata* = CD *'atakkata* to (wish) to gain time.

’ardā’ihu ’enza yebelewwo:

Fakker lana messālē za-kerdāda garāht.

(37) Wa-’awše’a wa-yebēlomu:

Za-yezarre‘ šannāya zar‘a walda ’eg^{w}āla ’emma-ḥeyāw we’etu; (38) wa-garāhtu-ni ‘ālam we’etu; wa-šannāy-ni zar‘ weluda mangešt ’emuntu; wa-kerdād-ni weludu la-’ekuy; (39) wa-ḍarrāwi-ni za-zar‘omu Diyābelos we’etu; wa-mā’rar-ni xelqata ‘ālam we’etu; wa-‘aḍadd-ni malā’ekt ’emuntu. (40) Kama-kē ya’arreyewwo la-kerdād wa-ba-’essāt yāwe‘‘eyewwo, kamāhu yekawwen ba-xelqata ‘ālam. (41) Yefēnnewomu walda ’eg^{w}āla ’emma-ḥeyāw la-malā’ektihu, wa-ya’arreyu ’em-mangeštu k^{w}ello ‘alāweyāna wa-’ella yegabberu ’abbasā, (42) wa-yewaddeyewwomu westa ’etona ’essāt, wa-ba-heyya yekawwen bekāy wa-ḥaqiya senan. (43) ’Amēhā yebarrehu ṣādeqān kama ḍaḥāy ba-mangešta ’abuhomu. Za-bo ’ezana sami‘a yesmā‘. (44) Kā‘eba, temassel mangešta samāyāt madfena za-xebu’ westa garāht, wa-rakibo be’si xab’a, wa-’em-feššeḥāhu ḥora, wa-šēṭa k^{w}ello za-bo, wa-tašāyaṭa we’eta garāhta. (45) Kā‘eba, temassel mangešta samāyāt be’sē šayāṭē za-yaxaššeš bāḥreya šannāya. (46) Wa-rakibo ’aḥatta bāḥreya ’enta bezux šēṭā, ḥora wa-šēṭa k^{w}ello za-bo wa-tašāyaṭā. (47) Kā‘eba, temassel mangešta samāyāt garifa ’enta tawadyat westa bāḥr, wa-’em-k^{w}ellu zamada ‘āšā ’astagābe’at, (48) ’enta mali’ā ’a‘ragu westa ḥayq, wa-nabiromu ’arayu šannāyo westa mudāy, wa-’ekuyo-sa gadafewwo ’af’a. (49) Kamāhu yekawwen ba-xelqata ‘ālam: yewaḍḍe’u malā’ekt wa-yefalleṭu ’ekuyāna ’em-mā’kalomu la-ṣādeqān, (50) wa-yewaddeyewwomu westa ’etona ’essāt xaba bekāy wa-ḥaqiya senan.

(51) Wa-yebēlomu ’Iyasus:

Labbawkemu-nu ’enka zanta k^{w}ello?

---

36. D *fakkara* to interpret, expound, explain. Dt *tafakkara* pass. *fekkārē* explanation, interpretation, exposition. *mafakker* interpreter, expounder; soothsayer, prophet.

42. *’eton* (pl. *-āt*) furnace, oven. G *ḥaqaya* to grind/grit/gnash the teeth; to chew. CG *’aḥqaya* caus.

44. G *dafana (yedfen)* to cover, hide, conceal. *madfen* treasure; sepulchre.

47. *garif* net.

Wa-yebēlewwo: 'Ewwa. (52) Wa-yebēlomu:

> Ba'enta zentu k^{w}ellu ṣaḥāfi za-yeḍḍammad la-mangešta samāyāt yemassel be'sē bā'la bēt za-yāwaḍḍe' 'em-mazgabu ḥaddisa wa-beluya.

(53) Wa-faṣṣimo 'Iyasus 'ellonta messāleyāta, tanše'a 'em-heyya. (54) Wa-ḥora hagaro, wa-maharomu ba-mek^{w}rābomu 'eska soba yeddammamu wa-yebelu:

> 'Em-'aytē la-zentu ze-k^{w}ellu ṭebab wa-xayl? (55) 'Akko-nu zentu we'etu waldu la-ṣarābi? 'Akko-nu 'emmu semā Māryām wa-'axawihu Yā'qob wa-Yosēf wa-Sem'on wa-Yehudā? (56) Wa-'axātihu k^{w}ellon xabēna hallawā? 'Em-'aytē 'enka lotu zentu k^{w}ellu?

(57) Wa-yāng^{w}aragg^{w}eru ba'enti'ahu. Wa-yebēlomu 'Iyasus:

> 'Albo ba-xaba 'i-yekabber nabiy za'enbala ba-hagaru wa-ba-bētu.

(58) Wa-'i-gabra ba-heyya xayla bezuxa ba'enta 'i-'aminotomu.

Chapter XIV

25. Ba'enta Yoḥannes wa-Hērodes

(1) Wa-ba-we'etu mawā'el sam'a Hērodes neguš nagaro la-'Iyasus. (2) Wa-yebē la-'agbertihu:

> Ze-we'etu Yoḥannes Maṭmeq. We'etu tanše'a 'em-mutān, wa-ba'enta zentu yetgabbarā xaylāt botu.

(3) 'Esma we'etu Hērodes 'axazo la-Yoḥannes, wa-moqeḥo ba-bēta moqeḥ ba'enta Hērodeyādā, be'sita Fileppos 'exuhu, (4) 'esma yebēlo Yoḥannes lotu:

> 'I-yekawwenaka tāwsebā laka.

(5) Wa-'enza yefaqqed yeqtelo, yefarreh 'aḥzāba, 'esma kama nabiy yerē''eyewwo la-Yoḥannes. (6) Wa-kawino 'elata ledatu la-Hērodes, zafanat walattā la-Hērodeyādā ba-mā'kalomu, wa-'addamato la-Hērodes. (7) Wa-maḥala lāti kama yahabā za-sa'alato. (8) Wa-'aqdamat 'a'mero ba-xaba 'emmā, wa-tebēlo:

---

55. G *ṣaraba* to hew, do carpentry. *ṣerbat* woodwork, stonework. *ṣarābi* carpenter, craftsman.

57. Q *'ang^{w}arg^{w}ara* to be angry, vexed; to murmur, mutter.

XIV 6. D *'addama* to please (someone: o.s.). CDt *'asta'addama* to be pleased with (a.d.o.), to find pleasing, pleasant. *'addām* pleasing, pleasant. *ma'addem* idem.

Habani ba-zeyya ba-ṣāḥl re'so la-Yoḥannes Maṭmeq.
(9) Wa-takkaza negūš ba'enta maḥalāhu wa-ba'enta 'ella yeraffequ meslēhu, wa-'azzaza yahabewwā. (10) Wa-fanniwo matara re'so la-Yoḥannes ba-bēta moqeḥ. (11) Wa-'amṣe'u re'so ba-ṣāḥl, wa-wahabewwā la-ye'eti walatt, wa-wasadat la-'emmā. (12) Wa-maṣ'u 'ardā'ihu, wa-naš'u badno, wa-qabarewwo, wa-maṣi'omu zēnawewwo la-'Iyasus.

26. Ba'enta xams xebest

(13) Wa-sami'o 'Iyasus, tageḥša 'em-heyya ba-ḥamar westa gadām 'enta bāḥtitu. Wa-sami'omu 'aḥzāb, talawewwo ba-'egr 'em-'ahgur. (14) Wa-waḍi'o, re'ya bezuxāna 'aḥzāba, wa-meḥromu, wa-'aḥyawa dewuyānihomu. (15) Wa-mesēta kawino, qarbu xabēhu 'ardā'ihu 'enza yebelu:

Gadām we'etu beḥēr, wa-sa'ātu-ni xalafa. Feteḥomu la-'aḥzāb kama yeḥuru westa 'ahgur wa-yeššāyaṭu la-re'somu mable'a.

(16) Wa-yebēlomu 'Iyasus:

'Akko maftew yeḥuru. Habewwomu 'antemu za-yeballe'u.

(17) Wa-yebēlewwo:

'Albena zeyya za'enbala xams xebest wa-kel'ē 'āšā.

(18) Wa-yebē:

'Amṣe'ewwon lita zeyya.

(19) Wa-'azzazomu la-sab' yerfequ diba šā'r. Wa-naš'a we'eta xamsa xebesta wa-kel'ē 'āšā, wa-naṣṣara xaba samāy, wa-bāraka, wa-fatito wahaba la-'ardā'ihu xabāweza, wa-'ardā'ihu la-'aḥzāb. (20) Wa-bal'u k^w^ellomu, wa-ṣagbu, wa-'agḥašu za-tarfa fetatāta 'ašarta wa-kel'ēta mazāre'a melu'a. (21) Wa-'ella-sa bal'u 'emuntu sab' kama xamsā me't za'enbala 'anest wa-daqq.

27. Ba'enta zakama ḥora diba bāḥr

(22) Wa-'agabbaromu sobēhā la-'ardā'ihu kama ye'ragu westa ḥamar wa-yeqdemewwo xaba mā'dot 'eska soba yefēnnewomu la-'aḥzāb. (23) Wa-'emze fatḥomu la-'aḥzāb, wa-'arga westa dabr 'enta bāḥtitu yeṣalli.

---

8. *ṣāḥl* dish, bowl, platter.

19. G *fatata* = D *fattata* to break (bread); to distribute, give out. Gt *tafatata* = Dt *tafattata* pass. *fett* (pl. *fetat*, *-āt*) part, portion, morsel; gift. *fetat* (pl. *-āt*) idem.

20. *mazāre'* (pl. only) baskets, containers.

21. *daqq* (coll.) children and/or servants.

Wa-mesēta kawino bāḥtitu hallo heyya. (24) Wa-ḥamar-sa nāhu mā'kala bāḥr hallo, wa-yethawwak 'em-mogadāt, 'esma 'em-qedmēhu we'etu nafās. (25) Wa-ba-rābe't sa'āta lēlit maṣ'a xabēhomu 'Iyasus 'enza yaḥawwer diba bāḥr. (26) Wa-soba re'yewwo 'ardā'ihu 'enza diba bāḥr yaḥawwer, tahawku 'enza yebelu: Methat we'etu. Wa-'em-gerremāhu 'awyawu. (27) Wa-ba-gizēhā tanāgaromu 'Iyasus 'enza yebel:

Ta'amanu. 'Ana we'etu. 'I-tefrehu.

(28) Wa-'awše'o Pēṭros wa-yebē:

'Emma-sa 'anta-hu, 'Egzi'o, 'azzezani 'emṣā' xabēka 'enta diba māy.

(29) Wa-yebēlo: Na'ā. Wa-warido Pēṭros 'em-diba ḥamar, ḥora diba māy yebṣāḥ xaba 'Iyasus. (30) Wa-soba re'ya nafāsa xayyāla, farha, wa-'axaza yessaṭam. Wa-'awyawa 'enza yebel: 'Egzi'o, 'adxenani. (31) Wa-sobēhā safḥa 'edēhu 'Iyasus, wa-'axazo, wa-yebēlo:

Wexuda hāymānot, ba-ment nāfaqqa?

(32) Wa-'arigomu westa ḥamar, ye'eta gizē xadaga nafās. (33) Wa-'ella westa ḥamar sagadu lotu 'enza yebelu:

'Amān walda 'Egzi'abḥēr 'anta.

(34) Wa-'adiwomu, baṣḥu westa medra Gēnessārēṭ. (35) Wa-'a'marewwo sab'a we'etu beḥēr, wa-fannawu xaba k^wellu 'adyām, wa-'amṣe'u lotu k^wello ḥemumāna. (36) Wa-'astabq^{w}e'ewwo kama yelkafu zafara lebsu, wa-k^wellomu 'ella lakafewwo yaḥayyewu.

Chapter XV

28. Ba'enta 'ella yaxaddegu te'zāza 'Egzi'abḥēr

(1) Wa-'emze qarbu xaba 'Iyasus 'ella maṣ'u 'em-'Iyarusālēm ṣaḥaft wa-Farisāweyān 'enza yebelu:

---

26. G *matha* to be deceptive in appearance. *methat* (pl. *-āt*) phantom, fantasy, spectre. G *garama* to be awesome, fear-inspiring. D *garrama* to frighten, terrify. Dt *tagarrama* to be terrible, threatening, fearful. *gerrum* awesome, terrible, fearsome, awe-inspiring. *germā/gerremā* terror, awe; awesome nature. *tegremt* threats, terrors.

30. CG *'asṭama* to submerge, immerse, flood. Gt *tasaṭma* to sink (intrans.). *seṭmat* submersion, sinking. *masṭem* adj. submerging, flooding.

36. G *lakafa (yelkef)* to touch. CG *'alkafa* to touch, cause to touch. Gt *talakfa* pass. *zafar ('azfār)* hem or fringe of a garment.

La-ment ’ardā’ika yet‘addawu šer‘ata liqānāt, ’esma ’i-yetxaḍḍabu ’edawihomu soba xebesta yeballe‘u?

(3) Wa-’awše’a wa-yebēlomu:

La-ment ’antemu-ni tet‘addawu te’zāza ’Egzi’abḥēr ba’enta šer‘atekemu? (4) Wa-’Egzi’abḥēr-sa yebē:

’Akber ’aba wa-’emma, wa-za-yāḥammi ’aba wa-’emma mota yemut.

(5) Wa-’antemu-sa tebelu:

Za-yebē la-’ab wa-la-’em "Habta za-’em-xabēya za-baq^{w}ā‘kuka" ’i-yākabber ’abāhu wa-’i-’emmo.

(6) Wa-sa‘arkemu qālo la-’Egzi’abḥēr ba’enta šer‘atekemu. (7) Madlewān, šannāya tanabbaya ’Isāyeyās lā‘lēkemu ’enza yebel:

Ze-ḥezb ba-kanāferihomu yākabberuni, wa-ba-lebbomu-sa nawwāxa yereḥḥequ ’emennēya; (9) wa-kanto yāmallekuni ’enza yemēhheru temherta šer‘atāta sab’.

(10) Wa-ṣawwe‘omu la-ḥezb, wa-yebēlomu:

Seme‘u wa-labbewu (11) kama ’akko za-yebawwe’ westa ’af za-yārakk^{w}eso la-sab’, ’allā za-yewaḍḍe’ ’em-westa ’af we’etu yārakk^{w}eso la-sab’.

(12) Wa-’emze qaribomu ’ardā’ihu, yebēlewwo:

Tā’ammer-hu kama Farisāweyān sami‘omu qālaka ’ang^{w}arg^{w}aru?

(13) Wa-’awše’a wa-yebē:

K^{w}ellu takl ’enta ’i-takalā ’abuya samāyāwi teššērraw. (14) Xedegewwomu. ‘Ewurān ’emuntu ’amreḥta ‘ewurān. ‘Ewur la-‘ewur la’emma marḥo, kel’ēhomu yewaddequ westa gebb.

(15) Wa-’awše’a Pēṭros, wa-yebēlo:

Negerana zanta messālē.

(16) Wa-yebēlomu ’Iyasus:

XV 4. G *ḥamaya (yeḥmi)* to curse, revile, slander. *ḥemuy* disgraceful, shocking. *ḥamēt* vn.

5. This is a difficult sentence. The Eth. appears to mean: It is a gift on my part that I have been of any profit to you." *habta* is in construct with the nominalized *za-’em-xabēya*. The *za-* of *baq^{w}ā‘kuka* may be compared with that of the construction treated on §29.3; it may be a simple relative, however: "That by which I have been a profit to you is a gift on my part."

8. *kanfar* (pl. *kanāfer*) lip, edge, hem.

ʿĀdi-hu ʾantemu-ni ʾi-labbāweyān ʾantemu? (17) ʾI-tāʾammeru-nu kama kʷellu za-yebawweʾ westa ʾaf westa karš yetgammar wa-ṣemma yetgaddaf? (18) Wa-za-sa yewaḍḍeʾ ʾem-westa ʾaf ʾem-lebb yewaḍḍeʾ, wa-ʾemuntu yārakkʷesewwo la-sabʾ. (19) ʾEsma ʾem-westa lebb yewaḍḍeʾ xellinnā ʾekuy: qatil, māḥzan, zemmut, serq, semʿ ba-ḥassat, wa-ḍerfat. (20) ʾEllu-kē za-yārakkʷesewwo la-sabʾ, wa-zaʾenbala taxaḍebo ʾedaw-sa baliʿ ʾi-yārakkʷeso la-sabʾ.

29. Baʾenta Kananāwit ʾenta walattā taʾabbed

(21) Wa-waḍiʾo ʾIyasus ʾem-heyya, tageḥša westa dawala Ṭiros wa-Sidonā. (22) Wa-nāhu beʾsit Kananāwit ʾem-weʾetu ʾadwāl waḍʾat ʾenza teṣarrex wa-tebel:

Maḥarani, ʾEgziʾo, walda Dāwit. Walatteya ʾekuy gānēn ʾaxazā.

(23) Wa-ʾi-ʾawšeʾa ʾIyasus qāla. Wa-qaribomu ʾardāʾihu, ʾastabqʷeʿewwo ʾenza yebelu:

Fannewā, ʾesma teṣarrex ba-dexrēna.

(24) Wa-ʾawšeʾa, wa-yebē:

ʾI-tafannawku zaʾenbala xaba ʾabāgeʿ za-tahagʷla za-bēta ʾEsrāʾēl.

(25) Wa-qaribo, sagadat lotu ʾenza tebel:

ʾEgziʾo, redeʾani.

(26) Wa-ʾawšeʾa, wa-yebēlā:

ʾI-kona šannāya našiʾa xebesta welud wa-wehiba la-kalabāt.

(27) Wa-tebē:

ʾEwwa, ʾEgziʾo, ʾesma kalabāt-ni yeballeʿu ʾem-ferfārāt za-yewaddeq ʾem-māʾeda ʾagāʾeztihomu.

(28) Wa-ʾemze ʾawšeʾa ʾIyasus, wa-yebēlā:

ʾO-beʾsito, ʿabiy hāymānoteki. Yekunki bakama tefaqqedi. Wa-ḥaywat walattā ʾem-yeʾeti saʿāt.

30. Baʾenta ʾaḥzāb ʾella tafawwasu ʾem-bezux dawēhomu

(29) Wa-xalifo ʾem-heyya ʾIyasus, baṣḥa xaba ḥayqa bāḥr za-Galilā, wa-ʿarigo dabra, nabara heyya. (30) Wa-qarbu xabēhu ʾaḥzāb bezuxān ʾenza bomu meslēhomu ḥankāsāna, ʿewurāna, ṣemumāna, ḍewwusāna, wa-

---

27. *ferfār/ferfur* (pl. *-āt*) crumb. *māʾed* (pl. *-āt*) table.

30. *ḍewwus* weak, crippled, maimed. CD *ʾaḍawwasa* to weaken,

bā'edāna bezuxāna, wa-gadafewwomu xaba 'egarihu la-'Iyasus, wa-fawwasomu, (31) 'eska soba 'aḥzāb yānakkeru 'enza yerē''eyu kama bahhāmān yetnāgaru, wa-ḥankāsān yaḥawweru, wa-'ewurān yerē''eyu. Wa-sabbeḥewwo la-'Amlāka 'Esrā'ēl.

31. Ba'enta sab'u xebest

(32) Wa-ṣawwe'omu 'Iyasus la-'ardā'ihu, wa-yebēlomu:

Yāmeḥḥeruni 'ellu 'aḥzāb, 'esma nāhu šalusa mawā'ela yeṣanneḥu xabēya, wa-'albomu za-yeballe'u. Wa-'i-y̓efaqqed 'efannewomu ṣewumāna kama 'i-yemaṣlewu ba-fenot.

(33) Wa-yebēlewwo 'ardā'ihu:

'Em-'aytē 'enka lana ba-gadām xebest za-yāṣaggeb la-za-maṭana-ze ḥezb?

(34) Wa-yebēlomu 'Iyasus:

Mi-maṭana xabāweza bekemu?

Wa-yebēlu:

Sab'u, wa-xedāṭ 'āšā.

Wa-'azzazomu la-ḥezb yerfequ diba medr. (36) Wa-naš'a sab'u xebesta wa-'āšā-ni, wa-ye'eta gizē 'a'k^{w}ito, fatata wa-wahaba la-'ardā'ihu, wa-'ardā'ihu la-ḥezb. (37) Wa-bal'u k^{w}ellomu wa-ṣagbu, wa-za-tarfa fetatāta 'agḥašu sab'ata 'asfāridāta melu'a. (38) Wa-'ella-sa bal'u 'edaw konu 'arbe'ā me't za'enbala 'anest wa-daqq. (39) Wa-fatiḥo 'aḥzāba, 'arga westa ḥamar, wa-ḥora westa dawala Magēdal.

Chapter XVI

(1) Wa-maṣ'u Farisāweyān wa-Saduqāweyān 'enza yāmēkkerewwo, wa-sa'alewwo te'merta 'em-samāy yār'eyomu. (2) Wa-'awše'a, wa-yebēlomu:

'Emkama masya wa-kona ḥawāya, tebelu: "Ṣeḥew beḥēr, 'esma yāqyaḥayyeḥ samāy." (3) Wa-'emkama ṣabḥa, tebel: "Yom-sa-kē yezannem, 'esma yāqyaḥayyeḥ samāy demmuna." Gaṣṣa samāy-nu

---

cripple, maim.

XVI 2. *ḥewāy* the red glow of the evening sky. *ṣeḥew* serene. Note that in speaking of the weather Eth. will use *beḥēr* (the land) as the subject where English has the impersonal "it." Q *'aqyāḥyeḥa* to grow reddish.

3. D *dammana* to cloud over, obscure; to become cloudy. CD *'adammana* idem. *demmun* cloudy. *damanmin* rather cloudy.

tā'ammeru fakkero, wa-ta'āmera mawā'el-sa 'i-tā'ammeru? (4) Wa-yebēlomu:

Tewledd 'elut wa-zammā te'merta taxaššeš, wa-te'mert 'i-yetwahhabā za'enbala te'merta Yonās nabiy.

Wa-xadagomu, wa-ḥora.

32. Ba'enta beḥu'a Farisāweyān

(5) Wa-baṣiḥomu 'ardā'ihu mā'dota, ras'u xebesta naši'a. (6) Wa-yebēlomu 'Iyasus-sa:

'Uqu wa-ta'aqabu 'em-beḥu'omu la-Farisāweyān wa-Saduqāweyān.

(7) Wa-xallayu babaynātihomu 'enza yebelu:

Xebesta 'i-nasā'na.

(8) Wa-'a'maromu 'Iyasus, wa-yebēlomu:

Menta texēlleyu babaynātikemu, ḥeṣuṣāna hāymānot, 'esma xebesta 'albekemu? (9) 'Ādihu 'i-telēbbewu-nu, wa-'i-tezzēkkaru za-'ama xams xebest 'ella la-xamsā me't, wa-mi-maṭana mazāre'a 'agḥaškemu? (10) Wa-sab'u xebest 'ella la-'arbe'ā me't, wa-mi-maṭana 'asfāridāta 'agḥaškemu? (11) 'Efo za-'i-telēbbewu kama 'akko ba'enta xebest za-'ebēlakemu? Ta'aqabu 'emenna beḥ'atomu la-Farisāweyān wa-Saduqāweyān.

(12) Wa-'emze labbawu kama 'akko za-yebē yet'aqabu 'emenna beḥ'ata xebesta 'allā 'emenna temherta Farisāweyān wa-Saduqāweyān.

33. Ba'enta za-tase''elomu ba-Qisāreyā

(13) Wa-baṣiḥo 'Iyasus beḥēra Qisāreyā za-Fileppos tase''elomu la-'ardā'ihu 'enza yebel:

Manna-hi yebelewwo yekun sab' la-walda 'eg^{w}āla 'emma-ḥeyāw?

---

5. G *ras'a (yersā')* to forget; to be negligent; to err; to be impious, wicked. CG *'arse'a* caus. Gt *taras'a* pass.; to fall into error/sin. *rāse'* forgetful, negligent, impious. *rasi'* impious, sinful. *res'at* forgetfulness, negligence, impiety. *res'ān, res'ennā* idem.

13. *behla* with direct object and object complement means "to call someone something." The *yekun*, however, necessitates a more complicated analysis: the object suffix of *yebelewwo* is anticipatory, and *yekun* belongs to a kind of result clause. There is undoubtedly a mixing of two constructions here, resulting from a slavish rendering

(14) Wa-yebēlu:

Bo-’ella Yoḥannes-hā Maṭmeqa, wa-kāle’ān ’Ēleyās-hā, wa-manfaqomu ’Ēremeyās-hā, wa-’emma ’akko ’aḥada ’em-nabiyāt.

(15) Wa-yebēlomu:

’Antemu-kē manna tebeluni kawina?

(16) Wa-’awše’a Sem‘on Pēṭros, wa-yebē:

’Anta we’etu masiḥ waldu la-’Egzi’abḥēr ḥeyāw.

(17) Wa-’awše’a ’Iyasus, wa-yebēlo:

Beḍu‘ ’anta, Sem‘on walda Yonā. ’Esma šegā wa-dam ’i-kašata laka, ’allā ’abuya za-ba-samāyāt. (18) Wa-’ane-sa ’ebelaka kama ’anta k^{w}ak^{w}ḥ, wa-diba zāti k^{w}ak^{w}ḥ ’aḥanneṣā la-bēta Keresteyān, wa-’anāqeṣa Si’ol ’i-yexēyyelewwā. (19) Wa-’ehubaka marāxuta mangešta samāyāt. Wa-za ’asarka ba-medr yekawwen ’esura ba-samāyāt, wa-za fatāḥka ba-medr yekawwen fetuḥ ba-samāyāt.

(20) Wa-’emze gaššaṣomu la-’ardā’ihu kama ’albo la-za yengeru kama we’etu ’Iyasus Kerestos. (21) Wa-’em-’amēhā ’Iyasus ’axaza yengeromu la-’ardā’ihu kama hallawo yeḥur ’Iyarusālēm, wa-bezuxa yāḥammemewwo rabbanāt wa-liqāna kāhenāt wa-ṣaḥaft, wa-yetqattal, wa-ba-šālest ‘elat yetnaššā’. (22) Wa-tasaṭwo Pēṭros, wa-’axaza yegaššeṣo ’enza yebel:

Ḥāsa laka ’Egzi’o. ’I-yekun lā‘lēka zentu.

(23) Wa-tamayeṭo, yebēlo la-Pēṭros:

Ḥur ’em-dexrēya Sayṭān. Mā‘qafeya lita ’anta, ’esma ’i-texēlli za-’Egzi’abḥēr za’enbala za-sab’.

(24) Wa-’emze yebēlomu ’Iyasus la-’ardā’ihu:

Za-yefaqqed yetlewani, yeslā’ nafso, wa-yāṭbe‘, wa-yenšā’ masqala motu wa-yetlewani. (25) Wa-za-yefaqqed yādxenā la-nafsu

---

of the Greek.

21. *rabbān* (pl. *-āt*, *rabbanāt*) teacher, leader (an Aramaic word).

22. Gt *tasaṭwa* to accept, receive, take; to respond (to: o.s.).

24. G *ṭab‘a* to be willing, ready (to do something). CG *’aṭbe‘a* to do something willingly (with foll. coordinated verb); to persevere, be constant, firm, undeterred; caus. of preceding meanings. *ṭebu‘* willing, quick, eager, ready, undeterred, bold, persevering. *wa-yāṭbe‘ wa-yenšā’* "and let him be willing to take up."

yegaddefā, wa-za-sa gadafā la-nafsu ba'enti'aya yerakkebā. (26) Wa-menta-nu yebaqq^{w}e'o la-sab' la'emma k^{w}ello 'ālama rabḥa wa-nafso hag^{w}la? Wa-menta 'em-wahaba sab' bēzāhā la-nafsu? (27) 'Esma hallawo la-walda 'eg^{w}āla 'emma-ḥeyāw yemṣā' ba-sebḥāta 'abuhu mesla malā'ektihu, wa-'amēhā ya'asseyo la-k^{w}ellu bakama megbāru. (28) 'Amān 'ebelakemu, bo-'ella hallawu 'em-'ella yeqawwemu zeyya 'ella 'i-yeṭe''emewwo la-mot 'eska 'ama yerē''eyewwo la-walda 'eg^{w}āla 'emma-ḥeyāw ba-sebḥāta 'abuhu.

Chapter XVII

34. Ba'enta zakama tawallaṭa ba-qedmēhomu 'Iyasus

(1) Wa-'emdexra sessu mawā'el naš'omu 'Iyasus la-Pēṭros wa-la-Yā'qob wa-la-Yoḥannes 'exuhu, wa-'a'ragomu westa dabr nawwāx 'enta bāḥtitomu. (2) Wa-tawallaṭa rā'yu ba-qedmēhomu, wa-'abreha gaṣṣu kama ḍaḥāy, wa-'albāsihu-ni kona ṣa'adā kama berhān. (3) Wa-nāhu 'astar'ayewwomu Musē wa-'Ēleyās 'enza yetnāgaru meslēhu. (4) Wa-'awše'a Pēṭros wa-yebēlo la-'Iyasus:

> 'Egzi'o, šannāy we'etu lana hallewo zeyya, wa-'emma-sa tefaqqed, negbar ba-zeyya šalasta saqālewa, 'aḥatta laka wa-'aḥatta la-Musē wa-'aḥatta la-'Ēleyās.

(5) Wa-'enza yetnāgar, nāhu dammanā beruh ṣallalomu, wa-nāhu qāl 'em-westa dammanā 'enta tebel:

> Ze-we'etu waldeya za-'āfaqqer, za-botu šamarku, wa-lotu seme'ewwo.

(6) Wa-sami'omu 'ardā'ihu, wadqu ba-gaṣṣomu, wa-farhu ṭeqqa. (7) Wa-qarba 'Iyasus wa-lakafomu, wa-yebē:

> Tanše'u, wa-'i-tefrehu.

(8) Wa-'anše'u 'a'yentihomu, wa-'albo za-re'yu wa-'i-manna-hi za'enbala 'Iyasus bāḥtito. (9) Wa-'enza yewarredu 'em-dabr, 'azzazomu 'Iyasus 'enza yebel:

> 'I-tengeru wa-'i-la-mannu-hi zā-rā'ya 'eska 'ama walda 'eg^{w}āla 'emma-ḥeyāw 'em-mutān yetnaššā'.

(10) Wa-tase''elewwo 'ardā'ihu 'enza yebelu:

> Wa-'efo yebelu ṣaḥaft: "'Ēleyās hallawo yemṣā' qedma?"

(11) Wa-'awše'a 'Iyasus wa-yebēlomu:

> 'Ēleyās yeqaddem maṣi'a wa-yāstarāte' k^{w}ello. (12) Wa-

XVII 4. *saqalā* (pl. *saqālew*) tabernacle, tent.

’ebelakemu bāḥtu kama ’Ēleyās wadde’a maṣ’a, wa-’i-ya’marewwo, wa-bāḥtu gabru lā‘lēhu k^{w}ello zakama faqadu, wa-kamāhu la-walda ’eg^{w}āla ’emma-ḥeyāw-ni hallawo yāḥmemewwo.

(13) Wa-’emze ’a’maru ’ardā’ihu kama ba’enta Yoḥannes Maṭmeq yebēlomu:

35. Ba’enta za-nagargār

(14) Wa-baṣiḥomu xaba ’aḥzāb, qarba xabēhu be’si, wa-sagada lotu ’enza yetmaḥallel wa-yebel:

(15) ’Egzi’o, tašāhal lita waldeya, ’esma ’ekuy gānēn ’axazo, wa-yāngaraggero, wa-mabzexto yewaddeq westa ’essāt wa-bo ’ama westa māy. (16) Wa-’amṣā’kewwo xaba ’ardā’ika, wa-se’newwo fawweso.

(17) Wa-’emze ’awše’a ’Iyasus, wa-yebē:

’O-tewledd ’i-’amānit wa-‘elut, ’eska mā’zē-nu ’ehēllu meslēkemu? ’Eska mā’zē-nu ’et‘ēggašakemu? ’Amṣe’ewwo lita zeyya.

(18) Wa-gaššaṣo ’Iyasus, wa-waḍ’a gānēnu ’em-lā‘lēhu, wa-ḥaywa ḥeḍān ba-ye’eti sa‘āt. (19) Wa-’emze qaribomu ’ardā’ihu ’enta bāḥtitomu, yebēlewwo la-’Iyasus:

Ba’enta ment neḥna se’enna ’awḍe’oto?

(20) Wa-yebēlomu ’Iyasus:

Ba’enta ḥeṣaṣa hāymānotekemu. ’Amān ’ebelakemu: ’Emma bekemu hāymānota maṭana xeṭṭat senāṗē, tebelewwo la-ze dabr "Feles ’emzeyya xaba kaḥa," wa-yefalles, wa-’albo za-yessa’’anakemu.

(21) Wa-za-kama-ze ’i-yewaḍḍe’ za’enbala ba-ṣom wa-ba-ṣalot.

(22) Wa-’enza yānsosewu westa Galilā, yebēlomu ’Iyasus:

Hallawo la-walda ’eg^{w}āla ’emma-ḥeyāw yāgbe’ewwo westa ’eda sab’, wa-yeqattelewwo, wa-’ama šālest ‘elat yetnaššā’.

Wa-takkazu ṭeqqa.

36. Ba’enta ’ella yese’’elu ṣabāḥta

(24) Wa-baṣiḥomu Qefernāhom, maṣ’u ’ella ṣabāḥta dinār yenašše’u xaba Pēṭros, wa-yebēlewwo:

---

14. Qt *tamāḥlala* to beseech, supplicate.

15. *mabzexto* adv. often, frequently.

20. *kaḥa*, *kaḥā*, *kaḥāka*, *kaḥaka*, *kaḥak* thither, to that place; further on.

Liqekemu-sa, ’i-yehub-nu ṣabāḥta?

(25) Wa-yebē: ’Ewwa. Wa-bawi’o westa bēt, ’aqdama ’Iyasus behiloto: Menta tebel, Sem‘on? Nagašta medr ’em-xaba mannu yenašše’u ṣabāḥta wa-gādā? ’Em-xaba weludomu-nu wa-mi-ma ’em-xaba nakir?

(26) Wa-yebē: ’Em-xaba nakir. Wa-yebēlo ’Iyasus: ’Engā ’ag‘āzeyān-nu ’emuntu weludomu? (27) Wa-bāḥtu, kama ’i-yāng^{w}arg^{w}eru, ḥur westa bāḥr, wa-day maqāṭena, wa-za-qadāmē ’ašgarka ‘āšā nešā’ wa-kešet ’afāhu, wa-terakkeb dināra seṭeṭirā. Kiyāhu nešā’, wa-habomu lita-hi wa-laka.

Chapter XVIII

37. Ba’enta ’ella yebelu mannu ya‘abbi

(1) Wa-ba-ye’eti sa‘āt qarbu xabēhu ’ardā’ihu la-’Iyasus ’enza yebelu: Mannu ’engā ya‘abbi ba-mangešta samāyāt?

(2) Wa-ṣawwe‘a ḥeḍāna wa-’aqamo mā’kalomu, (3) wa-yebē: ’Amān ’ebelakemu: ’Emma ’i-tamayaṭkemu wa-’i-konkemu kama ḥeḍānāt, ’i-tebawwe’u westa mangešta samāyāt. (4) Wa-za-’atḥata re’so kama-ze ḥeḍān ze-we’etu za-ya‘abbi ba-mangešta samāyāt. (5) Wa-za-hi tawakfa ’aḥada ḥeḍāna za-kama-ze ba-semeya, kiyāya tawakfa. (6) Wa-za-hi ’asḥatomu la-’aḥadu ’em-’ellu ne’usān ’ella ya’ammenu beya, yexēyyeso kama ye’seru ba-kesādu māḥraṣa ’adg wa-yāsṭemewwo westa legg^{w}ata bāḥr. (7) ’Alē-lo la-‘ālam ’em-mansut, ’esma gebr yemaṣṣe’ mansut, wa-bāḥtu ’alē-lo la-we’etu be’si za-botu yemaṣṣe’ mansut. (8) Wa-’emma ’edēka ’aw ’egreka tāseḥḥetaka, meterā wa-gedef ’em-lā‘lēka. Yexēyyesaka tebā’ westa ḥeywat ḥankāseka wa-ḍewwuseka ’em-’enza beka kel’ē ’eda wa-kel’ē ’egra tetwaday westa ’essāt za-la-‘ālam. (9) Wa-’emma-hi ‘ayneka tāseḥḥetaka, melexā wa-gedef ’em-lā‘lēka. Yexēyyesaka naqq^{w}āreka tebā’ westa ḥeywat

---

25. *gādā* gift (for a superior).

27. *maqāṭen* (pl. only) hooks, fish-hooks. *seṭeṭirā* stater (coin).

XVIII 6. *’adg* (f. *’adegt*; pl. *’a’dug*) ass. *legg^{w}at* (pl. *-āt*) depth of the sea, abyss.

7. *gebr* = *ba-gebr* adv. out of necessity, necessarily, surely, certainly.

9. *naqq^{w}ār* one-eyed, blind.

'em-'enza kel'ē ʻayna beka tetwaday westa Gahānnama 'essāt. (10) ʻUqu 'i-tāstāḥqerewwomu la-'aḥadu 'em-'ellu ne'usān. 'Ebelakemu kama malā'ektihomu ba-samāyāt watra yerē''eyu gaṣṣo la-'abuya za-ba-samāyāt. (11) 'Esma maṣ'a walda 'eg^{w}āla 'emma-ḥeyāw yexšeš wa-yādxen za-tahag^{w}la.

38. Ba'enta me't 'abāgeʻ

(12) Ment tebelu? 'Emma-bo be'si za-botu me'ta 'agābeʻa, wa-'emma tagadfa 'aḥadu 'em-westētomu, 'akko-hu yaxaddeg tasʻā wa-tasʻata westa 'adbār, wa-yaḥawwer yexšeš za-tagadfo? (13) Wa-'emkama rakabā, 'amān 'ebelakemu kama yetfēššāḥ ba'enti'ahā fadfāda 'em-tasʻā wa-tasʻatu 'ella 'i-tagadfu. (14) Kamāhu-kē 'i-yetfaqqad ba-qedma 'abuya za-ba-samāyāt kama yethag^{w}al 'aḥadu 'em-'ellu ne'usān. (15) Wa-'emma-ni 'abbasa laka 'exuka, ḥur wa-gaššeṣo ba-bāḥtitekemu, 'anta wa-we'etu, wa- emma samʻaka, rabāḥka 'exwāka. (16) Wa-'emma-sa 'i-samʻaka, nešā' meslēka ba-dāgem 'aḥada 'aw kel'ē kama ba-'afa kel'ē wa-šalastu samāʻt yequm k^{w}ellu qāl. (17) Wa-'emma-sa 'i-samʻomu lomu-hi, neger ba-bēta Kerestiyān, wa-'emma-sa la-bēta Kerestiyān 'i-samʻā, yekunka kama 'arami wa-maṣabbeḥāwi. (18) 'Amān 'ebelakemu: Za-'asarkemu ba-medr yekawwen 'esura ba-samāyāt, wa-za-fatāḥkemu ba-medr fetuḥa yekawwen ba-samāyāt. (19) Wa-ʻādi 'ebelakemu: La'emma xabru kel'ētu 'emennēkemu ba-westa medr ba'enta k^{w}ellu gebr za-sa'alu, yetgabbar lomu ba-xaba 'abuya za-ba-samāyāt. (20) 'Esma xaba hallawu kel'ētu wa-šalastu gubu'ān ba-semeya, heyya hallawku 'ana mā'kalomu.

(21) Wa-'emze qarba xabēhu Pēṭros, wa-yebēlo:
'Egzi'o, sefna 'emma 'abbasa lāʻlēya 'exuya 'exdeg lotu? 'Eska sebʻ-nu?

(22) Wa-yebē 'Iyasus:
'I-yebelaka "'Eska sebʻ" 'allā "ʻādi 'eska sabʻā ba-ba-sebʻ."

39. Ba'enta za-yefaddi 'elfa makāleya

(23) Ba'enta-ze temassel mangešta samāyāt be'sē negūša za-faqada yegbar ḥasāba mesla 'agbertihu. (24) Wa-'enza yetḥāsab,

---

21. *sefna* interrogative adv. how many times? how many?
23. G *ḥasaba* to compute, reckon; to think, believe, impute.

’amṣe’u lotu ’aḥada za-yefaddi ’elfa makāleya. (25) Wa-xaṭi’o za-yefaddi, ’azzaza ’egzi’u yešiṭewwo mesla be’situ wa-mesla weludu wa-k^{w}ello za-bo ’eska yefaddi. (26) Wa-wadqa ’enka we’etu gabr, wa-sagada ’enza yebel:

’Egzi’o, ta‘aggašani, wa-k^{w}ello ’efaddeyaka.

(27) Wa-maḥaro ’egzi’u la-we’etu gabr, wa-fatḥo, wa-‘edāhu-ni xadaga lotu. (28) Wa-waḍi’o we’etu gabr, rakaba ’aḥada gabra ’emenna ’abyāṣihu za-yefaddeyo me’ta dināra, wa-’axazo yexneqo ’enza yebel:

Hab, seleṭ za-tefaddi.

(29) Wa-wadqa we’etu gabra ’egzi’u, wa-’astabq^{w}e‘o ’enza yebel:

Ta‘aggašani, wa-k^{w}ello ’efaddeyaka.

(30) Wa-’abayo, wa-ḥora wa-’amoqeḥo ’eska yefaddeyo. (31) Wa-re’eyomu ’abyāṣihu zakama rassayo, takkazu ṭeqqa, wa-ḥawiromu nagarewwo la-’egzi’omu k^{w}ello zakama kona. (32) Wa-’emze ṣawwe‘o ’egzi’u, wa-yebēlo:

Gabr ’ekuy, k^{w}ello ‘edā xadaggu laka ’esma ’astabq^{w}ā‘kani. (33) ’Akko-hu maftew ’anta-hi temḥar biṣaka bakama ’ana maḥarkuka?

(34) Wa-tam‘e‘a ’egzi’u, wa-maṭṭawo la-’ella yek^{w}ēnnenu ’eska ’ama yesalleṭ k^{w}ello za-yefaddeyo. (35) Kamāhu-kē ’abuya-ni samāyāwi yegabber lakemu ’emma ’i-xadaggemu la-biṣekemu ’em-lebbekemu.

Chapter XIX

40. Ba’enta ’ella tase’’elu ’emma yekawwen xadiga be’sit

(1) Wa-kona ’emza faṣṣama ’Iyasus zanta nagara, tanše’a ’em-Galilā, wa-basḥa westa beḥēra Yehudā mā‘dota Yordānos. (2) Wa-talawewwo ’aḥzāb bezuxān, wa-fawwasomu ba-heyya. (3) Wa-maṣ’u xabēhu Farisāweyān ’enza yāmēkkerewwo wa-yebelu:

Yekawwen-hu la-be’si xadiga be’sit ba-k^{w}ellu za-’abbasat?

Gt *tahasaba* pass. Glt *taḥāsaba* to take up accounts with. *ḥasāb* computation, reckoning, account; quantity, price; portion, share. *gabra ḥasāba* to settle accounts.

24. *’elf* (pl. *’a’lāf*) myriad, 10000. *te’lefit*, *me’lefit* a vast number. *maklit* (pl. *makāley*) talent (wt.).

27. *‘edā* debt, guilt.

(4) Wa-'awše'a, wa-yebēlomu:

'I-yanbabkemu-nu kama za-faṭaromu 'em-tekāt be'sē wa-be'sita gabromu? (5) Wa-yebē: Ba'enta-ze yaxaddeg be'si 'abāhu wa-'emmo, wa-yetallewā la-be'situ, wa-yekawwenu kel'ēhomu 'aḥada šegā. (6) 'Enka-sa-kē 'i-konu kel'ē za'enbala 'aḥadu šegā 'emuntu. Za-'Egzi'abḥēr-kē ḍamara, sab' 'i-yefleṭ.

(7) Wa-yebēlewwo:

'Efo 'enka 'azzaza Musē yahabu maṣḥafa felṭān wa-yexdegewwā.

(8) Wa-yebēlomu:

Musē-sa bakama 'ekaya lebbekemu daxarakemu texdegu 'anesteyākemu, wa-'em-tekāt-sa 'akko kama-ze za-tagabra. (9) Wa-'ebelakemu bāḥtu kama 'emma-bo za-xadaga be'sito za'enbala ba-zemmut, wa-'awsaba kāle'ta, zammawa. Wa-'enta daḥarewwā za-'awsabā zammawa.

(10) Wa-yebēlewwo 'ardā'ihu:

'Emma kama-ze we'etu šer'ata be'si mesla be'situ, 'akko šannāy 'awsebo?

(11) Wa-yebēlomu:

'Akko k^{w}ellu za-yāgammero la-zentu qāl, za'enbala la-'ella tawehba. (12) 'Esma-bo xeṣewāna 'ella kamāhu tawaldu 'em-karša 'emmomu, wa-bo xeṣewān 'ella xaṣawomu sab', wa-bo xeṣewān 'ella xaṣawu re'somu ba'enta mangešta samāyāt. Wa-za-sa yekel faṣṣemo la-yefaṣṣem.

(13) Wa-'emze 'amṣe'u lotu daqqa kama yānber 'edēhu lā'lēhomu wa-yeṣalli, wa-gaššeṣewwomu 'ardā'ihu. (14) Wa-yebēlomu 'Iyasus:

Xedegu daqiqa, wa-'i-tekle'ewwomu maṣi'a xabēya, 'esma la-'ella kama-ze ye'eti mangešta samāyāt.

(15) Wa-'anbara 'edēhu lā'lēhomu, wa-xalafa 'em-heyya.

41. Ba'enta bā'el za-tase''elo la-'Egzi'ena

(16) Wa-nāhu maṣ'a 'aḥadu, wa-yebēlo:

XIX 6. G *ḍamara* = D *ḍammara* to join, affix, connect, attach. Glt *taḍāmara* to associate with (one another). *ḍemrat* joining, connection. *maḍāmer* (f. *-t*) partner, mate, companion, spouse.

8. G *daxara* to sanction, allow. *madxar* sanction, blessing.

9. G *daḥara (yedḥar)* to divorce, repudiate.

12. G *xaṣawa* to castrate. *xeṣew* castrated; n. eunuch.

Liq, ment-nu xēr za-'em-gabarku, ḥeywata za-la-'ālam ba-za 'ewarres?

(17) Wa-yebēlo:

Menta tessē''alani ba'enta xēr? 'Aḥadu we'etu xēr, wa-'emma-sa tefaqqed tebā' westa ḥeywat, 'eqab te'zāzāta.

(18) Wa-yebēlo: 'Ayyāta? Wa-yebēlo 'Iyasus:

'I-qatila nafs, 'i-tamāḥezo, 'i-sariq, 'i-ḥassewo sem'. (19) 'Akbero 'abuka wa-'emmeka, wa-'afqero biṣeka kama re'seka.

(20) Wa-yebēlo we'etu warēzā:

Zanta k^{w}ello 'aqabku 'em-ne'seya. Ment 'enka za-tarfani?

(21) Wa-yebēlo 'Iyasus:

'Emma-sa tefaqqed feṣṣuma tekun, ḥur, šiṭ ṭeritaka, wa-hab la-meskin, wa-tāṭarri mazgaba ba-samāyāt. Wa-na'ā, telewani.

(22) Wa-sami'o warēzā zanta nagara, xalafa 'enza yetēkkez, 'esma-bo bezuxa ṭerita. (23) Wa-yebēlomu 'Iyasus la-'ardā'ihu:

'Amān 'ebelakemu kama bā'el 'em-'eṣub ba'atu mangešta samāyāt. (24) Wa-kā'eba 'ebelakemu: Yeqallel ba'ata gamal 'enta seq^{w}rata marfe' 'em-bā'el bawi'a mangešta 'Egzi'abḥēr.

(25) Wa-sami'omu 'ardā'ihu, 'ankaru ṭeqqa 'enza yebelu:

Mannu 'engā yekel dexina?

(26) Wa-naṣṣaromu 'Iyasus, wa-yebēlomu:

Ba-xaba sab' 'i-yetkahhal-ze, wa-ba-xaba 'Egzi'abḥēr-sa k^{w}ellu yetkahhal.

(27) Wa-'emze 'awše'a Pēṭros, wa-yebēlo:

Nāhu neḥna xadagna k^{w}ello wa-talonāka. Menta 'engā nerakkeb?

(28) Wa-yebēlomu 'Iyasus:

'Amān 'ebelakemu, 'antemu 'ella talokemuni, 'ama dāgem ledat, 'ama yenabber walda 'eg^{w}āla 'emma-ḥeyāw diba manbara sebḥātihu, 'antemu-ni tenabber diba 'ašartu wa-kel'ētu manābert 'enza

---

18. Glt *tamāḥezo* to fall/be in love; to commit adultery. *maḥaz* (pl. *-ān*) lover (m. or f.). *maḥazā* (pl. *-t*) youth, a youth; lover (m. or f.). *māḥzen* illicit affairs.

23. *'em-'eṣub* adv. hardly, scarcely.

24. *seq^{w}rat* aperture, opening. G *saq^{w}ara (yesq^{w}er)* to pierce, dig out/through. Gt *tasaq^{w}ra* pass. *sequr* perforated, excavated, breached. G *raf'a* to sew. Gt *taraf'a* pass. *ref'at* suture, sewing. *rafā'i* tailor. *ref'o* sewn work. *marfe'* (pl. *marāfe't*) needle.

tek^{w}ēnnenu ʻašarta wa-kel'ēta ḥezba 'Esrā'ēl. (29) Wa-k^{w}ellu za-xadaga 'abyāta wa-'axawa wa-'axāta wa-'abā wa-'emma wa-be'sita wa-weluda wa-garāweha ba'enta semeya me'ta mekʻebita yenašše', wa-ḥeywata za-la-ʻālam yewarres. (30) Wa-bezuxān yekawwenu qadamt dexra, wa-daxart qedma.

Chapter XX

42. Ba'enta za-taʻāsaba gabā'ta

(1) 'Esma temassel mangešta samāyāt be'sē bāʻla bēt za-waḍ'a ba-nagh yetʻāsab gabā'ta la-ʻaṣada waynu. (2) Wa-takāhala mesla gabā't ba-ba-dinār la-ʻelat, wa-fannawomu westa ʻaṣada waynu. (3) Wa-waḍi'o gizē šalās saʻāt, re'ya kāle'āna 'enza yeqawwemu westa mešyāṭ ḍeruʻāna. (4) Wa-lomu-ni yebē:

Ḥuru 'antemu-ni westa ʻaṣada wayneya, wa-za-ba-retuʻ 'ehubakemu.

Wa-'emuntu-hi ḥoru. (5) Wa-kāʻeba waḍi'o gizē sessu wa-tasʻu saʻāt, gabra kamāhu kema. (6) Wa-gizē ʻašru wa-'aḥatti waḍi'o rakaba kāle'āna 'enza yeqawwemu, wa-yebēlomu:

Ment 'aqamakemu zeyya k^{w}ello ʻelata ḍeruʻānikemu?

Wa-yebēlewwo:

'Esma 'albo za-taʻāsabana.

(7) Wa-yebēlomu:

Ḥuru 'antemu-ni westa ʻaṣada wayneya, wa-za-ratʻani 'ehubakemu.

(8) Wa-'emza masya, yebē bāʻla ʻaṣada wayn la-maggābihu:

Ṣawweʻomu la-gabā't, wa-habomu ʻasbomu, wa-'axaz qedma 'em-daxart 'eska qadamt.

(9) Wa-maṣ'u 'ella ʻašru wa-'aḥatti saʻāt, wa-naš'u ba-ba dinār. (10) Wa-maṣ'u qadamt, wa-masalomu za-yāfadaffedu naši'a, wa-naš'u ba-ba dinār 'emuntu-hi. (11) Wa-naši'omu, 'ang^{w}arg^{w}aru lāʻlēhu la-bāʻla bēt 'enza yebelu:

---

29. *mekʻebit* n. double, the double amount. *mekʻebita* adv. twofold, doubly. *me'ta mekʻebita* a hundredfold.

XX 1. *gabā'i* (pl. *gabā't*) hireling, wage-worker.

2. Glt *takāhala mesla* to come to an agreement with.

5. *kema* a postpositive particle emphasizing the preceding word: "also, even, too."

(12) 'Ellu daxart 'aḥatta sa'āta taqanyu, wa-'asta'arraykomu meslēna la-'ella ṣorna kebadā wa-lāhbā la-'elat.

(13) Wa-'awši'o, yebēlo la-'aḥadu 'emennēhomu:

Kāle'eya, 'i-gafā'kuka. 'Akko-nu ba-dinār takāhalkuka? (14) Nešā' za-yerakkebaka, wa-ḥur. Faqadku 'ana la-ze daxāri 'ahabo kama laka. (15)'I-yekawwenani-hu 'egbar za-faqadku ba-newāyeya? 'Ayneka-nu ḥamāmi we'etu 'esma 'ana xēr 'ana?

(16) Kamāhu-kē yekawwenu daxart qedma wa-qadamt dexra, 'esma bezuxān 'emuntu ṣewwu'ān, wa-xedāṭān xeruyān.

(17) Wa-'enza ya'arreg 'Iyasus 'Iyarusālēm, naš'omu la-'ašartu wa-kel'ētu 'ardā'ihu 'enta bāḥtitomu, wa-'agḥašomu 'em-fenot, wa-yebēlomu:

(18) Nāhu na'arreg 'Iyarusālēm, wa-ye'exxezewwo la-walda 'eg^{w}āla 'emma-ḥeyāw, wa-yāgabbe'ewwo xaba liqāna kāhenāt wa-ṣaḥaft, wa-yek^{w}ēnnenewwo ba-mot, (19) wa-yemēṭṭewewwo la-ḥezb, wa-yessālaqu lā'lēhu, wa-yeqaššefewwo, wa-yesaqqelewwo, wa-ba-šālest 'elat yetnaššā'.

43. Ba'enta daqiqa Zabedēwos

(20) Wa-'emze maṣ'at xabēhu 'emmomu la-daqiqa Zabedēwos mesla daqiqā, wa-sagadat lotu 'enza tese''el 'em-xabēhu. (21) Wa-yebēlā: Ment tefaqqedi? (22) Wa-tebēlo:

Rassi lita kama yenbaru 'ellu daqiqeya kel'ēhomu 'aḥadu ba-yamāneka wa-'aḥadu ba-ḍagāmeka ba-mangešteka.

(22) Wa-'awše'a 'Iyasus wa-yebē:

'I-tā'ammeru za-tese''elu. Tekelu-ni sateya za-'ana hallawku ṣewā'a 'estay?

Wa-yebēlewwo: Nekel. (23) Wa-yebēlomu:

Ṣewā'eya-sa tesatteyu, wa-nabira ba-yamāneya-sa wa-ba-ḍagāmeya 'akko 'ana za-'ehub, za'enbala la-'ella 'astadālawa lomu 'abuya.

(24) Wa-sami'omu 'ašartu ḥazanu ba'enta kel'ēhomu 'axaw. (25) Wa-ṣawwe'omu 'Iyasus wa-yebēlomu:

Tā'ammeru-nu kama mak^{w}ānentihomu la-'aḥzāb ye'ēzzezewwomu, wa-'abaytomu yeššēllaṭu lā'lēhomu. (26) 'Akko-kē kama-ze za-yekun ba-xabēkemu-sa, bāḥtu za-yefaqqed 'em-westētekemu 'abiya yekun yekunkemu lā'ka; (27) wa-za-hi-yefaqqed 'emennēkemu yekun liqa yekunkemu gabra. (28) Bakama 'i-maṣ'a walda 'eg^{w}āla 'emma-ḥeyāw yetla'akewwo, za'enbala yetla'ak wa-yahab nafso bēzā bezuxān.

44. Ba'enta kel'ē 'ewurān

(29) Wa-'enza yewaḍḍe'u 'em-'Iyāriḥo, talawewwo sab' bezuxān. (30) Wa-nāhu kel'ētu 'ewurān yenabberu ṭeqqā mangad, wa-sami'omu kama 'Iyasus yaxallef, ṣarxu 'enza yebelu:

Tašāhalana 'Egzi'o, walda Dāwit.

(31) Wa-sab'-sa yegēššeṣewwomu kama yārmemu, wa-'a'bayu ṣarixa 'enza yebelu:

Tašāhalana 'Egzi'o, walda Dāwit.

(32) Wa-qoma 'Iyasus, wa-ṣawwe'omu, wa-yebē:

Menta tefaqqedu 'egbar lakemu?

(33) Wa-yebēlewwo:

'Egzi'o, kama yetkašatā 'a'yentina.

(34) Wa-'amḥarewwo la-'Iyasus, wa-lakafomu 'a'yentihomu, wa-ba-gizēhā naṣṣaru wa-talawewwo.

Chapter XXI

45. Ba'enta 'ewāl

(1) Wa-qaribo 'Iyarusālēm, baṣḥa Bēta Fāgē xaba Dabra Zayt. Wa-'emze fannawa 'Iyasus kel'ēta 'em-'ardā'ihu, (2) wa-yebēlomu:

Ḥuru hagara za-qedmēkemu, wa-ye'eta gizē terakkebu 'edegta 'eserta wa-'ewāla meslēhā. Feteḥu wa-'amṣe'u lita. (3) Wa-'emma-bo za-yebēlakemu menta tegabberu, balu, "'Egzi'omu yefaqqedomu," wa-ba-gizēhā yefēnnewomu.

(4) Wa-ze-kona kama yetfaṣṣam ba-nabiy za-tabehla:

(5) Balewwā la-walatta Ṣeyon: Nāhu negušeki yemaṣṣe' xabēki, yawwāh, 'enza yeṣṣē''an diba 'edegt wa-diba 'ewāl 'eg^{w}āla 'edegt.

(6) Wa-ḥawiromu 'ardā'ihu, gabru bakama 'azzazomu 'Iyasus. (7)

---

30. *ṭeqqā/ba-ṭeqqā* prep. near, beside. *mangad* public road, highway; trip, journey, pilgrimage. G *nagada* to make a journey, to travel on business. *negd* travel, trade. *nagd* (pl. *-ān*) a traveler, stranger, guest. *nagādi* traveler, merchant. Cf. *'engedā*.

XXI 2. *'ewāl* young of an animal, esp. the foal of an ass.

'Amṣe'u 'edegta wa-'ewāla, wa-raḥanu 'albāsihomu lā'lēhon, wa-taṣe''ena 'Iyasus. (8) Wa-za-yebazzex ḥezb naḍafu 'albāsihomu westa fenot, wa-kāle'ān-hi yematteru 'a'ṣuqa 'em-westa 'eḍaw wa-yenaḍḍefu westa fenot. (9) Wa-ḥezb-sa 'ella yaḥawweru qedmēhu wa-'ella-hi yetallewu yeṣarrexu 'enza yebelu:

Hosā'nā la-walda Dāwit. Buruk za-yemaṣṣe' ba-sema 'Egzi'abḥēr.
Hosā'nā ba-'aryām.

(10) Wa-bawi'o 'Iyasus 'Iyarusālēm, tahawkat k^wellā hagar 'enza tebel:

Mannu we'etu zentu?

(11) Wa-yebēlu 'aḥzāb:

Ze-we'etu 'Iyasus nabiy za-'em-Nāzerēt za-Galilā.

(12) Wa-bo'a 'Iyasus bēta maqdas, wa-sadada k^wellomu 'ella yešayyeṭu wa-yeššāyaṭu ba-bēta maqdas, wa-gafte'a mā'edātihomu la-mawalleṭān wa-manābertihomu la-'ella yešayyeṭu regba. (13) Wa-yebēlomu:

Ṣeḥuf: bēteya bēta ṣalot yessammay, wa-'antemu-sa terēsseyu ba'ata saraqt.

46. Ba'enta 'ewurān wa-seburān

(14) Wa-maṣ'u xabēhu 'ewurān wa-ḥankāsān ba-bēta maqdas, wa-'aḥyawomu. (15) Wa-'emza re'yu liqāna kāhenāt wa-ṣaḥaft mankera za-gabra, wa-daqiqa-ni 'enza yeṣarrexu ba-bēta maqdas wa-yebelu: "Hosā'nā la-walda Dāwit," 'i-ḥawwazomu. (16) Wa-yebēlewwo:

Tesamme'-nu za-yebelu 'ellu?

Wa-yebēlomu 'Iyasus:

'Ewwa. 'Albo-hu 'ama 'anbabkemu kama 'em-'afa daqiq wa-ḥeḍānāt 'astadālawka sebḥāta?

(17) Wa-xadagomu, wa-waḍ'a 'af'a 'em-hagar Bityāneyā-hā, wa-'aṣlala heyya.

---

7. G *raḥana* to spread (as a saddle), to saddle.

8. G *naḍafa/naṣafa* to spread, lay out. Gt *tanaṣfa* pass. *neṣuf* spread. *manṣaf* anything laid out: rug, covering.

9. *hosā'nā* (Hebrew) Save us! Hosanna!

12. Q *gafte'a* to overturn. Qt *tagafte'a* pass.

15. D *ḥawwaza* to please, delight, be pleasing to. CGt *'astaḥawaza* to be pleased. CDt *'astaḥawwaza* to regard as pleasing, acceptable; to please, delight. CGlt *'astaḥāwaza* idem. *ḥawwez* (pl. *-āt*) pleasure, delight. *ḥawwāz* pleasant, delightful, agreeable.

47. Baʼenta balas ʼenta yabsat

(18) Wa-ṣabiḥo ʼenza yaʻarreg ʼIyasus hagara, rexba. (19) Wa-reʼya ʻeḍa balas ba-mangad, wa-ḥora xabēhā, wa-ʼalbo za-rakaba westētā zaʼenbala q^{w}aṣl bāḥtitu. Wa-yebēlā:

ʼI-yekun ʼenka ferē ʼem-westēteki la-ʻālam.

Wa-yabsat ba-gizēhā yeʼeti balas. (20) Wa-reʼeyomu ʼardāʼihu, ʼankaru wa-yebēlu:

ʼEfo ba-gizēhā yabsat balas?

(21) Wa-ʼawšeʼa ʼIyasus, wa-yebēlomu:

ʼAmān ʼebelakemu, ʼemma bekemu hāymānota wa-ʼi-tenāfequ, ʼakko kema za-balas za-tegabberu, ʻādi la-zentu dabr ʼemma tebelewwo "Tanšeʼ wa-tawaraw westa bāḥr," yetgabbar. (22) Wa-k^{w}ello za-saʼalkemu ba-ṣalot ʼenza taʼammenu tenaššeʼu.

48. Baʼenta ʼella taseʼʼelewwo kāhenāt wa-rabbanāt la-ʼIyasus ba-mabāḥta mannu tegabber zanta

(23) Wa-bawiʼo bēta maqdas, qarbu xabēhu ʼenza yemēhher liqāna kāhenāt wa-malāheqta ḥezb ʼenza yebelu:

Ba-mabāḥta mannu zanta tegabber, wa-mannu wahabaka zanta šelṭāna?

(24) Wa-ʼawšeʼa ʼIyasus wa-yebēlomu:

ʼEssēʼʼalakemu ʼana-hi ʼaḥatta qāla za-ʼemkama nagarkemuni ʼana-hi ʼāyaddeʻakemu ba-ʼayy šelṭān ʼegabber zanta. (25) Ṭemqatu la-Yoḥannes ʼem-ʼaytē weʼetu? ʼEm-samāy-nu wa-mima ʼem-sabʼ-nu?

Wa-xallayu babaynātihomu, wa-yebēlu:

ʼEmma nebē za-ʼem-samāy, yebelana "Ba-ʼefo-kē za-ʼi-ʼamankemewwo?" (26) Wa-ʼemma-hi nebē za-ʼem-sabʼ, nefarrehomu la-ḥezb, ʼesma kama nabiy ba-xabēhomu Yoḥannes.

(27) Wa-ʼawšeʼewwo la-ʼIyasus, wa-yebēlu: ʼI-nāʼammer. Wa-yebēlomu weʼetu-hi:

ʼAna-hi ʼi-yāyaddeʻakemu ba-ʼayy šelṭān zanta ʼegabber.

---

24. CG *ʼaydeʻa* to inform, tell (someone: o.s.). Gt *tayadʻa* pass.

25. *mima* interrogative particle, here introducing the second part of a double question: Is it x or is it y?

49. Ba'enta kel'ē 'axaw messālē

(28) Wa-menta tebelu? Be'si botu kel'ēta weluda 'axawa, wa-yebēlo la-qadāmāwi:

Waldeya, ḥur taqanay yom westa ʻaṣada wayneya.

(29) Wa-'awše'a, wa-yebē "'Enbeya." Wa-'emdexra-ze tanasseḥa, wa-ḥora. (30) Wa-la-kāle'u-ni yebēlo kamāhu, wa-'awše'a wa-yebē: "'Oho, 'egzi'eya." Wa-'i-ḥora. (31) Mannu 'enka 'em-kel'ēhomu za-gabra faqāda 'abuhu?

Wa-yebēlewwo: "Qadāmāwi." Wa-yebēlomu 'Iyasus:

'Amān 'ebelakemu kama maṣabbeḥāweyān wa-zammāweyāt yeqaddemukemu westa mangešta 'Egzi'abḥēr, (32) 'esma maṣ'a xabēkemu Yoḥannes ba-fenota ṣedq, wa-'i-'amankemewwo, wa-maṣabbeḥāweyān-sa wa-zammāweyāt 'amnewwo. Wa-'antemu-sa re'eyakemu-hi, 'i-nassāḥkemu ṭeqqa 'emdexra la-'amin botu.

50. Ba'enta ʻaṣada wayn messālē

(33) Kāle'ta messālē seme'u. Be'si bā'la bēt, wa-takala ʻaṣada wayn, wa-gabra lotu ḍaq^{w}ana, wa-karaya westētu mekyāda, wa-ḥanaṣa māxfada, wa-wahabo la-ḥarast, wa-nagada. (34) Wa-'ama baṣḥa gizē ferēhu, fannawa 'agbertihu xaba ḥarast kama yenše'u ferēhu. (35) Wa-naš'ewwomu ḥarast la-'agbertihu, wa-bo za-zabaṭu, wa-bo za-qatalu, wa-bo za-wagaru. (36) Wa-'emze fannawa kāle'āna 'agberta 'ella yebazzexu 'em-qadamt, wa-kiyāhomu-ni kamāhu rassayewwomu. (37) Wa-dexra fannawa xabēhomu waldo, 'enza yebel:

Yaxafferewwo la-waldeya-sa.

(38) Wa-soba re'yewwo ḥarast la-waldu, yebēlu babaynātihomu:

Nawā ze-we'etu wāres. Ne'u, neqtelo wa-yekunana lana restu.

(39) Wa-naš'ewwo, wa-'awḍe'ewwo 'af'a 'em-ʻaṣada wayn, wa-

---

29. *'enbeya* exclamation: No! I refuse!

30. *'oho* exclamation of assent: Very well, I will (do so).

33. G *ḍaq^{w}ana* to surround with a fence or wall. *ḍaq^{w}an* fence, wall. *māxfad* tower.

34. G *ḥarasa (yeḥres)* to plow. Gt *taḥarsa* pass. *ḥarāsi* (pl. *ḥarast*) plowman, farmer, tenant farmer. *māḥras* (pl. *maḥāres*) plow.

qatalewwo. (40) 'Emkama 'enka maṣ'a 'egzi'a 'aṣada wayn, menta yerēsseyomu la-'ellek^{w}tu ḥarast?

(41) Wa-yebēlewwo:

Ba-ḥešum la-'ekuyān yeqattelomu, wa-wayno-hi yehub la-kāle'ān 'aqabt, la-'ella yehubewwo ferēhu ba-ba gizēhu.

(42) Wa-yebēlomu 'Iyasus:

'Albo-hu 'ama 'anbabkemu westa maṣāḥeft:

'Ebn 'enta mannanewwā nadaqt ye'eti konat westa re'sa mā'zent. 'Em-xaba 'Egzi'abḥēr konat zāti, wa-manker ye'eti la-'a'yentina.

(43) Ba'enta zentu 'ebelakemu kama yethayyad 'em-xabēkemu mangešta 'Egzi'abḥēr, wa-tetwahhab la-ḥezb za-yegabber ferēhā. (44) Wa-za-sa wadqa diba ye'eti 'ebn yetqaṭaqqaṭ, wa-la-za-hi wadqa dibēhu yedammeqo.

(45) Wa-sami'omu liqāna kāhenāt wa-Farisāweyān 'amsālātihu, 'a'maru kama ba'enti'ahomu yebel. (46) Wa-'enza yefaqqedu ye'xazewwo, farhu 'aḥzāba, 'esma kama nabiy we'etu ba-xabēhomu.

Chapter XXII

51. Ba'enta 'ella taṣawwe'u westa kabkāb

(1) Wa-'awše'a 'Iyasus dāgema, wa-nagara ba-messālē 'enza yebel:

(2) Temassel mangešta samāyāt be'sē negša za-gabra kabkāba la-waldu. (3) Wa-fannawa 'agbertihu yeṣawwe'ewwomu la-'ella ta'aššaru westa kabkāb, wa-'i-faqadu yemṣe'u. (4) Wa-dāgema fannawa kāle'āna 'agberta 'enza yebel:

Balewwomu la-'ella 'aššarnāhomu: Nāhu mesāḥeya

---

41. *ba-ḥešum* adv. phrase: vilely, wretchedly, without pity.

42. D *mannana* to reject, repudiate, despise. Dt *tamannana* pass. *mennun* rejected, despised; unsuitable, worthless, vile. *mennānē* repudiation, rejection; worthlessness, wickedness.

44. Q *qaṭqaṭa* to crush, grind up. Qt *taqaṭqaṭa* pass. *qeṭquṭ* crushed, ground. *qeṭqāṭē* vn. crushing, grinding, destruction. G *damaqa* to grind up, crush.

XXII 3. D *'aššara* to call a meeting, to invite. Dt *ta'aššara* pass. *'ašur/'aššur* feast, banquet.

4. G *masḥa* to dine, sup. CG *'amseḥa* caus. *mesāḥ* meal, dinner; banquet, feast. *magze'* (pl. *magāze't*) fattened cattle, fatlings.

'astadālawku, wa-ṭabāḥku magāze'teya wa-'aswāreya, wa-kʷellu delew; ne'u westa kabkābeya.

(5) Wa-'emuntu-sa tahayyayu wa-xalafu. Bo-za-ḥora westa garāhtu, wa-bo za-hora westa tagbāru. (6) Wa-'ella-sa tarfu 'axazu 'agbertihu wa-qatalewwomu, wa-kiyāhu-ni ṣa'alewwo. (7) Wa-tam'e'a neguš, wa-fannawa ḥarrāhu yeqtelewwomu la-'ellektu qatalt; wa-qatalewwomu, wa-hagaromu-ni 'aw'ayu. (8) Wa-'emze yebēlomu la-'agbertihu:

> Ba'āleya-sa delew we'etu, wa-bāḥtu la-'ella 'aššarnāhomu-sa 'i-kafalomu. (9) Ḥuru-kē 'enka westa marāḥebt wa-'anāqeṣ, wa-kʷello za-rakabkemu ṣawwe'u westa kabkāb.

(10) Wa-waḍi'omu 'emuntu 'agbert westa fenāw, 'astagābe'u kʷello za-rakabu 'ekuyāna wa-xērāna, wa-mal'a bēta ba'āl 'em-'ella yeraffequ. (11) Wa-bawi'o neguš yer'ayomu la-'ella yeraffequ, rakaba ba-heyya be'sē za-'i-labsa lebsa mar'ā. (12) Wa-yebēlo:

> Kāle'eya, 'efo bo'ka zeyya za'enbala telbas lebsa mar'ā?

Wa-tafaḍma we'etu. (13) Wa-'emze 'azzaza neguš la-gazā't:

> Ye'serewwo 'edawihu wa-'egarihu wa-yāwḍe'ewwo westa ṣanāfi ṣelmat westa bekāy wa-ḥaqiya senan,

(14) 'esma bezuxan 'emuntu ṣewwu'ān, wa-xedāṭān xeruyān.

52. Ba'enta 'ella tase''elu ba'enta dinār

(15) Wa-'emze ḥoru Farisāweyān wa-tamākaru kama yāsḥetewwo ba-qālu. (16) Wa-fannawu xabēhu 'ardā'ihomu mesla sab'a Hērodes, wa-yebēlewwo:

CQ *'amazge'a* to fatten. *sor* (pl. *'aswār*) ox, steer.

5. *tagbār* business, activity, task, job.

8. G *kafala (yekfel)* to divide (up); to apportion, distribute; to make someone a participant/partaker in; impersonally: to be one's portion (*'i-kafalomu* it was not their portion = they were not worthy of it). Gt *takafla* pass.; to divide up among (oneselves); to hesitate, be of divided mind. *keful* divided. *kefl* (pl. *-āt*) part, portion, share; section, category; chapter. *makfalt* part, portion, share.

12. G *faḍama* = D *faḍḍama* to stop up, obstruct, make speechless. Gt *tafaḍma* = Dt *tafaḍḍama* pass.; to be speechless.

13. G *gaz'a* to serve at a feast. *gez'/gaz'* feast, banquet. *gazzā'* = *gazā'i* (pl. *gazā't*) waiter, attendant (at feast).

Liq, nā'ammer kama rāte' 'anta wa-ba-ṣedq temēhher fenota 'Egzi'abḥēr, wa-'i-taḥasseb manna-hi, wa-'i-tādallu la-gaṣṣa sab'. (17) Negerana-kē 'enka za-yeratte'aka yekawwen-hu wehiba ṣabāḥta dinār la-neguš, wa-mima 'i-yekawwen-nu.

(18) Wa-'a'maromu 'Iyasus 'ekayomu, wa-yebēlomu:

Menta tāmēkkeruni, madlewān? (19) 'Ar'eyuni 'alāda dinār.

Wa-'amṣe'u lotu dinara. (20) Wa-yebēlomu 'Iyasus:

Za-mannu zentu malke'u wa-maṣḥafu?

(21) Wa-yebēlewwo: Za-nagāši. Wa-yebēlomu:

Habu za-nagāši la-nagāši, wa-za-'Egzi'abḥēr la-'Egzi'abḥēr.

(22) Wa-sami'omu, 'ankaru wa-xadagewwo wa-xalafu.

53. Ba'enta Saduqāweyān 'ella yebelu 'albo tenšā'ē mewutān

(23) Wa-ba-ye'eti 'elat maṣ'u xabēhu Saduqāweyān 'ella yebelu 'albo tenšā'ē mewutān. Wa-tase''elewwo 'enza yebelu:

Liq, Musē yebē: 'Emma-bo za-mota 'exuhu 'enza 'albo weluda, yāwseb be'sita 'exuhu wa-yāqem weluda la-'exuhu. (25) Hallawu 'enka xabēna sab'atu 'axaw, wa-za-yelehheq 'awsaba wa-mota, wa-'esma 'albo weluda, xadaga be'sito la-'exuhu. (26) Wa-kamāhu kāle'u-ni wa-šālesu-hi 'eska sab'atihomu. (27) Wa-dexra k^{w}ellomu motat ye'eti be'sit. (28) 'Ama yetnašše'u 'enka mewutān, la-mannu 'em-sab'atihomu tekawwen be'sita, 'esma k^{w}ellomu 'awsabewwā?

(29) Wa-'awše'a 'Iyasus, wa-yebēlomu:

Teseḥḥetu ba-'i-ya'mero maṣāḥeft wa-'i-xayla 'Egzi'abḥēr. (30) 'Ama-sa yaḥayyewu mewutān, 'i-yāwassebu wa-'i-yetwāsabu, 'allā kama malā'ekta 'Egzi'abḥēr ba-samāyāt 'emuntu. (31) Wa-ba'enta tenšā'ē mewutān-sa, 'i-yanbabkemu-hu za-tabehla lakemu 'em-xaba 'Egzi'abḥēr, za-yebē:

> 'Ana 'Egzi'abḥēr, 'amlāka 'Abrehām wa-'amlāka Yesḥaq wa-'amlāka Yā'qob.

---

16. lit.: "you regard/consider no one" = "You take no account of person, i.e. are impartial."

19. *'alād* coin.

20. G *lak'a* to impress (a seal), to inscribe. Gt *talak'a* pass.; to be affixed. *leku'* impressed, inscribed, affixed. *malke'* seal impression, likeness, figure.

'Amlāka ḥeyāwān-kē we'etu, wa-'akko 'amlāka mewutān. (33) Wa-sami'omu ḥezb, 'ankaru mehiroto.

54. Ba'enta ṣaḥāfi za-tase''elo 'ayy te'zāz ya'abbi

(34) Wa-sami'omu Farisāweyān kama faḍamomu la-Saduqāweyān, tagābe'u xabēhu. (35) Wa-tase''elo 'aḥadu 'em-westētomu ṣaḥāfē hagar 'enza yāmēkkero:

Liq, 'ayy-nu te'zāz ya'abbi ba-westa 'orit?

(37) Wa-yebēlo 'Iyasus:

'Afqer 'Egzi'abḥēr 'amlākaka ba-k^wellu lebbeka wa-ba-k^wellu nafseka wa-ba-k^wellu xayleka wa-ba-k^wellu xellinnāka. (38) Zāti te'zāz 'abāy wa-qadāmit. (39) Wa-kāle'tā-hi temasselā: 'Afqer biṣaka kama nafseka. (40) Ba-'ellāntu kel'ē te'zāz tasaqlu k^wellu 'orit wa-nabiyāt.

55. Ba'enta Farisāweyān zakama tase''elomu Kerestos walda mannu we'etu Kerestos

(41) Wa-'enza gubu'ān Farisāweyān, tase''elomu 'Iyasus, (42) 'enza yebel:

Menta tebelu ba'enta Kerestos? Walda mannu we'etu?

Wa-yebēlewwo: Za-Dāwit. (43) Wa-yebēlomu 'Iyasus:

'Efo 'enka lalihu Dāwit ba-manfas qeddus yebē:

(44) Yebēlo 'egzi' la-'egzi'eya: Nebar ba-yamāneya 'eska 'āgabbe'omu la-ṣalā'teka tāḥta makayyada 'egarika.

(45) Za-lalihu 'enka Dāwit 'egzi'eya yebēlo, 'efo 'enka yekawweno waldo?

(46) Wa-'albo za-kehla 'awše'oto qāla, wa-'albo za-ṭab'a 'em-ye'eti 'elat tase''eloto menta-ni.

Chapter XXIII

(1) Wa-'emze nagaromu 'Iyasus la-ḥezb wa-la-'ardā'ihu 'enza yebel:

(2) Diba manbara Musē nabaru ṣaḥaft wa-Farisāweyān. K^wello za-maharukemu gebaru wa-'eqabu. (3) Wa-bakama yegabberu-sa 'i-tegbaru, 'esma za-yemēhheru 'i-yegabberu. (4) Wa-ya'asseru ṣora 'abiya wa-kebuda, wa-yāsakkemewwo la-sab' diba matākeftu,

---

XXIII 4. G *sakama* to carry on the shoulders. CG *'askama* caus. Gt *tasakma* = G. *matkaf(t)* (pl. *matākeft*) shoulder.

wa-lalihomu-sa ’i-yelakkefewwo ba-’aṣbā‘tomu. (5) Wa-k^{w}ello megbāromu za-yegabberu la-‘ayna sab’ yegabberu, wa-yā‘abbeyu ’azfārihomu, (6) wa-yāfaqqeru re’sa merfāqāt ba-westa mesāḥāt, wa-nabira feṣṣuma ba-westa ’a‘wādāt, (7) wa-ta’āmex^{w}a ba-westa mešyāṭāt, wa-yebelomu sab’ "Rabbi." (8) ’Antemu-sa-kē ’i-tessamayu rabbi, ’esma ’aḥadu we’etu mamehherekemu, wa-’antemu-sa ’axaw k^{w}ellekemu. (9) Wa-’i-terasseyu ’aba ba-diba medr, ’esma ’aḥadu we’etu ’abukemu samāyāwi. (10) Wa-’i-tessamayu mamehherāna, ’esma ’aḥadu mamehherekemu we’etu Kerestos. (11) Wa-bāḥtu za-yelehheqakemu yekunkemu lā’ka, (12) ’esma za-’a‘baya re’so yaxasser, wa-za-’atḥata re’so yekabber.

56. Ba’enta ’alē-lomu la-ṣaḥaft wa-Farisāweyān

(13) ’Alē lakemu ṣaḥaft wa-Farisāweyān, madlewān, ’esma teballe‘u ’abyāta maballatāt wa-tāmakanneyu wa-tābazzexu ṣalota. Ba’enta zantu terakkebu fadfāda k^{w}ennanē. ’Alē lakemu ṣaḥaft wa-Farisāweyān, madlewān, ’esma ta‘aṣṣewu mangešta samāyāt westa gaṣṣu la-sab’. ’Antemu-hi ’i-tebawwe’u wa-la-’ella-hi yebawwe’u tekalle’ewwomu bawi’a. (15) ’Alē lakemu ṣaḥaft wa-Farisāweyān, madlewān, ’esma ta‘awwedu bāḥra wa-yabsa kama tāṭmequ ’aḥada falāsē. Wa-taṭamiqo, terēsseyewwo kā‘batakemu la-Gahānnam. (16) ’Alē lakemu ṣaḥaft wa-Farisāweyān, ’amreḥta ‘ewurān, ’ella tebelu: Za-maḥala ba-bēta maqdas dāxen we’etu, wa-za-sa maḥala ba-warqa bēta maqdas yegēgi. (17) ’Abdān wa-‘ewurān. ’Ayy ya‘abbi: warq-nu wa-mima bēta maqdas-nu za-yeqēddeso la-warq? (18) Wa-za-maḥala ba-mašwā‘t dāxen tebelu, wa-za-sa maḥala ṣenḥāḥo yegēgi tebelu. (19) ’Abdān wa-‘ewurān. ’Ayy ya‘abbi: ṣenḥāḥ-nu wa-mima mešwā‘ za-yeqēddeso la-we’etu ṣenḥāḥ? (20) Za-kē maḥala ba-mešwā‘ maḥala botu wa-maḥala ba-k^{w}ellu za-dibēhu. (21) Wa-za-hi maḥala ba-bēta maqdas

---

XXIII 4. G *sakama* to carry on the shoulders. CG *’askama* caus. Gt *tasakma* = G. *matkaf(t)* (pl. *matākeft*) shoulder.

13. *maballat* (pl. *-āt*) widow; nun. CQ *’amaknaya* to pretend, make excuses. *mekneyāt* (false) excuse, pretext; reason, cause.

15. *terēsseyewwo kā‘batakemu la-Gahānnam* You make him your double for Gehenna (i.e., twice as liable to Gehenna as yourselves).

18. *ṣenḥāḥ* sacrifice, offering.

maḥala botu wa-ba-za-yenabber westētu. (22) Wa-za-hi maḥala samāya maḥala manbara 'Egzi'abhēr wa-ba-za-yenabber dibēhu. (23) 'Alē lakemu ṣaḥaft wa-Farisāweyān, madlewān, 'ella tābawwe'u ʿăšerāta 'edēhu la-'azāb wa-la-selan wa-la-kamin, wa-xadaggemu za-yaʿabbi te'zāzāta 'orit: ṣedqa, wa-meṣwāta, wa-hāymānota. Ze-ni maftew tegbaru, wa-kiyāhu-ni 'i-texdegu. (24) 'Amreḥta ʿewurān, 'ella ṣāḍota tenaṭṭefu wa-gamala-sa tewexxeṭu. (25) 'Alē lakemu ṣaḥaft wa-Farisāweyān, madlewān, 'ella taxaḍḍebu ṣewāʿa wa-ṣāḥla 'enta 'af'ahu, wa-wesṭu-sa melu' hayda wa-ʿammaḍā wa-teʿgelta. (26) Farisāwi ʿewur, qedma xeḍebo la-ṣewāʿ wa-la-ṣāḥl 'enta wesṭu, kama yekun neṣuḥa 'enta 'af'ahu-ni. (27) 'Alē lakemu ṣaḥaft wa-Farisāweyān, madlewān, 'ella temasselu maqābera gebsusāna, 'ella 'enta 'af'ahomu yāstare''eyu šannāyāna, wa-'enta wesṭomu-sa melu'āna 'aʿṣemta wa-'abdenta wa-k^wello rek^wsa. (28) Kamāhu-kē 'antemu-ni 'enta 'af'akemu teṣṣēddaqu la-ʿayna sab', wa-'enta wesṭekemu-sa melu'ān 'antemu ʿammaḍā wa-hayda wa-'adlewo. (29) 'Alē lakemu ṣaḥaft wa-Farisāweyān, madlewān, 'ella tenaddequ maqāberihomu la-nabiyāt, wa-tāstašāneyu zexromu la-ṣādeqān, (30) wa-tebelu:

> Soba-sa hallawna ba-mawāʿela 'abawina, 'emma 'i-xabarna meslēhomu neqtel nabiyāta.

(30) Nāhu-kē lalikemu ta'ammenu kama daqiqomu 'antemu la-qatalta nabiyāt. (32) 'Antemu-hi faṣṣemu masfarta 'abawikemu. (33) 'Afʿot, tewledda 'arāwita medr, 'efo tekelu 'amšeṭo 'em-k^wennanē Gahānnam? (34) Ba'enta-ze nāhu 'ana 'efēnnu xabēkemu nabiyāta wa-ṭababta wa-ṣaḥafta, wa-teqattelu ba-westētomu, wa-tesaqqelu, wa-teqaššefu 'em-westētomu ba-mak^{w}ārebtihomu, wa-tesaddu 'em-hagar westa hagar, (35) kama yebṣāḥ lāʿlēkemu dama

---

23. *ʿăšerāta 'ed* a tithe. *'azāb/'azab/'azob* hyssop, mint. *selan* dill. *kamin* cummin.

24. *ṣāḍot/ṣāṣot* gnat, flea. G *naṭfa* to strain out. *neṭuf* strained, pure. *manṭaft* strainer, sieve. G *wexṭa/waxaṭa (yaxaṭ)* to swallow.

27. *gebses* gypsum, plaster. *gebsus* plastered. *ʿaḍm* (pl. *'aʿḍemt*) bone.

33. *'afʿot* vipers.

k^wellu ṣādeqān za-take‘wa diba medr ’em-dama ’Abēl ṣādeq ’eska dama Zakāreyās walda Barākeyu, za-qatalkemu ba-mā’kala bēta maqdas. (36) ’Amān ’ebelakemu: Yebaṣṣehā la-zāti tewledd ze-k^wellu. (37) ’Iyarusālēm, ’Iyarusālēm, ’enta teqattelomu la-nabiyāt wa-’enta tewēggeromu la-ḥawāreyāt la-’ella tafannawu xabēhā, mi-maṭana faqadku ’āstagābe’omu la-weludeki kama ’enta tāstagābe’ doreho ’afrextihā tāḥta kenafihā, wa-’abaykemu. (38) Nāhu yetxaddag lakemu bētekemu badwa. (39) ’Amān ’ebelakemu: ’I-terē’’eyuni ’em-ye’zē ’eska soba tebelu: Buruk za-yemaṣṣe’ ba-sema ’Egzi’abḥēr.

Chapter XXIV

57. Ba’enta xelqata ‘ālam

(1) Wa-waḍi’o ’Iyasus ’em-bēta maqdas, ḥora, wa-qarbu ’ardā’ihu, wa-’ar’ayewwo ḥenṣāhu la-mek^{w}rāb. (2) Wa-’awše’a, wa-yebēlomu:

Terē’’eyu-nu zanta k^wello? ’Amān ’ebelakemu, ’i-yetxaddag zeyya ’ebn diba ’ebn za-’i-yetnaššat.

(3) Wa-’enza yenabber ba-Dabra Zayt, qarbu ’ardā’ihu xabēhu ’enza yebelu ’enta bāḥtitomu:

Negerana mā’zē yekawwen-ze, wa-ment te’mertu la-meṣ’ateka wa-la-xelqata ‘ālam.

(4) Wa-’awše’a ’Iyasus wa-yebēlomu:

‘Uqu ’albo za-yāsḥetkemu, (5) ’esma bezuxān yemaṣṣe’u ba-sema zi’aya ’enza yebelu, "’Ana we’etu masiḥ," wa-bezuxāna yāseḥḥetu. (6) Wa-hallawakemu tesme‘u qatla wa-demḍa ḍabā’it. ‘Uqu ’i-tedangeḍu, ’esma gebr yekawwen kamāhu, wa-’akko ba-gizēhā za-yaxalleq. (7) Wa-yetnaššā’ ḥezb diba ḥezb wa-nagašt diba nagašt, wa-yemaṣṣe’ raxāb wa-bedbed wa-hakak ba-ba baḥāwertihu. (8) Wa-ze-k^wellu qadāmi māḥmam. (9) ’Amēhā yemēṭṭewukemu la-mendābē, wa-yeqaššefukemu wa-yeqattelukemu wa-yeṣalle’ukemu k^wellu ḥezb ba’enta semeya. (10) Wa-’amēhā ya‘allewu bezuxān,

---

37. *doreho* (pl. *dawāreh*) m.f. chicken, hen, rooster. *’afrext/’afxert* (coll.) chicks.

XXIV 2. G *našata (yenšet)* to destroy, overturn. Gt *tanašta* pass. *nešut* destroyed. *neštat* destruction.

6. *ḍabā’it/ṣabā’it* battle, fighting.

7. *hakak* tumult, chaos.

wa-yeṣalle'u babaynātihomu wa-yetqātalu. (11) Wa-bezuxān ḥassāweyāna nabiyāt yemaṣṣe'u, wa-bezuxāna yāseḥḥetu. (12) Wa-'em-bezxā la-'ekay tesēkk^{w}es feqra bezuxān. (13) Wa-za-sa 'azlafa te'gešto we'etu yedexxen. (14) Wa-yessabbak ze-wangēla mangešt westa k^{w}ellu 'ālam kama yekun sem'a lā'la k^{w}ellu 'aḥzāb, wa-ye'eta 'amira yebaṣṣeḥ xelqat. (15) Wa-'ama re'ikemu xasāro la-musenā za-tabehla ba-Dāne'ēl nabiy 'enza yeqawwem westa makān qeddus (za-yānabbeb yelabbu), (16) 'amēhā 'ella westa Yehudā yeg^{w}ayyu westa 'adbār, (17) wa-za-westa nāḥs 'i-yerad yenšā' za-westa bētu, (18) wa-za-westa garāht 'i-yetmayaṭ dexrēhu yenšā' lebso. (19) 'Alē lon bāḥtu la-ḍenusāt wa-la-'ella yaḥaḍḍenā ba-we'etu mawā'el. (20) Wa-ṣalleyu bāḥtu kama 'i-yekun g^{w}eyyākemu ba-keramt wa-ba-sanbat, (21) 'esma yekawwen ye'eta 'amira 'abiy ḥemām wa-mendābē za-'i-kona 'em-qedma 'ālam wa-'eska yom, wa-'i-yekawwen-hi. (22) Wa-soba 'akko-hu za-xaṣarā 'emāntu mawā'el, 'albo za-'em-dexna mannu-hi za-šegā, wa-bāḥtu ba'enta xeruyān yaxaṣṣerā 'emāntu mawā'el. (23) 'Amēhā 'emma-bo za-yebēlakemu "Nawā zeyya hallo Kerestos, wa-nawā kaḥak," 'i-te'manu, (24) 'esma yemaṣṣe'u ḥassāweyāna masiḥ wa-ḥassāweyāna nabiyāt, wa-yegabberu ta'āmera 'abayta wa-mankera la-'asḥeto, soba-sa yetkahhalomu, la-xeruyān-hi. (25) Nāhu qadamku nagirotakemu. (26) 'Emma-kē yebēlukemu "Nawā gadāma hallo," 'i-teḍā'u; wa-"Nawā westa 'abyāt," 'i-te'manu, (27) 'esma kama 'enta mabraq yewaḍḍe' 'em-ṣebāḥ, wa-yāstare''i 'eska 'arab, kamāhu meṣ'atu la-walda 'eg^{w}āla 'emma-ḥeyāw. (28) Xaba hallawa gadalā, heyya yetgābe'u 'ansert. (29) Wa-ba-gizēhā 'em-dexra ḥemāmon la-'emāntu mawā'el, ḍaḥāy-ni yeṣallem, wa-warx-ni 'i-yehub berhāno, wa-kawākebt yewaddequ 'em-samāy, wa-yānqalaqqel xayla samāyāt. (30) Wa-ye'eta 'amira yāstare''i ta'āmerihu la-walda 'eg^{w}āla 'emma-ḥeyāw ba-samāy. 'Amēhā yebakkeyu k^{w}ellu 'aḥzāba medr, wa-yerē''eyewwo la-walda 'eg^{w}āla 'emma-ḥeyāw ba-dammanāta samāy yemaṣṣe' mesla xayl wa-sebḥāt bezux. (31) Wa-yefēnnewomu la-malā'ektihu mesla qāla qarn

---

12. D *sakk^{w}asa* to cease, come to an end, die out.

28. *gadalā* corpse(s), cadaver(s).

29. CQ *'anqalqala* intrans.: to move, shake, quake; trans.: to move, shake, agitate. *naqalqāl* motion, shaking, agitation.

‘abiy, wa-yāstagābe’omu la-xeruyānihu ’em-’arbā‘tu makān ’em-’aṣnāfa samāy ’eska ’aṣnāfa samāy. (32) Wa-’em-balas ’a’meru ’amsālihu: ’emkama kona ‘aṣqā dekuma wa-q^{w}aṣlā lamlama, tā’ammeru kama qarba mā’raru. (33) Kamāhu-kē ’antemu-hi ’emkama re’ikemu zanta k^{w}ello, ’a’meru kama qarba wa-hallo xaba xoxt. (34) ’Amān ’ebelakemu kama ’i-taxallef zā-tewledd ’eska ze-k^{w}ellu yetgabbar. (35) Samāy wa-medr yaxallef wa-qāleya-sa ’i-yaxallef.

58. Ba’enta sa‘āt wa-‘elat

(36) Wa-ba’enta ye’eti-sa ‘elat wa-ye’eti sa‘āt ’albo za-yā’ammerā, wa-’i-malā’ekta samāy wa-’i-wald za’enbala ’ab bāḥtitu. (37) Wa-bakama kona ba-mawā‘ela Nox kamāhu yekawwen meṣ’atu la-walda ’eg^{w}āla ’emma-ḥeyāw. (38) Bakama ye’eta ’amira ’em-qedma ’ayx yeballe‘u wa-yesatteyu wa-yāwassebu wa-yetwāsabu, ’eska ’ama bo’a Nox westa tābot, (39) wa-’i-ya’maru ’eska soba maṣ’a māya ’axy wa-’aṭfe’a k^{w}ello, kamāhu-kē yekawwen meṣ’atu la-walda ’eg^{w}āla ’emma-ḥeyāw. (40) ’Amēhā kel’ē yehēllewu westa garāht: ’aḥada yenašše’u wa-kāle’o yaxaddegu. (41) Wa-kel’ēti yaḥarreṣā ba-’aḥadu māḥraṣ: ’aḥatta yenašše’u wa-kāle’tā yaxaddegu. Wa-kel’ē yesakkebu westa ’aḥadu ‘arāt: ’aḥada yenašše’u wa-’aḥada yaxaddegu. (42) Tegehu ’enka, ’esma ’i-tā’ammeru ba-’ayy sa‘āt yemaṣṣe’ ’egzi’ekemu. (43) Wa-zanta bāḥtu ’a’meru: soba yā’ammer-hu bā‘la bēt gizē yemaṣṣe’ sarāqi, ’em-taghā wa-’em-’i-xadaga yetkaray bētu. (44) Ba’enta-ze ’antemu-hi delewānikemu hallewu, ’esma ba-gizē ’i-tā’ammeru yemaṣṣe’ walda ’eg^{w}āla ’emma-ḥeyāw. (45) Mannu ’engā gabr mā’man wa-ṭabib za-yešayyemo ’egzi’u westa bētu kama yahabomu sisita ba-gizēhu? (46) Beḍu‘ we’etu gabr za-maṣi’o ’egzi’u yerakkebo ’enza zanta yegabber. (47) ’Amān ’ebelakemu kama diba k^{w}ellu ṭeritu yešayyemo. (48) Wa-’emma-sa yebē we’etu gabr ’ekuy ba-lebbu, "Yeg^{w}anaddi ’atiwa ’egzi’eya," (49) wa-yezabbeṭ ’abyāṣihu, wa-yeballe‘ wa-yesatti mesla sakart, (50) wa-yemaṣṣe’ ’egzi’u la-we’etu gabr ba-‘elat

---

49. G *sakra (yesker, yeskar)* to be intoxicated. CG *’askara* caus. *sekur* inebriated, drunk. *sakār* intoxicating drink; intoxication. *sekrat* intoxication. *sakāri* (pl. *sakart*) drunkard.

'i-taḥazzaba wa-ba-gizē 'i-y̓a'mara, (51) wa-yek^{W}ēnneno wa-yemattero wa-yāgabbe' makfalto mesla madlewān xaba bekāy wa-ḥaqiya senan.

Chapter XXV

59. Ba'enta 'as̆ru danāgel

(1) 'Amēhā temassel mangešta samāyāt 'as̆ru danāgela 'ella nas̆'ā maxātewihon wa-waḍ'ā westa qabbalā mar'āwi. (2) Wa-xams 'em-westēton 'abdāt 'emāntu, wa-xams ṭabābāt. (3) Wa-'abdāt-sa nas̆i'on maxātewihon 'i-nas̆'ā qeb'a meslēhon, (4) wa-ṭabābāt-sa nas̆'ā qeb'a ba-gamā'eyehon mesla maxātewihon. (5) Wa-g^{W}andeyo mar'āwi daqqasā k^{W}ellon wa-nomā. (6) Wa-mā'kala lēlit wewwe'ā kona:

Nāhu mar'āwi maṣ'a. Ḍā'u westa qabbalāhu.

(7) Wa-'emze tans̆e'ā 'elleku danāgel k^{W}ellon, wa-'as̆annayā maxātewihon. (8) Wa-'elleku 'abdāt yebēlāhon la-ṭabābāt:

Habāna 'em-qeb'eken, 'esma maxātewina ṭaf'ā.

(9) Wa-'aws̆e'āhon ṭabābāt 'enza yebelā:

'Emma-bo, kama 'i-ya'akkelana lana wa-laken. Ḥurā xabēhomu la-'ella yes̆ayyeṭu wa-tas̆āyaṭā laken.

(10) Wa-ḥawiron yes̆s̆āyaṭā, baṣ̈ḥa mar'āwi, wa-bo'ā meslēhu 'elleku delewāt westa kabkāb, wa-ta'aṣwa xoxt. (11) Wa-dexra maṣ'ā 'ellektu-hi danāgel, wa-yebēlā: 'Egzi'o, 'egzi'o, 'arxewana. (12) Wa-'aws̆e'on, wa-yebē:

'Amān 'ebelaken kama 'i-y̓ā'ammeraken.

(13) Tegehu-kē, 'esma 'i-tā'ammeru 'elata wa-sa'āta.

60. Ba'enta 'ella nas̆'u makāleya berur

(14) 'Esma kama be'si za-yenagged, wa-ṣawwe'a 'agbertihu,

---

50. G *ḥazaba* to think, believe, suppose. Gt *taḥazba* = Dt *taḥazzaba* = G; also: to expect; to fear, avoid; to care, be concerned. *teḥzebt* opinion, belief, expectation, fear.

XXV 1. *qabalā/qabbalā* a meeting, encounter; *westa qabbalā* prep. phrase: out to meet.

4. *gem'ē* (pl. *gamā'ey*) flask, container for oil.

6. D *wawwe'a* to shout. *wewwe'ā* a shout, cry.

9. *'emma-bo kama* perhaps.

wa-wahabomu newāyo yetgabbaru. (15) Wa-bo la-za wahabo xamesta maklita, wa-bo la-za kel’ē, wa-bo la-za ’aḥada: la-la ’aḥadu bakama yekelu. Wa-nagada ba-gizēhā. (16) Wa-ḥora zeku za-xamsa maklita naš’a, wa-tagabbara bontu, wa-rabḥa kāle’ta xamsa maklita. (17) Wa-kamāhu za-hi kel’ēta rabḥa kāle’ta kel’ēta. (18) Wa-za-’aḥatta-sa naš’a xalafa wa-karaya medra wa-xab’a warqa ’egzi’u. (19) Wa-’emdexra bezux mawā‘el ’atawa ’egzi’omu la-’elleku ’agbert, wa-taḥāsaba meslēhomu. (20) Wa-qarba za-xamsa makāleya naš’a, wa-’amṣe’a kāle’ta xamsa makāleya ’enza yebel:

> ’Egzi’o, xamsa makāleya wahabkani, wa-nāhu xamsa kāle’ta rabāḥku.

(21) Wa-yebēlo ’egzi’u:

> ’O-gabr xēr wa-me’man. Ba-ḥedāṭ konka me’mana. Westa bezux ’ešayyemaka. Bā’ westa tefšeḥta ’egzi’eka.

(22) Wa-maṣ’a za-kel’ēta-ni maklita naš’a, wa-yebē:

> ’Egzi’o, ’akko-hu kel’ēta makāleya wahabkani? Nāhu kel’ēta kāle’ta makāleya ’ella rabāḥku.

(23) Wa-yebēlo ’egzi’u:

> ’O-gabr xēr wa-me’man. Ba-ḥedāṭ konka me’mana. Westa bezux ’ešayyemaka. Bā’ westa feššeḥāhu la-’egzi’eka.

(24) Wa-maṣ’a za-’aḥatta-ni maklita naš’a, wa-yebē:

> ’Egzi’o, ’ā’ammeraka kama deruk be’si ’anta. Ta’arrer xaba ’i-zarā‘ka, wa-tāstagābe’ ’em-xaba ’i-zarawka. (25) Wa-fariheya ḥorku wa-xabā’ku maklitaka westa medr. Nāhu ’enka makliteka.

(26) Wa-’awše’o ’egzi’u, wa-yebēlo:

> ’Ekuy gabr wa-hakkāy. Tā’ammerani kama ’a’arrer xaba ’i-zarā‘ku wa-’āstgābe’ ’em-xaba ’i-zarawku. (27) ’Em-našā’ka warqeya, wa-’em-’agbā’ka westa mā’ed, wa-maṣi’eya ’em-’astagabbarkewwo laliya ba-redē. (28) Neše’u ’em-xabēhu maklita, wa-habewwo la-za-botu ‘ašarta maklita.

---

14. Note Dt *tagabbara* in the sense "to invest," and CDt (vs. 27 below) "to recover one's investment."

24. *deruk* harsh, savage.

27. *redē* interest (financial). Gt *taradya* to lend at interest, to receive interest. Glt *tarādaya* idem.

(29) ’Esma la-k^{w}ellu la-za-bo yehubewwo wa-yewēssekewwo, wa-la-za-sa ’albo ’ella-hi-bo yahayyedewwo. (30) Wa-la-gabr-sa ’ekuy ’awḍe’ewwo westa ṣanāfi ṣelmat xaba bekāy wa-ḥaqiya senan.

61. Ba’enta meṣ’atu la-Kerestos

(31) Wa-’ama yemaṣṣe’ walda ’eg^{w}āla ’emma-ḥeyāw ba-sebḥātihu, wa-k^{w}ellomu malā’ektihu meslēhu, ’amēhā yenabber westa manbara sebḥātihu. (32) Wa-yetgābe’u k^{w}ellomu ’aḥzāb qedmēhu, wa-yefalleṭomu za-za zi’ahomu kama nolāwi yefalleṭ ’abāge‘a ’em-’aṭāli. (33) Wa-yāqawwem ’abāge‘a ba-yamān wa-’aṭālē ba-ḍagām.
(34) ’Amēhā yebel neguš la-’ella ba-yamān:

Ne‘u burukānihu la-’abuya. Terasu mangešta za-’astadālawa lakemu ’em-qedma ‘ālam. ’Esma rexebku wa-’ablā‘kemuni, ṣamā’ku wa-’astaykemuni, wa-nagda konku wa-tawakafkemuni. (36) ‘Araqqu wa-’albaskemuni, dawayku wa-ḥawwaṣkemuni, tamoqāḥku wa-nababkemuni.

(37) ’Amēhā yāwašše’u ṣādeqān, wa-yebelu:

’Egzi’o, mā’zē re’ināka rexubaka wa-’ablā‘nāka, wa-ṣemu’aka wa-’astaynāka? (38) Wa-mā’zē re’ināka ’engedāka wa-tawakafnāka, wa-‘erāqaka wa-’albasnāka? (39) Wa-dewuyaka-ni wa-ḥawwaṣnāka, wa-muquḥaka wa-nababnāka?

(40) Wa-yāwašše’ neguš, wa-yebelomu:

’Amān ’ebelakemu: k^{w}ello za-gabarkemu la-’aḥadu ’em-’ellu ne’usān ’axaweya ’ella ya’ammenu beya, lita gabarkemu.

(41) Wa-’emze yebelomu la-’ella ba-ḍagām:

Ḥuru regumān westa ’essāt za-la-‘ālam za-delew la-sayṭān wa-la-malā’ektihu. (42) ’Esma rexebku wa-’i-y̓ablā‘kemuni, ṣamā’ku wa-’i-y̓astaykemuni, (43) wa-nagda konku wa-’i-tawakafkemuni, ‘araqqu wa-’i-y̓albaskemuni, dawayku wa-’i-ḥawwaṣkemuni, tamoqāḥku wa-’i-nababkemuni.

(44) ’Amēhā yāwašše’u ’ella ba-ḍagām ’enza yebelu:

’Egzi’o, mā’zē re’ināka rexubaka wa-ṣemu’aka wa-’engedāka wa-‘erāqaka wa-dewuyaka wa-tamoqiḥaka wa-’i-tale’eknāka?

(45) Wa-’emze yāwašše’omu neguš ’enza yebel:

---

32. *ṭali* (f. -*t*; pl. *’aṭāli*) goat.

'Amān 'ebelakemu: za-'i-gabarkemu la-'aḥadu 'em-'ellu ne'usān, lita 'i-gabarkemu.

(46) Wa-yaḥawweru 'ella-hi westa k^wennanē za-la-'ālam, wa-ṣādeqān-sa westa ḥeywat za-la-'ālam.

Chapter XXVI

(1) Wa-kona 'emza faṣṣama 'Iyasus zanta k^wello nagara, yebēlomu la-'ardā'ihu:

(2) Tā'ammeru kama 'eska kel'ē mawā'el yekawwen Fāsik, wa-ye'exxezewwo la-walda 'eg^{w}āla 'emma-ḥeyāw wa-yesaqqelewwo.

(3) Wa-'emze tagābe'u liqāna kāhenāt wa-liqānāta ḥezb westa 'aṣada liqa kāhenāt za-semu Qayāfā, (4) wa-tamākaru kama 'Iyasus-hā ba-ḥebl ya'axazewwo wa-yeqtelewwo. (5) Wa-yebēlu: Bāḥtu 'akko-kē ba-ba'āl, kama hakaka 'i-yekun westa ḥezb.

62. Ba'enta 'enta qab'ato la-'Egzi'ena 'efrata

(6) Wa-baṣiḥo 'Iyasus Bitānyā bēta Sem'on za-lamṣ, (7) maṣ'at xabēhu be'sit 'enza bāti beralē za-melu' 'efrata westētu za-bezux šēṭu, wa-soṭat diba re'su la-'Iyasus 'enza yeraffeq. (8) Wa-re'eyomu 'ardā'ihu, tame''u wa-yebēlu:

La-ment-nu maṭana-ze 'ahg^{w}alat? (9) Za-'em-tašayṭa ba-bezux wa-yahabewwo meṣwāta la-naddāyān.

(10) Wa-'a'mara 'Iyasus, wa-yebēlomu:

La-ment tāsarreḥewwā la-be'sit? Šannāya gebra gabrat lā'lēya. (11) Wa-naddāyān-sa zalfa terakkebewwomu, wa-kiyāya-sa 'akko zalfa za-terakkebuni. (12) Wa-zanta-sa 'efrata za-soṭat diba re'seya la-qabareya gabrat. (13) 'Amān 'ebelakemu: Ba-xaba tasabka ze-wangēl ba-westa k^wellu 'ālam yānabbebu za-gabrat zā-ni wa-yezakkerewwā.

(14) Wa-'emze ḥora 'aḥadu 'em-'ašartu wa-kel'ētu 'ardā'ihu za-semu Yehudā 'Asqorotāwi xaba liqāna kāhenāt, (15) wa-yebēlomu:

Mi-maṭana tehubuni wa-'ana lakemu 'āgabbe'o?

Wa-wahabewwo šalāsā berura. (16) Wa-'em-'amēhā yefaqqed yerkab šāxta kama yāgbe'o.

XXVI 7. *beralē/biralē* beryl, crystal; here = an alabaster vessel. *'efrat* unguent. G *soṭa (yesuṭ)* to pour. Gt *tasawṭa* pass. and reflex. *sewuṭ* poured. *suṭat* vn. pouring, emptying.

63. Ba'enta zakama tase''elewwo ba-xaba yāstadālewu lotu Fešḥa

(17) Wa-ba-qadāmit ‘elata Fešḥ qarbu 'ardā'ihu la-'Iyasus wa-yebēlewwo:

Ba-'aytē tefaqqed nāstadālu laka teblā‘ Fešḥa?

(18) Wa-yebēlomu 'Iyasus:

Ḥuru xaba 'egalē wa-balewwo: Yebē liq: "Gizēya qarba, wa-xabēka 'egabber Fāsikā mesla 'ardā'eya."

(19) Wa-gabru 'ardā'ihu bakama 'azzazomu 'Iyasus, wa-'astadālawu Fešḥa. (20) Wa-mesēta kawino, rafaqa mesla ‘ašartu wa-kel'ētu 'ardā'ihu. (21) Wa-'enza yeballe‘u, yebē:

'Amān 'ebelakemu kama 'aḥadu 'emennēkemu yāgabbe'ani.

(22) Wa-takkazu ṭeqqa wa-'axazu yebalu ba-ba 'aḥadu:

'Ana-hu 'engā 'Egzi'o?

(23) Wa-'awše'a, wa-yebē:

Za-ṣabxa meslēya 'edēhu westa maṣbex we'etu yāgabbe'ani. (24) Wa-walda 'egʷāla 'emma-ḥeyāw yaḥawwer bakama ṣeḥuf ba'enti'ahu, wa-bāḥtu 'alē lotu la-we'etu be'si za-ba-lā‘lēhu yetmēṭṭawewwo la-walda 'egʷāla 'emma-ḥeyāw. 'Em-xayyaso soba 'i-tawalda la-we'etu be'si.

(25) Wa-'awše'a Yehudā za-yāgabbe'o, wa-yebē: 'Ana-hu 'engā rabbi? Wa-yebēlo:

'Anta tebē.

64. Ba'enta šer‘ata mesṭir

(26) Wa-'enza yeballe‘u, naš'a xebesta 'Iyasus, wa-bāraka, wa-fatata, wa-wahaba la-'ardā'ihu, wa-yebē:

'Enkemu bele‘u. Ze-we'etu šegāya.

(27) Wa-naš'a ṣewā‘a, wa-'a'kʷata, wa-wahabomu 'enza yebel:

Setayu 'em-westētu kʷellekemu. (28) Ze-we'etu dameya za-ḥaddis šer‘at za-yetka‘‘aw ba'enta bezuxān kama yetxadag xaṭi'at. (29) Wa-'ebelakemu: 'I-ẏesatti 'enka 'em-ze ferē wayn 'eska 'entākti ‘elat 'ama 'esatteyo ḥaddisa meslēkemu ba-mangešta 'abuya.

---

17. *Fešḥ* Passover. *Fāsikā* idem.

23. G *ṣabxa* to dip. *ṣabx* sauce, gravy. *maṣbex* dish, bowl.

26. *'enkemu* = *'enka*. This particle is thus seen to be composed of an element *'en-* plus a second person pronominal element.

(30) Wa-'anbibomu, waḍ'u westa Dabra Zayt. (31) Wa-'emze yebēlomu 'Iyasus:

K^{w}ellekemu ta‘allewuni ba-zāti lēlit, 'esma yebē maṣḥaf:

'Eqattelo la-nolāwi, wa-yezzarraw 'abāge‘a mar‘ētu.

(32) Wa-'emkama tanšā'ku, 'eqaddemakemu Galilā.

(33) Wa-'awše'a Pēṭros, wa-yebēlo:

'Emma-hi k^{w}ellomu ‘alawuka, 'i-y̓a‘allewaka gemurā.

(34) Wa-yebēlo 'Iyasus:

'Amān 'ebelaka kama ba-zāti lēlit šelsa tekeḥḥedani za'enbala yenqu doreho.

(35) Wa-yebēlo Pēṭros:

'Emma-hi motku meslēka, 'i-y̓ekeḥḥedaka.

Wa-kamāhu yebēlu k^{w}ellomu 'ardā'ihu. (36) Wa-'emze ḥora meslēhomu ‘aṣada wayn za-semu Gētēsēmān, wa-yebēlomu la-'ardā'ihu:

Nebaru zeyya 'eska soba 'aḥawwer kaḥa wa-'eṣalli.

(37) Wa-naš'o la-Pēṭros wa-la-kel'ēhomu daqiqa Zabdēwos, wa-'axaza yetakkez wa-yeḥzen. (38) Wa-'emze yebēlomu:

Takkazat nafseya 'eska la-mawit. Nebaru zeyya, wa-tegehu meslēya.

(39) Wa-ta'atata ḥeqqa 'em-heyya, wa-sagada ba-gaṣṣu, wa-ṣallaya, wa-yebē:

'Abuya, 'emma-sa yetkahhal, yexlef 'emennēya ze-ṣewā‘. Wa-bāḥtu faqādaka yekun, wa-'akko faqādeya.

(40) Wa-ḥora xaba 'ardā'ihu, wa-rakabomu 'enza yenawwemu, wa-yebēlo la-Pēṭros:

Kama-ze-nu se'enkemu tagiha 'aḥatta sa‘āta meslēya? (41) Tegehu wa-ṣalleyu kama 'i-tebā'u westa mansut. Manfas-sa yefattu, wa-šegā dekum.

(42) Wa-kā‘eba ḥora dāgema, wa-ṣallaya, wa-yebē:

'Abuya, 'emma 'i-yetkahhal ze-xalifa za'enbala 'esteyo, yekun faqādaka.

(43) Wa-gab'a kā‘eba xaba 'ardā'ihu, wa-rakabomu 'enza yenawwemu, 'esma 'a‘yentihomu kebudāt. (44) Wa-ḥora kā‘eba ba-šāles, wa-ṣallaya kiyāhu kema qāla 'enza yebel. (45) Wa-gab'a kā‘eba xaba 'ardā'ihu,

---

39. *ḥeqqa* adv. a little, a little while, a short distance. *ba-ḥeqqa* sufficiently, enough; very much, altogether.

44. Note the emphatic use of *kiyā- kema*: the very same words.

wa-yebēlomu:

Numu ’enka-sa, wa-’a‘refu. Nāhu baṣḥa gizēhu, wa-yāgabbe’ewwo la-walda ’eg^{w}āla ’emma-ḥeyāw westa ’eda xāṭe’ān. (46) Tanše’u, neḥur. Nāhu qarba za-yāgabbe’ani.

65. Ba’enta geb’atu la-Kerestos

(47) Wa-’enza zanta yetnāgar, nāhu Yehudā ’em-‘ašartu wa-kel’ētu ’aḥadu maṣ’a, wa-meslēhu bezux sab’ mesla maṭābeḥ wa-‘eḍaw, ’em-xabēhomu la-liqāna kāhenāt wa-liqānāta ḥezb. (48) Wa-za-yāgabbe’o wahabomu te’merta ’enza yebel:

Za-sa‘amku we’etu. Kiyāhu ’axazu.

(49) Wa-qarba xaba ’Iyasus, wa-sa‘amo, wa-yebēlo: Bāḥa Rabbi. (50) Wa-yebēlo ’Iyasus:

Kāle’eya, maṣā’ka-nu?

Wa-’anše’u ’edawihomu, wa-’axazewwo la-’Iyasus. (51) Wa-nāhu ’aḥadu ’em-’ella meslēhu la-’Iyasus safḥa ’edēhu wa-malxa maṭbāḥto, wa-zabaṭo la-gabra liqa kāhenāt, wa-mataro ’ezno. (52) Wa-yebēlo ’Iyasus:

’Agbe’ maṭbāḥtaka westa bētu, ’esma k^{w}ellomu ’ella maṭbāḥta yānašše’u ba-maṭbāḥt yemawwetu. (53) Yemasselakemu-nu za-’i-yekel ’astabq^{w}e‘oto la-’abuya wa-yāqem lita fadfāda ’em-‘ašartu wa-kel’ētu sarāwita malā’ekt? (54) ’Efo ’enka yetfaṣṣam qāla maṣḥaf za-yebē kama-ze hallawo yekun?

(55) Wa-yebēlomu la-ḥezb ’Iyasus sobēhā:

Kama za-sarāqi tedēgenu maṣā’kemu ba-‘eḍaw wa-ba-maṭābeḥ ta’axazuni? Wa-zalfa ’enabber meslēkemu ba-mek^{w}rāb wa-’emēhher, wa-’i-’axazkemuni.

(56) Wa-ze-k^{w}ellu za-kona kama yebṣāḥ qāla nabiyāt. Wa-’emze k^{w}ellomu ’ardā’ihu xadagewwo wa-g^{w}ayyu. (57) Wa-’ella ’axazewwo la-’Iyasus wasadewwo xaba Qayāfā liqa kāhenāt xaba tagābe’u ṣaḥaft wa-liqānāt. (58) Wa-talawo Pēṭros ’em-reḥuq ’eska ‘aṣada liqa kāhenāt, wa-bo’a wesṭa, wa-nabara mesla wa‘āli yer’ay māxlaqto la-nagar. (59) Wa-yaxaššešu liqāna kāhenāt wa-ṣaḥaft wa-liqānāt wa-k^{w}ellu ‘awd samā‘ta ḥassat ba-za yeqtelewwo la-’Iyasus, wa-’i-rakabu. (60) Wa-

---

47. *‘eḍ* in the sense "club."

52. *bēt* in the sense "sheath."

55. *kama za-* like, as though, as it were.

maṣ'u bezuxān samā'ta ḥassat, wa-se'nu. Wa-dexra maṣ'u kel'ētu, (61) wa-yebēlu:

Yebē-ze: 'Ekelo našitoto la-bēta 'Egzi'abḥēr wa-ba-šālest 'elat 'anše'oto.

(62) Wa-tanše'a liqa kāhenāt, wa-yebēlo:

'I-tesamme'-nu za-maṭana-ze yāstawādeyuka?

(63) Wa-'i-y̓awše'o 'Iyasus. Wa-yebēlo liqa kāhenāt:

'Amḥalkuka ba-'Egzi'abḥēr ḥeyāw kama tengerani 'emma 'anta-hu Kerestos waldu la-'Egzi'abḥēr.

(64) Wa-yebēlo 'Iyasus:

'Anta tebē, wa-bāḥtu 'ebelakemu: 'Em-ye'zē-sa terē''eyewwo la-walda 'egʷāla 'emma-ḥeyāw 'enza yenabber ba-yamāna xayl wa-'enza yemaṣṣe' ba-dammanāta samāy.

(65) Wa-šaṭaṭa 'albāsihu liqa kāhenāt 'enza yebel:

Menta 'enka tefaqqedu lotu samā'ta? Nāhu ḍarfa, wa-samā'kemu ḍerfato. (66) Menta 'enka tebelu?

Wa-'awše'u, wa-yebēlu: Yeqtelewwo. (67) Wa-'emze taf'u westa gaṣṣu, wa-kʷar'ewwo, wa-ṣaf'ewwo 'enza yebelu:

Tanabbay lana Kerestos. Mannu we'etu za-ṣaf'aka?

66. Ba'enta zakama keḥda Pēṭros

(69) Wa-Pēṭros yenabber 'af'a westa 'aṣad. Wa-maṣ'at walatt, wa-tebēlo:

'Anta-hi mesla 'Iyasus Galilāwi hallawka.

(70) Wa-keḥda ba-gaṣṣa kʷellu 'enza yebel:

'I-y̓ā'ammero za-tebeli.

(71) Wa-waḍi'o xoxta, re'yato kāle't, wa-tebēlomu la-'ella heyya yeqawwemu:

Ze-ni hallo mesla 'Iyasus Nāzerāwi.

(72) Wa-keḥda kā'eba, wa-maḥala kama "'I-y̓ā'ammero la-we'etu be'si."

(73) Wa-ḥeqqa behilo, maṣ'u 'ella yeqawwemu wa-yebēlewwo la-Pēṭros:

'Amān 'anta-hi 'em-xabēhomu 'anta, wa-nagareka yā'awweqaka.

(74) Wa-maḥala, wa-taragma kama "'I-y̓ā'ammero la-we'etu be'si." Wa-ba-gizēhā naqawa doreho. (75) Wa-tazakkara Pēṭros qālo la-'Iyasus ze-yebēlo:

---

67. G *taf'a* to spit. *tef'at* spit. G *kʷar'a* or D *kʷarre'a* to strike someone's head with one's fists. Gt *takʷar'a* pass.

Šelsa tekeḥḥedani za’enbala yenqu doreho.
Wa-waḍ’a ’af’a, wa-bakaya marira.

Chapter XXVII

(1) Wa-ṣabiḥo tamākaru k^{w}ellomu liqāna kāhenāt wa-liqānāta ḥezb yeqtelewwo la-’Iyasus. (2) Wa-’asiromu, wasadewwo wa-maṭṭawewwo la-Pilāṭos Panṭanāwi la-mal’aka ’aḥzāb.

67. Ba’enta zakama nasseḥa Yehudā

(3) Wa-’emze soba re’ya Yehudā za-’agbe’o kama ’arseḥewwo, nasseḥa wa-’agbe’a šalāsā berura la-liqāna kāhenāt wa-la-liqāwenta ḥezb, (4) ’enza yebel:

’Abbasku za-’agbā’ku dama ṣādeq.

Wa-yebēlewwo:

Mi-lā‘lēna? ’Anta ’a’mer.

(5) Wa-gadafa we’eta berura westa mek^{w}rāb, wa-ḥora, wa-taxanqa. (6) Wa-naš’u liqāna kāhenāt we’eta berura, wa-yebēlu:

’I-yekawwen nedayo westa q^{w}erbān, ’esma šēṭa dam we’etu.

(7) Wa-tamākiromu, tašāyaṭu botu medra labḥāwi la-maqābera ’engedā. (8) Wa-tasamya we’etu medr medra dam ’eska yom. (9) Wa-ye’eta ’amira baṣḥa qāla ’Ēremeyās nabiy za-yebē:

Wa-naš’u šalāsā berura šēṭo la-kebur za-’akbaru ’em-daqiqa ’Esrā’ēl, (10) wa-wahabewwon la-garāhta labḥāwi bakama ’azzazani ’Egzi’abḥēr.

(11) Wa-qoma ’Iyasus qedmēhu la-mal’aka ’aḥzāb, wa-tase’’elo mal’aka ’aḥzāb, wa-yebēlo:

’Anta-hu negušomu la-’Ayhud?

(12) Wa-yebē ’Iyasus: ’Anta tebē. Wa-’enza yāstawādeyewwo liqāna kāhenāt wa-liqāwenta ḥezb, ’albo za-yāwašše’omu wa-’i-menta-hi. (13) Wa-’emze yebēlo Pilāṭos:

’I-tesamme‘-nu maṭana yāstawādeyuka?

(14) Wa-’i-yawše’o wa-’i-’aḥatta qāla ’eska yānakker mal’ak. (15) Wa-ba-ba‘āl yālammed mal’aka ’aḥzāb ’aḥyewo ’aḥada la-ḥezb ’em-westa muquḥān za-faqadu. (16) Wa-bo ’amēhā muquḥ za-semu Barbān, semu‘,

---

XXVII 7. *labḥāwi* potter.

15. G *lamada (yelmad)* to be accustomed (to do: inf.). CG *’almada* idem. *lemud* accustomed, usual. *lemād* custom, habit.

wa-yā'ammero k^{w}ellu. (17) Wa-'enza gubu'ān 'emuntu, yebēlomu Pilāṭos la-ḥezb?

Manna tefaqqedu 'āḥyu lakemu, Barbānhā-nu wa-mima 'Iyasushā-nu za-semu Kerestos?

'Esma yā'ammer kama la-qen'atomu 'agbe'ewwo. (19) Wa-'enza yenabber ʻawda, la'akat xabēhu be'situ 'enza tebel:

ʻUq 'i-ta'abbes lāʻla we'etu ṣādeq, 'esma bezuxa ḥamamku yom ba-ḥelm ba'enti'ahu.

(20) Wa-liqāna kāhenāt wa-liqāwent 'oho 'abalu ḥezba kama Barbānhā yes'alu wa-'Iyasushā yeqtelu. (21) Wa-'awše'a mal'aka 'aḥzāb 'enza yebelomu:

Manna tefaqqedu 'em-kel'ēhomu 'āḥyu lakemu?

Wa-yebēlu: Barbānhā. (22) Wa-yebēlomu Pilāṭos:

Menta 'enka 'erasseyo la-'Iyasus za-semu Kerestos?

Wa-yebēlu k^{w}ellomu: Seqelo. (23) Wa-yebēlomu mal'ak:

Menta 'ekuya gabra?

Wa-'afadfadu ṣarixa 'enza yebelu: Seqelo, seqelo. (24) Wa-'emza re'ya Pilāṭos kama 'albo za-yebaqq^{w}eʻ za'enbala kama ʻādi hakaka za-yekawwen, naš'a māya, wa-taxaḍba 'edēhu ba-qedmēhomu la-ḥezb 'enza yebel:

Neṣuḥ 'ana 'em-damu la-ze ṣādeq. 'Antemu 'a'meru.

(25) Wa-yebēlu k^{w}ellu ḥezb: Damu lāʻlēna wa-lāʻla weludena. (26) Wa-'emze fatḥa lomu Barbānhā, wa-qašafo la-'Iyasus, wa-maṭṭawomu yesqelewwo. (27) Wa-'emze mastarāteʻāta ḥarrā naš'ewwo la-'Iyasus 'em-mek^{w}ennān, wa-'astagābe'u māxbaromu. (28) Wa-'albasewwo kalamēdā za-layy. (29) Wa-ḍafaru 'aklila za-šok, wa-'astaqaṣṣalewwo westa re'su, wa-xellata westa yamānu. Wa-'astabraku qedmēhu, wa-yessālaqu lāʻlēhu, wa-yebēlewwo: Bāḥa, neguša 'Ayhud. (30) Wa-yewarrequ lāʻlēhu, wa-yek^{w}arreʻewwo ba-xellat re'so. (31) Wa-tasāliqomu lāʻlēhu, salabewwo we'eta kalamēdā, wa-'albasewwo 'albāsihu, wa-

---

27. *mastarāteʻ* a guard, soldier.

28. *kalamēdā za-layy* robe of purple.

29. G *ḍafara (yeḍfer)* to weave, plait. Gt *taḍafra* pass. *ḍefur* woven, plaited. *ḍefro* plaited work. *ḍefrat* vn. weaving, joining, plaiting. CDt *'astaqaṣṣala* to crown (someone: o.s.) with (a.d.o.). *qaṣṣalā* crown, diadem. *xellat* reed, cane. CGt *'astabraka* to kneel. *berk* (pl. *'abrāk*) knee.

wasadewwo yesqelewwo. (32) Wa-’enza yewaḍḍe’u, rakabu be’sē Qarēnāwē, za-semu Sem‘on, wa-‘abbaṭewwo yeṣur masqalo. (33) Wa-baṣiḥomu beḥēra za-semu Golgoltā, za-ba-terg^{w}āmēhu qarānyu, (34) wa-wahabewwo yestay wayna wa-ḥamota demmura, wa-ṭe‘imo ’abaya sateya. (35) Wa-’emze saqalewwo, wa-takāfalu ’albāsihu ’enza yet‘āḍawu. (36) Wa-nabaru ya‘aqqebewwo heyya. (37) Wa-’anbaru mal‘elta re’su ṣeḥifomu za-kona ’enza yebelu: Ze-we’etu negušomu la-’Ayhud ’Iyasus. (38) Wa-’emze tasaqlu meslēhu kel’ētu fayyāt, ’aḥadu ba-yamān wa-’aḥadu ba-ḍagām. (39) Wa-’ella yaxallefu yeḍarrefu lā‘lēhu ’enza yāḥawwesu re’somu, (40) wa-yebelu:

> Za-yenaššeto la-mek^{w}rāb wa-yaḥanneṣo ba-šālest ‘elat, ’adxen re’saka. ’Emma-sa walda ’Egzi’abḥēr ’anta, rad ’em-masqaleka.

(41) Wa-kamāhu liqāna kāhenāt-hi yessālaqu mesla ṣaḥaft wa-liqānāt ’enza yebelu:

> (42) Bā‘eda ’adxana wa-re’so ’i-yekel ’adxeno. ’Emma neguša ’Esrā’ēl we’etu, yerad ’em-masqal, wa-ne’man botu. (43) Za-ta’amna ba-’Egzi’abḥēr, nāhu ye’zē yādxeno ’emma yefaqqedo, ’esma yebel: Walda ’Egzi’abḥēr ’ana.

(44) Wa-kamāhu fayyāt-ni ’ella tasaqlu meslēhu yezanagg^{w}eg^{w}ewwo. (45) Wa-’em-sessu sa‘āt ṣalma k^{w}ellu ‘ālam ’eska tas‘u sa‘āt. (46) Wa-gizē sa‘āt tasu‘at ṣarxa ’Iyasus ba-qāl ‘abiy ’enza yebel.

> ’Ēlōhi, ’Ēlōhi, lamā sabaqtani?

Ze-we’etu behil: ’Amlākeya, ’Amlākeya, la-ment xadaggani? (47) Wa-sami‘omu ’ella yeqawwemu heyya, yebēlu: ’Ēleyās-hā yeṣēwwe‘ ze-sa. (48) Wa-we’eta gizē roṣa ’aḥadu ’em-xabēhomu, wa-naš’a sefnega wa-mal’o beḥi’a, wa-’asara westa xellat, wa-’aḥzazo. (49) Wa-bo ’ella yebēlu:

> Xedeg ner’ay ’emma yemaṣṣe’-nu ’Ēleyās yādxeno.

(50) Wa-ṣarxa kā‘eba ’Iyasus ba-‘abiy qāl, wa-waḍ’at manfasu. (51)

---

31. G *salaba (yesleb)* to take (a.d.o.) away (from: o.s.), deprive of, strip off. Gt *tasalba* reflex. and pass. *selbat* vn.

34. *ḥamot* gall.

35. *ta‘āḍawa* to cast lots. *‘eḍā* a lot. *‘eḍḍāwē/‘uḍāwē* vn. casting lots.

38. *fayyāt* thieves; *fayyātāwi* a thief.

48. *sefneg, sefnag* sponge. *beḥi’* vinegar. The meaning of the verb *’aḥzaza* is not clear.

Wa-tašaṭṭa manṭolā‘ta bēta maqdas ’em-lā‘lu ’eska tāḥtu, wa-kel’ēta kona. Wa-’adlaqlaqat medr, wa-naq‘a k^{w}ak^{w}ḥ. (52) Wa-takaštu maqāberāt, wa-tanše’u bezuxān ’abdentihomu la-ṣādeqān, (53) wa-waḍ’u ’em-maqāberihomu, wa-bo’u hagara qeddesta ’em-dexra tanše’u, wa-’astar’ayewwomu la-bezuxān. (54) Wa-mak^{w}annena me’t wa-’ella meslēhu ya‘aqqebewwo la-’Iyasus re’eyomu we’eta deleqleqa wa-zakama yekawwen, farhu ṭeqqa, wa-yebēlu: ’Amān walda ’Egzi’abḥēr we’etu-ze. (55) Wa-hallawā heyya bezuxāt ’anest ’ella yerē’’eyā ’em-reḥuq k^{w}ello za-kona, ’ella talawāhu la-’Iyasus ’em-Galilā, ’ella yetla’’akāhu: (56) Māryā Magdalāwit wa-Māryā ’enta Yā‘qob wa-’emmu la-Yosēf wa-’emmomu la-daqiqa Zabdēwos.

68. Ba’enta zakama sa’ala šegāhu la-’Egzi’ena Yosēf

(57) Wa-maseyo maṣ’a be’si bā‘el ’em-’Armāteyās za-semu Yosēf, wa-we’etu-hi taḍamdo la-’Iyasus. (58) Wa-ḥora xaba Pilāṭos, wa-sa’ala badno la-’Iyasus, wa-’azzaza Pilāṭos yahabewwo. (59) Wa-naši’o badno Yosēf, ganazo ba-sendun neṣuḥ, (60) wa-qabaro westa maqāber ḥaddis za-’awqara westa k^{w}ak^{w}ḥ, wa-’ank^{w}ark^{w}ara ’ebna ‘abiya diba xoxta maqāber, wa-xalafa. (61) Wa-hallawā heyya Māryā Magdalāwit wa-kāle’tā-hi Māryā yenabberā qedma maqāber. (62) Wa-ba-sānitā, ’enta ye’eti ’emdexra ‘arb, tagābe’u liqāna kāhenāt wa-Farisāweyān xaba Pilāṭos, (63) wa-yebēlewwo:

> Tazakkarna, ’egzi’o, za-yebē zeku giguy ’ama ḥeyāw we’etu: ’Ama šālest ‘elat ’etnaššā’. (64) ’Azzez ’enka ye‘qabu maqāberihu ’eska šalus mawā‘el, kama ’i-yemṣe’u ’ardā’ihu wa-’i-yesreqewwo lēlita wa-’i-yebalu la-ḥezb: Tanše’a ’em-mewutān. Wa-tekawwen daxārita gēgāyu ’enta ta’akki ’em-qadāmit.

(65) Wa-yebēlomu Pilāṭos:

> Neše’u šagarāta, wa-ḥuru, ’aṣne‘u bakama tā’ammeru.

(66) Wa-ḥoru, wa-qattaru maqābero, wa-’aṣne‘u, wa-xatamewwā la-ye’eti

---

51. *manṭolā‘t* (pl. *manṭawāle‘*) veil, covering.

59. *sendun/sendon* fine linen.

60. G *waqara* = D *waqqara* = CG *’awqara* to dig, excavate. N *’ank^{w}ark^{w}ara* to roll (trans. and intrans.). *nak^{w}ark^{w}ār* n. rolling. *mank^{w}arāk^{w}er* wheel.

65. *šagarāt* (pl.) guards.

66. D *qattara* to seal, lock. *qettur* locked, sealed.

'ebn mesla šagarāt.

Chapter XXVIII

(1) Wa-sarka sanbat la-ṣabiḥa 'eḥud, maṣ'at Māryā Magdalāwit wa-kāle'tā-ni Māryā yer'ayā maqābera. (2) Wa-nāhu kona deleqleq 'abiy, 'esma mal'aka 'Egzi'abḥēr warada 'em-samāy, wa-qarba, wa-'ankʷarkʷarā la-'ebn, wa-nabara dibēhā. (3) Wa-rā'yu kama za-mabraq, wa-lebsu ṣā'dā kama za-barad. (4) Wa-'em-ferhatu tahawku wa-konu kama 'abdent 'ella ya'aqqebu. (5) Wa-'awše'a mal'ak, wa-yebēlon la-'anest:

'I-tefrehā 'anten-sa, 'esma 'ā'ammer kama 'Iyasus-hā taxaššešā za-taqatla. (6) 'I-hallo zeyya. Tanše'a bakama yebē. Na'ā re'eyā xaba taqabra. (7) Wa-feṭuna ḥurā, negerāhomu la-'ardā'ihu kama tanše'a 'em-mewutān, wa-nāhu yeqaddemakemu Galilā, wa-ba-heyya terē''eyewwo. Nāhu 'aydā'kuken.

(8) Wa-xalafā feṭuna 'em-xaba maqāber ba-ferhat wa-ba-fešseḥā 'abiy, wa-roṣā yengerā la-'ardā'ihu. (9) Wa-nāhu 'Iyasus tarākabon, wa-yebē: Bāḥeken. Wa-qarbā, wa-'axazā 'egarihu, wa-sagadā lotu. (10) Wa-'emze yebēlon 'Iyasus:

'I-tefrehā. Ḥurā, negerāhomu la-'axaweya kama yeḥuru Galilā, wa-ba-heyya yerē''eyuni.

(11) Wa-xalifon 'emāntu, 'atawu šagarāt hagara wa-nagaru la-liqāna kāhenāt kʷello zakama kona. (12) Wa-tagābe'u, wa-makaru mesla liqāwent, wa-wahabewwomu bezuxa warqa la-šagarāt. (13) Wa-yebēlewwomu:

Balu: 'ardā'ihu lēlita maṣ'u wa-saraqewwo 'enza nenawwem. (14) Wa-'emkama tasam'a-ze ba-xaba mal'aka 'aḥzāb, neḥna nā'ammeno, wa-kiyākemu-ni 'ella za'enbala ḥazan nerēsseyakemu.

(15) Wa-naši'omu berura, xalafu, wa-gabru bakama maharewwomu. Wa-waḍ'a ze-nagar 'em-xaba 'Ayhud 'eska yom. (16) Wa-ḥoru Galilā 'ašartu wa-'aḥadu 'ardā'ihu dabra za-'azzazomu 'Iyasus, (17) wa-re'yewwo, wa-sagadu lotu, wa-nāfaqu. (18) Wa-qarba 'Iyasus, wa-tanāgaromu 'enza yebel:

Tawehba lita kʷellu kʷennanē samāy wa-medr. (19) Ḥuru, maharu kʷello 'aḥzāba 'enza tāṭammeqewwomu ba-sema 'ab wa-wald wa-

---

XXVIII 1. *sark* evening, twilight. *sarka Sanbat* Sabbath evening = beginning of the next day. *la-ṣabiḥa 'eḥud* at the dawn (inf.) of the first day of the week.

manfas qeddus. (20) Wa-maharewwomu k^wello ye‘qabu za-’azzazkukemu, wa-nāhu ’ana meslēkemu ba-k^wellu mawā‘el ’eska xelqata ‘ālam.

Matthew V, 1-24 in Ethiopic Script

ምዕራፍ ፡ ፭ ፤

፩ ፤ ፭ ፤ በእንተ ፡ ብፁዓን ። ወርእዮ ፡ አሕዛበ ፡ ዐርገ ፡ ውስተ ፡ ደብር ፡
፪ ፤ ወነቢሮ ፡ ቀርቡ ፡ ኀቤሁ ፡ አርዳኢሁ ። ወከሠተ ፡ አፉሁ ፡ ወመሀሮሙ ፡ እ
፫ ፤ ንዘ ፡ ይብል ። ብፁዓን ፡ ነዳያን ፡ በመንፈስ ፡ እስመ ፡ ሎሙ ፡ ይእቲ ፡ መን
፬ ፤ ግሥተ ፡ ሰማያት ። ብፁዓን ፡ እለ ፡ ይላሕዉ ፡ ይእዜ ፡ እስመ ፡ እሙንቱ ፡
፭ ፤ ይትፌሥሑ ። ብፁዓን ፡ የዋሃን ፡ እስመ ፡ እሙንቱ ፡ ይወርስዋ ፡ ለምድ
፮ ፤ ር ። ብፁዓን ፡ እለ ፡ ይርኅቡ ፡ ወይጸምኡ ፡ ለጽድቅ ፡ እስመ ፡ እሙንቱ ፡
፯ ፤ ይጸግቡ ። ብፁዓን ፡ መሐርያን ፡ እስመ ፡ እሙንቱ ፡ ይትመሐሩ ። ብፁዓ
፰ ፤ ን ፡ ንጹሓነ ፡ ልብ ፡ እስመ ፡ እሙንቱ ፡ ይሬእይዎ ፡ ለእግዚአብሔር ። ብፁ
፱ ፤ ዓን ፡ ገባርያነ ፡ ሰላም ፡ እስመ ፡ እሙንቱ ፡ ውሉደ ፡ እግዚአብሔር ፡ ይሰ
፲ ፤ መዩ ። ብፁዓን ፡ እለ ፡ ይሰደዱ ፡ በእንተ ፡ ጽድቅ ፡ እስመ ፡ ሎሙ ፡ ይእቲ ፡
፲፩ ፤ መንግሥተ ፡ ሰማያት ። ብፁዓን ፡ አንትሙ ፡ ሶበ ፡ ይሰድዱክሙ ፡ ወይዘን
ጕጉክሙ ፡ ወይነቡ ፡ ኵሎ ፡ እከየ ፡ ላዕሌክሙ ፡ እንዘ ፡ ይሔስዉ ፡ በእንቲ
፲፪ ፤ አየ ። ተፈሥሑ ፡ ወተሐሠዩ ፡ እስመ ፡ ዐስብክሙ ፡ ብዙኅ ፡ ውእቱ ፡ በሰ
ማያት ። እስመ ፡ ከመዝ ፡ ሰደድዎሙ ፡ ለነቢያት ፡ እለ ፡ እምቅድሜክሙ ።
፲፫ ፤ አንትሙ ፡ ውእቱ ፡ ጼው ፡ ለምድር ፡ ወእመሰ ፡ ጼው ፡ ለስኰ ፡ በምንትኑ ፡
ይትቄሰም ። አልቦኬ ፡ እንከ ፡ ለዘይበቍዕ ፡ ዘእንበለ ፡ ለገዲፍ ፡ አፍአ ፡ ወ
፲፬ ፤ ይከይዶ ፡ ሰብእ ። አንትሙ ፡ ውእቱ ፡ ብርሃኑ ፡ ለዓለም ። ኢትክል ፡ ሀገ
፲፭ ፤ ር ፡ ተኀብኦ ፡ እንተ ፡ መልዕልተ ፡ ደብር ፡ ትነብር ። ወኢያኀትዉ ፡ ማኀቶ
ተ ፡ ከመ ፡ ያንብርዋ ፡ ታሕተ ፡ ከፊር ፡ አላ ፡ዲበ ፡ ተቅዋማ ፡ ወታበርህ ፡
፲፮ ፤ ለኵሎሙ ፡ እለ ፡ ውስተ ፡ ቤት ። ከማሁ ፡ ይብራህ ፡ ብርሃንክሙ ፡ በቅድ
መ ፡ ሰብእ ፡ ከመ ፡ ይርአዩ ፡ ምግባሪክሙ ፡ ሠናየ ፡ ወይሰብሕዎ ፡ ለአቡክ
፲፯ ፤ ሙ ፡ ዘበሰማያት ። ኢይምሰልክሙ ፡ ዘመጻእኩ ፡ እስዐር ፡ ኦሪተ ፡ ወነቢያ
ተ ። ኢመጻእኩ ፡ እስዐሮሙ ፡ አላ ፡ እፈጽሞሙ ። አማን ፡ እብለክሙ ፡ ፲፰ ፤
እስከ ፡ የኀልፍ ፡ ሰማይ ፡ ወምድር ፡ የውጣ ፡ እንተ ፡ አሐቲ ፡ ቅርፀታ ፡ ኢ
ተኀልፍ ፡ እምኦሪት ፡ እስከ ፡ ሶበ ፡ ኵሉ ፡ ይትገበር ። ዘኬ ፡ ፈትሐ ፡ አሐ ፲፱ ፤
ተ ፡ እምእላ ፡ ትእዛዛት ፡ እንተ ፡ ተሐጽጽ ፡ ወይሜህር ፡ ከመዝ ፡ ለሰብእ ፡
ሕጹጸ ፡ ይሰመይ ፡ በመንግሥተ ፡ ሰማያት ፡ ወዘሰ ፡ ይሜህር ፡ ወይገብር ፡
ውእቱ ፡ ዐቢየ ፡ ይሰመይ ፡ በመንግሥተ ፡ ሰማያት ። ናሁ ፡ እብለክሙ ፡ ከ ፳ ፤
መ ፡ እመ ፡ ኢፈድፈደ ፡ ጽድቅክሙ ፡ ፈድፋደ ፡ እምጸሐፍት ፡ ወእምፈሪ
ሳውያን ፡ ኢትበውኡ ፡ ውስተ ፡ መንግሥተ ፡ ሰማያት ። ሰማዕክሙ ፡ ከ ፳፩ ፤
መ ፡ ተብህለ ፡ ለቀደምት ፡ ኢትቅትል ፡ ነፍሰ ፡ ወዘሰ ፡ ቀተለ ፡ ረስሐ ፡ ው
እቱ ፡ ለኵነኔ ። ወአንሰ ፡ እብለክሙ ፡ ኵሉ ፡ ዘያምዕዕ ፡ እኅዋሁ ፡ ረስሐ ፡ ፳፪ ፤
ውእቱ ፡ ለኵነኔ ፡ ወዘሂ ፡ ይቤ ፡ እኅዋሁ ፡ ዘፀርቅ ፡ ረስሐ ፡ ውእቱ ፡ ለዐው
ድ ። ወዘሂ ፡ ይቤ ፡ አብድ ፡ ረስሐ ፡ ውእቱ ፡ ለገሃነመ ፡ እሳት ። ወእምከመ ፳፫ ፤
ኬ ፡ ታበውእ ፡ አምኃከ ፡ ውስተ ፡ ምሥዋዕ ፡ ወበህየ ፡ ተዘከርከ ፡ ከመበ ፡
እኁከ ፡ ዘየሐይሰከ ። ኅድግ ፡ ህየ ፡ መበአከ ፡ ቅድመ ፡ ምሥዋዕ ፡ ወሑር ፡ ፳፬ ፤
ቅድመ ፡ ተኳነን ፡ ምስለ ፡ እኁከ ፡ ወእምዝ ፡ ገቢአከ ፡ አብእ ፡ አምኃከ ።

A Selected Bibliography

A. Grammars and Dictionaries

Chaine, Marius. *Grammaire éthiopienne*. Nouvelle édition. Beirut: Imprimerie Catholique, 1938.

Dillmann, August. *Lexicon linguae aethiopicae*. Leipzig: Weigel, 1865. Reprinted New York: Ungar, 1955, and Osnabruck, 1970.

________. *Ethiopic Grammar*. 2nd ed. enlarged and improved by C. Bezold, translated by J. A. Crichton. London: Williams and Norgate, 1907.

Grébaut, S. *Supplément au Lexicon linguae aethiopicae de A. Dillmann et édition du Lexique de Juste d'Urbin*. Paris: Imprimerie nationale, 1952.

Praetorius, F. *Grammatica aethiopica*. Karlsruhe and Leipzig: H. Reuther, 1886.

B. The Traditional Pronunciation of Ge'ez

Cohen, M. "La prononciation traditionelle du guèze (éthiopien classique)," *Journal Asiatique* (1921), 217-269.

Littmann, E. *Ge'ez-Studien I-II*. *Nachrichten von der k. Gesellschaft der Wissenschaften zu Göttingen*, phil.-hist. Klasse, 1917, pp. 672-702. *III*, ibid., 1918, pp. 318-339.

Mittwoch, Eugen. *Die traditionelle Aussprache des Äthiopischen*. Berlin: W. de Gruyter, 1926.

Trumpp, E. "Über den Akzent im Äthiopischen," *ZDMG* 28 (1874), 515-561.

C. Miscellaneous Grammatical and Lexical Studies

Hetzron, Robert. *Ethiopian Semitic: Studies in Classification*. *Journal of Semitic Studies*, Monograph No. 2. Manchester: Manchester University Press, 1972.

Leslau, Wolf. "South-east Semitic: Ethiopic and South Arabic," *JAOS* 72 (1943), 4-14.

________. "Arabic Loanwords in Geez," *Journal of Semitic Studies* 3 (1958), 146-168.

Littmann, E. "Die äthiopische Sprache," *Handbuch der Orientalistik, vol. III: Semitistik* (Leiden: E. J. Brill, 1954), pp. 350-375.

Nöldeke, Th. "Lehnwörter in und aus dem Äthiopischen," *Neue Beiträge zur semitischen Sprachwissenschaft* (Strassburg, 1910), pp. 31-66.

Schneider, R. *L'expression des compléments de verbe et de nom et la place de l'adjective épithète en guèze.* Paris, 1959.

Ullendorff, E. *The Semitic Languages of Ethiopia. A Comparative Phonology.* London: Taylor's Press, 1955.

D. Bibliographies and Surveys

Guidi, I. *Breve storia della letteratura etiopica.* Rome, 1932.

Leslau, Wolf. *Bibliography of the Semitic Languages of Ethiopia.* New York: New York Public Library, 1946.

________. *An Annotated Bibliography of the Semitic Languages of Ethiopia.* The Hague: Mouton, 1965.

________. "Ethiopia and South Arabia," in *Current Trends in Linguistics* (ed. T. Sebeok), Vol. 6: *Linguistics in South West Asia and North Africa*, pp. 467-527. The Hague: Mouton, 1970.

Littmann, E. *Geschichte der äthiopischen Literatur.* Leipzig, 1909.

Simon, J. "Bibliographie éthiopienne 1 (1946-51)," *Orientalia* n.s. 21 (1952), 44-66; 209-30.

Ullendorff, E. *The Ethiopians: An Introduction to Country and People.* 3rd ed. Oxford: Oxford University Press, 1973.

E. Some Sources for Published Texts

The hundreds of published Ethiopic texts are scattered among many journals, series, and individual books. The following is merely a sampling of some major sources.

1. Biblical and Related

Boyd, J. O., ed. *The Octateuch in Ethiopic.* Leiden, 1909-11.

Charles, R. H. *The Ethiopic Version of the Book of Enoch.* Oxford, 1893.

________. *The Ethiopic Version of the Hebrew Book of Jubilees.* Oxford, 1895.

Dillmann, A. *Biblia Veteris Testamenti Aethiopica.* Leipzig, 1835-94.

Platt, T. P. *Novum Testamentum Domini nostri et servatoris Jesu Christi aethiopice.* London, 1830.

Wangēl Qeddus za-ʾEgziʾena wa-Madxenena ʾIyasus Kerestos wa-maṣāḥeftihomu la-ḥawāreyātu qeddusān. Leipzig, 1899. Reprinted in 1949 and distributed by the American Bible Society.

2. Non-Biblical

Bezold, C. *Kebra Nagašt: Die Herrlichkeit der Könige. Abhandlungen der k. Bayerischen Akademie* XXIII, 1. Munich, 1909.

Corpus Scriptorum Christianorum Orientalium. Scriptores aethiopici. This major source contains over sixty volumes devoted to Ethiopic texts.

Dillmann, A. *Chrestomathia aethiopica.* Leipzig, 1866. Reprinted Berlin, 1950.

Patrologia Orientalis. Paris.

Note should also be taken of the many major texts published by A. E. W. Budge.

Glossary

The words in the Glossary are arranged according to consonantal roots in the following alphabetic order:

ʾ ʿ b d ḍ f g h ḥ k l m n p q r s š ṣ t ṭ w x y z

By standard convention, words not properly derivable from a consonantal root, such as loanwords and certain proper names, are listed by consonant structure alone, with initial *Ci-/Cē-* and *Cu-/Co-* taken as *CY-* and *CW-* respectively. Thus,

ʾadmās	is alphabetically	*ʾdm-*
ʾOrit	"	*ʾwr-*
diyāqon	"	*dyy-*

The labiovelars (k^w, g^w, q^w, and x^w) are not distinguished in the alphabetical ordering from their plain counterparts.

The subjunctive form of all G verbs, when known, is given in parentheses:

ʾabaya G *(yeʾbay)* to refuse

The plural suffixes *-āt/-t* and *-ān* are to be attached directly to the preceding word. E.g.

teʾmert (pl. *-āt*, *taʾāmer*, *-āt*) is to be read as
teʾmert (pl. *teʾmertāt*, *taʾāmer*, *taʾāmerāt*).

Because some words containing *ḍ* or *ṣ* have not always been normalized in the texts, the reader should remember to check each possibility in locating a word.

In his *Grammar* and *Lexicon* A. Dillmann uses a numerical system for identifying the various conjugational types of verbs. That system corresponds to ours as follows:

	1	2	3
I	G	D	L
II	CG	CD	CL
III	Gt	Dt	Lt/Glt
IV	CGt	CDt	CLt/CGlt
V	designates N verbs (see §50.3)		

Thus II,2 designates a CD verb; III,1 a Gt verb, etc.

-ʾ*a* suffix denoting direct quotation. It is added to the first few words of a quotation and to the last, or, more rarely, to every single word of the text.

ʾ*ab* (w. pron. suff.: ʾ*abu*-, acc. ʾ*abā*-; pl. ʾ*abaw*) father; forefather, ancestor; *bēta* ʾ*ab* family.

ʾ*abbā* an honorific title applied to venerated men of any station in religious life.

ʾ*abda* G *(yeʾbad)* to be mad, to rage. CG ʾ*aʾbada* caus. CGt ʾ*astāʾbada* to regard as or treat as a fool; to despise, ridicule. ʾ*abd* (f. ʾ*abedd*; pl. ʾ*abdān*, ʾ*abdāt*) foolish, stupid, ignorant, imprudent; mad, insane; n. fool. ʾ*ebud* idem.

ʾ*abāl* (pl. -*āt*) limb or member of the body; body, self, person.

ʾ*ebn* (pl. ʾ*eban*, ʾ*aʾbān*) m.f. stone. ʾ*ebna barad* hailstone(s).

ʾ*abbasa* D to commit a crime or sin (against: *lāʿla*, *la*-). ʾ*ebbus* wicked, criminal. ʾ*abbāsi* = *maʾabbes* sinner, criminal. ʾ*abbasā* (pl. -*t*) sin, crime, guilt.

ʾ*abaya* G *(yeʾbay)* to refuse, be unwilling (to do: inf.); to spurn, disobey, say no to (a.d.o.).

ʾ*ed* (w. pron. suff.: ʾ*edē*-; pl. ʾ*edaw*) f.m. hand; *diba* ʾ*edawa* through the agency of.

ʾ*adg* (f. ʾ*adegt*; pl. ʾ*aʾdug*) ass.

ʾ*admās* the hardest substance (Gk. *adamas*).

ʾ*addama* D to please (someone: o.s.). CDt ʾ*astaʾaddama* to be pleased with (a.d.o.), to find pleasing, pleasant. ʾ*addām* pleasing, pleasant. *maʾaddem* idem.

ʾ*adim* leather.

ʾ*adawa* G to sweep. ʾ*edew* swept. ʾ*edāw* sweepings, refuse.

ʾ*af* (w. pron. suff. ʾ*afu*-, acc. ʾ*afā*-; pl. ʾ*afaw*) mouth.

ʾ*afʾa*/ʾ*afʾā* adv. outside, on or to the outside; ʾ*afʾa* ʾ*em*- prep. on or to the outside of.

ʾ*afʿot* vipers.

ʾ*Afrenj* the Romans.

ʾ*efo* interrog. adv. how? in what way? why?

ʾ*agadā* large bone of the leg; tibia, shin-bone.

ʾ*egalē* indef. pron./adj. a certain (person), such-and-such (a person).

ʾ*eg*ʷ*āl* (pl. -*āt*) coll. and sing.: the young of any animal or fowl, including humans; ʾ*eg*ʷ*āla* ʾ*emma-ḥeyāw* mankind, man.

ʾegr (pl. *ʾegar*, *ʾaʾgār*) f.m. foot; *ʾegra ḍaḥāy* ray of sunlight; *westa/xaba ʾegara* at the feet of; *ba-ʾegr* on foot.

ʾEgziʾabḥēr God.

ʾaḥadu (acc. *ʾaḥada*) m. one, a certain (one); *ʾaḥatti* (acc. *ʾaḥatta*) f. idem. *ʾaḥatta* adv. once, one time. *ʾeḥud* the first day of the week or month.

ʾakala G *(yeʾkal/yeʾkel)* to be sufficient for, to satisfy (o.s. or *la-*); to be approximately. CG *ʾaʾkala* = Gt *taʾakla* to be satisfied, have enough. *ʾekul* sufficient, enough. *māʾkala* prep. (w. pron. suff.: *māʾkalē-*, but see § 10.1) among, in the midst of; *ba-māʾkala* idem; *ʾem-māʾkala* from among.

ʾakāl (pl. *-āt*) body, limbs, stature; substance, hypostasis, person. *lehqa ba-ʾakālu* he reached maturity.

ʾaʾkʷata CG to praise. Gt *taʾakʷta* pass. *ʾekut* praised, lauded. *ʾaʾkʷāti* one who renders praise or thanks. *ʾaʾkʷatēt* praise, glory, thanksgiving.

ʾakko neg. no, not, it is not (see §29.3).

ʾakya G *(yeʾkay)* to be evil, bad, wicked. CG *ʾaʾkaya* to make (something: a.d.o.) bad; to act badly (toward: *lāʿla/diba*). *ʾekuy* (f. *ʾekit*) evil, bad, wicked. *ʾekay* (pl. *-āt*) evil, wickedness. *ʾekit* n. idem; *ba-ʾekit* direly, without pity.

ʾalbo neg. of *bo*: there is/ are not (see §§28.2,3,5).

ʾalād a coin.

ʾelf (pl. *ʾaʾlāf*) myriad, ten thousand. *teʾlefit*, *meʾlefit* a vast number.

ʾallā conj. but, rather; except, unless.

ʾella rel. pron. c. pl. (§25.1); *ʾella mannu* pl. of *mannu*.

ʾellā dem. pron. f.pl. these; *ʾellu* idem m. pl. these.

ʾellāntu (acc. *ʾellānta*) dem. pron. f.pl. these; *ʾellontu* (acc. *ʾellonta*) idem m.pl.

ʾalē la- exclam.: Woe unto ....

ʾem-/ʾemenna prep. (w. pron. suff. *ʾemennē-*) from. *ʾemze* adv. then, next, thereupon. *ʾem-kama* conj. as soon as. *ʾemza* conj. when.

ʾem- conditional particle. See §§51.1,2.

ʾem- ... *ʾem-* conj. either ... or.

ʾama (1) prep. at the time of (see §25.2); (2) conj. when; (3) rel. adv. when. *ʾamēhā* adv. at that time, then, next; *ʾem-ʾamēhā* from that time onward.

ʾemma, la-ʾemma conj. if. *ʾemma-bo kama* perhaps. *ʾemma-hi* ... *ʾemma-hi* either ... or. *ʾemma-ʾakko* adv. otherwise, if that were not so.

ʾemm (pl. *-āt*) mother; *ʾemma-ḥeyāw* the mother of the living (Eve).

ʾemmat (pl. *-āt*) cubit; forearm.

ʾamna G *(yeʾman)* to be true; to believe (a.d.o. or *la-*, esp. with persons); to believe in *(ba-)*, have faith in. Gt *taʾamna/taʾamana* to be believed; to believe in (a.d.o. or *ba-*); to confess (sins: a.d.o.); to be confident, sure. CG *ʾaʾmana* to convert (a.d.o., in religious sense); to profess, assert, confirm as a fact. *ʾemun* faithful, trustworthy, true; *ʾemuna* adv. truly, in truth. *ʾamāni* one who believes; adj. faithful. *ʾemnat* faith, belief. *ʾamin* idem. *ʾamān* truth; as adj. (read ? *ʾammān*) true, faithful; *ʾamāna, ba-ʾamān* adv. truly, in truth. *māʾman, meʾman, māʾmen* (f. *-t*) adj. faithful, believing; true, trustworthy; n. a believer.

ʾaʾmara CG to know, understand, comprehend, realize, learn. Gt *taʾamra* pass. D *ʾammara* to tell, show, indicate, make known (something: a.d.o.; to: o.s.). Dt *taʾammara* pass. of D; to give a sign, to signal. CD *ʾaʾammara* = D. *ʾemmur* known, recognized. *ʾaʾmero* knowledge; *ʾi-yaʾmero* ignorance. *māʾmer* skilled, knowing; n. soothsayer. *teʾmert* (pl. *-āt, taʾāmer, -āt*) m.f. sign, omen; miracle.

ʾamir m.f. day. Only in fixed expressions: *ʾem-/ʾeska weʾetu/yeʾeti ʾamir* from/until that day (past or future); *weʾeta/yeʾeta ʾamira* on that day; *k^wello ʾamira* all day, every day.

ʾemāntu pron. f.pl. they; *ʾemuntu* idem m. pl. they.

ʾammexa D to greet, pay respect to. Glt *taʾāmexa* to greet one another, to kiss (in greeting). *ʾammexā* a greeting, kiss; a gift offered out of respect.

ʾamēkalā a thorny plant.

ʾana pron. I.

ʾanbaṭā (pl. *ʾanābeṭ*) locust(s).

ʾenbala, za-ʾenbala (w. pron. suff.: *ʾenbalē-*) prep. without, except for, excepting. See §28.5.

ʾenbeya interj. No. I refuse.

ʾanadā m. skin, hide, leather; *ḥabla ʾanadā* thong.

ʾengā part. used esp. in questions to mark an inference from a preceding statement, often with a nuance of doubt (see §51.4d).

taʾangada Qt to be a stranger/guest. *ʾengedā* (pl. *ʾanāged*) stranger, guest.

ʾenka, *ʾenkemu* part. so, then, therefore (see §51.4e).

ʾanqaṣ/ʾanqaḍ (pl. *ʾanāqeṣ*) m.f. gate (of city, temple, or other large structure).

ʾanest (pl. of *beʾsit*) women; *ʾanestiyā* (coll.) the women, the womenfolk.

taʾansasa Qt to become like a brute animal. *ʾensesā* animals, beasts, cattle. *ʾensesāwi* adj. animal, bestial.

ʾanta pron. you (m.s.); *ʾanti* idem (f.s.); *ʾantemu* idem (m.pl.); *ʾanten* idem (f.pl.).

ʾenta (1) rel. pron. f. s. (or poetic for m.s.), see §25.1; (2) prep. via, by way of.

ʾenza conj. while, when, as; see §31.2, §32.3.

ʾaraft (pl. *ʾarafāt*) m.f. wall, partition.

ʾaragāy (f. -*t*, *ʾaragit*; pl. *ʾaʾrug*) old person. *ʾaragāwi* (f. -*t*) idem.

ʾarami (coll.) pagans, heathens, non-Christians. *ʾaramāwi* adj. idem.

ʾarara G *(yeʾrer/yeʾrar)* to harvest. *māʾrar* harvest.

ʾarāray a style of church singing for certain feast-days and happy occasions.

ʾarwē (pl. *ʾarāwit*) m.f. animal, wild beast; *ʾarwē medr* snake, serpent.

ʾaraya G *(yeʾri)* to pick, gather, pluck up/out.

ʾasfarēdā (pl. -*t*) basket.

ʾasḥatyā m.f. ice, hail, snow, frost.

ʾeska prep. up to, until, as far as; conj. until; to the extent that, with the result that; *ʾeska soba* conj. idem.

ʾesma conj. (1) because, since, for; (2) that, the fact that (+ n. clause). *ʾem-weʾetu ʾesma* an example of this is ....

ʾasara G *(yeʾser)* to tie up, bind (a.d.o.); to tie something (a.d.o.; to: *ba-/westa*). Gt *taʾasra* pass. *ʾesur* bound, tied, captive, restricted. *ʾesrat* n. binding, tying. *māʾsar*, *māʾser*, *māʾsart* (pl. *maʾāser*, -*t*) m.f. bond, fetter; vow.

ʾasāreyon a small coin. (Gk. *assarion*).

ʾessāt m.f. fire.

ʾatata G *(yeʾtet)* to go away, be removed. CG *ʾaʾtata* to remove, take away. Gt *taʾatata* = Dt *taʾattata* = G or pass. of CG. *ʾetut* remote, distant.

ʾatawa G *(yeʾtu/yeʾtaw)* to go home; to depart (for home). CG *ʾaʾtawa* to send home, let go home; to bring home/indoors. *ʾetwat/ʾetot* n. return (home); return, yield (of crops). *meʾtāw* home, place to which one returns; act of returning.

ʾeton (pl. *-āt*) furnace, oven.

ʾaw conj. or.

ʾo- voc. part. O! Oh! Usually prefixed, as in *ʾo-negš*, but with *ʾEgziʾ* it is regularly suffixed: *ʾEgziʾo* O Lord! It may also express wonder or grief.

ʾewwa adv. surely, indeed, even; yes.

ʾoho exclam. of assent: Very well, I will (do so).

ʾOrit the Mosaic Law, the Pentateuch.

ʾex^w (acc. *ʾexwa* or *ʾex*^{w}*a*; w. pron. suff.: *ʾexu-*, acc. *ʾex*^{w}*ā-* or *ʾexwā-*; pl. *ʾaxaw*) brother.

ʾext (pl. *ʾaxāt*) sister.

ʾaxaza G (*yeʾxaz/yaʾaxaz* §39.1) to seize, grasp, hold (a.d.o. or *ba-*); to take captive; to possess, control, occupy; to begin (to do: subj. ± *kama*). Gt *taʾexza* pass. CG *ʾaʾxaza* to order (someone: a.d.o.) held. Glt *taʾāxaza* to be involved in a battle or similar activity (with: *mesla*). *ʾexuz* captive, held; possessed by (e.g. *ʾexuza ʾagānent*); joined, continuous. *ʾaxāzi* owner, possessor; master, lord. *ʾaxaz/ʾāxz* m. fist.

ʾi- neg. not (prefixed directly to element negated).

ʾēpis qopos (pl. *-āt*) bishop. *liqa ʾēpis qoposāt* archbishop.

ʾiyor, *ʾayar* (pl. *-āt*) air, atmosphere (Gk. *aēr*).

ʾaytē interr. adv. where? *ba-ʾaytē* idem. *ʾem-ʾaytē* whence? from where?

ʾItyopyā Ethiopia.

ʾayx the Deluge.

ʾayy (pl. *-āt*) interr. adj. which?

ʾazāb, *ʾazab*, *ʾezob* hyssop, mint.

ʾezn (pl. *ʾezan*, *ʾaʾzān*) f. ear. *māʾzen(t)*, *māʾzan(t)* (pl. *maʾāzen*) corner.

ʾazēb the south.

ʾazzaza D to order, command (someone: o.s.; to do: subj.). Dt *taʾazzaza* pass.; to obey (someone: *la-*). *ʾezzuz* commanded, ordered (of person or thing); *ʾezzuz weʾetu kama* + subj.: it has been commanded that ...; *ba-kama ʾezzuz ba-xaba* ... as has been commanded by. *te'zāz* (pl. *-āt*) f.m. command, order; edict, law, commandment; *ba-te'zāza* at the command of.

mā'bal/mā'bel (pl. *-āt*) m.f. wave, flood.

'Ebrāwiyān the Hebrews.

'abbaṭa D to compel, force, coerce.

'abya G *(ye'bay)* to be big, large, great, important. CG *'a'baya* to make great, increase, augment; to extol, exalt. Dt *ta'abbaya* to be boastful, arrogant. *'abiy* (f. *'abāy*; pl. *'abayt*) big, great, large, important; *ba-'abiy qāl* in a loud voice. *'ebbuy* arrogant, boastful, insolent, haughty. *'ebay* (pl. *-āt*) greatness, size; magnificence, majesty. *te'bit* arrogance, insolence.

'ed (pl. *-aw*) coll. men, males; the menfolk (of a given community); also used as the pl. of *be'si*.

'ādi adv. still, yet, again, moreover, still more. With pron. suff. = to still be, as in *'enza 'ādina zeyya* while we are still here; *'ādiya ḥeyāw* I am still alive. With foll. time word: more, as in *'ādi xamus* five days more.

'edew (pl. *-ān*) enemy.

'adawa G *(ye'du/ye'daw)* to cross (a.d.o. or acc. of goal or prep. phrase). Gt *ta'adawa* to transgress (a law: *'em-*; against a person: *lā'la*); also = G. CG *'a'dawa* to bring/lead/take across. *mā'dot* (pl. *ma'ādew*) the opposite side (of river, mountain etc.); *mā'dota* prep. across, to the opposite side of, beyond. See §43.1(e). *'edā* debt, guilt.

'eḍ (pl. *-aw*) m.f. tree; grove, woods; wood (material); a club.

'aḍada G *(ye'ḍed)* to harvest. Gt *ta'aḍḍa* pass. *'aḍādi* harvester. *mā'ḍad* sickle.

'aḍm (pl. *'a'ḍemt*) bone.

ta'āḍawa to cast lots. *'eḍā* a lot. *'eḍḍāwē/'uḍāwē* n. casting lots.

'aḍaya/'aḍya G to putrify, get wormy. *'eḍē* (pl. *-yāt*, *'eḍayāt*) worm, caterpiller.

'efrat unguent, ointment.

ta'aggala Dt to cheat, defraud; to oppress, treat unjustly, rob. *te'gelt* fraud, defrauding, robbing; injury, damage.

ta'aggaša Dt to be patient, persevere; to practice restraint, abstinence. CDt *'asta'aggaša* caus. of Dt; to bear patiently. *ta'aggāši* patient, persevering. *te'gešt* temperance, continence, patience, tolerance. *masta'aggeš* temperant, patient, long-suffering.

'ālam (pl. *-āt*) m.f. world, this world, the secular world; the universe, all creation; eternity; all time past, present, and future. *la-'ālam* forever. *'eska la-'ālam, la-'ālama 'ālam* idem. *'ālamāwi* (f. *-t*) adj. worldly, of this world.

'alawa G *(ye'lu)* to pervert; to act perversely, to transgress (laws etc.); to be rebellious, evil, refractory, apostate, heretical. CG *'a'lawa* caus.; to translate (from one language into another); to copy or transcribe. *'elew* (f. *'elut*) crooked, perverse, evil; rebellious, heretical. *'elwat* disaster; perversity, heresy, apostacy; copy, transcription. *'alāwi* wicked, perverse; infidel, heretical.

'ām, 'āmat (pl. *'āmatāt*) f.m. year; *la-la-'āmu* adv. yearly, every year.

'am'am mud, slime.

'amd (pl. *'a'mād*) column, pillar.

'ammaḍa D to sin, act unjustly or wickedly; to harm, injure. *'ammāḍi* unjust, wicked, criminal. *'ammaḍā* injustice, wickedness. *ma'ammeḍ* = *'ammāḍi*.

'amaqa G *(ye'meq/ye'maq)* to be deep. CG *'a'maqa* to make deep, to penetrate deeply. *'emuq* deep. *'emaq* depth. *mā'meq* (pl. *ma'āmeq*) the deep, abyss.

'anbari whale.

'anzara Q to pipe, play a musical instrument. *'enzirā* a musical instrument of any sort. *ma'anzer* musician, piper, flute-player.

'aqaba G *(ye'qab)* to guard, keep watch on; to take care of, preserve, keep safe; to observe, keep (e.g. the law). Gt *ta'aqaba* pass. of G; to guard one's self (against: *'emenna* or o.s.). CG *'a'qaba* to hand (a.d.o.) over to (someone: o.s. or *xaba*) for safekeeping. *'equb* (1) under guard, in custody; (2) set aside, reserved (for: *la-*); (3) cautious, guarded; *'eqebt* (pl. *'equbāt*) concubine, harem-woman. *'aqābi* (pl. *'aqabt*) guard; *'aqābē ('aṣada) wayn* vintner, one in charge of the wine; *'aqābē re's/šegā* body-guard; *'aqābē nabib* speaker, spokesman; *'aqābē gannat* gardener; *'aqābē šerāy* doctor, physician. *'eqbat* n. guarding, observing, keeping; watch, vigil. *mā'qab* (pl. *ma'āqeb, -t*) guard, guard-post.

ta'aqfa to be hindered, impeded; to stumble, knock against. CG

ʾaʿqafa to impede, present an obstacle to (o.s.). *ʿeqeft* (pl. *-āt*) impediment, obstacle, hindrance. *māʿqaf/māʿqef* idem.

ʾaʿqala CG to collect water in a basin or reservoir. *meʿqāl* (pl. *-āt*) basin, reservoir.

ʿaqqama D to define, set limits to. *ʿaqm* (or *ʿaqqem*) measure, degree, extent; moderation; end, completion, maturation; *ba-ʿaqm* moderately. *ʿaqma werzāwē* maturity, manhood. *ʿeqqum* limited, defined, determined. *ʿeqqāmē* determination, definition.

ʿaraba/ʿarba (yeʿrab/yeʿreb) to set (of heavenly bodies). CG *ʾaʿraba* to cause to set. *ʿarab* west; Arabia. *ʿarb* Friday; *ʿelata ʿarb*, *ʿarb ʿelat* idem. *ʿerbat* n. setting. *ʿarabi* western; Arabian. *ʿarabāwi* idem. *meʿrāb* the west; *meʿrāba ḍaḥāy* idem.

ʾaʿrafa CG (1) intrans.: to rest, find rest, come to rest; to die; (2) trans.: to give rest (to: o.s.; from: *ʾemenna*). *ʿeruf* adj. resting, still; dead. *ʿeraft* (pl. *-āt*) f.m. rest, peace, quiet; death. *meʿrāf* (pl. *-āt*) a quiet place, resting-place; one's final resting-place; a measure of length, a stade; chapter of a book.

ʿarga G *(yeʿreg/yeʿrag)* to ascend, come/go up, climb. CG *ʾaʿraga* to bring/lead/take up; to offer up (a sacrifice). *ʿergat* ascent, ascension; assumption (into heaven); elevation (of the Host). *māʿreg* (pl. *maʿāreg*, *-āt*) m.f. (place of) ascent; grade, degree, level, class; stairs, ladder. *meʿrāg* idem.

taʿāraka Glt to become friends (with). *ʿark* (f. *ʿarekt*; pl. *ʾaʿrekt*, *ʿarkān/ʿarkāt*) friend.

ʿarqa/ʿaraqa to be naked, empty; to be orphaned. CG *ʾaʿraqa* to strip bare; to empty out. Gt *taʿarqa* to be stripped, denuded, emptied. *ʿeruq* naked, empty. *ʿerāq* (appositional pron. suff. obligatory) naked, empty, alone. *ʿerqān* nakedness; shame (the sexual parts).

ʿarāt (pl. *-āt*) bed.

ʿarraya D (rarely G *ʿaraya*, *yeʿri*) to be level, smooth; to be equal (to: *la-*, *mesla*, *kama*); to make equal, level; to share (a.d.o.) equally. CD *ʾaʿarraya* to make (something: a.d.o.) equal (to: *mesla*). Dt *taʿarraya* pass. of CD. *ʿerruy* (fem. *ʿerrit*) equal (to: *la-*, *mesla*), the same (as); *ʿerruya* = *ba-ʿerruy* adv. equally, to the same extent. *ʿerreyennā/ʿerrinnā* equality.

ʿarraza D to prepare or furnish clothing. *ʿarāz* (or *ʿarrāz*) (pl. *-āt*) clothing, vestments.

ʿasaba G *(yeʿseb)* to hire for wages. *ʿasb* wages, hire, pay, reward.

ʿassāb hireling, mercenary.

ʿasaya G *(yeʿsi)* to repay. Gt *taʿasya* to be repaid, accept payment. *ʿesēt* payment, reward.

ʿāšā (pl. *-t*) fish.

ʿašru (acc. idem) f. ten. *ʿašartu* (acc. *ʿašarta*) m. ten. *ʿāšer* (f. *-t*) adj. tenth. *ʿāšerāwi* (f. *-t*) idem. *ʿāšerāy* (f. *ʿāšerit*) idem. *ʿašur* the tenth day (of the month); ten days. *ʿašr/ʿešr* f. ten; *ʿešra* adv. ten times. *ʿešrā* twenty. *ʿāšerāt* a tenth, tithe.

ʿaššara D to call a meeting; to invite (a.d.o.). Dt *taʿaššara* pass. *ʿašur/ʿaššur* feast, banquet.

ʿaṣaba/ʿaṣba G *(yeʿṣeb/yeʿṣab)* to be hard, harsh, difficult (for: o. s.); to be necessary. *ʿeṣub* harsh, difficult, onerous; difficult (to do: *la-* + inf.); *ba-ʿeṣub*, *ʾem-ʿeṣub* adv. with difficulty. *ʿeṣab*, *ʿaṣāb* harshness, difficulty; need, want.

ʿaṣad (pl. *ʾaʿṣād*, *-āt*) m.f. any circumscribed area: courtyard, atrium; pen, stall; field, farm; village; *ʿaṣada wayn* vineyard.

ʿaṣf (pl. *-āt*, *ʾaʿṣeft*) m. tunic, cloak, mantle.

ʿaṣq (pl. *ʾaʿṣuq*, *-āt*) m.f. branch, palm-branch.

ʿaṣawa/ʿaḍawa *(yeʿṣew)* to close, shut, lock, bolt. Gt *taʿaṣwa* pass. *ʿeṣew* locked, closed, bolted. *ʿaṣāwi* doorkeeper. *māʿṣo* (pl. *maʿāṣut*) door, gate; lock, bolt.

ʿaṭana G *(yeʿṭen)* to burn incense. *ʿeṭān* incense. *māʿṭant* (pl. *maʿāṭen*) censer, thurible.

ʿoda G *(yeʿud)* trans.: to go around, surround; to avoid, circumvent (a.d.o.); intrans.: to go around, circulate, tour. CG *ʾaʿoda* to lead/take around, cause to circulate. *ʿudat* circle, circuit, orbit. *ʿawādi* messenger, herald, preacher. *ʿawd* (pl. *ʾaʿwād*) environs, neighborhood, vicinity; area in general; a court of law; a circuit, period of time; threshing-floor. *ʿawda* prep. around, surrounding (suffixes added as to an acc. noun).

ʿof (pl. *ʾaʿwāf*) bird; fowl.

ʿewāl young of an animal, esp. the foal of an ass.

ʿom (pl. *ʾaʿwām*, *-āt*) tree(s), dense grove, woods.

ʿoqa G *(yeʿuq)* to beware of, take care for, be cautious of (*lāʿla*, *la-*, or acc.); esp. common in the imperative with a neg. subjunctive: take care not to, be careful not to (*ʿuq kama ʾi...*). CG *ʾaʿoqa* to make known, show (a.d.o.; to: o.s.). Gt *taʿawqa* to be noticed, perceived, recognized; to be made known, revealed. *ʿewuq* familiar, well-known.

ʿora G *(yeʿur)* to be blind. CG *ʾaʿora* to blind. Dt *taʿawwara* to neglect, overlook, let pass unnoticed; to despise. *ʿewur* blind. *ʿurat* blindness.

ʿawyawa Q to wail in mourning. *ʿawyāt* n. wailing.

taʿayyana Dt to set up camp, to camp; with *lāʿla*: to besiege. *ʿayn* (pl. *ʾaʿyent*) f. eye; *sabʾa ʿayn* spies, scouts. *teʿyent* (pl. *-āt*, *taʿāyen*) army, host; camp, encampment; tent(s); gathering, congregation.

ʿezl a mode of church singing used during Lent and for funerals and certain feast-days.

ʿazaqt (pl. *-āt*, *ʿazaqāt*) f.m. well, cistern.

B

ba- prep. in, into; by, with (of agent). With pron. suff.: §28.1. Expressing possession: §28.2. Expressing existence: §28.3. *bo za-* as indef. pron.: §28.4.

baʾenta (w. pron. suff.: *baʾentiʾa-*) prep. about, concerning; because of, on account of; for the sake of. *baʾenta ment* why? *baʾenta-ze* thus, therefore. *baʾenta za-* because.

beʾsi (pl. *sabʾ*) man, husband, person. *beʾsit* (pl. *ʾanest*) woman, wife.

baʿada G to change, alter. Gt *tabaʿada* = Glt *tabāʿada* to move away, emigrate; to be changed, altered, alien, unfamiliar. *beʿud* different, alien, strange. *bāʿed* (f. *bāʿedd*) other, different; strange, alien. *beʿdennā* change, difference.

beʿla G *(yebʿal)* to be rich, wealthy. CG *ʾabʿala* to make rich. *beʿul* (f. *beʿelt*) rich, wealthy. *bāʿel* (f. *-t*; pl. *ʾabʿelt*) rich, wealthy. *bāʿl* (f. *bāʿelt*; pl. *ʾabʿelt*) owner, possessor, master. *baʿʿāl* idem. *baʿāl* (pl. *-āt*) m.f. feast, festival; *gabra baʿāla* to hold/celebrate a festival; *baʿāl tekelt* a fixed festival; *baʿāl ʾi-tekelt* a movable festival. *beʿl* wealth, riches.

badbada Q to die. *bedbed* plague, fatal illness.

badn (pl. *ʾabdent*) m. corpse.

badara G *(yebder)* to hurry, precede, arrive first. CG *ʾabdara* to prefer, choose, select, favor; with foll. inf.: to do something eagerly, willingly, with undivided attention. Gt *tabadra* pass. of CG. Glt *tabādara* to compete with (in running), to race. *badr* contest, race.

badwa G to be desert, wasteland. CG *'abdawa* caus. *badw*, *badā* desert, wasteland, uncultivated area.

baḍ'a/baṣ'a G *(yebḍā')* to vow. CG *'abḍe'a* to make or declare blessed; to obtain a vow; to become happy, blessed. *beḍu'/beṣu'* fortunate, blessed; vowed, dedicated. *beḍ'at* vow. *beḍu'āwi* beatific, blessed. *beḍ'ān* beatification, blessedness.

bag' (pl. *'abāge'*) sheep.

behla G (imperf. *yebel*, subj. *yebal*; special preterite *yebē-l*; see § 39.2) to say, speak; to call (someone: o.s.; something: a.d.o.). Gt *tabehla* to be spoken, said; to be mentioned, named, spoken of. Glt *tabāhala* to speak (debate, discuss, argue) with one another *(mesla, babaynāt-*, acc.).

behma G *(yebham)* to be mute. *bahhām* mute. *behmat* muteness.

bāḥ/bāḥa (w. or without pron. suff. of the 2nd pers.) exclam. Greetings! *bāḥa beḥla* to greet.

beḥ'a G to ferment (intrans.). CG *'abḥe'a* to ferment (trans.). Gt *tabeḥ'a* = G. *beḥu'* fermented; leaven, yeast. *beḥi'* vinegar. *beḥ'at* fermentation.

beḥēr (pl. *baḥāwert*) m. region, province, district.

bāḥr (pl. *'abḥert*) f.m. sea, ocean. *bāḥrey* (pl. *-āt*) pearl.

bāḥtit- adj./adv. alone, sole, only; used appositionally, always with a pron. suff., e.g. *'ana bāḥtiteya* I alone; *rakabkewwo bāḥtito* I found him alone (or: him only). *'enta bāḥtit-* by one's self, alone; e.g. *nabara 'enta bāḥtitu* he sat by himself. *bāḥtu* adv. but, however. May occur first in the clause as *wa-bāḥtu* or be placed after the first main element of the clause, esp. if this is an element preposed for emphasis.

tabāḥtawa Qt to take up a life of solitude. *beḥtew* adj. alone, solitary. *bāḥtāwi* anchorite, one who lives in solitude. *beḥtewennā* anchoritism.

tabak^{w}ra Gt to be the firstborn; to give birth for the first time. *bak^{w}r* firstborn; the usual construction of this word is with a pronominal suffix, as in *waldā za-bak^{w}rā* her firstborn son (lit. her son which was her firstborn). *bek^{w}rennā* status of firstborn.

bakaya G *(yebki)* to weep, mourn (over: *diba, lā'la, ba'enta*). Glt *tabākaya* to weep together, mourn mutually. CG *'abkaya* to move to tears. *bekāy* m. weeping, lamentation. *mabkey* mourner (professional).

bāleḥa L to rescue, save, liberate. Lt *tabāleḥa* pass. *bālāḥi* liberator, protector.

maballat (pl. *-āt*) widow, widowhood; nun.

balas/balasā (pl. *-t*, *ʾablās*) fig(s), fig-tree.

balya G *(yebli)* to be old, worn out, decrepit, obsolete. CG *ʾablaya* caus. *beluy* (f. *belit*) old, etc.; *Ḥegg Belit* the Old Testament. *balāyi* old, wearing out.

balxa G *(yeblāx)* to be sharp. CG *ʾablexa* to sharpen. *balix* sharp. *belx* sharp point or edge.

baq^{w}*ʿa* G *(yebq*^{w}*āʿ)* to be useful, of benefit, profitable, suitable, appropriate (to a person: o.s. or *la-*); *beq*^{w}*eʿani* Please. CGt *ʾastabq*^{w}*eʿa* to plead, beseech, pray (with, to: o.s.). *bāq*^{w}*eʿ* useful, beneficial. *baq*^{w}*āʿi* idem; also: benefactor. *baq*^{w}*ʿēt* use, usefulness. *baq*^{w}*ʿ* idem.

baq^{w}*ala/baq*^{w}*la* G *(yebq*^{w}*el/yebq*^{w}*al)* to sprout, grow. CG *ʾabq*^{w}*ala* caus. *baq*^{w}*l* (pl. *-āt*) plant, herb, vegetation. *baqalt* date-palm.

berʿ (pl. *ʾabrāʿ*) reed; arm of a candelabrum.

barbara Q to pillage. *sabʾa barbār* barbarians, plunderers.

barad m. hail.

barha G *(yebrāh)* to shine, be bright, be light. CG *ʾabreha* to illuminate, cause to be bright; to emit light. *beruh* bright, shining; cheerful, happy. *berhān* (pl. *-āt*) m. light (lit. and fig.). *berhānāwi* (f. *-t*) of or pertaining to light, esp. in heavenly or spiritual sense.

ʾastabraka CGt to kneel. *berk* (pl. *ʾabrāk*) knee.

bāraka L to bless (a.d.o. or *lāʿla*). Lt *tabāraka* pass. *buruk* (f. *burekt*) blessed; fortunate, happy; excellent, outstanding. *barakat* (pl. *-āt*) m.f. blessing. *burākē* (pl. *-yāt*) idem.

beralē/biralē beryl, crystal; alabaster vessel.

baraqa G *(yebreq)* to lightning, flash like lightning. CG *ʾabraqa* caus. *mabraq* (pl. *mabāreqt*) m. lightning.

berur (pl. *-āt*) m. silver.

bert m. copper.

tabāraya Glt to follow successively, to do by turns. *ʾebrēt* alternation, successive turn(s); round or tour of duty or office. *ba-ʾebrēta* during the administration of; *ba-ba-ʾebrētomu* each in his own turn.

besrāt/besserāt good news, gospel.

baṣḥa G *(yebṣāḥ)* to arrive; to happen (to: o.s. or *lāʿla, diba*). CG *ʾabṣeḥa* caus. Glt *tabāṣeḥa* to bring (someone: a.d.o.) before a judge. *beṣḥat* arrival.

bataka G *(yebtek)* to break (trans.). Gt *tabatka* to break (intrans.). *betuk* broken. *betkat* fracture, rupture, breaking.

batr (pl. *ʾabter*) staff, branch.

boʾa G *(yebāʾ)* to enter *(westa, ba-)*. CG *ʾabeʾa* to bring/lead/take in; to introduce, insert. Glt *tabāweʾa* to intrude, slip in uninvited (into, among: acc.). *baʾat* (pl. -*āt*) entry, entrance, entering; cave, lair, den, cell. *mubāʾ/mebwāʾ* (pl. -*āt*) place of entry; act of entering. *mabāʾ* (pl. -*āt*) offering.

ʾabeḥa CG to allow, permit (o.s. of person + subj. of verb). Gt *tabawḥa* pass.; to have power over *(lāʿla, diba, ba-)*. CGt *ʾastabawḥa* to ask for permission. *bewuḥ la-* it is permitted for (*la-*: someone) to do (subj.). *mabāḥt* power, authority, permission.

bayyana D to discern, distinguish, make out. CD *ʾabayyana* to make clear, evident. *ba-baynāti-* (pron. suff. required) prep. among, between (used mainly with verbs denoting reciprocal activity. See Voc. 24)

bayyaṣa D to separate, distinguish, discern. Glt *tabāyaṣa* to become companions. *biṣ* (sing. or coll.; pl. *ʾabyāṣ*) friend, comrade, companion; neighbor; single individual.

bēt (pl. *ʾabyāt*) m.f. house; room; sheath.

bēzawa Q to redeem. CQ *ʾabēzawa* caus. Qt *tabēzawa* to redeem for one's self; to be redeemed. *bēzā* ransom; as prep.: in exchange for. *bēzāwi* redeemer, savior. *mabēzāwi* idem.

bazxa G *(yebzāx)* to be many, much, numerous, abundant. CG *ʾabzexa* to multiply, make numerous; to produce a lot of, have a lot of. *bezux* (f. *bezext*) many, much, numerous, abundant. *bezx* multitude, large number or amount. *mabzext* major part, majority; most of; *mabzexto* adv. often, frequently.

D

dāʾemu adv. just, merely, only; furthermore, moreover; rather, but, on the contrary.

tadbāb roof, top, summit, pinnacle. *dabub* the north.

dabr (pl. *ʾadbār*) m. mountain; monastery.

dabtarā (pl. *dabāter*) tent, tabernacle.

dābēlā (pl. *-t*) male of any animal, esp. ram, he-goat.

dafana G *(yedfen)* to cover, hide, conceal. *madfen* treasure; sepulchre.

dagama G *(yedgem)* with inf. or coordinated verb: to do again. *dāgem* (f. *-t*) adj. second, other, further; *dāgema* adv. again, a second time; further, moreover.

daḥara G *(yedḥar)* to divorce, repudiate.

dakma (yedkem/yedkam) to be tired, weary, weak, feeble, ill. CG *ʾadkama* caus. *dekum* (f. *dekemt*) tired, etc. *dekām* weariness, infirmity, weakness.

ʾadlaqlaqa Q to shake, quake, tremble; also caus. of the same. *deleqleq* violent motion, storm, tempest; earthquake.

dalawa G *(yedlu)* to weigh (a.d.o.; out to: o.s.); to be useful, suitable, proper, correct (for someone: o.s.; to do something: subj. ± *kama*). CG *ʾadlawa* to please, satisfy (someone: a.d.o. or *la-*); to adulate, fawn over, flatter. Dt *tadallawa* to prepare one's self, get ready; to live in luxury. CDt *ʾastadallawa* to prepare, make ready (trans.). CGlt *ʾastadālawa* idem. *delew* (f. *delut*) adj. worthy (to do: subj.), deserving; proper; weighed. *delwat* weight, worthiness, propriety. *madlew* (pl. *-ān*) hypocrite, fawner; an unjust official or judge. *madālew* (pl.) scales, balance. *tadlā* preparation; propriety, appropriateness, worthiness; luxury, affluence.

dam (pl. *-āt*) m.f. blood.

damḍa G *(yedmeḍ/yedmaḍ)* to sound. CG *ʾadmaḍa* caus. *demḍ* sound, noise.

ʾadmama CG (rare) to astonish, stupify. Gt *tadamma* = Dt *tadammama* to be astonished, amazed, stupified. *madmem* marvelous, astonishing; n. miracle, marvel.

dammana D to cloud over, obscure; to become cloudy. CD *ʾadammana* idem. *demmun* cloudy. *dammanā* (pl. *-t*) m.f. cloud(s). *damanmin* rather cloudy.

damaqa G to grind up, crush.

dammara D to insert, mix in, join together, unite. Dt *tadammara* pass.; to be married. *demmur* mixed, united, joined. *demmārē* union, joining, uniting. *tedmert* union, marriage.

dangaḍa Q to be astonished, stupified, amazed, disturbed in mind, terrified. CQ *ʾadangaḍa* to astonish etc. *denguḍ* astonished, etc. *dengāḍē* astonishment, etc. *madangeḍ* adj. astonishing, etc.

dengel (pl. *danāgel*) virgin; as applied to men: monk, celibate. *dengelennā* virginity.

danqawa Q to be hard of hearing. *denqew* hard of hearing; slow-witted, dense.

daqiq (coll.) children; offspring, progeny; *Daqiqa ʾEsrāʾēl* the Israelites. *daqq* (coll.) children and/or servants.

daqqasa D to sleep. *deqqās* sleep.

dergeḥā a patch.

deruk harsh, savage.

dasēt (pl. *dasayāt*) island.

dexna G *(yedxan)* to escape safely (from: *ʾemenna*); to be safe, unharmed; to be saved (in the religious sense). CG *ʾadxana* to save, keep safe, rescue; to save (rel. sense). *dexun* safe, unharmed; saved (rel. sense); immune to, free of *(ʾemenna)*. *dāxen* safe, whole, sound, unharmed. *dāxn* safety, well-being, security. *dāxnā/dexnā* idem. *madxen* = *madxani* savior, redeemer. *madxanit* m.f. salvation, safety, redemption.

dexra adv. afterward. *dexra* (w. pron. suf.: *dexrē-*) prep. behind, in back of; *ba-dexra* idem; *ʾem-dexra* from behind, after (of time); *ʾem-dexra-ze* after this, afterwards; *ʾem-dexra* conj. after. *dax(x)ārit* end.

daxara G to allow, sanction. *madxar* sanction, blessing.

dawal (pl. *ʾadwāl*) region, district, territory.

doreho (pl. *dawāreh*) m.f. chicken, hen, rooster.

dawaya G *(yedway)* to be sick, ill. Dt *tadawwaya* to feign illness. CG *ʾadwaya* to make ill. *dewuy/dewey* (f. *deweyt*) sick, ill. *dawē* (pl. *-yāt*) f.m. sickness, illness, disease.

diba (w. pron. suff.: *dibē-*) prep. on, upon, onto, against; *ba-diba* idem; *ʾem-diba* from on, from upon.

dēgana Q/L to pursue, chase (a.d.o. or *dexra*, *ʾem-dexra*).

ʾadyām (pl.; pl. *-āt*) area, region, environs, neighborhood, adjacent district.

dayyana D to judge, condemn, punish. Dt *tadayyana* = Gt *tadayna* pass. *dayn* judgment, punishment, condemnation, esp. of the Last Judgment.

diyāqon (pl. *-āt*) deacon. *diqunā* diaconate, office of deacon.

Ḍ

ḍab'a/ṣab'a G *(yeḍbā')* to fight, make war (with: a.d.o.). Glt *taṣābe'a* to fight one another (a.d.o. or *mesla*). *ṣab'* (pl. *'aṣbā'*, *-t*) m.f. war, battle; *ḥora ṣab'a* to go out to battle. *ṣabā'i* warrior, soldier. *ṣabā'it* f.m. army, troops; battle, fighting.

'aḍbara/'aṣbara ṣebura to work clay. *ḍebur/ṣebur* clay, mud.

ḍāḍē moth, worm.

ḍafara G *(yeḍfer)* to weave, plait. Gt *taḍafra* pass. *ḍefur* woven, plaited. *ḍefro* plaited work. *ḍefrat* n. weaving, joining, plaiting.

'astaḍāge'a CLt to place on a bed or litter. *ḍeg'*, *ḍegā'* pillow, mattress. *maḍāg^{w}e'* a paralytic.

ḍagām the left hand or side; *ḍegm* idem.

ḍaḥāy/ḍaḥay (pl. *-āt*) m.f. sun. *Hagara Ḍaḥāy* Heliopolis.

'aḍme'a CG to listen to, to hear.

ḍamada G *(yeḍmed)* to join, bind together, yoke. Gt *taḍamda* pass.; to dedicate one's self to, pursue assiduously, submit one's self to, minister to. *ḍemud* joined, connected; zealous, assiduous; as n.: devoté, disciple, servant. *ḍemd* yoke, pair. *ḍammād* sectarian, zealot, devoté. *maḍmad* rope, thong.

ḍamara G = *ḍammara* D to join, affix, connect, attach. Glt *taḍāmara* to associate with (one another). *ḍemrat* n. joining, connecting. *maḍmer/maḍmar* (pl. *maḍāmer*, *-t*) partner, mate, companion, spouse.

ḍamr m.f. wool.

meḍnegā' railing, railed enclosure; a place where one leans or reclines.

ḍansa G *(yeḍnes/yeḍnas)* to become pregnant (by: *'em-*); to conceive (a child: a.d.o.). Gt *taḍansa* to be conceived. *ḍenest* (f.) pregnant. *ḍens* pregnancy.

ḍaq^{w}ana G *(yeḍq^{w}en)* to surround with a fence or wall. *ḍaq^{w}an/ḍaq^{w}n* fence, wall.

'aḍre'a CG (intrans.) to cease, stop, be at rest; (trans.) to bring to a stop. Gt *taḍar'a* = CG intrans. *ḍeru'* inert, at rest, brought to a stop. *ḍer'at* cessation, rest; *za'enbala ḍer'at* without ceasing, without interruptions.

ḍarfa/ḍarafa G *(yeḍref)* to blaspheme (against: *lā'la*, *la-*, or acc.). *ḍeruf* blasphemous, wicked, impious. *ḍarāfi* blasphemer. *ḍerfat* blasphemy.

ḍarq (pl. *'aḍreqt*) patch, tatter. *za-ḍarq* patched, threadbare.

'aḍrara CG to be hostile. Glt *taḍārara* to act hostilely toward, be an enemy of. *ḍarr* (pl. *'aḍrār*) enemy, adversary. *ḍarrāwi* adj. enemy, hostile.

ḍoga G to be savage, wild, perverse, evil, malignant. *ḍewug* = *ḍawwāg* savage, etc. *ḍug* perverseness etc.

'aḍawwasa CD to weaken, cripple, maim. *ḍewwus* weak, crippled, maimed.

ḍēwawa Q/L to take captive, lead away captive, deport, exile. Qt *taḍēwawa* pass. *ḍēwew/ḍiwew* captive, exiled. *ḍēwā*, *ḍēwāwē*, *ḍiwāwē* captivity, exile.

F

fadfada Q to become numerous, abundant, to increase; to surpass, be superior; *wa-za-yefadaffed 'em-zentu* and what's more. CG *'afadfada* caus.; to surpass (someone in: two acc.). *fadfāda* adv. exceedingly, very much, greatly.

fadaya G *(yefdi)* to pay back, to pay a debt. Gt *tafadya* to exact payment or punishment; to receive payment or punishment, to be paid back. *fedā* repayment, retribution; punishment, revenge. *fadāy(i)* one who pays back. *mafdē* money; reward, payment.

faḍama G = *faḍḍama* D to stop up, obstruct. Gt *tafaḍma* = Dt *tafaḍḍama* pass.; to be speechless.

faḍana G to have a fever. *faḍant* fever.

feḥm (pl. *'afḥām*) carbon, coal.

fakkara D to interpret, expound, explain. Dt *tafakkara* pass. *fekkārē* explanation, interpretation, exposition. *mafakker* interpreter, expounder; soothsayer, prophet.

falag (pl. *'aflāg*) river.

falasa G *(yefles)* to separate, go away, depart, emigrate; to secede, split off (from: *'emenna*); *falasa xaba* to go over to the side of; *falasa 'em-zentu ʿālam* to die. CG *'aflasa* to send away, deport, exile, remove. Glt *tafālasa* to wander as exiles from one place to another; to pass from one generation to another. *felus* exiled, in exile. *felsat* wandering, travel; exile; death; assumption (into heaven). *Felsata Bābilon* the Babylonian Exile. *falāsi* an exile, alien, pilgrim.

falaṭa G *(yefleṭ)* to separate, divide, segregate, put into a separate group or category; to distinguish, discern. Gt *tafalṭa* pass. CG

ʾaflaṭa to speak distinctly, to make a distinction. Glt *tafālaṭa* to separate from one another. *feluṭ* separate, distinct. *felṭat* separation, division, distinction.

fannawa D to send. Dt *tafannawa* pass. Glt *tafānawa* to bid farewell to (o.s.). *fennew* sent. *fenot/fennot* (pl. *fenāw/fennāw, -ē*) f.m. road, way, path. *fennā* (1) = *fenot*; (2) *fennā sark* early evening.

faqada G *(yefqed)* to want, wish, desire, require; freq. with subj. ± *kama*. Gt *tafaqda* pass. *faqād* (pl. *-āt*) m.f. desire, wish, will; *ba-faqādu* of his own accord; *mašwāʿta faqād* voluntary offering; *zaʾenbala faqād* involuntarily. *faqādi* one who actively seeks something (e.g. mercy, revenge); (pl. *faqadd*) necromancer.

ʾafqara CG to love. Gt *tafaqra* pass. Glt *tafāqara* to love one another; to love (someone: *mesla*). *fequr* (f. *feqert*) beloved, loved. *feqr* love.

ferfār, ferfur (pl. *-āt*) crumb.

farha G *(yefrāh)* to be afraid; to fear (a.d.o. or *ʾem-*). Gt *tafarha* to be feared. CG *ʾafreha* to frighten. *farāhi* fearful, reverent. *farrāh* fearful, timid. *ferhat* (pl. *-āt*) fear, dread, awe; fearfulness, timidity. *mafreh* fear-inspiring, dreadful.

faras (pl. *ʾafrās*) m.f. horse. *sabʾa ʾafrās* horsemen.

ʾafrext/ʾafxert (coll.) chicks.

faraya G *(yefray)* to bear fruit, be fruitful. CG *ʾafraya* caus.; also = G. *ferē* (pl. *-yāt, fereyāt*) m. fruit (lit. and fig.), blossom, bud; *gabra/wahaba ferē* to produce fruit. *màfrey* fruitful.

tafaššeḥa Dt to rejoice (in: *ba-, baʾenta, lāʿla, diba*). *feššuḥ* happy, joyous, rejoicing. *feššeḥā* joy, happiness. *tefšeḥt* (pl. *-āt*) idem.

Fesḥ Passover.

faṣṣama D to complete, finish, end; to fulfill, accomplish; with foll. inf.: to finish doing something. Dt *tafaṣṣama* pass. *feṣṣum* done, accomplished, completed, fulfilled, consummated; perfect, whole, complete. *feṣṣāmē* consummation, end, completion, perfection. *tafṣāmēt* idem.

fatḥa G *(yeftāḥ)* to untie, loosen, open; to let loose, set free; to forgive (sins: a.d.o.); to pass judgment. Gt *tafatḥa* pass. CG *ʾafteḥa* to bring to judgment. Glt *tafāteḥa* to engage in a legal case (with: *mesla* or acc.). *fetuḥ* open; forgiven (persons or sins). *fatāḥi* (pl. *fatāḥt*) judge. *fetḥ* judgment (act or fact).

fatala G *(yeftel)* to twist, spin. Gt *tafatla* pass. *fetul* spun, twisted. *fatl* (pl. *'aftāl, 'aftelt*) thread, cord. *fetlo* twisted work.

fatana G *(yeften)* to investigate, explore; to examine, test. CG *'aftana* to hand over for examination. Gt *tafatna* pass. of G. *fetun* investigated, examined, tested. *fatāni* examiner, tester.

fatata G = *fattata* D to break (bread); to distribute, give out. Gt *tafatata* = Dt *tafattata* pass. *fett* (pl. *fetat*) part, portion, morsel; gift. *fetat* (pl. *-āt*) idem.

fatawa G *(yeftaw)* to desire strongly (often, but not necessarily, in bad sense: to lust for, be greedy for). CG *'aftawa* caus.; to please, satisfy. *fetew* desired, desirable, pleasing, pleasant. *fetwat* (pl. *-āt*) desire, lust, craving; the thing desired, pleasure. *fetwatāwi* libidinous, given to excessive desires. *maftew* it is necessary, fitting, proper, obligatory (foll. by subj. ± *kama*).

faṭana G *(yefṭen)* to be quick, swift. CG *'afṭana* to hurry, hasten; freq. with inf. or coord. verb: to hurry to do, to do quickly. *feṭun* swift, quick.

faṭara G *(yefṭer)* to create, produce; to devise, fabricate. Gt *tafaṭra* pass. *feṭur* created. *feṭrat* the act of creation; what is created, creatures; nature, character; kind, species. *faṭāri* creator (always refers to God).

fawwasa D to cure, heal (a.d.o. of person or disease; a.d.o. of person, from: *'em-*). Dt *tafawwasa* pass. *fawwes* (pl. *-āt*) cure, healing; medicine, medication. *mafawwes* physician.

faxara G *(yefxar)* to espouse, become engaged to (a.d.o. woman). Gt *tafaxara/tafexra* pass. *fexert* fiancée. *faxāri* fiancé.

fayyāt (coll.) thieves; *fayyātāwi* a thief.

G

ge'za G *(yeg'az)* to migrate; to be free (i.e. not enslaved). CG *'ag'aza* caus. *ge'z* (1) (pl. *-āt*) mode of life, manner; nature, quality, essential nature; *ba-ge'za* prep. in accord with the view of; (2) ordinary mode of church singing; (3) *Ge'z/'Ag'āzi* the Ethiopians; *beḥēra Ge'z/'Ag'āzi* Ethiopia.

gab'a G *(yegbā')* to come/go back, to return. CG *'agbe'a* to bring/lead/take back; to turn back, deflect; to hand over, betray (a.d.o.; to: *westa 'eda*). Glt *tagābe'a* to gather, assemble (intrans.).

CG1t *'astagābe'a* to gather, assemble (trans.); *'astagābe'a māxbara lā'la* to convene an ecclesiastical council against. *geb'at* return; conversion (to: *westa*); betrayal. *gabā'i* (pl. *gabā't*) mercenary, hired worker. *gubu'* gathered, collected. *megbā'* refuge, place to return to.

gebb (pl. *gebab*, *'agbāb*) hole, cave, lair.

gabra G *(yegbar)* to act, work, function; to make, create, fashion, produce; to do, perform, enact, carry out. Gt *tagabra* pass. CG *'agbara* to make or order (someone: a.d.o.) to do or make (something: a.d.o.). Dt *tagabbara* to work, do work; to work something, esp. in agricultural sense: to work land; to transact business (with: *mesla*); to invest. CD *'agabbara* = CG. CDt *'astagabbara* to recover one's investment. *gabr* (pl. *'agbert*) servant. *gebr* (pl. *-āt*, *gebar*) m.f. deed, act; work, task, business; religious service, liturgy; product, artifact, creation; as adv.: necessarily, out of necessity; *ba-gebr* idem. *gabāri* (pl. *gabart*) maker, fashioner, craftsman; this word shares many of the idioms associated with G *gabra*. *gabbār* (coll.) workers, laborers; *liqa gabbār* foreman. *megbār* (pl. *-āt*) action, practice, behavior, custom(s); business, activity. *tagbār* business, activity, task, job.

gebses gypsum, plaster. *gebsus* plastered.

Gabaza 'Aksum Guardian of Aksum, epithet of the Mother Church at Aksum.

gādā gift (for a superior).

gadafa G *(yegdef)* to throw, cast; to throw away, discard; to lose by waste or neglect. Gt *tagadfa* pass. *geduf* thrown, cast; discarded; lost, rejected.

g^wadg^{w}ada Q to knock (on a door).

tagādala G1t to struggle, contend, esp. in religious sense of struggling against temptation. *gadl* (pl. *-āt*) a struggle, contest, esp. of saints and martyrs; title of works dealing with the lives of saints and ascetics. *mastagādel* a contender, "soldier of Christ."

gadalā corpse(s), cadaver(s).

gadām (pl. *-āt*) wilderness; any remote, uninhabited area. *gedm* (pl. *gedam*) width, breadth.

gaf'a G *(yegfā')* to harm, injure, oppress. Gt *tagaf'a* pass. *gefu'* injured, harmed; violent. *gef'* harm, injury; violence; oppression. *gafā'i* oppressor, tyrant.

gafteʾa Q to overturn. Qt *tagafteʾa* pass.

ʾaghada CG to make public, show openly, make manifest; to act or speak openly. Gt *tagehda* pass. *gehud* (f. *gehedd*) clear, manifest, open, obvious. *gahhād* idem.; *gahhāda* adv. openly, manifestly, publicly. *gehdat* openness.

ʾagḥaša CG to take aside, divert; to remove, take away. Gt *tageḥša* to depart, withdraw.

galʿ (pl. *-āt*, *ʾagleʿt*) a pot.

gemʿē (pl. *gamāʿey*) flask, container for oil.

gamal (pl. *-āt*, *ʾagmāl*) m.f. camel.

ʾagmara CG to perfect, finish, consummate; to include completely, to comprehend. Gt *tagamra* pass. *gemurā* adv. always, altogether, completely; common with neg.: (not) at all. *la-gemurā* adv. forever, always.

Genbot Eth. month name: May 9 - June 7.

g^w*end* (pl. *-āt*, *ʾag*^{w}*nād*) trunk of a tree; a restraining device, stock.

g^w*andaya* Q to last, remain; to delay, tarry, be slow in coming; with inf.: to be tardy or late in doing, to be too long in doing. CQ *ʾag*^{w}*andaya* to put off, delay, defer. Q1t *tag*^{w}*anādaya* to delay in doing (*lāʿla*, *lāʿla* + inf., or inf. alone).

gānēn (pl. *ʾagānent*) demon, evil spirit; *za-gānēn* (pl. *ʾella ʾagānent*) one possessed by an evil spirit.

gannat (pl. *-āt*) f. garden; the Garden of Eden.

ganaya G *(yegnay)* to bow down; to submit, be submissive; to render humble thanks. CG *ʾagnaya* to subject. G1t *tagānaya* to confess one's sins, to seek pardon. *genāy* humble thanks.

ganaza G *(yegnez)* to prepare (a body) for burial. Gt *taganza* pass. CG *ʾagnaza* caus. *genuz* prepared for burial. *genzat* preparation for burial. *magnaz* materials used in preparing a body for burial.

tag^w*arʿaya* to strangle (or hang) one's self. g^w*erʿē* (pl. g^w*arāʿit*) throat, neck.

garif net.

garāht (pl. *garāweh*) field, arable land.

garama G to be awesome, fear-inspiring. D *garrama* to frighten, terrify. Dt *tagarrama* to be terrible, threatening, fearful. *gerrum/gerum* awesome, terrible, fearsome, awe-inspiring. *gerremā/germā* terror, awe; awesome nature. *tegremt* threats, terrors.

gasasa G *(yegses)* to touch. Gt *tagassa* pass. *gessat* touch, touching.

gaššaṣa D to rebuke, reproach; to instruct. Dt *tagaššaṣa* pass. *geššuṣ* well instructed, learned. *magaššeṣ* teacher, instructor. *tagšāṣ* (pl. *-āt*) rebuke, reproach, admonition, instruction.

gaṣṣ (pl. *-āt*) face; aspect, appearance; type, sort.

gēgaya Q/L to err, go astray, get lost; to sin, commit error. N *ʾangēgaya* to wander back and forth, hither and yon. *giguy* lost, erring; sinful, wicked. *gēgāy* (pl. *-āt*) error, sin, crime, guilt.

gēsa G *(yegis)* to do something early in the day. *gēsam(a)* adv. tomorrow.

g^{w}ayya G *(yeg^{w}yay/yeg^{w}yi)* to flee. CG *ʾag^{w}yaya* to put to flight. *g^{w}ayāy(i)* fugitive. *g^{w}eyyā* flight. *meg^{w}yāy* refuge, asylum.

gizē (pl. *-yāt*) m.f. time: (1) the specific time of or for an event; (2) time in a more general durative sense. Frequent in set phrases: *weʾeta/yeʾeta·gizē* at that time; *(ba-)gizē ṣebāḥ/mesēt* etc. in the morning/evening; *ba-gizēhu* at its/the proper time; *ba-gizēhā* immediately, straightway; *ba-k^{w}ellu gizē* always. *Gizē* is also equivalent to a conjunction before verbal clauses: when, whenever, e.g. *gizē ṣawwāʿkani* when you summoned me. The same is true of the compounds *ba-gizē*, *ʾem-gizē*, and *ʾeska gizē*.

gazʾa G to serve at a feast. *gezʾ/gazʾ* feast, banquet. *gazzāʾ* = *gazāʾi* (pl. *gazāʾt*) waiter, attendant (at feast).

ʾegziʾ (pl. *ʾagāʾezt*, *ʾagāʾest*) lord, master, leader, chief. *ʾEgziʾena* Our Lord. *ʾegzeʾt* lady, mistress. *ʾEgzeʾtena* Our Lady (Mary). *ʾEgziʾabḥēr* God.

gazfa G *(yegzef)* to be dense, stupid, dull, stout. *gezf*, *gezaf* density, dullness, stupidity.

gazama G *(yegzem)* to cut down (a tree); to fell; to cut, hew (wood). Gt *tagazma* pass.

H

hadʾa G *(yehdāʾ)* to be quiet, tranquil. CG *ʾahdeʾa* to pacify, calm, make tranquil. *heduʾ* quiet, tranquil, placid. *hedʾat* peace, tranquillity.

hag^{w}la/hag^{w}ala G *(yehg^{w}al/yehg^{w}el)* to perish, die; to lose, suffer a loss (of: a.d.o.). CG *ʾahg^{w}ala* to destroy. Gt *tahag^{w}la* to perish, die, be destroyed. *hegul* lost, destroyed. *hag^{w}l* destruction, end. *māhg^{w}el* = *māhg^{w}ali* destroyer; adj. destructive.

hagar (pl. *ʾahgur*) f.m. city; sometimes used vaguely for region, district; *Xams ʾahgur* Pentapolis. *hagarit* town, city.

hakak tumult, chaos.

tahakaya Gt to be idle, lazy, negligent, remiss; to cease, stop, be inactive. CG *ʾahkaya* caus. *hakkāy* lazy, idle, etc. *hakēt* laziness, idleness, etc.

hallawa D to exist, be; see §44.2 for details on meaning and constructions. *hellāwē* being, essence, nature, substance. *tamayṭa xaba hellāwēhu* he returned to his normal state.

-hu interrog. particle; see §8.3.

hoka G *(yehuk)* to move, agitate, disturb. Gt *tahawka* pass. *hawk* motion, movement, agitation, disturbance; mob, crowd, tumult. *hukat* idem.

hosāʿnā (Heb.) Save us. Hosanna.

-hi encl. part. even, the very (see §51.4b); added to interrog. pron. to form indef. pron. (see §29.2).

hēda G *(yehid)* to take by force. Gt *tahayda* pass. and reflex. (i.e. for one's self). *hayd* violence, taking by force; booty, prey. *hayādi* a violent person, plunderer.

hāymānot m.f. faith (esp. Christian). *mahaymen* (f. *-t*) adj./n. faithful (in the religious sense); a believer.

ʾahyaya CG to cause to forget, to induce amnesia. Dt *tahayyaya* to neglect, skip, be unconcerned about. *heyyat* negligence, forgetfulness, amnesia.

heyya adv. there, in that place; *ba-heyya* idem; *ʾem-heyya* from there, thence. *heyyanta* (w. pron. suff.: *heyyantē-*) prep. in place of, instead of.

Ḥ

ḥabl (pl. *ʾaḥbāl*) m.f. rope, cord.

ʾaḥbara CG to clean, polish. *ḥebr* (pl. *-āt*, *ḥebar*) color. *ḥebur* variegated.

taḥabaya Gt to assume responsibility for (o.s.), stand as guarantor for (o.s.) to (a third party: *ʾemenna*). *ḥabi* (pl. *ḥabayt*) prefect, governor, procurator; *ḥabē meʾt* centurion.

ḥaddasa D to renew, renovate, restore. Dt *taḥaddasa* pass. *ḥaddis* (f. *ḥaddās*, pl. *ḥaddast*) new. *Ḥegg Ḥaddis* the NT.

ḥaḍana G *(yeḥḍen)* to nurse, nourish, foster, cultivate; to take care of (one's young). Gt *taḥaḍna* pass. *ḥeḍn* (pl. *ḥeḍan*) bosom, embrace. *ḥeḍnat* n. nourishing, nursing. *ḥeḍān* (pl. -*āt*) infant, very young child. *māḥḍan* (pl. -*āt*, *maḥāḍen*) womb; *bā westa māḥḍanā* she is pregnant.

māḥḍē/māḥṣē axe.

ḥegg (pl. *ḥegag*) m.f. law; the Law (scriptural sense); *gabra ḥegga* to perform/carry out the law; *ba-ḥegg* legally, lawfully.

ḥagāy summer.

ḥalaba G *(yeḥleb)* to milk. *ḥalib* milk, juice.

ḥalama G to dream. Dt *taḥallama* to dream dreams, see visions. *ḥelm* (pl. *ḥelam*, *ʾaḥlām*) dream, vision.

ḥalaya G *(yeḥli)* to sing, make music; to sing about (a.d.o.). *ḥalāyi* (f. -*t*; pl. *ḥalayt*) singer. *māḥlēt* (pl. -*āt*, *maḥāley*) song, singing, music. *māḥlētāy* musician, singer.

ḥamda G = Gt *taḥamda* to be burned to ashes. *ḥamad* ash(es).

ḥaml (pl. *ʾaḥmāl*) vegetation, shrubs.

Ḥamlē Eth. month name, July 8 - Aug. 6.

ḥamma/ḥamama (yeḥmam/yeḥmem) to be ill, suffer illness, pain or distress. CG *ʾaḥmama* to afflict with illness, pain, distress. Glt *taḥāmama* to hate one another. CGlt *ʾastaḥāmama* to take pains with, give careful attention to, devote one's self to. *ḥemum* ill, afflicted, distressed. *ḥemām* (pl. -*āt*) illness, pain, disease, affliction. *māḥmem* grievous, afflicting with grief or pain.

ḥemmat soot. *māya ḥemmat* ink.

ḥamar (pl. *ʾaḥmār*) f.m. boat, ship.

taḥāmawa Glt to acquire an in-law. *ḥam* (w. pron. suff.: *ḥamu-*, acc. *ḥamā-*; pl. *ʾaḥmāw*) father-in-law, son-in-law. *ḥamāt* mother-in-law, daughter-in-law. *tāḥmā* in-law relationship.

ḥamot gall.

ḥamaya G *(yeḥmi)* to curse, revile, slander. *ḥemuy* disgraceful, shocking. *ḥamēt* n. cursing, reviling, slander.

ḥankasa Q to limp, be lame. *ḥankās* lame, crippled. *ḥenkāsē* lameness.

ḥanaṣa G *(yeḥneṣ)* to build, construct. Gt *taḥanṣa* pass. CG *ʾaḥnaṣa* caus. *ḥenuṣ* built, constructed. *ḥanāṣi* architect, builder. *ḥenṣ*, *ḥenṣat*, *ḥenṣā* building, construction.

ḥaql (pl. *ʾaḥqul*, *ʾaḥqāl*, *ʾaḥqelt*) field; any vast and empty tract. *ḥaqqāl* farmer.

ʾastāḥqara/ʾastaḥaqara CGt to revile, ridicule. *ḥequr* vile, despicable.

ḥeqqa adv. a little, a little while, a short distance. *ba-ḥeqqu* sufficiently, enough; very much, altogether.

ḥaqaya G to grind/gnash the teeth. CG *ʾaḥqaya* caus.

ḥaq^{w}*ē* (pl. *-yāt*) loins.

ḥaraḍa G *(yeḥreḍ)* to grind (flour). Gt *taḥarḍa* pass. *ḥariḍ* flour, dough. *māḥraḍ* mill, mill-stone.

ḥarama G to set aside as sacred, to dedicate (a.d.o.) to a deity; to regard as taboo. D *ḥarrama* to anathematize. CG *ʾaḥrama* = G; also: to make or declare as taboo. Dt *taḥarrama* to be taboo, prohibited; to abstain from for reasons of taboo; to be superstitious. *ḥerum/ḥerrum* sacred, forbidden, taboo, anathematized; abstinent. *ḥermat* (pl. *-āt*) anything sacred; ritual, ceremony. *meḥrām* (pl. *-āt*) sacred precinct, temple. *teḥremt* abstinence, devotion.

ḥarra/ḥarara G *(yeḥrar/yeḥrer)* to burn (intrans.), be ablaze. CG *ʾaḥrara* to burn (trans.). *ḥarur* heat, fervor, passion, ardor.

ḥarrā (coll.) army, troops, soldiers.

ḥarasa G *(yeḥres)* to plow. Gt *taḥarsa* pass. *ḥarāsi* (pl. *ḥarast*) plowman, farmer, tenant farmer. *māḥras* (pl. *maḥāres*) a plow.

ḥarāweyā (pl. *ʾaḥrew*) pig, sow, swine.

ḥāsa interj. Heaven forbid! Let it not be so!

ḥassawa D to lie, be deceitful, false. CD *ʾaḥassawa* to accuse of falsehood. Dt *taḥassawa* to be accused of falsehood, be found out a liar. *ḥassat* a lie. *ḥessew* false, deceitful. *ḥassāwi* a liar.

ḥašama G to be bad, foul, evil. CG *ʾaḥšama* to act wickedly; to make foul, evil; to harm, damage. *ḥešum* bad, foul, evil, harmful. *ḥešam* (pl. *-āt*) wickedness, evil; crime, harm. *ba-ḥešum* adv. vilely, wretchedly, without pity.

ḥašar chaff, piece of straw.

taḥašaya/taḥašya Gt to rejoice (in, at: *ba-*, *baʾenta*). *ḥašēt* happiness, joy.

ḥasaba G to compute, reckon; to think, believe, impute. Gt *taḥasaba* pass. Glt *taḥāsaba* to take up accounts with. *ḥasāb* computation, reckoning, account; quantity, price; portion, share. *gabra ḥasāba* to settle accounts.

ḥaṣaṣa/ḥaṣṣa G *(yeḥṣeṣ)* to decrease (in quantity), become inferior (in quality), be deficient; to be subtracted. CG *ʾaḥṣaṣa* to diminish, make less, worse, inferior; to be deficient (in doing: inf.; in: acc. or *ʾemenna*); to subtract, cause a loss of (a.d.o.

with o.s. of person so affected). *ḥeṣuṣ* minor, less, small, inferior, deficient, lacking. *ḥeṣaṣ*, *ḥeṣṣat* decrease, diminution, deficiency, lack.

ḥaṣ (pl. *ʾaḥṣā*, *-t*) arrow.

ḥatata G *(yeḥtet)* to investigate, examine, scrutinize; to question, interrogate. Gt *taḥatata* pass. *ḥatatā* investigation, interrogation. *māḥtat* testimony; a witness, testifier.

ḥora G *(yeḥor, yeḥur)* to go. *ḥurat* (pl. *-āt*) n. going, manner of going; departure, journey; way of life, manners, customs. *ḥawāreyā* (pl. *-t*) apostle. *meḥwār* (pl. *-āt*) the distance one may travel in a given time (e.g. *meḥwāra šalus* a three-day's journey); course, orbit.

ʾaḥosa CG to move, shake, agitate (trans.). Gt *taḥawsa* idem intrans. or pass.; *za-yetḥawwas* reptiles, "creeping things." *ḥusat* motion, movement. *ḥewās* (pl. *-āt*) a physical sense. *ḥawisā* exclam. of wonder or admiration.

ḥawwaṣa D to inspect, look at (a.d.o.); to look in on, visit (a.d.o.); to look after (good and bad senses). Dt *taḥawwaṣa* pass. *ḥewwāṣē* visit, visitation, attention.

ḥewāy the red glow of the evening sky.

ḥawwaza D to please, delight, be pleasing to. CGt *ʾastaḥawaza* to be pleased. CDt *ʾastaḥawwaza* to regard as pleasing, acceptable; to please, delight. CGlt *ʾastaḥāwaza* idem. *ḥawwez* (pl. *-āt*) pleasure, delight. *ḥawwāz* pleasant, delightful, agreeable.

ḥayq (pl. *-āt*) shore (of sea or lake).

ḥēsa G *(yeḥis)* to scold, reprove. Gt *taḥaysa* pass. *ḥis* reproach, scolding.

ḥaywa G *(yeḥyaw)* to live, be alive; to revive, come back to life; to recover, get well. CG *ʾaḥyawa* to restore to life; to heal, cure; to let live. *ḥeyāw* (f. *-t*) alive, living; *ʾemma-ḥeyāw* Mother of the Living (i.e. Eve). *ḥeywat* m.f. life, lifetime. *māḥyew*, *māḥyawi* life-giving, salvific.

ḥazaba G to think, believe, suppose. Gt *taḥazba* = Dt *taḥazzaba* = G; also: to expect; to fear, avoid; to care, be concerned. *teḥzebt* opinion, belief; fear, expectation.

ḥezb (pl. *ʾaḥzāb*, *ḥezab*) people, nation; crowd; NT the Gentiles.

ḥazana G *(yeḥzen/yeḥzan)* to be sad. CG *ʾaḥzana* to make sad; often used impersonally: *ʾaḥzano* he was saddened. *ḥazan* sadness, grief.

ḥezun (f. *ḥezent*) sad. *māḥzen*, *māḥzani* saddening, provoking sadness; also = *māḥzan* cause of sadness. See also *māḥzen* sub *mḥz*.

K

kāʿeb (f. *-t*) adj. second, other; *kāʿeba* adv. again, a second time; further, moreover. *mekʿebit* n. double, the double amount; *mekʿebita* adv. twofold, doubly; *meʾta mekʿebita* a hundredfold.

kaʿawa (yekʿaw) to pour out, spew out (trans.). Gt *takeʿwa* idem intrans.

kabda G to be heavy, serious. CG *ʾakbada* to make heavy; to be burdensome. *kebud* (f. *kebedd*) heavy. *kebad* heaviness. *kabd* the liver; the stomach.

kabkāb wedding, wedding feast.

kabra G *(yekbar)* to be glorious, magnificent, great, famous, illustrious. CG *ʾakbara* to make or regard as glorious, etc. *kebur* (f. *kebert*) glorious, etc. *kebr* glory, honor; splendor, magnificence.

kadana G *(yekden)* to cover, protect; to pardon (sins). Gt *takadna* pass. *kedun* covered, protected. *kedān* (pl. *-āt*) covering; esp. tunic, garment. *kednat* protection. *kadāni* protector.

kafala G *(yekfel)* to divide (up); to apportion, distribute; to make someone a participant/partaker in/of; impersonally: to be one's portion (e.g. *ʾi-kafalomu* it was not their portion = they were not worthy of it). Gt *takafla* pass.; to divide up among oneselves; to hesitate, be of divided mind. *keful* divided. *kefl* (pl. *-āt*) part, portion, share; section, category; chapter. *makfalt* part, portion, share.

kafar (pl. *ʾakfār*) container for measuring, a bushel.

kehla G (imperf. *yekel*, subj. *yekhal*) to be able (to do: inf.); to prevail against (o.s. or *mesla*). Gt *takehla* (1) = *kehla*, esp. when used, by attraction, with a foll. inf. of a Gt verb; (2) impersonal: to be possible (for someone: o.s.; to do: inf.). CG *ʾakhala* to enable, make able. *kahāli* powerful, strong, capable; *kahālē* k^{w}*ellu* omnipotent; *kahāli la-* + inf. or v.n.: capable of (doing). Glt *takāhala mesla* to come to an agreement with.

kāhen (pl. *-āt*) priest; *liqa kāhenāt* chief priest. *kehnat* priesthood.

kaḥa, *kaḥaka*, *kaḥak*, *kaḥā(ka)* adv. thither, to that place; further on.

keḥda G *(yekḥad)* to deny, repudiate; intrans.: to lack faith, be an unbeliever. Glt *takāḥada* to argue with, contradict (someone: o.s.;

concerning: *baʾenta*). CG *ʾakḥada* to contradict, not believe (someone: a.d.o.); to lead (someone: a.d.o.) from the faith. *kaḥādi* infidel, unbeliever; rebel. *kāḥd* lack of faith, impiety, heresy; disobedience, rebellion; *zaʾenbala kāḥd* without doubt, without fear of contradiction. *keḥdat* denial, apostacy, rebellion.

k^{w}*ak*^{w}*ḥ* rock(s), stone(s).

kalʾa G *(yeklāʾ)* to prevent (someone: o.s.; from doing: inf.); to withhold (something: a.d.o.; from: *ʾemenna*). Gt *takalʾa* pass.; to abstain (from: *ʾemenna*). *kelʾat* prohibition, prevention.

kāleʾ (f. -*t*) adj. other, another, second; n. companion. *kelʾē* m.f. two. *kelʾētu* (acc. *kelʾēta*) m. two; *kelʾēti* (acc. *kelʾēta*) f. two.

kalb (pl. *kalabāt*, *ʾaklebt*, *ʾaklāb*) dog.

kalleḥa D to cry out, shout. *kellāḥ* a cry, shout.

kallala D to crown, to surround like a crown. Dt *takallala* to be crowned (with: acc., e.g. *takallala kebra* he was crowned with glory; or *ba-*). *kellul* crowned (with: *ba-*). *kellālē* n. crowning, coronation. *ʾaklil* (pl. -*āt*) crown, diadem.

k^{w}*ell-* quantifier: all, each, every (see §10.3). *k*^{w}*ellantā-* (w. pron. suff.) all of, the whole of. *k*^{w}*ello* adv. altogether, completely; (not) at all. *k*^{w}*ellahi*/*k*^{w}*ellehi* adv. everywhere, wherever; *ba-k*^{w}*ellahi* idem.

kalamēdā robe, vestment.

kelsest (pl. *kalāsest*) bundle, sheaf.

maklit (pl. *makāley*) talent (wt.).

kama (w. pron. suff.: *kamā-*) (1) prep. like, as; *kama-ze* like this, thus, in this way; *kamāhu* idem; (2) conj. that (introducing a noun clause); so that, in order that (+ subj.); *kama ʾi-* so that not, lest (+ subj.). *ba-kama* (1) prep. according to, in accordance with; (2) conj. according as, as. *za-kama* conj. how. *ʾem-kama* conj. as soon as, when.

kema postpositive part.: also, even, too.

kamin cummin.

kanfar (pl. *kanāfer*) lip; edge, hem.

k^{w}*annana* D to judge, condemn, punish; to rule, have power (over: acc. or *ba-*). CD *ʾak*^{w}*annana* to put (someone: o.s.) in charge of (acc. or *lāʿla*). Dt *tak*^{w}*annana* pass. of D. Glt *tak*^{w}*ānana* to become reconciled (with: *mesla*). *k*^{w}*ennun* judged, condemned, subject to punishment. *k*^{w}*ennanē* (pl. -*yāt*) judgment, condemnation, punishment. *makʷannen* (pl. *makʷānent*) judge, administrator, high official.

kantu vanity, emptiness; freq. in constr. phrases, e.g. *xellinnā kantu* vain thoughts. *ba-kantu* = *kanto* adv. in vain; fortuitously, without purpose, without reward or result.

kʷarʿa G = D *kʷarreʿa* to strike someone's head with one's fists. Gt *takʷarʿa* pass.

karabo basket.

kirubēl cherub, cherubim. *kirub* idem. *kirubāwi* adj. cherubic.

karbē myrrh.

mekʷrāb (pl. *-āt*) temple, shrine, synagogue.

kerdād weed(s).

karama/karma G to spend the winter; to belong to the previous year. *keramt* winter; rainy season; year. *karāmi* of or pertaining to the previous year.

Kerestiyān Christian; *bēta Kerestiyān* (pl. *-āt*, *ʾabyāta Kerestiyānāt*) church; the Church. *Kerestiyānāwi* (f. *-t*) a Christian; adj. Christian. *Kerestennā* Christianity.

karš (pl. *-āt*) belly, stomach.

kertās parchment, paper.

karaya G *(yekri)* to dig (e.g. a well), dig in (the ground), dig through (a wall). Gt *takarya* pass. *karāyi* (pl. *karayt*) in *karāyē maqāber* grave-digger.

kesād/kešād (pl. *-āt*, *kesāwed*, *kasāwed*) m.f. neck.

kašata G *(yekšet)* to reveal, uncover, lay bare; to open (esp. lips, mouth, eyes); to reveal, make manifest. Gt *takašta* pass. *kešut* uncovered, bare; open (esp. of the eyes).

kokab (pl. *kawākebt*) m. star; *kokaba mesēt/ṣebāḥ* evening/morning star.

kona G *(yekun)* to be, become. See Voc. 8. *wa-kona soba* and when, and while. *makān* (pl. *-āt*) m.f. place, locale.

-kē (± *ʾenka*) encl. part. therefore (see §51.4c).

kēda G *(yekid)* to tread, trample (on: a.d.o.); to thresh (by treading). CG *ʾakēda* to cause to tread; to thresh. Gt *takayda* pass. of G. *mekyād* sole of the foot, footprint; base; threshing floor. *makayyad/makyad* idem; footstool.

takāyada Glt to make a treaty, pact, covenant (with: *mesla* or o.s.); to promise. *kidān* (pl. *-āt*) m.f. (1) pact, treaty, covenant; (2) will, testament. *Kidān Belit* OT; *Kidān Ḥaddis* NT. *gabra/šēma/*

takāyada kidāna mesla/xaba to make a treaty, etc. with. *Kidān* is also used of the benefit promised by God to those who celebrate the commemoration of a particular saint.

L

la- prep. to, for (dative); for forms with suffixes, see §20.1; cf. also §10.2.

la'aka G *(yel'ak)* to send (message/messenger: a.d.o.; to: *la-*, *xaba*). Gt *tale'ka* to serve, administer to (a.d.o.). *le'uk* sent; n. apostle, messenger. *lā'k* (pl. *-ān*) servant. *mal'ak* (pl. *malā'ekt*) angel, messenger. *mal'ekt* (pl. *-āt*) epistle, letter; legate, legation; ministry, service, office, function.

la-'emma-nu conj. whether.

la'ala G to be high, superior. CG *'al'ala* = CD *'ala''ala* to raise up, elevate, exalt. Dt *tala''ala/tale''ela* pass. of CD; to be higher (than: *'emenna*). *le'ul/le''ul* high, lofty, superior, exalted. *lā'la* prep. (w. pron. suff.: *lā'lē-*) on, upon; (motion) down onto; over, above; about, concerning. *lā'lu* adv. above; freq. in the adj. phrase *za-lā'lu* upper, esp. in the sense "celestial, heavenly"; *'em-X wa-lā'lu 'emennēhu* from X onward (in enumerations); *ba-lā'lu* above, on high; *'em-lā'lu* from above, from on high. *mal'elt* upper part or surface of anything; *mal'elta* prep. above.

lebb (pl. *'albāb*) m.f. heart; mind, intellect.

labḥāwi potter.

labsa G *(yelbas)* to dress (intrans.); to don (a garment: a.d.o.). CG *'albasa* to clothe, dress (trans.), with acc. of person and acc. of garment. Gt *talabsa* pass. and reflex. *lebus* dressed, clothed. *lebs* (pl. *'albās*) m. clothes, clothing; a garment. *lebsat* v.n. dressing, clothing, donning. *malbas(t)* (pl. *malābes*) garment, tunic.

labbawa D to comprehend, understand; to be intelligent; to be aware, conscious (of: *'emenna*). CD *'alabbawa* caus. Dt *talabbawa* to be comprehended, understood. *lebbew* intelligent, comprehending. *labbāwi* idem. *lebbāwē* mind, intellect. *lebbunnā* idem; skill, cleverness.

lafē wa-lafē adv. this way and that, back and forth. *mangala lafē wa-lafē* idem. *mā'dota lafē* on the other side, opposite.

legg^{w}*at* (pl. -*āt*) depth of the sea, abyss.

lahaba G to flame, burn. CG *ʾalhaba* to burn, ignite (trans.). *lāhb* flame, heat.

lehqa G *(yelhaq)* to grow up; to grow old; (rarely) to increase in size/quantity. CG *ʾalhaqa* to raise, rear (e.g. child, plants). *lehqat* old age. *lehqennā* idem. *lehiq* (f. *leheqt*) grown up, adult; old, eldest. *liq* (pl. -*ān*, *liqāwent*, *liqānāt*) elder, chief. *malheqt* (coll.; pl. -*āt*, *malāheqt*, -*āt*) elders, seniors (in rank or age).

lāhm (pl. *ʾalhemt*) m.f. bull, cow. *ʿaṣada ʾalhemt* stockyard.

lāḥawa L to mourn, grieve. *luḥew/leḥew* adj. grieving. *lāḥ* grief, mourning.

laḥosas whispering; a style of singing.

laḥaya G to be beautiful. *lāḥey* (f. -*t*) beautiful.

lakʾa G to impress (a seal), to inscribe. Gt *talakʾa* pass.; to be affixed. *lekuʾ* impressed, inscribed, affixed. *malkeʾ* a seal impression, likeness, figure.

lakafa G *(yelkef)* to touch. CG *ʾalkafa* to touch, cause to touch. Gt *talakfa* pass.

lamada G *(yelmad)* to be accustomed (to do: inf.). CG *ʾalmada* idem. *lemud* accustomed, usual. *lemād* custom, habit.

lamlama Q to bloom, grow green; to be tender. *lemlāmē* verdure, tenderness.

lamṣ leprosy; *za-lamṣ* leper.

laqqeḥa D to lend. Dt *talaqqeḥa* to borrow. *leqqāḥ* a loan.

lasḥa G *(yelsāḥ)* to be unseasoned, insipid, tasteless, fatuous. *lesuḥ* insipid, etc.

lesān (pl. -*āt*) m.f. tongue, language. *lesāna Yonānāwiyān* Greek; *lesāna ʿEbrāyesṭ* Hebrew; *lesāna ʾAfrenj* Latin; *lesāna ʿArabi* Arabic; *lesāna Geʿz* Geʿez.

ʾalṣaqa CG to be near, approach; with *la-* + inf.: to be about to. Glt *talāṣaqa* to stick together, be connected. CGlt *ʾastalāṣaqa* to glue together, join, connect. *leṣuq* joined, adhering; connected, continuous.

maltāḥt (pl. *malāteḥ*) jaw, cheek.

lēlit (pl. *layāley*) m.f. night.

layy purple cloth.

M

-ma encl. part. See §51.4f.

mā'ed (pl. *-āt*) table.

mā's/mā's (pl. *'am'est, 'am'est*) m.f. skin, hide, leather.

me't (pl. *'am'āt*) hundred.

mā'zē interr. adv. when?

tam'e'a/tame''a/tam'a Gt to become angry, enraged (see §21.1). Glt *tamā'e'a* to get mad at one another. CG *'am'e'a* to enrage. *ma''at* m.f. wrath.

me'ra adv. once, one time.

ma'ār honey. *ma'ar'ir* sweet. CQ *'amā'rara* to sweeten.

me'za G to smell good, be fragrant. CG *'am'aza* to scent, perfume. Dt *tame''eza* to be scented, fragrant. *me'uz* fragrant, sweet. *ma'azā* (pl. *-t*) fragrance.

medr (pl. *-āt, 'amdār*) f.m. the earth; earth, ground, soil; land, district, country. *medra ṣebāḥ* eastern country; *'arwē medr* (pl. *'arāwita medr*) snake. *medrāwi* (f. *-t*) worldly, of the world.

maggaba D to administrate, be in charge of (a.d.o.); to surround and protect (with: *ba-*). CD *'amaggaba* to place (someone: a.d.o.) in charge of (a.d.o. or *lā'la, diba, ba-*). Dt *tamaggaba* to be placed in charge of. *meggeb/megb* office, post, duty, ministry. *maggābi* (pl. *-yān, maggabt*) administrator, guardian; a general designation for various types of rulers: prefect, proconsul, satrap, governor.

Maggābit Eth. month name: Mar. 10 - Apr. 8.

'amagze'a CQ to fatten (cattle). *magze'* (pl. *magāze't*) fattened cattle, fatlings.

mahara G *(yemhar)* or *mahhara* D to teach (someone: o.s.; something: a.d.o. or *ba-, ba'enta*). Dt *tamahhara/tamehhera* to be taught (subject is either person taught or matter taught); to learn (a.d.o.). *mehur/mehhur* learned, expert (in: acc. or *ba-* or constr.). *mamehher/mamher* (f. *-t*) teacher. *temhert* (pl. *-āt*) what is taught, doctrine, teaching; study, learning.

māhraka Q to take captive, take as booty. *mehrekā* booty, spoils.

maḥala G *(yemḥal)* to swear (an oath). CG *'amḥala* to beswear, adjure. Glt *tamāḥala* to take a mutual oath, to conspire. *maḥalā* oath, treaty.

tamāḥlala Qt to beseech, supplicate. *meḥlelā* supplication(s).

meḥra G *(yemḥar)* to have mercy, pity (on: *la-* or o.s.). CG *ʾamḥara* to move to pity. Gt *tameḥra* to be shown pity/mercy. CGt *ʾastamḥara* to be merciful; to move to pity. *meḥrat* (pl. *-āt*) mercy, pity; *gabra meḥrata la-/mesla/lāʿla* to have pity on, show mercy toward. *maḥāri* (one who is) merciful.

maḥawa G *(yemḥaw)* to pluck. Gt *tameḥwa* pass.

tamāḥaza Glt to fall/be in love; to commit adultery. *maḥaz* (pl. *-ān*) lover (m. or f.). *maḥazā* (pl. *-t*) youth, a youth; lover (m. or f.). *māḥzen* illicit affairs.

tamakkeḥa Dt to boast. *mekkeḥ* n. boasting. *temkeḥt* idem. *makkāḥ* boastful.

makana G *(yemken)* to be sterile, childless. D *makkana* = CG *ʾamkana* to orphan. *makān* (f. of unattested **makin*) sterile, childless, barren. *meknat* childlessness.

ʾamaknaya CQ to pretend, make excuses. *mekneyāt* (false) excuse, pretext; reason, cause.

makara G *(yemker)* to plan, propose, decide on (a.d.o. or subj.); to take counsel (with: *mesla*); to test, choose by testing. CG *ʾamkara* to advise, give counsel to (o.s.). Glt *tamākara* to take counsel together (with: *mesla*); to deliberate and decide (to do: subj.). Dt *tamakkara* to be tested, tempted, tried. CD *ʾamakkara* to test, try, tempt, examine. *mekr* plan, counsel, advice; consideration, deliberation; prudence, wisdom; opinion, point of view. *makāri* counselor, advisor. *mamker* (pl. *mamākert*) idem. *mekkur* tempted, tried. *makkarā* (pl. *-t*) temptation, testing, trying, examination.

malʾa G *(yemlāʾ)* (1) trans.: to fill (x with y: two acc. or acc. + *lāʿla/westa/ba-*); (2) intrans.: to be full, filled (of/with: acc. or *ʾemenna*); to be fulfilled, completed; to abound, be abundant. Gt *tamalʾa* to be filled (with: acc. or *ba-*). *meluʾ* full (of: *ʾem-* or acc.); abundant, copious; filling (acc.). *melʾ* what fills (e.g. *melʾa ʾed* a handful); *ba-melʾu* (or w. other suff.) in toto, completely.

malaka G *(yemlek)* to take possession of, occupy, rule. Gt *tamalka* pass. CG *ʾamlaka* to worship God, to worship as a god (a.d.o. or *la-*). Gt *tamalka* to be made lord or divine. *meluk* occupied, possessed, subject; pious. *malāki* owner, ruler, heir. *melkennā* dominion, power, authority. *ʾAmlāk* the Lord. *ʾamlākāwi* divine.

malakot lordship, deity, divinity. *malakotāwi* divine. *mamlaki* one who worships God or gods.

malxa G *(yemlāx)* to tear out, uproot, draw out. Gt *tamalxa* pass. *melux* uprooted, torn out.

ʾamandaba CQ to afflict, oppress (a.d.o.). Qt *tamandaba* pass. *mendābē* m.f. affliction, torment.

mangala prep. (w. pron. suff. *mangalē-*) to, toward, in the direction of. *ba-mangala* idem. *ʾem-mangala* from the direction of; on the part of.

mank^{w}asa Q to become a monk, live a monastic life. *manakos* (pl. *-āt*) monk, nun. *manakosāyt* nun. *menk^{w}esennā* monasticism.

mannana D to reject, repudiate, despise. Dt *tamannana* pass. *mennun* rejected, despised; unsuitable, worthless, vile. *mennānē* repudiation, rejection; worthlessness, wickedness.

ʾamansawa CQ to lead to destruction/temptation. Qt *tamansawa* pass. *mensew* liable to temptation/punishment. *mansut* (pl. *manāsew*) temptation, danger; calamity, divine punishment. *mensāwē* idem.

ment (acc. *menta*) interrog. pron. what? *la-ment*, *baʾenta ment* why? *ment-hi/ni* anything, nothing (see §29.2).

mannu (acc. *manna*) interrog. pron. who? *mannu-hi/ni* anyone, no one (see §29.2).

tamarʿawa Qt to get married (to a woman: o.s.). *marʿā* wedding, marriage. *marʿāwi* groom, son-in-law. *marʿāt* (pl. *marāʿew*) bride, daughter-in-law.

maraga G to plaster. *merug* plastered. *marg* plaster.

tamarg^{w}aza Qt to lean upon. *merg^{w}ez* staff.

marḥa G *(yemrāḥ)* to lead, guide; to show (the way: a.d.o.; to: o.s.). Gt *tamarḥa* pass. *marāḥi* leader. *marḥ* (pl. *ʾamreḥt*) leader, guide.

marra/marara G *(yemrar/yemrer)* to be bitter (lit. and fig.). CG *ʾamrara* to be bitter; to make bitter, exacerbate, aggravate; to behave bitterly or sharply. *marir* (f. *marār*) bitter. *merar* (pl. *-āt*) bitterness. *merrat* idem.

marēt dirt, dust. *marētāwi* adj. dust, of dust.

tamarraya Dt = Glt *tamāraya* to divine, practice divination, soothsaying. *māri* (pl. *māreyān*, *māreyāt*, *mārayt*) heathen priest, soothsayer.

masḥa G to dine, sup. CG *ʾamseḥa* caus. *mesāḥ* meal, dinner; banquet, feast.

masiḥ the Anointed, the Messiah; *masiḥāwi* adj. Christian.

meskin pauper, poor person. *meskinat* poverty.

Maskaram Eth. month name: Sept. 11-Oct. 10.

masala G *(yemsal)* to resemble, be like (a.d.o.); to seem, appear as (acc. of pred. n. or adj.; o.s. of person perceiving; also foll. by *kama* and n. clause; exx. in Voc. 35); often used impersonally: it seems (o.s. of person; + *kama/za-* and n. clause). CG *ʾamsala* to regard as, hold as equivalent to (two acc. or acc. + *kama*). Gt *tamasla* = Dt *tamassala* (1) to become or be made like/similar to (a.d.o. or *la-/ba-/kama*); (2) to imitate; (3) to transform one's self, change (into: a.d.o. or *ba-/la-/kama/ba-ʾamsāla*); (4) to be represented (by a likeness). *mesl* (pl. *-āt*, *mesal*, *ʾamsāl*) m. likeness, form, image; proverb. *ʾamsāl* (pl. *-āt*) idem. *mesla* prep. with, in the company of (w. obj. suff.: *meslē-*). *messālē* (pl. *-yāt*) parable, proverb, similitude.

māsana L to be ruined, destroyed; to perish; to become corrupt, rotten. CL *ʾamāsana* to corrupt, destroy, wipe out. Lt *tamāsana* pass. of CL. *musun* corrupt(ed). *musenā* corruption (physical, moral), destruction. *māsāni* perishable, corruptible.

mesṭir (pl. *-āt*) m.f. mystery; the Eucharist.

mesēt (pl. *-āt*) evening, twilight.

mašaṭa G *(yemšeṭ)* to snatch, snatch away, seize and carry off by force. CG *ʾamšaṭa* to flee, escape. Gt *tamašṭa* pass. and reflex. of G. *mešuṭ* seized, snatched. *mašāṭi* (pl. *mašaṭṭ*) rapacious, violent. *mamšaṭ* handle, lever.

maṣʾa G *(yemṣāʾ)* to come; with *diba/lāʿla* or o.s.: to happen to, to occur to, come upon. CG *ʾamṣeʾa* to bring, offer; to cause to happen, bring about. *meṣʾat* arrival, advent, coming. *memṣāʾ* place of origin.

maṣlawa Q to wilt, wither. CQ *ʾamaṣlawa* caus. Qt *tamaṣlawa* to become withered; to wrinkle the face. *meṣlew* wilted, withered, wrinkled.

maṣaw/maḏaw spring (season).

maṣwata Q to give alms, practice charity. Qt *tamaṣwata* to receive alms. *meṣwāt* act of charity, benefaction.

met (pl. *ʾamtāt*) husband.

matha G to be deceptive in appearance. *methat* (pl. *-āt*) phantom, fantasy, spectre.

matara G *(yemter)* to cut, cut off (lit. and fig.); to decree. Gt *tamatra* pass. D *mattara* = G. Dt *tamattara* = Gt. *metur* cut off, amputated; decided, decreed. *metrat* n. cutting (off). *metār* fragment, segment.

maṭana prep. during, for/to the extent of. *ba-mi-maṭan* for how much? *'amṭāna* conj. as long as.

maṭṭawa D to surrender, hand over (a.d.o.; to: o.s. or *la-*). Dt *tamaṭṭawa* pass.; to accept, receive (§22.1). *meṭṭew* handed over, delivered.

mo'a G *(yemā')* to conquer, defeat, subdue. Gt *tamaw'a* pass. CG *'amo'a/'ame'a* to make (someone: a.d.o.) victorious (over: *lā'la/ ba-*). *mu'at* victory (for self); defeat (for another). *mawā'i* victorious.

moqa G *(yemuq)* to grow hot; to become intense (of the heat). CG *'amoqa* caus. CGlt *'astamāwaqa* to cause to become hot. *moq* heat. *muqat* heat. *mewuq* hot.

moqeḥa Q to put into chains/bonds, cast into prison. Qt *tamoqeḥa* pass. CQ *'amoqeḥa* caus. *moqeḥ* (pl. *mawāqeḥt*) bonds, fetters, chains. *'asara/wadaya westa moqeḥ* to cast into bonds/prison. *bēta moqeḥ* prison.

mota G *(yemut)* to die. CG *'amota/'amata* to let die; to put to death; to have killed. *mot* m.f. death. *mewut/mewet* (f. *mewett*; pl. *mewutān, mewetān, mutān*) dead. *mawāti* mortal. *māweta* corpse; the dead; *'eg^{w}āla māwetā* orphan(s).

māy (pl. *-āt*) m. water; liquid.

mima coordinating part. either, or, whether (see §51.4f).

mēṭa G *(yemiṭ)* trans.: to turn away, divert; to turn, direct (e.g. face; toward: *xaba*); to return (a.d.o.) to its original place; to convert, transform (a.d.o.; into: *la-, westa*). Gt *tamayṭa* pass.; intrans.: to turn around, return, come back; to be converted (relig. sense). *miṭat* (pl. *-āt*) a turning (to or from); return; change.

Miyāzyā Eth. month name: Apr. 9 - May 8.

N

na- introd. part. used to prepose and emphasize a pronominal element; inflected: *naya* as for me, *nayo* ... him, *nayā* ... her, *nayana* ... us, *nayomu* ... them (m.), *nayon* ... them (f.).

ne'sa G *(yen'as)* to be small, little (in size or importance); to be young. CG *'an'asa* caus. *ne'us* (f. *ne'est*) small, little, young. *na'ās* a young girl. *ne's* childhood, infancy. *nestit* a little, a small amount; used in construct (e.g. *nestita xebest*) or appositionally as an adj. (e.g. *hagar nestit*); *nestita* adv. a little, for a little while; *ba-ba-nestit* little by little.

ne'- Imptv. base: come. Inflected: m.s. *na'ā*, f.s. *ne'i*, m.pl. *ne'u*, f.pl. *na'ā*.

na'awa G *(yen'aw)* to hunt; to catch birds. *na'āwi* hunter. *na'awē/nā'wē* hunting.

'anbe'a CG to weep. *'anbe'* (pl. *'anābe'*) tear(s).

nababa G *(yenbeb)* to speak, tell (a.d.o.; to *la-* or o.s.). Gt *tanabba* to be read, recited. Glt *tanābaba* to speak with (*mesla, xaba,* or acc.). CG *'anbaba* to read, recite; to study, meditate. *nebāb* speech; what one says, manner of speaking. *nabābi* garrulous, talkative, boastful; capable of speech, rational.

'anbalbala Q/N to flame. *nabalbāl* flame.

nabara G *(yenbar)* to sit, sit down; to stay, remain; to continue; to live, dwell. CG *'anbara* to set, place, deposit; to settle, cause to dwell. *nebur* sitting, seated, situated; residing; n. resident. *nebrat* n. sitting down; session; position; condition, state; manner or mode of life; dwelling, abode. *manbar* (pl. *manābert*) m.f. throne, seat, chair. *manbart* state, condition, mode of life. *menbār* place where something is put; place of residence; base, foundation.

nabiy (pl. *-āt*) prophet. Dt *tanabbaya* to prophesy (to: *la-*; against: *lā'la*). *tenbit* prophecy.

nad'a G *(yendā')* to drive (as cattle). Gt *tanad'a* pass. *nadā'i* one who drives, expels.

nadda G *(yended/yendad)* to burn (subject is fire, flame, anger, etc.). CG *'andada* to set afire, ignite (a.d.o.). Glt *tanādada* to burn with a mutual passion. *nedud* adj. burning, flaming. *neddat* flame, burning. *nadd* m. flame; *nadda 'essāt* idem. *nadādi* adj. burning, blazing (of fire, wrath, lust). *mendād* furnace, oven, fireplace.

nadaqa G *(yendeq)* to build, erect. Gt *tanadqa* pass. *nedq* building, structure, wall. *nadāqi* builder.

nadya G *(yendi)* to be poor, destitute; to be deficient (in: *ba-*). CG *'andaya* to reduce to poverty. *nedēt/nedyat* poverty. *naddāy* poor, destitute; n. poor person.

naḍafa/naṣafa G to spread, lay out. Gt *tanaṣfa* pass. *neṣuf* spread. *manṣaf* anything laid out: rug, covering.

naḍxa G *(yenḍāx)* to strike, beat, knock down, trample. Gt *tanaḍxa* pass.

nafaqa G *(yenfeq)* to divide, separate. L *nāfaqa* to divide (usually in half, into two parts or factions); to be hesitant, doubtful, skeptical. Lt *tanāfaqa* to divide (intrans.), break up into factions. Gt *tanafqa* idem. *nefuq* divided, split. *nufuq* hesitant, doubtful. *nafq* compartment, box. *nefq* half, one of two parts. *nufāqē* division, dissention, skepticism. *manfaq* half, one of two parts; faction, sect, splinter-group; the half-way point.

nafsa G to blow (of the wind). CG *ʾanfasa* to breathe (something: a. d.o.) out; to rest, take a breather, find relief (from: *ʾemenna*); to give rest or relief to. *nafs* (pl. *-āt*) m.f. soul, spirit, breath, vital life-force; a person; self. *nafās* (pl. *-āt*) m.f. wind. *manfas* (pl. *-āt*, *manāfest*) m.f. spirit; the Spirit of God; a spirit or demon (good or bad); *Manfas Qeddus* the Holy Spirit. *manfasāwi* (f. *-t*) spiritual, of the spirit.

nafaṣa G *(yenfeṣ)* to flee, escape. CG *ʾanfaṣa* to put to flight. *nafāṣi* fugitive. *nafāṣit* remnant, what survives.

nafxa G *(yenfāx)* to blow, breath; to blow into, inflate; *nafxa baqarn* to blow a horn. Gt *tanafxa* to be inflated, to swell. *nefxat* inflation, blowing.

nagada G *(yenged)* to make a journey, to travel on business. *negd* travel, trade. *nagd* (pl. *-ān*) a traveler, stranger, guest. *nagādi* traveler, merchant. *mangad* public road, highway; trip, journey, pilgrimage. Cf. *ʾengedā*.

nag^{w}*adg*^{w}*ād* (pl. *-āt*) thunder.

nagafa G *(yengef)* to knock off, shake off, dispel. CG *ʾangafa* idem. Gt *tanagfa* pass.; to lose leaves. *neguf* deciduous.

nagha G to dawn, grow light. CG *ʾangeha* to do something early in the day. *nagh* early morning.

nagara G *(yenger)* to say, tell (a.d.o.; to: dat. suff. or *la-*). Gt *tanagra* to be told, spoken. Glt *tanāgara* to speak with (*mesla*, *xaba*, or acc.; about: *ba-/baʾenta* or acc.); to speak (a language: *ba-*). *nagar* (pl. *-āt*) speech, account, narrative; thing, affair, situation.

ʾangargara Q/N to roll, spin (trans. and intrans.). *nagargār* a type of epilepsy; rolling, spinning.

ʾang^{w}*arg*^{w}*ara* Q/N to be angry, vexed; to murmur, mutter.

nagša G *(yengeš/yengaš)* to become king, ruler; to rule (over: *la/lāʿla/diba*). CG *ʾangaša* to make someone (a.d.o.) king (over: *la/lāʿla*). *negš* reign, rule. *neguš* (pl. *nagašt*) king, ruler. *negešt* (pl. *-āt*) queen. *nagāši* (pl. *nagašt*) king, ruler. *mangešt* (pl. *-āt*) m.f. kingdom; kingship, majesty; *mangešta samāyāt* the Kingdom of Heaven; *zamada/weluda mangešt* the royal family.

nāhu introductory particle, usually rendered as "behold." It calls attention to the immediacy (spatial or temporal) of what follows. If used alone with a following noun, it may be taken as a full predication: "Here, now, is X." Usually, however, it introduces and emphasizes a preposed noun, e.g. *nāhu malʾak maṣʾa xabēya*, where it may be omitted in English or rendered by such expressions as "suddenly, to my surprise, of all things" or as "It was/is X who ..." Clauses introduced by *nāhu* may sometimes be translated as subordinate in English: "now that ..."

neḥna we.

nāḥs (pl. *ʾanḥest*) roof, rooftop.

Naḥasē/Naḥasē Eth. month name: Aug. 7 - Sept. 5.

ʾankara CG to wonder, marvel, be amazed (at: a.d.o. or *ʾemenna/baʾenta/ba-*); to regard as strange or marvelous. Gt *tanakra* pass. Glt *tanākara* to repudiate, be alienated from (o.s.). *nakir* (f. *nakār*; pl. *nakart*) adj. strange, alien, foreign; other, different; marvelous, wonderful. *manker* (pl. *-āt*) miracle, marvel, wonder; adj. (f. *-t*) marvelous, wondrous.

ʾank^{w}*ark*^{w}*ara* Q/N to roll (trans. and intrans.). *nak*^{w}*ark*^{w}*ār* n. rolling. *mank*^{w}*arāk*^{w}*er* wheel.

naqʿa G *(yenqāʿ)* trans. and intrans.: to split, burst, rupture. CG *ʾanqeʿa* = G trans. *nequʿ* split, ruptured, cracked. *naqʿ* (pl. *ʾanqeʿt*) fountain, source, spring. *neqʿat* split, crack, fissure. *manqeʿt* thigh.

naqha G *(yenqāh)* to wake up, be awake, be alert. CG *ʾanqeha* to awaken, revive. *nequh* awake, watchful, alert. *neqhat* watchfulness, alertness.

ʾanqalqala Q/N intrans.: to move, shake, quake; trans.: to shake, agitate. *naqalqāl* motion, shaking, agitation.

naqq^{w}*ār* one-eyed, blind.

naqawa G = D *naqqawa* to emit its appropriate sound (subject may be bird or animal). *neqāw* animal sounds.

nasseḥa D to repent (of: *ʾemenna/baʾenta*). Dt *tanasseḥa* idem. CD *ʾanasseḥa* caus. *nessuḥ* repentant. *nassāḥi* one who is repentant. *nesseḥā* repentance, regret, penitence.

nesr (pl. *ʾansert*) eagle, vulture.

ʾansosawa Q/N to walk, stroll.

našʾa G *(yenšāʾ)* to raise, lift, pick up; to take, receive, accept; to capture; to take as a wife. Gt *tanašʾa* pass.; *tanšeʾa* to arise, get up; to rise (from the dead); to rise up against *(lāʿla)*. CG *ʾanšeʾa* to raise, cause to rise (from a seated or lying position). *tenšāʾē* resurrection; *Baʿāla Tenšāʾē* Feast of the Resurrection (Easter).

našata G *(yenšet)* to destroy, overturn. Gt *tanašta* pass. *nešut* destroyed. *neštat* destruction.

naṣḥa G *(yenṣāḥ)* to be pure, clean. CG *ʾanṣeḥa* caus. *neṣuḥ* pure, clean; innocent, uncorrupted, sincere. *neṣḥ* purification, etc. *neṣḥennā* purity, chastity, innocence. *manṣeḥi* one who purifies.

ʾanṣafṣafa Q/N to ooze, drip; trans.: to exude in drops. *naṣafṣāf* juice, drops. *ṣafṣāf* idem.

naṣṣara D to look, look at (a.d.o. or *westa, xaba*). Glt *tanāṣara* to look at one another. CG *ʾanṣara* to look (*mangala*: toward). *neṣṣārē* look, glance, viewing; sight (ability to see).

ʾanṭeʿa CG to tear off/apart.

naṭafa G to strain out. *neṭuf* strained, pure. *manṭaft* strainer, sieve.

manṭolāʿt (pl. *manṭawāleʿ*) veil, covering.

-nu interrog. part. See §8.3.

nawā introd. part. equivalent to *nāhu* (q.v. above).

tanolawa Qt to function as a shepherd, to tend flocks. *nolāwi* (pl. *nolot*) shepherd.

noma G *(yenum)* to sleep. CG *ʾanoma/ʾanama* to put to sleep. *newām* m. sleep.

newāy (pl. *-āt*) m. vessel, utensil, instrument; property, possessions, wealth.

noxa G *(yenux)* to be high, lofty; to be tall, long; to be distant, far off. CG *ʾanoxa/ʾanexa* to extend, put forth (e.g. one's hand);

to lengthen, make long(er); to raise high, elevate, exalt; *ʾanexa manfasa lāʿla* he was patient about. *nawix* (f. *nawāx*; *nawāxt*) adj. high, etc. *nawwāx* idem. *nux* m. length (of time, space); height.

nexla G *(yenxal)* to collapse, fall into ruin, be destroyed. CG *ʾanxala* to knock down, destroy, devastate, topple.

-ni encl. part. even, the very (see §51.4b); added to interrog. pron. to form indef. pron. (see §29.2).

naya see *na-* above.

nāzaza L to console. Lt *tanāzaza* pass. *nāzāzi* consoler. *nuzāzē* consolation.

P

Pāg^{w}emēn Eth. month name: Sept. 6 - Sept. 10.

pāppās (pl. *-āt*) bishop, archbishop, metropolitan; *liqa pāppasāt* patriarch (of the Church). *peppesennā* the office of *pāppās*: episcopacy, see.

Q

q^{w}āʿ (pl. *-āt*) raven, crow.

qabʾa G *(yeqbāʾ)* to smear, anoint. Gt *taqabʾa* pass. and reflex. *qebuʾ* smeared, anointed. *qebʾ* (olive) oil, ointment, butter. *qebʾat* anointing.

taqabbala Dt to go out to meet; to welcome, accept, receive. *qabalā/qabbalā* a meeting, encounter; *westa qabbalā* prep. out to meet.

qabara G *(yeqber/yeqbar)* to bury, inter. Gt *taqabra* pass. CG *ʾaqbara* caus. *qebur* buried. *qabar* burial, funeral. *maqbart* (pl. *maqāber*, *-āt*) m. grave, tomb, sepulchre; pl. also = sing.

qabṣa G *(yeqbeṣ/yeqbaṣ)* to be discouraged, be in distress; *qabaṣa tasfā* to lose hope, to despair; to abandon, give up on. CG *ʾaqbaṣa* to cause to despair. *qebuṣ* discouraged, despairing. *qebṣat* despair.

qadḥa G *(yeqdāḥ)* to draw water. Gt *taqadḥa* pass. *qadāḥi* drawer of water; cupbearer. *maqdeḥt* water-jar.

qadama G *(yeqdem)* to go before, precede (o.s. or *la-/ʾemenna*); with inf. or coord. verb: to do beforehand, to do first. CG *ʾaqdama* to put or place first; to happen/exist first/previously/beforehand; with inf. or coord. verb = G in same usage. Gt *taqadma* to occur first/beforehand. Glt *taqādama* to go/come out to meet. *qadāmi* adj.: first, previous, prior, antecedent; n.: beginning, first or best of anything; (pl. *qadamt*) the ancients, men of old, those who came before; nobles, princes; as adv. at first, in the beginning, previously. *qadāmē*, *qadāmihu* adv. idem. *qadāmit* n. beginning. *qedma* prep. before (of place), in the presence of; *ba-qedma* idem; *ʾem-qedma* from before, from the presence of; before (of time), prior to; as conj. (with subj.) before. *qedma* adv. previously, beforehand. *qadimu* adv. first, at first, previously, before this; *ʾem-qadimu* idem; also used as a noun in a few fixed expressions: *mawāʿela qadimu* days of old; *za-qadimu* things of old. *maqdem* n. beginning; *maqdema* adv. first, beforehand.

qaddasa D to sanctify, make or regard as holy; to perform sacred offices. Dt *taqaddasa* pass. *qeddus* (f. *qeddest*) holy, sacred; as n.: saint, esp. in titles, e.g. *Qeddus Mārqos* Saint Mark. *qeddesāt* holiness, sanctity, sacredness; frequent in constr. phrases, e.g. *hagara qeddesāt* holy city. *qeddesennā* idem. *qeddāsē* (pl. *-yāt*) sanctification, consecration; the sacred service or liturgy. *maqdas* temple, sanctuary; *Bēta Maqdas* the Temple in Jerusalem.

qāl (pl. *-āt*) m.f. voice, sound, word, saying.

q^{w}*elʿē* (f. *-t*; pl. *-yāt*) servant, domestic.

qalala G to be light, easy, swift, slight. CG *ʾaqlala* to lighten, diminish a burden; to make swift, agile; to scorn, disdain, make light of. CD *ʾaqallala* to consider light, to lighten. CGlt *ʾastaqālala* to lighten; to scorn, disdain, despise, revile. *qalil* (f. *qalāl*) light, etc. *maqlali* one who lightens or alleviates.

qanʾa G *(yeqnāʾ)* to be zealous, eager; to envy, be jealous of (person: *la-*; thing: *ʾemenna*); to emulate, imitate (a.d.o.). CG *ʾaqneʾa* to incite to zeal or imitation. Glt *taqāneʾa* to be jealous of one another. CGlt *ʾastaqāneʾa* to cause to be mutually envious. *qanʾ* = *qenʾat* jealousy; zeal; emulation, intense hate or love. *qanāʾi* (one who is) jealous, zealous.

q^{w}*enq*^{w}*enē* moth, worm.

q^{w}*enṣel* (pl. q^{w}*anāṣel*) wolf, fox.

qenāt (pl. *-āt*, *qenāwet*) m. belt, cincture.

qanaya G *(yeqni)* to reduce to servitude, to subject, rule; to force to work. CG *ʾaqnaya* idem. Gt *taqanya* pass. of G; to serve, minister to (a person); to work (e.g. a field). *qenuy* subject, servant, slave. *qenē* servitude; service, ministry; task, office, function. *qenyat* domination, dominion, subjection.

qenē church singing, church music.

qarba G *(yeqrab)* to draw near, approach *(xaba, westa, la-)*. Glt *taqāraba* to approach one another, come close together; to have sexual intercourse. CG *ʾaqraba* to cause to approach, to bring near, to offer. *qerub* near, nearby, adjacent (to: *la-/xaba*); at hand, nigh (of time); *ba-qeruba* prep. near (suff. added as to noun in the acc. q^w*erbān* (pl. *-āt*) offering, sacrifice; spec. the eucharist. *meqrāb* neighborhood, vicinity.

qaraḍa/qaraṣa G to incise, sculpt. Gt *taqarṣa* pass. *qerḍat/qerṣat/*q^w*erṣat* the stroke of a letter; stroke, mark, incision.

taqārana Glt to oppose, resist. *qarn* (pl. *ʾaqrent*) horn (of animal), horn (blown in battle, etc.); tip, end. *taqārāni* contrary, resisting, opposing. *mastaqāren* idem.

q^w*arra/*q^w*arara* to be cold, cool; to cool (of anger). CG *ʾaq*^{w}*rara* caus. q^w*arir* (f. q^w*arār*) cold, cool. q^w*err* cold, coldness.

qassama D to season, make tasty. Dt *taqassama* pass. *qessum* well seasoned, tasty. *maqsem* (pl. *maqāsem*) highly seasoned food.

qasis/qassis (pl. *qasāwest*) presbyter, elder.

qašafa G *(yeqšef)* to beat, whip; to afflict, punish. Gt *taqašfa* pass. *qešuf* beaten, whipped, afflicted. *qešfat* punishment, affliction. *maqšaft* (pl. *-āt*) m.f. punishment, beating, whipping; divine punishment.

qašama G *(yeqšem)* to pick (fruit), gather, collect, harvest. Gt *taqašma* pass. *qašm* harvest, picking; the crops harvested (pl. *ʾaqšām*). *qašāmi/qaššām* a picker of fruit.

ʾastaqaṣṣala CDt to crown (someone: o.s.) with (a.d.o.). *qaṣṣalā* crown, diadem.

q^w*aṣl* (pl. *ʾaq*^{w}*ṣel*) m.f. leaf, foliage.

qaṣara G to enclose or fortify with a wall. *qeṣr/qaṣr* (pl. *ʾaqṣār*) wall, enclosure, fortification wall.

qatala G *(yeqtel)* to kill, murder. Gt *taqatla* pass. CG *ʾaqtala* caus. Glt *taqātala* to fight or kill one another; to fight (with: *mesla* or acc.). *qetul* slain. *qatl* n. killing, murder; battle, fighting; *gabra qatla mesla* to fight a battle with. *qetlat* murder, killing. *qatāli* (pl. *qatalt*) murderer, killer.

qattara D to seal, lock. *qettur* locked, sealed.

qatr noon, midday; *gizē qatr* idem.

qaṭin (f. *qaṭān*; pl. *qaṭant*) fine, delicate; n. fine clothes. *qaṭin* (coll.) servants, domestics. *qeṭnat* fineness, delicacy. *maqāṭen* (pl. only) hooks, fish-hooks.

qaṭqaṭa Q to grind; to break. Qt *taqaṭqaṭa* pass. *qeṭquṭ* ground, broken. *qeṭqāṭē* n. grinding, breaking, destruction.

qobar (pl. *-āt*) blackness, darkness.

qoma G *(yequm)* to arise, stand; to stand, take a position; to come to a halt, stop. Glt *taqāwama* to oppose, withstand, take a stand against (a.d.o. or *mesla/lāʿla/qedma*); to stand up for *(la-)*. CG *ʾaqama* to set up, establish; to confirm the truth of; to carry out the terms of; to cause to cease (e.g. rain). *qom* m. stature, height. *qumat* nature, state, condition. *qawāmi* standing, stable; n. patron, protector. *meqwām* (pl. *-āt*) location, place where one stands or stops; *meqwāma māy* pool. *taqwām* pedestal, lamp-stand.

qēḥa G to grow red. *qayeḥ/qayiḥ* (f. *qayāḥ*) red. *qiḥat* redness. Q *ʾaqyaḥyeḥa* to make/become reddish.

R

reʾs (pl. *ʾarʾest*) m.f. head; top, summit; chief, leader; with pron. suff.: self.

reʾya G *(yerʾay)* to see. Gt *tareʾya* to appear, seem (pred. n. or adj. may be in the acc.). Glt *tarāʾaya* to look at one another, see one another *(gaṣṣa ba-gaṣṣ* face to face). CG *ʾarʾaya* to show (something: a.d.o.; to someone: o.s.); to reveal, make manifest. CGt *ʾastarʾaya* to appear, become visible, manifest (unto: o.s.); to make visible. *rāʾy* (pl. *-āt*) vision, revelation; appearance, form, aspect. *reʾyat* appearance, form, aspect. *ʾarʾayā* image, form, likeness, appearance; type, standard, norm, pattern; copy. transcription. *raʾāyi* (pl. *-yān/-yāt*; *raʾayt*) observer, seer; *raʾāyē xebuʾāt* soothsayer; *raʾāyē kokab* astrologer.

ʾarʿut yoke.

reʿya G *(yerʿay)* to pasture, tend (herds, flocks); to graze (subject: flocks). Gt *tareʿya* to graze, be tended. *marʿēt* (pl. *-āt*, *marāʿey*) cattle, flock, herd; pasture. *marʿay* idem. *merʿāy* a pasture.

ʾarbāʿ (acc. *-a*) f. four; *ʾarbāʿtu* (acc. *ʾarbāʿta*) m. four. *rābeʿ*

(f. -*t*) adj. fourth. *rābeʿāwi* (f. -*t*) idem. *rābeʿāy* (f. *rābeʿit*) idem. *rebʿ* f. four; *rebʿa* adv. four times. *ʾarbeʿā* forty.

rababa G to expand, extend, spread out (trans.). Gt *tarabba* pass. and intrans. *rebbat* expansion, extension. *marbabt* net.

rabbān (pl. -*āt*, *rabbanāt*) teacher, leader.

rabḥa G *(yerbāḥ)* to gain (as) profit; to be profitable. CG *ʾarbeḥa* to make profitable, to make (someone) profit. *rebāḥ/rabāḥ* profit, interest, gain.

radʾa G *(yerdāʾ)* to help (someone: o.s.). Gt *taradʾa* pass. Glt *tarādeʾa* to render mutual aid, to help (a.d.o. or *mesla*). *radāʾi* helper, assistant. *radʾēt* help, assistance; helper, assistant. *radʾ* (pl. *ʾardāʾ*, *ʾardeʾt*) helper, assistant; disciple, follower.

taradya Gt to lend at interest, receive interest. Glt *tarādaya* idem. *redē* interest.

rafʾa G to sew. Gt *tarafʾa* pass. *refʾat* suture, sewing. *rafāʾi* tailor. *refʾo* sewn work. *marfeʾ* (pl. *marāfeʾt*) needle.

rafaqa G *(yerfeq)* to recline at a meal. CG *ʾarfaqa* caus. *merfāq* a place to recline; a meal, party, symposium. *marfaq* threshhold.

regb (pl. *ʾargāb*) dove.

ragama G *(yergem)* to curse, execrate. Gt *taragma* pass. Glt *tarāgama* pass. *regum* cursed, execrated. *ragāmi* curser, execrator. *margam* (pl. -*āt*) curse, execration.

reḥba G *(yerḥab)* to be wide, spacious, ample. CG *ʾarḥaba* caus. *reḥub* wide, spacious. *reḥib* (f. *raḥāb*) idem. *reḥb* width, breadth. *rāḥb*, *reḥbat* idem. *marḥeb* (pl. *marāḥebt*) a wide place, street, forum, marketplace.

raḥana G to spread (a.d.o.) as a saddle, to saddle.

reḥqa G *(yerḥaq)* to be distant, remote, far off (both spatial and temporal). CG *ʾarḥaqa* to remove, put at a distance; to delay. Glt *tarāḥaqa* to separate (mutually; from: *ʾemenna/mesla*/o.s.). *reḥuq* far away, remote, distant; *reḥuqa maʿʿat* slow to anger. *reḥuqa* = *ba-reḥuq* adv. at a distance; *ʾem-reḥuq* from afar. *reḥqat* period of time or interval of space.

rakaba G *(yerkab)* to find, come upon; to acquire. Gt *tarakba* to be found, to be (pred. adj. or n. may be in the acc.). CG *ʾarkaba* caus. Glt *tarākaba* to congregate; to join, associate with (*mesla* or acc.). CGt *ʾastarkaba* to be at leisure (for); to be busy with, involved in; to be ready, convenient, opportune. *rekbat* n.

finding; acquisition. *merkāb* acquisition; pay, stipend.

rak^{w}sa G *(yerk^{w}es/yerk^{w}as)* to be unclean, impure, polluted, contaminated; to be bad (in general). CG *ʾark^{w}asa* to pollute, defile. *rekus* (f. *rek^{w}est*) unclean, etc. *rek^{w}s* uncleanness, pollution; anything unclean, vile.

ʾarmama CG to be silent; to make silent. Gt *taramma* to be passed over in silence. CGlt *ʾastarāmama* to make silent, quiet down, make tranquil. *marmem* silent. *ʾarmāmi* silent, not speaking.

rasʿa G *(yersāʿ)* to forget; to be negligent; to err; to be impious, wicked. CG *ʾarseʿa* caus. Gt *tarasʿa* pass.; to fall into error/sin. *rāseʿ* forgetful, negligent, impious. *rasiʿ* impious, sinful. *resʿat* forgetfulness, negligence, impiety. *resʿān*, *resʿennā* idem.

rasḥa G to be subject or liable (to: *la-*), to be in danger of; to be a defendant; to be unclean, dirty. CG *ʾarseḥa* to condemn; to make dirty, pollute, contaminate. *resuḥ* dirty, etc.; the accused, defendant. *resḥat* (pl. *-āt*) dirt, filth, pollution; crime, guilt.

rassaya D to put, place, set; to impute (something: a.d.o.) to (someone: *lāʿla*, *la-*); to make/regard (something: a.d.o.) as/into (something: a.d.o. or *kama/westa/la-*); to make (someone: a.d.o.) do something (subjunctive). *ressuy* prepared, made ready, equipped. *tersit* adornment, equipment; adoption.

rašʾa G *(yeršāʾ)* to grow old. CG *ʾaršeʾa* caus. *rešʾ*, *rešʾennā*, *rešʾān* old age.

ratʿa G *(yertāʿ)* to be just, righteous, truthful, sincere. CG *ʾarteʿa* to make right, correct, straight, stable. *retuʿ* (f. *reteʿt*) just, righteous; straight, level, even; correct, proper, orthodox; *hāymānot reteʿt* the orthodox faith. *rāteʿ* (f. *-t*) just, righteous, truthful, sincere. *retʿ* justice, what is right; truth. *mastarāteʿ* soldier, guard.

roṣa G *(yeruṣ)* to run. Glt *tarāwaṣa* to run as a group. CG *ʾaroṣa* to cause to run (esp. horses). *rawāṣi* swift, running. *merwāṣ* distance run, course; race.

rexba G *(yerxab)* to be hungry. CG *ʾarxaba* caus. *rexub* hungry, starving. *raxab/raxāb* hunger, famine.

ʾarxawa CG to open (trans.). Gt *tarexwa* to open (intrans.), be opened. *rexew* open. *marxo* (pl. *marāxut*) m.f. key.

ʾaryām (pl. only) highest heaven, the heavenly heights; *māḥlēta ʾaryām* a musical term.

S

-sa encl. part. but, however, on the other hand.

sa'ala G *(yes'al)* to ask for (a.d.o.; from someone: *xaba*, *'em-*, o.s.). Glt *tasā'ala* to find out by asking around. Dt *tase''ela* to ask (someone: o.s. or *ba-xaba*; about something: a.d.o. or *ba'enta*). *se'lat* request, prayer, petition.

se'na G to be unable (to do: inf.). Gt *tase'na* to be impossible (impersonal + o.s. and inf.). *se'un* impotent, powerless. *se'nat* impotence, inability.

sa'at/sa'āt (pl. *-āt*) hour, time.

sa'ama G *(yes'am)* to kiss. Gt *tase'ma* pass. Glt *tasā'ama* to kiss one another. *se'mat* a kiss.

sa'ara G *(yes'ar)* to destroy, violate, annul, dissolve, bring to an end. G *se'ra* = Gt *tase'ra* pass. of trans. G. *se'rat* destruction, violation, annulment; dismissal, removal from office.

tasabbe'a Dt to become man, be incarnate. *sab'* (pl.) people, men (pl. of *be'si*); man, mankind. *tesbe't* incarnation.

sab'u (acc. idem) f. seven. *sab'atu/sabā'tu* (acc. *sab'ata*) m. seven. *sābe'* (f. *-t*) adj. seventh. *sābe'āwi* (f. *-t*) idem. *sābe'āy* (f. *sābe'it*) idem. *sabu'* the seventh day (of week or month); seven days. *seb'* f. seven; *seb'a* adv. seven times. *sab'ā* seventy.

sabbeḥa D to praise, laud, glorify. Dt *tasabbeḥa* pass. *sebbuḥ* praised, glorified. *sebbāḥē* praise, glorification, hymn. *sebḥat* (pl. *-āt*) praise, glory, majesty; *lotu sebḥat* To Him be praise (formula after divine names). *sebbeḥāt* idem.

sabaka G *(yesbek)* to preach (a.d.o. or *ba-*). Gt *tasabka* pass. *sebkat* n. preaching, proclamation; a preaching mission. *sabāki* preacher.

sabara G *(yesber)* to break (into pieces). Gt *tasabra* pass.; to be overcome by disaster. *sebur* broken. *sebr* fragment, piece. *sebār* idem. *sebrat* n. breaking.

sadada G *(yesded)* to persecute; to drive out, banish, expel; to excommunicate; to divorce (a wife). Gt *tasadda* pass. *sedud* expelled, exiled, excommunicated. *seddat* exile, expulsion; persecution. *sadādi* persecutor; exorcist.

sedestu (acc. *sedesta*) m. six. *sessu* (acc. idem) f. six. *sādes* (f. *-t*) adj. sixth. *sādesāwi* (f. *-t*) idem. *sādesāy* (f. *sādesit*) idem. *sadus* the sixth day (of the week or month); six days. *seds* f. six;

sedsa adv. six times. *sessā* sixty.

safḥa G *(yesfāḥ)* trans.: to spread out, extend, expand; intrans. idem. Gt *tasafḥa* idem intrans. *sefuḥ* spread out, extended; wide, spacious, ample; open, sincere, guileless; generous. *sefḥ* expansion, extension; width, expanse; sincerity; warp (of a loom). *sefḥat* extension, width, capacity. *masfeḥ* hammer, mallet; anvil.

safana G *(yesfen)* to become strong, powerful; to exercise control, rule (over: *diba/lāʿla/la-* or a.d.o.). *safāni* ruler, controller, governor. *masfen* (pl. *masāfent*) ruler, governor, prefect, high official, judge; *masfena meʾt* centurion. *mesfenā* the office or status of a *masfen*.

sefna interrog. adv. how many? how many times?

sefneg/sefnag sponge.

safara G to measure out. Gt *tasafra* pass. Glt *tasāfara* to mete out, distribute. *sefur* measured. *masfart* (pl. *masāfer*) a measure, specific amount.

ʾasfaṭa CG to persuade, entice, seduce, deceive. Gt *tasafṭa* pass. *sefṭat* seduction, lure, enticement. *safāṭi* seducer, deceiver.

ʾasaffawa CD to promise (something: a.d.o.; to someone: o.s. or *la-*). Dt *tasaffawa* to hope for, expect, look forward to (a.d.o.). *tasfā* (pl. *-t*) m.f. hope, expectation, promise.

safaya G *(yesfi)* to sew. Gt *tasafya* pass. *safāyi* sewer, tailor, cobbler. *masfē* awl.

sagada G *(yesged)* to bow down (to: *la-/qedma*). *segud* prostrate (in a position of worship/adoration). *segdat* prostration, act of adoration. *mesgād* place of worship, shrine, mosque.

ʾasgala CG to divine, practice augury. CGt *ʾastasagala* idem; to consult diviners. *sagal* divination. *masaggel* (pl. *-ān*) diviner, magician, soothsayer.

saḥaba G *(yesḥab)* to pull, drag, draw; to attract (to: *xaba*); to protract *(qāla, nagara)*. Gt *teseḥba* pass.

seḥta G *(yesḥat)* to err, get lost; to stray (from a path or doctrine). CG *ʾasḥata* to lead astray; to lead into sin or error. *seḥut* erring, led into error. *seḥtat* (pl. *-āt*) error, sin; *zaʾenbala seḥtat* without error.

sakaba G *(yeskeb/yeskab)* to lie down. CG *ʾaskaba* caus. *sekub* adj. lying down. *meskāb* (pl. *-āt*) place to lie down; bed, couch.

ʾaskāl (pl. *-āt*) grape(s).

sakama G to carry on the shoulders. CG *'askama* caus. Gt *tasakma* = G.

sakra G *(yesker/yeskar)* to be intoxicated. CG *'askara* caus. *sekur* inebriated, drunk. *sakār* intoxicating drink; intoxication. *sekrat* intoxication. *sakāri* (pl. *sakart*) drunkard.

sakk^{w}asa D to cease, come to an end, die out.

sak^{w}at/sakot (pl. *'ask^{w}āt*) street, quarter.

maskot (pl. *masākew*) m.f. window.

salaba G *(yesleb)* to take (a.d.o.) away (from: o.s.), deprive of, strip off. Gt *tasalba* reflex. and pass. *selbat* n. depriving, taking away.

salām m.f. safety, peace; *ba-salām* safely, in peace; *gabra salāma mesla* to make peace with; *salām laka* Greetings! *Lā'lēhu salām* May peace be upon him!

selan dill.

tasālaqa Glt to joke, sport, play; to mock, make fun of *(lā'la)*. *selāq* sport, play, mockery. *mastasāleq* mocker, scorner.

salaṭa G (1) to be whole, perfect; (2) to accept/bring back (something: a.d.o.) whole/complete/in its entirety; to pay back; (3) to consummate, finish up/off. D *sallaṭa* = G(2) and G(3); also: to be effective, to accomplish results. Gt *tasalṭa* = Dt *tasallaṭa* to be finished, consummated. *sellāṭē* completion.

sem (pl. *'asmāt*) m. name; fame, reputation.

sam'a G *(yesmā')* to hear, hear of, hear about; to heed, obey, listen to (acc. or *la-*). Gt *tasam'a* pass. CG *'asme'a* caus.; to summon (a.d.o.) as a witness. Glt *tasāme'a* to hear and understand one another, each other's language. *semu'* famous, illustrious; notorious. *samā'i* adj. hearing, listening to, obedient; n. (pl. *samā't*) witness, martyr. *sem'* (pl. *-āt*) m.f. rumor, report; testimony; martyrdom, martyrs.

'asmaka CG to lean; to prop up, cause to lean. *masmak(t)* prop, support. *mesmāk* idem.

samēn the south.

samāni (acc. idem) f. eight. *samānitu, samāntu* (acc. *samānta*) m. eight. *sāmen* (f. *-t*) adj. eighth. *sāmenāwi* (f. *-t*) idem. *sāmenāy* (f. *sāmenit*) idem. *samun* the eighth day (of the month); eight days, a week. *semn* f. eight; *semna* adv. eight times. *samāneyā* eighty.

samaya G *(yesmi)* to name (for constructions see Voc. 16). Gt *tasamya* pass. (pred. n. in the acc.). CG *ʾasmaya* to be well known, famous, outstanding. *semuy* named, called; famous, illustrious.

samāy (pl. *-āt*) m.f. heaven, sky. *samāyāwi* (f. *-t*) heavenly, divine, celestial.

tasanāʾawa Q1t to come to an agreement, be in accord.

ʾasanbata CQ to observe the sabbath or Sunday. *sanbat* (pl. *-āt*, *sanābet*) sabbath; Sunday *(sanbata Kerestiyān)*; week.

sendon/sendun fine linen.

senn (pl. *senan*, *ʾasnān*) tooth.

tasannana Dt = G1t *tasānana* to enter into litigation with, to contend with. *tasnān* lawsuit, litigation, controversy.

senāp̣ē mustard.

sanuy (f. *sanit*) the second day (of week or month), two days; *sānit (ʿelat)* the next day; *sānitā* idem; *ba-sānitā* on the next day (or night).

saqala G *(yesqel)* to suspend, hang up; to crucify. Gt *tasaqla* pass.; to depend (on: *ba-/xaba*); to adhere, cling (to: *westa*). *sequl* hanging, suspended, crucified; dependent. *seqlat* crucifixion. *masqal* (pl. *masāqel*) m. cross.

saqalā (pl. *saqālew*) tent, tabernacle.

saq^{w}*ara (yesq*^{w}*er)* to pierce, dig out/through. Gt *tasaq*^{w}*ra* pass. *sequr* perforated, excavated, breached. *seq*^{w}*rat* aperture, opening.

ʾasqoqawa Q to lament, sing a dirge. *saqoqāw* dirge, lamentation. *masqoqew* mourner; adj. lamenting, mourning.

ʾasrāb (pl. only) cataracts, downpours.

saragalā (pl. *-t*) cart, wagon, chariot.

ʾasargawa CQ to adorn, deck out, beautify. Qt *tasargawa* pass. and reflex. *sergew* adorned, decorated, made beautiful. *sarg*^{w} (pl. *-āt*) adornment, beautification.

sarḥa G *(yesrāḥ)* to labor to the point of exhaustion, to be afflicted with difficult tasks or duties. CG *ʾasreḥa* to tire, exhaust; to cause or impose labor/misery. *seruḥ* vexed, exhausted. *serāḥ* (pl. *-āt*) labor, bother, exhaustion, affliction.

sark evening, twilight; *sarka Sanbat* Sabbath evening.

saraqa G *(yesreq)* to steal. CG *ʾasraqa* caus. Gt *tasarqa* pass. *sarāqi* (pl. *saraqt*) thief. *serq/sarq* stolen object; theft.

sarara G *(yesrer)* to fly. *serur* adj. flying, in flight. *serrat* flight, flying. *sarāri* = *serur*.

sarwē (pl. *sarāwit*) troops, army, cohorts; a military leader.
saraya G *(yesray/yesri)* to forgive, excuse, pardon. Gt *tasarya* pass. CGt *'astasraya* to seek pardon (from: *'emenna*).
tasātafa Lt to associate with (acc. or *mesla*); to share (something: *ba-*) with (someone: acc.) *sutuf* companion, partner. *sutāf/sutāfē* m.f. sing. and coll., companion, associate, consort.
satya G *(yestay)* to drink. CG *'astaya* caus. Gt *tasatya* pass. *setē* = *satāy* = *mastē* a drink (the act or what is drunk). *satāy(i)* a drinker, one who is fond of drinking. *mestāy* a place for drinking, a watering place.
'asṭama CG to submerge, immerse, flood. Gt *tasaṭma* to sink (intrans.). *seṭmat* submersion, sinking. *masṭem* adj. submerging, flooding.
seṭeṭirā a stater (coin).
tasaṭwa Gt to accept, receive, take; to comply with; to respond.
soba conj. when; *wa-kona soba* and when. *ye'eta sobē* at that time. *sobēhā* adv. immediately, then, thereupon.
sawwara D to hide, cover over, conceal, protect. Dt *tasawwara* reflex. and pass. *sewwur* hidden, covered, concealed. *mesewwār* hidden place, hiding place.
sor (pl. *'aswār*) ox, steer.
surāfēl seraph, seraphim.
soṭa G *(yesuṭ)* to pour. Gt *tasawṭa* pass. and reflex. *sewuṭ* poured. *suṭat* n. pouring, emptying.
sexin frankincense
sayf (pl. *'asyāf*, *'asyeft*) m.f. sword.
sēsaya Q/L to nourish, sustain, provide for. Qt/Lt *tasēsaya* pass. *sisāy* sustenance, food, provisions. *sisit* idem.
sayṭān (pl. *-āt*) Satan; a devil, demon, adversary.

Š

šā'n (pl. *'aš'en*, *'aš'ān*, *'ašā'en*) shoe, sandal.
še'ra G to grow green, to grow. *šā'r* (pl. *'aš'ert*) herbage, vegetation, grass. *še'ur* grassy, covered with vegetation. *še'ert* (pl. *'aš'ert*) hair (of head or body).
ša'aya G to winnow. *maš'ē* winnowing-fork.
šegā (pl. *-t*) m. flesh, meat (human or animal); body; the flesh as opposed to the spirit. *šegāwi* of the flesh (not spiritual); carnal.

ʾašgara CG = CD *ʾašaggara* to cast nets, fish, capture by trapping. Gt *tašagra* to be captured, ensnared. *mašagger* (pl. *-ān*) fisherman. *mašgart* (pl. *mašāger*) snare, net, trap. *šagarāt* (pl.) guards. *ʾašgāri* hunter, fisherman.

tašāhala Glt to show mercy (to: a.d.o.); to forgive. *šāhl* mercy, kindness. *mastašāhel* merciful, lenient; seeking mercy or forgiveness.

šaḥaqa/šeḥqa G *(yešḥaq)* to ridicule (a.d.o. or *lāʿla*). CG *ʾašḥaqa* caus. *šāḥq/šaḥaq* ridicule. *mešḥāq* comedy theater.

šalās (acc. *-a*) f. three; *šalastu* (acc. *šalasta*) m. three. *šāles* (f. *-t*) adj. third. *šālesāwi* (f. *-t*) idem. *šālesāy* (f. *šālesit*) idem. *šalus* the third day (of week or month); three days. *šels* f. three; *šelsa* adv. thrice. *šalāsā* thirty. *mašlest* (pl. *mašāles*) a kind of measure.

šallaṭa D to have power, authority. CD *ʾašallaṭa* = CG *ʾašlaṭa* to give power to. Dt *tašallaṭa* = Gt *tašalṭa* to acquire power, authority; to rule. *šeluṭ/šelluṭ* powerful, in power. *šelṭān* (pl. *-āt*) power, authority.

šamra G *(yešmar)* to take delight, be pleased (with/in: *ba-*). CG *ʾašmara* to please, delight, give pleasure to (o.s. or *la-*). *šemur* pleasing (to: *la-/ba-xaba/ba-qedma*), nice, pleasant. *šemrat* favor, approval, consent; *ba-šemrata* with the consent of. *mašmer/mašmari* pleasing (to: *xaba/la-*).

Šenē/Senē Eth. month name: June 8 - July 7.

šannaya D to be beautiful, fine, excellent, good, fitting, appropriate. CD *ʾašannaya* to adorn, deck out, array; to make (a.d.o.) good; to do (something: inf.) well. *šennuy* adorned, decked out, lovely. *mašanney* the best (of), the best part (of). *šenn* beauty. *mešennāy* = *mašanney*. *šannāy* (f. *-t*) beautiful, fine, excellent, good (both physical and moral senses).

šaqq (pl. *-āt*, *ʾašqāq*) sack, sack-cloth.

šāqaya L to afflict, vex, torment. Lt *tašāqaya* pass. *šeqāy* vexation, torment. *mašqē* goad; weaver's comb.

šarʿa G *(yešrāʿ)* to put into order, arrange; to establish, set up, ordain. Gt *tašarʿa* pass. *šeruʿ* arranged, ordered, established, ordained. *šerʿat* (pl. *-āt*) order, arrangement, disposition; decree, edict, command; law, statute; treaty, pact, testament; custom, habit, any fixed pattern.

šaraba G to drink in, absorb.

šernāy/sernāy wheat.

šārara L to found, establish. Lt *tašārara* pass. *šerur/šurur* founded, established. *šurārē* founding, foundation. *šārāri* founder. *mašarrat* (pl. *-āt*) foundation, firmament, bottom. CQ *'amašrata* to found. Qt *tamašrata* pass.

šaraqa G *(yešreq)* to rise, shine (of the sun). CG *'ašraqa* caus. *šarq* (pl. *'ašrāq*) rising (of heavenly bodies); the east; the new moon, the calends. *šerqat* rising, appearance. *šaraqāwi* eastern. *mešrāq* (pl. *-āt*) the east.

šaraṣa/šarṣa G *(yešreṣ/yešraṣ)* to sprout. CG *'ašraṣa* caus. *šarṣ* a sprout, sprouting.

šarawa G = D *šarrawa* to eradicate, extirpate. Gt *tašarwa* = Dt *tašarrawa* pass. *šerw* (pl. *-āt*, *šeraw*, *'ašrāw*) root; nerve, muscle, tendon. *šerrāwē* eradication.

šarwē (pl. *šarāwit*) beam, timber.

šerāy (pl. *-āt*) medicine, herbs, etc.; incantations, spells, magic; *za-/'alla šerāy*, *sab'a šerāy* dealers in magic and spells.

šaṭaqa G *(yešṭeq)* to cut, split. Gt *tašaṭqa* pass. *šeṭuq* cut, split. *šeṭqat* n. cutting, splitting; a cut, split.

šaṭaṭa G *(yešṭeṭ)* to tear (apart), rend. Gt *tašaṭṭa* pass. *šeṭuṭ* torn, rent. *šeṭṭat* n. tearing, rending; the part torn off, tatter, fragment.

šuʿ/suʿ flax, tinder.

šawʿa G *(yešuʿ)* to sacrifice, offer (a.d.o.; to: *la-*). Gt *tašawʿa* pass. *šawāʿi* (pl. *šawāʿt*) priest, sacrificer. *mašwāʿt* (pl. *-āt*, *mašāweʿ*) m. sacrifice; altar. *mešwāʿ* (pl. *-āt*) altar.

šok (pl. *'ašwāk*) thorn, sting.

šawaya G to ripen (of grain). *šawit* ear of grain.

šēma G *(yešim)* to appoint (to an office), designate (a.d.o. ± obj. compl. in acc.); to put, place, set. Gt *tašayma* pass. (pred. n. in acc.). *šeyum* appointed, set, placed; n. appointee, official, governor, prefect. *šimat* (pl. *-āt*) m.f. ordination; office, position. *mašāyemt* (pl.) container(s), basket(s).

šēṭa G *(yešiṭ)* to sell (to: *xaba*, *la-*). Gt *tašayṭa* pass. Glt *tašāyaṭa* to buy. *šēṭ* price, value. *šayāṭi* (pl. *šayaṭṭ*) seller, merchant. *mešyāṭ* (pl. *-āt*) marketplace.

šaxata/šexta G to be at ease, at rest, comfortable, well off. D

šaxxata to put at ease, allow to rest. CD ʾašaxxata = D. Dt
tašexxeta pass. of D. šexut relaxed, at rest, at ease. šāxt
tranquility, relaxation, rest.

Ṣ

ṣāᶜdawa Q to be white. CQ ʾaṣāᶜdawa caus. ṣeᶜdew adj. white.
ṣāᶜdā/ṣaᶜadā (pl. ṣaᶜādew) adj. white. ṣeᶜdāwē whiteness.
ṣaᶜadᶜid whitish.
ṣaᶜala G (yeṣᶜal) to curse, revile. D ṣaᶜᶜala idem. Dt taṣeᶜᶜela/
taṣaᶜᶜala pass. ṣeᶜul/ṣeᶜᶜul despised. ṣeᶜlat n. cursing, reviling. ṣaᶜāli curser, reviler.
ṣaᶜᶜana D to load (an animal or vehicle). Dt taṣeᶜᶜena to mount,
ride on (animal or vehicle); also of a demon possessing a person.
ṣeᶜᶜun laden; riding, mounted. maṣtaṣeᶜᶜen horseman.
ʾaṣᶜaqa CG to press in on, to confine. ṣeᶜuq narrow, confined. ṣāᶜq
confinement, press; need. maṣᶜeq adj. pressing, confining.
ṣeᶜra G to be grieved, pained, afflicted. CG ʾaṣᶜara = CD ʾaṣaᶜᶜara
to inflict grief or pain upon. Dt taṣeᶜᶜera pass. of CD. ṣeᶜur/
ṣeᶜᶜur grieved, pained, afflicted. ṣāᶜr pain, torment, grief,
affliction.
ṣabʾa G. See ḍabʾa.
ʾaṣbāᶜt (pl. ʾaṣābeᶜ) f.m. finger, toe.
ṣabba/ṣababa G (yeṣbeb) to be (too) narrow; to narrow, confine. CG
ʾaṣbaba caus. ṣabib (f. ṣabāb) narrow, confined. ṣebbat narrowness. maṣbeb a narrow place, pass.
ṣabḥa G (yeṣbāḥ) to grow light, to dawn; ṣabiḥo at dawn. Glt
taṣābeḥa to greet early in the day. ṣebāḥ (pl. -āt) m.f. early
morning; the east.
ṣabbeḥa D to exact/collect taxes or tribute. CD ʾaṣabbeḥa caus.
ṣabbāḥt tribute, taxes. maṣabbeḥ tax-collector. maṣabbeḥi idem.
meṣebbāḥ tax office.
ṣabal dust. ṣebul dust.
ṣabxa G to dip. ṣabx sauce, gravy. maṣbex dish, bowl.
ṣadfa G to rush, plunge headlong. CG ʾaṣdafa caus. ṣadf (pl. ʾaṣdāf)
precipitous place, precipice, abyss.
ṣadala G to shine, be splendid. CG ʾaṣdala to shine, emit light,
gleam. ṣedul shining, splendid. ṣadāl splendor, light, gleam.
ṣadqa G (yeṣdeq/yeṣdaq) to be righteous, just, true, faithful. Dt

taṣaddaqa to give the appearance (falsely) of being righteous. CG *'aṣdaqa* to make righteous, just; to declare just or innocent. *ṣādeq* (f. *-t*) righteous, etc. *ṣedq* (pl. *-āt*) justice; rightness, truth; *ba-ṣedq* legally, rightfully.

ṣadāy autumn.

ṣāḍot/ṣāṣot gnat, flea.

ṣaf'a G *(yeṣfā')* to strike, slap, box. Gt *taṣaf'a* pass. *ṣef'at* a blow, slap.

ṣefnat pack, wallet.

'aṣfaqa to make dense; to do something frequently (+ inf.). Gt *taṣafqa* to be dense, crowded. *ṣefuq* dense, thick, crowded; frequent.

ṣagba G to be sated, filled, satisfied; to be sick of something. CG *'aṣgaba* to satiate, satisfy. *ṣegub* sated, full, satisfied. *ṣegāb* satiety, abundance.

ṣegg^{w} (pl. *ṣeg*^{w}*ag*^{w}) street, market-place.

ṣag^{w}*r* hair (human or animal); fur, feathers, plumage.

ṣaggawa D to show grace or favor (to: o.s. or *la-*); to bestow gifts. Dt *taṣaggawa* to be shown grace or favor. *ṣagā* (pl. *-t*) m.f. grace, favor, kindness; gift, payment, reward; *ba-ṣagā* gratis, as a gift. *ṣaggāwi/ṣagāwi* liberal, generous.

ṣagaya G to flower. *ṣeguy* adj. flowering, adorned with flowers. *ṣegē* (pl. *-yāt*) flower.

ṣehqa G *(yeṣhaq)* to desire; to be eager for, pursue diligently; to take care of. CG *'aṣhaqa* caus. *ṣehuq* desirous, eager, concerned. *ṣāhq* desire, eagerness.

ṣaḥafa G *(yeṣḥaf)* to write. Gt *taṣeḥfa* pass. CG *'aṣḥafa* caus. *ṣeḥuf* written. *ṣeḥfat* writing (act or product). *ṣaḥāfi* (pl. *ṣaḥaft*) scribe; learned person. *maṣḥaf* (pl. *maṣāḥeft*) m.f. book, document; writing, inscription.

ṣāḥl dish, bowl, platter.

ṣeḥew serene.

ṣal'a G *(yeṣlā')* to hate, be hostile toward (a.d.o.). Gt *taṣal'a* pass. and reflex. Glt *taṣāle'a* to behave in a hostile way toward one another. *ṣelu'* hated, hateful. *ṣel'/ṣal'* hatred, hostility, enmity. *ṣalā'i* (pl. *ṣalā't*) enemy, hater, detracter.

ṣalḥawa Q to act treacherously. *ṣelḥew* treacherous, guileful. *ṣelḥut* treachery, guile, malice.

ʾaṣlala CG to furnish shade; to seek the shade; to sit, live, dwell. D *ṣallala* to shade, cover. Dt *taṣallala* to be shaded, dark. *ṣalalo* lampblack, soot. *ṣelālot/ṣellālot* shade, shadow(s), darkness. *meṣlāl/meṣellāl* a shady place, arbor, pavilion. *maṣallat* tabernacle, tent; *Baʿāla Maṣallat* Feast of Tabernacles.

ṣalma/ṣalama G *(yeṣlam/yeṣlem)* to grow dark, be black; of eyes: to grow blind; *ṣalma gaṣṣu* he became angry. CG *ʾaṣlama* caus. *ṣelum* dark, obscured, blinded. *ṣalim* (f. *ṣalām*) black. *ṣelmat* m.f. darkness; the days of the month after the 15th are known as *mawāʿela ṣelmat* (days of wane); note the formula *ʾama X-u la-ṣelmata Y* on the X day (using *qatul* form) of the second half of the month Y.

ṣallaya D to pray (to: *xaba/qedma*; for: *baʾenta/lāʿla/diba*), to pray for (something: a.d.o.). *ṣalot* (pl. *-āt*) prayer(s). *meṣellāy* place to pray, chapel.

ṣamʾa G *(yeṣmāʾ)* to be thirsty (for: *la-*). CG *ʾaṣmeʾa* caus. *ṣemuʾ* thirsty. *ṣemʾ* thirst.

ṣamhayaya Q to wither, dry up.

ṣamma G to be deaf and dumb. CG *ʾaṣmama* to make deaf, dumb. Gt *taṣamama* to be made deaf, to feign deafness. *ṣemum* deaf and/or dumb. *ṣemma, ṣemmita, ba-ṣemmit* adv. secretly, in secret, in private.

ṣāmawa L *(yeṣāmu)* to labor, toil. CL *ʾaṣāmawa* to inflict harsh labor on; to mortify (the flesh, as an ascetic practice). *ṣāmā/ḍāmā* (pl. *-t*) m.f. labor, toil, work; device, artifice.

ṣanʿa G *(yeṣnāʿ)* to be strong, powerful, firm, sure; lasting, enduring; hard, harsh, severe. CG *ʾaṣneʿa* to make strong, etc.; to grasp firmly *(ba-)*; to learn by heart *(ba-lebb-)*. *ṣenuʿ* (f. *ṣeneʿt*) strong, etc. *ṣanāʿi* (pl. *sanāʿt*) strong, firm; fortified. *ṣenʿ*, *ṣenʿat* hardness, firmness; strength, power, force; *ṣenʿa samāy* the firmament of the sky. *meṣnāʿ* (pl. *-āt*) firm base; firmament.

ṣenf (pl. *ʾaṣnāf, ṣenaf*) m. edge, margin, hem; shore, bank; end, limit. *ʾaṣnāfa medr* the ends of the earth. *ṣanāfi* adj. exterior, extreme, outer.

ṣanḥa G *(yeṣnāḥ)* to wait, await, expect; to be imminent (to: o.s. or *la-*); to lie in wait for. CG *ʾaṣneḥa* to set traps or snares for; to promise (i.e. cause to expect); to prepare (something: a.d.o.;

for: *la-*). *ṣenuḥ* waiting, expectant; put aside, reserved.

ṣenḥāḥ sacrifice, offering.

taṣannasa Dt to be impoverished, reduced to poverty. *ṣennus* poor, indigent, wretched. *taṣnās* poverty, wretchedness; lack, deficiency.

Ṣerʿ Greece, the Greeks. *ba-Ṣerʿ* in Greek. *Ṣerʿāwi* adj. Greek.

ṣaraba G to hew, do carpentry. *ṣerbat* woodwork, stonework. *ṣarābi* carpenter, craftsman.

ṣerḥ (pl. *ʾaṣrāḥ*, *ʾaṣreḥt*) room, chamber, house; bedroom.

ṣariq copper, small coin. *ṣariqat* thin disk, cake.

ṣarxa G *(yeṣrāx)* to cry out. *ṣerāx* a cry, shout.

ṣawweʿa D to call, summon; to invite; to proclaim. Dt *taṣawweʿa* pass. *ṣewwuʿ* summoned, invited. *ṣewweʿā* call, summons, invitation. *ṣewwāʿē* idem.

ṣewāʿ (pl. *-āt*) cup.

ṣolāʿ (pl. *-āt/-t*) rock(s).

ṣoma G *(yeṣum)* to fast. *ṣewum* adj. fasting. *ṣom* (pl. *ʾaṣwām*, *-āt*) fast, fasting.

ṣomāʿt (pl. *-āt*) monk's cell.

ṣora G *(yeṣor/yeṣur)* to carry, bear (lit. and fig.). CG *ʾaṣora/ʾaṣara* caus. Gt *taṣawra* pass. *ṣewur* adj. bearing, burdened (with: acc.). *ṣor* (pl. *ʾaṣwār*) burden. *ṣawwār* carrier(s), porter(s). *ṣawāri* (f. *-t*; pl. *ṣawart*) one who carries, bears (e.g. *ṭebab*, *zēnā*).

ṣēʾa G to rot. *ṣeyuʾ* rotten, decayed. *ṣiʾat* rot, decay.

ṣēḥa G *(yeṣiḥ)* to make level, to pave (a road). Gt *taṣēḥa* pass. *ṣeyuḥ* level, even, paved; easy. *maṣyāḥt* highway.

ṣēw salt.

T

tābot (pl. *-āt*) ark (of Noah, of the Covenant).

tabʿa to be brave, manly. *tebʿ*, *tebʿat* bravery, courage, virtue. *tabāʿt* (pl. *ʾatbuʿ*) n. a male. *tabbāʿ* = *tabāʿi* (pl. *tabāʿt*) adj. male, strong. *tabāʿtāwi* (or *-āy*) adj. male, masculine.

tafʾa G to spit. *tefʾat* spit, saliva.

tagha G to be wakeful, watchful, vigilant, attentive. *teguh* wakeful, etc. *tegāh* vigilance, watchfulness.

teḥta G to be humble. CG *ʾatḥata* to make humble, to subject. Dt *tateḫḫeta* to humble one's self, be submissive, to act or be inferior, lowly. *teḫḫut* humble, modest, obedient; lowly, ignoble. *teḫḫetennā* humility, humbleness. *tāḥta* prep. under, below, beneath; adv. below, from below. *mataḥett* lower or inferior part; *mataḥetta* prep. below, under, beneath.

matkaf(t) (pl. *matākeft*) shoulder.

takala G *(yetkel)* to plant; to fix in, implant. Gt *tatakla* pass. CD *ʾatakkala* to push, shove, hit. *tekul* planted; implanted, fixed. *takl* (pl. *-āt*, *ʾatkelt*) a plant, tree; *ʿaṣada ʾatkelt* orchard, grove; also fig.: *takla ṣedq*, *takla hāymānot*. *matkal* (pl. *matākel*) stake, peg. *matkel* idem.

takʷlā (pl. *-t*, *takʷālut*) wolf.

ʾatkata CG to wish to gain time. CD *ʾatakkata* idem. *tekāt* antiquity, yore; *za-tekāt* ancient, old, primeval, pristine; *ʾem-tekāt(u)* from of old, hitherto, once, formerly.

takkaza D to be sad, distressed, troubled in mind, to be concerned. CD *ʾatakkaza* caus. *tekkuz* sad, etc. *tekkāz* (pl. *-āt*) sadness, grief, care, concern; business, task.

talawa G *(yetlu)* to follow, accompany (a.d.o. or *la-*). CG *ʾatlawa* caus. Glt *tatālawa* recipr. *telwat/telot* n. following; dowry. *talāwi* follower; disciple, pupil; sectarian, successor. *matlew* adj. following. *matlew/matlo* that which follows, succession; rest, remainder. *matlewa* adv. then, immediately thereafter, in succession.

tarfa/tarafa G *(yetref/yetraf)* to be left over, remain, survive. CG *ʾatrafa* to leave (as a remainder). *teruf* left, remaining; abundant; excellent, outstanding. *tereft* (pl. *terufāt*) virtue, excellence, perfection. *terāf* remainder, residue; overflow, abundance; *Terāfāta Nagašt* the OT book of Chronicles (lit. the remainder or overflow from Kings). *taraf/tarf* idem. *tarāfi* survivor.

targʷama Q to translate (from ... into: *ʾemenna ... xaba/la-*). Qt *tatargʷama* pass. *tergʷāmē* (pl. *-eyāt*) m.f. translation, interpretation; *za-ba-tergʷāmēhu*, *ze-weʾetu tergʷāmēhu* the interpretation of which is ... *matargʷem* translator, interpreter.

tesʿu/tasʿu (acc. idem) f. nine. *tesʿatu/tasʿatu*, *tasāʿtu* (acc. *-ta*) m. nine. *tāseʿ* (f. *-t*) adj. ninth. *tāseʿāwi* (f. *-t*) idem. *tāseʿāy* (f. *tāseʿit*) idem. *tasuʿ* the ninth day (of the month); nine days. *tesʿ* f. nine; *tesʿa* adv. nine times. *tesʿā/tasʿā* ninety.

totān (pl. -*āt*) thong, lace; *totāna šā'n* shoelace, sandal-thong.

Tāxšāš Eth. month name: Dec. 10 - Jan. 8.

Ṭ

ṭā'ot (pl. -*āt*) m. heathen idol(s).

ṭe'ma/ṭa'ama G *(yeṭ'am/yeṭ'em)* to taste, to experience (e.g. death); to be tasty, delicious. CG *'aṭ'ama* caus.; to make sweet, pleasant. *ṭe'um* tasty, delicious, sweet, pleasant. *ṭā'm* (pl. -*āt*) m.f. taste, flavor; sweet taste, pleasant taste; reason, good sense.

ṭe'ya G *(yeṭ'ay)* to be healthy, well. CG *'aṭ'aya* to make healthy, well, cause to recover. *ṭe'uy* (f. *ṭe'it*) well, healthy (of person or place). *ṭe'innā* good health.

ṭab'a G to be willing, ready (to do something). CG *'aṭbe'a* to do something willingly (with foll. coord. verb); to persevere, be constant, firm, undeterred; caus. of same meanings. *ṭebu'* willing, quick, eager, ready, undeterred, bold, persevering.

ṭabba G *(yeṭbab/yeṭbeb)* to be wise, prudent; to be skilled, expert. Dt *taṭabbaba* to be crafty, cunning. CG *'aṭbaba* to make wise, etc. *ṭabib* (f. *ṭabāb*; pl. *ṭababt*) wise, etc. *ṭebab* (pl. -*āt*) wisdom, prudence, skill.

ṭabḥa G to make an incision; to sacrifice. Gt *taṭabḥa* pass. *ṭebḥ* sacrifice, sacrificial victim. *ṭebḥat* sacrifice. *maṭbāḥt* (pl. *maṭābeḥ*) knife, sword.

ṭaf'a G *(yeṭfā')* to go out (of a light or fire); to perish, vanish. CG *'aṭfe'a* to extinguish; to destroy, annihilate. *ṭef'at* extinction, destruction, loss.

ṭafara G to roof over, put up a ceiling. *ṭafar* roof, ceiling.

ṭalla G to be moist. CG *'aṭlala* to moisten, bedew. *ṭelul* moist, rich, fat, prosperous. *ṭall* dew. *maṭlali* adj. moistening, refreshing.

ṭali (f. -*t*; pl. *'aṭāli*) goat.

'aṭmaqa CG to baptize. Gt *taṭamqa* pass. *ṭemuq* baptized. *ṭemqat* baptism. *maṭmeq* baptizer, esp. *Yoḥannes Maṭmeq* John the Baptist. *meṭmāq* place for baptizing; baptistry; pool.

ṭaqaba G to sew, attach by sewing. *ṭeqbat* n. sewing, stitch.

Ṭeqemt Eth. month name: Oct. 11 - Nov. 9.

ṭeqm wall, city wall, fortification wall. *'arafta ṭeqm* fortification walls; *'ahgura ṭeqm* fortified cities.

ṭeqqa adv. very, extremely; exactly, accurately; still, even. *ṭeqqā*, *ba-teqqā* prep. near, beside.

Ṭerr Eth. month name: Jan. 9 - Feb 7.

'aṭraya CG to acquire, possess. Gt *taṭarya* pass. *ṭerit* possession, property, wealth.

ṭerāz (pl. *-āt*) fragment, fascicle of a book.

ṭayyaqa D to examine, observe closely, scrutinize, investigate, explore; to ascertain by examining. CD *'aṭayyaqa* to inform (someone: o.s.) of something (a.d.o.). Dt *taṭayyaqa* to seek certainty, try to make sure; also passive: to be ascertained, found out for sure. *ṭeyyuq* precise, accurate; certain, sure; *ṭeyyuqa* adv. precisely, accurately, for a certainty.

ṭēsa G *(yeṭis)* to smoke. CG *'aṭēsa* caus. *ṭis* smoke.

W

wa- conj. and.

we'etu (acc. *we'eta*) m.s. pron. he; that one, that (pron. and adj.).

wa'ala/we'la G *(ya'al)* to pass the day, remain. *wa'āli* attendant, servant. *'elat* (pl. *-āt*, *mawā'el*) day; time (see Voc. 10). *ma'ālt* (pl. *mawā'el*) m.f. day, daytime; *ma'ālta* during the day; pl. also = period, era.

we'ya G *(ya'ay)* to be burned up, consumed by fire. CG *'aw'aya* to burn up (trans.); to burn, scorch. *we'uy* hot, burning. *wā'y* fire, heat, burning. *we'yat* n. burning, conflagration.

wadde'a D to finish, complete; used as an auxiliary verb in the sense of "already": e.g. *wadde'a yenabber* already sits, is already positioned. Dt *tawadde'a* pass.

wadqa G *(yedaq)* to fall, fall down, collapse. CG *'awdaqa* to drop, let fall; to throw down, cast down; to fell, hew down. *weduq* fallen, lying fallen. *deqat* fall, ruin, collapse. *denqata* adv. suddenly, unexpectedly.

wadaya G *(yeday)* to put, place, set. Gt *tawadya* pass. CGlt *'astawādaya* to bring charges against, to accuse. *wedēt* charge, accusation. *mudāy* (pl. *-āt*) a container of any sort; basket, hamper.

waḍ'a G *(yeḍā')* to go/come forth, emerge; with *'em-*: to leave, depart from, to spring from, originate in. CG *'awḍe'a* to bring/lead/take forth; to expel; to put forth, produce. *weḍu'* adj. departing; emerging; lacking (in: *'em-*); alien (to: *'em-*). *ḍa'at* exit, departure; *'em-X ḍa'atu* he is a native of X. *muḍā'* place of exit, source.

wafara G *(yewfer, yufar)* to go out into the country. *wafr* the countryside, fields, farms, farmland. *mufār* farmland, pasture.

mogad (pl. *mawāged*) wave.

wagara G *(yegar, yewger)* to throw, cast; to stone (someone: o.s. ± *ba-'ebn*). Gt *tawagra* to be stoned. Glt *tawāgara* to throw stones at one another. D *waggara* = G. Dt *tawaggara* = Gt. *wagr* (pl. *'awger*, *-āt*) heap, mound, hill. *mogart* sling.

'awgaza CG to excommunicate, anathematize, curse. Gt *tawagza* pass. Glt *tawāgaza* to alienate one's self from (a.d.o.). *weguz* excommunicated, cursed. *wegzat/gezat* excommunication.

wahaba G (imperf. *yehub*, subj. *yahab*) to give (something: a.d.o.; to: dat. suff.) Gt *tawehba* pass. *habt* (pl. *-āt*) gift. *wahābi* one who gives, donor; adj. generous.

weḥza G *(yewḥaz/yaḥaz)* to flow. CG *'awḥaza* to cause to flow (esp. tears). *weḥiz* (pl. *-āt*, *waḥāyezt*) river, stream; flow, current. *weḥzat* flow, flowing. *muḥāza māy* aqueduct, canal.

tawakfa Gt to accept, receive, take unto one's self; also passive of same. Dt *tawakkafa* idem. *wekuf/wekkuf* accepted, acceptable, agreeable, pleasant.

tawakkala Dt to trust or have faith (in: *ba-/diba* or o.s.). *wekkul* trusting, confiding, dependent. *tewkelt* trust, faith, confidence.

walada G *(yelad)* to bear (a child); to beget (a child: a.d.o.; by: *ba-xaba*). Gt *tawalda* pass. Glt *tawālada* to procreate; to increase or flourish by procreation. CG *'awlada* to beget; to cause to bear. *wald* (pl. *welud*) son, child, boy, lad; pl. also used as singular. *walatt* (pl. *'awāled*) daughter, girl. *welud* (1) pl. of *wald*; (2) syn. of *wald* in singular; (3) adj. born, begotten. *ledat* birth. *walādi* (f. *-t*) parent. *mulād* place of birth, native land. *tewledd* (pl. *-āt*) offspring, family; race, tribe, family, species; generation.

wallaṭa D to change, alter, transform. Dt *tawallaṭa* pass. *welluṭ* changed, transformed, different. *wellāṭē* change, alteration, transformation. *tawlāṭ* change; exchange, price.

wangēl m.f. gospel. *wangēlāwi* (f. *-t*) adj. gospel; n. evangelist.

waqara G = D *waqqara* = CG *ʾawqara* to dig, excavate.

warada G *(yerad)* to descend, come down, go down. CG *ʾawrada* to bring/send/lead down. *redat* descent. *murād* place of descent, downward slope.

warq m. gold, money.

waraqa G *(yewreq)* to spit. *merāq* spittle, saliva.

warasa G *(yeras)* to inherit. CG *ʾawrasa* to make someone an heir. Gt *tawarsa* to gain by inheritance. Glt *tawārasa* to inherit (jointly or singly), gain possession of. *warāsi* heir. *rest* (pl. *-āt*) inheritance. *mawārest* (pl.) heirs. *wāres* heir (very rare).

warx (pl. *ʾawrāx*) m.f. moon, month. *warxāwi* lunatic.

warwa G *(yewru)* to throw, cast. Gt *tawarwa* pass. and reflex.

warēzā (pl. *warāzut*) a youth, young man. *werzāwē* manhood, maturity. *werzut* idem.

ʾawsaba CG to marry (subj. man; obj. woman). CGlt *ʾastawāsaba* to give someone in marriage, to marry off. *sabsāb* marriage.

wasada G *(yesad/yesed/yewsed)* to lead, conduct, bring, take (a.d.o.; to: *xaba/westa/la-*).

wassaka D to add (a.d.o.; to: *diba/lāʿla*); to increase, augment (a.d.o.). Dt *tawassaka* to be added (to: *westa/xaba* or o.s.). *tawsāk* addition.

wassana D to delimit, mark off, define. Dt *tawassana* pass. *wassan* boundary, limit.

westa (w. pron. suff.: *westēt-*) prep. in, into, to; *ba-westa* idem; *ʾem-westa* from in, from within.

wessāṭē interior, middle.

ʾawšeʾa CG to respond, answer; to take up a discourse. Glt *tawāšeʾa* to speak against, contradict; to dispute, argue (with: o.s. or *la-*). *šāʾšāʾ* eloquence, refined manner of speaking.

ʾawtara CG to continue, persevere in, be assiduous in (a.d.o. or inf.); to direct (hands, eyes) to *(xaba/lāʿla/la-)*. *watra* adv. always, perpetually, continuously, assiduously.

waṭana G *(yeṭan/yewṭen)* to begin (a.d.o. or subj. or inf.). Gt *tawaṭna* pass. *ṭent* n. beginning; *ʾem-ṭent* from the beginning.

wawweʿa D to shout. *wewweʿā* a shout, cry.

wexda G to be few, small. *wexud* few, small, scanty. *wexdat* paucity, scantiness.

wexṭa/waxaṭa G *(yaxaṭ)* to swallow.

wayn (pl. *ʾawyān*) m. vine, wine. *ʿaṣada wayn* vineyard.

X

xaba (w. pron. suff.: *xabē-*) prep. by, with, at, near; to, toward, unto; *ba-xaba* idem; *ʾem-xaba* from with, from the presence of; through the agency of, by means of. As rel. adv. where, see §25.2.

xabʾa G *(yexbāʾ)* to hide, conceal. Gt *taxabʾa* reflex. and pass. *xebuʾ* hidden, concealed; secret, arcane; *ba-xebuʾ* secretly, in secret. *mexbāʾ* (pl. *-āt*) hiding place, hidden place; receptacle.

xabra/xabara G *(yexbar)* to be connected or associated (with: *mesla*); to join, associate (with: *mesla*); to conspire (against: *lāʿla*); to be in accord with, agree with (*mesla, ba-*; subject usually words, things, stories); to share something (a.d.o.) with *(mesla)*; with inf. or coord. verb: to do jointly, together. CG *ʾaxbara* to associate (someone: a.d.o.; with: *mesla*); to make a conspiracy; to be in agreement, accord. Gt *taxabara* to be associated (with: *mesla*). *xebur* joined, associated; *xebura* adv. together, jointly, at one and the same time. *xebrat* union, joining, association; consensus, accord. *māxbar* m.f. congregation, gathering; crowd, tumult; council; colleagues, associates; monastery, convent.

xabaza G *(yexbez)* to bake. *xabāzi* baker. *xebest* (pl. *xabāwez*) m. bread, piece of bread.

xadaga G *(yexdeg)* (1) to leave, abandon, desert; (2) to divorce (a wife); (3) to forgive (someone: *la-*; of or for sins or debts: a.d. o.); (4) to neglect, ignore; (5) to renounce, give up; (6) to let, allow, permit (someone: o.s. or *la-*; to do: subj.); (7) to stop, cease, desist. Gt *taxadga* pass. Glt *taxādaga* to divorce (someone: *mesla*). *xedug* left, abandoned, deserted; divorced. *xedgat* remission (of sins or debts). *xedgāt/xedāgāt* divorce; *maṣḥafa xedgāt* divorce document.

xadara G *(yexder)* to reside, dwell, inhabit (usually with a prep. phrase, but sometimes with the acc.); *xadara lāʿla* to reside in, possess (said of demons or spirits in a person). CG *ʾaxdara* caus. Gt *taxadra* to be inhabited. Glt *taxādara* to live together, cohabit (with: *mesla*). *xedur* adj. residing, dwelling. *xedrat* n. residing, dwelling. *māxdar* (pl. *maxāder*) dwelling-place, residence; room, cell.

Xedār Eth. month name: Nov. 10 - Dec. 9.

xedāṭ a small amount, a little; adj. (pl. *-āt*) few.

xaḍaba G *(yexḍeb)* to wash, wash away. Gt *taxaḍba* to wash one's self (a part of the body may be added as a.d.o.). *xeḍub* washed. *xeḍbat* washing, ablution. *mexḍāb* (pl. *-āt*) bath, bathing place.

māxfad tower.

xafara/xafra G *(yexfar)* to be ashamed (of: *ba'enta*; to do something: inf. or verbal noun or subj.; before, in the presence of: *gaṣṣa*, *'emenna*); to fear, revere (someone: *gaṣṣa*, *'emenna*). Gt *taxafra* to be ashamed, put to shame. *xafrat* (pl. *-āt*) shame, impropriety, turpitude. *xefur* ashamed. *xafāri* ashamed; shameful.

xalafa G *(yexlef)* to pass (by: *'enta*, *'enta xaba*; through: *'enta westa*; among: *'enta mā'kala*; away from, i.e. to leave: *'em-*, *'em-xaba*); to perish. Glt *taxālafa* to wander to and fro. CG *'axlafa* to cause to pass; to pass (time). *xeluf* adj. crossing, passing. *xalāfi* (pl. *xalaft*) passer-by; adj. transitory. *xalāfit* (coll.) those passing by. *mexlāf* place for crossing or passing through.

xellat reed, cane.

xalqa G *(yexlaq/yexleq)* to come to an end, be finished, consummated; to perish, disappear. CG *'axlaqa* to destroy, finish, consummate. *xelqat* end, consummation, completion; death. *māxlaqt* end, completion; consummation, climax, death; performance, execution.

$x^{w}allaq^{w}a$ D to count, number, reckon. Dt $tax^{w}allaq^{w}a$ pass. $x^{w}elluq(^{w})$ counted, numbered, reckoned. $x^{w}elq^{w}/x^{w}alq^{w}$ (pl. $x^{w}elaq^{w}$) number, sum. $x^{w}ell\bar{a}q^{w}\bar{e}$ n. numbering, counting. *'albo* $x^{w}elq^{w}a$ *N* there is no limit to N, N is boundless.

xallaya D to think, ponder, meditate (about: a.d.o. or *ba'enta*); to think up, devise; to decide (to do: *kama* + subj.); to take thought of, to take care of, look after (someone: o.s. or *ba'enta/la-*). CD *'axallaya* to cause (someone: o.s.) to think about or decide to do. Dt *taxallaya* to be thought of, conceived. *xellinnā* (pl. *-t*) mind, thought, intellect; product of thought, idea; process of thought, thinking, cogitation; proposal, advice, opinion.

xams (acc. *-a*) f. five. *xamestu* (acc. *xamesta*) m. five. *xāmes* (f. *-t*) adj. fifth. *xāmesāwi* (f. *-t*) idem. *xāmesāy* (f. *xāmesit*) idem. *xamus* the fifth day (of week or month); five days. *xems* f. five; *xemsa* adv. five times. *xamsā* fifty.

xanaqa G *(yexneq)* to choke, throttle. Gt *taxanqa* pass. and reflex.

xaraya G *(yexray)* to choose, select. Gt *taxarya* pass. *xeruy* chosen, selected; pleasing, acceptable; an arbiter, mediator; *xeruyān* the Elect (i.e. those who will be saved at the Last Day). *xeryat* choice, selection.

xasra G *(yexsar)* to be in bad straits, wretched, miserable; to suffer loss, be reduced to poverty; to be dishonored, vilified, despised. CG *ʾaxsara* to cause/inflict/afflict (with) any of the preceding states (a.d.o. of person). *xesur* wretched, impoverished, afflicted, vile, despised. *xasār* (pl. *-āt*) m.f. wretchedness, poverty, ignominy.

xašaša G *(yexšeš)* to seek, look for; to demand, require (from: *ba-xaba/ʾemenna*); to study, pursue diligently. Gt *taxašša* pass. and reflex. (for one's self). Glt *taxāšaša* to inquire collectively, discuss with one another (something: o.s.). *xašašā* (pl. *-t*) wish, desire.

xaṣin (pl. *xaṣāwent*) m. iron; sword, weapon; tool, implement.

xaṣara G *(yexṣer)* to be short. CG *ʾaxṣara* to shorten, diminish, subtract from. *xeṣur* short, shortened. *xaṣir* (f. *xaṣār*) idem.

xaṣawa G to castrate. *xeṣew* castrated; n. eunuch.

xaṭʾa G to lack, not have, not find; (rarely) to sin. CG *ʾaxṭeʾa* to deprive (someone: a.d.o. or o.s.; of: a.d.o.), to cause to lack; to cause to sin. Gt *taxaṭʾa* to withdraw, go away; to be absent, lacking. *xeṭuʾ* not having, deprived. *xaṭiʾat* (pl. *xaṭāweʾ*, *xaṭāyeʾ*) m.f. sin(s). *xāṭeʾ* (f. *-t*) sinful, wicked; n. sinner.

xeṭṭat grain, seed.

xatama G *(yextem)* to seal, close and seal. Gt *taxatma* pass. *xetum* sealed, signed, *xatāmi* one who seals, signer. *māxtam(t)* a seal.

xatawa G to burn, be alight. CG *ʾaxtawa* to light (a lamp); to burn, emit light. *māxtot* (pl. *maxātew*) lamp.

xoṣā sand.

xoxt (pl. *xoxāt*, *xawāxew*) m.f. door, doorway.

xēla G to become well, strong. D *xayyala* to be strong, mighty, powerful; to prevail over, be superior to (a.d.o.). CD *ʾaxayyala* to make strong, etc. Dt *taxayyala* to be strengthened, strong; to prevail, dominate; to act with force (good or bad sense) against. *xeyyul* strong, etc. *xayyāl* idem. *xayl* (pl. *-āt*) strength, power, might; army, troops.

xēr (f. *-t*) good, excellent. *xirut* excellence, goodness, virtue.

xayyasa D to be better, more outstanding. Often impersonal:

yexēyyesani kama + subj. it is better for me that ... CD
'axayyasa to make better, more pleasing. *xisān* excellence.

Y

ye'eti (acc. *ye'eta*) f.s. she; that, that one (pron. or adj.).
ye'ezē(± ni) adv. now. *'em-ye'ezē* from now on. *'eska ye'ezē* up until now.
yabsa G *(yeybas)* to be dry, arid. CG *'aybasa* caus. *yebus* dry, arid. *yabs* dry land, the dry ground.
'ayde'a to inform, tell (someone: a.d.o.). Gt *tayad'a* pass.
Yakātit Eth. month name: Feb. 8 - Mar. 9.
yamān the right side or hand. *yemn* idem; *yemna* adv. on/to the right. *yemuna* adv. rightly, correctly.
yogi adv. perhaps, by chance, perchance.
yawha G to be gentle, mild, modest, submissive, innocent, simple; to please, charm, persuade, entice. D *yawweha* idem. *yawhat* mildness, etc. *yawwāhat* idem. *yawwāh* adj. mild, gentle, etc. *yawhennā* mildness, etc.
yom adv. today; on this day (of the year).
Yonānāwiyān the Greeks.
yawṭā the Gk. letter iota.

Z

za- rel. pron. m.s. §25.1; absolute rel. §25.1 e-f; prep. of §25.1g; conj. that, the fact that (introducing noun clause after verbs of speaking, etc.). *ba'enta za-* conj. because. *za-* in cleft sentences §29.1, §29.3. *za-* in questions §29.1.
zā- f.s. this (adj. and pron.).
ze- (acc. *za-*) m.s. this (adj. and pron.).
zabaṭa G *(yezbeṭ)* to beat, whip (a.d.o.; the part of the body may be specified with *diba/westa/lā'la*). Gt *tazabṭa* pass. Glt *tazābaṭa* recipr. *zabāṭi* ruffian, fighter. *zebuṭ* beaten. *zebṭat* n. beating, whipping.
zafana G to dance. *zafan* n. dancing. *zafāni* (f. *-t*) dancer. *mezfān* place for dancing.
zafar (pl. *'azfār*) hem or fringe of a garment.
zagaba G *(yezgeb)* to store up, accumulate, hoard; to store away, hide. Gt *tazagba* pass. *mazgab* (pl. *mazāgebt*) treasure, wealth; store-

room, magazine.

zeḥna G to be calm, tranquil. CG *ʾazḥana* caus. *zeḥun* calm, tranquil. *zāḥn* calm, tranquility.

zakara G *(yezker)* to remember, mention. Gt *tazakra* pass. D *zakkara* = G. Dt *tazakkara* = G. *zekur* mentioned, remembered. *zekr* mention, memory; commemoration. *tazkār* memorial service or holiday, commemoration; memory; memorandum, notation; *gabra tazkāra* to celebrate a commemoration; *ʿelata tazkār* day of commemoration.

zeku (acc. *zek*^{w}*a*) m.s. that (adj. or pron.); *zektu, zek*^{w}*tu* Idem §8.4.

ʾazlafa CG to continue (doing), persevere in (doing), followed by acc. verbal noun or acc. inf. *zelufa, la-zelufu* adv. continuously, continually, perpetually, forever. *zalfa* adv. idem; always, regularly, frequently, often. *ʾi- ... zalfa* never. *za-zalf* adj. perpetual. *la-zalāfu, la-zelāfu* = *la-zelufu.*

zalgasa Q to be afflicted with a dreadful disease (leprosy, elephantiasis). *zelgus* leprous. *zelgāsē* leprosy, elephantiasis.

tazamda Gt to be related. *zamad* (pl. *ʾazmād*) m. family, kin, relatives, clan; tribe, kind, sort, species. Sing. and pl. forms are used interchangeably. *tezmedd* family, tribe, race, species.

zammara D (1) to make music; to play instruments, sing; (2) to state or proclaim authoritatively, to bear witness to. CG *ʾazmara* = D (2). *zemmur* authority, witness. *zemmārē* psalm, hymn. *mazammer* psalmist, church singer. *mazmur* (pl. *-āt*) psalm, the psalter; chorus of singers. *mezmār* authority, witness.

zammawa D to commit adultery; to have illicit intercourse (with: *mesla* or a.d.o.). CD *ʾazammawa* caus. *zemmut* adultery, hárlotry. *zammā* whore, adulterer, fornicator. *zammāwi* idem. These terms applied to both males and females.

zanma G to rain. CG *ʾaznama* to bring rain, cause to rain. *zenām* (pl. *-āt*) m.f. rain.

zangeʿa Q to be insane, mad, crazy. *zenguʿ* mad, raving; stupid, inept.

zang^{w}*ag*^{w}*a* Q to ridicule, hold in scorn. *zeng*^{w}*āg*^{w}*ē* scorn, ridicule.

zentu (acc. *zanta*) m.s. this (pron. or adj.).

zēnawa L/Q to inform. Qlt *tazēyānawa* recipr. *zēnā* (pl. *-t*) m.f. news, report; narrative, story, account; pronouncement.

zeqq (pl. *-āt*) wineskin.

zarʾa G to sow, scatter (seed). Gt *tazarʾa* pass. *zarʾ* (pl. *ʾazreʾt*) seed; progeny.

zar'ạ G alternate spelling for the preceding.

mazāre' (pl.) baskets, containers.

zarawa G *(yezru)* to scatter, disperse, distribute. Gt *tazarwa* pass. *zerew* scattered, dispersed. *zerwat* dispersion. *zarāwi* (one) who scatters, disperses; prodigal, extravagant.

zāti (acc. *zāta*) f.s. this (pron. and adj.).

tazaxxara/tazexxera Dt to boast; to brawl. *zexxur* boastful, arrogant; quarrelsome. *tezxert* n. boasting, insolence; strife, brawling.

zexr tomb, monument.

zēmā melody, tune, song. *le''ul zēmā* a style of singing.

zeyya adv. here; *ba-zeyya* idem. *'em-zeyya* from here, hence.

The Principal Parts of G Verbs

The numbers in parentheses refer to lessons in the grammar where the given form and its inflection are discussed.

a. Standard Types

Root Type	Perfect	Imperfect	Subjunctive	Imperative
Sound	*qatala* (11)	*yeqattel* (32)	*yeqtel* (33)	*qetel* (34)
	nabara (11)	*yenabber* (32)	*yenbar* (33)	*nebar* (34)
	gabra (11)	*yegabber* (32)	*yegbar* (33)	*gebar* (34)
I-Guttural	*'asara* (11)	*ya'asser* (38)	*ye'ser* (38)	*'eser* (38)
	'amna (11)	*ya'ammen* (38)	*ye'man* (38)	*'eman* (38)
II-Guttural	*sa'ala* (12)	*yese''el* (39)	*yes'al* (39)	*sa'al* (39)
	keḥda (12)	*yekeḥḥed* (39)	*yekḥad* (39)	*kaḥad* (39)
III-Guttural	*maṣ'a* (13)	*yemaṣṣe'* (40)	*yemṣā'* (40)	*meṣā'* (40)
I-W	*warada* (11)	*yewarred* (41)	*yerad* (41)	*rad* (41)
	wadqa (11)	*yewaddeq* (41)	*yedaq* (41)	*daq* (41)
	wagara (11)	*yewagger* (41)	*yewger/yegar* (41)	*weger/gar* (41)
II-W	*qoma* (15)	*yeqawwem* (42)	*yequm* (42)	*qum* (42)
	ṣora (15)	*yeṣawwer* (42)	*yeṣor/yeṣur* (42)	*ṣor/ṣur* (42)
II-Y	*šēma* (15)	*yešayyem* (42)	*yešim* (42)	*šim* (42)
III-W	*fatawa* (14)	*yefattu* (43)	*yeftaw* (43)	*fetaw* (43)
III-Y	*bakaya* (14)	*yebakki* (43)	*yebki* (43)	*beki* (43)
	satya (14)	*yesatti* (43)	*yestay* (43)	*setay* (43)

b. Mixed Types and Irregular Verbs

Perfect	Imperfect	Subjunctive	Imperative	Meaning
re'ya (14)	*yere''i/yerē''i* (43)	*yer'ay* (43)	*re'i* (43)	to see
šawʿa (15)	*yešawweʿ* (42)	*yešuʿ* (42)	*šuʿ* (42)	to offer up
'axaza (12)	*ye'exxez* (39)	*ye'xaz/ya'axaz* (39)	*'axaz* (39)	to seize
kehla (12)	*yekel* (39)	*yekhal* (39)	*kahal* (39)	to be able
behla (12)	*yebel* (39)	*yebal* (39)	*bal* (39)	to say
wahaba (12)	*yehub* (41)	*yahab* (41)	*hab* (41)	to give
waḍ'a (13)	*yewaḍḍe'* (40)	*yeḍā'* (41)	*ḍā'* (41)	to go out

Perfect	Imperfect	Subjunctive	Imperative	Meaning
weḥza (12)	*yeweḥḥez* (39)	*yaḥaz* (41)	---	to flow
boʾa (15)	*yebawweʾ* (42)	*yebāʾ* (42)	*bāʾ* (42)	to enter
ḥora (15)	*yaḥawwer* (42)	*yeḥor/yeḥur* (42)	*ḥor/ḥur* (42)	to go
weʿya (14)	*yeweʿʿi* (43)	*yaʿay* (43)	---	to burn
ʾakya (14)	*yaʾakki* (43)	*yeʾkay* (43)	---	to be bad
wadaya (14)	*yewaddi* (43)	*yeday* (43)	*day* (43)	to place
ḥaywa (14)	*yeḥayyu* (43)	*yeḥyaw* (43)	*ḥeyaw* (43)	to live
ʾatawa (14)	*yaʾattu* (43)	*yeʾtu/yeʾtaw* (43)	*ʾetu/ʾetaw* (43)	to go home

Synopsis of the Sound Triliteral Verb

The numbers refer to the lessons where details on a given form and its inflection may be found. Forms in brackets are rare. Consonantal doubling found in the tradition, but not adopted in our transliteration, is indicated by parentheses.

	Perfect	Imperfect	Subjunctive	Imperative
G	*qatala*	*yeqattel*	*yeqtel*	*qetel*
	gabra	*yegabber*	*yegbar*	*gebar*
CG	*ʾaqtala* (26,27)	*yāqattel* (45)	*yāqtel* (45)	*ʾaqtel* (45)
Gt	*taqatla* (21)	*yetqattal* (44)	*yetqatal* (44)	*taqatal* (44)
CGt	*ʾastaqtala* (49)	*yāstaqattel* (49)	*yāstaqtel* (49)	*ʾastaqtel* (49)
Glt	*taqātala* (24)	*yetqā(t)tal* (44)	*yetqātal* (44)	*taqātal* (44)
CGlt	*ʾastaqātala* (49)	*yāstaqāt(t)el* (49)	*yāstaqātel* (49)	*ʾastaqātel* (49)
D	*qattala* (11)	*yeqēttel* (46)	*yeqattel* (46)	*qattel* (46)
CD	*ʾaqattala* (26,27)	*yāqēttel* (48)	*yāqattel* (48)	*ʾaqattel* (48)
Dt	*taqattala* (22)	*yetqēttal* (48)	*yetqattal* (48)	*taqattal* (48)
CDt	*ʾastaqattala* (49)	*yāstaqēttel* (49)	*yāstaqattel* (49)	*ʾastaqattel* (49)
L	*qātala* (11)	*yeqāt(t)el* (49)	*yeqātel* (49)	*qātel* (49)
	dēgana (11)	*yedēg(g)en* (49)	*yedēgen* (49)	*dēgen* (49)

	Perfect	Imperfect	Subjunctive	Imperative
	moqeḥa (13)	*yemoq(q)eḥ* (49)	*yemoqeḥ* (49)	*moqeḥ* (49)
CL	*ʾaqātala* (26,27)	*yāqā(t)el* (49)	*yāqātel* (49)	*ʾaqātel* (49)
Lt	Like Glt above (49)			
CLt	Like CGlt above (49)			

	Infinitive (Lesson 30)	Perfective Participle (Lesson 31)	Verbal Adjective	Agent Noun
G	*qatil(ot-)*	*qatil-*	*qetul* (35), *qatil* (18), *qātel* (17)	*qatāli* (34)
CG	*ʾaqtelo(t-)*	*ʾaqtil-*	[*ʾeqtul*]	*maqtel*, *maqtali*, *ʾaqtāli* (45)
Gt	*taqat(e)lo(t-)*	*taqatil-*	[*teqtul*]	[*taqatāli*]
CGt	*ʾastaqatelo(t-)*	*ʾastaqatil-*	[*ʾesteqtul*]	*mastaq(a)tel* (49)
Glt	*taqātelo(t-)*	*taqātil-*		[*taqātāli*]
CGlt	*ʾastaqātelo(t-)*	*ʾastaqātil-*		*mastaqātel* (49)
D	*qattelo(t-)*	*qattil-*	*qettul* (47), *qattil* (18)	*qattāli*, *maqattel* (47)
CD	*ʾaqattelo(t-)*	*ʾaqattil-*		
Dt	*taqattelo(t-)*	*taqattil-*		
CDt	*ʾastaqattelo(t-)*	*ʾastaqattil-*		*mastaqattel*
L	*qātelo(t-)*	*qātil-*	*qutul* (49)	*qātāli*, *maqātel* (49)
CL	*ʾaqātelo(t-)*	*ʾaqātil-*		
Lt	Like Glt above.			
CLt	Like CGlt above.			

Verbal Nouns:

G	*qetl*, *qetlat*, *qetal*, *qetāl*, *qatāl*, *qatl*, [*qatalā*], [*qatal*] (36).
CG	[*ʾaqtalā*], [*ʾeqtelā*] (45).
CGt	[*ʾesteqtāl*]
D	*qattel*, *qettel*, *qettālē*, *qettalē*, *qettelā* (47).
Dt	*teqtelt*, *taqtāl* (48).
L	*qutālē*, *qutelā* (49).

For all Quadriliteral and Quinquiliteral verbs see Lesson 50.